T0399008

THE OXFORD HANDBOOK OF

THE LATIN BIBLE

THE OXFORD HANDBOOK OF

THE LATIN

BIBLE

Edited by

H. A. G. HOUGHTON

OXFORD
UNIVERSITY PRESS

UNIVERSITY PRESS

Oxford University Press is a department of the University of Oxford. It furthers
the University's objective of excellence in research, scholarship, and education
by publishing worldwide. Oxford is a registered trade mark of Oxford University
Press in the UK and certain other countries.

Published in the United States of America by Oxford University Press
198 Madison Avenue, New York, NY 10016, United States of America.

© Oxford University Press 2023

Library of Congress Cataloging-in-Publication Data
Names: Houghton, H. A. G., author.
Title: The Oxford handbook of the Latin Bible / H.A.G. Houghton.
Description: New York : Oxford University Press, [2023] |
Series: Oxford handbooks series |
Includes bibliographical references and index. |
Identifiers: LCCN 2022037330 (print) | LCCN 2022037331 (ebook) |
ISBN 9780190886097 (hardback) | ISBN 9780190886127 |
ISBN 9780190886110 (epub)
Subjects: LCSH: Bible. Latin—History. | Bible. Latin—Versions—History.
Classification: LCC BS68 .H68 2022 (print) | LCC BS68 (ebook) |
DDC 220.4/7—dc23/eng/20221129
LC record available at https://lccn.loc.gov/2022037330
LC ebook record available at https://lccn.loc.gov/2022037331

DOI: 10.1093/oxfordhb/9780190886097.001.0001

Printed by Sheridan Books, Inc., United States of America

Contents

List of Figures

Acknowledgments

First of all, I would like to express my gratitude to Steve Wiggins for his invitation to edit this handbook and his prompt and helpful assistance throughout its creation. I am delighted that such a distinguished international team of contributors, from a variety of academic traditions, readily agreed to participate in the volume. It is particularly good to include papers from colleagues for whom English is not their normal language of publication, and I acknowledge the aid of Google Translate and the DeepL software for the English translation of chapters 10, 14, 17, 18, 22, 23, 24, and 25. Thanks go to the Royal Irish Academy, Trinity College Dublin, Corpus Christi College Cambridge, the Biblioteca Medicea Laurenziana (and the Ministero per i beni e le attività culturali), the Archive of Mariendonk Abbey, and Anthony Forte for permission to reproduce pictures, and in particular to the British Library for its generous policy of placing images from the Catalogue of Illuminated Manuscripts in the public domain. I would also like to thank the College of Arts and Law at the University of Birmingham for contributing to the cost of some reproductions. Peter Stotz died in 2020, having delivered the full text of his chapter, and I am grateful that it has been possible to include it as originally planned.

Although it is not customary to include a dedication in a handbook such as this, it provides an opportunity to honor two of the leading figures in this field, both now in their ninth decade. Pierre-Maurice Bogaert and Roger Gryson are among the few whose expertise spans the breadth of this volume, and each has made an incomparable contribution to scholarship on the Latin Bible. Although neither was in a position to participate, the importance of their work is evident throughout these chapters, and I hope that they will accept this collection as a grateful tribute.

H. A. G. Houghton
Institute for Textual Scholarship
and Electronic Editing
University of Birmingham

List of Abbreviations

AGLB	*Aus der Geschichte der lateinischen Bibel*
ANTF	*Arbeiten zur neutestamentlichen Textforschung*
BAV	Bibliotheca Apostolica Vaticana
BCE	Before Common Era
BETL	*Bibliotheca Ephemeridum Theologicarum Lovaniensium*
BL	British Library
BLB	Badische Landesbibliothek
BM	Bibliothèque Municipale
BML	Biblioteca Medicea Laurenziana
BN	Biblioteca Nazionale
BNC	Biblioteca Nazionale Centrale
BnF	Bibliothèque nationale de France
BNM	Biblioteca Nazionale Marciana
BSB	Bayerische Staatsbibliothek
BTT	*Bible de tous les temps*
BUC	Biblioteca Universidad Complutense
CBL	*Collectanea Biblica Latina*
CCCM	*Corpus Christianorum Continuatio Medievalis*
CCSL	*Corpus Christianorum Series Latina*
CE	Common Era
CISAM	Centro italiano di studi sull'alto medioevo
CLA	*Codices Latini Antiquiores* (ed. E. A. Lowe, 1934–1972)
CSEL	*Corpus Scriptorum Ecclesiasticorum Latinorum*
CSIC	Consejo Superior de Investigaciones Científicas
CT	Concilium Tridentinum (Council of Trent)
ed.	edition
ff.	folios
FIDEM	Fédération Internationale des Instituts d'Études Médiévales
fol.	folio

GA	Gregory-Aland
GCS	*Die griechischen christlichen Schriftsteller der ersten Jahrhunderte*
HAB	Herzog August-Bibliothek
KB	National Library (Kongelige Bibliotek/Koninklijke Bibliotheek/Kungliga Biblioteket)
LXX	Septuagint
MGH	*Monumenta Germaniae Historica*
NLR	National Library of Russia
NRSV	New Revised Standard Version
ns	new series
NTTSD	New Testament Tools, Studies, and Documents
ÖNB	Österreichische Nationalbibliothek
PG	*Patrologia Graeca* (ed. J.-P. Migne, 1857–1866)
PL	*Patrologia Latina* (ed. J.-P. Migne, 1844–1855)
SC	*Sources chrétiennes*
TECC	*Textos y estudios 'Cardenal Cisneros'*
T&S	Texts and Studies
UB	Universitätsbibliothek
UL	University Library
USTC	Universal Short Title Catalogue
Vg	Vulgate
VL	*Vetus Latina*
vols.	volumes
WUNT	*Wissenschaftliche Untersuchungen zum Neuen Testament*

LIST OF CONTRIBUTORS

Alexander Andrée is a Latinist and Director of Research at the Museum of the Middle Ages in Stockholm. He was formerly Professor of Latin and Palaeography at the Centre for Medieval Studies, University of Toronto. He has published extensively on the medieval schools, particularly in the twelfth century, and is the author of critical editions of Gilbertus Universalis's *Glossa ordinaria* on Lamentations (2005), Anselm of Laon's *Glosae super Iohannem* (2014), and Peter Abelard's *Historia calamitatum* (2015, repr. 2017). His research now focuses on Greek and Latin literature of earlier periods, including publications on Liudprand of Cremona and Lucan's *De bello ciuili*.

Thomas Johann Bauer is Professor of New Testament Exegesis and Theology in the Catholic Theology Faculty of the University of Erfurt. Since 2014, he has been the Academic Director of the Vetus Latina Institute at the Archabbey of Beuron, and he is also Dean of Theology in the Bavarian Benedictine Academy. His publications include a literary critical study of the Book of Revelation (2007) and an analysis of the Epistles to the Galatians and Philemon (2011).

Ashley Beck is a Roman Catholic priest and Associate Professor at St. Mary's University, Twickenham, where he is responsible for the master's program in Catholic Social Teaching and the foundation degree in Pastoral Ministry. He recently published a new edition and translation of *De Athanasio* by Lucifer of Cagliari (2021), and short biographies of Pope Benedict XV and St. Oscar Romero. He is a former president of the Catholic Theological Association of Great Britain.

Shari Boodts is Senior Researcher of Medieval History at Radboud University, Nijmegen. She specializes in Latin patristic literature and its medieval reception and manuscript transmission, with a particular interest in late-antique sermons. She produced a critical edition of Augustine's *Sermones ad populum 157–183* (2016), and was co-editor of *Preaching in the Patristic Era. Sermons, Preachers, Audiences in the Latin West* (2018).

Michelle P. Brown was formerly the Curator of Medieval and Illuminated Manuscripts at the British Library, and Professor of Medieval Manuscript Studies at the School of Advanced Study, University of London. She is a Lay Canon of Truro Cathedral, a Patron of the Society of Bookbinders, and a Trustee of the Hereford Mappa Mundi. Her publications include books on the Luttrell Psalter, the Holkham Picture Bible, the Book of Cerne, and the Lindisfarne Gospels, as well as *In The Beginning: Bibles Before the Year*

1000 (2006), *The Lion Companion to Christian Art* (2008), and *Art of the Islands: Celtic, Pictish, Anglo-Saxon, and Viking Visual Culture* (2016).

José Manuel Cañas Reíllo is an academic researcher at the Instituto de Lenguas y Culturas del Mediterráneo y Oriente Próximo of the Spanish National Research Council (CSIC, Madrid, Spain). His research focuses on the textual criticism of the Septuagint and the *Vetus Latina*, as well as other versions such as the Syrohexapla, Ethiopic, Coptic, Armenian, and Georgian. In 2013, he was appointed editor of the volume of Judges for the Göttingen Septuagint.

Gilbert Dahan is an emeritus Director of Research at the French National Centre for Scientific Research (CNRS) and Director of Studies at the École pratique des hautes études (Paris). He specializes in the Christian exegesis of the Bible in the Middle Ages. Among his numerous books are *L'exégèse chrétienne de la Bible en Occident médiéval* (1999), *Lire la Bible au moyen âge* (2009), and *Étudier la Bible au moyen âge* (2021). He has convened many conferences and is one of the organizers of the *Journées d'histoire de l'exégèse*.

Siobhán Dowling Long is a College Lecturer in Education at University College Cork, Ireland. She is the author of *The Sacrifice of Isaac: The Reception of a Biblical Story in Music* (2013), *The Bible in Music: A Dictionary of Songs, Works and More* (2015) with John F. A. Sawyer, and co-editor of *Reading the Sacred Scriptures: From Oral Tradition to Written Documents and their Reception* (2018) with Fiachra Long. She has contributed numerous articles on the Bible and Music to the *Encyclopedia of the Bible and its Reception*.

Oliver Dy is Professor of Systematic Theology at the Loyola School of Theology, Philippines. Among his research interests are the study of Vatican II and the philosophy of translation. He has published on the use of the Latin Vulgate in liturgical translation in *Questions Liturgiques* (2016), and contributed to *"Res opportunae nostrae aetatis": Studies on the Second Vatican Council offered to Mathijs Lamberigts* (2020).

J. K. Elliott is Professor Emeritus of New Testament Textual Criticism at the University of Leeds. He continues to sit on the Council of Devonshire Hall, Leeds, and on the Brotherton Library's committee on the Holden Library in the University of Leeds.

Wim François is Professor of Early Modern Church and Theology at KU Leuven. He is also the Academic Librarian of the Maurits Sabbe Library in the Faculty of Theology and Religious Studies. His research interests include vernacular Bible reading, scholarly Bible commentaries, and other areas of early modern biblical culture. His publications include books on Erasmus of Rotterdam (2012), religious reform in the Middle Ages and Early Modern era (2017), and the Council of Trent (3 volumes, 2018).

Edmon L. Gallagher is Professor of Christian Scripture at Heritage Christian University (Florence, Alabama). He studies the reception of biblical literature in ancient Judaism and Christianity. His books include *Hebrew Scripture in Patristic Biblical Theory* (2012), *The Biblical Canon Lists from Early Christianity* (2017, with John D. Meade), and *Translation of the Seventy* (2021).

David Ganz taught Palaeography at the University of North Carolina at Chapel Hill and at King's College London. He is a corresponding member of the *Monumenta Germaniae Historica* who works on Latin manuscripts copied before 1000. His publications include *Corbie in the Carolingian Renaissance* (1990), and *Einhard and Notker the Stammerer, Two Lives of Charlemagne* (2008).

Antonio Gerace is senior fellow at the Fondazione per le Scienze religiose "Giovanni XXIII" in Bologna (FSCIRE), working on the education of clergy and the translations of the Creed in the Early Modern era. He is also a voluntary research fellow at KU Leuven, and is qualified in Italy as Associate Professor in Religious History Sciences. His publications include *Biblical Scholarship in Louvain in the "Golden" Sixteenth Century* (2019), and articles on figures such as Girolamo Seripando, Francis Lucas of Bruges, Thomas Stapleton, Nicholas Tacitus Zegers, and Adam Sasbout.

H. A. G. Houghton is Professor of New Testament Textual Scholarship and Director of the Institute for Textual Scholarship and Electronic Editing (ITSEE) at the University of Birmingham, and a member of the Research Unit Biblical Studies at KU Leuven. He serves on the Editorial Committee for the United Bible Societies' *Greek New Testament* and Nestle-Aland *Novum Testamentum Graece*, and is a corresponding editor of the Vetus Latina Institute. He has published numerous articles and books on the Latin manuscripts and text of the New Testament.

Adam Kamesar is Professor of Judaeo-Hellenistic Literature at Hebrew Union College in Cincinnati. His book *Jerome, Greek Scholarship, and the Hebrew Bible* was published in 1993, and his later work on the Latin biblical tradition and exegesis has appeared in the *Journal of Early Christian Studies*, *Adamantius*, *Vigiliae Christianae*, and *The New Cambridge History of the Bible*. His commentary on Philo's *Quod deterius potiori insidiari soleat* is to be published soon.

Christina M. Kreinecker is Research Professor at KU Leuven and an Associate Fellow of ITSEE (University of Birmingham). She studied classics, theology, and philosophy in Salzburg and Rome. She is one of the editors of *The Principal Pauline Epistles: A Collation of Old Latin Witnesses* (2019), and the author of two books: the *Papyrological Commentary on 2 Thessalonians* (2010), and a text-critical analysis of the Coptic Resurrection accounts (2008).

Guy Lobrichon was a Lecturer at the Collège de France and then Professor at the University of Avignon. Among his many publications are *La Bible au Moyen Âge* (2003), *Romanesque Burgundy* (2013/2015), and contributions to *The New Cambridge History of Christianity* (2008), and *The New Cambridge History of the Bible* (2012). His current academic activity focuses on the history of manuscripts and the application of the Bible in Latin and Old French in the Middle Ages.

Paul Mattei was a student at the École Normale Supérieure de Saint-Cloud, and then Agrégé des Lettres and Professor of Latin Language and Literature at the Université Lumière (Lyon 2). He is a visiting professor at the Istituto Patristico "Augustinianum" in Rome and a member of the Pontificia Academia Latinitatis, the Accademia Ambrosiana (Milan) and the Pontificio Comitato delle Scienze Storiche. His research and publications span the fields of Latin patristics, philology (including editions and translations of Tertullian, Cyprian, Novation, Ambrose, and Augustine), and the history of doctrine.

Martin McNamara is Emeritus Professor of Sacred Scripture in the Milltown Institute of Theology, Dublin. He studied at the Gregorian University and Pontifical Biblical Institute in Rome, and the École Biblique, Jerusalem. He has written on the Palestinian Targum and its relation to the New Testament, and the text and study of the Psalter and the Apocrypha in the early Irish Church, including several recent volumes of collected essays.

Paul Needham is Scheide Librarian Emeritus, Princeton University Library. He has published extensively on topics of bibliography and book history, with a special emphasis on fifteenth-century printing.

Annie Noblesse-Rocher is Professor of the History of Medieval and Modern Christianity at the Protestant Theological Faculty of the University of Strasbourg, where she researches the history of exegesis. She has organized numerous international colloquia on the Bible in the sixteenth century. She is the author of a book on the sermons of the twelfth-century Guerric of Igny (2005) and numerous articles on exegetical practices in the Middle Ages and among the Rhenish Reformers.

Oliver W. E. Norris is a postdoctoral researcher on the *Vetus Latina* tradition. He was Research Fellow on the "Critical Editions of the Hebrew Bible" project at the University of Oxford, and is currently preparing a new digital edition of the Verona Psalter at ITSEE, University of Birmingham. He holds a doctorate from King's College London on the gospel sources of the fifth-century Christian poet Sedulius, and has published on the psalm text of Fortunatianus of Aquileia (2017) and the Milan Psalter (2018).

Anna Persig is a postdoctoral researcher at the Faculty of Theology and Religious Studies at KU Leuven, Belgium. She holds a doctorate from the University of Birmingham on the textual tradition and linguistic features of the Vulgate and *Vetus Latina* Catholic Epistles. Her publications include an article on the biblical quotations in the *Liber de fide* attributed to Pseudo-Rufinus the Syrian (2020) and a monograph on the Vulgate text of the Catholic Epistles (2022).

Ulrich B. Schmid is a Professor at the Kirchliche Hochschule Wuppertal/Bethel, and Research Associate at the Göttingen Academy of Sciences and Humanities and the Institute for New Testament Textual Research in Münster (INTF). He is the author of books on Marcion's text of the Pauline Epistles (1995) and the Latin version of Tatian's

Diatessaron (2005). He has published widely on the textual tradition of the New Testament, and is a co-editor of the *Editio Critica Maior* of the Gospel according to John.

Peter Stotz was emeritus Professor of Medieval Latin Philology at the University of Zurich. His research on Latin language and literature included contributions to the Middle Latin Dictionary, and work on critical editions of Zwingli and Bullinger. In addition to books on the Latin poetry of St. Gall (1972), and a monograph on the Bible in Latin (2011/2015), he was author of a five-volume handbook on the Latin language of the Middle Ages (1996–2004).

Kevin Zilverberg is Assistant Professor of Sacred Scripture at Saint Paul Seminary School of Divinity and the University of St. Thomas in St. Paul, Minnesota. He is the founding director of Saint Paul Seminary Press and the general editor of the Catholic Theological Formation Series. His recent monograph, *The Textual History of Old Latin Daniel from Tertullian to Lucifer* (2021), like most of his publications, concerns the Bible and the Latin language.

Books of the Latin Bible

NRSV	Stuttgart Vulgate	Other Latin Forms	Pentateuchus	Heptateuchus	Octateuchus
Genesis	Genesis				
Exodus	Exodus				
Leviticus	Leuiticus				
Numbers	Numeri				
Deuteronomy	Deuteronomium				
Joshua	Iosue	Iesu Naue			
Judges	Iudicum				
Ruth	Ruth				
1 Samuel	Samuhel/I Regum	I Regnorum			
2 Samuel	Samuhel/II Regum	II Regnorum			
1 Kings	Malachim/III Regum	III Regnorum			
2 Kings	Malachim/IV Regum	IV Regnorum			
1 Chronicles	Verba Dierum/ I Paralipomenon				
2 Chronicles	Verba Dierum/II Paralipomenon				
Ezra	Ezras/I Esdrae	II Esdras 1–10 (LXX)			
Nehemiah	Ezras/II Esdrae	II Esdras 11–23 (LXX), Nehemias			
Esther	Hester				
Job	Iob				
Psalms	Psalmi				
[Odes]	–	Odae			
Proverbs	Prouerbia				
Ecclesiastes	Ecclesiastes				
Song of Songs	Canticum Canticorum				
Isaiah	Isaias	Esaias			
Jeremiah	Hieremias	Ieremias			

NRSV	Stuttgart Vulgate	Other Latin Forms	
Lamentations of Jeremiah	Threni	Lamentationes	
Ezekiel	Hiezechiel	Ezechiel	
Daniel	Danihel		
Hosea	Osee		
Joel	Iohel		
Amos	Amos		
Obadiah	Abdias		
Jonah	Ionas		
Micah	Micha	Micheas	*XII Prophetae*
Nahum	Naum		
Habakkuk	Abacuc		
Zephaniah	Sofonias	Sophonias	
Haggai	Aggeus		
Zechariah	Zaccharias		
Malachi	Malachi	Malachias	
Tobit	Tobias	Tobit, Thobis	
Judith	Iudith		
Additions to Esther	Hester 10:4–16:24		
Wisdom of Solomon	Sapientia Salomonis		
Ecclesiasticus	Sirach (Liber Iesu Filii Sirach)	Ecclesiasticus, Siracides	
Baruch	Baruch		
Letter of Jeremiah	Baruch 6	Epistula Ieremiae	
Azariah and the Three Jews	Danihel 3:24–90		
Susannah	Danihel 13:1–64	Susanna	
Bel and the Dragon	Danihel 13:65–14:41	Bel et Draco	
1 Maccabees	I Macchabaeorum		
2 Maccabees	II Macchabaeorum		
1 Esdras	Ezrae III/III Esdras	I Esdras (LXX), Esra I	
Manasseh	Oratio Manasse		
3 Maccabees	–	III Macchabaeorum	

NRSV	Stuttgart Vulgate	Other Latin Forms		
2 Esdras	Ezrae IIII/IV Esdras			
4 Maccabees	–	IV Macchabaeorum		
[Psalm 151]	Psalmus CLI			
Matthew	Secundum Mattheum	*Euangelia*		
Mark	Secundum Marcum			
Luke	Secundum Lucam			
John	Secundum Iohannem			
Acts of the Apostles	Actus Apostolorum			
Romans	Ad Romanos	*Epistulae Pauli*		
1 Corinthians	Ad Corinthios I			
2 Corinthians	Ad Corinthios II			
Galatians	Ad Galatas			
Ephesians	Ad Ephesios			
Philippians	Ad Philippenses			
Colossians	Ad Colossenses			
1 Thessalonians	Ad Thessalonicenses I			
2 Thessalonians	Ad Thessalonicenses II			
1 Timothy	Ad Timotheum I			
2 Timothy	Ad Timotheum I			
Titus	Ad Titum			
Philemon	Ad Philemonem			
Hebrews	Ad Hebraeos			
James	Iacobi	*Epistulae Catholicae*	*Epistulae Canonicae*	
1 Peter	I Petri			
2 Peter	II Petri			
1 John	I Iohannis			
2 John	II Iohannis			
3 John	III Iohannis			
Jude	Iudae			
Revelation	Apocalypsis			
[Laodiceans]	Ad Laodicenses			

INTRODUCTION

H.A.G. HOUGHTON

THE LATIN BIBLE

THE Latin Bible stands at the heart of Western culture. For almost fifteen hundred years, it was the principal source for scholars, philosophers, and theologians to reflect on the ideas and narratives which shaped society in Europe and beyond. Its impact was not just in the religious sphere. The translation of the Bible had a major influence on the development of the Latin language in Late Antiquity and the Middle Ages. Its words were chanted in monasteries and churches and continue to be sung in modern concert halls and cathedrals. Explaining and studying its contents was a central part of the school curriculum, and one of the key factors in the creation of the university. Textual revisions were undertaken under the patronage of popes and emperors, sometimes as a means of promoting religious reform. Copies of the Bible embody developments in art and technology. Some manuscripts are artistic masterpieces, with richly colored pictures and jeweled bindings reflecting both the prestige of those who commissioned them and the pinnacles of contemporary creative skills and techniques. The first book to be produced with the printing press was Gutenberg's Latin Bible. Since then, this collection of writings has been the focus of monumental editing projects, from the Renaissance humanist polyglots to scholarly endeavors of the late nineteenth and twentieth centuries, and it has found new life in recent decades with the creation of the *Nova Vulgata* and the advance of digitization. Many of its manuscripts have an iconic value for the cultural history of the places in which they were created (and in some cases from which they take their name), and the locations in which they have evoked the admiration of medieval pilgrims and modern tourists.

The present handbook seeks to provide an introduction to many of the facets of the tradition and history of the whole Latin Bible. The scope of such a project, spanning domains such as art history, philology and Romance linguistics, palaeography and codicology, cultural history, patristic and medieval theology, textual criticism and editorial technique, as well as liturgy, music, early vernacular works, and several classics of literature, is beyond the capability of any individual scholar or standard monograph.[1] There is currently no volume that covers the breadth of subjects treated here, and much of the scholarly literature related to the Latin Bible is in European languages other than English. It is hoped that these chapters will offer an orientation for Anglophone readers to topics that are, at the same time, the preserve of academic specialists and of more general interest, both to those studying neighboring fields and to those who identify with the religious tradition of Christianity in the West. Several of the contributions in their entirety—as well as quotations and technical terms, including those in Latin— have been translated for the benefit of a broader readership. The latter part of this Introduction provides a guide to some of the specialist vocabulary, the standard editions and resources for scholarly work on the Latin Bible, and the conventions employed in this handbook.

The chapters are arranged in broadly chronological order, with groupings according to particular themes. Chapter 1 (Houghton) introduces the earliest Latin biblical translations, known as the *Vetus Latina* ("Old Latin"). The evidence for these has to be pieced together from a few surviving manuscripts, many of which are fragmentary, and biblical quotations in early Christian writers. The characteristics shared by multiple early revisions appear to point to a single form of text underlying the extant witnesses, although the extant material is often scarce. Chapter 2 (Cañas Reíllo) explains the importance of the Latin Bible for the text of the Old Testament. The Old Latin versions were translated from manuscripts which no longer survive of the Greek version known as the Septuagint. This means that there are many cases where the Latin supports very early readings, and may even sometimes preserve the oldest form of text. The Old Latin Bible was, eventually, replaced by a text associated with the scholar Jerome and later known as the Vulgate. Chapter 3 (Kreinecker) explores the nature of Jerome's revision of the Gospels, carried out in 382–84. Chapter 4 (Kamesar) considers Jerome's approach to the books of the Hebrew Scriptures, for which he produced a new translation based on Hebrew sources at the end of the fourth and beginning of the fifth century. Chapter 5 (Norris) examines the three versions of the Psalter associated with Jerome (known as the Roman Psalter, Gallican Psalter, and Hebrew Psalter) as well as their Old Latin precursor. The use of the psalms during Christian worship means that these were some of the best-known texts of the Latin Bible, with earlier versions continuing to have currency for many centuries. Chapter 6 (Persig) offers new insights into the books of the Vulgate New Testament outside the Gospels, whose reviser is unknown. Jerome also played less of a part in the revision of apocryphal writings: Chapter 7 (Gallagher) enumerates the sources and significance of the Latin texts of the deuterocanonical books of the Bible.

---

[1] Recent years have seen the publication of two complementary introductions to different parts of the field: van Liere 2014, with a focus on the Middle Ages and the Old Testament, and Houghton 2016, which is restricted to the New Testament in the first millennium.

The oldest extant manuscripts of the Latin Bible were produced in the fourth and fifth centuries. Chapter 8 (Ganz) describes the characteristics of these documents and their successors up to the year 800. In addition to their physical details and style of script, paratextual details such as prefaces, chapter lists, annotations, and glosses are also considered. Chapter 9 (Mattei) investigates the role of the Bible in the early Latin Church and the development of interpretative approaches such as allegory. It sets out the exegetical practices and writings of fourth-century writers such as Hilary of Poitiers, Ambrose of Milan, Jerome, and, especially, Augustine of Hippo. Distinctive features of Latin interpretation are identified, where possible, as well as the individual scriptural books which are most commonly discussed. Chapter 10 (McNamara) sheds light on the biblical documents and practices characteristic of insular tradition. Irish scribes and teachers from the fifth century onward found the Latin Bible a rich stimulus for creative and ingenious scholarly activity. Chapter 11 (Houghton) considers Latin biblical tradition as juxtaposed with other languages, as found in bilingual manuscripts from the fourth to the thirteenth century and beyond. Although the most frequent companion text is Greek (particularly in the Gospels and Psalms), Gothic, Old English, Old High German, and Arabic all attest to specific linguistic and cultural contexts behind the production and use of these documents.

The Carolingian era, inaugurated by the political and religious activity of Charlemagne, proved a high point in the development of the Latin Bible and prepared the ground for medieval scholarship. Chapter 12 (Boodts) examines the biblical revisions of Alcuin of York and Theodulf of Orleans, and the technical innovations that led to the creation of pandects with the whole Bible in a single volume. The number of commentaries on Scripture also increased significantly in the years 750–1000, with an evolution in the way in which they drew on earlier sources. Chapter 13 (Lobrichon) offers an overview of the principal formats of Bibles produced in the eleventh to fifteenth century. In addition to luxury Bibles and portable Bibles, this period also saw the rise of the illustrated Bible. The contents and sequence of writings also provide evidence for how these books were used. Chapter 14 (Andrée) covers the development of a distinctive type of medieval Bible, with the scriptural text surrounded and interspersed with a commentary known as a "gloss." Although the best known of these is the *Glossa ordinaria*, other types were also in circulation. Chapter 15 (Schmid) deals with Latin gospel harmonies, in which the four canonical Gospels are combined into a single narrative. Although the oldest surviving example was produced in the middle of the sixth century, this type of manuscript was popular in the medieval period: the chapter draws attention to the interaction between these texts and those of the gloss, which appears to be responsible for variant biblical readings in vernacular harmonies. Chapter 16 (Dahan) explains how Paris became the centre of biblical scholarship in the twelfth and thirteenth centuries. In addition to the typical single-volume "Paris" Bibles, tools for interpretation were created such as lists of alternative readings (*correctoria*), section divisions, and concordances. Important roles were played by religious orders such as the Franciscans and Dominicans, the school of Saint-Victor, and individuals such as Peter Lombard, Peter Comestor, and Peter the Chanter. Chapter 17 (Dahan) presents the exegesis of the Middle Ages, including the contrast between the literal and spiritual sense of Scripture. Further procedures and techniques were developed with the aim of characterizing biblical interpretation as a science.

Chapter 18 (Needham) introduces the first one hundred years of printed Bibles (*incunabula*). Gutenberg's pioneering Latin Bible of 1455 was followed by a series of further innovations which determined the features of printed Bibles. Key figures in this include the printer Robert Estienne (latinized as Stephanus) and the humanist scholar Desiderius Erasmus, but others made important contributions. Chapter 19 (Gerace) explores how the Council of Trent identified and addressed problems with the contemporary use and form of Scripture. Its decrees on the Vulgate prompted several decades of activity to establish an official text of the Latin Bible, first in Louvain and later in pontifical committees, culminating in the Sixto-Clementine Vulgate of 1592. Chapter 20 (François) provides more information on biblical scholarship during the Humanist period. Important and extensive contributions were made both by Roman Catholic and by Protestant scholars. The sixteenth and seventeenth centuries saw a balancing of the formal authority of the Vulgate with philological investigations of original language scriptural texts in Hebrew and Greek, as well as other ancient biblical translations. Chapter 21 (Noblesse-Rocher) reveals how, despite the emphasis of the Protestant Reformation on the translation of the Bible into vernacular languages, new editions and revisions of the Latin Bible were also produced by Protestants including Martin Luther. Although these fresh translations were intended to bring out elements from the original languages, they also demonstrate the ongoing currency and importance of Latin texts of Scripture for the Reformers. Chapter 22 (Dahan) documents the place of the Latin Bible in Jewish tradition in the medieval period. The eleventh-century Rabbi Solomon (Rashi), based in Northern France, served as an authority, but there were numerous other connections between Christians and Jews, and converts were often important sources of information. Hebrew grammars and the translation of Jewish commentaries into Latin multiplied significantly in the sixteenth century.

Chapter 23 (Bauer) covers scholarship on the Latin Bible from the seventeenth to the twentieth century. This comprises many of the major editions that remain in use, such as Sabatier's edition of the Old Latin, the Oxford Vulgate, and the Roman Vulgate. Studies of individual manuscripts also contribute to modern research and the present shape of the discipline. A leading role has been played by the Vetus Latina Institute, founded in 1949. Chapter 24 (Bauer) describes its efforts to prepare a comprehensive edition of the surviving Old Latin evidence, to replace that of Sabatier, and involvement in the Stuttgart Vulgate. Chapter 25 (Zilverberg) details the creation of a new Latin Bible following the Second Vatican Council. The *Nova Vulgata* was intended to be a more accurate representation of modern editions of the original language sources but to retain the ecclesiastical authority of the Latin text. Notwithstanding the rise of vernacular liturgies after the same Council, this translation continues to be the official text of the Vulgate in the Roman Catholic Church. Chapter 26 (Dy and François) examines the role of Latin source texts in the creation of vernacular translations of Scripture, with particular reference to German, French, English, and Dutch. In English tradition, this goes back to the fourteenth-century Wycliffe Bible, although the standard example is the Douay-Rheims Bible of 1609. Even the translators of the latter, however, also made reference to Hebrew and Greek sources, a practice which was not uncommon. Chapter 27 (Elliott) sets out the presentation of Latin evidence in modern editions of the Greek New Testament, including synopses. This includes lists of the manuscripts cited and the limitations of this material.

The final chapters investigate the broader cultural significance of the Latin Bible. Chapter 28 (Stotz) explores the effect of the Bible on the Latin language of Late Antiquity and the Middle Ages. Claims that the early Church used a special type of "Christian Latin" (*Sondersprache*) have been largely dismissed. Nevertheless, the translation of the Scriptures influenced not only the vocabulary but even the linguistic structures of subsequent Christian writings, as its innovations became part of religious discourse. Chapter 29 (Beck) treats the use of the Latin Bible in Christian worship, from liturgical lessons and biblical canticles to the effect of scriptural language on newly written texts. The ongoing offering of public worship in Latin by the Roman Catholic Church continues to draw on multiple versions of the Latin Bible. Chapter 30 (Dowling Long) offers a chronological overview of musical settings of biblical texts in Latin. Although this continues to be a common practice in the context of worship, the performance of larger-scale works such as oratorios, passions, and requiems in a secular setting have created a new domain in which scriptural texts find currency. Chapter 31 (Brown) considers the importance of the Latin Bible in art history. The material record provided by the continuous production of Latin Bibles for more than sixteen centuries bears witness to the evolution of artistic practices and technological innovations. It further reflects the changing sociohistorical circumstances in which these artifacts were used. The decoration and illumination of biblical manuscripts can also be seen as a form of visual exegesis, reflecting the interplay of text and context.

TERMINOLOGY

Over the course of the centuries covered by this handbook, the terms used to refer to the Latin Bible have changed in form and application.[2] Nowhere is this clearer than in the term **Vulgate**, from the Latin *Vulgata* "common" (edition or version). In its earliest attestation, Augustine and Jerome use *Vulgata* to signify the Old Latin translation from the Septuagint—in contrast to Jerome's new version. The identification of *Vulgata* with the text of the version produced by Jerome and others at the end of the fourth century appears only to have been formally made at the Council of Trent in 1546 (Bogaert 2012:

---

[2] The goal of this section is to consider key terms related to the present volume: explanations of other specialist vocabulary may be found in standard reference works or online.

69; see also chap. 19). By the end of that century, however, the authoritative edition of the Vulgate was the medieval text of the Sixto-Clementine edition of 1592. Scholarly editions of the nineteenth and twentieth centuries nonetheless sought to recover the fourth-century text. The situation grew yet more complicated with the creation of the *Nova Vulgata* in 1979, which took over as the official Latin text of the Roman Catholic Church, although it has rarely been adopted elsewhere. In general usage, then, Vulgate with no further qualifier refers to the texts as revised by Jerome and others which are found in the majority of Latin Bibles: these are presented in the Stuttgart Vulgate, Roman Vulgate, and Oxford Vulgate (see below). There are differences between this and the Carolingian editions of Alcuin and Theodulf, as well as the Sixto-Clementine text, although all are in broad continuity. In contrast, substantial revisions or fresh translations, including the *Nova Vulgata* (sometimes called the Neo-Vulgate), should be specified as such. To use Vulgate as a synonym for the Latin Bible obscures this development, as well as the important pre-Vulgate tradition.

The earliest Latin versions of the Bible, preceding the revisions from the end of fourth century, are known as the **Old Latin**, or *Vetus Latina* (although this Latin phrase does not seem to have been used in antiquity). Augustine mentions a form of text which he identifies as *Itala* ("Italian"), which is occasionally found in older scholarship as a synonym for Old Latin, yet it does not refer to the tradition as a whole. The term *Afra* ("African") sometimes appears in opposition to *Itala*, and Old Latin texts often continue to be described as "African," "Italian," or "European," based on the witnesses in which they are attested. Further precision may be offered by the editorial text types reconstructed as part of the modern *Vetus Latina* edition (see chap. 1, 2, and 24), although these are not available for all books and are too detailed for most contexts. It has sometimes been suggested that the plural, *Veteres Latinae*, would be a better reflection of the variety of early texts in the early period, but there is a unity both in the textual tradition and the chronological period which means that the singular is sufficient.

The Old Latin books of the Old Testament are translations of the version known as the **Septuagint** (sometimes abbreviated by the Latin or Greek numerals for 70, **LXX** and *o′*). This was a translation of the Hebrew Scriptures into Greek made in the third and second centuries BCE, attributed to seventy translators. The Septuagint was one of the texts in the **Hexapla**, a scholarly edition in six columns created by the third-century Christian scholar Origen, which included other Greek Old Testament translations by Symmachus, Aquila, and Theodotion. Thoroughgoing revisions of the biblical text are known as **recensions**, one of the most important of which is attributed to the third-century Lucian of Antioch. The selection of approved biblical books (the **canon** of Scripture) varies in different traditions: the additional books included in the Greek Old Testament are known as the **deuterocanonical books**. Books which are not accepted into the canon are often described as **apocryphal**. The first five, six, seven, and eight books of the Old Testament are sometimes described, respectively, as the **Pentateuch**, **Hexateuch, Heptateuch,** and **Octateuch** (see the table of *Books of the Latin Bible* at the beginning of this volume). The **Hexameron** refers to the six days of Creation.

The combination of passages from the four Gospels into a single continuous text is a **gospel harmony**. The most famous example of this in Antiquity is the *Diatessaron* of the second-century author Tatian. An individual episode or passage of Scripture may be termed a **pericope** (from the Greek for "section"). The extracts from the Bible which are read during Christian worship are known as **lections** (or, less commonly, **lessons**). A **lectionary** is a book that contains these texts (normally in the order in which they are read during the year) rather than a continuous biblical text. **Bilingual** manuscripts have the same text in two languages: printed scholarly editions which feature the biblical text in multiple languages are known as **polyglots**. A manuscript containing the whole Bible is a **pandect**; one whose original text has been erased for copying another work is a **palimpsest**. A book produced during the first century of printing may be called an **incunable**.

All manuscript copies of the Latin Bible are in **codex** format, as are printed books, consisting of pages (**folios**) written on both sides and bound along one edge (or through the central fold). The right-hand page of each double-page spread (or **opening**) is known as the *recto* and the left-hand as the *verso*. In the system of **pagination**, a different number is written on the *recto* and on the *verso*; in the system of **foliation**, the number is only written on the *recto* and a suffix is added to identify each side (e.g., fol. 148r and fol. 148v). The groups of pages which make up the manuscript are known as **quires** or **gatherings**. The size of pages in printed books is described based on the number of times the basic sheet of paper has been folded: a single fold (providing two pages) is known as **folio**; a further fold (providing four pages) is **quarto**; a further fold (providing eight pages) is **octavo**; other, smaller formats are also found. Where possible, the size of pages has also been provided in millimeters, with the height given first and the width second. A distinction is sometimes made between the size of the whole page, including margins, and that of the **text block**, the written or printed area of the page consisting of one or more columns.

The immediate document from which a manuscript was copied is known as the **exemplar**; more distant ancestors may be described as **antigraphs**. The German word *Vorlage* is often used for "source manuscript." Two manuscripts copied from the same exemplar are **siblings**. A copy of a particular work normally contains a variety of **paratextual material**, from prefaces, prologues, chapter titles, and cross-reference systems to commentaries and notes by later users. There is a type of abbreviation specific to Christian manuscripts called a *nomen sacrum* (plural *nomina sacra*, "sacred names [or nouns]"), usually identified by a line above the word. Among these is Jesus Christ, written as IHS XPS in Latin tradition (using several Greek letters).

The academic discipline of **textual criticism** examines the differences between versions of the same writing, often with the aim of establishing the earliest form of its text. The entirety of evidence is the **textual tradition**, which may be divided into **direct tradition** (copies of the work in its original language) and **indirect tradition** (translations of the work, quotations or extracts from the work). In biblical tradition, the word **version** is often specifically used to mean "translation." Quotations of the

Bible in early Christian authors (sometimes known as the Fathers of the Church, or **patristic** writers) are also called **citations**.[3] The wording of a source is its **reading**; units of wording which differ are **variant readings**, or simply **variants**. The words chosen for a translation may be described as **renderings**. Where renderings differ, further analysis is required to establish whether they are based on the same reading, or reflect differences between their sources. The process of comparing witnesses is **collation**: a list of variant readings is a (**critical**) **apparatus**, in which witnesses may be identified by an abbreviation (**siglum**, plural **sigla**). Scholarly editions (also called **critical editions**) which include such information come in several sizes: a **hand edition** typically only provides a selection of the evidence, while an *editio maior* ("larger edition") is more comprehensive. *Correctoria* are lists of variant readings compiled in the medieval period.

The explanation of the meaning of the Bible is **exegesis**. This often takes place in an oral setting as **sermons** or **homilies** delivered by a preacher during Christian worship (**liturgy**) or, in a later educational context, as a series of classes or lectures. **Hermeneutics** are the principles of biblical interpretation. Chapter 17 provides an explanation of the different "senses of Scripture," with oppositions between "literal" and "spiritual" or "literal," "allegorical," "tropological," and "anagogical." **Commentaries** or **expositions** are writings that treat a biblical text in sequence, often in great detail. Sometimes these were originally delivered orally and transcribed for publication. The units of biblical text quoted in commentaries are referred to as **lemmata** (singular **lemma**). In the medieval period, the word **postil** (Latin *Postilla*, "after these [words of Scripture]") initially referred specifically to biblical commentaries but was later used more generally for sermons. The biblical extracts in compilations of verses on a particular theme or topic are *testimonia*. A **concordance** is a list of biblical words, usually in alphabetical order, with an indication of the verse in which they appear.

Certain geographical or chronological terms appear frequently in the description of Latin Bibles. **Insular** refers to the British Isles and Ireland (sometimes including Brittany) from roughly the sixth to the ninth century. The **Merovingian** kings ruled the Franks (an area including most of modern France, Belgium, and West Germany) from the fifth century. They were followed by Charlemagne (Charles the Great), a Frankish ruler who gave his name to the ninth-century **Carolingian** empire. The **Ottonian** period, in the tenth and eleventh centuries, was named after a dynasty of Saxon emperors. Much of modern Spain and southern France was ruled by the **Visigoths** until the Arab conquest in the middle of the eighth century. Those who continued to practice Christianity under Muslim rule during the Middle Ages were known as **Mozarabs**. Many of these terms are also used to describe styles of handwriting (or **scripts**). In addition, a distinction is made between scripts consisting solely of capital letters (**uncial** or **majuscule**) and those with different forms for smaller letters (**cursive** or **minuscule**).

---

[3] The phrase "patristic citation" is ambiguous: only the context will clarify whether it is a quotation of the Bible made by a patristic writer or a quotation of that patristic writer in another source.

EDITIONS AND RESOURCES

The standard hand edition of the text of the Vulgate, which aims to present the text of the fourth-century revision, is the **Stuttgart Vulgate**, now in its fifth edition.[4] This has a minimal apparatus (although it notes all differences from the Sixto-Clementine Vulgate) and presents the text in sense-lines. It draws on the two major editions of the twentieth century, the **Roman Vulgate** (or **Benedictine Vulgate**) of the Old Testament and the **Oxford Vulgate** of the New Testament.[5] These provide extensive text-critical information in their apparatus: Chapter 23 provides further details of the projects behind them. It should be noted that a hand edition of the Oxford Vulgate was released in 1911, although its text sometimes differs from the subsequent volumes of the main edition.

The **Sixto-Clementine Vulgate** was published in 1592, although corrected versions were issued in 1593 and 1598. The original printings are available online, in the public domain.[6] For academic purposes, however, a modern edition with details of variant readings is often preferred, such as those of Hetzenauer or Colunga and Turrado, both of which have been reprinted many times.[7] More than a millennium lies between this version and the text of the Stuttgart Vulgate: identifying the forms of biblical text available to scholars in the intervening period is fraught with difficulty, although the apparatus of the Roman and Oxford Vulgates may be of assistance, along with the increasing numbers of digitized manuscripts and early printed books. The full text of the second edition of the **Nova Vulgata** (1986) has been released on the Vatican website.[8] In printed form, it appears in the Nestle-Aland *Novum Testamentum Latine* (third edition 2014) and their bilingual *Novum Testamentum Graece et Latine*. Different Vulgate texts can be identified by their treatment of particular names, such as Eve in Genesis or the Matthaean genealogy (Houghton 2016: 133).

For the books that have so far been published, the *Vetus Latina* edition offers the most comprehensive presentation of the remains of the Old Latin Bible, with the extant evidence organized into text types and a very detailed apparatus (see chap. 1 and 24). For other books, recourse to Sabatier's eighteenth-century edition may be necessary, although more recent presentations are available of the Gospels and principal Pauline

---

[4] Robert Weber and Roger Gryson (eds.), *Biblia Sacra Iuxta Vulgatam Versionem* (5th ed., Stuttgart, Germany: Deutsche Bibelgesellschaft, 2007). An open access online text is available at <https://www.academic-bible.com/en/online-bibles/biblia-sacra-vulgata/read-the-bible-text/>.

[5] Abbey of St. Jerome, *Biblia Sacra Iuxta Latinam Vulgatam Versionem* (18 vols.) (Rome: Vatican Polyglot Press, 1926–95); J. Wordsworth, Jerome, and H. J. White (eds.), *Nouum Testamentum Domini Nostri Iesu Christi* (3 vols.) (Oxford: Clarendon Press, 1889–1953).

[6] E.g., the 1592 edition at <https://archive.org/details/bub_gb_sIwgf1mnUoUC> and <https://books.google.co.uk/books?id=wtv21mSctwsC>.

[7] Michael Hetzenauer (ed.), *Biblia Sacra Vulgatae editionis* (Innsbruck: Wagner, 1906); Alberto Colunga and Laurentio Turrado (eds.), *Biblia Vulgata* (Madrid: Editorial Católica, 1946).

[8] <https://www.vatican.va/archive/bible/nova_vulgata/documents/nova-vulgata_index_lt.html>.

Epistles.[9] The collection of material made by the Vetus Latina Institute and released online as the *Vetus Latina Database* (**VLD**) is a useful first port-of-call for information about Old Latin forms of text: it should be noted that it is not complete for the parts of the edition which had been published before 1999, and the patristic evidence may need to be verified according to the most recent edition.[10] The first two volumes of the edition, also known as the *Register* and *Repertorium*, provide full details about the Old Latin manuscripts and Christian writings which are cited in the edition: the Vetus Latina siglum (VL) is usually provided in brackets when a manuscript is mentioned in this handbook.[11] There is no single catalogue of Latin biblical manuscripts, which number in the thousands. Fischer (2010: 137–44) provides a list of around 450 gospel books copied in the first millennium. Information about editions and studies of Latin Christian texts is also given in the *Clavis Patrum Latinorum* (**CPL**) of the *Corpus Christianorum* (see below). This is now openly accessible online as part of the *Clavis Clavium* (**ClaCla**), which also includes medieval and hagiographical works.[12]

The classic edition of early Latin Christian writings is Migne's *Patrologia Latina* (**PL**), presenting texts from Tertullian to Pope Innocent III (d. 1216). Its 217 volumes were published between 1844 and 1855 but mostly reproduce earlier editions. They are all available online, along with four volumes of indices.[13] Most modern critical editions have appeared in one of the three main series. The *Corpus Scriptorum Ecclesiasticorum Latinorum* (CSEL, sometimes known as **VC** from its designation as the "Vienna Corpus") has published 106 volumes of Latin Christian writings up to the eighth century since its foundation in 1864. *Sources chrétiennes* (**SC**), founded in 1942, provides the texts of Greek, Latin, and other authors with a facing-page French translation. Its monastic series includes writings from members of religious orders from the eleventh to the fourteenth centuries. The Latin section of the *Corpus Christianorum* (1953–) is divided in two: the *Series Latina* (**CCSL**) covering works of Late Antiquity, and the *Continuatio Medievalis* (**CCCM**) which currently consists of 365 volumes from the Carolingian era to the end of the Middle Ages. The same publishers are also behind the most comprehensive

---

[9] Pierre Sabatier (ed.), *Bibliorum sacrorum latinae versions antiquae seu vetus Italica* (3 vols.) (Rheims, France: Florentain, 1743–49); Adolf Jülicher, Walter Matzkow, and Kurt Aland (eds.), *Itala. Das Neue Testament in altlateinische Überlieferung* (4 vols.) (Berlin: De Gruyter, 1938–63); Adolf Jülicher, Walter Matzkow, and Kurt Aland (eds.), *Itala. Das Neue Testament in altlateinische Überlieferung* (2nd ed., Berlin: De Gruyter, 1970–76); H. A. G. Houghton, C. M. Kreinecker, R. F. MacLachlan, and C. J. Smith, *The Principal Pauline Epistles: A Collation of Old Latin Witnesses* (NTTSD 59) (Leiden: Brill, 2019).

[10] The VLD is hosted at <www.brepolis.net>. Although there is no online counterpart to the *Vetus Latina* edition, further information is available at <www.vetus-latina.de> and <www.vetuslatina.org>. Transcriptions of Old Latin manuscripts of John, Acts, and some Pauline Epistles are available online (see the information provided in chap. 1).

[11] Roger Gryson, *Altlateinische Handschriften/Manuscrits Vieux Latins* (VL 1/2) (2 vols.) (Freiburg, Germany: Herder, 1999–2004); Roger Gryson, *Répertoire général des auteurs ecclésiastiques latins de l'antiquité et du haut moyen-âge* (VL 1/1) (2 vols.) (5th ed., Freiburg, Germany: Herder, 2007).

[12] <https://clavis.brepols.net/clacla/>.

[13] Links may be found at <http://patristica.net/latina/>. There is also a subscription database at <http://pld.chadwyck.co.uk/>.

database of Latin writings, the **Brepols Library of Latin Texts** (LLT), stretching from classical antiquity to the Second Vatican Council. This contains not only the critical texts of the writings published in the *Corpus Christianorum* but also many of those from *Sources chrétiennes* and other venues.[14] Numerous independent collections of Latin writings are also available online, along with some translations.[15] Further information about electronic tools and resources related to Christian texts is available in the Instrumenta Studiorum chapter of the *Oxford Handbook of Early Christian Studies*.[16] Many official documents of the Roman Catholic Church related to the Bible are collected in the *Enchiridion Biblicum*.[17]

CONVENTIONS

Any handbook that spans as many centuries and academic traditions as this one faces the challenge of harmonizing multiple sets of conventions and practices. It is therefore important to set out the practices that have been adopted in the present volume, and to express gratitude for the forebearance of contributors from whose preferred system these differ.

Biblical books are identified by their name in the New Revised Standard Version (NRSV; see the list of *Books of the Latin Bible* at the beginning of this volume). Alternative forms are sometimes provided in brackets (e.g., Sirach and the Apocalypse). Note that the Song of Songs, sometimes called Canticles, should be distinguished from the Canticles which are known in Greek tradition as the biblical Odes. The apocryphal work known as 1 Esdras in the Septuagint (and NRSV) is identified as 3 Ezra (or 3 Esdras) in the Vulgate. Chapter and verse numbering in all books follows the Stuttgart Vulgate. This occasionally differs from that of modern translations, the *Vetus Latina, Nova Vulgata*, and the standard editions of the Greek New Testament. In the case of the Psalms, for which the Stuttgart Vulgate provides both the Gallican Psalter (based on the Septuagint) and the Hebrew Psalter, the former is adopted with the indication LXX. Table 1.1 provides an overview of the two systems of psalm numbering. However, the verse numbers sometimes differ between the Vulgate and the Septuagint depending on whether the psalm title is counted as the first verse.[18]

---

[14] The LLT is available through subscription at the BREPOLiS platform (<www.brepolis.net>), which also hosts the electronic texts of the *Monumenta Germaniae Historia*, the *Archive of Celtic-Latin Literature*, the *Vetus Latina Database* and the *Database of Latin Dictionaries*.

[15] Particular mention should be made of the writings of Augustine at <www.augustinus.it> and the Christian section of *The Latin Library* (<http://www.thelatinlibrary.com/christian.html>).

[16] Available at <https://doi.org/10.1093/oxfordhb/9780199271566.003.0047>.

[17] Erminio Lora and Alfio Filippi (eds.), *Enchiridion Biblicum: Documenti della chiesa sulla Sacra Scrittura* (3rd ed., Bologna: Dehoniane, 2004).

[18] In addition, Bogaert (2013: 522) notes that the oldest Latin numbering of the Psalms differs from that in modern editions of the Septuagint.

Table 1.1 Differences in Psalm Numbering

Gallican Psalter/LXX	Masoretic Text/NRSV
1–8	1–8
9	9–10
10–112	11–113
113	114–15
114	116:1–9
115	116:10–19
116–45	117–46
146	147:1–11
147	147:12–29
148–50	148–50

Place names are given in an Anglicized form, when this remains in common usage. Thus Louvain is used for Leuven, Basle for Basel or Bâle, Rheims for Reims, and Lyons for Lyon. The same is true of other proper nouns, with Jerome rather than Hieronymus, and Hilary for Hilarius. In the case of medieval writers, who may often be identified in numerous ways (e.g., Gilbertus Porretanus, Gislebertus Porretanus, Gilbertus Pictaviensis, Gilbert de la Porrée, Gilbert of Poitiers), the English form in the *Oxford Encyclopedia of the Middle Ages* or the *Oxford Dictionary of the Christian Church* has been preferred, with an attempt to ensure consistency between chapters.[19]

Classical Latin does not have the letters *j* and *v*, but these are customary for consonantal *i* and *u* in the medieval period. As a broad rule of thumb, consonantal *i* and *u* have been maintained in chapters relating to Latin texts of the first millennium, and *j* and *v* used after the year 1000. This has also been applied in the titles of Latin works (e.g., Augustine's *Tractatus in Iohannis euangelium*), but in bibliographical references the form on the title page has been reproduced (e.g. Migne's edition of *Tractatus in Joannis Evangelium*). In keeping with most early Latin manuscripts, however, *V* rather than *U* is used for initial capitals (hence *Vetus Latina*, not *Uetus Latina*).

Where a writing is cited as a primary source in the body of a chapter, details are provided in a footnote, and the final bibliography is restricted to secondary literature. This means, for example, that Sabatier's edition normally appears in the bibliography but is treated as a primary source in chapter 24, "Modern Scholarship on the Latin Bible." Occasional exceptions may include editions which include extensive secondary

---

[19] André Vauchez (ed.), *Oxford Encyclopedia of the Middle Ages* (Cambridge: James Clark, 2002), also at <https://doi.org/10.1093/acref/9780227679319.001.0001>; F. L. Cross and E. A. Livingstone (eds.), *Oxford Dictionary of the Christian Church* (3rd ed., Oxford: Oxford University Press, 2005), <https://doi.org/10.1093/acref/9780192802903.001.0001. Both are available at <www.oxfordreference.com>. Sometimes, bibliographic indications differ from the form adopted.

material, such as an editor's introduction, or frequently cited texts. Where a Latin text is quoted, details are given of the edition from which it has been taken; this is not provided for more general references to ancient writings, which may be identified in the series mentioned above or through the use of a search engine. Latin titles have been preferred for original Latin works, with the exception of biblical commentaries.

BIBLIOGRAPHY

Bogaert, Pierre-Maurice. 2012. "The Latin Bible, c. 600 to c. 900." In *New Cambridge History of the Bible: Vol. 2. From 600 to 1450*, edited by Richard Marsden and E. Ann Matter, 69–92. Cambridge: Cambridge University Press.

Bogaert, Pierre-Maurice. 2013. "The Latin Bible." In *New Cambridge History of the Bible: Vol. 1. From the Beginnings to 600*, edited by James C. Paget and Joachim Schaper, 505–26. Cambridge: Cambridge University Press.

Fischer, Bonifatius. 2010. "Die lateinischen Evangelien bis zum 10. Jahrhundert. Zwei Untersuchungen zum Text." *Zeitschrift für die neutestamentliche Wissenschaft* 101: 119–44.

Houghton, H. A. G. 2016. *The Latin New Testament: A Guide to Its History, Texts and Manuscripts*. Oxford: Oxford University Press.

van Liere, Frans. 2014. *An Introduction to the Medieval Bible*. Cambridge: Cambridge University Press.

CHAPTER 1

··

THE EARLIEST LATIN TRANSLATIONS OF THE BIBLE

··

H. A. G. HOUGHTON

THE OLD LATIN VERSION AND ITS ORIGINS

··

THE earliest Latin texts of the Bible are known collectively as the "Old Latin version" or *Vetus Latina [uersio]*. This appellation should not be taken to indicate a single identifiable form of text for each book, a common place or time of origin, or a uniformity of translation or editorial practice. Rather, it is applied to all biblical books in Latin prior to the creation of the version later known as the Vulgate, and beyond that to variant forms of Latin text which continued to circulate in the following centuries. It thus extends from the first written evidence for the Latin biblical text in the late second century to nonstandard versions of particular books incorporated in single-volume Bibles produced more than a millennium later at the end of the High Middle Ages. It embraces not only translations made directly from Greek manuscripts but also subsequent revisions or adjustments based on different source texts, and numerous reworkings prompted by internal considerations of Latin language or style.

The multiplicity of Latin biblical texts was already identified as a problem at the end of the fourth century. In the preface to his revision of the Gospels, Jerome claimed that there were almost as many versions as there were manuscripts; Augustine explained the variety in Latin Bibles as arising from fresh translations being created piecemeal by early Christians with limited competence in Greek and Latin.[1] Nevertheless, it appears that all the Old Latin evidence which survives today derives from one translation of each biblical book. These were not necessarily produced at the same place or

---

[1] Jerome, *Praefatio in quattuor euangelia*; Augustine, *De doctrina christiana* 2.11.16.

time, although the majority were in circulation by the beginning of the third century. It was revisions of these, carried out in various ways, often independent of each other, which led to the subsequent proliferation of texts. These may be separated into different geographical groups (e.g., "Italian" or "North African") based on the affiliation of biblical quotations in Christian authors who were active in a particular location. It should, however, be remembered that books as well as individuals traveled widely around the Mediterranean in this period. Even before the production of the texts which became incorporated into the Vulgate, it seems that a form associated with North Italy had gained a certain prominence. This provided the basis for the revision of the New Testament according to Greek manuscripts by Jerome and others (see chap. 3 and 6). In the case of the Old Testament, there is a much sharper disjunction: the Old Latin was translated from the Greek Septuagint (see chap. 2), whereas most of the Vulgate consists of Jerome's new Latin version based on Hebrew (see chap. 4). Certain books, however, especially the deuterocanonical writings and others for which a Hebrew source was not available, preserve an Old Latin version: for example, the Vulgate contains the oldest surviving Latin text of the Wisdom of Solomon and Ecclesiasticus (Sirach).

Parallels with other languages, as well as some evidence from antiquity, suggest that the first Latin translations of the Bible would have been oral versions produced ad hoc during the course of religious meetings. Greek was the *lingua franca* of the Mediterranean in Roman times, and—thanks to the influential role of the Septuagint—was also extensively used by Jews in the Diaspora. The composition of the entire New Testament in Greek, as well as the writings of authors such as Philo and Josephus, bears witness to this. At some point, however, when Christian or Jewish assemblies were held in communities where spoken Greek was not universally understood, it was necessary to provide translations of the portions addressed to those attending. Oral renderings of Greek homilies and scriptural readings into Syriac and Latin during Christian services in fourth-century Jerusalem are described by the pilgrim Egeria.[2] For the recitation of longer biblical passages in the vernacular, a written translation would have been invaluable. It has been suggested on linguistic grounds that the Latin text of the Passion Narrative in Matthew represents an earlier stratum than the rest of the Gospel (Burton 2000: 40–44). This would accord with the reading of this lengthy account during the observances of Holy Week; later on, the translation of the remaining material would have provided a complete Latin version of this and other biblical books. Differences in the Latin texts of the Heptateuch have also been attributed to the initial translation of certain sections for liturgical use (Fischer 1951–54: 17*). Once a translation had been written down, it would have been far simpler for communities in a similar linguistic context to commission or make copies than to produce a new rendering of their own.

The translation of biblical books into Latin appears to have taken place in a Christian rather than a Jewish context. There is no evidence for a Latin translation based on

---

[2] Egeria, *Itinerarium/Peregrinatio*, 47.3–4.

Hebrew prior to that of Jerome: although the predominance of Greek and Latin in a particular area would have been the same regardless of religion, the characteristic features of Latin scriptural manuscripts correspond to Christian usage. These include the adoption of the codex rather than the scroll, and the use of *nomina sacra* abbreviations. The oldest surviving Latin biblical codices are almost entirely New Testament writings, in particular gospel books. Certain technical terms in the Latin translation of the Old Testament, such as *angelus* or *propheta*, reflect Christian practise and, sometimes, theology (Kedar 1988: 311–13). This is not to say that there was no Jewish influence on the earliest Latin translations or some of the later revisions. The indication of the "Day of Preparation" as *cena pura* rather than *praeparatio* (Greek παρασκευή) in the Old Latin Gospels and Judith indicates a familiarity with Jewish practice. At 2 Timothy 3:8, *Mambres* rather than *Iambres* derives from Hebrew tradition rather than the Greek Septuagint, and there are other occasions when the Old Latin is independent of this translation and even reflects misreadings of the Hebrew, although these are likely to have been mediated through a lost Greek form (Kedar 1988: 306, 309; Kraus 2003; see also chap. 2). A reference to a list of feasts at Judith 8:6 in a text-form attested in Rome at the end of the fourth century may indicate its use in Jewish circles, while some additions in Jeremiah 17 resemble rabbinic commentary. The sporadic nature of such details, however, along with the fact that several are found in clusters, suggests that they were introduced as corrections at a later stage, perhaps by converts (Kedar 1988: 310). The earliest evidence for Jewish use of a Latin Bible comes from the fifth and sixth centuries, and appears to indicate that they used Jerome's version (Kraus 2003: 511–13).

The origin of most, if not all, of the earliest Latin translations of biblical writings appears to have been in North Africa.[3] Christians in Europe at the turn of the third century, such as Irenaeus of Lyons and Hippolytus of Rome, continued to write and worship in Greek. The same was true of communities in the eastern Mediterranean provinces of Syria, Palestine, and Egypt. In contrast, Greek was not so well established in Roman North Africa or Mauretania, where it competed with indigenous languages such as Berber or Punic. The majority of the first Christian writers in Latin, including Tertullian, were born or active in North Africa. The earliest form of the biblical text in Latin normally matches quotations made by Cyprian of Carthage and his compatriots: the most ancient form of the gospels is transmitted in a fourth-century manuscript which was probably copied in Africa (Houghton 2020: 30–32). Further evidence for the early use of Latin by religious groups in these provinces is found in the accounts of court proceedings transmitted as the Acts of the Martyrs, as well as inscriptions. Situated at one of the narrowest points of the Mediterranean, Carthage is close to Sicily and not far by boat from Rome and the rest of mainland Italy: new writings and other innovations from this region could be quickly disseminated

---

[3] Frede (1975–82: 146) considers that the earliest version of the Pauline Epistles is of Italian rather than African origin. No African evidence survives for the book of Esther.

throughout Western Europe, as is shown in the surviving correspondence of many Christian authors.

The Old Latin version is sometimes criticized as a poor translation, and even non-sensical in certain places. Although some examples might be cited in support of this, ancient reports of its inadequacy (like those of its origins) should not be taken at face value. In practice, anyone in antiquity able to produce a written translation possessed a reasonable degree of education. If the main purpose of the earliest Latin version was for liturgical use, replacing a simultaneous oral translation, deficiencies in language or sense were unlikely to have been tolerated; once it began to circulate in book form, infelicities or inaccuracies would soon have been eliminated by readers in the same way as for any other written text in antiquity. It is true that the translation of the Old Testament caused puzzlement in places, but this was also true of its source, the Septuagint. Nor were copies of biblical writings in Latin solely the preserve of Christian congregations: Augustine, who famously described his conversion after reading the Pauline Epistles, encouraged non-Christians to go to booksellers and "buy a manuscript and read it: we are not ashamed."[4] The translation technique of the Old Latin version displays considerable linguistic sensitivity and more care and creativity than the literal approach of later revisers, including Jerome (Burton 2000; Kedar 1988: 307). Of course, certain manuscripts are poorly written and contain numerous copying errors and nonsense readings, but the same is true in Greek New Testament tradition and many other works: such scribal mistakes are not a reflection of the quality of the text being transmitted.

Sources for the Old Latin Version: Manuscripts

One of the problems facing research on the earliest Latin translations of the Bible is the lack of surviving evidence.[5] The later prevalence of the Vulgate means that few manuscripts of the older versions have been preserved. Most have perished through age, being well over a thousand years old, and many were no doubt destroyed during invasions and other periods of instability in Late Antiquity. A significant proportion of Old Latin texts are found as the undertext of palimpsest manuscripts: not only did the biblical text-form become obsolete, but so did the majuscule script in which older documents were written, leading to the repurposing of the parchment. Other witnesses are predominantly Vulgate manuscripts in which certain sections have an Old Latin affiliation, including lectionaries containing biblical passages read during worship. In the case of pandects of a whole or partial Bible assembled from several sources, certain

---

[4] Augustine, *Sermo* 198.20 (Dolbeau 26; *Recherches augustiniennes* 26 [1992]: 90–141), referring to the Bible; see also *Sermo* 114B.15 (Dolbeau 5).

[5] For further details of the extant Old Latin manuscripts, identified using their VL number, see the *Vetus Latina Register* (Gryson 1999–2004) and, for the New Testament, Houghton 2016: 210–54; many are described in chapter 8.

books may have been copied from an exemplar with an earlier version of the biblical text, perhaps unnoticed by the compiler. On a smaller scale, if the book to be copied lacked a few pages, or was damaged in some other way, the missing portion could have been supplemented from another manuscript with a different textual affiliation (Bogaert 2012: 78 describes the case of VL 102). This phenomenon is known as "block mixture." In both cases, the resulting discrepancy would rarely have been noticed without careful comparison by later users. Another type of "mixed text" manuscript presents an amalgam of Old Latin and Vulgate texts resulting from the partial incorporation of adjustments toward one version or another. Extensive corrections can still be seen in some Old Latin manuscripts, although these are often restricted to a few passages rather than present throughout: it is likely that multiple layers of correction across several generations of copies underlie some texts which, although Vulgate in many places, still retain readings from the earlier version as "fossils." Alternatively, Old Latin forms may have been inserted into Vulgate manuscripts because they reflected texts used in liturgy, quoted in commentaries, or familiar in some other way.

The most ancient extant Old Latin codices are gospel books. Some of these may owe their preservation to their association with a famous religious figure and subsequent veneration as relics, such as the late fourth-century Codex Vercellensis (VL 3, *a*). The earliest form of text is preserved in Codex Bobiensis (VL 1, *k*), copied in Africa around the same time. Several of the oldest Italian gospel books are written in gold and silver ink on purple parchment: Codex Palatinus (VL 2, *e*), Codex Veronensis (VL 4, *b*), Codex Brixianus (VL 10, *f*), Codex Vindobonensis (VL 17, *i*) and Codex Sarzanensis (VL 22, *j/z*). Other fifth-century manuscripts of the Old Latin gospels include a set of fragments from a gospel book which may have been copied in Rome (VL 16, *n/o/a²*), Codex Corbeiensis secundus (VL 8, *ff²*), Matthew in Codex Claromontanus (VL 12, *h*), and the bilingual Codex Bezae (VL 5, *d*), possibly produced in Berytus, which also contains the Acts of the Apostles and part of the Catholic Epistles.[6] Fragments of Revelation, Acts, and the Catholic Epistles are preserved in the fifth-century Fleury Palimpsest (VL 55, *h*). The earliest complete witness to the Pauline Epistles is the bilingual Codex Claromontanus (VL 75, *d*), although an Old Latin text is also transmitted in the sixth-century Freising Fragments (VL 64, *r*). Some later manuscripts also provide important Old Latin evidence for the New Testament, among which are the ninth-century Corbey St. James (VL 66, *ff*), the "Anonymous Budapest" commentary on Paul (VL 89, *b*), and, in Acts and Revelation, the thirteenth-century Codex Gigas (VL 51, *gig*).

Because Jerome's Gallican Psalter, based on the Septuagint, was adopted in Carolingian times in preference to his translation from Hebrew, this is by far the most common type of Old Latin manuscript (VL 300–485). The oldest complete Psalter, which has an Old Latin text predating Jerome's three versions, is the Psalter of St. Germain (VL 303, *γ*), copied on purple parchment in the sixth century. A trio of palimpsests containing parts of the Pentateuch date from the fifth century and were probably produced in Italy: the

---

[6] For more on Codex Bezae and other bilingual manuscripts, see chap. 11.

Palimpsestus Vindobonensis (VL 101), with pages of Genesis, Exodus, and Leviticus; the Palimpsestus Wirceburgensis (VL 103), which also has some text from Deuteronomy; and the Palimpsestus Monacensis (VL 104), with parts of Exodus to Deuteronomy. The most substantial witness to the Old Latin Heptateuch is the Codex Lugdunensis (VL 100), copied in Lyons in the second half of the sixth century. There are two fifth-century Old Latin manuscripts containing portions of the four books of Kings (Samuel and Kings): another Palimpsestus Vindobonensis originally written in Africa (VL 115), and the illustrated Quedlinburg Itala (VL 116), which has minimal biblical text. The Constance or Weingarten Fragments (VL 175) preserve an Old Latin text for parts of eight books of the Prophets, copied in Italy in the fifth century. Other early Old Testament manuscripts are very small fragments: the key witnesses are later whole or part Bibles which transmit an Old Latin version of particular books. These include Codex Complutensis Primus, also known as the First Bible of Alcalá (VL 109, X), a tenth-century Spanish manuscript with Old Latin texts of Ruth, 2 Chronicles, and Hebrews, and two eleventh-century Italian Bibles: one now in Vercelli (VL 123) which is Old Latin in Tobit, Judith, Esther, Ezra, and Nehemiah, and one in Madrid (VL 129) which preserves the earliest version of 1 Esdras (3 Ezra).

Sources for the Old Latin Version: Biblical Quotations

The scarcity of direct manuscript evidence for the Old Latin Bible, especially outside the Gospels and Psalms, means that the indirect testimony of biblical quotations in Christian writers plays a key role in the reconstruction of the earliest Latin versions of the Bible.[7] Authors such as Cyprian, Hilary of Poitiers, Ambrose of Milan, and even Jerome and Augustine composed numerous works prior to the textual revisions which were incorporated into the Vulgate and therefore relied on manuscripts with an Old Latin text. Given that the adoption of the revised texts was by no means immediate, and witnesses to the earlier versions continued to be copied in subsequent generations, later writers also preserve Old Latin evidence. These include Cassiodorus and Gildas, who both used biblical manuscripts with an Old Latin affiliation in the sixth century. At the beginning of the eighth century, Bede examined several copies of the Acts of the Apostles, including at least one Old Latin witness, for his commentary.

One of the advantages of quotations is that it is often possible to establish the time and place at which the author was active. This allows editors to trace the chronological development and geographical diffusion of particular versions, and even reconstruct different forms of text associated with individual authors or locations (see below). However, in order to provide a secure foundation for the biblical text, it needs to be established both that the author is citing accurately from a scriptural manuscript and also that the citation has been faithfully transmitted. The majority of quotations were made

---

[7] Details of the patristic writings used in the *Vetus Latina* edition and the system of abbreviations are given in the *Vetus Latina Repertorium* (Gryson 2007); see also chap. 24.

from memory, and in many cases the exact form of text was not important: authors may have paraphrased their biblical source or quoted inaccurately. There are exceptions to this: collections of *testimonia* (biblical extracts assembled on particular topics), scriptural commentaries, and other exegetical works must have drawn from a written source; lengthy passages or series of quotations which occur in their original biblical sequence are more likely to have been made with reference to a manuscript; writers sometimes insist on specific readings or refer to the use of a codex. In contrast, some citations may derive from another patristic writing, or an ad hoc translation from Greek, rather than a Latin version of the Bible. Certain authors used different biblical codices depending on the time or place: when preaching, Augustine normally took his text from the manuscripts belonging to the local church (Houghton 2008: 32–38). In terms of the fidelity of transmission, the text of biblical quotations may have been adjusted subconsciously, by copyists familiar with a different form, or deliberately, by an editor seeking to bring it into conformity with a current version. Exegetical works such as commentaries are particularly vulnerable to this. Nevertheless, manuscripts of early Christian writings transmit extensive nonstandard forms of Latin biblical text, many of which may plausibly be taken to reflect Old Latin versions used by the authors (Houghton 2014, 2017).

The amount of remaining evidence for the Old Latin Bible therefore varies widely from book to book, and even from verse to verse. Some passages are frequently cited, whereas others are barely mentioned or rarely treated in commentaries: for example, there are hardly any verbatim quotations of Ruth. The preservation of manuscripts is dependent on particular historical circumstances, and the biblical passages transmitted by fragments or in sections of block mixture are also haphazard. In the Gospel according to John, the range of Old Latin versions in extant manuscripts is significantly broader than those attested in biblical quotations (Houghton 2013); in other books, indirect evidence provides the sole testimony for pre-Vulgate texts. The task of the modern editor is therefore to assemble and analyze the available material, in order to reconstruct individual forms of text and determine what can be known about the history of the tradition.

Textual Traditions

Latin biblical texts can be categorized in a number of ways. The most frequent difference is between Old Latin and Vulgate, which is also the principal way of relating this tradition to differing strands in the Greek New Testament. Scholarly work on the Old Latin, however, also leads to the reconstruction of different text-types in earliest tradition.

Old Latin and Vulgate

The extent to which versions of the biblical text may be identified as Old Latin can vary. Although the textual tradition of the Vulgate is by no means unanimous, it offers a generally consistent form against which it is possible to identify differences that typify Old Latin versions. When the Vulgate text of a biblical book is a revision of an existing Old Latin one, including the whole of the New Testament, there is often considerable overlap between all forms of text: it is therefore better to characterize such Latin tradition as a single continuum, comprising multiple revisions, rather than two distinct textual streams. In the case of the Old Testament books for which Jerome used Hebrew texts to produce a new translation, the division between Old Latin and Vulgate is more clearly marked. Certain paratextual features are character-istic of manuscripts with the revised texts found in the Vulgate: Jerome's prefaces, the use of sense-lines in particular Old Testament books, the Eusebian Apparatus, the *Primum quaeritur* prologue to the Pauline Epistles, and certain sequences of writings (such as the order of the Gospels). It is worth noting that the Old Latin follows the Septuagint in treating Samuel and Kings as four books of Kings (or Kingdoms).[8] There have also been attempts to isolate vocabulary or other linguistic details char-acteristic of Jerome's revisions as a means of identifying text with a Vulgate affiliation (see chap. 3).

Variety in Vulgate witnesses and continuing editorial activity after the fifth century means that not every deviation from a standard text should be identified as an Old Latin form. For example, adjustments to Latin texts and even attempts to produce new translations in bilingual manuscripts may have been made long after the Vulgate be-came established (see chap. 11). In addition, the restricted range of Latin words to render Greek or serve as synonyms means that later editorial choices may coincide with Old Latin forms even if they were introduced independently. Only if a reading is attested in early quotations, or manuscripts that consistently match these quotations, is it proper to identify it as Old Latin. If early attestation is lacking, it is more accurate to designate nonstandard readings by a term such as "non-Vulgate," to acknowledge that although such forms differ from editorial texts of the Vulgate, they may not have been present in an Old Latin version.

Relationship to Greek Tradition

The overall movement in the text of the Latin Bible appears to have been from an initial looseness to a more exact, word-for-word correspondence with a Greek text. Oral translations would have involved a significant element of paraphrase, possibly with occasional expansions to gloss unusual words or concepts. These characteris-tics seem also to have influenced the early written Latin rendering: the oldest texts often display more creativity and periphrasis while lacking certain phrases, espe-cially incidental observations (see Houghton 2016: 144). There are a number of cases

---

[8] A list of Latin names for biblical books is provided in the table of *Books of the Latin Bible* at the beginning of this volume.

in which the underlying Greek has influenced Latin usage, especially when it reflects Hebrew constructions (see chap. 28). Although there are some examples of the borrowing of Greek words (such as *agape* for "love" and *cata* for "according to"), the first translators seem to have made a particular effort to find Latin equivalents (e.g., *benenuntiare* rather than *euangelizare* for "spread the good news," or *tinctio* rather than *baptisma*). In contrast, the tendency of later revisions, including that of Jerome, is to adjust the Latin text to match the structure and form of the Greek more closely. This included the reintroduction of Greek words which had become established as Christian technical terms, as well as the alteration of word order: earlier Latin versions depart more frequently from the sequence in Greek tradition, which is then reinstated by revisers.

As well as being a very valuable witness to the Septuagint and sometimes other Greek texts of the Old Testament (see chap. 2), the Old Latin version is often associated with the strand of Greek New Testament tradition known as the "Western" text. This diverges from what is generally identified as the earliest Greek text, as well as from the later, Byzantine form in the majority of manuscripts. Most scholars characterize "Western" readings as the result of redactional activity at an early point in the history of the New Testament tradition, and they do not necessarily form a coherent group (Burton 2013: 190–91). Their frequency varies from book to book: in the Acts of the Apostles, "Western" witnesses—especially Codex Bezae—offer a significantly longer form with expansions of the narrative; in the Gospels and Pauline Epistles, the differences are less common and tend to involve substitutions. A number of "Western" forms are typical of adjustments which might be made during translation: in this respect, their association with bilingual manuscripts may be significant. During the third and fourth centuries, however, many "Western" readings were eliminated from Latin versions, bringing them more into line with mainstream Greek tradition, as is the case with the Vulgate. In practice, the nature of the Greek text available to each translator or reviser will have depended entirely on the individual copies to which they had access, although Augustine notes that certain churches were renowned for the quality of their biblical codices.[9]

Variations in Latin do not necessarily reflect variations in Greek. Many different Latin renderings can be derived from the same underlying term, and changes in the choice of words (even for connectives or other *uerba minora*) may have been introduced without reference to a Greek text. Only when a Latin variant clearly represents a different source reading might it be the result of comparison with Greek (cf. Burton 2000: 11–13), although harmonization either to the context or to parallel passages should also be considered, as well as the possibility of copying errors. By the same token, agreement between Latin witnesses rarely constitutes independent testimony to the same Greek reading: in most cases, such text will have been inherited from an existing translation. Only if a Latin text has undergone a thorough comparison with Greek (as was Jerome's

---

[9] *De doctrina christiana* 2.15.22.

intention when revising the gospels) should it be taken as confirmation of a particular reading.

The Initial Translation and Subsequent Revisions

The characteristics of the underlying Greek text constitute one of several reasons that all extant Old Latin evidence has been deemed to derive from a single original translation. Consistent reflection of the same Greek source, including some poorly-attested forms, is best explained as an indication of the dependence of Latin tradition on the same point of contact with a particular Greek exemplar. For example, after Matthew 20:28, almost all Old Latin witnesses include an additional saying of Jesus which resembles Luke 14:8–10. Likewise, at Luke 9:62, Old Latin versions have "looking backwards" before "putting his hand to the plough," a reordering unlikely to have happened independently in multiple early translations: it would soon have been adjusted following comparison with another Greek source (as in the Vulgate). Old Latin witnesses share apparent misreadings of Greek (e.g., προσχαίροντες, "rejoicing," rather than προστρέχοντες, "approaching," at Mark 9:15), or other errors, such as "at his entrance" rather than "at his word" in Luke 1:29. Internal Latin features also support the origin of surviving texts from the same translation. There is a surprising lack of variation in the rendering of rare or unusual Greek words, such as *immarcescibilem* ("unfading") for ἀμαράντινον at 1 Peter 5:4, or *cottidianum* ("daily") for ἐπιούσιον at Matthew 6:11 and Luke 11:3. Patterns of apparently spontaneous variation are also widely attested. For example, ὁ λίθος ("stone") is rendered by *lapis* throughout Matthew, yet at Matthew 27:60 all Latin translations use *saxum* to refer to the stone which, six verses later, is once again rendered by *lapis*. The omissive nature of the earliest version, with certain words or phrases left out (especially if they appeared to be redundant), has already been mentioned above: it is more difficult to explain the introduction of paraphrases into later texts than their removal in favor of a Latin form that corresponds more closely to a Greek source.

Although comparison with Greek undoubtedly played a part in revisions of the Latin biblical text, such as the insertion of omitted phrases or the replacement of paraphrases, most of the differences between surviving Old Latin versions reflect internal linguistic considerations. An ongoing process of adjusting the Latin translation in order to replace words felt to be outdated, quaint, or inapposite; to "correct" constructions that did not correspond to current usage; and to introduce consistency within and between biblical books, accounts for much of the variation to be found in Old Latin tradition. The choice of Latin rendering for the same underlying Greek word has led to the differentiation of textual forms according to their "translation coloring" (*Übersetzungsfarbe*; see Burton 2000; Vogels 1928). The earliest texts usually render the Greek words for "commandment," "disciple," "light," "people," and "word" by *mandatum, discens, lumen, plebs*, and *sermo*, while later forms prefer *praeceptum, discipulus, lux, populus*, and *uerbum* (further examples in Houghton 2020: 24–25). The first set of renderings are normally present in the biblical quotations of Christian writers in North Africa. They do not represent a Latin dialect peculiar to Africa but, rather, reflect the probable origin of the Latin translation: later authors throughout the Roman Empire cite biblical verses in this wording without demur, yet different sets of Latin renderings are preferred and become established in subsequent versions. In several cases, there may be three or more possible renderings of the same Greek word, such as *clarificare*, *magnificare*, and *glorificare* for "glorify" (δοξάζειν) or *diuersorium*, *hospitium*, and *refectio* for "inn" (κατάλυμα).

The geographical distribution of the attestation of certain renderings has led to the association of textual forms with particular locations (see the section "Old Latin Text-Types"). There is some support for this in antiquity: in a famous passage, Augustine states his preference for a translation of the Old Testament associated with North Italy (which he calls *Itala*), and elsewhere refers to African witnesses (*Afra*).[10] The former gave rise to the custom of using the term *Itala* to refer to all Old Latin versions, which has rightly been abandoned. The practice of dividing Old Latin texts into "African," "Italian," and sometimes also "European" still has currency, although it can be difficult to maintain: while the earliest African evidence tends to reflect the most ancient Latin form, text-forms found in later African authors are often more widespread (e.g., in Spain or Sardinia), and Augustine's comment demonstrates that different versions were available across the Mediterranean by the end of the fourth century. It is therefore important to combine geographical labels with chronological indications, as well as recognizing that the attestation of different versions may not be the same as their origin.

The variation between different terms in the revisions of the Old Latin Bible reflects the process of the establishment of specialist vocabulary in early Latin Christianity (see further chap. 28). As noted above, early translators frequently offered a Latin rendering for a technical term which was later replaced by a Greek borrowing. Thus the initial rendering of παραβολή ("parable") was *similitudo*, which later gave way to *parabola*. Similarly, παράκλητος ("paraclete") appears first as *aduocatus* and then as *paracletus*. Elsewhere, the alternation is between two Latin renderings, such as *bene sentire* and *complacere* for "approve" (εὐδοκέω) or *nequam* and *malus* for "evil" (πονηρός). Sometimes, the sense of an existing word was extended to cover a Christian usage, perhaps on a model in Greek: one such example is *salus*, which originally just signified "health" or "safety" but also took on the meaning of "salvation" (like the Greek σωτηρία). In certain cases, there may be a theological or societal significance to lexical choices, with a preference for terms that marked Christianity out as a new development rather than one in continuity with other religious practice. For example, the classical Latin word for "temple" *fanum*, is restricted to pagan temples, whereas *templum* is used both in this sense (e.g., 1 Kings 16:32, 2 Kings 5:18) and, principally, for the Jewish temple. Despite references in early Christian writers to *sermo noster* ("our discourse"), attempts during the twentieth century to identify a special form of language (*Sondersprache*) that was peculiar to Christian communities have not resulted in wide acceptance. Although

---

[10] *De doctrina christiana* 2.15.22; *Retractationes* 1.21. On *Itala*, see also Burton 2000: 5–6.

"Christian Latin" is often characterized by particular theological and ecclesiastical vocabulary and its use or imitation of phrases from the Latin Bible, it is an overstatement to
describe this as a separate form of language (Fredouille 1996).

Revision of the Latin Bible continued throughout the fourth and fifth centuries. Some
alterations will have taken the form of punctual adjustments (perhaps based on comparison with Greek), or the emendation of a particular passage; others may have been more
extensive. The creation of a series of textual divisions, accompanied by a set of chapter
titles (*capitula*), is indicative of a new edition of a biblical book: although these are
rarely attested in the oldest surviving manuscripts, multiple forms have been preserved
which are based on Old Latin texts. Evidence for a fourth-century Donatist edition of
the Bible is seen in *capitula* reflecting the theology of this group, as well as other scriptural paratexts known as the *Compendium*, which includes stichometric indications
of the length of each book, a collection of prophecies, and lists of Hebrew names and
their interpretation (Rouse and McNelis 2000). Augustine's concern for obtaining high-
quality scriptural texts is clear in the second book of *De doctrina christiana*: when he
learned of Jerome's revision of the Septuagint, he was keen to acquire copies, and wrote
to Jerome expressing approbation of his work on the text of the Gospels.[11] However, the
story Augustine relates about the riot in the church at Oea when Jerome's new translation of Jonah was read during the liturgy, introducing the detail that Jonah sheltered
under some ivy (*hedera*) rather than a gourd (*cucurbita*), shows that biblical revisions
were not always well received. Another example of fourth-century conservatism is seen
in the preference expressed by the anonymous writer known as Ambrosiaster for the
earliest Latin translations, hallowed by the usage of Tertullian, Victorinus of Poetovio,
and Cyprian, rather than those based on contemporary Greek texts.[12] It is therefore
not surprising that Old Latin texts were still copied and used for several hundred years.
Moreover, readings from the earlier version continued to be present in the biblical text
of Christian communities on the geographical or ecclesiastical margins, such as Ireland,
Mozarabic Spain, and the Cathars in Languedoc (see Houghton 2016: 96–104).

Old Latin Text-Types

Given the scarcity of material for much of the Old Latin Bible, the practice followed in
the *Vetus Latina* edition is to group the surviving evidence into a series of text-types in
addition to citing individual witnesses in the apparatus (see further chap. 24). Such editorial reconstructions are not without problems (e.g., Burton 2013: 184–86), but they
provide a relatively straightforward means of indicating how the extant sources may be
located within the broader tradition despite its incomplete preservation. Texts from later
revisions are normally more extensively preserved, meaning that whereas the earliest

[11] *Epistula* 71 (which also relates the story of the congregation at Oea) and *Epistula* 82; see also *Epistula*
28 (Houghton 2008: 10–13).
[12] *Commentary on Romans* 5.14 (see Houghton 2016: 25–26).

translations may often no longer be attainable, it remains possible to identify differing Old Latin forms which circulated in particular contexts. Although early Christian writers are the principal sources for identifying the circulation of textual forms, it should be remembered that one writer can attest to multiple types, deriving from the manuscripts available to them. The text-types not only reflect the attestation of the surviving evidence but also, ideally, represent stages at which a substantial revision was carried out by an editor, whether that was based on comparison with Greek or purely internal criteria. Where textual forms cannot be distinguished, or the tradition is invariant, the Latin version is sometimes simply described as **Type L** (e.g., Ruth, for which the sole Old Latin text is that of the tenth-century Codex Complutensis Primus [VL 109]).

Early witnesses that stand outside a fixed Latin translation are indicated by **Type X**. These are usually biblical quotations which appear to have been translated ad hoc from a Greek Bible. The author most regularly indicated in this way is Tertullian, although there are Latin versions of Greek writings in which biblical material was translated as part of the main text, such as Irenaeus of Lyons's *Aduersus Haereses*, or Theodore of Mopsuestia's commentary on the Pauline Epistles.[13] The citations of Genesis in the early Latin form of the Book of Jubilees and Pseudo-Philo are classified in this way, as is Jerome's text of 2 Peter (identified as a direct translation from Greek). In 1 Esdras, Type X represents the anonymous Donatist *Liber genealogus*, preserving traces of a different translation to the rest of the extant tradition. **Type Y** is another siglum for early evidence not connected to a written Latin version: it is used in Revelation for specific readings in the biblical text of the commentary of Victorinus of Poetovio, who cites very loosely and also made reference to Greek.

The most ancient translation is normally designated **Type K**, although in 1 Esdras a form of text identified as the initial translation (*Urübersetzung*) is classified as **Type U** (VL 129). Type K is attested primarily in the writings of Cyprian (the German for Carthage is *Karthago*), which display a consistency of text and translation style consistent with a written version. It is also found in Codex Bobiensis (VL 1; parts of Matthew and Mark) and the Fleury Palimpsest (VL 55; Acts and Revelation). There are other early African witnesses to this text, including the body of writings pseudonymously attributed to Cyprian, and a set of lengthy gospel *capitula* from the third century. A revision of this text used by later African writers is known as **Type C**. Its sources include Optatus of Milevis, Quodvultdeus, and Augustine's Donatist opponents. In 1 John, it indicates the citations of the Donatist Tyconius, while it is attested by Augustine himself in his early writings on Genesis as well as in Judith. Type C in Revelation is the lemma text of the sixth-century African commentator Primasius of Hadrumetum. This form is present in Codex Palatinus (VL 2; Gospels) even though it is believed to have been copied in North Italy.

Type D usually indicates an early European revision of the initial translation, often associated with the older Greek-Latin bilingual manuscripts, although in the Gospels the

---

[13] A summary of scholarship on the biblical texts available to Tertullian is provided by Dunn (2020: 87–91), who concludes that he used a variety of sources to suit his argument.

principal witness is Codex Vercellensis (VL 3). The main patristic source for this form is Lucifer of Cagliari, the fourth-century bishop of the capital of Sardinia. It is also found in the lemma text of the contemporary "Anonymous Budapest" commentary on Paul (VL 89) and Gregory of Elvira's commentary on the Song of Songs. In the Wisdom of Solomon and Ecclesiasticus, it is attested by the Old Latin *testimonia* collection known as the *Liber de diuinis scripturis* (Pseudo-Augustine *Speculum*). The significance of Type D is different in Revelation, where it is used occasionally for Old Latin readings in the mixed text of the ninth-century Book of Armagh (VL 61, *D*). **Type E** is used as a generic description for multiple European forms in the volumes on Genesis and Isaiah.

The majority of surviving Old Latin witnesses have a text corresponding to **Type I**. This was current in North Italy from the late third century, although its readings are often present in biblical citations by Novatian, an Italian contemporary of Cyprian. This widespread form may reasonably be identified with Augustine's *Itala*, and seems to have been the basis for the revision of the New Testament incorporated into the Vulgate. It occurs in sources such as Marius Victorinus, the anonymous Ambrosiaster, Jerome, Filastrius of Brescia, Ambrose of Milan, and the three writers from Aquileia (Fortunatianus, Rufinus, and Chromatius), as well as the more distant Hilary of Poitiers. Surviving Old Latin manuscripts with this form include several copied in North Italy in the fifth century (see above), as well as some much later productions (VL 123 in Judith and Esther, Codex Gigas [VL 51] in Acts and Revelation). A series of subtypes are constituted by readings peculiar to individual witnesses. These include **Type J** (readings in Codex Veronensis of the gospels), **Type R** (forms unique to Lucifer of Cagliari), and **Type M** (a text typical of the area around Milan, including the citations of Ambrose). In Esther and Judith, however, Type R is the earliest surviving text, preserved in VL 130, 151, and 155 as well as the *testimonia* in the *Liber de diuinis scripturis*. As his observations on the text make clear, Augustine had access to multiple biblical manuscripts with differing affiliations: where his text is not paralleled by another type, it is indicated as **Type A**.

Several other fourth-century text-types are reconstructed in certain books. The most frequent is **Type S**, associated with Spanish writers such as Gregory of Elvira as well as late African sources. This connection is unsurprising given that many North African Christians took refuge in Spain in the fifth and sixth centuries, some of them even founding monasteries there (Houghton 2016: 62). Type S is found in Spanish manuscripts of the Vulgate (e.g., VL 67), sometimes in the form of marginal glosses (VL 91–96). In Genesis, it is attested by VL 100 and 101. It is also the form of the lemma text of Tyconius's commentary on Revelation, although this is mediated through the reworking by Beatus of Liébana. **Type T** also has some Spanish connections. This is a widely circulating text which appears to be another revision of Type I made around the same time as the Vulgate. In the Catholic Epistles, it is transmitted in the Fleury Palimpsest (VL 55) and the Spanish supplementary pages to the Freising Fragments (VL 64), as well as VL 32, VL 65, and VL 67. **Type F** is the text of James in VL 66, which appears to represent a revision made in Rome around the year 400. A text of similar origin for Esther, Judith, and Tobit is found in VL 109 and the citations of Ambrosiaster: this may have been produced in a Jewish context. **Type G**, only reconstructed in James, is constituted by Old Latin readings in pre-Carolingian Gaul.

Jerome's revision of a Latin version of the Septuagint, based on Origen's Hexapla, is identified as **Type O** (from the Greek numeral for seventy). **Type H** indicates his translation from Hebrew. The Vulgate text of other books is presented as **Type V**. In the Wisdom of Solomon and Ecclesiasticus (Sirach), Type V is the earliest surviving text (with the exception of a few citations of Type K), preceding Types D and I. In 1 Esdras, it was thought to be the oldest version until the discovery of Type U, of which it is a revision.[14]

EDITIONS AND SCHOLARSHIP

The only complete edition of the Old Latin Bible to have been published is that of Pierre Sabatier in the eighteenth century, which is now largely outdated.[15] Since the middle of the twentieth century, the Vetus Latina Institute in Beuron has been engaged on a comprehensive edition of the surviving Old Latin material, conceived as a "new Sabatier" (see chap. 24). The volumes which have so far appeared are:

1.	*Register/Repertorium* (Gryson 1999–2004, 2007)
2.	Genesis (Fischer 1951–54)
4/5.	Ruth (Gesche 2005)
6/2.	1 Esdras (Gesche 2008–16)
7/2.	Judith (Bogaert & Haelewyck 2001–2020)
7/3.	Esther (Haelewyck 2003–8)
10/3.	Song of Songs (Introduction only: Schulz-Flügel 1992)
11/1.	Wisdom of Solomon (Thiele 1977–1985)
11/2.	Ecclesiasticus [Sirach] (Ch. 1–28: Thiele 1987–2005, Forte 2014–21)
12.	Isaiah (Gryson 1987–97)
14/1.	Daniel (Haelewyck 2021)
17.	Mark (Haelewyck 2013–18)
19.	John (Ch. 1–9: Burton, Houghton, MacLachlan, and Parker 2011–13)
21.	Romans (Introduction only: Eymann 1996)
22.	1 Corinthians (Introduction only: Fröhlich 1995–98)
24.	Ephesians, Philippians, Colossians (Frede 1962–4, 1966–71)
25.	Thessalonians, Timothy, Titus, Philemon, Hebrews (Frede 1975–82, 1983–91)
26/1.	Catholic Epistles (Thiele 1956–69)
26/2.	Revelation (Gryson 2000–3).

---

[14] For an example and discussion of the different Latin text-types reconstructed at Genesis 3:17, see chap. 2; an account of the Old Latin evidence for each section of the New Testament is provided in Houghton 2016: 154–83.

[15] Petrus Sabatier, ed., *Bibliorum Sacrorum Latinae versiones antiquae* (3 vols., Rheims: Florentain, 1743–49); see further chap. 23.

Material gathered for the remaining books is available online in the *Vetus Latina Database*, with other sites for Acts and the Pauline Epistles.[16] The edition of gospel manuscripts by Jülicher, Matzkow, and Aland (1963–76) is still useful for the portions which have not yet appeared in the *Vetus Latina* edition. Many of the editions of individual manuscripts produced in the late nineteenth and early twentieth centuries as part of the *Oxford Old Latin Biblical Texts*, the *Collectanea Biblica Latina*, and the Beuron *Texte und Arbeiten* series continue to be important: Old Latin evidence based on these is presented in the apparatus of the major Vulgate editions (the Roman Vulgate for the Old Testament and the Oxford Vulgate for the New Testament; see further chap. 23). The *Vetus Latina Hispana* project (Ayuso Marazuela 1953–67) produced editions of Spanish witnesses for the Psalter and the Octateuch. More recent Spanish scholarship has focused on the marginal glosses of the Old Testament, especially in the historical books (see chap. 2). Studies of Latin biblical texts continue to appear in the series *Aus der Geschichte der lateinischen Bibel* (AGLB) and the *Revue bénédictine*, which also provides a list of recent publications on the Latin Bible (the biennial *Bulletin de la Bible latine*). Much work remains to be done in order to complete the *Vetus Latina* edition and come to a fuller understanding of the history and significance of the earliest Latin translations, but it is to be hoped that the impetus and assistance provided by computer tools and digital resources will stimulate new research and discoveries in this rich field of study.

BIBLIOGRAPHY

Ayuso Marazuela, Teófilo. 1953–67. *La Vetus Latina Hispana*. 3 vols. Madrid: CSIC.

Billen, A. V. (1927). *The Old Latin Texts of the Heptateuch*. Cambridge: Cambridge University Press.

Bogaert, Pierre-Maurice. 2012. "The Latin Bible, c. 600 to c. 900." In *New Cambridge History of the Bible: Vol. 2. From 600 to 1450*, edited by Richard Marsden and E. Ann Matter, 69–92. Cambridge: Cambridge University Press.

Bogaert, Pierre-Maurice. 2013. "The Latin Bible." In *New Cambridge History of the Bible: Vol. 1. From the Beginnings to 600*, edited by James Carleton Paget and Joachim Schaper, 505–26. Cambridge: Cambridge University Press.

Bogaert, Pierre-Maurice, and Jean-Claude Haelewyck, eds. 2001–20. *Judith*. VL 7/2. Freiburg, Germany: Herder.

Burton, Philip H. 2000. *The Old Latin Gospels. A Study of their Texts and Language*. Oxford: Oxford University Press.

Burton, Philip H. 2013. "The Latin Version of the New Testament." In *The Text of the New Testament in Contemporary Research*, edited by Bart D. Ehrman and Michael W. Holmes, 167–200. 2nd ed. NTTSD 42. Leiden: Brill.

Burton, Philip H., H. A. G. Houghton, R. F. MacLachlan, and D. C. Parker, eds. 2011–13. *Evangelium secundum Iohannem*. VL 19. Freiburg: Herder.

---

[16] <https://brepolis.net/vld> (subscription required); material for Acts is presented at <https://nttf.klassphil.uni-mainz.de/> and for Romans to Galatians at <www.epistulae.org/XML/compaul.xml>; see also <www.iohannes.com/vetuslatina> for John.

Dunn, Geoffrey D. 2020. "Scripture in Tertullian's Polemical and Apologetic Treatises." In *The Bible in Christian North Africa. Part 1: Commencement to the Confessiones of Augustine (ca. 180 to 400 CE)*, edited by Jonathan P. Yates and Anthony Dupont, 80–99. Handbooks of the Bible and Its Reception 4/1. Berlin: De Gruyter.

Eymann, Hugo, ed. 1996. *Epistula ad Romanos* (Einleitung). VL 21. Freiburg: Herder.

Fischer, Bonifatius, ed. 1951–54. *Genesis*. VL 2. Freiburg: Herder.

Forte, Anthony J., ed. 2014–21. *Sirach: pars altera*. VL 11/2. Freiburg: Herder.

Frede, Hermann Josef, ed. 1962–64. *Epistula ad Ephesios*. VL 24/1. Freiburg: Herder.

Frede, Hermann Josef, ed. 1966–71. *Epistulae ad Philippenses et ad Colossenses*. VL 24/2. Freiburg: Herder.

Frede, Hermann Josef, ed. 1975–82. *Epistulae ad Thessalonicenses, Timotheum*. VL 25/1. Freiburg: Herder.

Frede, Hermann Josef, ed. 1983–91. *Epistulae ad Titum, Philemonem, Hebraeos*. VL 25/2. Freiburg: Herder.

Fredouille, Jean-Claude. 1996. "'Latin chrétien' ou 'latin tardif'?" *Recherches augustinennes* 29: 5–23.

Fröhlich, Uwe, ed. 1995–98. *Epistula ad Corinthios 1* (Einleitung). VL 22. Freiburg: Herder.

Gesche, Bonifatia, ed. 2005. *Ruth*. VL 4/5. Freiburg: Herder.

Gesche, Bonifatia, ed. 2008–16. *Esra I*. VL 6/2. Freiburg: Herder.

Gryson, Roger, ed. 1987–97. *Esaias*. VL 12; Freiburg: Herder.

Gryson, Roger. 1999–2004. *Altlateinische Handschriften/Manuscrits vieux latins*. 2 vols. VL 1/2. Freiburg: Herder.

Gryson, Roger, ed. 2000–3. *Apocalypsis Iohannis*. Vetus Latina 26/2. Freiburg: Herder.

Gryson, Roger. 2007. *Répertoire général des auteurs ecclésiastiques latins de l'antiquité et du haut moyen-âge*. 5th ed. 2 vols. VL 1/1. Freiburg: Herder.

Haelewyck, Jean-Claude, ed. 2003–8. *Hester*. VL 7/3. Freiburg: Herder.

Haelewyck, Jean-Claude, ed. 2013–18. *Evangelium secundum Marcum*. VL 17. Freiburg: Herder.

Haelewyck, Jean-Claude, ed. 2021. *Danihel*. VL 14/1. Freiburg: Herder.

Houghton, H. A. G. 2008. *Augustine's Text of John. Patristic Citations and Latin Gospel Manuscripts*. Oxford: Oxford University Press.

Houghton, H. A. G. 2013. "Patristic Evidence in the New Edition of the Vetus Latina Iohannes." In *Biblical Quotations in Patristic Texts*, edited by Laurence Mellerin, H. A. G. Houghton, and Markus Vinzent, 69–85. Studia Patristica 54. Leuven: Peeters.

Houghton, H. A. G. 2014. "The Biblical Text of Jerome's Commentary on Galatians." *Journal of Theological Studies* 65, no. 1: 1–24.

Houghton, H. A. G. 2016. *The Latin New Testament: A Guide to Its Early History, Texts, and Manuscripts*. Oxford: Oxford University Press.

Houghton, H. A. G. 2017. "The Layout of Early Latin Commentaries on the Pauline Epistles and their Oldest Manuscripts." In *Studia Patristica vol. XCI: Including Papers Presented at the Seventeenth International Patristics Conference*, edited by Markus Vinzent, 71–112. Leuven: Peeters.

Houghton, H. A. G. 2020. "Scripture and Latin Christian Manuscripts from North Africa." In *The Bible in Christian North Africa. Part 1: Commencement to the Confessiones of Augustine (ca. 180 to 400 CE)*, edited by Jonathan P. Yates and Anthony Dupont, 15–50. Handbooks of the Bible and Its Reception 4/1. Berlin: De Gruyter.

Jülicher, Adolf, Walter Matzkow, and Kurt Aland, eds. 1963–76. *Itala. Das Neue Testament in altlateinischer Überlieferung*. 4 vols. 2nd ed. (Matthew–Luke). Berlin: De Gruyter.

Kedar, Benjamin. 1988. "The Latin Translations." In *Mikra: Text, Translation, Reading and Interpretation of the Hebrew Bible in Ancient Judaism and Early Christianity*, edited by Martin Jan Mulder and Harry Sysling, 299–338. Assen: Van Gorcum.

Kraus, Matthew. 2003. "Hebraisms in the Old Latin Version of the Bible." *Vetus Testamentum* 53: 487–513.

Rouse, Richard H., and Charles McNelis. 2000. "North African Literary Activity: A Cyprian Fragment, the Stichometric Lists and a Donatist Compendium." *Revue d'Histoire des Textes* 30: 189–238.

Schulz-Flügel, Eva, ed. 1992. *Canticum canticorum* (Einleitung). VL 10/3. Freiburg: Herder.

Thiele, Walter, ed. 1956–69. *Epistulae Catholicae*. VL 26/1. Freiburg: Herder.

Thiele, Walter, ed. 1977–85. *Sapientia Salomonis*. VL 11/1. Freiburg: Herder.

Thiele, Walter, ed. 1987–2005. *Sirach: pars prima*. VL 11/2. Freiburg: Herder.

Vogels, Heinrich Joseph. 1928. "Übersetzungsfarbe als Hilfsmittel zur Erforschung der neutestamentlichen Textgeschichte." *Revue bénédictine* 40: 123–29.

Yates, Jonathan P., and Anthony Dupont, eds. 2020. *The Bible in Christian North Africa. Part 1: Commencement to the Confessiones of Augustine (ca. 180 to 400 CE)*. Handbooks of the Bible and Its Reception 4/1. Berlin: De Gruyter.

CHAPTER 2

THE LATIN BIBLE AND THE SEPTUAGINT

JOSÉ MANUEL CAÑAS REÍLLO

THE *VETUS LATINA* AS A VERSION OF THE SEPTUAGINT

SECONDARY versions, the old translations of the Septuagint into other languages such as Latin, Coptic, Armenian, Georgian, Ethiopic, Syriac, and Arabic, have great relevance for the textual criticism of the Old Testament (Cañas Reíllo 2021: 132–33).[1] Among these, textual criticism gives preference to the *Vetus Latina*. It is the oldest translation of the Septuagint into another language. Tertullian's quotations bear witness to its existence at the end of the second century, and Cyprian of Carthage's writings attest that in the middle of the third century there was a complete Latin Bible in North Africa. As a translation, the *Vetus Latina* is a faithful and literal version of the Greek Bible, in which each Greek word has its Latin correspondence. Even the word order of the Greek *Vorlage* has been kept in the Latin translation. Both languages, Greek and Latin, are very close to each other: they share an Indo-European origin and grammatical categories which make it possible to translate almost every peculiarity of the Greek language into Latin (Ulrich 1985: 76–80).

Latin Bibles from the third to the fifth centuries shaped their canon and book order on the model of the Septuagint—that is, the Alexandrian canon, which is broader and

---

[1] Greek manuscripts are cited with the abbreviation LXX followed by the siglum in Rahlfs (1914) and Rahlfs–Fraenkel (2004), e.g., LXX^A = Codex Alexandrinus; for more than one manuscript or text-type, a simplified abbreviation is used, for example LXX^{LO} = LXX^L (Lucianic recension) and LXX^O (Origen's Hexaplaric text). Latin manuscripts are cited using the *Vetus Latina* sigla (Gryson 1999).

more inclusive than the Hebrew Bible.[2] The Latin canon included the greater part of the deuterocanonical books, for instance Tobit, Judith, the Greek additions to Esther, 1–2 Maccabees, Wisdom of Solomon, Ecclesiasticus (Sirach), Baruch, the Letter of Jeremiah and the Greek additions to Daniel; it also included some of the apocryphal texts of the Septuagint, such as the Prayer of Manasseh and Psalm 151, but not 3–4 Maccabees and the Psalms of Solomon (see chap. 7). The *Vetus Latina* also reproduces the sequence of books in the Septuagint, as opposed to the Hebrew Bible (Trebolle Barrera 2016: 319).

For most books, it appears that there was a unique original translation into Latin. However, the evidence attested in manuscripts and quotations by the Church Fathers is rich and varied, for the texts were subjected to revisions in two ways:

1. Accommodation to a Greek text, because the Septuagint was the authoritative text for the Latin Bible. However, the Greek text also had its own revisions, and they left traces in the Latin Bible.
2. Linguistic revision, because the language of the oldest Latin translation was tinged with popular elements of spoken Latin, and with Hellenisms and Semitisms. There was thus a tendency to bring its language to a normative Latin, removing popular influence and Semitic traces as much as possible.

Quotations by the Church Fathers permit the stratification of the biblical text from the point of view of chronology and of geography of the variety resulting from these processes. In this way, it is easy to follow the evolution of the *Vetus Latina* from the mid-third century to the sixth century, when it began to be supplanted by Jerome's translations.

The purpose of the editions of the Vetus Latina Institute of Beuron (see chap. 24) is to provide not only a critical edition of texts but also their evolution in relation to the Greek tradition. Taking as an example the book of Genesis (Fischer 1951–54), several text-types are distinguished (see also chap. 1):

K = The oldest text (Carthage, mid-third century).
C = An African text (late third century).
E = European text, with the following subtypes:
S = Late African text used in Spain.
I = Italian text (fourth/fifth century).
A = Revised text (Augustine).
M = Revised text (Ambrose of Milan).
O = Hexaplaric text.
P = Text influenced by the Hexaplaric edition and by the Vulgate
X = Remains of an old Latin translation of the *Libri Iubilaeorum* (*Parva Genesis*).
H = Jerome's translation.

---

[2] For the additional material (known as "plusses") in the Septuagint compared to the Masoretic Text and divergences in their canons, see Lust (2003: 44–48).

Not all these text-types are attested in the whole book of Genesis. At the most, there is material for two or three textual types in any one verse. Genesis 3:17 offers an illustration of the evolution of *Vetus Latina* texts:[3]

LXX ἐν λύπαις φάγῃ αὐτὴν πάσας τὰς ἡμέρας
   K *in tristitia et gemitu edes ex ea omnibus diebus*
   E *in maeroribus manducabis eam omnes dies*
   H *in laboribus comedes ex ea cunctis diebus*

Leaving aside the H-text, differences are evident in K and E in accordance with the tendencies mentioned above:

1. Regarding linguistic change, the use of different Latin words for the same Greek word is observed. For λύπη, "pain," "grief," "sadness," K has *tristitia et gemitu* attested from the third century (Cyprian of Carthage). However, *gemitus* is the Latin word for στεναγμός in the previous verse. E has *maeror* (Ambrosiaster), but *tristitia* (Augustine) and *dolor* (Hilary of Poitiers) are also attested. The verb ἐσθίω is translated by *edo* in the oldest text (K) but by *manduco* in E; H has *comedo*. K has *ex ea* for αὐτήν, attested in Cyprian of Carthage, which survives in later periods, even in H, although variant readings are attested: *ex illa* (Pseudo-Augustine), *eam* (E) and *illam* (Augustine).

2. Regarding accommodation to the Greek text, there is just one case of difference in Latin which might be explained as arising in this way. The Greek λύπαις corresponds to *maeroribus, tristitiis,* and *doloribus,* while *tristitia et gemitu* (K) depends on a singular (as in Armenian and Coptic). A singular form is also attested in Theodotion (μετὰ μόχθου).

The schema of text-types can differ from book to book. For instance, in 1 Esdras, Gesche (2008–16: 25) reconstructed four text-types:

U = Oldest Latin text used in Europe.
V = Revision of U.
I = Early revision of U.
X = Text not very close to an unspecified African text.

For Ruth, only three text-types are found (Gesche 2005: 33):

L = Old Latin text in Codex Complutensis Primus (VL 109).
M = Ambrose of Milan's quotations.
H = Jerome's translation.

---

[3] For the Greek text and its variant readings, see Wevers (1974).

This shows how editors are dependent on the extant evidence, which is often very slim, to reconstruct the textual history of the earliest Latin version.

The Septuagint continued to influence the Latin Bible beyond the living period of the *Vetus Latina*, through Jerome's translation and the medieval tradition of the Latin Bible in its Vulgate edition. Jerome initially made a revision of the *Vetus Latina* version based on the Septuagint Psalter, which could perhaps be identified with the Roman Psalter (Graves 2017: 279; see further chap. 5). The second step was the revision of *Vetus Latina* texts according to Origen's Hexaplaric edition, described below. In a third step Jerome made a new Latin translation from the *Hebraica ueritas* ("Hebrew truth"), which refers not only to the Hebrew text and the Jewish exegetical tradition but also to the versions of the three Jewish translators Aquila (α'), Symmachus (σ'), and Theodotion (θ') that Jerome found in Origen's Hexapla. Jerome also translated books and sections of the Septuagint that are not part of the Masoretic Text. Examples of this include the books of Judith, Tobit, and the Greek additions to Esther and to Daniel, the last two with the obeli taken from Origen's Hexapla (see below). In the canon and sequence of books, the influence of the Septuagint is obvious in the Latin Bibles of the Middle Ages and in the Vulgate edition.

Vetus Latina, Septuagint, and Qumran: Problems of Textual Criticism

The manuscript tradition of the Septuagint is relatively late compared to the chronological period covered by its textual history, from the oldest translation from Hebrew until the period of the major Greek majuscule codices. The oldest Greek manuscripts were copied in the fourth and fifth centuries, but the evidence of papyri and fragments prior to this time shows that the textual tradition was richer and broader. Each book of the Septuagint poses a particular problem of textual criticism. There are books translated from a Hebrew *Vorlage* in different periods and with different translation techniques; for other books, the original text was written in Greek. In consequence, chronology, language, and textual history differ from one to another.

The textual criticism of the Septuagint aims to reconstruct the oldest Greek text, that is, the Old Greek (often indicated as "OG"), so called to differentiate it from later strata of the Greek textual tradition. The task of reaching the Old Greek is arduous. From its early stages, it was revised following two tendencies. One is the accommodation to a Hebrew text that may have differed from the Hebrew *Vorlage* of the Old Greek. For instance, the Greek Pentateuch is a translation from a Hebrew *Vorlage* very close to the Dead Sea Scrolls, but later revisions used a Hebrew text close to the Masoretic Text as reference. The other is the linguistic and stylistic improvement to bring the text up to date with linguistic changes that occurred after the initial translation. Both trends of change are inseparable, as is shown in the Greek manuscripts of the main revisions (Lucianic, Hexaplaric, Kaige: see below).

The distinction between "pre-Hexaplaric" and "Hexaplaric" is of primary importance to evaluate the role of the *Vetus Latina* in Septuagint textual criticism. At the beginning of the third century, Origen of Alexandria undertook the most important and influential edition of the Bible, known as the Hexapla. It comprised six different texts arranged in six columns: the Hebrew text, its transliteration into Greek, the translations of Aquila and Symmachus, Origen's edition of the Septuagint (Hexaplaric Greek or *Quinta*), and Theodotion's translation. In the post-Hexapla period, Origen's Greek edition contaminated almost all branches of the Septuagint textual tradition. For textual criticism this distinction is a crucial point: pre-Hexaplaric stages are closer to the Old Greek, while Hexaplaric stages show influence from Origen's edition. The first step in reaching the Old Greek is therefore to detect pre-Hexaplaric stages within the Greek tradition.

An internal analysis of the texts offers a reverse way to reach the Old Greek text prior to the influence of revisions. However, the Greek manuscripts are not enough in this endeavor; external comparisons are needed, and in this the *Vetus Latina* is fundamental in accessing early stages of the Septuagint (i.e., pre-Hexaplaric strata), for the reasons already mentioned concerning its early chronology, its extraordinary fidelity to the Greek text, and its evolution. The value of the *Vetus Latina* in the textual criticism of the Septuagint varies from book to book. It is conditioned by the quality and quantity of Latin witnesses, by their textual history, and by their relationship with the Greek textual tradition. The place of each book in the canon is also a factor to take into account. The *Vetus Latina* text is fragmentarily preserved in the books that are part of the Hebrew Bible, because Jerome's translations gradually displaced them from the sixth century onward. But Jerome did not translate the books outside the Hebrew canon; in consequence, the old texts of the *Vetus Latina* were not displaced and they were part of the Latin Bibles of the Middle Ages. Thus, for Wisdom, Eccesiasticus, Baruch, 1–2 Maccabees, and other books, the *Vetus Latina* evidence is rich and pluriform, and complete books have been preserved in more than one text-type.

The *Vetus Latina* also makes it possible to go back in time to the moment of translation of the Bible from Hebrew into Greek. Before the discovery of the Dead Sea Scrolls, text-critical studies of the Septuagint had as their sole reference point the Masoretic Text, which shows great uniformity and is only transmitted in manuscripts of the Middle Ages: it is a standardized text. As the Septuagint is a literal translation of the Hebrew text older than the Hebrew extant manuscripts, its testimony might allow one to reach stages of the Hebrew text that are older than the Masoretic Text. For Greek books that are close to Masoretic Text, this is relatively straightforward, but in other books there is a striking lack of symmetry between the Septuagint and the Masoretic Text that could be explained by a free translation or a nonextant Hebrew *Vorlage*. For example, Greek Jeremiah is shorter than the Masoretic Text and in other books it has a sequence of chapters that differs from the Masoretic Text.

The discovery of the Dead Sea Scrolls in 1947 brought about the greatest revolution in history for biblical textual criticism. Its consequences affected not only the Hebrew Bible but also the Septuagint and the secondary versions (see Tov 2012: 4–13;

Fernández Marcos 1998a: 82–83). Since the Dead Sea Scrolls date from the period 250 BCE–68 CE, they are older than the Masoretic Text and the Septuagint manuscripts. They show that in pre-Christian times, the Hebrew text was not standardized, that different editions of some books were known, and that there were differences from the Masoretic Text. The relevance for the textual criticism of the Septuagint lies in its similarity to the Dead Sea Scrolls and not to the Masoretic Text. As the *Vetus Latina* is a faithful translation of the Septuagint, it is also an indirect piece of evidence related the Dead Sea Scrolls, and it can thus play an important role in the textual criticism of the Old Testament. However, the coincidence of the Septuagint with the Dead Sea Scrolls is not absolute. Three different levels of agreement can be established: close relationship, occasional agreements, and sporadic but significant agreements (Tov 2012: 6–13).

Five years later, in 1952, the discovery of scrolls in Nahal Hever copied in the first century CE also had a significant impact on textual criticism of the Septuagint. They preserved fragments of the books of Jonah, Micah, Nahum, Habakkuk, Zephaniah, and Zechariah with a revised Greek text closer to the Masoretic Text than the Septuagint (see Kreuzer 2018: 139–44; Fernández Marcos 1998b: 83–87). The revision is characterized by some recurrent literal translations, such as וְגַם / καί γε (which provides the name Kaige by which this revision is known), אָנֹכִי / ἐγώ εἰμί, אִישׁ / ἀνήρ for the expression of distributives, and אֵין / οὐκ ἔστι (Barthélemy 1963: 31–80). As later research has shown, the Kaige revision is only one aspect of a broad movement in pre-Christian times with the purpose of harmonizing the Greek text to a Hebrew *Vorlage* close to the Masoretic Text. Although Kaige research was initially based on the fragments of Nahal Hever, further examination has identified the following ways in which this tradition may be detected in the Septuagint:

- To explain similar Hebraizing tendencies (proto-Theodotion) detected by previous research in other books, for instance, in Lamentations, Ruth, Song of Songs, in the Theodotionic complements of Jeremiah and Job, in the *Quinta* (i.e., Origen's Septuagint edition in the Hexapla), and in the Psalter.
- To delimit the so-called Kaige sections in Samuel–Kings.[4]
- To explain the role of the Theodotionic text ($LXX^{\theta'}$) in the textual history of Daniel.
- To place the B-text in the textual history of LXX Judges, and especially to highlight its features (Fernández Marcos 2012).

In the same way, Kaige and proto-Theodotion have been fundamental to understanding how the Greek Jewish translators Aquila, Symmachus, and Theodotion fit into the Septuagint text tradition. Currently, the Kaige revision is one of the main topics in Septuagint research.

---

[4] See Barthélemy 1963: 46–47. The Kaige sections are βγ (2 Samuel 10:1–1 Kings 2:11) and γδ (1 Kings 22 and 2 Kings).

THE *VETUS LATINA* AS EVIDENCE FOR THE OLD GREEK

In the third century, *Vetus Latina* texts were in use in North Africa. This implies that its early stages offer an older witness than most of the Greek manuscripts. It therefore makes it possible to reach old strata of the Septuagint that are prior to the main Greek revisions, sometimes with the support of the Dead Sea Scrolls. The following examples show how the relationship of the Septuagint and the *Vetus Latina* in relation to the Dead Sea Scrolls and the Masoretic Text may be described in two ways: first, when the *Vetus Latina* is a witness of a lost Greek *Vorlage*; second, when the *Vetus Latina* is a witness to variant readings in Greek manuscripts (sometimes with the Dead Sea Scrolls) against the Masoretic Text.

The *Vetus Latina* as a Witness to a Lost Greek Vorlage

The *Vetus Latina* is especially striking when it bears witness to a Greek *Vorlage* which differs from the text of surviving Greek manuscripts. It has sometimes provided the basis for editorial conjectures in the Greek text, as in the case of 1–2 Maccabees. De Bruyne, who edited the Latin versions of these books in 1932, noted that some readings and omissions in them are not attested in extant Greek manuscripts. For instance, at 1 Maccabees 5:66, the Latin manuscripts VL 146, VL 109, VL 7 and VL 195 (text-types *L* and *B* in the edition) have *Marisan*, as found also in Josephus (Μάρισαν: *Antiquitates* XII.353). The reading attested by Greek manuscripts is Σαμαριαν, supported by the Latin Vulgate and two Syriac versions (SyI and SyII). De Bruyne explained the Latin reading as coming from a lost Greek text that had Μάρισαν, a conjecture adopted in the critical edition of the Septuagint text of 1 Maccabees (Kappler 1990).

Similarly, at 2 Maccabees 3:4, Greek manuscripts state that Simon, the captain of the Temple, was of the tribe of Benjamin: in consequence, he was neither a priest nor a Levite, which would have been a problem for exercising that role (De Bruyne 1932: X). De Bruyne conjectured *Balgea*, taking as the basis the variant readings *balcea* (VL 146), *belgaa* (VL 95), and Zohrab's edition of the Armenian. This name is attested in other Latin text-types, with small changes: *bargea* in X, *balgei* in B, and the doublets in M (*de tribu benjamin [de] balgei cognatione*) and P (*balgeus [e tribu] benjamin*) also attested in Armenian manuscripts *mgd*. In the Hebrew Bible, the name is found in Nehemiah 12:5–8, בִּלְגָּה, among the priestly families that had returned from captivity, as De Bruyne pointed out. In his 1976 edition of the Greek text of 2 Maccabees, Hanhart adopted the reading Βαλγεα based on this evidence.

Numerous examples of similar cases are found in the *Vetus Latina* and the Septuagint, as discussed by Trebolle Barrera (2016: 327). For instance, the Latin manuscript VL 104 differs from the Septuagint in Exodus 36–40, offering an older form of text; in Job, quotations in patristic writers attest a shorter text than the Masoretic Text, which is very close to the Old Greek; in Ezra-Nehemiah (Esdras B in the Septuagint) variant readings in the *Vetus Latina* are not attested in the Greek manuscripts. Among the deuterocanonical books, the *Vetus Latina* has the original order of Ecclesiasticus (Sirach), placing 33:13b–36:10 before 30:25–33:15a.

The *Vetus Latina* as a Witness to Greek Variants against the Masoretic Text

In other cases, the *Vetus Latina* supports variant readings in Greek manuscripts which have no correspondence with the Masoretic Text. Some of the best-known examples (discussed further in Trebolle Barrera 2015: 18, 2016: 327) are as follows:

- Deuteronomy: at 27:4, the Latin translation *in monte Garzin* of VL 100 is only attested in Greek by the Giessen fragment[5] (αρ γαρ[ι]ζιμ) and, in other versions, in the Samaritan Pentateuch. The remaining Greek manuscripts mostly have Γαιβάλ (= Masoretic Text עֵיבָל); see further Wevers (1995: 417).
- Ezekiel: Papyrus LXX[967] frequently has the support of Old Latin witnesses. VL 177 agrees with it against the Masoretic Text in the chapter sequence 38-39-37, which appears to be original, and the omission of Ezekiel 36:23c–28.
- Samuel and Jeremiah: 4QSam[a] and 4QJer[b.d] show text-types very close to the Hebrew *Vorlage* of the Septuagint. In Samuel the *Vetus Latina* supports a proto-Lucianic stage that differs from the Masoretic Text. Jeremiah 39(46):1–2 is absent from both VL 177 and the Septuagint, and both verses are marked with asterisks in Origen's edition. It is almost certain that these verses were neither in Old Greek Jeremiah nor in its Hebrew *Vorlage*. For more examples, see Bogaert (2013: 226–40).
- Daniel: Quodvultdeus's quoted text of this book has the same chapter arrangement as LXX[967] (1–4, 7–8, 5–6 and 9–12) with the sequence Daniel—Bel and the Dragon—Susanna.
- Esther: The Greek *Vorlage* (GrIII) of the *Vetus Latina* is the first and oldest Greek translation from Hebrew, prior to GrII (LXX[L]) and GrI (LXX). For further information, see Haelewyck (2003–8: 70–72).
- Judges: The Latin manuscript VL 100 (sometimes with Lucifer of Cagliari's quotations) supports the Lucianic revision attested in the Greek manuscripts LXX[54] [59 75 458 127 314 537 44 106 314 344] (see Cañas Reíllo 2020a: 549–50; Cañas Reíllo 2020b: 181–86), this stage being a pre-Hexaplaric text-type.[6] Also in Judges, 4QJudg[a], the

---

[5]   Giessen, Universitätsbibliothek, P. 13.19.22.26; fifth/sixth century; see Wevers (1977: 16).

[6]   The references to manuscripts of LXX Judges are based on the collations preserved at the *Septuaginta Unternehmen* in Göttingen. For classification and text-types, see Fernández Marcos (2011: 7*). For the value of secondary versions in the textual criticism of LXX Judges, see Cañas Reíllo (2018: 234–37); an overview of text-critical problems in LXX Judges is given by Fernández Marcos (2016: 189–92) and Trebolle Barrera (2014).

Septuagint and Old Latin witnesses omit 6:7–10 against the Masoretic Text (see Trebolle Barrera 2014: 53–54).

- Joshua: 4QJosh[a], Septuagint and the *Vetus Latina* represent the same text-type against the Masoretic Text (García Martínez 2012: 148).

The *Vetus Latina* and the Proto-Lucianic and Lucianic/Antiochian Recensions

The Lucianic recension relies on an older revision of the Greek text undertaken in accordance with a Hebrew text. This separated from the Septuagint majority at an early stage, possibly the first century CE (Fernández Marcos 2013: 59–60). This old revision is called proto-Lucianic and is the basis for another revision, that of the historical Lucian of Antioch (ca. 240–312). A proto-Lucianic text was known by Flavius Josephus and is the basis for Old Testament quotations in the New Testament (Spottorno 2013: 76–83; Meiser 2013: 195). Therefore, in the Lucianic/Antiochian revision two stages are found:

1. An old revised stage, or proto-Lucianic, that preserves a great number of readings of the Old Greek that were lost in other branches of the Greek manuscript tradition.
2. The Lucianic recension with editorial changes (Fernández Marcos 1994: 33–34).

The Lucianic/Antiochian revision shows some recurrent traits, such as corrections to avoid Semitisms in the Old Greek, variations of synonyms that gave rise to several variant readings, a tendency to replace Hellenistic forms with Attic ones and the adjustment of the text for public reading (Fernández Marcos 1994: 31–32; Fernández Marcos and Busto Sáiz 1989: xxix–xxxii). This text is found in quotations by Antiochian writers of the fourth and fifth centuries, such as Theodoret of Cyr, Asterius, John Chrysostom, Eustathius, and Theodore of Mopsuestia, hence its description as "Antiochian." So far, this revision has been identified as the Antiochian recension in the historical books 1–2 Samuel, 1–2 Kings and 1–2 Chronicles; it might also be employed for the Lucianic text of other historical books, such as Joshua and Judges, but there is not enough text quoted in the Antiochian Fathers to permit this identification. For these other books, the term "Lucianic" is preferred.

As the *Vetus Latina* translation was made before Lucian's activity, it and the quotations in Flavius Josephus provide key evidence to identify proto-Lucianic variant readings in the Lucianic revision. For example, in Judges 5:7, Greek manuscripts have three translations, supported by various secondary versions, of the Hebrew פְּרָזוֹן, a collective noun with the meaning "villagers," "dwellers in the open" (Fernández Marcos 2011: 56*):

LXX^{AO}: φαραζων, φραζων (Syrohexapla, Armenian).
LXX^{L}:   οἱ κρατοῦντες (VL 100 *potentes*).
LXX^{MV}: οἱ κατοικοῦντες (VL 91–96 *commorantes*, Augustine *habitantes*, Georgian).
LXX^{B}:   δυνατοί (Coptic).

These readings may be stratified as follows. The earliest Greek form, attested in LXX^{L}, is οἱ κρατοῦντες (LaMontaigne 2013:45). The support of VL 100 shows that the Greek reading might be pre-Hexaplaric, very close to the Old Greek (or maybe the Old Greek itself?), although VL 100 sometimes shows secondary readings and corruptions. This Greek form is the basis for οἱ κατοικοῦντες (LXX^{MV}), as paralleled in later Latin witnesses. Schenker (2013: 209–10) has shown that in Samuel and Kings the text of VL 91–95 is old but also has late variant readings, while in Judges they "represent mostly the B (Kaige) text" (Trebolle Barrera 2014: 57–58; on these manuscripts see further Morano 1999). The reading δυνατοί in LXX^{B} comes from a revision based on a Hebrew text close to the Masoretic Text: its Hebrew *Vorlage* is close to that of the Vulgate (*fortes*). Finally, φαραζων, φραζων in LXX^{AO} is a Hexaplaric revision based on the Hebrew, which formed the *Vorlage* of the Syrohexapla.

The *Vetus Latina* is also a fundamental key to identify pre-Hexaplaric strata in the Antiochian recension of Samuel, Kings, and Chronicles, as may be seen in the critical apparatus of the editions of Fernández Marcos and Busto Sáiz (1989–96).[7] This positive apparatus only includes Old Latin readings that support the Antiochian text (LXX^{Ant}) against the non-Antiochian text (LXX^{rel}), as in the following examples:

2 Sam. 6:12 VL 91–95: *et dixit Dauid: reuocabo benedictionem in domum meam*
          LXX^{Ant}:   καὶ εἶπε Δαυίδ·Ἐπιστρέψω τὴν εὐλογίαν εἰς τὸν οἶκόν μου
          LXX^{rel}:   omits
2 Sam. 10:15 VL 115: *et uiderunt fili Ammon quoniam Syrus*
          LXX^{Ant}:   καὶ εἶδον οἱ υἱοὶ Ἀμμὼν ὅτι ὁ σύρος
          LXX^{rel}:   εἶδεν Συρία ὅτι
2 Kings 21:8 VL^{LUC}: *sed si audierint me per omnia, quae mandaui eis*
          LXX^{Ant}:   πλὴν ἐὰν ἀκούσωσι κατὰ πάντα ἃ ἐνετειλάμην αὐτοῖς
          LXX^{rel}:   οἵτινες φυλάξουσιν πάντα, ὅσα ἐνετειλάμην κατὰ πᾶσαν
1 Chr. 5:10 VL 91–95: *super omnem faciem orientis*
          LXX^{Ant}:   ἐπὶ πάντος προσώπου ἀνατολῶν
          LXX^{rel}:   ἕως πάντες κὰτ᾽ ἀνατολάς
2 Chr. 9:18 VL 109: *et scabellum posuit in auro selle*
          LXX^{Ant}:   καὶ ὑποπόδιον ὑπέθηκεν ἐν χρυσῷ τῷ θρόνῳ
          LXX^{rel}:   omits

---

[7] The text of VL 91–95 has been edited by Morano (1989) for 1–2 Samuel, and by Moreno (1992) for 1–2 Kings.

In these books, the Antiochian text usually represents a Hebrew text-type that differs from the Masoretic Text. When the Dead Sea Scrolls have preserved enough text to draw conclusions, they generally agree with the Antiochian text.[8] The same line continues to be found in part of the Old Latin tradition, as in the following example:

1 Sam. 1:23	VL 91–95, 115:	*dominus* (+ *omne verbum* VL 91–95) *quod exiit de ore tuo*
	LXX:	κύριος (+ πᾶν LXX^Ant) τὸ ἐξελθὸν ἐκ τοῦ στόματός σου
	4QSamᵃ:	מפיך היוצא ה]יהו
	Masoretic Text:	יְהוָה אֶת־דְּבָרוֹ

However, in other instances the *Vetus Latina* text is closer to the Masoretic Text than to 4QSamᵃ. As Fernández Marcos has pointed out, the use of the *Vetus Latina* in the textual criticism of the Septuagint requires a previous analysis of its textual history, because its testimony is not uniform (1994: 48). One of the main areas of current Septuagint research is the Lucianic/Antiochian text because of its importance as a key to reconstruct the Old Greek (Kreuzer 2013).

THE *VETUS LATINA* AND HEBRAIZING REVISIONS

The discovery of the Kaige revision contributed to the understanding of Hebraizing revisions in different biblical books as phenomena belonging to the same trend of adapting the Greek text to a pre-Masoretic Hebrew form that is very close to the Masoretic Text. The impact of research on Kaige is not limited to the Septuagint text; it also allows the reinterpretation of the position of the *Vetus Latina* in the textual history of some books (see further Kreuzer 2016: 54–61; Wirth 2016: 13–21).

One example of this is Daniel, in which two Greek text-types are known: the Old Greek (LXXᵒ') and the Theodotionic text (LXXᶿ') (see Zilverberg 2017 and 2021: 17–20). Textual evidence for LXXᵒ' is fragmentary and scarce, the most important testimonies being manuscript LXX⁸⁸ and Papyrus LXX⁹⁶⁷ (Ziegler and Munnich 1999: 9–17 and 63–76) with the support of the Syrohexapla. LXXᶿ' is a revision based on an older Hebraizing text (proto-Theodotionic) related to Kaige, which replaced LXXᵒ' in the third century. It was accepted by the Christian churches as the reference text for Greek Daniel and is attested by the greater part of Greek evidence, such as the fourth-century Codex Vaticanus (LXX^B). Most of the Latin evidence supports LXXᶿ' (especially LXX^L),

---

[8] See, for Samuel, Fernández Marcos and Busto Sáiz (1989: xxxi–xxxiv), and for Kings, Fernández Marcos and Busto Sáiz (1992: xxx–xxxii). The Dead Sea Scrolls preserve very little material for 1–2 Chronicles (Fernández Marcos and Busto Sáiz 1996: xxix).

such as quotations in Lucifer of Cagliari and Augustine. However, some Latin witnesses represent LXX°ʹ, including Tertullian, Cyprian of Carthage, Victorinus of Poetovio (*scholia* on Revelation), the *Consultationes Zacchaei et Apollonii,* Hilarianus and some Latin manuscripts (Cañas Reíllo 2019: 154–55, 2017: 576). The following two examples illustrate this:

> Daniel 1:17 Tertullian: *dedit enim deus adolescentulis*
> > LXX°ʹ: καὶ τοῖς νεανίσκοις ἔδωκεν ὁ κύριος
> > LXXᶿʹ: καὶ τὰ παιδάρια ταῦτα, οἱ τέσσαρες αὐτοί, ἔδωκεν αὐτοῖς ὁ θεὸς (= MT)
> Daniel 14:4 (Bel 5) Cyprian: *nihil colo ego nisi dominum deum meum*
> > LXX°ʹ: οὐδένα σέβομαι ἐγὼ εἰ μὴ κύριον τὸν θεὸν
> > LXXᶿʹ: οὐ σέβομαι εἴδωλα χειροποίητα, ἀλλὰ τὸν ζῶντα θεὸν

Cyprian's quotations show that the *Vorlage* of his Latin Daniel text was LXX°ʹ, but he sometimes matches readings of LXXᶿʹ: the latter is also the source behind his quotations of Susanna (Zilverberg 2017: 36).

The problem of the double text in Judges (A and B in Rahlfs-Hanhart 2007) has also been reinterpreted in the light of the Kaige revision. The A-text includes the manuscript LXXᴬ, the Hexaplaric revision (LXX°), the Lucianic revision (LXXᴸ) and other manuscripts, such as the uncial LXXᴹⱽ. The B-text is represented in the manuscript LXXᴮ and numerous minuscule manuscripts, which seems to be part of the Kaige revision or a revision related to Kaige. This duality is reflected in the *Vetus Latina*: VL 100 mostly supports a pre-Hexaplaric Greek stratum represented by the group LXXᴬ, while VL 91–96 largely agree with LXXᴮ (Trebolle Barrera 2014: 59).

Finally, there is a set of variant readings in the *Vetus Latina* that are closer to the Masoretic Text than to the Septuagint. These have been the object of debate since Blondheim (1925), who saw in them a direct link with the Hebrew text. Such variant readings might be linked to Jewish Latin-speakers or are result of a revision based on the Hebrew. Recent research has considered them the result of the influence of Greek variant readings close to the Masoretic Text that were lost in Septuagint manuscripts, for example, in VL 91–95 for Samuel–Kings (Fernández Marcos 1994: 84). Kraus (2003: 512) reexamined some examples of such Hebraizing variant readings and concluded that they either have their origin in Greek tradition or must be explained as the result of the influence of Jerome. There are three groups of variant readings of this type in Kings (Moreno Hernández 1992: 201–4):

1. Those supported by the Masoretic Text but not by the Septuagint in Kaige sections: 2 Kings 4:42 VL 91– 95 *chremel zecalin* = MT בְּצִקְלֹנוֹ כַּרְמֶל, MT/LXX παλάθας βακελέθ.

2. Those that are the result of an alternative interpretation of the Masoretic Text: 2 Kings 5:19 VL 91–95 *in gopheram terram*, cf. MT כִּבְרַת־אָרֶץ, LXX χαβραθὰ τῆς γῆς.

3. Variant readings with no support in the Septuagint or the Masoretic Text: 2 Kings 3:26 VL 91–95 *Syriae* (from *אָרָם) but MT אֱדוֹם and LXX Ἐδώμ.

The opposite situation occurs in 2 Chronicles 20:2. VL 109 and other Latin witnesses have *de trans mare de Edom* for מֵעֵבֶר לַיָּם מֵאֲרָם (MT) but the Septuagint reads ἐκ πέραν τῆς θαλάσσης ἀπὸ Συρίας (from אֲרָם) (Kraus 2003: 495–96). This type of Hebraizing variant has also been found in other books, such as Judges. VL 91–96 (see Ayuso Marazuela 1967: 284) have *happarsdona* (Judges 3:22) and *ehudhammasdrona* (Judges 3:23), corresponding to הַפַּרְשְׁדֹנָה (MT: "hole," "hollow"?) and אֵהוּד הַמַּסְדְּרוֹנָה, where אֵהוּד is a proper name and מִסְדְּרוֹן has the doubtful meaning "porch," "entrance," but LXX^AB read ἐκ τῆς κοιλίας (Judges 3:22) and LXX^A Αωδ εἰς τὴν προστάδα / LXX^B τοὺς διατεταγμένους (Judges 3:23). A fuller explanation of this reading is provided by Fernández Marcos (1998b: 418).

THE *VETUS LATINA* AND THE HEXAPLA

Among the texts in Origen's six-column Bible known as the Hexapla, the fifth column (the so-called *Quinta*) contained his edition of the Septuagint. Origen compared the Septuagint text with the Hebrew Bible of his time and highlighted the differences between them. For text in the Septuagint lacking in Hebrew, he put an obelus at the beginning and a metobelus at the end; for Septuagint text with no equivalent in Hebrew, he added the Greek equivalent taken from Theodotion in the fifth column and marked it with an asterisk at the beginning and with a metobelus at the end. This edition had a great influence, contaminating most of the Greek textual tradition, although it had little effect on some revisions such as Kaige. In the seventh century the Hexapla was lost, with only the fifth column (the unique component of the Hexapla) being transmitted through separate copying. Fragments of other columns of the Hexapla have been preserved and have been published by Field (1867–75). The *Quinta* was translated into Syriac by Paulus of Tella at the beginning of the seventh century; he also incorporated into his text the Aristarchian symbols used by Origen (i.e., asterisks and obeli). This is the Syrohexapla, of primary importance for the knowledge of the position of obeli and asterisks in the original text of the Hexapla.

Starting in 389, Jerome made a revision of an Old Latin text using Origen's edition (i.e., the *Quinta*). Of this revision, only the Psalter, Job, and fragments of the Song of Songs remain; the prologues survive for other books such as Proverbs, Ecclesiastes (Qoheleth), and 1–2 Chronicles (Graves 2017: 279). In addition, many traces of the Hexaplaric text remain in Jerome's biblical commentaries (e.g., the Song of Songs; see Ceulemans 2009: 375). The survival of the Hexaplaric text of the Psalter (i.e., the *Psalterium ex Graeco*) is especially relevant. It circulated widely in the Middle Ages, and was named the "Gallican Psalter" because of its diffusion in French manuscripts. Alcuin of York incorporated it as the Psalter of his Latin Bible edition in the eighth century, and it has been part of the *textus receptus* since the first printed edition of the Vulgate (Mainz 1454/55).

In the editions of the Vetus Latina Institute the letter O is used for Latin text-types based on the Hexaplaric edition. For the most part, these have been preserved in Jerome's writings. For example, in Genesis, this text-type is found in Jerome's *Quaestiones Hebraicae in Genesim*. This has relevance for the reconstruction of lost text of the *Quinta*, which can be a very important complement to the reconstruction of sections of the lost Hexaplaric edition. In some cases, text-types O and H (Jerome's translation from Hebrew) are unique, as in Genesis 19:36:[9]

> LXX: καὶ συνέλαβον αἱ δύο θυγατέρες Λὼτ ἐκ τοῦ πατρὸς αὐτῶν
> O: *et conceperunt duae filiae Lot de patre suo*
> H: *conceperunt ergo duae filiae Loth de patre suo*

In Isaiah, text-type O is found in Jerome's *Explanationum in Esaiam libri octo*, which differs from H. Isaiah 5:17 reads:

> LXX: καὶ βοσκηθήσονται οἱ διηρπασμένοι ὡς ταῦροι
> O: *et pascentur direpti quasi tauri*
> H: *et pascentur agni iuxta ordinem suum* (cf. α' and σ')[10]

In Esther, Jerome translated the Greek supplements from a Hexaplaric form of the Septuagint, i.e. LXX^O (Haelewyck 2003–8: 64–65), as shown in the following examples:

> A 17 LXX: Βουγαῖος
> LXX$^{O(-93)}$: ἐβουγαῖος = O *ibugeus* (ms. Q) (12:6)
> 4:8 LXX: περὶ τοῦ λαοῦ
> LXX$^{O(-58)}$: + καὶ τῆς πατρίδος = O *pro populo suo et pro patria sua* (15:1)
> C 16 LXX: ἤκουον ἐκ γενετῆς μου ἐν φυλῇ πατριᾶς μου
> LXX$^{O(-58)}$: ἤκουον τοῦ πατρός μου = O *audiui a patre meo* (14:5)

The Hexapla also influenced the *Vetus Latina* text, although in such a camouflaged way that this is very difficult to detect. The Latin manuscript VL 100 preserves textual materials from various sources in Joshua 5:4–6, including the Hexaplaric Greek (Sipilä 2014: 261–71). Traces of Jerome's Hexaplaric edition are also found in other Christian writings, such as the exegesis of the Song of Songs by Ambrose of Milan. This shows similarities with the translations of α' and σ' transmitted in the Hexapla (Ceulemans 2009: 377–82).

---

[9] The Greek text is from Wevers (1974: 201). For O and H text-types, see Fischer (1951–54: 223).
[10] See the Hexaplaric apparatus in Ziegler (1939: 139).

CONCLUSION: THE RELEVANCE OF THE *VETUS LATINA* FOR TEXTUAL CRITICISM

Current research considers the Latin Bible as essential evidence for the textual criticism of the Septuagint. Being the oldest and most faithful translation of the Septuagint, it provides evidence that allows a clear distinction to be made between pre-Hexaplaric and Hexaplaric stages of the Greek Bible. In the pre-Hexaplaric stage, it offers a key to reaching a Greek text very close to the original translation, linking its textual tradition with Hebrew. This Hebrew text is not always related to the Masoretic Text; instead, it shows similarities to the Dead Sea Scrolls, making the *Vetus Latina* an indirect witness to an older Hebrew text than the Masoretic Text. The evolution of the Greek Bible also left its traces in Latin tradition: as most surviving Greek manuscripts are later than the *Vetus Latina*, the latter is a witness of great importance in detecting different strata in the textual history of the Septuagint. In, general, the Latin textual tradition is richer and more complicated than the Greek and Hebrew, making it a necessary tool for textual criticism when data are lacking from the Septuagint.

ACKNOWLEDGMENTS

This study has been carried out within the framework of the Research Project *Edición y estudio de textos bíblicos y parabíblicos* (FFI2017-86726-P), with funding by the Ministerio de Ciencia, Innovación y Universidades of the Government of Spain. I would like to thank Kevin Zilverberg for his assistance in revising the English.

BIBLIOGRAPHY

Ausloos, H., B. Lemmeljin, and J. Trebolle Barrera, eds. 2012. *After Qumran. Old and Modern Editions of the Biblical Texts—The Historical Books*. BETL 246. Leuven: Peeters.

Ayuso Marazuela, Teófilo. 1967. *La Vetus Latina Hispana. II. El Octateuco*. Madrid: CSIC.

Barthélemy, Dominique. 1963. *Les devanciers d'Aquila. Première Publication intégrale du texte des fragments du Dodécaprophéton*. Supplements to Vetus Testamentum 10. Leiden: Brill.

Blondheim, David S. 1925. *Les parlers judéo-romans et la Vetus Latina: étude sur les rapports entre les traductions bibliques en langue romane des juifs au Moyen âge et les anciennes versions*. Paris: Champion.

Bogaert, Pierre-Maurice. 2013. "De la *Vetus Latina* à l'hébreu pré-massorétique en passant par la plus ancienne Septante: Le livre de Jérémie, exemple privilégié." *Revue théologique de Louvain* 44: 216–43.

Cañas Reíllo, José Manuel. 2017. "Daniel: 18.4 Secondary Translations, 18.4.1. Vetus Latina." In *The Hebrew Bible*, Vol. 1C: *Writings*, edited by A. Lange & E. Tov, 575–78. Leiden: Brill.

Cañas Reíllo, José Manuel. 2018. "Septuagint-Judges: The Value of Secondary Translations for Its Textual History." In *Die Septuaginta—Geschichte, Wirkung. Relevanz*, edited by

M. Meiser, M. Geiger, S. Kreuzer, and M. Sigismund, 230–43. WUNT 405. Tübingen: Mohr Siebeck.

Cañas Reíllo, José Manuel. 2019. "Latin. 3. Daniel, Additions to." In *Textual History of the Bible, Vol. 2B: The Deuterocanonical Scriptures*, edited by F. Feder and M. Henze, 153–57. Leiden: Brill.

Cañas Reíllo, José Manuel. 2020a. "Manuscripts and Recensions in LXX-Judges." In *Die Septuaginta—Themen, Manuskripte, Wirkungen*, edited by E. Bons, M. Geiger, F. Ueberschaer, M. Sigismund, and M. Meiser, 544–60. WUNT 444. Tübingen: Mohr Siebeck.

Cañas Reíllo, José Manuel. 2020b. "Recensions, Textual Groups, and Vocabulary Differentiation in LXX-Judges." In *The Legacy of Soisalon-Soininen. Towards a Syntax of Septuagint Greek*, edited by T. Kauhanen and H. Vanonen, 175–88. De Septuaginta Investigationes 13. Göttingen: Vandenhoeck & Ruprecht.

Cañas Reíllo, José Manuel. 2021. "The Septuagint and Textual Criticism of the Greek Versions." In *T&T Clark Handbook of Septuagint Research*, edited by W. A. Ross and W. E. Glenny, 123–34. London: Bloomsbury T&T Clark.

Ceulemans, Reinhart. 2009. "The Latin Patristic Reception of the Book of Canticles in the Hexapla." *Vigiliae Christianae* 63: 369–89.

De Bruyne, Donatien, 1932. *Les anciennes traductions latines des Machabées*. Anecdota Maredsolana 4. Maredsous: Abbey.

Fernández Marcos, Natalio. 1994. *Scribes & Translators. Septuagint & Old Latin in the Books of Kings*. Leiden: Brill.

Fernández Marcos, Natalio. 1998a. *Introducción a las versiones griegas de la Biblia* [The Septuagint in Context: Introduction to the Greek Version of the Bible]. 2nd ed. TECC 64. Madrid: CSIC. Repr., translated by W. G. E. Watson, Atlanta: Society of Biblical Literature, 2010.

Fernández Marcos, Natalio. 1998b. "The Textual Context of the Hexapla: Lucianic Texts and Vetus Latina." In *Origen's Hexapla and Fragments. Papers presented at the Rich Seminar on the Hexapla*, edited by A. Salvesen, 408–20. Tübingen: Mohr Siebeck.

Fernández Marcos, Natalio. 2011. *Judges*. Biblia Hebraica Quinta 7. Stuttgart: Deutsche Bibelgesellschaft.

Fernández Marcos, Natalio. 2012. "The B-Text of Judges. *Kaige* Revision and Beyond." In *After Qumran. Old and Modern Editions of the Biblical Texts—The Historical Books*, edited by H. Ausloos, B. Lemmeljin, and J. Trebolle Barrera, 161–69. BETL 246. Leuven: Peeters.

Fernández Marcos, Natalio. 2013. "The Antiochene Edition in the Text History of the Greek Bible." In *Der Antiochenische Text der Septuaginta in seiner Bezeugung und seiner Bedeutung*, edited by Sigfried Kreuzer and Marcus Sigismund, 57–73. De Septuaginta investigationes 4. Göttingen: Vandenhoeck & Ruprecht.

Fernández Marcos, Natalio. 2016. "Kritai/Iudices/Das Buch der Richter." In *Einleitung in die Septuaginta*, edited by S. Kreuzer, 188–98. Gütersloh: Gütersloher Verlagshaus.

Fernández Marcos, Natalio, and José Ramón Busto Sáiz. 1989. *El texto antioqueno de la Biblia Griega. I. 1-2 Samuel*. TECC 50. Madrid: CSIC.

Fernández Marcos, Natalio, and José Ramón Busto Sáiz. 1992. *El texto antioqueno de la Biblia Griega. II. 1-2 Reyes*. TECC 53. Madrid: CSIC.

Fernández Marcos, Natalio, and José Ramón Busto Sáiz. 1996. *El texto antioqueno de la Biblia Griega. III. 1-2 Crónicas*. TECC 60. Madrid: CSIC.

Fischer, Bonifatius, ed. 1951–54. *Genesis*. VL 2. Freiburg: Herder.

Field, Frederick. 1867–75. *Origenis Hexaplorum quae supersunt*. Oxford: Clarendon Press.

García Martínez, Florentino. 2012. "Light on the Joshua Books from the Dead Sea Scrolls." In *After Qumran. Old and Modern Editions of the Biblical Texts—The Historical Books*, edited by H. Ausloos., B. Lemmeljin, and J. Trebolle Barrera, 146–59. BETL 246. Leuven: Peeters.

Gesche, Bonifatia. ed. 2005. *Ruth*. VL 4/5. Freiburg: Herder.

Gesche, Bonifatia. ed. 2008–16. *Esra I*. VL 6/2. Freiburg: Herder.

Graves, Michael. 2017. "1.3. Primary translations. 1.3.5. Vulgate." In *The Hebrew Bible*, vol. 1C: *Writings*, edited by A. Lange & E. Tov, 278–89. Leiden: Brill.

Gryson, Roger. 1999. *Altlateinische Handschriften/Manuscrits vieux latins. Répertoire descriptif. Première Partie: Mss 1–275*. VL 1/2A. Freiburg: Herder.

Haelewyck, Jean-Claude, ed. 2003–8. *Hester*. VL 7/2. Freiburg: Herder.

Hanhart, Robert, ed. 1976. *Maccabaeorum liber II*. Septuaginta IX/2. 2nd reimpr., Göttingen: Vandenhoeck & Ruprecht.

Kappler, Werner. ed. 1990. *Maccabaeorum liber I*. Septuaginta IX/1. 3rd reimpr., Göttingen: Vandenhoeck & Ruprecht.

Kraus, Matthew. 2003. "Hebraisms in the Old Latin Version of the Bible." *Vetus Testamentum* 53: 487–513.

Kreuzer, Siegfried. 2013. "Der Antiochenische Text der Septuaginta. Forschungsgeschichte und eine neue Perspective." In *Der Antiochenische Text der Septuaginta in seiner Bezeugung und seiner Bedeutung*, edited by Sigfried Kreuzer and Marcus Sigismund, 23–56. De Septuaginta investigationes 4. Göttingen: Vandenhoeck & Ruprecht.

Kreuzer, Siegfried. 2016. "Entstehung und Überlieferung der Septuaginta." In *Einleitung in die Septuaginta*, edited by S. Kreuzer, 29–88. Gütersloh: Gütersloher Verlagshaus.

Kreuzer, Siegfried. 2018. "Zur Relevanz editorischer Prinzipien." In *Die Septuaginta—Geschichte. Wirkung, Relevanz*, edited by M. Meiser, M. Geiger, S. Kreuzer, and M. Sigismund, 130–45. WUNT 405. Tübingen: Mohr Siebeck.

Kreuzer, Siegfried, and Marcus Sigismund, eds. 2013. *Der Antiochenische Text der Septuaginta in seiner Bezeugung und seiner Bedeutung*. De Septuaginta investigationes 4. Göttingen: Vandenhoeck & Ruprecht.

LaMontagne, Nathan. 2013. "The Song of Deborah. Judges 5: Meaning and Poetry in the Septuagint." PhD diss., Catholic University of America, Washington, DC.

Lust, Johan. 2003. "Septuagint and Canon." In *The Biblical Canons*, edited by J.-M. Auwers and H. J. De Jonge, 39–55. BETL 158. Leuven: University Press.

Meiser, Martin. 2013. "Antiochenische Textformen in neutestamentlichen Psalmzitaten in der Rezeption der christlichen Antikee—eine textkritische Spurensuche." In *Der Antiochenische Text der Septuaginta in seiner Bezeugung und seiner Bedeutung*, edited by Sigfried Kreuzer and Marcus Sigismund, 179–96. De Septuaginta investigationes 4. Göttingen: Vandenhoeck & Ruprecht.

Morano Rodríguez, Ciriaca. 1989. *Glosas marginales de Vetus Latina en las Biblias Vulgatas españolas. 1-2 Samuel*. TECC 48. Madrid: CSIC.

Morano Rodríguez, Ciriaca. 1999. "La historia textual de las glosas marginales de *Vetus Latina* del *Codex Gothicus Legionensis*." In *Codex Biblicus Legionensis. Veinte estudios*, 281–302. León: Real Colegiata de San Isidoro.

Moreno Hernández, Antonio. 1992. *Las glosas marginales de Vetus Latina en las Biblias Vulgatas españolas. 1-2 Reyes*. TECC 49. Madrid: CSIC.

Rahlfs, Alfred. 1914. *Verzeichnis der griechischen Handschriften des Alten Testaments, für das Septuaginta-Unternehmen*. Göttingen: Weidmann.

Rahlfs, Alfred, and Detlef Fraenkel. 2004. *Verzeichnis der griechischen Handschriften des Alten Testaments. Bd. 1.1: Die Überlieferung bis zum VIII. Jahrhundert*. Septuaginta Supplementum. Göttingen: Vandenhoeck & Ruprecht.

Rahlfs, Alfred, and Robert Hanhart, eds. 2007. *Septuaginta. Id est Vetus Testamentum graece iuxta Septuagint interpretes*. 2nd ed. Stuttgart: Deutsche Bibelgesellschaft.

Schenker, Adrian. 2013. "Der Platz der altlateinischen Randlesarten des Kodex von León und der Valvanera-Bibel in der biblischen Textgeschichte. 1-2Kgt)." In *Der Antiochenische Text der Septuaginta in seiner Bezeugung und seiner Bedeutung*, edited by Sigfried Kreuzer and Marcus Sigismund, 199–210. De Septuaginta investigationes 4. Göttingen: Vandenhoeck & Ruprecht.

Sipilä, Seppo. 2014. "Old Latin Text of Josh 5:4-6 and Its Contribution to the Textual History of the Greek Joshua." In *In the Footsteps of Sherlock Holmes. Studies in the Biblical Text in Honour of Anneli Aejmelaeus*, edited by K. de Troyer, T. M. Law, and M. Liljeström, 257–72. Leuven: Peeters.

Spottorno, Victoria. 2013. "The Status of the Antiochene Text in the First Century A.D." In *Der Antiochenische Text der Septuaginta in seiner Bezeugung und seiner Bedeutung*, edited by Sigfried Kreuzer and Marcus Sigismund, 74–83. De Septuaginta investigationes 4. Göttingen: Vandenhoeck & Ruprecht.

Tov, Emmanuel. 2012. "The Qumran Hebrew Texts and the Septuagint—An Overview." In *Die Septuaginta—Entstehung, Sprache, Geschichte*, edited by S. Kreuzer, M. Meiser, and M. Sigismund, 3–17. WUNT 286. Tübingen: Mohr Siebeck.

Trebolle Barrera, Julio. 2014. "The Textual History and the Text Critical Value of the Old Latin Version in the Book of Judges." In *Die Septuaginta—Text, Wirkung, Rezeption. 4. Internationale Fachtagung veranstaltet von Septuaginta Deutsch*, edited by W. Kraus & S. Kreuzer, 53–72. WUNT 325. Tübingen: Mohr Siebeck.

Trebolle Barrera, Julio. 2015. "The Text-Critical Contribution of the Antiochean Greek and Old Latin Texts—Case Study: 2 Kings 8:10-11." In *Essays on the Composition, Redaction, and Transmission of the Bible in Honor of Zipi Talshir*, edited by C. Werman, 17–35. Winona Lake: Eisenbrauns.

Trebolle Barrera, Julio. 2016. "1.4. Secondary Translations. 1.4.1. Vetus Latina." In *Textual History of the Bible*: vol. 1A. *The Hebrew Bible: Overview Articles*, edited by A. Lange & E. Tov, 319–31. Leiden: Brill.

Ulrich, Eugene. 1985. "Characteristics and Limitations of the Old Latin Translation of the Septuagint." In *La Septuaginta en la investigación contemporánea*, edited by N. Fernández Marcos, 67–80. TECC 34. Madrid: CSIC.

Wevers, John William, ed. 1974. *Genesis*, Septuaginta I. Göttingen: Vandenhoeck & Ruprecht.

Wevers, John William, ed. 1977. *Deuteronomium*. Septuaginta III/2. Göttingen, Germany: Vandenhoeck & Ruprecht. 2nd ed., adiuvante U. Quast, 2006.

Wevers, John William. 1995. *Notes on the Greek Text of Deuteronomy*. Septuagint and Cognate Studies 39. Atlanta: Scholars.

Wirth, Raimund. 2016. *Die Septuaginta der Samuelbücher. Untersucht unter Einbeziehung ihrer Rezensionen*. De Septuaginta investigationes 7. Göttingen: Vandenhoeck & Ruprecht.

Ziegler, Joseph, and Olivier Munnich, eds. 1999. *Susanna, Daniel, Bel et Draco, Editio secunda Versionis iuxta Septuagint interpretes, Versionis iuxta "Theodotionem" fragmenta adiecit* D. Fraenkel. Septuaginta XVI/2. Göttingen: Vandenhoeck & Ruprecht.

Ziegler, Joseph, ed. 1939. *Isaias*. Septuaginta XIV. Göttingen: Vandenhoeck & Ruprecht.

Zilverberg, Kevin. 2017. *The Textual History of Old Latin Susanna*. Paper presented for the *lectio coram publico* of the preparatory doctoral year. Rome: Pontifical Biblical Institute.

Zilverberg, Kevin. 2021. *The Textual History of Old Latin Daniel from Tertullian to Lucifer*. Madrid: CSIC.

CHAPTER 3

JEROME AND THE
VULGATE GOSPELS

CHRISTINA M. KREINECKER

INTRODUCTION

THE Latin text of the Bible, known as the Vulgate, is a complex combination of individual writings of varying types. Only the Old Testament and the New Testament gospels can be attributed to Jerome (Fischer 1972: 21; Metzger 1977: 356–62; see also chap. 1). Yet, whereas the text of the Vulgate Old Testament is a new translation from Hebrew, the New Testament gospels are a revision of existing Old Latin texts according to Greek. This revision was commissioned by Pope Damasus in 382 CE, most likely coinciding with the change from Greek to Latin as the official language used in liturgy in the West (Mülke 2015: 50–56).

Knowledge of Jerome's life, education, and personal connections is vital for a thorough understanding of his revisional activity. This chapter therefore begins by highlighting key moments in his background. Second, the purpose and methods of the revision of the gospels are discussed by analyzing Jerome's own preface in relation to his actual revised text. Third, the challenge of identifying possible Latin and Greek templates for Jerome's revision will be met by looking at the underlying methodological assumptions of previous suggestions, often based on now outdated text-critical methods. Subsequently, characteristics of Jerome's revisional technique are discussed and examples are given of textual changes from the Old Latin to the Vulgate. Finally, as the Vulgate gospels were not immediately successful but gained their popularity gradually over the centuries, the shift from the Old Latin to the general acceptance of the Vulgate gospels is traced by favoring a broad approach to textual transmission which takes into account new digital technologies and quotations in contemporaneous Christian writings alongside biblical manuscripts. This chapter aims to highlight how research on the Latin Bible and the affiliation of Old Latin and Vulgate gospels has come to a turning point due to new discoveries and recent developments in New Testament textual criticism. It is every-thing but a closed matter.

SOPHRONIUS EUSEBIUS HIERONYMUS:
THE MAN BEHIND THE REVISION

Jerome's excellent education, his travels between West and East, and his various acquaintances made him the perfect candidate to undertake a revision of the Latin bib-lical text (Fürst 1998: 324). Jerome was born to wealthy Christian parents around the year 347 in Stridon in Dalmatia, a place somewhere in the region of modern Slovenia, Croatia, and Montenegro.[1] His full Latin name was Sophronius Eusebius Hieronymus. He was sent to Rome to study the classical triad of grammar, rhetoric, and philosophy around 360. His teacher, the grammarian Aelius Donatus, made Jerome familiar with the classical authors, including rhetors, philosophers, historians, and poets, a knowledge he would later use in his work of revision. After his studies, Jerome moved to Trier. Here he was introduced to an ascetic lifestyle, which he continued in Aquileia in Northern Italy. In 373/374 he made a pilgrimage to Jerusalem and fell ill in Syrian Antioch. He stayed there with Apollinaris of Laodicea to study Greek, exegesis, and theology. Subsequently, he lived as a hermit in the desert of Chalcis on the estate of his friend Evagrius, where he befriended a monk of Jewish origin who taught him Hebrew. Jerome thereby became a man of three languages (*trilinguis*), which was essential to his later revisions of the Latin Bible.[2] In 381, he went to Constantinople to study with Gregory of Nazianzus and Gregory of Nyssa and became familiar with Origen's works, of which he would translate several into Latin. He attended the Synod in Rome in 382 as part of a delegation from Constantinople, perhaps as a reflection of his translation activities. Pope Damasus made Jerome his secretary and, in view of his excellent linguistic skills, asked him to revise the Latin Bible. Jerome finished the revision of the gospels by 384 and began his first revision of the psalter. Yet his time in Rome was of mixed blessings: his ascetic lifestyle found some support among the wealthy Roman aristocracy, including the wealthy Marcella and Paula with her daughter Eustochium, but he was nevertheless criticized for this and his revisional work on the Bible (Greschat 1984: 149; Moreschini and Norelli 2007: 424). After the death of Damasus, his supporter, in 384, his life in Rome became increasingly difficult. In 385, he moved first to Antioch and subsequently to Alexandria to study with

---

[1] Drobner 2011: 344 locates Stridon close to Emona, modern Ljubljana in Slovenia, while Metzger 1977: 331 identifies it with Grahovo Polje in Montenegro.

[2] Jerome was proud of his trilingualism, as can be seen in his apology against Rufinus (*Apol.* 3.6, PL 23: 483A): *ego philosophus, rhetor, grammaticus, dialectus, Hebraeus, Graecus, Latinus, trilinguis.*

Didymus the Blind. In 386, he continued on to Bethlehem where he would stay until his death on September 30, 419 or 420.

The Purpose and Methods of the Vulgate Gospels: Jerome's Preface

Jerome's Latin version of the four gospels is preceded by a literary preface addressed to its commissioner, Pope Damasus.[3] Jerome provides information therein on the reasons, methods, and intentions behind his work and addresses some of the anticipated criticisms. According to Jerome, it was the great variety of Old Latin readings in the fourth century that necessitated a standardized Latin text. He famously observed that there are "almost as many Latin versions as there are manuscripts" (*tot sunt paene quot codices*), due mainly to incorrect translations in the first place, alterations for the worse, and inattentive scribes. As Damasus had asked him to "make a new book out of an old" (*nouum opus facere me cogis ex ueteri*), Jerome is clear about the character of his work: it is a revision, not a new translation.

Methodologically, the Latin was revised according to a Greek source. The aim was to establish those readings from the Old Latin texts which "correspond to the Greek truth" (*cum graeca consentiant ueritate*) and to correct the Latin accordingly. Jerome's preface matches scholarly assessments of his biblical text, which is neither a new translation nor a systematically consistent revision. His corrections largely concern various errors and incorrect readings as well as occasional changes of style (see below). His adaptations include presenting the four gospels in the order of the old Greek codices (*codicum graecorum emendata conlatione sed ueterum*), that is, Matthew–Mark–Luke–John. This allows Jerome to extend his edition by the addition and explanation of the Eusebian Canon Tables.[4] In terms of the criticism he expects, Jerome evokes the topos of modesty by claiming that he is uneasy to be set as judge over the great variety of old and venerable textual readings. He fears misunderstanding and the accusation of arrogance and expects a general dismissal of his new, unfamiliar text which replaces a well-known, beloved version. Such charges were already leveled against Jerome during his time in Rome. After Damasus's death, ecclesiastical approval for this text was not given until Pope Gregory (590–604), and Old Latin readings would stay prominent until the ninth century. The name "Vulgate" (*uulgata editio*, "commonly accepted edition") did not become popular until the thirteenth century (see the "Introduction," in this volume).

---

[3] Critical edition in Weber and Gryson 2007: 1515–16.

[4] These tables are a synoptic system developed and explained by Eusebius of Caesarea in his *Letter to Carpianus*. It is based on Ammonius's section numbers and presents parallel sections in ten tables which allow for a synoptic comparison. See further Crawford 2019.

JEROME'S OLD LATIN AND GREEK
TEMPLATES

The text of the Vulgate gospels is a revision of an Old Latin text with regard to a Greek source. Any attempt to identify the changes introduced by Jerome has to take into consideration one or more Old Latin texts and at least one Greek text according to which Jerome made his corrections. The textual outcome is therefore heavily dependent on presuppositions about Jerome's Latin and Greek templates. The hermeneutical circle and methodological problems of this are instantly evident: almost all extant Latin manuscripts date from a time after Jerome and are mixed texts that contain both Old Latin and Vulgate readings. In addition, the frequency of contamination and commixture of Old Latin and Vulgate readings can and does vary, not only between individual biblical books contained in the same codex but also within one individual book itself.[5] Likewise, our understanding of the early Greek gospel tradition is incomplete. Only a handful of manuscripts have survived from the early centuries and—as in the Latin tradition—manuscripts from later centuries may well carry an old text but bear signs of contamination (Fischer 1972: 22). Any attempt to reconstruct a Vulgate text can therefore only produce an approximation, not an accurate account of Jerome's revision.

Over the centuries, a variety of texts and manuscripts have been identified as possible templates. Most of these suggestions were based on a text-critical understanding which has now become outdated. Even so, once possible templates have been established, the methodological steps to identify Vulgate readings remain the same in principle. First, a reading is considered to be Vulgate when it does not match those from established Old Latin manuscripts: a reading that can be explained as a correction from an Old Latin attestation has a strong claim to be Vulgate. Second, a reading is more likely to be Vulgate when it corresponds to a Greek reading attested in the fourth century. These rules have to be applied tentatively, not absolutely. It is currently agreed that no extant individual manuscript can be identified as one of Jerome's templates, either for Latin or for Greek. Instead, the entire Old Latin and early Greek tradition must be taken into account. Modern technology and full digital descriptions, and the possibilities they hold for further analyses, play a vital part in this development.

Latin Templates

The text of Codex Brixianus (VL 10, Italy, sixth century) was proposed by Wordsworth and White as a possible Latin template used by Jerome: they printed this in full in their

---

[5] This is, for example, the case in Codex Corbeiensis primus (VL 9, Italy, eighth century), where the first nine chapters of Matthew show Vulgate readings while the later chapters contain Old Latin text.

Oxford Vulgate (1889–98; cf. Fischer 1955). Codex Vercellensis (VL 3, Italy, second half of the fourth century) was another suggested candidate (Souter 1911). Vogels (1928) abandoned the idea that any one extant manuscript represents Jerome's Old Latin text and instead suggested a text close to five codices: Vercellensis, Corbeiensis secundus (VL 8, Italy, fifth century), Veronensis (VL 4, Italy, end of fifth century), Vindobonensis (VL 17, Italy, end of fifth century), and Monacensis (or Valerianus, VL 13, Illyria or Italy, sixth or seventh century).[6] Fischer (1955: 193, 195) observes that, due to the long-standing contamination of manuscripts, the entire known Old Latin tradition should be considered. In terms of the reconstructed Old Latin text types, it is currently agreed that Jerome's revision was based on a manuscript of the text type I, which circulated in Italy in the middle of the fourth century (Houghton 2016a: 33, 120–21; see also chap. 1). The edition of all four gospels in the *Vetus Latina* series and the application of new technologies and reliable full digital transcriptions will allow for new observations and insights in the future. Likewise, increased understanding and thorough critical analysis of the biblical quotations in Christian writers before Jerome will extend our knowledge significantly: for example, the Old Latin text in Fortunatianus of Aquileia's recently rediscovered commentary on the gospels still awaits a detailed study in respect to Jerome's revision.[7]

Greek Templates

Various suggestions of possible Greek templates have been made, yet all are based on the outdated methodological approach of classifying Greek texts according to geographical types (see Parker 2008: 174). The opinion that Jerome preferred the so-called Alexandrian text type over the so-called Western text type has long prevailed (see Elliott 1992: 223; Metzger 1977: 355–56; Fischer 1972: 63–64). Wordsworth and White (1889–98) suggested a Greek text close to that of the fourth-century codices Vaticanus and Sinaiticus (GA 03, 01) and the eighth-century Codex Regius (GA 019). Subsequently, Hermann von Soden (1902–13) favored a Greek text that formed the archetype of his supposed three "recensions," text types he connected to Jerusalem, Hesychius, and Lucian. Vogels (1928) suggested a Koine or Byzantine type of Greek text. All these suggestions met with heavy criticism and, again, no individual manuscript can be identified as Jerome's source. The use of digital tools to make and compare full-text transcriptions of Greek New Testament manuscripts offers new possibilities in reconstructing Jerome's source (e.g., Wasserman and Gurry 2017; Mink 2004).

---

[6] All of these codices have the order Matthew–John–Luke–Mark. For further details, see Houghton 2016a.

[7] This was rediscovered in 2012 and critically edited by Dorfbauer (2017). Houghton (2017: 236) has determined that it shows no Vulgate influence and corresponds to other fourth-century Italian texts.

Typical Vulgate Features and
Textual Changes

According to his own preface, Jerome corrected only "errors which seemed to change the sense and allowed the rest to remain as it had been" so that his text "would not differ greatly from the customary Latin reading"[8] He revised an existing Latin translation by adapting it to a Greek text he considered authoritative (*Graeca ueritas*). As multiple layers of corrections had already been made to Old Latin texts prior to Jerome, deciding whether a specific reading was introduced by Jerome or was already present in his template is a methodologically challenging task.[9] Nevertheless, differences of various kinds are obvious between predominantly Old Latin and predominantly Vulgate texts. It should also be kept in mind that corrections to the Old Latin text were not made consistently. The following paragraphs illustrate tendencies of the Vulgate text and counterexamples could be given (see further Harrison 1986; Vogels 1928: 34–36).

Jerome's ordering of the gospels into the Greek sequence Matthew–Mark–Luke–John is a clear characteristic of the Vulgate, as is the presence of initial Eusebian canon tables and the corresponding marginal apparatus. However, textual adjustments were not made consistently in material paralleled in more than one gospel, and there are fewer instances in the Vulgate of harmonization than in Old Latin texts (Harrison 1986: 236; Vogels 1928: 9). For example, the Greek word for High Priest, ἀρχιερεύς, is primarily rendered as *princeps sacerdotum* in Matthew, but as *summus sacerdos* in Mark and often as *pontifex* in John. Another famous example is the treatment of the Greek noun γεωργός ("farmer") in the so-called Parable of the Wicked Tenants in Matthew 21:33–44 with parallels in Mark 12:1–11 and Luke 20:9–18. The Old Latin reads *colonus*, which is consistently replaced by *agricola* in Matthew in the Vulgate. Yet in the same story in Mark, *colonus* is only occasionally altered to *agricola* in the Vulgate, while in Luke *colonus* is completely retained. On one hand, this illustrates that Jerome did not make a thoroughgoing revision of the Old Latin and left much of the earlier version unaltered (Metzger 1977: 354; Harrison 1986: 233–36). On the other hand, it exemplifies the observation that the Gospel according to Matthew shows more changes than Mark, Luke, and John, indicating that Jerome revised them in the new sequence which he implemented (Houghton 2016a: 34; Harrison 1986: 236). The reason for this decline in interventions is hard to determine, but it has been presumed that Jerome had more enthusiasm at the beginning of his work and may later have changed his approach in order to focus on corrections (Vogels 1928: 49).

Although Old Latin texts generally tend to a rather loose translation, Jerome sought a more literal rendering of the Greek even at the expense of Latin idiom (Burton 2000:

---

[8]   Weber and Gryson 2007: 1515–16. The English translation follows Houghton 2016a: 32.

[9]   See Fischer 1972: 12. Vogels 1928: 55 identified approximately 3,500 changes introduced by Jerome (813 changes in Matthew, 873 in Mark, 1021 in Luke, and 780 in John), a number that has been challenged as too high (Houghton 2016a: 33).

197–99). This led to a particular Latin style which may have been considered "sacred" yet not entirely "correct" in idiom (see Fischer 1972: 16, 83–87). Various analyses have shown that the Vulgate tends to be more loose and idiomatically Latin in passages where Greek linguistic phenomena without Latin equivalents are paraphrased. Among these are grammatical, syntactic, and rhetorical elements such as the aorist, the perfect active and present passive participles, the lack of the definite article, a higher frequency of particles and participles in the Greek language, and double negatives, for which a literal translation would result in the opposite meaning (Fischer 1972: 87; Harrison 1986: 237).

There are numerous changes in vocabulary from the Old Latin to the Vulgate. Famous among these are changes from *quod* to *quia* (ὅτι, "that"), from *etiam* to *uero* or *autem*, from *rememorari* to *recordari* ("recollect"), from *adpropiare* to *adpropinquare* ("approach"), from *absconsus* to *absconditus* ("hidden"), from *manducare* to *comedere* or *edere* ("eat," perhaps reflecting Jerome's personal preference), from *attendere* to *cauere* ("beware"), and from *deludere* with the accusative to *inludere* ("mock") with the dative. Vulgate texts often have the pronoun *is* instead of *ille* or *ipse*. Furthermore, there is a tendency to translate ἐκβάλλειν ("throw out") with the Latin word *eicere* instead of Old Latin *expellere*. Likewise, the adverbs εὐθύς and εὐθέως ("immediately") are rendered by *statim* in the Vulgate when the Old Latin texts prefer *continuo*.

Among the many instances in which Old Latin renderings are made to conform more closely to the Greek form in the Vulgate, such as the imperative *memento* in Luke 23:42 instead of the Old Latin *memor esto* for the Greek μνήσθητι ("remember"), the rendering of Greek participles stands out. The following seven examples are seen in just one chapter. In Matthew 2:4 the Old Latin *congregauit . . . et* is changed to *congregans* (συναγαγών, "gathering"); in Matthew 2:7 *uocauit magos et* becomes *uocatis magis* (καλέσας τοὺς μάγους, "calling the Magi"); in Matthew 2:8 *ueniam et* is corrected to *ueniens* (ἐλθών, "coming") and the same holds true for *uenit et* in Matthew 2:9 and Matthew 2:23; in Matthew 2:16 the Greek participles ἰδών ("seeing") and ἀποστείλας ("sending") are rendered as *uidens* and *mittens* in the Vulgate, whereas most Old Latin witnesses read *ut uidit* and *misit et*. This Vulgate characteristic is also seen in the alteration of Old Latin word order to match that of Greek. It may be noted that, when it came to Scripture, Jerome considered that "even the word order is a sacred mystery" (*et uerborum ordo mysterium est*), as he wrote in his letter to Pammachius.[10] Three examples from Luke 22 suffice to illustrate this. In Luke 22:48 the Old Latin *dixit autem illi Iesus* is replaced by *Iesus autem dixit ei* (Ἰησοῦς δὲ εἶπεν αὐτῷ, "but Jesus said to him"), which also shows the preference for *ei* rather than *ille*, as mentioned above. In Luke 22:53 the Vulgate *manus in me* corresponds to the Greek τὰς χεῖρας ἐπ' ἐμέ ("hands on me"), while Old Latin texts read *in me manum*. Finally, the Vulgate word order *alius uidens eum* in Luke 22:58 matches the Greek ἕτερος ἰδὼν αὐτόν ("another, seeing him"), unlike *uidens eum alius* in Old Latin witnesses.

---

[10] *Epistula* 57.5, *De optimo genere interpretandi* (PL 22: 571); Harrison 1986: 161.

A host of examples could be given of individual corrections introduced in the Vulgate, of which a few may suffice.

1. Attention is paid to the semantics of Latin words which differ from their Greek counterparts, as in the rendering of the Greek adverb λάθρᾳ ("concealed," "aside"). Different renderings are chosen in the Vulgate according to context. In Matthew 1:19, *occulte* expresses privacy, while in Matthew 2:7 *clam* has the sense of willful concealment (it is possible that Jerome deliberately replaced the Old Latin *occulte* to picture Herod in a negative light). In John 11:28, λάθρᾳ is rendered by *silentio* because there it simply denotes quietness and calmness (Harrison 1986: 204–206). On the other hand, πλήν ("except") is mostly given as *uerumtamen* in the Vulgate, correcting various inconsistencies in the Old Latin (Harrison 1986: 212–213).

2. Other inconsistencies were adapted as well. The Old Latin singular *per prophetam*, for example, was transferred to the plural *per prophetas* (διὰ τῶν προφητῶν, "through the prophets") in Matthew 2:23, just as the Old Latin plural *radices* was changed to the singular *radicem* (τὴν ῥίζαν, "root") in Matthew 3:10.

3. Jerome's classical education and his high appreciation for Greek are even reflected in the Latin spelling of the Greek letter φ. During the time of Cicero, "ph" was standard in terms borrowed from Greek, but by the fourth century the Latin "f" had replaced it. Jerome reinstated the classical spelling in the gospels, in words such as *pharisaei* or *cophinus* (Harrison 1986: 32). Likewise, his preference for Greek can be seen in his introduction of Greek technical terms such as *anathematizare* ("to curse") in Mark 14:71 and *parasceue* (the "day of preparation") in John.

4. Not all changes are for the better, as in Jerome's introduction of etymologizing renderings which closely match the Greek. A well-known example occurs in the Lord's Prayer at Matthew 6:11. Instead of the Old Latin *panem nostrum cottidianum* ("our daily bread") the Vulgate imitates the problematic Greek ἐπιούσιον which is translated as *supersubstantialem*, a Latin word which remains as obscure as the Greek (Burton 2000: 196).

THE TRANSMISSION OF THE VULGATE

As mentioned above, Jerome's work was not immediately successful. It neither superseded the Old Latin readings nor was it granted official status by the church. Only in the latter half of the sixth and early seventh century did this change, beginning with the shift from Old Latin to Vulgate readings in Rome seen in several extant gospel books and in Spain with John, Bishop of Zaragoza, and Isidore of Seville (Houghton 2016a: 49–50, 63). From the ninth century onwards the Vulgate text, still heavily mixed with Old Latin, became the primary Latin version.

Early Transmission

The fifth century is still predominantly characterized by Old Latin codices, but one early Vulgate copy survives. This is Codex Sangallensis 1395, which was produced in the early fifth century in Italy, possibly still during Jerome's lifetime. Only half of the manuscript survives, but it is clearly Vulgate in its affiliation. Augustine has been shown to have acquired Jerome's revision around the year 403 and used it when writing *De consensu euangelistarum* (*On the Agreement of the Evangelists*) and his tractates on John (Houghton 2008). The widespread reading and copying of his works may have helped the Vulgate gain an initial circulation. The sixth and seventh centuries gave rise to mixed texts and contamination: some manuscripts copied from an Old Latin base were corrected toward the Vulgate, while Old Latin readings were inserted into manuscripts deriving from the Vulgate revisions. This mixture, along with the fact that features typical of Jerome's revision such as the Eusebian canons, the sequence of books, and even Jerome's preface can be found also in manuscripts with extensive Old Latin readings, makes studying the early transmission of the Vulgate a complicated yet fascinating task.[11]

An early sixth-century Italian revision of Jerome's version formed the basis for a series of gospel books associated with the missionary endeavors of Pope Gregory the Great. Gradually, a recognizably Vulgate text became known, quoted, and spread outside Italy. Spain, Ireland, Britain, and France mark the main areas for the early transmission of the Vulgate gospels. Traditionally, "types" or "groups" of Vulgate manuscripts have been identified according to these geographical areas (the so-called Italian, Spanish, Irish, and French types; Elliott 1992: 232; Metzger 1977: 334–41). However, such a pigeonholing of the manuscript tradition into geographical groups is inadequate: even if individual manuscripts may be allocated to a certain time, place, and style of writing, this does not automatically answer the question of their textual status and their mutual connections and influences. The first traces of the transmission of the New Testament text are found not in actual biblical manuscripts from various places but rather in writings by bishops and monks. The study of early Christian writers and their biblical quotations is therefore vital for a thorough understanding of the Latin transmission and correlations of readings, manuscripts, and places of production (Houghton 2014). To handle the complexity of a contaminated tradition, approaches are needed which point out connections between individual readings across the boundaries of biblical manuscripts and biblical quotations in the writings of contemporaneous Christian authors.[12]

---

[11] Examples of this mixture include: the sixth-century Burchard Gospels (Vulgate with extensive Old Latin readings which were later corrected); Codex Forojuliensis (J), copied in Aquileia in the sixth or seventh century, which contains Jerome's preface but not the Eusebian canon tables; Codex Aureus Holmiensis, sometimes described as Old Latin (VL 15) but with a strong Vulgate base, copied in Canterbury toward the end of the eighth century.

[12] An example of such an approach is Houghton (2016a: 43–95).

Revisions of the Vulgate

Because of the contamination of Jerome's text, several attempts to restore his version were made over the centuries, yet none had a long-lasting effect (Metzger 1977: 341–48). Prominent among these is Cassiodorus's alleged revision in the sixth century for his monastery at Vivarium, which seems not to have survived. The most significant revisions are by Theodulf of Zaragoza, who was Abbot of Fleury and Bishop of Orleans from 788 to 821, and of Alcuin of Northumbria, who undertook his revision while he was Abbot of Tours in response to Charlemagne's capitulary *Admonitio Generalis* in 789 (see chap. 12). Further examples of attempts to purify the Vulgate text are lists of variant readings (*correctoria*). The most influential ones are the *Correctorium Parisinense*, the *Correctorium Sorbonicum*, the *Correctorium* of Hugh of Saint-Cher, and the *Correctorium Vaticanum* of William de la Mare, all from the thirteenth century (see chap. 16).

Printed Editions of the Vulgate

The invention of printing did not bring an end to diversity or contamination in the transmission of the Latin Vulgate text (Metzger 1977: 348–52; see also chaps. 18 and 19). The first printed critical edition was that of Stephanus in 1528, which later became the base for an official ecclesiastical version as decided at the Council of Trent in 1546. Subsequently, the so-called Sixtine edition of 1590 was commissioned by Pope Sixtus V. After Pope Clement VIII introduced around three thousand changes to this, the so-called Sixto-Clementine edition (1592) became the official biblical text of the Roman Catholic Church. The most important critical editions of the Vulgate New Testament today are the Oxford Vulgate (Wordsworth and White 1889–98) and the Stuttgart edition (Weber and Gryson 2007).

CONCLUSION

This contribution has revisited key issues of past Vulgate gospel research, including Jerome as a trilingual reviser with an excellent classical education, as well as traditional solutions and methodological considerations concerning possible Old Latin and Greek templates for Jerome's revision. Various examples of Jerome's revisional technique were discussed. These have shown that the methodology and aims described by Jerome in his preface are indeed reflected in his revised Latin text of the gospels. Yet the main questions concerning the textual affiliations of Old Latin and Vulgate readings are still open. This is partly due to the volume of material, including new discoveries and findings which still await detailed analysis in respect to the Vulgate gospels. First and foremost, however, traditional approaches to the Vulgate gospels have become obsolete due to major shifts within New Testament textual criticism over the last decades, including the development of new technologies and the application of digital tools.

Research on the Latin Bible transmission and the Vulgate Gospels has therefore come to a turning point: full digital transcriptions of manuscripts (Old Latin, mixed texts as well as primarily Vulgate ones) together with the full revision of the Greek gospel tradition as part of the work on the *Editio Critica Maior* will allow for new insights and can be expected to extend our knowledge of textual correlations between Old Latin and Vulgate readings. The best is yet to come.

Acknowledgments

Work on this contribution has been funded by Internal Funds KU Leuven (StG 3H190608: "New Testament in Translation").

Bibliography

Bogaert, Pierre-Maurice. 2013. "The Latin Bible." In *New Cambridge History of the Bible: Vol. 1. From the Beginnings to 600*, edited by J. Carleton Paget and J. Schaper, 505–26. Cambridge: Cambridge University Press.

Burton, Philip. 2000. *The Old Latin Gospels: A Study of Their Texts and Language*. Oxford: Oxford University Press.

Burton, Philip. 2014. "The Latin Versions of the New Testament." In *The Text of the New Testament in Contemporary Research: Essays on the Status Quaestionis*, 2nd ed., edited by Bart D. Ehrman and Michael W. Holmes, 167–200. Leiden: Brill.

Crawford, Matthew R. 2019. *The Eusebian Canon Tables: Ordering Textual Knowledge in Antiquity*. Oxford: Oxford University Press.

Dorfbauer, Lukas, ed. 2017. *Fortunatianus Aquileiensis. Commentarii in evangelia.* CSEL 103. Berlin: De Gruyter.

Drobner, Hubertus R. 2011. *Lehrbuch der Patrologie.* 3rd ed. Frankfurt am Main and Berlin: Peter Lang.

Elliott, J. Keith. 1992. "The Translations of the New Testament into Latin: The Old Latin and the Vulgate." In *Aufstieg und Niedergang der Römischen Welt II.26.1, Religion*, edited by Wolfgang Haase and Hildegard Temporini, 198–245. Berlin: De Gruyter.

Fischer, Bonifatius. 1955. "Der Vulgata-Text des Neuen Testaments." *Zeitschrift für die neutestamentliche Wissenschaft* 46, no. 3: 178–96.

Fischer, Bonifatius. 1972. "Das Neue Testament in lateinischer Sprache: Der gegenwärtige Stand seiner Erforschung und seine Bedeutung für die griechische Textgeschichte." In *Die alten Übersetzungen des Neuen Testaments, die Kirchenväterzitate und Lektionare*, edited by Kurt Aland, 1–92. ANTF 5. Berlin: De Gruyter.

Fürst, Alfons. 1998. "Hieronymus." In *Lexikon der Antiken Christlichen Literatur*, 3rd ed., edited by Siegmar Döpp and Wilhelm Geerlings, 323–30. Freiburg: Herder.

Fürst, Alfons. 2003. *Hieronymus. Askese und Wissenschaft in der Spätantike.* Freiburg: Herder.

Greschat, Martin. 1984. *Alte Kirche II.* Gestalten der Kirchengeschichte 2. Stuttgart: Kohlhammer.

Harrison, Rebecca. 1986. "Jerome's Revision of the Gospels." PhD diss., University of Pennsylvania. ProQuest (AAI8614809). https://repository.upenn.edu/dissertations/AAI8614809.

Houghton, H. A. G. 2008. "Augustine's Adoption of the Vulgate Gospels." *New Testament Studies* 54, no. 3: 450–64.

Houghton, H. A. G. 2014. "The Use of the Latin Fathers for New Testament Textual Criticism." In *The Text of the New Testament in Contemporary Research: Essays on the Status Quaestionis*, 2nd ed., edited by Bart D. Ehrman and Michael W. Holmes, 375–405. Leiden: Brill.

Houghton, H. A. G. 2016a. *The Latin New Testament: A Guide to Its Early History, Texts, and Manuscripts*. Oxford: Oxford University Press.

Houghton, H. A. G. 2016b. 'The Text of John in Fortunatianus of Aquileia's Commentary on the Gospels." In *Studia Patristica 74: Including Papers Presented at the Fifth British Patristics Conference*, edited by Markus Vinzent and Allen Brent, 263–79. Leuven: Peeters.

Houghton, H. A. G. 2017. "The Divisions and Text of the Gospels in Fortunatianus' Commentary on the Gospels." In *Fortunatianus redivivus: Bischof Fortunatian von Aquileia und sein Evangelienkommentar*, edited by Lukas J. Dorfbauer and Victoria Zimmerl-Panagl, 215–37. CSEL Extra Seriem. Berlin: De Gruyter.

Jay, Pierre. 2006. "Jerome (ca. 347–419/420)." In *Handbook of Patristic Exegesis*. The Bible in Ancient Christianity 1, edited by Charles Kannengiesser, 1094–133. Leiden: Brill.

Kelly, J. N. D. 1975. *Jerome: His Life, Writings, and Controversies*. New York: Harper & Row.

Meershoek, G. Q. A. 1966. *Le Latin biblique d'après Saint Jérôme: Aspects linguistiques de la rencontre entre la Bible et le monde classique*. Nijmegen: Dekker & Van de Vegt.

Metzger, Bruce M. 1977. "The Latin Versions." *The Early Versions of the New Testament: Their Origin, Transmission, and Limitations*, 285–362. Oxford: Clarendon Press.

Mink, Gerd. 2004. "Problems of a Highly Contaminated Tradition: The New Testament: Stemmata of Variants as a Source of a Genealogy for Witnesses." In *Studies in Stemmatology II*, edited by Pieter van Reenen, August den Hollander, and Margot van Mulken, 13–85. Amsterdam: John Benjamins.

Moreschini, Claudio, and Enrico Norelli. 2007. *Handbuch der antiken christlichen Literatur*. Gütersloh: Gütersloher Verlagshaus.

Mülke, Markus. 2015. "Damasus und Hieronymus: Die lateinische Evangelienrevision und ihre papstgeschichtliche Bedeutung." In *Bibelübersetzung und (Kirchen-)Politik*, edited by Markus Mülke and Lothar Vogel, 41–68. Kirche–Konfession–Religion 64. Göttingen: Vandenhoek & Ruprecht.

Parker, David C. 2008. *An Introduction to the New Testament Manuscripts and Their Texts*. Cambridge: Cambridge University Press.

Souter, Alexander. 1911. "The Type or Types of Gospel Text Used by St Jerome as the Basis of his Revision: With Special Reference to St Luke's Gospel and Codex Vercellensis (a)." *Journal of Theological Studies* 12: 583–92.

Stummer, Friedrich. 1928. *Einführung in die lateinische Bibel: Ein Handbuch für Vorlesungen und Selbstunterricht*. Paderborn: Ferdinand Schöningh.

Vogels, Heinrich Joseph. 1928. *Vulgatastudien: Die Evangelien der Vulgata untersucht auf ihre lateinische und griechische Vorlage*. Neutestamentliche Abhandlungen 14. Münster: Aschendorff.

von Soden, Hermann. 1902–13. *Die Schriften des Neuen Testaments in ihrer ältesten erreichbaren Textgestalt hergestellt auf Grund ihrer Textgeschichte*. 4 vols. Göttingen: Vandenhoeck & Ruprecht.

Wasserman, Tommy, and Peter J. Gurry. 2017. *A New Approach to Textual Criticism: An Introduction to the Coherence-Based Genealogical Method*. Atlanta: SBL.

Weber, Robert, and Roger Gryson, eds. 2007. *Biblia Sacra: Iuxta Vulgatam Versionem*. 5th ed. Stuttgart: Deutsche Bibelgesellschaft.

Wordsworth, John, and Henry Julian White, eds. 1889–98. *Nouum Testamentum Domini nostri Iesu Christi latine secundum editionem sancti Hieronymi. I. Quattuor Evangelia*. Oxford: Clarendon Press.

CHAPTER 4

JEROME AND THE HEBREW SCRIPTURES

ADAM KAMESAR

THE EDUCATION OF JEROME AND THE *HEBRAICA UERITAS*

One might gain the impression, from some details of his biography, that Jerome's discovery of the *Hebraica ueritas*, the "Hebrew truth" as he would have said, and his promotion of it in his various editorial enterprises, is connected with his residence in Syria and Palestine. Certainly, by his own account, he took up the study of Hebrew with a convert to Christianity from Judaism during his stay in the "desert" of Chalcis, east of Antioch, perhaps in the middle to late 370s (*Epistula* 125.2; see Rebenich 2002: 13–20). And he began his famous translation "according to the Hebrew" only around the year 390, after he had settled permanently in Bethlehem. Nevertheless, the recognition of the importance of the Hebrew text on the part of Jerome, and the decision to make a new Latin translation directly from it, must be understood within the broader context of his background and education. The outstanding feature of that education is its cosmopolitan character. From his home in Stridon, perhaps in present-day Croatia, he traveled to Rome, Trier, Antioch, Constantinople, and Alexandria and studied with some of the finest scholars of his day. There can be little doubt that his familiarity with a wide variety of traditions of learning helps to explain his achievement and also contributed to the sophistication of his approach. In the following survey, we examine three of those traditions.[1]

---

[1] For a more linear and chronological summary of Jerome's education, insofar as it relates to his biblical studies, see Kamesar 2013: 653–57. The present discussion takes a detailed look at a few key elements.

The Apologetic Tradition and the Parity of Hellenism and Judaism

From the time of Alexander the Great onward, Greek came to be the *lingua franca* of the Mediterranean world, and Greek and Hellenistic culture gradually acquired a position of dominance. Even after the Roman conquest, Greek cultural hegemony continued, because the Romans acknowledged the superiority of the Greeks in matters of science and the arts. Accordingly, it is hardly surprising that with the spread of Christianity throughout the Roman Empire, the Greek translation of the Old Testament, called the Septuagint, held the preeminent place.[2] It is unlikely that potential converts would bother with an obscure language of just one of many peoples of the eastern part of the empire, and one which was not particularly celebrated, at least in the first and second centuries CE, for its contributions to human civilization.[3] However, over time, the Christian apologetic movement was able to change that perception, and bring Hellenism and Judaism, or as some would put it, Hebraism, into positions of approximate parity in the cultural sphere. In due course, we shall see the relevance of this change for Jerome's endeavors.

In the New Testament, we already find antecedents of the idea that Jews and Greeks constitute the principal groups of humanity.[4] This idea of course reflects a Jewish or Christian perspective and was developed by early apologists. In the second century, Christians began to speak of themselves as a "third race," distinct from their Jewish and Greek predecessors and contemporaries (Gruen 2017; Harnack 1924: 1.281–89). But as the Christian movement came to gain greater prominence and influence, the threefold division was taken over even by pagan opponents of Christianity, such as Porphyry and Julian.[5] This construct indirectly elevates the position of the Jews, vis-à-vis the Greeks, in regard to the significance of their historical roles.

In the earliest texts, the *Kerygma Petri* and the *Apology* of Aristides, the threefold distinction relates to religious observances and theological belief (Gruen 2017: 241–43). However, the construct, as it evolved over the next two centuries, came to encompass the entire cultural and literary legacy of the Jews or Hebrews, and set them in a position of parity, or even superiority, in comparison to the Greeks. This may be seen especially in Eusebius' *Praeparatio euangelica*. Here we learn that the Greek alphabet is derived from the Hebrew (10.5), that the Hebrews employed the appropriate literary forms (11.5), and that the "philosophy" of Moses and the prophets, duly divided into physics, ethics, and

---

[2] In this article, the term "Septuagint" indicates the text of the Greek translation, whereas the word "Seventy" is used to refer to the translators as persons.

[3] For the lack of significant achievements on the part of the Jewish *ethnos*, see the view of Celsus as quoted by Origen, *Contra Celsum* 4.31; compare also the earlier views cited by Josephus, *Contra Apionem* 2.135, 148.

[4] See especially 1 Corinthians 10:32, 12:13; Galatians 3:28; Colossians 3:11.

[5] Porphyry, *Contra Christianos* (Harnack fr. 1 = Becker fr. 88D); Julian, *Contra Galilaeos* (Masaracchia 1990: fr. 3).

logic, stands in a favorable light when compared to that of Plato and the Greeks (11.1.1, 28.18–19). Indeed, Eusebius upholds the position that Plato was dependent on Moses and the Hebrew prophets for various views (11.8, 16). In undertaking these comparisons, Eusebius speaks of and relies on biblical literature as a whole, as well as on later Judaeo-Hellenistic writings.

Such a perspective on the history of culture would potentially change the relevance of the Hebrew Bible in the eyes of the educated Christian of the fourth century. If the ancient Hebrew books are on a par with the classic works of Greek literature, they certainly would be worthy of study in their own right. And this would be particularly the case for Latin Christians. Those educated in the Latin schools were well aware that much of their literary culture was derived from the Greek. Latin writers of poetry and prose took over the genres of the Greeks and looked to the most eminent Greek authors as models. In other words, the "sources" of Latin literature were often Greek. Consequently, if Hebrew literature were to be set alongside the Greek as a basis for doctrine and culture, this would be a parallel phenomenon, and it would hardly be unreasonable for one to seek access to the original sources.

This is an essential part of the background that accounts for Jerome's interest in Hebrew, and it may be further illuminated by his use of a favorite image. Recent scholars have emphasized that in his advocacy of the use of the Hebrew text, Jerome likes to speak of the *fons* ("source" or "spring") and *riuuli* ("streamlets") (Kamesar 1993: 45; Fürst 2016: 328–29 with n. 7; Weigert 2016: 30–31). The former is the original text, whereas the latter are translations and/or interpretations based on them. The point is often that we gain greater knowledge, and are in a better position to interpret the text, when we examine the original rather than derivative forms of it.[6] This same imagery had been employed by Cicero in a similar context. After quoting Plato to the effect that philosophy is the greatest gift of the gods to humans, he says that he tells those who would study it to go to the Greeks, "so that they may draw from the sources rather than pursue the streamlets" (*ut ex fontibus potius hauriant quam riuulos consectentur*). It is clear from the context that by *riuuli*, he means works about philosophy in Latin.[7] In another passage, Cicero indicates that his own translations or adaptations [sc. of Greek works] will have the aim of "opening the sources of philosophy."[8] The source takes on, obviously, a privileged position.

The use of this imagery by Jerome in the way that has been described is noteworthy, and it tells us that for him, and no doubt for much of his readership, the endeavor to gain access to and familiarity with the Hebrew text has full legitimacy within the history of Latin culture. The way for this step, however, had been prepared by the apologists,

---

[6] For this, see especially *Epistula* 20.1–2; *Epistula* 34.3–4.

[7] *Academica* 1.8. The words are put into the mouth of Varro.

[8] *Tusculanae Disputationes* 1.5–6. Cf. also *Tusculanae Disputationes* 5.36 and *De Officiis* 1.6, for similar language with regard to adaptations of Greek philosophical works. These passages show, contrary to the notion of Weigert (2016: 31 n. 83), that Cicero did employ the image of the *fons* when speaking of translation and adaptation.

especially Eusebius, who had elevated the status of Hebrew Bible to the same level as that of Greek literature.

The Origenian Tradition and the Hexapla

Just as the change in the esteem of the Hebrew Bible prepared the way for Jerome's innovations, so did the advances made in Greek scholarship concerning it. It must be remembered that even for those Jews and Christians reading the Bible in the version of the Septuagint, Hebrew had a certain relevance. This is due to the presence in the Greek text of etymological explanations, of words that are transliterated rather than translated, and of various Hebrew literary devices. In the period between Philo and Origen, Greek scholarship on the Hebrew Bible had achieved significant progress. Philo did not know Hebrew, and had access to only one resource, the *onomastica* or lists of proper names with the corresponding Greek translation (Grabbe 1988: 101–9, 111–13). By the time of Origen, however, Greek-speaking Jews had produced a number of artful translations or revisions. Most notable are those of Aquila and Symmachus, composed in the second century CE. The version of Aquila is quite literal, that of Symmachus more free. But both versions rely on systematic translation techniques and are highly sophisticated literary achievements. It is the merit of Origen to have understood the relevance of these versions for biblical study and to have placed them in his Hexapla. This was a multicolumned Bible that contained the Hebrew text in both Hebrew letters and in Greek transliteration, and the various Greek translations in parallel columns (Dorival 2013: 608–11; see also chap. 2).

The Hexapla led to a greater awareness on the part of Christians of the difficulties connected with the reading and exegesis of the books of the Old Testament. In the first place, they came to understand in a more concrete fashion than before that their sacred texts were not originals, but translations. The translations in the Hexapla often differed among themselves, which created perplexities about what the Law, the Prophets, and the other books really meant. Moreover, for those who were better informed, the Hexapla allowed them to get a sense of the major differences between the Septuagint and the Hebrew text that was in circulation at the time. In addition to problems of translation, there were those of textual transmission.

It is generally believed that Jerome had his first direct contact with the works of Origen, including the Hexapla, or more probably exegetical writings relying on it, during his first stay in the East, in the middle to late 370s (Nautin 1986: 304). This is probably true, but in the present context, it must be emphasized that he had already encountered the Origenian exegetical tradition a number of years earlier. Indeed, in Trier, in 367 or 368, when he was about twenty, he read Hilary of Poitiers's *Tractatus super Psalmos*. This commentary, as Jerome would later say, was based on the work of Origen, although it also included Hilary's original contributions. Jerome will have known the work very well, because he tells us that he copied it with his own hand.[9]

---

[9] *Epistula* 5.2. For Hilary's dependence on Origen, see *De uiris illustribus* 100; cf. also *Epistulae* 61.2, 112.20.

Hilary's discussions contain clear acknowledgements of the importance of the Hebrew source for anyone wishing to gain an in-depth understanding of Scripture. Already near the beginning of his commentary, in his discussion of Psalm 2, Hilary sets out a unique version of the story of the origin of the Septuagint and explains the reasons for the differences between it and the renderings of "those who translated later" (i.e., Aquila and the other *recentiores*). He also provides an actual example, employing transliteration, of the "ambiguity" of the Hebrew language, no doubt alluding to the fact that it was written only in consonants (see further Kamesar 2005a). Also important is Hilary's large commentary on Psalm 118. Hilary explains clearly in his introduction how this psalm is organized according to the order of the Hebrew alphabet, and he makes other important observations in the course of the commentary. On one occasion, he indicates that the force of a Hebrew and a Greek word cannot be fully conveyed in Latin, and elsewhere he comes back to the matter of the "ambiguity" of the Hebrew, explaining it by citing the differing translations of the Seventy and the other translators (*Tractatus in Psalmum* 118.5.1, 13). On another occasion, he cites the same kind of difference between the translations in order to account for the varying views held by interpreters with regard to verse 28 of the Psalm (*Tractatus in Psalmum* 118.4.6). Also worthy of note is his decision to follow the Greek edition(s) of the Psalms "emended according to the Hebrew," a probable allusion to the versions of the *recentiores* or the corrected Septuagint, with regard to the placement of verse 57 (*Tractatus in Psalmum* 118.8.1).

It is hard to imagine that these kinds of observations on the part of Hilary did not stimulate Jerome to investigate the later translations further, and we know that by the end of his first stay in the East he had a thorough knowledge of them. In the preface to his version of Eusebius's *Chronicon*, probably written at Constantinople around 380, he speaks of the fact that Aquila, Symmachus, and Theodotion produced "practically a different work in the same work," while following different methods of translation. Perhaps even more telling is his comment that even the anonymous versions have their own "legitimate diversity" (Helm 1984: 3). Just a few years later, in 383 or 384, in the preface to a translation of two of Origen's homilies on the Song of Songs, he intimates that the differences in the various Greek translations do not only relate to matters of style or minor detail but are closely connected with the deepest meanings of the text. Speaking of Origen's larger commentary on the same biblical book, Jerome says that he so magnificently and clearly explained the Septuagint, the versions of Aquila, Symmachus, and Theodotion, and the anonymous *Quinta* that the verse "the king has brought me into his chamber" (Song of Songs 1:4) seems to be fulfilled in him (Baehrens 1925: 26). The implication is clear. Close study of the different versions, in their variety, gives one the opportunity to penetrate into the inner recesses of the Scripture and appreciate its deepest nuances.[10] Indeed, Jerome may be alluding here to

---

[10] The Song of Songs was thought to be concerned with *epoptikē*, the discipline by which one advances to the highest mysteries and contemplation of the divine. See Origen, *Commentarius in Cantica*, prol. 3.1–3, 14–16; Basil, *Homilia in principium Prouerbiorum* 1 (PG 31: 388A–B).

Origen's view, learned from a Jewish or Jewish Christian informant, that Scripture is like a house with many rooms.[11]

Knowledge of the versions in the Hexapla is closely connected, in Jerome, with the study of Hebrew. We know this from his letters (e.g., *Epistulae* 20.3, 32.1) and later commentaries, in which discussions of Hebrew philology often rely on views derivable from the later translations. One might wonder why the Hexapla did not stimulate a similar sustained and systematic interest in the Hebrew text on the part of the Greek Fathers, and that it took a Latin scholar to recognize and bring to fruition the full implications of that work. The answer to this question is most likely connected with the circumstance noted above. Jerome was an heir of Latin literary culture, in which there was, at least up until his time, an important component of bilingualism. A fuller discussion of the importance of that tradition may now be provided.

The Latin Tradition and the Discipline of Grammar

It is well known that Jerome, when he studied in Rome as a youth, had Aelius Donatus as his schoolmaster. Donatus was one of the greatest teachers of his age, and wrote influential works in each of the two areas into which Latin *grammatice* was divided in the imperial age: normative grammar and the study of literary texts, or in the terminology of Quintilian, *recte loquendi scientia* and *poetarum enarratio*.[12] These are his grammatical textbook in two parts, an *Ars minor* and an *Ars maior*, and his commentaries on Vergil and Terence.

Jerome knew the Latin grammatical tradition not only from his studies with Donatus but from his own reading. He had a thorough knowledge of Quintilian, the first book of whose *Institutio oratoria* included a significant section on *grammatice*. And he also had close familiarity with Suetonius's *De grammaticis et rhetoribus*, which he had employed already in his adaptation of Eusebius's *Chronicon*. We may highlight just one element from each of these works that is of importance for Jerome's use and study of a Hebrew text. In Quintilian's grammatical chapters, as in the whole work, we see the importance of bilingualism, to which we have already alluded. The significance of the Greek language and Greek literature emerges at every turn. As for the book of Suetonius, although best known for saucy anecdotes, one may gain from it a clear sense of the varied tasks that had been undertaken by the *grammatici* in the classical age. The discipline of *grammatice* had become highly professional and systematic, and Jerome would apply this same kind of sophistication to the study of biblical literature.

That Jerome himself had great confidence in *grammatice* as a distinct field of inquiry will be clear from the comments he makes on Titus 1:1. Discussing the phrase "knowledge of the truth that is in accord with piety," Jerome asks whether there might be a truth that is not in accord with piety, and answers in the affirmative. He cites

---

[11] *Philocalia* 2.3. Perhaps the informant was inspired by John 14:2.
[12] *Institutio Oratoria* 1.4.2. For the significance of these areas in the age of Jerome, see Kaster 1988: 17–18.

grammatice, dialectic, and other liberal arts as examples of disciplines that might possess it. Knowledge [sc. of the truth] according to piety is then identified with knowledge of the Scriptures, but that which involves belief and the reward of eternal life (*Comm. in Titum* 1:1b–4 [CCSL 77C: 8]).

Naturally, then, the question arises about the *Hebraica ueritas*, "Hebrew truth." Does it fall within the truths *grammatice* might possess, or does it require a "knowledge of the truth according to piety"? Some recent scholars, notably Eva Schulz-Flügel, seem to imply that the latter might also be involved, with the claim that in speaking of the *Hebraica ueritas*, Jerome also had in view the truth of revelation or "the truth in its theological sense" (Schulz-Flügel 2000: 42; Weigert 2016: 32–33). Although not disputing the view that the phrase has the sense of "original Hebrew text," she believes that the primary explanation for Jerome's use of it had to do with a specific philosophy of language. As she sees it, Jerome, in contrast to Augustine, would be an adherent of the view advocated by Cratylus in the Platonic dialogue of that name, according to which the name of a thing is in correspondence with its "being." The words (*onomata*) are indicative of "things as they are" (*ta onta*). Such an approach would privilege the Hebrew text, because it is the words in their Hebrew form that would express the essences of the things (Schulz-Flügel 1996: 660–62; 2014: 753–57).

One need not deny that Jerome may have accepted some elements of such a theory of language, especially in regard to the significance of etymologies, for these ideas were known in early Christianity.[13] Nevertheless, it seems overambitious to appeal to the theory, interpreted in a manner to accord with biblical revelation, to explain the formula *Hebraica ueritas*. In the first place, Jerome employs the word *ueritas* of texts that do not contain original biblical revelations. In *Epistula* 124.1, he speaks of the Greek text of Origen's *De principiis* as a *Graeca ueritas*, and in *Ep.* 106.46, referring to the Greek translation of the Psalms, he mentions the *hexaplorum ueritas* (i.e., the text in its Hexaplaric recension).[14] Augustine, following Jerome's lead, speaks of a *Latina ueritas*, no doubt referring to a (would-be) reliable Latin translation of the Old Testament (*Epistula* 71.6). Moreover, as a synonym or equivalent of *ueritas*, Jerome appears to use the word *fides*, of the New Testament in *De uiris illustribus* 135, and of the Old in *Epistula* 71.5. This would refer simply to the authenticity or fidelity of the document.[15] The term *auctoritas* is also used with the same intent.[16] Finally, *ueritas* in the sense of "correct text form" is found in a contemporary pagan source, Symmachus, *Epistula* 1.24.

---

[13] Schulz-Flügel (1996, 2014) suggested Origen, Donatus (in connection with Lucretius, *De rerum natura* 5.1028–90), and ancient Near Eastern and Jewish conceptions as possible sources for Jerome. But the more obvious source would be Eusebius, *Praeparatio euangelica* 11.6.

[14] For the reading *hexaplorum* in *Epistula* 106, see Marti 1974: 289.

[15] For this use of *fides* in a source of the same era, see Firmicus Maternus, *Mathesis* 6.24.7; cf. 1.2.10. The usage may derive from the legal sphere. Cf. Paulus, *Digesta* 22.4.2.

[16] See especially *Praefatio in libros Salomonis (iuxta LXX)* 1.1–3, where it is used with reference to the version of the Seventy translators. (The prefaces of Jerome's translations and revisions of the Bible are cited, sometimes with the line number, according to Weber and Gryson 2007. The three prefaces of the revision "according to the Septuagint" not included in this edition are cited according to Canellis 2017.)

The origin of the formula *Hebraica ueritas* is more likely to be sought in the Latin grammatical tradition. For the word *ueritas* occurs in a number of sources, notably Varro, Cicero, and Quintilian, where it refers to the principle(s) of analogy and/or etymology as criteria for determining correctness in grammar, as opposed to that of usage or *consuetudo*. The *ueritas* is a kind of standard that allows one to make choices within the variations that are the result of *consuetudo* (Ax 1990: 8–10). It is much more probable that Jerome's predilection for the term *ueritas* in the context of textual criticism derives from this linguistic use of the word than from some philosophical or theological intention. One should note his statement in *Praefatio in libros Salomonis (iuxta LXX)* 1.7–9, that he corrected the mistranslations *curiosissima ueritate* (i.e. by applying the strictest standard). And we may say more generally that he is attempting to highlight an original, authentic form of a text, as opposed to those forms that may represent *consuetudo* but have strayed from or moved beyond the original form on account of translation and textual transmission.[17]

The natural conclusion would be that it is possible to arrive at this kind of textual truth by means of the knowledge that is in accord with grammatical science and not necessarily with piety. Indeed, Jerome indicates to Rufinus that one may separate matters of faith and matters of erudition (*Aduersus Rufinum* 1.13). We should therefore reckon with an element of secularism in Jerome's advocacy of the Hebrew text.

THE MAKING OF THE HEXAPLARIC REVISION AND THE VERSION *IUXTA HEBRAEOS*

Jerome's formation in these three traditions had reached maturity certainly by about 380, the time of his translation of Eusebius's *Chronicon*, for this work attests to his deep familiarity with all of them. Accordingly, it is hardly surprising to find that his most intensive work and most notable progress in Hebrew studies, as far as we can determine, took place during the years in Rome, ca. 382–85. If one may speak of a "conversion" to the Hebrew text, it should probably be dated to this period (Kamesar 1993: 41–43). Why then, one may ask, did Jerome undertake a revision of at least some books of the Old Testament, based on Origen's Hexaplaric Septuagint text, sometime during the years 386–88, and only afterward begin the translation "according to the Hebrew," in 390–91? The most widespread explanation of this fact is that, contrary to what has just been stated, his "conversion" to the Hebrew text took place only around 390. Such a position holds that until that time, Jerome believed in the inspiration of the Septuagint, and it was through a gradual disillusionment with that version, gained in the course of his

---

[17] For Jerome's awareness of *consuetudo*, see *Praefatio in euangelia* 30–32; *Praefatio in Iob (iuxta LXX)* 1.9–11; *Epistula* 106.12.

work on the revision, that he abandoned the latter project and decided to turn directly to the Hebrew.[18] It is easier to explain the Hexaplaric revision, however, by appeal to more practical and concrete circumstances.

Around 383, Jerome was commissioned by Damasus to produce a revision of the text of the Latin Gospels because they were circulating in too many different forms (see chap. 1, 3). There was a need for a standard text. It is in all probability the same practical need that led to the Hexaplaric revision. Jerome was well aware that the Latin text of the Old Testament was based on the Septuagint, and a proper corrected version of that text would need to be based on the Greek. This was an action different from the translation of the Hebrew text, but for Jerome it represented a step in the right direction. This is because, in his view, of the various recensions of the Septuagint that were in circulation, the Hexaplaric one was the closest to the Hebrew.[19]

Revision and translation were distinct activities. Jerome made a clear differentiation between the two in the description of his own work: "I restored the New Testament to the Greek original, I translated the Old according to the Hebrew."[20] The task of emendation and revision had a venerable and independent place in the Latin tradition of *grammatice*. Suetonius, in his *De grammaticis*, speaks of the fact that the great Marcus Valerius Probus (first century CE) devoted himself exclusively to the part of the discipline that consisted of *emendare, distinguere, adnotare* (24.2). Most likely, this refers to emendation and punctuation of texts, and marking them with critical signs.[21] For his part, Jerome is usually careful to describe his revision as an emendation, and he gives detailed indications about the use of the critical signs in the prefaces to those books of the revision that survive.[22]

The readers and sponsors of Jerome's revisions will also have been cognizant of what was involved in emendation. His friends like Paula, Eustochium, Domnio, and Heliodorus were Roman and Italian aristocrats, among whom the emendation of classical texts was a kind of learned hobby. Vettius Agorius Praetextatus, a pagan city prefect whose death in 384 is the subject of Jerome's comments in *Epistula* 23, was celebrated by his wife in an epitaph as one who "made better" the texts he took in hand. It can hardly be doubted that this refers to the coherence or readability of the text as judged

---

[18] For this view, see most recently Canellis 2017: 89, 93; Schulz-Flügel 1996: 650–653; 2014: 747–749; cf. also Weigert 2016: 36.

[19] The most explicit statement to this effect comes in *Epistula* 106.2 (the letter is generally dated to the period 404–10; see Fürst 2016: 246). Cf. *Comm. in Isaiam* 16.21 (on Isaiah 58:11).

[20] *Nouum testamentum graecae fidei reddidi, uetus iuxta hebraicum transtuli* (*De uiris illustribus* 135 [PL 23: 717–19]).

[21] See the translation of and commentary on Suetonius's text in Kaster 1995: 29, 260–62. It may be acknowledged that *adnotare* might have a broader meaning here and elsewhere, including in Jerome, and that the placing of the signs might be indicated by *distinguere* in Jerome (Arns 1953: 71–72), but this does not detract from the pertinence of the passage from Suetonius in this context.

[22] *Praefatio in Paralipomenon (iuxta Heb.)* 35–36; *Praefatio in libros Salomonis (iuxta Heb.)* 22–23; *Praefatio in Psalmos (iuxta Heb.)* 31–33; *Aduersus Rufinum* 2.24, 3.25; *Praefatio in Psalmos (iuxta LXX)* 9–14; *Praefatio in Iob (iuxta LXX)* 2.1–6; *Praefatio in libros Salomonis (iuxta LXX)* 1.1–6.

from "internal" criteria, something which was also a focus of Jerome's efforts.[23] A very ambitious project to emend the entire text of Livy was promoted by the family of the Symmachi, perhaps in the 390s.[24] Even the more modest efforts of *emendatio*, to which many subscriptions in Latin manuscripts attest, have their place in the cultural milieu.[25]

In short, Jerome's work on the Hexaplaric revision is best understood in light of the role of emendation in the Latin grammatical tradition, and against the background of contemporary scholarly activity. It is a project in its own right, not a preparatory step toward the translation from the Hebrew. This explains why he never spoke of it with disparagement as an immature effort, unlike some of his other projects.[26] To the contrary, he always maintained pride in it. We know that he revised six books according to the Hexaplaric Greek text: Psalms, Chronicles, Job, and the three books of Solomon, Proverbs, Ecclesiastes, and the Song of Songs. Whether he completed other books remains uncertain. In *Epistula* 134.2.3, he implies that he did, but this cannot be verified as nothing of them has been preserved.[27]

We are much better informed about the translation "according to the Hebrew," in which Jerome invested a greater commitment and effort. This also appeared in installments, during the approximate period 390–405. There is a general consensus among scholars on this point, although there are differences of opinion on the precise order of publication, and on the dates that may be assigned to individual books.[28] In general, it may be noted that Jerome often produced his works in response to requests from sponsors and correspondents, and did not follow biblical sequence. The basic data are as follows. In *Epistula* 48, generally dated to 393 or 394, Jerome indicates that he had already completed sixteen books of the Prophets (four major and twelve minor), Job, and Samuel and Kings. From chapter 134 of *De uiris illustribus*, a work now generally dated to 393, we learn that Jerome's friend Sophronius had already translated his versions of the Psalms and the Prophets into Greek. Whether the books of Samuel and Kings were the first to appear is uncertain, but they did have a certain importance: Jerome prefixed to them what he calls his *prologus galeatus*, or "prologue with a helmet," and says that it may serve as a preface to all of the books of the translation. The books of Chronicles were probably finished in 396 or 397, because in the preface Jerome refers to his *De optimo genere interpretandi* (= *Epistula* 57) as recent, and this work seems to have appeared in

---

[23] For the epitaph, see *Inscriptiones Latinae Selectae* 1259 (*in tergo*) 8–12, also available in Courtney 1995: 58–59. Cameron has recently argued that "make better" should be taken to mean "annotate" (2011: 478–80). This is an unconvincing attempt to deny the obvious meaning of the text (see Courtney 1995: 254). For Jerome's objectives, see *Praefatio in Iob (iuxta LXX)* 2.7–9; *Praefatio in libros Salomonis (iuxta LXX)* 1.7–11. For more learned forms of *emendatio* in the Latin environment, cf. Ps.-Horace, *Sermo* 1.10.2–3; Aulus Gellius, *Noctes Atticae* 1.15.18.

[24] See Symmachus, *Epistula* 9.13; for the date and further discussion of this and related efforts, see Roda 1981: 119–22.

[25] The significance of the subscriptions has been subject to some debate. For a recent assessment, see Zetzel 2018: 206.

[26] See *Commentarius in Abdiam*, prol.; cf. *Epistula* 27*.2.

[27] On this matter, see Fürst 2016: 88. The date of the letter is 416.

[28] For a fuller summary of the *status quaestionis* in regard to chronology, see Canellis 2017: 93–98.

396 (Bona 2007: 32–33 n. 76). By 398, the date of *Epistula* 71, Jerome had translated the entire Hebrew canon with the exception of the Octateuch and probably Esther. He then turned his attention to the Pentateuch, and finally, to Joshua, Judges, Ruth, and Esther. At the end of the preface to Joshua, which no doubt served also for Judges and Ruth, he mentions the death of his beloved friend and sponsor Paula, which occurred in 404.

How are we to assess the two different editions? In producing the Hexaplaric revision, Jerome was acting the churchman and paying attention to practical reality. With the version *iuxta Hebraeos*, however, he was following his own instincts and, as he says of Origen, giving the "full sails of his talent (*ingenium*) to the blowing winds. "[29] In the case of Jerome, this would apply not to exegesis but to translation. Indeed, in *Praefatio in Pentateuchum* 4–6, he teases his detractors by saying that they judge *ingenium* like wine, when criticizing him for producing the new (i.e., his own version) to replace the old (i.e., the Septuagint). The implication here is that translation is a matter of *ingenium*, in the case of both himself and the Seventy. Jerome confirms this later on when he intimates that the "inspiration" of translators is not to be understood in any prophetic or biblical sense but, citing the example of Cicero, only in the Graeco-Latin sense of natural talent. This way of speaking reveals the artistic pretensions he had for his version, and that he did intend it to be used in church, at least in a best-case scenario. He did not see its function limited to aid in exegesis, or to being a tool for scholars, as is sometimes claimed.[30] His statement in *Epistula* 106.46 that the (Latin version of the) Septuagint was to be sung in church may perhaps be restricted to the book of Psalms. But in any case, declarations of this sort probably only indicate that Jerome was not attempting to *constrain* anyone or any community to use his translation in church, not that he did not envisage a liturgical role for it. His composition of the version *iuxta Hebraeos* in stylistic continuity with the previous translations, and the claims that he makes for it as a literary work, suggest that he did. To these matters we now turn.

THE VERSION *IUXTA HEBRAEOS* AS A LITERARY ENDEAVOR

Jerome's attention to the literary quality of the biblical text emerges early on and is attested in the all-important text we have mentioned above, the preface to the translation of Eusebius's *Chronicon*. Within the context of a discussion of translation in general, he comes to speak of the translations of the Bible. He says that the Septuagint does not preserve the same "flavor" (*sapor*) of the original, and it was this circumstance that led Aquila, Symmachus, and the others to make new translations. He goes on to

---

[29] *Praefatio in Origenis Homilias in Ezechielem* (Baehrens 1925: 318). For such nautical imagery, cf. Curtius 1990: 128–30.

[30] Most recently by Schulz-Flügel 2014: 757–58; cf. Weigert 2016: 43.

say that the same circumstance (i.e. the poor quality of the Septuagint) has led educated persons who do not know that the biblical books are translated from the Hebrew
to be dismayed by their literary "dress." Such persons would not be in a position to appreciate the poetry of the Psalter, the songs of Moses or Isaiah, or the *grauitas* of (the
books of) Solomon.[31]

We learn from this text that, according to Jerome, there was already dissatisfaction
with the Septuagint as a literary entity in Jewish Hellenistic circles. The versions of
Aquila, Symmachus, and the rest represent attempts to fix the problem. Such a view of
the matter would be perfectly natural for one who had been trained in the classical Latin
tradition of translation and adaptation of Greek works, in which the focus tended to be
on the target language and on the artistic quality of the version, which was in a kind of
competition with the original (Traina 1993: 93–96). Indeed, in *Epistula* 57.5.3–5 Jerome
cites Cicero and refers to the example of the Latin comic poets to make the point that
one of the chief aims of a translator should be, in addition to rendering the sense, to
achieve stylistic fidelity to the original (Bartelink 1980: 54, 57–58; Mülke 2008: 153–63).
This means that, from his perspective, when dealing with the biblical corpus, Jerome
was confronted not just with a text-critical problem, as illustrated in the previous discussion, but with a literary problem.

Jerome's attempt to address this problem in the creation of the version *iuxta Hebraeos*,
at least to a certain extent, is evident from its earliest installments. The Prophets, as
noted above, were among the first books to appear in the new translation. In the prefaces
to the three Major Prophets, Jerome gives brief stylistic assessments of each. Isaiah has
an "urbane elegance," which cannot be reproduced in translation. Jeremiah, for his part,
exhibits more "rusticity" than one finds in Isaiah or in Hosea, and this is to be explained
by his origins in the small village of Anathoth. The style of Ezekiel, finally, is somewhere
between the two. In all likelihood, Jerome is applying the theory of the three levels of style
or three styles, known from Hellenistic literary criticism, to the corpus of the Hebrew
prophets. It was common to ascribe the three styles to different members of a canon of
authors. For example, among the Greek historians, Thucydides personifies the elevated
style, Xenophon the plain, and Herodotus the middle. It is possible that Jerome's knowledge of Hebrew was not quite at a level to appreciate the differing styles, and he may
have relied on his Jewish reading partners for guidance: similar characterizations of the
manner of expression of the different prophets are found in the Babylonian Talmud and
in the *Pesiqta deRav Kahana*. However, it was no doubt Jerome himself who interpreted
what he learned from his informants on the basis of his own education in *grammatice*
and rhetoric. He found the theory of the three styles to be a most helpful model in this
instance (see further Kamesar 2005b).

---

[31] For the text, see Eusebius, *Chronicon* (Helm 1984: 2–4). As Marti (1974: 175) points out, the sentence
that begins with *inde* on p. 3, l. 12, refers back to what Jerome says about the version of the Seventy in lines
1–4. His interpretation may be confirmed by the fact that the dismay of the "literate men" would not stem
from the versions of Aquila and the rest, because if they (the literate men) knew of the multiple versions,
they would know that the books were translations and not originals.

Despite the modesty he shows in saying that a translation cannot properly convey the eloquence of Isaiah (*Praefatio in Isaiam* 8–9), Jerome probably believed that he had achieved at least a partial measure of success in producing a version that imparted the "flavor" of the original. This may be discerned from his letter to Pammachius, written in 393 or 394, in which he refers to a number of his recent translations. He speaks first of the versions of the Prophets, and says that if Pammachius reads and takes pleasure (*delectari*) from this work, he (Jerome) will give him additional works (*Epistula* 48.4.1). It is the use of the term *delectari* that is significant. In Hellenistic literary criticism, there was much discussion about the goal or *telos* of literature. There was often an argument about whether pleasure (*hēdonē*) or benefit and instruction (*ōpheleia, didaskalia*) should be the primary objective. Horace, for example, took the view that the poet should aim to do both (*Ars Poetica* 333–34, 343–44). In some circles, however, the idea seems to have developed that pleasure was more closely connected with the form or language of a work, and benefit or instruction with its content.[32] One finds this view implicit in Seneca, *Epistula* 75.5: "Our words should provide not pleasure, but benefit. Nevertheless, if eloquence can be attained without trouble, if it is ready at hand or may be produced with little effort, then let it be present and accompany the worthiest subject." Here we see that "providing pleasure" is set in parallel to "eloquence." A similar notion is found in some patristic commentaries on the Psalms, to the effect that their melodious form provides pleasure or enchantment, and this is an aid for gaining beneficial moral instruction.[33] Consequently, it seems highly likely that Jerome, when speaking of Pammachius' "taking pleasure" in his translations, is alluding to his adaptation and rendering of their style, or even, as he would have it, styles.

This interpretation seems to be confirmed by what Jerome says about his version of Samuel and Kings later in the same letter. He tells Pammachius that he will be able to determine by reading it that texts that, by the fault of the translators, teem with defects *apud nos* (i.e., in Greek and Latin), glide along with a pure flow of discourse *apud suos* (i.e., in Hebrew).[34] Since Pammachius was able to read only Greek and Latin, and not Hebrew, his appreciation of the "flowing" of the Hebrew text would be the result of his reading Jerome's new version, not the original text. Jerome is therefore making a claim of the highest order about the stylistic fidelity of his own translation. He is saying, in effect, when one takes into account what he had said about the version of the Seventy in the preface to the *Chronicon*, that he has succeeded where they have failed.

Jerome continued to make this claim as he progressed with the publication of the translation. In the preface to the books of Solomon, generally dated to 398, he again

---

[32] Cf. Jensen 1923: 123; Michel 1960: 155–56. For the linkage between pleasure and form in Cicero, see also *Tusculanae Disputationes* 1.6, 2.7.

[33] Theodoret, *Commentarius in Psalmos*, praef. (PG 80: 857a–60a); Ambrose, *Expositio Psalmi* 1.10.

[34] *Epistula* 48.4.2. In the sentence that begins, *quae si legere uolueris*, it seems logical to take the first part (*quantae difficultatis . . .*) to refer to the commentaries on the prophets, and the second part (*et interpretum uitio . . .*) to refer to the translation of Samuel and Kings, both of which had been mentioned previously, in the same order.

compares his version from the Hebrew to the edition of the Seventy, as emended by himself (i.e., in Latin form). But he asserts that any careful reader will find that it is the former that is more comprehensible (*magis nostra intellegi*), and that, having been poured directly from the press into a very clean vessel, has preserved the original flavor (*sapor*). Here again, as in *Epistula* 48.4, the implication is that an educated student of the Bible will be able to make such an assessment solely on "internal" grounds, without access to the original Hebrew.

It may be that Jerome's statement about the greater comprehensibility of his version can provide us with a clue about his thinking, and explain why his claims are perhaps not as outlandish as one might think. We know from his commentaries, on the prophets in particular, that of the translators, he gave the highest marks to Symmachus, especially for clarity (Ziegler 1971: 142–48). We have seen too from the preface to Eusebius's *Chronicon* that he indeed appreciated the versions of the *recentiores* as stylistic enterprises. This is quite comprehensible when one remembers that the Septuagint, as modern scholarship has shown, is in actual fact a collection of translations by different people from different periods, and exhibits a variety of translation techniques. By contrast, Symmachus and the others produced homogeneous versions with literary design. Accordingly, it seems likely that Jerome had a real sense of the progress that had been made by the later Greek translators, and that he saw himself as building upon that. If he could lay claim to one aspect of style (i.e., clarity), it is not surprising that he does so with respect to another, fidelity.

In general, Jerome sought to create his translation in continuity with the previous tradition but, at the same time, to improve upon it. He wanted to show respect for the "simplicity" of biblical language (Weigert 2016: 62–64). Despite this, he also aimed for a modest elegance in Latin. As he says at the conclusion of his letter to Pammachius, one need not seek the eloquence of Cicero in his translation. An "ecclesiastical" rendering may have elegance (*uenustas*), even while needing to conceal it and shun it (*dissimulare eam debet et fugere*; *Epistula* 48.4.3). This is just another way of saying, as Seneca put it in *Epistula* 75.5, that eloquence should not aim to parade itself (*sit* [sc. *eloquentia*] *talis ut res potius quam se ostendat*). Statements of this sort are of course common in the Graeco-Latin tradition, but the simplicity of biblical style lent itself particularly well to this kind of defense.

Ultimately, Jerome was successful in his great act of cultural and literary mediation. It would of course take several hundred years for biblical language to become naturalized in the Latin world, and for his version to be recognized as a classic of literature (Auerbach 1965: 45–47). Nevertheless, the beginnings of the process are discernible within his own lifetime and just afterward. Jerome's younger contemporary Augustine, as is well known, had serious reservations about the new version from the Hebrew. However, by the time he came to write the fourth book of the *De doctrina christiana*, in the late 420s, he had a different view. In a section of this book he attempts to show that the biblical writers were not only wise but also eloquent, and that the Bible could be recommended not only for what it said but also for its manner of expression. In providing an example from the prophet Amos, he makes explicit his preference for the version of Jerome over that of the Seventy (*De doctrina christiana* 4.7.15). This is a clear acknowledgement of the literary quality of Jerome's version on the part of one of the masters of Latin Christianity. Others would follow suit in due course.

BIBLIOGRAPHY

Arns, Paulo Evaristo. 1953. *La Technique du livre d'après saint Jérôme*. Paris: de Boccard.

Auerbach, Erich. 1965. *Literary Language and Its Public in Late Latin Antiquity and in the Middle Ages*. Princeton: Princeton University Press.

Ax, Wolfram 1990. "Aristophanes von Byzanz als Analogist: Zu Fragment 374 Slater. (= Varro, de lingua Latina 9, 12)." *Glotta* 68: 4–18.

Baehrens, Wilhelm A., ed. 1925. *Origenes, Werke*, viii, *Homilien zu Samuel I, et alia*. GCS 33. Leipzig: J. C. Hinrichs.

Bartelink, Gerard J. M., ed. 1980. *Hieronymus, Liber de optimo genere interpretandi. Epistula 57: Ein Kommentar*. Leiden: Brill.

Bona, Edoardo, ed. 2007. *La libertà del traduttore: L'epistola de optimo genere interpretandi di Gerolamo*. Rome: Bonanno.

Cameron, Alan. 2011. *The Last Pagans of Rome*. New York: Oxford University Press.

Canellis, Aline, ed. 2017. *Jérôme, Préfaces aux livres de la Bible*. SC 592. Paris: Cerf.

Courtney, Edward. 1995. *Musa Lapidaria: A Selection of Latin Verse Inscriptions*. Atlanta: Scholars Press.

Curtius, Ernst Robert. 1990. *European Literature and the Latin Middle Ages, With a New Afterword*. Princeton: Princeton University Press.

Dorival, Gilles 2013. "Origen." In *New Cambridge History of the Bible: Vol. 1, From the Beginnings to 600*, edited by James Carleton Paget and Joachim Schaper, 605–28. Cambridge: Cambridge University Press.

Fürst, Alfons. 2016. *Hieronymus: Askese und Wissenschaft in der Spätantike*. 2nd ed. Freiburg: Herder.

Grabbe, Lester L. 1988. *Etymology in Early Jewish Interpretation: The Hebrew Names in Philo*. Atlanta: Scholars Press.

Gruen, Erich S. 2017. "Christians as a 'Third Race': Is Ethnicity at Issue?" In *Christianity in the Second Century: Themes and Developments*, edited by James Carleton Paget and Judith Lieu, 235–49. Cambridge: Cambridge University Press.

Harnack, Adolf von. 1924. *Die Mission und Ausbreitung des Christentums in den ersten drei Jahrhunderten*. 4th ed. Leipzig: J. C. Hinrichs.

Helm, Rudolf ed. 1984. *Eusebius, Werke*, vii, *Die Chronik des Hieronymus*. 3rd ed. GCS 47. Berlin: Akademie.

Jensen, Christian, ed. 1923. *Philodemos, Über die Gedichte, fünftes Buch*. Berlin: Weidmann.

Kamesar, Adam. 1993. *Jerome, Greek Scholarship, and the Hebrew Bible*. Oxford: Oxford University Press.

Kamesar, Adam. 2005a "Hilary of Poitiers, Judeo-Christianity, and the Origins of the LXX: A Translation of *Tractatus super Psalmos* 2.2-3 with Introduction and Commentary." *Vigiliae Christianae* 59: 264–85.

Kamesar, Adam. 2005b. "S. Gerolamo, la valutazione stilistica dei profeti maggiori ed i *genera dicendi*." *Adamantius* 11: 179–83.

Kamesar, Adam. 2013. "Jerome." In *New Cambridge History of the Bible: Vol. 1, From the Beginnings to 600*, edited by James Carleton Paget and Joachim Schaper, 653–75. Cambridge: Cambridge University Press.

Kaster, Robert A. 1988. *Guardians of Language: The Grammarian and Society in Late Antiquity*. Berkeley: University of California Press.

Kaster, Robert A., ed. 1995. *C. Suetonius Tranquillus, De Grammaticis et Rhetoribus*. Oxford: Oxford University Press.

Marti, Heinrich 1974. *Übersetzer der Augustin-Zeit: Interpretation von Selbstzeugnissen*. Munich: Wilhelm Fink.

Masaracchia, Emanuela, ed. 1990. *Giuliano Imperatore, Contra Galilaeos*. Rome: Ateneo.

Michel, Alain. 1960. *Rhétorique et philosophie chez Cicéron: Essai sur les fondements philosophiques de l'art de persuader*. Paris: Presses Universitaires de France.

Mülke, Markus. 2008. *Der Autor und sein Text: Die Verfälschung des Originals im Urteil antiker Autoren*. Berlin: De Gruyter.

Nautin, Pierre. 1986. "Hieronymus." *Theologische Realenzyklopädie* 15, no. 1–2, 304–15.

Rebenich, Stefan. 2002. *Jerome*. London: Routledge.

Roda, Sergio. 1981. *Commento storico al libro IX dell' epistolario di Q. Aurelio Simmaco*. Pisa: Giardini.

Schulz-Flügel, Eva. 1996. "The Latin Old Testament Tradition." In *Hebrew Bible/Old Testament: The History of Its Interpretation*, i, *From the Beginnings to the Middle Ages*, 1. *Antiquity*, edited by Magne Sæbø, 642–62. Göttingen: Vandenhoeck & Ruprecht.

Schulz-Flügel, Eva. 2000. "Hieronymus, Feind und Überwinder der Septuaginta? Untersuchungen anhand der Arbeiten an den Psalmen." In *Der Septuaginta-Psalter und seine Tochterübersetzungen*, edited by Anneli Aejmelaeus and Udo Quast, 33–50. Göttingen: Vandenhoeck & Ruprecht.

Schulz-Flügel, Eva. 2014. "Hieronymus—Gottes Wort: Septuaginta oder hebraica veritas." In *Die Septuaginta—Text, Wirkung, Rezeption*, edited by Wolfgang Kraus and Siegfried Kreuzer, 746–58. Tübingen: Mohr Siebeck.

Traina, Alfonso. 1993. "Le traduzioni." In *Lo spazio letterario di Roma antica*: ii. *La circolazione del testo*. 2nd ed., edited by Guglielmo Cavallo, P. Fedeli, and A. Giardina, 93–123. Rome: Salerno.

Weber, Robert, and Roger Gryson, eds. 2007. *Biblia Sacra iuxta Vulgatam Versionem*, 5th ed. Stuttgart: Deutsche Bibelgesellschaft.

Weigert, Sebastian. 2016. *Hebraica veritas: Übersetzungsprinzipien und Quellen der Deuteronomiumübersetzung des Hieronymus*. Stuttgart: Kohlhammer.

Zetzel, James E. G. 2018. *Critics, Compilers, and Commentators: An Introduction to Roman Philology, 200 BCE—800 CE*. New York: Oxford University Press.

Ziegler, Joseph. 1971. "Die jüngeren griechischen Übersetzungen als Vorlagen der Vulgata in den prophetischen Schriften." In *Sylloge: Gesammelte Aufsätze zur Septuaginta*, 139–228. Göttingen: Vandenhoeck & Ruprecht. First published 1943/1944.

CHAPTER 5

....

THE LATIN PSALTER

....

OLIVER W. E. NORRIS

No book of the Old Testament was more important than the Psalter both as a scriptural authority for Christian writers and in the daily life of the early Church and its successors. We learn from Tertullian that psalm chanting was already a part of Christian liturgy at the turn of the third century (*Ad uxorem* 2.8; Lamb 1962: 27). The Psalter was the subject of the greatest number of patristic commentaries in Latin as in Greek, as well as being the most copied book of the Latin Bible by medieval scribes after the Gospels (Schirner 2016: 1; Gryson 2004: 11). Yet whether it was due to the widespread need of a single text for chanting, or perhaps due to the realization by apologists that a widely varying text was of little use as a scriptural authority, the Latin Psalter went through a period of thorough standardization from the third to the fifth centuries and, by the end of Late Antiquity, the variety seen in the early psalter texts of the time of Tertullian, Cyprian, and Novatian had largely disappeared.

Nevertheless, the Latin Psalter is by no means a single-text tradition. As a translation of the Septuagint Psalter, four traditions, the Roman, Mozarabic, Milan or Ambrosian, and the Hexaplaric or Gallican Psalter were still widely found in bibles or the liturgy until the Council of Trent in the sixteenth century and in restricted use in specific dioceses until the Second Vatican Council in 1962.[1] By the far the most widely diffused of these traditions was the Hexaplaric Psalter: manuscript copies of it number in the thousands and its presence can be detected in nearly every copy of the Latin Psalter. In addition to these four Old Latin traditions, Jerome's *Iuxta Hebraeos*, a Latin version based on the Hebrew Psalter rather than the Septuagint, was widespread in early Bible pandects without ever being adopted for liturgical purposes.

---

[1] The term "Hexaplaric" is increasingly preferred to "Gallican" to avoid confusion with the Gallic group of psalters used in France prior to the dominance of the Gallican. The term "hexaplaric" without capitalization refers in this chapter to readings from the Jewish Greek *recentiores* translations of Aquila, Symmachus, and Theodotion that have entered the Latin Psalter tradition via Origen's Hexapla (see also chap. 2).

THE EARLY DEVELOPMENT OF THE
LATIN PSALTER

The early Latin Psalter tradition was simple. Translations may initially only have been made of those psalms needed for liturgical purposes or the instruction of the faithful (Kedar 1988: 301–2). The oldest sources preserve a different numbering scheme to that found in the Septuagint: the first two Psalms were numbered as a single psalm; then, as found in Bodmer Papyrus XXIV, Psalm 113 was divided into two and Psalms 116–17 again counted as a single psalm (Bogaert 2000: 55–57).[2] As the Latin liturgical tradition developed, so the Psalter began to acquire more elements, such as canticles and collects or psalm prayers. The first evidence of Latin *tituli* or superscriptions is found in Hilary of Poitiers. These Hebrew titles, already poorly translated in the Septuagint, became even more obscure in Latin. From the fourth century, they were supplemented by a series of Christian *tituli* of which six traditions were identified by Salmon (1959).

The oldest securely datable text in an extant Latin Psalter is that of the Verona Psalter (Verona, Biblioteca Capitolare I [1]; α; VL 300), a Greek-Latin double psalter copied in North Italy in the seventh century.[3] An almost identical form of text is cited by Augustine from about 395 (De Bruyne 1931: 563). For the development of the text prior to this date, we are largely dependent on indirect tradition. The development of the Latin Psalter is one of progression from a single translation to multiple traditions, followed by textual stabilization and the dominance of one or two textual forms, similar to that described by Tov for the development of the Septuagint (1988: 167–68). The exact date and location of the creation of the first Latin Psalter is unknown. In Capelle's study of the African Psalter, he concludes that the countless points of contact between Tertullian's psalm citations and later texts, especially those of Cyprian, support the existence of a Latin version of the Psalms by the end of the second century (Capelle 1913: 180–81). There is no proof that the first Latin Psalter translation came from Africa, but, given the African Church's transition from Greek to Latin by the third century, the need for a Latin Psalter for the liturgy was greater there than in Rome, where the Church used Greek until the time of Pope Damasus (366–84) (Klauser 1965: 25–26; see also chap. 1). Nonetheless, there is also evidence in the writings of Novatian that a Latin Bible text was available in Italy in the third century (Mattei 1995: 278–79). Novatian's text is the first evidence of the "European" revision of the Psalms with renderings such as *uerbum* and *laetitia* (Psalm 44:2, 8 [LXX]) where Cyprian has *sermo* and *exultatio*.

Although there is general agreement that the Latin Psalter stems from a single translation that underwent multiple revisions (Vaccari 1952: 253; Ongaro 1954: 450, 473–74;

---

[2] See further table 1.1 in the Introduction. As in the volume as a whole, psalm numbering in the present chapter follows the Septuagint.

[3] Manuscripts are given with library reference, the siglum used in Weber 1953, and the Vetus Latina number in Gryson 1999–2004. On bilingual psalters, see also chap. 11.

Botte 1958: 91–92; Bogaert 2000: 64; Allgeier 1931: 482; De Bruyne 1931: 546), scholars are divided over the path taken by the text from its archaic form to that preserved in surviving psalters. For Capelle (1913: 117), Allgeier (1931: 482) and Botte (1958: 91–92), the Psalter had an African base with an overlay of "European" vocabulary. On the other hand, Vaccari (1952: 253), Weber (1953: xii) and Ongaro (1954: 473–74), saw its text as a European, more specifically Italian, translation that had replaced the version used in Africa. For proponents of the first theory, readings from the psalm citations of Tertullian and Cyprian found in the later psalter text are relics of the archaic base; for those of the second, they are contaminations perhaps stemming from liturgical sources conserving the archaic text.

The somewhat sporadic presence of readings found in Tertullian or Cyprian in later psalter texts lends support to the latter view. Only the twelfth-century quadruple Monte Cassino Psalter (Archivio della Badia, 557 A; VL 136) preserves a text with a persistent archaic element (Amelli 1912: xix–xxiv; Capelle 1920: 126–27). This is obscured through its revision against an unidentified Hebrew text, with Hebraizing readings that cannot be explained through use of Origen's Hexapla (Ammassari 1987: 894). Cyprian's Psalter remained in use throughout the third century and can be seen in pseudo-Cyprianic texts such as *De montibus*; a similar text, which has undergone some revision, is also found in the fourth-century writings of Pacian of Barcelona and Donatists such as Tyconius, Petilian, and Parmenian (Capelle 1913: 19, 56, 221–25). Thereafter, the fate of the Cyprianic text is unknown, although traces can be found in later writers such as Fulgentius and Quodvultdeus.

The publication of the Latin Sinai Psalter in 2010 by Thibaut (Sinai, St Catherine's Monastery, Slavonic 5; VL 460) has shed further light on the psalter tradition in North Africa. Discovered at St Catherine's Monastery in 1950, this ninth-century manuscript probably came from a Latin-speaking North-African Christian community (Vezin 1995: 347–48). It supports Cyprian on several occasions where he follows a Latin text with a different Greek *Vorlage* to that found in Tertullian and the other Latin witnesses. For example, the reading *iniustiam* at Psalm 44:8 (LXX) is dependent on ἀδικίαν ("injustice") as found in Codex Alexandrinus, Rahlfs 2013, and the Sahidic version, while the Vulgate has *iniquitatem* from ἀνομίαν ("lawlessness") in the remaining Greek witnesses; at Psalm 81:1 (LXX) the Sinai Psalter and Cyprian alone support the participle κρίνων, an apparent Symmachian reading, with all other witnesses preserving a finite form of the verb (Field 1875: 234). This is one of a number of Hebraisms listed by Capelle (1913: 205) that are found in Cyprian's Psalter. Elsewhere the Sinai Psalter renders δόξα ("glory") by *claritas* at Psalm 25:8 (LXX) (supported by Parmenian in Augustine, *Contra epistulam Parmeniani* 3.5.25), βοηθεῖν ("help") by *auxiliare* at Psalm 43:27 (LXX) (supported by Quodvultdeus, *Liber Promissionum* 1.3.13), ἀνομία ("lawlessness") by *facinus* at Psalm 50:4 (LXX), and ἀνομεῖν by *facinus mittere* at Psalm 105:6 (LXX). These readings contribute to a text that is the most "African" of any extant psalter witness.

As in other patristic writings, the biblical citations of Cyprian's *Testimonia* underwent many textual alterations from a very early stage, as the biblical text was adapted to that of different localities (Bevenot and Weber 1972: liv). This can be seen in Cyprian's text of Psalm 44:10 (LXX), which in the Latin Psalter tradition ends with the addition *circumamicta uarietate*, an interpolation found in all the Septuagint witnesses but not the Masoretic Text or the *recentiores* (Norris 2017: 301–3). The manuscripts with Cyprian's text can be placed in four recensions, from the omission of the interpolation as attested by the Lorsch manuscript (Vienna, ÖNB, lat. 962) to the Sessorianus (Rome, BNC Vittorio Emanuele II, Sessorianus 58 [2106]), which preserves the Vulgate text. The citations of this psalm in early patristic witnesses reflect these recensions: Pacian's citations of the verse (*Epistula* 3.2.4, 3.25.1) contain an early revision present in the now-lost sixth-century Verona manuscript; Fortunatianus, writing around 350 CE, preserves a form found in the Angers manuscript (Angers, BM 148 [140]); finally, the Vulgate form is first found in Ambrose's *De uirginibus* (1.7.36), albeit with a reversed word order, and a later manuscript with excerpts from Fortunatianus' commentary also shows the citation with a Vulgate text. Thus the process seen in successive revisions of Cyprian's *Testimonia* can be used to explain the differences between Cyprian's Psalter and the text of the later psalter manuscripts: such an evolution of the text is likely to have been far greater in documents that were frequently copied and revised due to their importance in the daily life of the Church.

THE PSALTER AT THE TIME OF JEROME

The Latin Psalter at the time of Jerome is more securely attested in direct tradition. Three traditions have been transmitted that make up the backbone of the Old Latin Psalter: the Roman tradition, the Gallic/Mozarabic tradition, and the North-Italian/African tradition. The texts transmitted by the Roman and Verona Psalters were known to Jerome, while that of the Saint-Germain Psalter (see below) contains a number of readings paralleled by the Hexaplaric Psalter that are possible evidence of a common source (Thibaut 1959: 108; Rahlfs 1979: 43–44). In his study of Rufinus's Psalter, Gribomont classified these texts according to their predominant Greek traditions: the Roman and Saint-Germain Psalters follow a Greek text that has affinities with the Upper-Egyptian and "proto-Lucianic" traditions whereas the Verona Psalter is closer to the Greek portion of the Verona Psalter, a text identified as "R" (Gribomont and Merlo 1972: 6).

The earliest tradition is represented primarily by the Roman Psalter. Although the first citations of the Roman Psalter are not found before the *Regula magistri* in the sixth century, followed soon after by the Rule of Benedict, Cassiodorus and Gregory the Great (Adriaen 1958: xix; de Vogüé 1964: 211), an early form of the Roman Psalter text can be found in Rufinus's writings (Gribomont and Merlo 1972: 106). The name *Psalterium Romanum* comes from the ninth-century German triple psalters that place its text alongside Jerome's *Gallicanum* (Hexaplaric) and the *Hebraicum* (*Iuxta Hebraeos*) (Bogaert 2000: 60). A tradition arose in Carolingian times which associated this psalter with Jerome's first revision of the Old Latin, done hurriedly in Rome against the Septuagint in 383 or 384, as mentioned in the preface to his Hexaplaric Psalter. In an article published in 1930, De Bruyne cast serious doubt on the veracity of this tradition, highlighting a number of mistranslations and harmonizations in the Roman Psalter that he felt would not have escaped the notice of Jerome. Although vigorously contested by Allgeier (1931), who underlined the similarities between the Roman Psalter and Jerome's Hexaplaric Psalter, there is no conclusive argument to support Jerome's involvement in the Roman Psalter beyond perhaps his selection of this text for use at Rome.

A close relative to the Roman Psalter is the Milan Psalter, whose text is preserved in more than forty manuscripts and three recensions, the oldest of which date to the ninth century. Nohe (1936: 165–66) suggests that the Milanese text is based on one of Ambrose's psalters, subsequently revised against other Old Latin versions, especially the Roman Psalter, as well as independently against the Septuagint. The vast majority of corrections find parallels in the Greek minuscule manuscripts rather than the majuscule tradition (Rahlfs 1907: 73; Nohe 1936: 132). Some corrections based on Greek sources are of particular interest, such as the addition of *libera* at the start of the last stich of Psalm 34:17 (LXX), unparalleled elsewhere in Latin tradition, which is a rendering of ῥῦσαι ("save") found in the fifth (Septuagint) column of the Mercati Hexapla fragments (Rahlfs 1098), Rahlfs 55 and Theodoret (Estin 1984: 83).

The Gallic tradition is preserved by the Saint-Germain Psalter (Paris, BnF, lat. 11947; γ; VL 303) written on purple vellum. This was edited by Sabatier, who published it in 1743 with the variants from the *uetus* column of the Corbie Triple Psalter (St. Petersburg, NLR, F.v.I.5; δ; VL 325) and its close copy the now-illegible Chartres Psalter (Chartres, BM, 22 [30]; VL 326). The final member of this family is the first Reichenau fragment (Karlsruhe, BLB, Aug. CCLIII; κ; VL 301), a sixth-century palimpsest published by Dold and Capelle in 1925. Although there is some evidence to suggest that the psalm texts of Hilary precede those of the Saint-Germain Psalter, the tradition is closest to the psalm citations of Eucherius of Lyons in the fifth century (Jeannotte 1917: 41–43; Dold and Capelle 1925: 222).

A second palimpsest fragment, (Karlsruhe, BLB, Aug. CCLIII; λ; VL 302) was discovered in the same Reichenau manuscript and found by Capelle to belong to a separate tradition close to that of the Mozarabic Psalter. Together with the seventh-century Greco-Latin double psalter fragment known as the Coislin Psalter (Paris, BnF, Coislin 186; ε; VL 333) and the Psalter of Zeno of Verona (Vatican, BAV, Vat. lat. 5359; ζ; VL 306), these manuscripts represent a subgroup of Gallic texts that lie very close to the Roman tradition, as can be seen by their almost identical rendering of the Greek δέ by *autem* or *uero*. The text from this tradition is closest to that found in number of fourth- to sixth-century writers from Southern Gaul, such as Salvian, Faustus of Riez, Ruricius of Limoges, and Caesarius of Arles (Dold and Capelle 1925: 222).

The Mozarabic Psalter is a recension found in several Spanish psalter manuscripts, liturgical books, and two Bibles. Like the Milan Psalter, it is related to the Roman Psalter but has a number of characteristic readings that can be attributed to local variation rather than a systematic revision of the Old Latin text against the Greek (Ayuso Marazuela 1962: 102–5). The text exists in two recensions, the older of which, according to Ayuso Marazuela (1962: 92) is preserved principally by the ninth-century

Codex Cavensis (Cava dei Tirreni, Archivio della Badia; moz^c; VL 189). The principal representative of the younger recension is the tenth-century Bible of Alcalá (Madrid, BUC, Complutensis 31 [1]; moz^x; VL 109). The age of the Mozarabic text is difficult to gauge: the Bible of Alcalá is a copy of a manuscript produced at least three hundred years earlier, which places the text in at least the seventh century (Houghton 2016: 97). However, Ayuso Marazuela (1959: 158–59) sees an affinity between the text of Gregory of Elvira, writing in the second half of the fourth century, and the Mozarabic Psalter. This, however, is only in the kernel of an Old Latin text common to his psalm text, the Mozarabic Psalter and the Roman Psalter.

The final tradition comprises witnesses that largely follow the Greek form found in the Verona Psalter. The Latin portion of the Verona Psalter, the Sinai Psalter, and the sixth-century North Italian palimpsest Saint-Gall Psalter (St. Gall, Stiftsbibliothek, Cod. Sang. 912; β; VL 304), along with one papyrus fragment which only survives as a typed transcription (see below), bear witness to a revision that was possibly made in North Italy. The text is first found in some of the writings of Ambrose and Tyconius's Commentary on the Apocalypse, and is closely related to that used for the majority of Augustine's *Enarrationes in Psalmos*. In addition to readings paralleled in this form in Greek tradition, the corresponding Latin version is characterized by a more literal translation (Ongaro 1954: 456; De Bruyne 1931: 562). Vaccari (1952: 254–55, 1958: 236–38) took the Saint-Gall Psalter as the oldest member of this group, but this was rebutted by Gribomont who saw it as a later, romanized witness (Gribomont and Merlo 1972: 5).

The Sinai Psalter has often been placed in the Verona Psalter group due to readings that suggest a similar revision in comparison with Greek (Thibaut 2010: 16; Gribomont and Merlo 1972: 5). Its text appears to be a mix of three sources: readings from the Mozarabic/Roman tradition, the Verona tradition, and the Cyprianic tradition. As noticed by Gribomont, it occasionally matches Augustine against the Verona or Saint-Gall Psalters (Gribomont and Merlo 1972: 46–47). In addition to the Cyprianic readings discussed above, the Sinai Psalter also contains a high proportion of archaisms such as the rendering of a second person aorist in a μη-clause by a perfect subjunctive in a *ne*-clause that betrays the literal renderings of early translations (Mohrmann 1961: 96–97). A further feature of this text is its readings shared with the Roman Psalter, including a number of serious errors such as the omission through haplography of the third stich of Psalm 27:4 (LXX), an error also found in Zeno's Psalter and the Coislin Psalter. However, it does not follow the Roman Psalter's characteristic rendering of ῥύεσθαι by *eripere* or the distinctive use of *eruere* in the Verona Psalter, instead generally preferring *liberare*, a characteristic of Cyprian's psalter (Capelle 1913: 120–21; Allgeier 1931: 475–78; De Bruyne 1931: 572). Where *eruere* is found in the Sinai Psalter, it is possibly the result of contamination from the Verona tradition. This is seen at Psalm 17:20 (LXX), where it has both *liberare* and *eruere*, the former being its usual rendering, the latter the result of an addition from the Verona tradition to bring the Sinai text in line with the uncials, where the Roman Psalter and the minuscule tradition omit the stichs. Readings such as these point to the Sinai Psalter being a witness, albeit a late one, to an earlier textual tradition than the Verona.

Alongside these witnesses, there is a typescript transcription of a now-lost papyrus amulet (P. Heidelberg Inv. Lat. 5), recovered from Fustat and dated to the fifth or sixth century, containing fragments of Psalms 15 and 20 (LXX) (Daniel and Maltomini 1988: 254). The readings of this tradition have been noted in the writings of Ambrose and Augustine as well as fifth-century Southern Italian texts such as Quodvultdeus's *Liber Promissionum* (Capelle 1913: 112, 188) and a series of homilies tentatively attributed to John of Naples, also known as the Latin Pseudo-Chrysostom homilies (Vaccari 1952: 250 n.1). Among liturgical sources, the African psalter collects are based on a fifth-century psalm text related to this group that eventually found its way into Gaul (Brou 1949: 21 n.1). Finally, the possible dependence of a number of Roman offertories on this text has been shown by both Pfisterer (2007: 45) and Maloy (2010: 39). This wide range of witnesses suggests that this text was more widespread than previously thought.

The distribution of the psalter manuscripts in the above three groups, Gallic, Roman, and African, can therefore be approximately represented as shown in Figure 5.1.

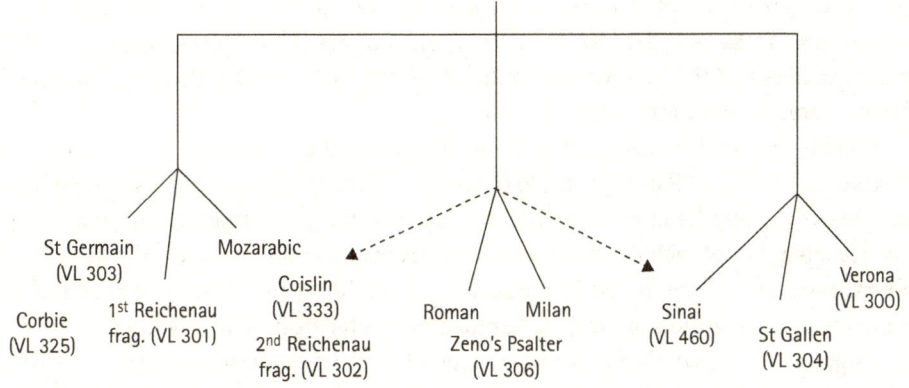

FIGURE 5.1. A simplified stemma of Latin Psalters.

JEROME'S PSALTERS

Jerome's Hexaplaric Psalter should be seen as a continuation of the improvement and revision of the original Latin translation of the Septuagint Psalter that took place over the preceding century. Despite eventually forming the basis of the Sixto-Clementine Vulgate, it is usually considered an Old Latin witness to the Septuagint translation (see chap. 2). It was by no means revolutionary to correct the Latin Psalter against the best available Greek text, or even against a hexaplaric text; as seen above, there is some evidence that the Jewish Greek revisions of the Septuagint were employed by revisers as early as Cyprian's time. However, the impact of Jerome's second revision on the Latin Psalter can be seen by the fact that it eventually become the primary psalter of Medieval Western Europe (Goins 2014: 192). This can partly be attributed to the personality of

Jerome: it is unlikely that any Latin Psalter had ever had such an eloquent defense as that found in Jerome's Epistle 106, where he analyzes 178 variants between the Hexaplaric Psalter and the Greek text in the possession of the Gothic Bishops Sunnia and Fretela. This, together with his preface *Psalterium Romae dudum*, acts as a sort of user's manual to the Hexaplaric Psalter (*Praefatio in Psalmos*, Weber and Gryson 2007: 767). In the former, he underlines his conviction that, when the different Greek recensions disagree, recourse should be made to the Hebrew tradition for the correct reading; in the latter he outlines his adoption of Origen's diacritical signs, the obelus and the asterisk, the former to mark superfluous passages in the Septuagint not found in the Hebrew and the latter those found in the Hebrew restored to the Greek largely with the aid of Theodotion's revision (Canellis et al. 2017: 68).

In the preface *Psalterium Romae dudum*, Jerome termed his second revision a *noua emendatio* ("new emendation") of the Greek text, and even a cursory glance at the text reveals that it is a revision rather than a translation. As his base, he took a text close to the Roman Psalter (Vaccari 1952: 219; Estin 1984: 275), perhaps so that his revision would gain widespread acceptance. The Roman Psalter lies at the center of the entire psalter tradition and was described by Weber (1953: x) as a sort of "common ancestor" to all the other psalters and the best witness to the primitive psalter text. It therefore would have been a natural choice for Jerome's base text.

There is a general consensus that Jerome produced the Hexaplaric Psalter within four years of his arrival in Palestine in 386 (Canellis et al. 2017: 98). He first visited the library at Caesarea where he consulted Origen's Hexapla, but since fragmentary witnesses to the Hexapla do not include the diacritical signs (as these are not needed where the different texts can be compared in parallel) it seems likely that Jerome also consulted a separate critical edition of Origen's Septuagint Psalter from which he took the diacritical signs (Estin 1984: 28–29). Thibaut's study (1959: 111–20, 149) summarized Jerome's method as correcting the Latin text in a four-stage process: he first removed transmission errors that had crept into the Latin tradition, then made the Latin text conform to his Hexaplaric textual model before removing translation errors and superfluous words from the Latin text. Finally, he conservatively modernized the style of the Latin text. The result was a text that contains far fewer errors than any other Old Latin Psalter text. It was, however, far from perfect: there are still a number of passages where the sense of the text is obscure and Jerome admitted in Epistle 106 the occasional translation error that he partly blamed on his haste in executing the work.[4]

Jerome's belief in the authority of the Hebrew tradition led to his move away from the Septuagint toward the *Hebraica ueritas* ("Hebrew truth"), an expression that he uses in his letter to Sophronius that prefaces the *Iuxta Hebraeos*. Whereas the Hexaplaric Psalter was an *emendatio*, the *Iuxta Hebraeos* was the result of Sophronius's request that he translate (*transferre*) into Latin in the manner of Aquila, Symmachus, and Theodotion (Weber and Gryson 2007: 768). Given its use of the *Hebraica ueritas* as its authority, the

---

[4] *Si quid uel transferentis festinatione uel scribentium uitio deprauatum est* (CSEL 55: 253).

Iuxta Hebraeos justifies the title of a new translation. Yet Jerome often maintains the text as found in the Old Latin Psalter, perhaps subconsciously, even sometimes employing Old Latin formulations that he had rejected in the composition of the Hexaplaric Psalter (Estin 1984: 205).

It is clear from the preface that the primary purpose of the *Iuxta Hebraeos* was polemical: the text was designed to provide Sophronius with an accurate representation of the Hebrew tradition so that he could "respond to Jewish arguments over every single word of the Psalms" (Weber and Gryson 2007: 769). To produce such an edition, Jerome studied and copied, or had copied, the Hebrew manuscripts from the Bethlehem Synagogue and began work on his translation which he composed between 390 and 392 (Canellis et al. 2017: 93). The full extent of Jerome's knowledge of Hebrew is unknown, but it seems likely that he was able to read it and he certainly employed a number of Jewish scholars to aid him in his translation (Rebenich 1993: 62–63). In addition, Jerome made substantial use of the *recentiores* found in Origen's Hexapla: following comparison with the Mercati Hexapla Fragments, Estin (1984: 205) concluded that on the rare occasions that Jerome felt the need to depart from the text in Origen's Septuagint column, he showed a marginal preference for Aquila's text over that of Symmachus.

Jerome's Psalters faced a mixed reception at first in the face of the popularity of the Roman Psalter, which, thanks in part to its adoption at Rome, had become the dominant recension of the Old Latin Psalter in Italy by the sixth century. Augustine adopted the Hexaplaric text in his *Enarrationes in Psalmos* from 415 CE in place of his Verona-type text, albeit with his own corrections (De Bruyne 1931: 564–67), as did Cassian in Southern Gaul (Stewart 1999: 35). It is from Southern Gaul that the oldest Hexaplaric Psalter hails, the late fifth-century Lyons Psalter (Lyons, Bibliothèque de la Ville, 425 [351]; η; VL 421), although this also contains an Old Latin Gallic text in parts. The second oldest Hexaplaric Psalter is the early seventh-century Cathach of St. Columba (Dublin, Royal Irish Academy 12.R.33; VL 420; see fig. 31.1) which points to the adoption of the Hexaplaric Psalter in Ireland at some point in the sixth century (McNamara 1973: 260; see also chap. 10). Perhaps under Irish influence it was later introduced by Alcuin in the ninth century both into his recension of the Tours Bible and the Carolingian liturgy (Bogaert 2000: 58–59). Its widespread diffusion eventually saw it adopted as the Latin Psalter of the Vulgate and the basis for the Roman Breviary at the Council of Trent (1546).

While Jerome's Hebrew translation of the Old Testament gradually became the dominant Latin Bible text over the course of the first millennium, his *Iuxta Hebraeos* never matched the popularity of the Hexaplaric Psalter. It is, however, found in some of the early biblical pandects, such as the Codex Amiatinus, and was included in the other Carolingian Bible recension, that of Theodulf of Orleans. Spain resisted the acceptance of Alcuin's recension: here alone the *Iuxta Hebraeos* enjoyed continued transmission as the biblical psalm text counterpart to the Mozarabic text used in the liturgy (Ayuso Marazuela 1962: 185). Its later transmission was principally restricted to single psalters or alongside other psalm texts in double, triple, or quadruple psalters (de Sainte-Marie 1954: v). One of these, the ninth-century Saint-Gall Psalter (Stiftsbibliothek, Cod. Sang.

19), preserves the name *Psalterium Iuxta Hebraeos* which was taken by Lagarde for his 1874 edition.

The Roman Psalter tradition remained popular in England prior to the Norman Conquest as well as in Germany and until much later in Central and Southern Italy (Rahlfs 1979: 53; Fischer 1975: 22). As for the other Old Latin traditions, the Gallic tradition was still being used in Ireland at the time of Patrick before yielding to the Hexaplaric (McNamara 1973: 260) and in France until the mid-eighth century (Fischer 1975: 24–25). By the sixth century the other Old Latin traditions had all but disappeared, only surviving where local churches maintained a conservative liturgy, such as in Spain and at Milan, or in isolated communities such as the Christians of North Africa who used the Sinai Psalter. Much like the Cyprianic Psalter before them, only traces of the earlier traditions can be found in later patristic citations and in some liturgical forms obscured by the normalization of the text against the dominant traditions.

BIBLIOGRAPHY

Adriaen, Marcus. 1958. *Magni Aurelii Cassiodori Expositio Psalmorum*. CCSL 97. Turnhout: Brepols.

Allgeier, Arthur. 1931. "Die erste Psalmenübersetzung des heiligen Hieronymus und das Psalterium romanum." *Biblica* 12, no. 4: 447–82.

Ammassari, Antonio. 1987. *Il salterio latino di Pietro*. Rome: Città Nuova.

Amelli, Ambrogio M. 1912. *Liber Psalmorum iuxta antiquissimam latinam versionem nunc primum ex Casinensi cod. 557 curante D. Ambrosio M. Amelli . . . in lucem profertur*. CBL 1. Rome: Pustet.

Ayuso Marazuela, Teófilo. 1959. "El salterio de Gregorio de Elvira y la Vetus Latina Hispana." *Estudios Bíblicos* 18: 135–59.

Ayuso Marazuela, Teófilo. 1962. *La vetus latina hispana. Vol. 5. El salterio. Parte 1*. Madrid: CSIC.

Bevenot, Maurice, and Robert Weber. 1972. *Sancti Cypriani Episcopi Opera. Pars I*. CCSL 3. Turnhout: Brepols.

Bogaert, Pierre-Maurice. 2000. "Le Psautier latin des origines au XIIème siècle. Essai d'histoire." In *Der Septuaginta-Psalter und Seine Tochterübersetzungen: Symposium in Göttingen 1997*, edited by Anneli Aejmelaeus and Udo Quast, 51–81. Göttingen: Vandenhoeck & Ruprecht.

Botte, Bernard. 1958. "Les anciennes versions de la Bible." *La Maison-Dieu* 53: 89–109.

Brou, Louis. 1949. *The Psalter Collects from V–VIth Century Sources: Three Series*. London: Henry Bradshaw Society.

Canellis, Aline, Robert Weber, and Roger Gryson. 2017. *Préfaces aux livres de la Bible*. SC 592. Paris: Cerf.

Capelle, Paul. 1913. *Le texte du psautier latin en Afrique*. CBL 4. Rome: Pustet.

Capelle, Paul. 1920. "L'élément africain dans le psalterium casinense." *Revue bénédictine* 32: 113–31.

Daniel, Robert W., and Franco Maltomini. 1988. "From the African Psalter and Liturgy." *Zeitschrift für Papyrologie und Epigraphik* 74: 253–65.

De Bruyne, Donatien. 1930. "Le problème du psautier romain." *Revue bénédictine* 42: 101–26.

De Bruyne, Donatien. 1931. "Saint Augustin reviseur de la Bible." In *Miscellanea agostiniana; testi e studi*, edited by Germain Morin and Antonio Casamassa, 521–606. Rome: Vatican.

Dold, Alban, and Bernard Capelle. 1925. "Deux psautiers gaulois dans le cod. Aug. CCLIII." *Revue bénédictine* 37: 181–203.

Estin, Colette. 1984. *Les psautiers de Jérôme: à la lumière des traductions juives antérieures.* CBL 15. Rome: Vatican.

Field, Frederick. 1875. *Origen Hexapla.* Oxford: Clarendon Press.

Fischer, Bonifatius. 1975. "Zur Überlieferung altlateinischer Bibeltexte im Mittelalter." *Nederlands archief voor kerkgeschiedenis / Dutch Review of Church History* 56, no. 1: 19–34.

Goins, Scott. 2014. "Jerome's Psalters." In *The Oxford Handbook of the Psalms*, edited by William P. Brown, 185–98. Oxford: Oxford University Press.

Gribomont, Jean, and Francesca Merlo. 1972. *Il salterio di Rufino.* CBL 14. Rome: Vatican.

Gryson, Roger. 2004. *Altlateinische Handschriften/Manuscrits vieux latins: répertoire descriptif. Deuxième partie.* VL 1/2B. Freiburg: Herder.

Houghton, H. A. G. 2016. *The Latin New Testament: A Guide to Its Early History, Texts, and Manuscripts.* Oxford: Oxford University Press.

Jeannotte, Henri. 1917. *Le Psautier de St. Hilaire de Poitiers.* Paris: Gabalda.

Kedar, Benjamin. 1988. "The Latin Translations." In *Mikra: Text, Translation, Reading and Interpretation of the Hebrew Bible in Ancient Judaism and Early Christianity*, edited by Martin Jan Mulder and Harry Sysling, 299–338. Assen: Van Gorcum.

Klauser, Theodor. 1965. *Kleine abendländische Liturgiegeschichte.* Bonn: Hanstein.

Lamb, John Alexander. 1962. *The Psalms in Christian Worship.* London: Faith.

Lowe, Elias Avery. 1955. "An Unknown Latin Psalter on Mount Sinai." *Scriptorium* 9, no. 2: 177–99.

Maloy, Rebecca. 2010. *Inside the Offertory: Aspects of Chronology and Transmission.* Oxford: Oxford University Press.

Mattei, Paul. 1995. "Recherches sur la Bible à Rome vers le milieu du IIIe s: Novatien et la Vetus Latina." *Revue bénédictine* 105: 255–79.

McNamara, Martin. 1973. *Psalter Text and Psalter Study in the Early Irish Church: A. D. 600–1200.* Dublin: Royal Irish Academy.

Mohrmann, Christine. 1961. "L'Étude de la latinité chrétienne." In *Études sur le latin des chrétiens 1.* 2nd ed., 83–102. Rome: Storia e letteratura.

Norris, Oliver. 2017. "Tracing Fortunatianus' Psalter." In *Fortunatianus Redivivus: Bischof Fortunatian von Aquileia und Sein Evangelienkommentar*, edited by Lukas J. Dorfbauer and Viktoria Zimmerl-Panagl, 283–306. Berlin: De Gruyter.

Nohe, Anton. 1936. *Der mailänder Psalter: seine Grundlage und Entwicklung.* Freiburg: Herder.

Ongaro, Giovanni. 1954. "Saltero veronese e revisione agostiniana." *Biblica* 35, no. 4: 443–74.

Pfisterer, Andreas 2007. "Super Flumina Babylonis: On the Prehistory of a Roman Offertory." In *Offertory and Its Verses: Research, Past, Present and Future*, edited by Roman Hankeln, 41–56. Trondheim: Tapir.

Rahlfs, Alfred. 1907. *Septuaginta-Studien. Der Text des Septuaginta-Psalters.* Vol. 2. Göttingen: Vandenhoeck & Ruprecht.

Rahlfs, Alfred. 1979. *Psalmi cum Odis.* Göttingen: Vandenhoeck & Ruprecht.

Rebenich, Stefan. 1993. "Jerome: The 'Vir Trilinguis' and the 'Hebraica Veritas'." *Vigiliae Christianae* 47, no. 1: 50–77.

Sainte-Marie, Henri de. 1954. *Sancti Hieronymi Psalterium iuxta Hebraeos.* CBL 11. Rome: Vatican.

Salmon, Pierre. 1959. *Les Tituli Psalmorum des manuscrits latins.* CBL 12. Rome: Vatican.

Schirner, Rebekka. 2016. "Textkritische Anmerkungen zu Psalm 118 in den Psalmenkommentaren des Hilarius, Ambrosius und Augustinus: Eine vergleichende Analyse." In *Traditio et Translatio:*

Studien zur lateinischen Bibel zu Ehren von Roger Gryson, edited by Thomas Johann Bauer, 1–30. AGLB 40. Freiburg: Herder.

Stewart, Columba. 1999. *Cassian the Monk*. New York: Oxford University Press.

Thibaut, André. 1959. "La révision hexaplaire de Jérome." In *Richesses et déficiences des anciens psautiers latins*, edited by Pierre Salmon, 107–49. CBL 13. Rome: Vatican.

Thibaut, André. 2010. *Le psautier latin du Sinaï*. AGLB 39. Freiburg: Herder.

Tov, Emanuel. 1988. "The Septuagint." In *Mikra: Text, Translation, Reading & Interpretation of the Hebrew Bible in Ancient Judaism & Early Christianity*, edited by Martin Jan Mulder and Harry Sysling, 161–88. Assen: Royal Van Gorcum.

Vaccari, Alberto. 1952. "I salteri di S. Girolamo e di S. Agostino." In *Scritti di erudizione e di filologia 1*, 207–55. Rome: Storia e letteratura.

Vaccari, Alberto. 1958. "S. Augustin, S. Ambroise et Aquila." In *Scritti di erudizione e di filologia 2*, 229–43. Rome: Storia e letteratura.

Vezin, Jean. 1995. "A propos des manuscrits latins du Sinaï." *Bulletin de la société nationale des antiquaires de France* 1993, no. 1: 347–49.

Vogüé, Adalbert de. 1964. *La Règle du Maître. 1*. SC 105. Paris: Cerf.

Weber, Robert. 1953. *Le psautier romain et les autres anciens psautiers latins: édition critique*. CBL 10. Rome: Vatican.

Weber, Robert, and Roger Gryson, eds. 2007. *Biblia Sacra Iuxta Vulgatam Versionem*. 5th ed. Stuttgart: Deutsche Bibelgesellschaft.

CHAPTER 6

THE VULGATE NEW TESTAMENT OUTSIDE THE GOSPELS

ANNA PERSIG

THE attribution of the revision of the latter books of the New Testament to Jerome is probably a posthumous extension of his work on the Gospels (see chap. 3). Doubts on Jerome's authorship have been cast on the basis of his discordant affirmations concerning the extent of the revision, the disagreement between the Vulgate and Jerome's citations in his commentaries on the Pauline Epistles, the absence of a preface for the whole Vulgate corpus, and stylistic divergences between the Gospels and the other books. These objections have been followed by alternative attributions to two contemporaries of Jerome: Pelagius and Rufinus the Syrian. This chapter discusses the arguments that have been used to support these attributions and gives particular attention to the first writers who cite the Vulgate New Testament: Jerome, Augustine, and the followers of Pelagius. It is essential to pinpoint the earliest sources that attest the Vulgate of the Acts, Epistles, and Apocalypse in order to reconstruct the textual transmission of the revision and identify the moment when the name of Jerome was associated with the Vulgate corpus.

EARLY ATTESTATIONS IN THE MANUSCRIPT TRADITION

The first attestation in the manuscript tradition of books of the Vulgate New Testament apart from the Gospels dates back to the sixth century: Codex Fuldensis (Fulda, Hochschul- und Landesbibliothek, Codex Bonifatianus 1), copied for and corrected by Victor of Capua in the years 546–47, contains the Pauline Epistles preceded by the

Primum quaeritur, the Epistle to the Laodiceans, Acts, Catholic Epistles, and Revelation, in a version close to the Vulgate, and a harmony of the Gospels based on Jerome's revision (Fischer 1985: 57–66; see also chap. 15). The slightly later Palimpsest of León (León, Archivo Catedralicio, 15; VL 67), from the seventh century, is the oldest surviving pandect of the Old and New Testament with the Vulgate Pauline Epistles, a mixed text in Acts, and Old Latin in the Catholic Epistles (Houghton 2016: 63). In the sixth century, Cassiodorus stated that he owned a small pandect with the Vulgate Old and New Testament organized *per cola and commata* (*Institutiones* 1.12.3; Fischer 1985: 12). There is a high degree of uncertainty about the origin of an edition of Priscillian's canons of the Pauline Epistles, preserved in three Spanish pandects, supposedly edited in the middle of the fifth century by a certain Peregrinus on the basis of an early Vulgate manuscript of Italian origin (Houghton 2016: 62–63).

The oldest source in the manuscript tradition, which names Jerome as the reviser of the Vulgate New Testament, probably going back to the middle of the fifth century, is the colophon at the end of the Epistle to the Hebrews in the ninth-century Bible of Saint-Germain-des-Prés (Paris, BnF, lat. 11553; VL 7), a Vulgate pandect with Old Latin elements in the Gospels (Fischer 1985: 81–89). Bogaert (2013: 519) supposed that the union of the Vulgate Gospels with the other revised books antedated the sixth century and was the product of an editorial initiative by booksellers who wanted to sell a complete New Testament attributed to an authoritative figure, such as Jerome. The union of the Vulgate New Testament by the fifth century is not plausible according to Fischer (1985: 68), who identified a different origin and quality in the texts of the Vulgate in Codices Fuldensis and Amiatinus, which had different manuscripts as models and not a single Vulgate pandect. In fact, early manuscripts that transmit the Vulgate New Testament in a pure form are uncommon because of the frequent contamination of Old Latin and Vulgate within individual books, and the alternation of Old Latin and Vulgate books within a single manuscript (see chap. 1). The Vulgate did not immediately replace the *Vetus Latina*: the mixed versions remained widespread until the Carolingian age when the Vulgate finally became predominant, and the attribution to Jerome was strengthened by the employment of Jerome's *Epistula* 53 as the preface of the corpus (Bogaert 2012: 83–84). The *uetus et uulgata editio* was then recognized as the authoritative version of the scripture at the Council of Trent in the light of its established use (Sutcliffe 1948: 37).

THE ATTRIBUTION TO JEROME

The attribution of the entire Vulgate New Testament to Jerome stems largely from the internal evidence of his own writings. Evidence from the affiliation of the biblical quotations in his commentaries on New Testament epistles and matters of translation style can be interpreted in a variety of ways.

Internal Evidence

The attribution of the latter books of the Vulgate New Testament to Jerome derives from the fact that he revised the Gospels between the years 382–384 CE, as claimed in the *Nouum Opus* preface, and from Jerome's affirmations on the extent of his work. In the following passages, Jerome takes credit for the revision of the whole New Testament:

> *De uiris illustribus* 135 (393 CE): *nouum testamentum graecae fidei reddidi, uetus iuxta hebraicum transtuli* ("I have translated the New Testament, faithful to the Greek; I have translated the Old Testament in accordance with the Hebrew" [Halton 2010: 168]).
>
> *Epistula* 71.5 to Lucinius (397–400 CE): *nouum testamentum graecae reddidi auctoritati* ("The New Testament I have restored to the authoritative form of the Greek original" [Schaff and Wace 1996: 378]).

Nonetheless, it may be taken as suspicious that Jerome never mentions the Acts, the Epistles, and Revelation but refers generally to the New Testament. In addition, Jerome's revision of the Old Testament had not been completed by this point, and his claim to have revised the whole New Testament may be a similar exaggeration. In contrast to the previous affirmations, Jerome twice restricts his revision to the Gospels:

> *Nouum opus* (384 CE): *haec praesens praefatiuncula pollicetur quattuor tantum euangelia* ("I therefore promise in this short Preface the four Gospels only." [Schaff and Wace 1996: 1040]).
>
> *Epistula* 27.1 to Marcella (384 CE): *in euangeliis emendare temptauerim* ("I had endeavored to correct passages in the gospels." [Schaff and Wace 1996: 147]).

However, the significance of these references is weakened by the fact that they are contemporary with the revision of the Gospels, when in all likelihood Jerome could not have accomplished the work on the other books (Chapman 1933: 33).

Other statements useful in assessing the extent of Jerome's revision can be drawn from Jerome and Augustine's correspondence. Augustine thanks Jerome for his revision of the Gospels but Jerome makes reference to the New Testament in his reply:

> Augustine, *Epistula* 71.6 to Jerome (397–400 CE): *proinde non paruas deo gratias agimus de opere tuo, quod euangelium ex graeco interpretatus es* ("At the same time, we are in no small measure thankful to God for the work in which you have translated the Gospels from the original Greek." [Schaff 1886: 327]).
>
> Jerome, *Epistula* 112.20 to Augustine (402 CE; *Epistula* 75.20 in Augustine's corpus): *Et si me, ut dicis, in noui testamenti emendatione suscipis* ("And since you approve of my labours in revising the translation of the New Testament, as you say." [Schaff 1886: 342]).

The evidence derived from Jerome and Augustine's writings is inconsistent and does not provide any clue to resolve the problem of the attribution of the Vulgate New Testament outside the Gospels.

Jerome's Citations in the Commentaries on the Pauline Epistles

The comparison between the text of the Vulgate and Jerome's quotations in his commentaries on Galatians, Ephesians, Philemon, and Titus, dated to the year 386, is another approach taken to investigate the authorship of the Vulgate Pauline Epistles. In the sixteenth century, Jacques Lefèvre d'Etaples made a list of the renderings of the Vulgate criticized by Jerome in his commentaries to prove that he was not the reviser of the Pauline Epistles. This position, which initially found little support, was reevaluated at the beginning of the twentieth century (Vaccari 1915). The fact that the citations in the commentaries differ from the Vulgate led first to the conclusion that Jerome was not the reviser of the Pauline Epistles (Cavallera 1920; De Bruyne 1915). This idea was supported by Jerome's allusions to the incorrectness of the *codices latini* ("Latin manuscripts") or *codices nostri* ("our manuscripts"), his consultation of the translation by a *Latinus interpres* ("Latin translator"), and the absence from the Vulgate of the corrections suggested by Jerome in the commentaries (Cavallera 1920: 284–85).

On the other hand, alternative hypotheses can be advanced to explain the discrepancy between the Vulgate and Jerome's citations. The differences could be due to citation from memory, direct translation from Greek, contamination, replacement of the biblical text, or simply because the Pauline Epistles were revised after the year 386. Jerome is rarely consistent when quoting from the Gospels, for instance, in his commentary on Matthew (Chapman 1933: 123; Lagrange 1918: 254). Considering that Jerome's quotations disagree slightly with the Vulgate, a two-stage process of revision was assumed: in the commentaries, Jerome could have quoted a partial revision of an Old Latin text, which was later refined around 392 and became the Vulgate (Chapman 1933: 297–98; Lagrange 1917: 444). If this was the case, Jerome should have quoted from the Vulgate in his later works. However, the analysis of Jerome's citations of the Catholic Epistles casts doubt on this being the case (Persig 2022: 7–9).

Stylistic Differences

The presence of stylistic differences between the Gospels and the other books was taken as proof against the attribution of the rest of the Vulgate New Testament to Jerome (Rebenich 1993: 51; Birdsall 1970: 374). However, this claim is not supported by specific studies and probably arose from superficial impressions. The presence of insignificant corrections in the Vulgate New Testament outside the Gospels was explained as Jerome's decreasing interest in the revision and his will to conclude the work as fast as possible in order to concentrate on the translation of the Old Testament from Hebrew (Elliott 1992: 221). This tendency is noticeable in the Gospels, in which the highest number of interventions is attested in Matthew, the first book in order (Houghton 2016: 34; see also chap. 3). However, its extension to the other books of the New Testament was rejected by Fischer (1972: 21), who believed that the principles of revision were so different in the Gospels in comparison with the other writings that it is erroneous to attribute the revision of the Acts, Epistles, and Revelation to Jerome. On the other hand, Chapman (1933: 283–34) claimed to have identified identical criteria of revision in all the books of the Vulgate New Testament. Without a stylistic analysis of the whole Vulgate New Testament, or at least a clarification of what different styles or principles of revision mean, it is impossible to determine whether the Vulgate New Testament is stylistically unitary or not and decide whether it can be attributed to Jerome or to one or more other revisers. Differences in the lexicon, the rendering of participles, and the word order between the Catholic Epistles indicate that the Vulgate versions of these letters were possibly revised by more than one reviser (Persig 2022) but this conclusion cannot be applied *a priori* to other books of the New Testament, whose language needs to be studied in detail.

THE ABSENCE OF THE PROLOGUE

The *Nouum Opus* preface refers only to Jerome's revision of the Gospels. An early prologue which introduces the whole New Testament, or at least the books outside the Gospels, is lacking. Nonetheless, general prologues to the Pauline and Catholic Epistles, Acts, and Revelation, and specific prologues to individual Pauline epistles are transmitted through the manuscript tradition.[1] The earliest of these, the *Primum quaeritur* prologue to the Pauline Epistles, provides insights into the dating of the revision and for this reason will be extensively described in a separate section. Later prologues to the Pauline Epistles are dependent on the *Primum quaeritur*: the *argumentum* to Romans *Romani ex Iudaeis* (PROL Rm Arg [S 674]) was not written by the author of the *Primum quaeritur* (Frede 1975–82: 101); *Primum intellegere nos oportet* (PROL Paul 3 [S 669]), first attested in Cassiodorus's revision of Pelagius's commentary, is based on PROL Rm Arg and has the secondary order of the letters with Thessalonians preceding Colossians, whereas *Epistulae Pauli ad Romanos causa* (PROL Paul 4 [S 651]) presents the original order Colossians–Thessalonians.

The prologue to the Catholic Epistles, *Non ita ordo est* (PROL cath [S 809]), is a pseud-epigraphic letter from Jerome to Eustochium and imitates the beginning of Jerome's

---

[1] The abbreviations used for the prologues in this section follow the *Vetus Latina* system for patristic writings and the numbers in Stegmüller's *Repertorium Biblicum* (S).

prologue to the Minor Prophets (Berger 1904: 11). It was not written by the reviser of the Vulgate. This is also the case for the prologue to Acts (PROL Act Mo), composed in the fifth century (Houghton 2016: 168), and that to Revelation (PROL Apc Mo [S 834/835]), written between the second half of the fifth century and the beginning of the sixth century, both dependent on other sources (Houghton 2016: 168, 181; Gryson 2000–3: 58–59). PROL Apc Spa, composed in Spain, adds further information about the biography of John and the Apocalypse. Jerome's *Epistula* 53.9.6, *De uiris illustribus* 9, and Isidore (IS pro 106–9) were also used as prefatory material to Revelation (Gryson 2000–2003: 61).

The *Primum Quaeritur*

The prologue to the Pauline Epistles, the *Primum quaeritur*, is commonly attributed to the reviser of the Vulgate because of its antiquity. In consideration of the content of the prologue, in which the Epistle to the Hebrews is deemed to be canonical and the letters appear in the order Colossians–Thessalonians, the *Primum quaeritur* cannot be attributed to Pelagius, who did not comment on Hebrews and followed the order Thessalonians–Colossians in his Expositions (Frede 1975–82: 100). Jerome cannot be considered to be the author of the *Primum quaeritur* either, because he excluded Hebrews from the canon in *De uiris illustribus* 5, characterizing the different character of Hebrews with the same arguments employed in the *Primum quaeritur* (stylistic differences due to the composition of the epistle in Hebrew by Paul; the absence of Paul's signature; the lack of chronological organization of the letters). Such similarities point to a relationship between the *Primum quaeritur* and *De uiris illustribus*: according to Frede (1975–82: 99–100), the *Primum quaeritur* depends on *De uiris illustribus*, written in 393 CE, which then becomes the *terminus post quem* for the composition of the prologue. The *terminus ante quem* derives from Pelagius's knowledge of the *Primum quaeritur* when he wrote his Expositions in 404–10 CE, in which he modified the sequence of the letters as presented in the prologue to the secondary order, with Thessalonians preceding Colossians. The timeframe proposed by Frede for the composition of the prologue (393–410 CE) fits the attribution to Rufinus the Syrian, who was in Rome at that time (Scherbenske 2013: 184; Fischer 1972: 73). However, there is no strong proof to demonstrate the dependence of the author of the prologue on *De uiris illustribus*: conversely, if Jerome was dependent on the *Primum quaeritur*, the composition of the prologue would predate the year 393 CE, invalidating the attribution to Rufinus the Syrian.

Pelagius

The textual transmission of Pelagius's Expositions of thirteen epistles of Paul, a commentary in short notes written between 406 and 410 CE, is not linear and the affiliation of its biblical text is uncertain. The commentary was enlarged by a follower of Pelagius and then attributed to Jerome after Pelagius's condemnation as a heretic. Later, Cassiodorus and his circle undertook a revision of the Expositions, which were attributed in Cassiodorus's copy to Pope Gelasius, in order to expurgate the Pelagian elements: this version was then edited under the name of Primasius (Souter 1922–31: 318–26).

De Bruyne's attribution of the Vulgate Pauline Epistles to Pelagius marked the beginning of the twentieth-century debates on the authorship of the Vulgate. A three-stage process of composition was assumed by De Bruyne (1915): Pelagius wrote a commentary consisting of marginal extracts, from which an anonymous editor extrapolated the biblical text and then published it independently with the addition of the *Primum quaeritur* and the Epistle to the Hebrews. In the middle of the fifth century the biblical text was revised, becoming the current Vulgate. However, this theory was abandoned because of its foundation on premises which turned out to be mistaken: De Bruyne followed Souter's initial assertion that the biblical text of Pelagius was affiliated to the Vulgate, but this hypothesis was later retracted by Souter in his edition of Pelagius's Expositions (1922–31).

Souter reassessed his idea that Pelagius commented on the Vulgate after having found similarities between the biblical text of manuscript B of Pelagius's commentary (Oxford, Balliol College, 157, fifteenth century), the Book of Armagh (VL 61), and the writers Gildas and Sedulius Scottus. Souter concluded that Pelagius's text was Old Latin as transmitted by B, which contains an Old Latin text partially contaminated with the Vulgate. His consideration that it was improbable that a scribe replaced the Vulgate with an Old Latin version is, however, not without counterexamples (Houghton 2017: 98). Frede (1961: 27–28) considered that Pelagius's biblical text was Vulgate, taking manuscript A (Karlsruhe, BLB, Codex Augiensis CXIX, eighth–ninth century) as the most reliable manuscript of Pelagius. Frede held B to be a Vulgate text with Old Latin readings, and that the links between B and the other sources do not point to a common model but are due to the presence of elements of text-type I, a pre-Vulgate text of Italian origin (see chap. 1). Frede's theory that Pelagius commented on a Vulgate text with Old Latin readings has two limitations: Frede's analysis concerns only the Epistle to the Ephesians and doubts on the foundation of text type I have been cast in view of its heterogeneity (Nellessen 1968).

More moderate suppositions, which do not label Pelagius's biblical text as Vulgate or Old Latin but considered it to be an Old Latin text close to the Vulgate, have been made by Lagrange (1917: 444) and Schäfer (1962: 366). They believed that Pelagius's text was used as the basis of Jerome's revision and that it gradually became the Vulgate and reached this final stage once it had been revised according to Greek. Similarly, de Plinval (1964: 848) affirmed that B contains a pre-Vulgate text, which was replaced in A by the Vulgate, revised by Jerome. A different theory is that of Charlier (1963: 267–70), who assumed that the biblical text of Pelagius was not Vulgate and Cassiodorus revised the biblical text during his reworking of Pelagius's Expositions. Recently, Frede's premises for the reconstruction of the biblical text of

Pelagius were supported by De Bruyn (1993) and Stelzer (2018) in their editions of Romans and 2 Corinthians. Stelzer concluded that the biblical text is in agreement with the Vulgate in 97 percent of the cases and is "the earliest representative of the Pauline Vulgate that we possess today" (2018: 136). The investigation of the character of Pelagius's biblical text is by no means complete, but it is safe to conclude that Pelagius commented on a biblical text very close to the Vulgate which at the same time retained an Old Latin influence.

Rufinus the Syrian

The discussions about the role of Pelagius in the composition of the Vulgate, although inconclusive, steered scholarly attention to members of the Pelagian circle as possible revisers of the Acts, the Epistles, and Revelation. Rufinus the Syrian was considered by the members of the Vetus Latina Institute in Beuron to be the likeliest candidate in light of the biographical details and the correspondence of his citations with the Vulgate (Fischer, 1972: 74; Frede, 1966–71: 42; Thiele, 1956–69: 100–101). However, there are multiple reasons to reconsider this attribution.

Rufinus the Syrian's biography is reconstructed from various sources: Augustine (*De gratia Christi et de peccato originali* 2.3) stated that Rufinus was hosted in Rome by Pammachius, while according to Marius Mercator (*Liber subnotationum in uerba Iuliani, praefatio* 2), Rufinus of Syria introduced Pelagianism to Rome under Pope Anastasius I (399–402 CE). Jerome (*Contra Ioannem Hierosolymitanum* 42, *Aduersus Rufinus* 3.24, *Epistula* 81) affirmed that he sent the monk Rufinus from Bethlehem to Rome via Milan to defend a certain Claudius, and asked him to greet Rufinus of Aquileia. If the evidence of Augustine, Marius Mercator, and Jerome refers to the same person, Rufinus the Syrian was acquainted with both Jerome and Pelagius and was in Rome between 399 and 402 CE, the timeframe during which the *Primum quaeritur* seems to have been composed. The decisive proof in favor of Rufinus the Syrian's attribution would be the presence of citations according to the Vulgate in the *Liber de fide*, but neither the attribution of this writing to Rufinus nor the original language (Greek or Latin) in which it was written is certain.

Various methodological inconsistencies undermine the hypothesis of the Beuron editors, who followed Miller's claim that Rufinus cited the Vulgate despite the presence of slight differences (Miller 1964: 14–15). Dunphy (2012: 227) showed that Miller's analysis is not reliable in that the quotations from the *Liber de fide* were compared with the Clementine Vulgate, which differs from the fourth-century text reconstructed in the Stuttgart Vulgate. An attentive analysis of the citations shows that the biblical text of the *Liber de fide* agrees mostly with the *Vetus Latina*, in particular with Ambrosiaster and other witnesses grouped under the sigla J and I, representing versions of the Pauline Epistles in circulation in Northern Italy in the mid-fourth century (Persig 2020; Fröhlich 1995–98: 221).

THE PELAGIAN CIRCLE

Although the members of the Pelagian circle—that is, John Cassian, Caelestius, Eucherius of Lyons, Julian of Eclanum, Rufinus the Syrian, and their opponent Prosper of Aquitaine—are supposed to cite a text close to the Vulgate (Frede 1975–82: 155; Fischer 1972: 74; Thiele 1956–69: 64, 72, 77, 85, 96), a study of this has not yet been carried out (Dunphy 2012: 222). Partial attention to the matter was given by Thiele in the sections dedicated to the Vulgate in his introduction to the Catholic Epistles (1956–69). A close examination of the citations of these writers shows that the affiliation of the biblical text changes according to both the letters and the writings in which the citations are contained (Persig 2022: 11–12). Pseudo-Jerome *Epistula* 41, from the year 384, is the earliest instance of the Vulgate text of James at 1:12 and 5:1–5, contemporary with Jerome's revision of the Gospels. Readings of the Vulgate version of 1 Peter are attested in the citations of Caelestius transmitted by Augustine and in the Pseudo-Pelagian Epistle 148, both from the years 413–14. The Vulgate text of 2 Peter is cited in the Caspari corpus (408–16 CE) and in Pseudo-Augustine, *De uita christiana* (written before 413) while 1 John agrees with the Vulgate in Julian of Eclanum's quotations reported by Augustine (428–30 CE). The anti-Pelagian writing *Hypomnesticon contra Pelagianos siue Caelestianos haereticos*, written at the beginning of the fifth century, has a biblical text affiliated to the Vulgate in most of the epistles with sporadic Old Latin elements. On balance, the followers of Pelagius attest a form of text close to the Vulgate, although often mixed with the *Vetus Latina* and unique readings, in the first half of the fifth century. With the exception of the early citations of James in *Epistula* 41, the attestations of the Vulgate in the quotations from the other epistles are later than those present in Jerome's writings.

JEROME AND AUGUSTINE'S QUOTATIONS OF THE CATHOLIC EPISTLES

Several citations from Jerome and Augustine's writings predate those of the followers of Pelagius, but it is uncertain whether the Vulgate readings attested in them are original, replacements by later copyists, or from a pre-Vulgate text which served as a source for the Vulgate or was later incorporated in the manuscripts of the Vulgate. If these forms of text are original, the attribution of the revision of the Vulgate Catholic Epistles to Rufinus the Syrian has to be questioned: Rufinus is supposed to have revised the Epistles when he was in Rome, around 399 CE, yet the citations from the Vulgate Catholic Epistles in Jerome's writings prove that the revision was in circulation before the year 399. This is shown by the presence of Vulgate quotations in the second book of *Aduersus Iouinianum* (for instance, James 1:12–15, 17; 2 Peter 2:17–18 and 1 John 2:2–6; 3:9; 4:13, 15; 5:16, 18), *De uiris illustribus* (1 Peter 5:13; 1 John 1:1; 2 John 1:1; 3 John 1:1) and *Commentariorum in Abacuc prophetam* (1 Peter 2:20, 27), all from 393 CE; *Epistula* 50 (James 3:2) of 394; *Contra Ioannem Hierosolymitanum* (1 Peter 3:15) and *Epistula* 52 (1 Peter 5:2–4), written in 397. Citations according to the Vulgate are also present in later works, although in a mixed form, for example, in *Dialogi contra Pelagianos*, dated to 415–16 CE. Particularly significant is a long quotation of Jude 5–7 in *Epistula* 46 of the year 386, which is the earliest citation of Jerome containing renderings distinctive of the Vulgate: not only does Jerome agree with the lexicon of the Vulgate against the *Vetus Latina* text-types, for instance, in the renderings *conmonere* against *admonere* (R) and *conmemorare* (T), *saluans* instead of *saluum fecit* (R) and *liberans* (T), *principatum* opposed to *ordinem* (D) and *dignitatem* (T), *domicilium* versus *habitaculum* (D, T), but he also translates the same Greek variants, such as *Iesus* instead of *deus* (R, T), the addition of *aeternis*, absent from the *Vetus Latina*, and the rendering of ἡμέρας ("days") as *diei* rather than the scribal error *dei* (D, T). Jerome's citations also follow the word order and syntax of the Vulgate, for example, in the participial rendering *exfornicatae* translating ἐκπορνεύσασαι ("indulged in sexual immorality"), rendered with different constructions in the *Vetus Latina*: *cum adulterium fecissent* (D) and *fornicatae sunt* (T).

As a consequence, the revision of the Catholic Epistles appears to precede that of the Pauline Epistles, which are not cited according to the Vulgate in Jerome's commentaries. Thiele (1956–69: 100) believed that the Catholic Epistles could have been revised by Rufinus the Syrian before the Pauline Epistles, following the Greek sequence in which the Catholic Epistles come first. Fischer (1972: 74) justified the attribution to Rufinus the Syrian with a hypothesis which is not entirely plausible: Rufinus revised the Catholic Epistles in Bethlehem, where the revision was consulted by Jerome; while in Rome, he published the Vulgate Pauline Epistles and left the revision of the Catholic Epistles incomplete. It is improbable that Jerome is the reviser either: the affiliation of the citations of Jerome is inconsistent and varies within and between the citations. Numerous unique features are also present, in particular in the first book of *Aduersus Iouinianum*, which is at the base of text-type X in 2 Peter, corresponding to Jerome's biblical text. Although the Vulgate is attested in early works of Jerome from the end of the fourth century, the citations of the Catholic Epistles in agreement with the Vulgate represent only 35 percent of Jerome's corpus (206 of 777) (Persig 2022: 9).

The biblical text of Augustine in the Catholic Epistles is also inconsistent: it has similarities with the African text type C, with the European type T, and is often unique. In James, Augustine cites the Vulgate in a number of writings dated between 400 and 430 CE. The citations of James 1:14 and 2:14 in *De continentia* are not as early as was once believed: the composition of the writing in the year 395 proposed by the Maurists was rejected by La Bonnardière (1959), who suggested a dating after 412, probably between 416 and 418; Gryson (2007: 210) dates the work to 418–20. Nevertheless, the number of citations with features of the Vulgate and their degree of consistency are impressive in James, while the biblical text of Augustine is Old Latin in the other letters.

CURRENT RESULTS AND NEW APPROACHES

At present, it may be stated that the revision of the Acts, the Epistles, and Revelation was carried out by a still unidentified reviser between the end of the fourth and the beginning of the fifth centuries, a dating reconstructed in light of the earliest citations and attestations of the Vulgate in the manuscript tradition. Not much later, the other books of the New Testament were attributed to the reviser of the Gospels, Jerome, perhaps for commercial reasons. Although the attribution to Jerome seems to be conventional and his comments on the extent of his revision are controversial, some of the other criteria followed by twentieth-century scholarship to deny Jerome's involvement in the revision appear to be weak: the presence of stylistic differences or divergent principles of revision between the Gospels and the other writings have not yet been ascertained. If, on one hand, Jerome does not cite the Pauline Epistles according to the Vulgate in his commentaries, on the other, he quotes the Vulgate Catholic Epistles in early writings dated between 386 and 397. It remains to be verified whether in these citations the Old Latin text has been replaced with the Vulgate or the biblical text is authentically Vulgate. However, the fact that the majority of Jerome's citations disagree with the Vulgate suggests that he is not the reviser of the Vulgate Catholic Epistles. Considering that Jerome cites the Vulgate Catholic Epistles in *De uiris illustribus* of the year 393, he might have also quoted the *Primum quaeritur* in the same writing and not vice versa, as Frede hypothesized. Both the revision of the Epistles and the composition of the *Primum quaeritur* could have been accomplished before 393.

Attributing the revision to Pelagius has been unsuccessful because of the incorrect premises on which it is based: attempts to define his biblical text as Vulgate or Old Latin remain inconclusive. Similarly, the imprecise comparison between the citations of the *Liber de fide* and the Clementine Vulgate, as well as Frede's dating of the *Primum quaeritur*, which fits the revision of the Pauline Epistles but is later than that of the Catholic Epistles, are not solid arguments to sustain the authorship of Rufinus the Syrian. The citations of Jerome and the quotations of James in Pseudo-Jerome *Epistula* 41, which are in agreement with the Vulgate, predate Rufinus's arrival in Rome in the year 399, where he supposedly undertook the revision of the Vulgate Epistles. The biblical text of the *Liber de fide* appears to be affiliated to the Old Latin text types I and J rather than to the Vulgate. There are therefore multiple indications that Rufinus the Syrian did not revise the Vulgate Epistles. The citations of the followers of Pelagius attest the Vulgate at the beginning of the fifth century, but a detailed study of their biblical text is still needed.

Until now, scholarly attention has been focused on the identification of a single reviser for Acts, the Epistles, and Revelation. However, the activity of multiple revisers is not unlikely, as the absence of a common prologue to the rest of the Vulgate New Testament and the existence of prologues to the single books or epistles may demonstrate. A study of the Latin language and style of the Vulgate New Testament outside the Gospels is necessary to test this hypothesis. The stylistic and linguistic analysis may point to the activity of a single author, if the books of the Vulgate New Testament share the same principles of revision, language, and style. Otherwise, several revisers could have collaborated or worked independently on these writings, as seems to be the case in the Catholic Epistles. The data derived from these complementary approaches, namely, a complete review of the earliest citations of the Vulgate New Testament outside the Gospels and an analysis of the language and style of these texts, will help to move forward in identifying the reviser or revisers of the Vulgate, clarifying the role played by the main figures of the fourth and fifth centuries in the composition and transmission of the revision and, generally speaking, improving our knowledge of the text, origin and spread of the Vulgate New Testament outside the Gospels.

ACKNOWLEDGMENTS

The research leading to this chapter was funded by the Midlands4Cities Doctoral Training Partnership and the Arts and Humanities Research Council.

BIBLIOGRAPHY

Berger, Samuel. 1893. *Histoire de la Vulgate pendant les premiers siècles du moyen age*. Nancy: Berger-Levrault.

Berger, Samuel. 1904. "Les préfaces jointes aux livres de la Bible dans les manuscrits de la vulgate." In *Mémoires présentés par divers savants à l'Académie des inscriptions et belles-lettres de l'Institut de France*, 1–78. Première série, Sujets divers d'érudition, Tome 11, 2e partie. Paris: Imprimerie Nationale.

Birdsall, J. N. 1970. "The New Testament Text." In *The Cambridge History of the Bible. I. From the Beginnings to Jerome*, edited by P. R. Ackroyd and C. F. Evans, 308–77. Cambridge: Cambridge University Press.

Bogaert, Pierre-Maurice. 2012. "The Latin Bible, c. 600 to c. 900." In *New Cambridge History of the Bible: Vol. 2. From 600 to 1450*, edited by Richard Marsden and E. Ann Matter, 69–92. Cambridge: Cambridge University Press.

Bogaert, Pierre-Maurice. 2013. "The Latin Bible." In *New Cambridge History of the Bible: Vol. 1. From the Beginnings to 600*, edited by James C. Paget and Joachim Schaper, 505–26. Cambridge: Cambridge University Press.

Cavallera, Ferdinand. 1920. "Saint Jérôme et la Vulgate des Actes, des Épîtres et de l'Apocalypse." *Bulletin de littérature ecclésiastique* VI, no. 11: 269–92.

Chapman, H. J. 1933. "St. Jerome and the Vulgate New Testament." *Journal of Theological Studies* 24: 33–51, 113–25, 283–99.

Charlier, Célestin. 1963. "Cassiodore, Pélage et les origines de la vulgate paulinienne." In *Studiorum Paulinorum Congressus Internationalis Catholicus 1961*, II:461–70. Rome: Pontifical Biblical Institute.

De Bruyn, Theodore S. 1993. *Pelagius' Commentary on St Paul's Epistle to the Romans*. Oxford: Clarendon Press.

De Bruyne, Donatien. 1915. "Étude sur les origines de notre texte latin de Saint Paul." *Revue Biblique* 12: 358–92.

Dunphy, Walter. 2012. "Ps-Rufinus, the 'Syrian', and the Vulgate. Evidence wanting!" *Augustinianum* 52: 219–56.

Elliott, J. K. 1992. "The Translations of the New Testament into Latin: The Old Latin and the Vulgate." In *Aufstieg und Niedergang der Römischen Welt* II.26.1, Religion, edited by Wolfgang Haase and Hildegard Temporini, 198–245. Berlin: De Gruyter.

Fischer, Bonifatius. 1972. "Das Neue Testament in lateinischer Sprache. Der gegenwärtige Stand seiner Erforschung und seine Bedeutung für die griechische Textgeschichte." ' In *Die alten Übersetzungen des Neuen Testaments, die Kirchenväterzitate und Lektionare*, edited by Kurt Aland, 1–92. ANTF 5. Berlin: De Gruyter.

Fischer, Bonifatius. 1985. *Lateinische Bibelhandschriften im frühen Mittelalter*. AGLB 11. Freiburg: Herder.

Frede, Hermann Josef. 1961. *Pelagius, der irische Paulustext, Sedulius Scottus*. AGLB 3. Freiburg: Herder.

Frede, Hermann Josef, ed. 1966–71. *Epistulae ad Philippenses et ad Colossenses*. VL 24/2. Freiburg: Herder.

Frede, Hermann Josef, ed. 1975–82. *Epistulae ad Thessalonicenses, Timotheum, Titum, Philemonem, Hebraeos*. VL 25/1. Freiburg: Herder.

Fröhlich, Uwe. 1995–98. *Epistula ad Corinthios: Einleitung*. 3 fasc. VL 22. Freiburg: Herder.

Gryson, Roger, ed. 2000–3. *Apocalypsis Johannis*. VL 26/2. Freiburg: Herder.

Gryson, Roger, 2007. *Répertoire général des auteurs ecclésiastiques latins de l'antiquité et du haut moyen âge*. 2 vols; VL 1/1. Freiburg: Herder.

Halton, Thomas P., trans. 2010. *St. Jerome, On Illustrious Men*. Fathers of the Church 100. Washington, DC: Catholic University of America.

Houghton, H. A. G. 2008. "Augustine's Adoption of the Vulgate Gospels." *New Testament Studies* 54, no. 3: 450–64.

Houghton, H. A. G. 2016. *The Latin New Testament. A Guide to Its Early History, Texts, and Manuscripts*. Oxford: Oxford University Press.

Houghton, H. A. G. 2017. "The Layout of Early Latin Commentaries on the Pauline Epistles and their Oldest Manuscripts." In *Studia Patristica* 91, edited by Markus Vinzent, 71–112. Leuven: Peeters.

La Bonnardière, Anne-Marie. 1959. "La date du «De Continentia» de saint Augustin." *Revue des études augustiniennes* 5: 121–7.

Lagrange, M.-J. 1917. "La Vulgate latin de l'Épître aux Galates et le texte grec." *Revue Biblique* 14: 424–50.

Lagrange, M.-J. 1918. "La révision de la Vulgate par S. Jérome." *Revue Biblique* 15: 254–57.

Miller, Mary William. 1964. *Rufini presbyteri Liber de Fide. A Critical Text and Translation with Introduction and Commentary*. Patristic Studies 96. Washington, DC: Catholic University of America.

Nellessen, Ernst. 1968. "Der lateinische Paulustext im Codex Baliolensis des Pelagius-kommentars." *Zeitschrift für die neutestamentliche Wissenschaft* 59: 210–30.

Persig, Anna. 2020. "The Affiliation of the Quotations from the New Testament Epistles in the *Liber de Fide*." In *At One Remove: The Text of the New Testament in Early Translations and Quotations*, edited by H. A. G. Houghton and P. Montoro, 287–310. T&S 3.24. Piscataway: Gorgias.

Persig, Anna. 2022. *The Vulgate Text of the Catholic Epistles: Its Language, Origin and Relationship with the Vetus Latina*. AGLB 42. Freiburg: Herder.

Plinval, Georges de. 1964. "Le problème des versions pélagiennes du texte de S. Paul." *Revue d'Histoire Ecclésiastique* 59: 845–53.

Rebenich, Stefan. 1993. "Jerome: The 'Vir Trilinguis' and the 'Hebraica Veritas.'" *Vigiliae Christianae* 47: 50–77.

Schäfer, K. T. 1962. "Pelagius und die Vulgata." *New Testament Studies* 9: 361–66.

Schaff, Philip, trans., 1886. *A Select Library of Nicene and Post-Nicene Fathers of the Christian Church, First Series. I. The Confessions and Letters of St. Augustin, with a sketch of his life and work*. Buffalo: Christian Literature Company.

Schaff, Philip, and Henry Wace, trans. 1996. *A Select Library of Nicene and Post-Nicene Fathers of the Christian Church, Second Series. VI, St. Jerome: Letters and Select Works*. Edinburgh: T&T Clark. Repr., Grand Rapids: Eerdmans.

Scherbenske, Eric W. 2013. *Canonizing Paul: Ancient Editorial Practice and the Corpus Paulinum*. Oxford: Oxford University Press.

Souter, Alexander. 1922–31. *Pelagius' Expositions of Thirteen Epistles of St. Paul*. 3 vols. Cambridge: Cambridge University Press.

Stelzer, Wilbert P. 2018. *A New Reconstruction of the Text of 2 Corinthians in Pelagius's Commentary on the Pauline Epistles*. T&S 3.17. Piscataway: Gorgias.

Sutcliffe, Edmund F. 1948. "The Council of Trent on the *Authentia* of the Vulgate." *Journal of Theological Studies* 49: 35–42.

Thiele, Walter, ed. 1956–69. *Epistulae Catholicae*. VL 26/1. Freiburg: Herder.

Vaccari, A. 1915. "Alle origini della Volgata, II. La Volgata del Nuovo Testamento." *La civiltà cattolica* 4: 160–70.

....

CHAPTER 7

DEUTEROCANONICAL BOOKS IN LATIN TRADITION

....

EDMON L. GALLAGHER

WHEN Johannes Gutenberg issued the *editio princeps* of the Latin Bible (1455), he included a rather fulsome collection of Old Testament scriptures, whereas he limited his New Testament to the standard canon of twenty-seven books. About a decade and a half earlier, the Council of Florence became the first ecumenical council to issue a list of biblical books, in a bull of union with the Copts, *Cantate Domino*, dated February 14, 1442, although the previous departure of the Greek delegation casts into doubt the ecumenical nature of the council at the time of the bull (Bedouelle 1984: 262). Beyond the books of the Jewish canon, the Old Testament approved at Florence included also Tobit, Judith, Wisdom of Solomon, Ecclesiasticus (Sirach), Baruch, and 1–2 Maccabees (text and translation in Tanner 1990: 572). Gutenberg's Bible included the entirety of the Florentine biblical canon along with the Prayer of Manasseh, 3 Ezra (known in the Septuagint and most English Bibles as 1 Esdras), and IV Ezra (= 5–4–6 Ezra, often known in English Bibles as 2 Esdras). Gutenberg's Bible conformed in content and sequence more or less with the Paris Bibles of the thirteenth century, although these latter usually omitted IV Ezra. A century after Gutenberg, the Roman Catholic Council of Trent (April 8, 1546) definitively settled the biblical canon (for Christians in communion with Rome) by putting under anathema anyone who would reject the list of books as formulated at Florence (Tanner 1990: 663–64). From that time, Latin Bibles sponsored by the Roman Catholic Church have adhered to this biblical canon, though starting with the Sixto-Clementine edition of the Vulgate (1592) and continuing with today's Stuttgart Vulgate (Weber and Gryson 2007), an appendix has included additional books: the Prayer of Manasseh, 3 Ezra, IV Ezra, and (in the Stuttgart Vulgate) Laodiceans and Psalm 151. Many of the Old Testament texts are also available in the major edition of the Roman Vulgate.[1]

---

[1] Abbey of St Jerome, *Biblia Sacra Iuxta Latinam Vulgatam Versionem* (18 vols., Rome: Vatican Polyglot Press, 1926–95).

TERMINOLOGY AND CORPUS

The Old Testament writings outside the Jewish canon were called "apocrypha" by Martin Luther, echoing the much earlier description by Jerome.[2] These books received the name "deuterocanonical" from Sixtus of Siena in his explanation of the Tridentine canons.[3] The term "deuterocanonical" usually now applies to the seven books considered canonical by Roman Catholics and apocryphal by Protestants and Jews—Tobit, Judith, Wisdom of Solomon, Ecclesiasticus, Baruch, 1–2 Maccabees—along with the Additions in Esther and Daniel. Sixtus actually labeled the entire book of Esther deuterocanonical, and gave this label to several New Testament books and passages: Mark 16:9–20; Luke 22:43–44; John 7:53–8:11; the Epistle to the Hebrews; James; 2 Peter; 2–3 John; Jude; and Revelation. This chapter omits discussion of all these New Testament writings but considers here some Christian writings found in some Latin manuscripts but not labeled deuterocanonical by Sixtus or usually by subsequent Christian tradition: Laodiceans, 3 Corinthians, and the Gospel of Nicodemus. Finally, the Odes (also known in Latin tradition as Canticles) will also form a part of the discussion.

The major representatives of the Latin Bible shown in Table 7.1 for the most part omit the Christian apocrypha while including most of the Old Testament

Table 7.1 Presence of Apocryphal Books in Latin Bibles

	Codex Amiatinus	Tours Bibles	Theodulf	Paris Bibles	Gutenberg	Trent	Sixto-Clementine	Stuttgart Vulgate
Tobit	•	•	•	•	•	•	•	•
Judith	•	•	•	•	•	•	•	•
1 Maccabees	•	•	•	•	•	•	•	•
2 Maccabees	•	•	•	•	•	•	•	•
Wisdom	•	•	•	•	•	•	•	•
Ecclesiasticus (Sirach)	•	•	•	•	•	•	•	•
Baruch			•	•	•	•	•	•
3 Ezra (1 Esdras)			•	•			appendix	appendix
IV Ezra				•			appendix	appendix
Prayer of Manasseh			•	•			appendix	appendix
Psalm 151	•	•						appendix

---

[2] Martin Luther, *Biblia, das ist, Die gantze Heilige Schrifft deudsch* (Wittemberg: Hans Lufft, 1534); see further Fricke 1991. The reference in Jerome's *Prologus Galeatus* is found in Weber and Gryson 2007: 365 l. 54.

[3] Sixtus of Siena, *Bibliotheca Sancta* (Venice: Franciscus Franciscius Senensis, 1566), 10.

deuterocanonical literature, although Laodiceans does sometimes appear in later Tours Bibles (Ganz 1994: 57).

The Latin Text of the Old Testament Deuterocanonical Books

Much of the Latin Bible exists—or once existed—in two major textual forms: the *Vetus Latina* and the translation by Jerome. As Jerome's translations became increasingly dominant in the Middle Ages, they often pushed the *Vetus Latina* into near obscurity, so that for many biblical books we rely primarily on patristic citations rather than manuscript copies for an understanding of the Old Latin text. But Jerome mostly ignored the deuterocanonical literature, so that the Old Latin editions of these books did not have to compete with other versions. We are thus in the fortunate position that for most of this literature we have complete manuscript copies of the *Vetus Latina* edition.

The deuterocanonical books of the Old Testament appeared in Latin at the same time as the initial Latin translations of the protocanonical books. In the mid-third century, Cyprian of Carthage quotes in Latin from Tobit, 1–2 Maccabees, Wisdom of Solomon, Ecclesiasticus (Sirach), Baruch (under Jeremiah's name), the Epistle of Jeremiah, and 3 Ezra/1 Esdras (Saxer 1985: 344–45, 367–69). Up-to-date studies of the Latin texts for all of the Old Testament deuterocanonical books are available in Feder and Henze (2019–20).

Additions to Daniel

Jerome produced a translation of the book of Daniel based on the Hebrew/Aramaic— or, as Jerome would say, Hebrew/Chaldean—text, complete with the Additions to Daniel, prefixed with an obelus. He mentions these Additions in his preface, explaining their absence from the Jewish version of the book and his consequent use of the obelus to "slay" (*iugulo*) them (Weber and Gryson 2007: 1341). He followed the Hexaplaric order by positioning Susanna and Bel and the Dragon at the end of the book (instead of putting Susanna at the front of the book), whereas the Prayer of Azariah and the Hymn of the Three Young Men appear in their usual position after Daniel 3:23. The Vulgate Daniel is available in the Stuttgart Vulgate and the Roman Vulgate (vol. 16, 1981).

The *Vetus Latina* Additions to Daniel are not as well preserved as the *Vetus Latina* of the other deuterocanonical books. VL 176 (ninth century) preserves Susanna and Bel and the Dragon, which are also partially extant in VL 177 (palimpsest, fifth century). These two manuscripts also partially preserve the Prayer of Azariah and the Song of the Three Young Men (VL 176, Daniel 3:36–60; VL 177, Daniel 3:24–50), but neither of them preserve the last thirty verses of this section (verses 61–90), a lack mostly remedied by liturgical manuscripts, particularly VL 251 (ca. 700). The edition of Daniel by Jean-Claude

Haelewyck, fascicles of which are now appearing, replaces the edition by Sabatier (1743–49: 2.855–89).[4]

Additions to Esther

Jerome translated the Hebrew text of Esther and included under an obelus the six Additions to Esther known in the Greek tradition. According to Haelewyck (2003–8: 64–65), Jerome translated these Additions from a Hexaplaric Greek text. He did not leave the Additions in their natural location in the text of Esther but gathered all the Additions at the end of the book with prefixed notes indicating where in the text they belonged. After Esther 10:3 (the end of the Hebrew book), a note appears in Vulgate manuscripts (reproduced in Weber and Gryson 2007: 724) explaining that the following material appears in Greek. Aside from the Stuttgart Vulgate, the text is available in the Roman Vulgate (vol. 9, 1951).

The *Vetus Latina* Esther has one extra Addition beyond those available in the Septuagint: a prayer of the Jews inserted after 3:15. As for the *Vetus Latina* Esther, we have four manuscripts of the complete text (VL 109, 123, 130, 151), the best of which is VL 151, the manuscript used by Sabatier (1743–49: 1.796–825). The *Vetus Latina* text has been edited for the Beuron Institute by Haelewyck, who argues that *Vetus Latina* Esther was translated from a lost Greek text, earlier than the extant Greek texts.[5]

Baruch/Epistle of Jeremiah

The book of Baruch as it exists in the Latin Vulgate today consists of six chapters. The sixth chapter was formerly an independent work known as the Epistle of Jeremiah, as it still is in Greek and as it is in our earliest Latin manuscripts, those of Theodulf's Bible in the early ninth century. In these Bibles, Baruch ends with an *explicit* and the Epistle of Jeremiah immediately follows with an *incipit*. Already some of the twelfth-century Giant Bibles treated Baruch and the Epistle of Jeremiah as a single book (Bogaert 2005: 325 n.166), and this union became complete in the Paris Bibles. These books early on formed part of the corpus of Jeremiah books. Our earliest manuscript containing Baruch, a Theodulf Bible now in Stuttgart (Θ^S), joins Baruch directly to Jeremiah without a break, and only after Baruch do we find the *explicit* for Jeremiah.[6]

Jerome's refusal to translate Baruch and the Epistle of Jeremiah (cf. his *Praef. Jer.* in Weber and Gryson 2007: 1166) meant that Bibles containing his version of Jeremiah, such

---

[4] Jean-Claude Haelewyck, ed., *Danihel* (VL 14/1) (Freiburg: Herder, 2021–).

[5] Jean-Claude Haelewyck, ed., *Hester* (VL 7/3) (Freiburg: Herder, 2003–8); on the Greek *Vorlage*, see Haelewyck 2006.

[6] Stuttgart, Württembergische Landesbibliothek, HB.II.16: digital images are available online at <http://digital.wlb-stuttgart.de/purl/bsz353338028>. Baruch starts on fol. 82r and the *explicit* appears on 82v.

as Codex Amiatinus and the Tours Bibles, omitted these additional works (Bogaert 2005: 332–36). Perhaps due to the continuing importance of Baruch in the liturgy (Feuerstein 1997: 42, 205), Theodulf incorporated into his Bibles a *Vetus Latina* form of Baruch and the Epistle: his version was received into the Italian Giant Bibles and the Paris Bibles, and thus became Vulgate. Scholars have identified three other Latin forms of Baruch (Bogaert 2005; Kabasele Mukenge 2000): one preserved only in the ninth-century Codex Cavensis (Mattei-Cerasoli 1935), another in some Spanish manuscripts attesting a peculiar order (Baruch 1:1–4; 3:9–5:9; 1:5–3:8; Hoberg 1902), and finally the short, Gallican recension printed by Sabatier (2.737–49), this latter omitting the Epistle of Jeremiah. The Jeremiah volume of the Roman Vulgate (vol. 14, 1972) prints the Theodulf version of Baruch (ch. 1–6) with variants among its manuscripts treated in the first apparatus, while readings from the other textual forms are noted in a lower apparatus.

The Biblical Odes

The Odes (or Canticles) is a collection of biblical songs. Similar collections are known in a variety of languages. There was no standard version. The Latin Odes/Canticles often appear in manuscripts of the Psalter or other liturgical collections (Gryson 2004: 15–19; Houghton 2016: 90–91). Schneider (1938) associated four major forms of Latin Odes/Canticles with Rome, Milan, Spain, and Ireland. All of these forms include the Song of the Sea (Exodus 15:1–19); the Song of Moses (Deuteronomy 32:1–43); the Prayer of Hannah (1 Samuel 2:1–10); Habakkuk's Prayer (Habakkuk 3:2–19); and the Hymn of the Three Young Men from the Additions to Daniel (Daniel 3:57–88, sometimes also with vv. 52–56). Other songs are also included, but not as consistently: Isaiah 5:1–7, 12:1–6, 26:9–20, 38:10–20; Jonah 2:3–10; Luke 1:46–55, 68–79; and the Prayer of Manasseh. The Greek Odes, recently studied by Harl (2014), appears first as a collection in the fifth-century Codex Alexandrinus (GA 02). The collection of Latin Odes/Canticles is just as early. An edition appears in Sabatier (1743–49), and the Spanish (Mozarabic) form has been printed based on VL 411.[7] The individual songs are being edited by the Vetus Latina Institute within the editions of the biblical books to which these passages originally belonged.

Ecclesiasticus

The book of Ben Sira (or Sirach) was translated into Latin during the second or third century; Cyprian quotes Ecclesiasticus 24:3–7 as coming from a book called Ecclesiasticus written by Solomon (*Ad Quirinum* 2.1). The translation was based on a Greek *Vorlage*

[7] J. P. Gilson, *The Mozarabic Psalter, MS. British Museum, Add. 30, 851* (London: Harrison and Sons, 1905). Digital images of this manuscript are available online: <http://www.bl.uk/manuscripts/FullDisplay.aspx?ref=Add_MS_30851>.

no longer extant, one which corresponds neither to the shorter nor longer Greek texts, and one that maintained the correct sequence of Ecclesiasticus 30:25–36:13a, a sequence altered in all extant Greek manuscripts. The character of the translation makes it useful for understanding its Greek base text; as its current editor has written, "the Latin text of Sirach is sometimes so slavishly literal that it is at times unintelligible" (Forte 2014: 72).The Latin Ecclesiasticus exists in nine text forms, the earliest (K) preserved for only small portions, while the Vulgate is the only form preserved complete. This Vulgate form is available in the Stuttgart Vulgate and the Roman Vulgate (vol. 12, 1964). The Beuron edition is currently in progress. It reached Ecclesiasticus 24:47 under the editorship of Walter Thiele, and is now being continued by Anthony J. Forte.[8]

3 Ezra (1 Esdras)

The book known in the LXX tradition as 1 Esdras eventually came to be known in the Latin tradition as 3 Ezra. Alcuin and Theodulf omitted 3 Ezra from their editions. The Paris Bibles usually refer to this book as 2 Ezra, following Ezra (= 1 Ezra) and Nehemiah. Gutenberg labeled Nehemiah "Ezra II," so that our book became Ezra III. The book itself is an alternative version of protocanonical Ezra. Latin patristic authors usually cite Ezra material from 3 Ezra rather than from protocanonical Ezra (Denter 1962: 53–67; Bogaert 2000a). The translation probably dates to the second century in North Africa. Gesche (2014) has identified three primary forms of the text, which are set out in the *Vetus Latina* edition.[9]

IV Ezra

The book known in Gutenberg's Bible as Ezra IV with sixteen chapters is a composite work, bringing together three originally distinct writings known to scholars under the following names: 5 Ezra (= IV Ezra 1–2), 4 Ezra (= IV Ezra 3–14), 6 Ezra (= IV Ezra 15–16), each having separate origins and histories. 4 Ezra was probably written in Hebrew at the end of the first century, then translated into Greek, and thence into Latin and other languages (Stone 1990: 1–9). Both the Hebrew and the Greek texts are completely lost, except for some citations in Greek authors (e.g., Clement of Alexandria, *Stromateis* 3.16, quoting 4 Ezra 5:35). 4 Ezra was especially influential due to its story of the burning of the scriptures by the Babylonians and Ezra's subsequent inspired restoration of them (4 Ezra 14; Bogaert 2015: 270–73). Ambrose cites 4 Ezra 6:41 as coming from the third book of Ezra (*De Spiritu Sancto* 2.6), probably meaning that Ambrose considered our 3 Ezra to be the first book of Ezra, while our Ezra-Nehemiah was his second book of Ezra (thus

[8] Walter Thiele, ed., *Sirach, Ecclesiasticus* (VL 11/2) (Freiburg: Herder, 1987–2005); Anthony J. Forte, ed., *Sirach, Ecclesiasticus: pars altera.* (VL 11/2) (Freiburg: Herder, 2014–).
[9] Bonifatia Gesche, ed., *Esra I.* (VL 6/2) (Freiburg: Herder, 2008–16).

in accordance with the presentation in LXX manuscripts). 5 Ezra may have been composed in Greek, in the second or third century, but only the Latin text (and derivative translations) is extant; it is clearly a Christian text (Bergren 2010). 6 Ezra was likely composed not in a Semitic language but in Greek—we have a fourth-century Oxyrhynchus fragment (P.Oxy. 1010)—and probably by a Christian (Bergren 1998); the Latin text, alone fully extant, is already attested by an allusion in the fifth-century *Apocalypse of Thomas* (Wright 2016). The Latin manuscripts of the composite IV Ezra are divided into a French family and a Spanish family (Bogaert 2015). Alcuin and Theodulf omitted IV Ezra from their Bibles, as did the Italian Giant Bibles and most of the Paris Bibles, but there are still 134 manuscripts transmitting the text, copied between 1200 and 1450 (Bogaert 2015: 292–302). The most readily available edition of IV Ezra is in the appendix to the Stuttgart Vulgate, which prints the French recension; a more complete edition is provided by Klijn.[10]

Judith

The *Vetus Latina* Judith was produced in the third century from a Hexaplaric Greek text, branching out from there into several families. We still have nineteen manuscripts of the complete *Vetus Latina* Judith, the earliest being from the eighth century (VL 145). Two manuscripts preserve *Vetus Latina* Judith side by side with Jerome's translation (VL 62, 132). As with Tobit, Jerome says that his translation was based on a Chaldean text (Weber and Gryson 2007: 691), but he clearly made use of the Old Latin and contributed certain passages of his own (cf. Judith 15:11; see Gallagher 2015). One of his motivations for producing a translation was to unify "the terrible variety of the many codices" (*multorum codicum uarietatem uitiossissimam*; Weber and Gryson 2007: 690). The Beuron edition of the *Vetus Latina* Judith is now complete.[11] The Vulgate Judith is available in the Stuttgart Vulgate and the Roman Vulgate (vol. 8, 1950).

1–2 Maccabees

The first two books of Maccabees were translated into Latin early enough to be cited by Cyprian. Since Jerome did not produce his own translation, all of our Latin manuscripts attest an Old Latin text form. The Latin tradition of 1 Maccabees essentially evinces two main branches: the older branch—as judged by, for example, patristic citations and vocabulary—is transmitted by three ninth-century manuscripts, VL 7, 109, and 146. De Bruyne labeled this branch L. The second branch, labeled B and represented especially by VL 195, presents a much freer translation with consistent revision from the Greek.

---

[10] A. Frederik J. Klijn, *Der lateinische Text der Apokalypse des Esra* (Berlin: Akademie, 1983).
[11] P.-M. Bogaert and Jean-Claude Haelewyck (eds), *Judith* (VL 7/2) (Freiburg: Herder, 2001–20).

The Vulgate represents the earlier L family with some corrections from the Greek and influence from the B family. The second book of Maccabees is preserved by mostly the same witnesses. Kappler and Hanhart (1959: 26–29) show that the Latin tradition attests readings probably original but now lost in the Greek tradition. The *Vetus Latina* of 2 Maccabees often stands close to the Antiochian Greek text, but the Latin texts also contain unique doublets (Kappler and Hanhart 1959: 34–36). The Old Latin versions have been edited by De Bruyne.[12] The Vulgate is available in the Stuttgart Vulgate and the final volume of the Roman Vulgate (vol. 18, 1995).

Prayer of Manasseh

This prayer was probably composed in Greek, and in the Septuagint tradition, the Prayer of Manasseh is included among the Odes, as in Codex Alexandrinus. It was as a part of such a collection that the Prayer first appeared in Latin, as attested by the commentary on the Canticles by Verecundus, bishop of Junca in the mid-sixth century (Schneider 1938: 17–21; Demeulenaere 1976: 148–61). It continued to be transmitted in liturgical manuscripts, but by the thirteenth century it had become the concluding piece to 2 Chronicles, where it remained in Gutenberg's edition. It is printed in the appendix to the Stuttgart Vulgate.

Psalm 151

It is unclear whether Jerome included this Psalm in his Gallican Psalter, but it does appear in dozens of manuscripts of the Gallican Psalter, such as Alcuin's Bibles, as well as in other editions (Bogaert 2000b). The Psalm also appears in Codex Amiatinus, which otherwise features Jerome's Hebrew Psalter. Psalm 151 is printed in the appendix to the Stuttgart Vulgate and in the Roman Vulgate (appendix to vol. 10, 1953).

Tobit

Of the two main Greek forms of Tobit—GI (shorter text) and GII (longer text)—the *Vetus Latina* Tobit provides an important witness to the longer text, otherwise attested mainly by the Greek Codex Sinaiticus. In his preface to Tobit, Jerome says that he translated the book at the request of bishops Chromatius and Heliodorus from a Chaldean *Vorlage* (Weber and Gryson 2007: 676). Close textual analysis reveals that he also used the *Vetus Latina* heavily, though he also seems to have contributed passages

---

[12] Donatien De Bruyne, ed., *Les anciennes traductions latines des Machabées* (Anecdota Maredsolana 4) (Maredsous: Abbaye de Maredsous, 1932).

of his own in order to promote topics important to him (cf. Tobit 8:4; Skemp 2000). Fortunately, Jerome's translation did not completely displace the Old Latin Tobit, which is complete in a dozen manuscripts, the earliest being eighth century. Two manuscripts preserve *Vetus Latina* Tobit side by side with Jerome's version (VL 62, 134). The *Vetus Latina* is currently being edited for the Beuron Institute by Jean-Marie Auwers (see Auwers 2006). The Vulgate text is available in the Stuttgart Vulgate and the Roman Vulgate (vol. 8, 1950). For a synopsis of the most prominent text forms of Tobit, see Weeks, Gathercole, and Stuckenbruck (2004).

Wisdom of Solomon

The Wisdom of Solomon was translated into Latin late in the second century. According to Thiele, the original translation branched off in several directions, the earliest of which (K) is attested in the Cyprianic literature. Later branches evince revision toward the Greek. One of these later branches became the Vulgate, which is the only text preserved in its entirety. This latter text contains various additions (usually a word, sometimes a clause) in comparison with the Greek, which the Vulgate seems to have inherited from the Latin tradition and may provide evidence for a Greek text not otherwise available. The Vulgate Wisdom is available in the Stuttgart Vulgate and the Roman Vulgate (vol. 12, 1964), while the *Vetus Latina* edition was edited by Thiele.[13]

THE LATIN TEXT OF THE NEW TESTAMENT DEUTEROCANONICAL BOOKS

This section considers the Latin text of *Laodiceans*, *3 Corinthians*, and the *Gospel of Nicodemus*.

Laodiceans

The Epistle to the Colossians in the New Testament contains a reference (Colossians 4:16) to a letter from Paul to the church at Laodicea. A letter ostensibly from Paul to the Laodiceans is found not infrequently in medieval Latin Bibles, widely believed by modern scholars to be a translation of a Greek document. The earliest manuscript containing the Latin text is the sixth-century Codex Fuldensis, but the Greek text (Lightfoot 1884: 274–300) may go back to the late second century. The Muratorian Fragment, traditionally located in second- or third-century Rome, mentions a forged

---

[13] Walter Thiele, ed., *Sapientia Salomonis* (VL 11/1) (Freiburg: Herder, 1977–85).

Pauline letter to the Laodiceans (ll. 63–65; see Gallagher and Meade 2017: 180–81), perhaps referring to our document.[14] Despite Jerome's declaration that everyone rejected Laodiceans (*De uiris illustribus* 5), it was well received in the West. Gregory the Great seems to have regarded it as genuinely Pauline, though he did not include it among the canonical fourteen epistles of the Apostle (*Moralia in Job* 35.48; see Lightfoot 1884: 295). In addition to Codex Fuldensis, Laodiceans found its way into some Tours Bibles (Bogaert 2012: 83) and several other copies of the New Testament (Bogaert 2012: 90; Houghton 2016: 194–95), such as Codex Cavensis (ninth century) and the First Bible of Alcalá (VL 109, tenth century).

3 Corinthians

This apocryphal correspondence between Paul and the Corinthians, forming part of the Acts of Paul, appears independently of that text in five Latin manuscripts, all from the tenth to the thirteenth centuries. One of these, the Vulgate manuscript B (the Bible of Biasca), places 3 Corinthians between Hebrews and Laodiceans (Hovhanessian 2000: 6–9). The Monza Bible (VL 86) includes a reference to 3 Corinthians in the table of contents. According to Bogaert, 3 Corinthians "nearly became part of the Latin Bible" (2012: 90).

Gospel of Nicodemus

This Gospel concentrates on the end of Jesus's life and his resurrection. The Greek text, which often goes under the name of the Acts of Pilate, was composed perhaps in the fourth century (Gounelle 2012: 82). The earliest manuscript of the Latin translation (Vienna, ÖNB, lat. 563; cf. VL 43) is a fifth-century palimpsest (Izydorczyk 1997a: 44–46). This Latin version became extraordinarily important in medieval Western Christianity, especially for its description of the Harrowing of Hell. The Latin text survives today in more than 450 manuscripts, all from the ninth century and later, except for the earlier Vienna palimpsest (Izydorczyk 2012: 100–101). Most of these manuscripts have been described by Izydorczyk (1993). The Gospel sometimes appears in the company of canonical texts, such as in ms 157 in Izydorczyk's catalogue (1993; see Izydorczyk 1997a: 75–83). The manuscript tradition was quite fluid, and the Latin text exists in three major forms, labeled A, B, and C (Izydorczyk 1997a: 46–53). These Latin texts became the basis for the many vernacular translations in Europe (see the articles in Izydorczyk 1997b). In his most recent update of his work on the Latin transmission, Izydorczyk described the complexity of the editing task, lamenting, "In its long manuscript history,

---

[14] See Clare K. Rothschild, *The Muratorian Fragment: Text, Translation, Commentary* (Tübingen: Mohr Siebeck, 2022).

the [*Euangelium Nicodemi*] does not seem to have ever had a single authoritative textual form" (2012: 113). The most widely available editions include that based on a tenth-century manuscript of Version A edited by Kim and the eclectic text of Tischendorf.[15]

THE RECEPTION OF THE
DEUTEROCANONICAL BOOKS IN THE
LATIN BIBLE

Most of the writings surveyed above have been considered important and spiritually edifying throughout the history of Latin-speaking Christianity, though not every writer favored receiving these writings into the biblical canon. As mentioned earlier, the Council of Trent in 1546 attached an anathema to its proclamation of the biblical canon, thus bringing to an end disputes about the seven deuterocanonical books of the Old Testament (i.e., Tobit, Judith, Wisdom of Solomon, Ecclesiasticus, Baruch, 1–2 Maccabees). These disputes had intensified during the sixteenth century, not merely as a result of the Protestant Reformation, and the deliberations at Trent had been somewhat contentious (see Jedin 1961: chap. 2). Both sides in the debate cited patristic authority in their favor.

More than a thousand years earlier, Jerome and Augustine advocated differing positions on this issue. For much of the ancient period and the Middle Ages, six deuterocanonical books were under discussion, omitting Baruch, which was either considered a part of Jeremiah or discarded altogether under the influence of Jerome. Augustine accepted all six deuterocanonical books within his biblical canon (*De doctrina christiana* 2.8.12; text and translation in Gallagher and Meade 2017: 226–29), while Jerome rejected them, endorsing the Jewish Bible for the Christian Old Testament. Near the end of his *Prologus Galeatus* (i.e., the preface to his translation of Samuel and Kings), Jerome listed the six deuterocanonical books (and the Shepherd of Hermas), labeling them "apocrypha" and declaring them noncanonical (Weber and Gryson 2007: 364–66; Gallagher and Meade 2017: 198–203). Jerome could cite previous authorities, especially among the Greeks, who also doubted the canonicity of the deuterocanonical books. But Augustine's position was in harmony with the major Latin tradition, affirmed at several North African councils during Augustine's lifetime (see Gallagher and Meade 2017: 222–25 on the *Breviarium Hipponense*).

These two great figures of fourth/fifth-century Latin Christianity set the agenda for subsequent discussion over the next millennium and more (see Gallagher 2020). These disputes could not fail to have an impact on Latin biblical manuscripts. The Codex

---

[15] H. C. Kim, ed., *The Gospel of Nicodemus: Gesta Salvatoris* (Toronto Medieval Latin Texts; Toronto: Pontifical Institute of Mediaeval Studies, 1973); Constantin Tischendorf, ed., *Evangelia apocrypha* (2nd ed.) (Leipzig: Mendelssohn, 1876), 333–432.

Amiatinus (Florence, Biblioteca Medicea Laurenziana, Amiatino 1; ca. 700 CE) contains the six deuterocanonical books intermixed with the other Old Testament books, along with the expanded editions of Esther and Daniel, and Psalm 151. The front matter of the codex reports the canon lists of Jerome (fol. 4r), Augustine (fol. 8r), and Hilary and Epiphanius (fol. 7r), each containing a different list of books. But a concluding statement assures readers that "although these things appear divergent in calculations, nevertheless by the teaching of the fathers, they all lead harmoniously to the instruction of the heavenly church" (fol. 4r).[16]

In the early ninth century, Theodulf, Bishop of Orleans, produced a series of Bibles that conformed more or less to the arrangement that Jerome had promoted in his *Prologus Galeatus*, following the Jewish tradition of arranging the Hebrew Bible into three sections: Law, Prophets, Writings (Chevalier-Royet 2007; see also chap. 12). Theodulf (following Isidore, *Etymologiae* 6.1) added a fourth section, containing the six deuterocanonical books and titled "Order of those books which are in the Old Testament outside the canon of the Hebrews."[17] Theodulf also reintegrated Baruch into his Bibles, after a period in which Baruch had disappeared from Bibles under the influence of Jerome.

Alcuin of Tours did not include Baruch in his Bibles, and neither did he group the deuterocanonical books together in the manner of Theodulf (Ganz 1994). The earliest Tours Bible, St Gall Stiftsbibliothek 75 (Φ^T), locates Wisdom of Solomon and Ecclesiasticus with the other Wisdom books, while the other four deuterocanonical books conclude the Old Testament without a preceding note signaling their absence from the Hebrew Bible.[18] The sequence of books at the end of the Old Testament (with the page reference in Φ^T) is as follows: Job (p. 447), Psalms (p. 463), Proverbs (p. 498), Ecclesiastes (p. 515), Song of Songs (p. 521), Wisdom (p. 524), Hiesu Filii Sirach/Ecclesiasticus (p. 536), Chronicles (p. 566), Ezra (= Ezra-Nehemiah, p. 606), Esther (p. 622), Tobit (p. 631), Judith (p. 638), 1 Maccabees (p. 648), and 2 Maccabees (p. 673). The Gospels immediately follow (p. 689). Alcuin included Psalm 151 at the end of the Psalter (p. 498), with the acknowledgement that this psalm is *extra numerum*. The book of Daniel ends with Susanna and Bel and the Dragon (p. 412), preceded by a note that the following material is derived from Theodotion's version and not from the Hebrew. There are no obeli here. But the Prayer of Azariah and the Song of the Three Young Men in Daniel 3 feature obeli before many of the lines (pp. 402–3). The additional material begins after Daniel 3:23, with the note, "what follows I did not find in the Hebrew volumes" (as in Weber and Gryson 2007: 1348). Likewise, the Additions to Esther (p. 628) are preceded by the same note that appears after Esther 10:3 in Weber and Gryson (2007: 724) acknowledging that

---

[16] Digital images of Codex Amiatinus are available at <http://opac.bmlonline.it/Record.htm?record= 120012494829>.

[17] This note is visible in the earliest preserved Theodulf Bible (Θ^S) at fol. 140v (see note 6 above); it is much clearer in the online images of the second-earliest Theodulf Bible, the Saint Hubert Bible (London, BL, MS Add. 24142), at fol. 165v; <http://www.bl.uk/manuscripts/Viewer.aspx?ref=add_ms_24142_f108r>.

[18] Digital images are available at <https://www.e-codices.unifr.ch/en/list/one/csg/0075>.

the following material appears "in the common edition" (*in editione uulgata*) (i.e., the Septuagint in contrast to the Hebrew). The note also mentions obeli, which actually appear only on page 629.

The Paris Bibles of the thirteenth century featured a new sequence of books and incorporated additional content (Light 2012: 384; see also chap. 16). The Old Testament concludes with this sequence: 1–2 Chronicles (with the Prayer of Manasseh as a conclusion), 1 Esdras (= Hebrew/Aramaic Ezra), Nehemiah, 2 Esdras (= 3 Ezra), Tobit, Judith, Esther, Job, Psalms, Proverbs, Ecclesiastes, Song of Songs, Wisdom of Solomon, Ecclesiasticus, Isaiah, Jeremiah, Lamentations, Baruch (6 chapters), Ezekiel, Daniel, Minor Prophets, and 1–2 Maccabees. This order is still found in modern editions of the Vulgate (e.g., Weber and Gryson 2007), with the exception that the works excluded from the canon at the Council of Trent—the Prayer of Manasseh (which was separated from Chronicles in Gutenberg's Bible) and 3 Ezra—have been relegated to the appendix.

BIBLIOGRAPHY

Auwers, Jean-Marie. 2006. "La tradition vieille latine du livre de Tobie: Un état de la question." In *The Book of Tobit. Text, Tradition, Theology*, edited by Géza G. Xeravits and József Zsengellér, 1–21. Leiden: Brill.

Bedouelle, Guy. 1984. "Le canon de l'Ancien Testament dans la perspective du Concile de Trente." In *Le Canon de l'Ancien Testament: Sa formation et son histoire*, edited by Jean-Daniel Kaestli and Otto Wermelinger, 253–82. Geneva: Labor et Fides.

Bergren, Theodore A. 1998. *Sixth Ezra. The Text and the Origin*. Oxford: Oxford University Press.

Bergren, Theodore A. 2010. "The Structure and Composition of 5 Ezra." *Vigiliae Christianae* 64: 115–39.

Bogaert, Pierre-Maurice. 2000a. "Les livres d'Esdras et leur numérotation dans l'histoire du canon de la Bible latine." *Revue bénédictine* 110: 5–26.

Bogaert, Pierre-Maurice. 2000b. "Le psautier latin des origins au XIIe siècle. Essai d'histoire." In *Der Septuaginta-Psalter und seine Tochterübersetzungen*, edited by Anneli Aejmelaeus and Udo Quast, 51–81. Göttingen: Vandenhoeck & Ruprecht.

Bogaert, Pierre-Maurice. 2005. "Le livre de Baruch dans les manuscrits de la Bible latine. Disparition et reintegration." *Revue bénédictine* 115: 286–342.

Bogaert, Pierre-Maurice. 2012. "The Latin Bible, c. 600 to c. 900." In *New Cambridge History of the Bible: Vol. 2. From 600 to 1450*, edited by Richard Marsden and E. Ann Matter, 69–92. Cambridge: Cambridge University Press.

Bogaert, Pierre-Maurice. 2015. "IV Esdras (2 Esdras; 4-5-6 Ezra) dans les Bibles latines." *Revue bénédictine* 125: 266–304.

Chevalier-Royet, Caroline 2007. "Les révisions bibliques de Théodulf d'Orléans et la question de leur utilization par l'exégèse carolingienne." In *Études d'exégèse carolingienne: autour d'Haymon d'Auxerre*, edited by Sumi Shimahara, 237–56. Turnhout: Brepols.

Demeulenaere, R. 1976. *Verecundi Iuncensis: Commentarii super Cantica Ecclesiastica*. CCSL 93. Turnhout: Brepols.

Denter, Thomas 1962. *Die Stellung der Bücher Esdras im Kanon des Alten Testaments: Eine kanongeschichtliche Untersuchung*. Marienstatt: Buch- und Kunsthandlung.

Feder, Frank, and Matthias Henze, eds. 2019–20. *Textual History of the Bible:* Vol. 2. *The Deutero-Canonical Scriptures.* Leiden: Brill.

Feuerstein, Rüdiger. 1997. *Das Buch Baruch: Studien zur Textgestalt und Auslegungsgeschichte.* New York: Peter Lang.

Forte, Anthony J. 2014. "Veteris Latinae Ecclesiastici: Apologia pro interprete latino." *Journal of Septuagint and Cognate Studies* 47: 69–92.

Fricke, Klaus Dietrich 1991. "The Apocrypha in the Luther Bible." In *The Apocrypha in Ecumenical Perspective: The Place of the Late Writings of the Old Testament among the Biblical Writings and Their Significance in the Eastern and Western Church Traditions,* edited by Siegfried Meurer, 46–87. New York: United Bible Societies.

Gallagher, Edmon L. 2015. "Why Did Jerome Translate Tobit and Judith?" *Harvard Theological Review* 108: 356–75.

Gallagher, Edmon L. 2020. "The Latin Canon." In *Textual History of the Bible*: Vol. 2. *The Deutero-Canonical Scriptures,* edited by Frank Feder and Matthias Henze, 166–90. Leiden: Brill.

Gallagher, Edmon L., and John D. Meade. 2017. *The Biblical Canon Lists from Early Christianity: Texts and Analysis.* Oxford: Oxford University Press.

Ganz, David. 1994. "Mass Production of Early Medieval Manuscripts: The Carolingian Bibles from Tours." In *The Early Medieval Bible: Its Production, Decoration and Use,* edited by Richard Gameson, 53–62. Cambridge: Cambridge University Press.

Gesche, Bonifatia. 2014. "Die älteste lateinische Übersetzung des Buches Esdras A: eine neue Entdeckung." *Vetus Testamentum* 64: 401–15.

Gounelle, Rémi. 2012. "Editing a Fluid and Unstable Text. The Example of the *Acts of Pilate* (or *Gospel of Nicodemus.*" *Apocrypha* 23: 81–97.

Gryson, Roger. 2004. *Altlateinische Handschriften/Manuscrits vieux latins: Répertoire descriptif. 2. Manuscrits du psautier.* VL 1/2B. Freiburg: Herder.

Haelewyck, Jean-Claude. 2006. "The Relevance of the Old Latin Version for the Septuagint, With Special Emphasis on the Book of Esther." *Journal of Theological Studies* ns 57: 439–73.

Harl, Marguerite. 2014. *Voix de louange: Les cantiques bibliques dans la liturgie chrétienne.* Anagôgê 8. Paris: Les belles lettres.

Hoberg, Gottfried. 1902. *Die älteste lateinische Übersetzung des Buches Baruch.* Freiburg: Herder.

Houghton, H. A. G. 2016. *The Latin New Testament. A Guide to Its Early History, Texts, and Manuscripts.* Oxford: Oxford University Press.

Hovhanessian, Vahan 2000. *Third Corinthians: Reclaiming Paul for Christian Orthodoxy.* New York: Peter Lang.

Izydorczyk, Zbigniew. 1993. *Manuscripts of the Evangelium Nicodemi: A Census.* Toronto: Pontifical Institute of Mediaeval Studies.

Izydorczyk, Zbigniew. 1997a. "The *Evangelium Nicodemi* in the Latin Middle Ages." In *The Medieval Gospel of Nicodemus: Texts, Intertexts, and Contexts in Western Europe,* edited by Zbigniew Izydorczyk, 43–101. Tempe: Medieval and Renaissance Texts and Studies.

Izydorczyk, Zbigniew, ed. 1997b. *The Medieval Gospel of Nicodemus: Texts, Intertexts, and Contexts in Western Europe.* Tempe: Medieval and Renaissance Texts and Studies.

Izydorczyk, Zbigniew 2012. "On the *Evangelium Nicodemi* before Print: Towards a New Edition." *Apocrypha* 23: 99–116.

Jedin, Hubert. 1961. *A History of the Council of Trent*: vol. 2. *The First Sessions at Trent, 1545–47.* London: Thomas Nelson and Sons.

Kabasele Mukenge, André. 2000. "Les particularités des témoins latins de Baruch." *Revue Biblique* 107: 24–41.

Kappler, Werner, and Robert Hanhart, eds. 1959. *Maccabaeorum liber II*. Septuaginta: Vetus Testamentum Graecum 9.2. Göttingen: Vandenhoeck & Ruprecht.

Light, Laura. 2012. "The Thirteenth Century and the Paris Bible." in *New Cambridge History of the Bible: Vol. 2. From 600 to 1450*, edited by Richard Marsden and E. Ann Matter, 380–91. Cambridge: Cambridge University Press.

Lightfoot, J. B. 1884. *Saint Paul's Epistles to the Colossians and to Philemon*. 7th ed. London: Macmillan.

Mattei-Cerasoli, Leo. 1935. *Liber Baruch secondo il testo del codice Biblico cavense*. Monte Cassino: Badia di Cava.

Sabatier, Pierre, ed. 1743–49. *Bibliorum sacrorum latinae versiones antiquae seu vetus Italica*. 3 vols. Rheims: Florentain.

Saxer, Victor 1985. "La Bible chez les Pères latins du IIIᵉ siècle." In *Le monde latin antique et la Bible*, edited by Jacques Fontaine and Charles Pietri, 339–69. BTT 2. Paris: Beauchesne.

Schneider, Heinrich 1938. *Die altlateinischen biblischen Cantica*. Beuron: Beuroner Kunstverlag.

Skemp, Vincent T. M. 2000. *The Vulgate of Tobit Compared with Other Ancient Witnesses*. Atlanta: Society of Biblical Literature.

Stone, Michael Edward. 1990. *Fourth Ezra: A Commentary*. Hermeneia. Minneapolis: Fortress.

Tanner, Norman P. 1990. *Decrees of the Ecumenical Councils*. 2 vols. Washington, DC: Georgetown University.

Weber, Robert, and Roger Gryson, eds. 2007. *Biblia sacra iuxta vulgatam versionem*. 5th ed. Stuttgart: Deutsche Bibelgesellschaft.

Weeks, Stuart D., Simon Gathercole, and Loren T. Stuckenbruck. 2004. *The Book of Tobit: Texts from the Principal Ancient and Medieval Traditions, with Synopsis, Concordances, and Annotated Texts in Aramaic, Hebrew, Greek, Latin, and Syriac*. Berlin: De Gruyter.

Wright, Charles D. 2016. "6 Ezra and *The Apocalypse of Thomas*: With a Previously Unedited 'Interpolated' Text of *Thomas*." *Apocrypha* 26: 9–55.

CHAPTER 8

··

EARLY MANUSCRIPTS OF THE LATIN BIBLE

··

DAVID GANz

SOME 363 manuscripts of the Latin Bible which may be dated before 800 CE have survived.[1] A total of 160 are gospel books, forty-one of which are datable before 600 CE and 119 datable between 600 and 800 CE. Thirty-nine Old Testament texts may be dated before 600 CE, and 113 between 600 and 800 CE. Of these, there are ten copies of the Pentateuch written before 600 CE and twenty-five dating between 600 and 800 CE, while five Psalters were copied before 600 CE and thirty-one between 600 and 800 CE (McGurk 1994:1). Twenty-six of the ninety-three biblical manuscripts copied before 600 CE were palimpsested, with other texts copied over them before 900 CE. Such palimpsests were more likely to be of Old Latin texts.

In the early Middle Ages single-volume manuscripts of the Bible were very rare, and the text was generally read in separate volumes. The canon of biblical books was determined by Church Councils (Gallagher and Meade 2017), and also set out in the so-called Gelasian decree, a sixth-century document (von Dobschütz 1912). Cassiodorus included several groupings of biblical books in his *Institutiones*, and diagrams of these groupings were copied in the first quire of the Codex Amiatinus (Chazelle 2006). Most of the surviving biblical manuscripts contain traces of their use in the liturgy for readings during the Mass or the Office (Dyer 2012), and many of these liturgical annotations have been edited. Biblical passages for the church year read at Vigils at St. Peter's in Rome are listed in *Ordo Romanus* XIV, an account of the custom at St. Peter's so that it might be imitated north of the Alps. The second recension of this text, *Ordo Romanus* XIII, gives the order of Catholic books placed in the cycle of the year in the Roman church (Andrieu

---

[1] For general introductions, see Bogaert 1988, Petitmengin 1985, and for manuscripts copied between 600 and 800, McGurk 1994; the New Testament is considered in Houghton 2016. Palaeographical descriptions and photographs of all of the manuscripts may be found in *Codices Latini Antiquiores* (CLA: Lowe 1934–71), also online at <https://elmss.nuigalway.ie/>.

1948; Jeffrey 2013).[2] The Bible was read in the Benedictine Office and at mealtimes in the monastic refectory. Monks also spent time in private study of the Bible and some manuscripts contain exegetical notes.

MANUSCRIPT PRODUCTION

Augustine urged his congregation to buy and read the Bible stating that the manuscripts were daily on sale.[3] A colophon copied into a ninth-century gospel book (Angers, BM, 24) reads: "from the workshop of Gaudiosus the *librarius* by the Chains of St. Peter in the city of Rome":[4] Gaudiosus was presumably a professional bookseller in charge of production. The stichometric list dated by Mommsen to 359 records the number of lines in each book of the Bible and in the works of Cyprian based on an estimation of sixteen syllables per line (Mommsen 1886, 1890; Berger 1893; Rouse and McNelis 2001; Bogaert 2003). The list was made in North Africa to establish the proper price for copies. There is another Latin list in the bilingual Codex Claromontanus of the Pauline Epistles (Paris, BnF, grec 107 [CLA 521; VL 75], ff. 467v–68v) and stichometric indications have also been preserved in Munich, BSB, Clm 6436 (CLA 1286; VL 64) at the end of the first epistle of John; in the Ashburnham Pentateuch for Genesis and Leviticus (the end of Exodus is missing); for the Pauline Epistles in St. Gall 70; for the Gospels of Luke and John in the ninth-century Tours gospel book Paris, BnF, lat. 260; in Tours Bibles for all of the biblical books. A tool designed for professional scribes was taken over by monastic scriptoria, where it served a different function.

Very few manuscripts have clear signs of who made them. Some were copied for bishops: Munich, BSB, Clm 6212 is a ninth-century copy of a Gospel book made for Ecclesius, Bishop of Ravenna from 521 to 534 (Wallenwein 2017: 293), while St. Gall, Stiftsbibliothek, 44 (CLA 899), containing Ezekiel and the minor prophets, was written for John, Bishop of Konstanz from 760 to 782. According to a later colophon copied by Aldred in the 970s, the Lindisfarne Gospels (CLA 187) were produced by Eadfrith, Bishop of Lindisfarne, before his death in 722 (Newton et al. 2013). London, BL, Add. MS 5463 (CLA 162) is a gospel book written by a monk Lupus for abbot Ato between 736 and 760. Toward the end of the eighth century, Abbot Maurdramnus of Corbie commissioned a multivolume Bible, of which five volumes have survived (CLA 707), with a colophon stating that one of the volumes was copied "for the convenience of

---

[2] Jeffrey gives strong arguments for the priority of *Ordo* XI. This *ordo* was copied into the Carolingian Rheims Bible (Rheims, BM, 1), and a Rheims copy of Acts, Revelation, and parts of the Old Testament (Douai, BM, 14).

[3] *Cottidie codices dominici uenales sunt, legit lector, eme tibi et tu lege quando uacat* (*Sermo* 114, cf. Houghton 2016: 22).

[4] *De statione Gaudiosi librarii* (the manuscript reads *Gaudii libri*) *ad uincula Sancti Petri ciuitate Romana.* See De Bruyne 1913, with plate and discussion in Wallenwein 2017: 36.

readers" (*propter compendium legentium*). Bishop Arn of Salzburg commissioned a multivolume Bible. The monk Winithar copied the Pauline Epistles, Numbers, Deuteronomy, Acts, and Revelation for St. Gall (CLA 893, 894, 903). Gundohinus copied a gospel book in 754 for a lady named Fausta at the demand of the monk Fulculfus at the unidentified monastery of Vosevio (CLA 716; see Nees 1987).

Scribes frequently asked for prayers, and some clearly regarded the copying of a biblical manuscript as a pious activity: *ora pro me* ("pray for me") colophons are found in the Codex Amiatinus, the Burchard Gospels, the Book of Durrow, and the Valerianus Gospels. Longer requests for prayers which name the scribe include *In dei nomine Maurinus hacse indignus presbiter ora pro me* ("in the name of God, Maurinus this unworthy priest: pray for me") in the tiny copy of John's Gospel from Chartres (Paris, BnF, lat. 10439 [CLA 600; VL 33]). Vatican City, BAV, Ottob. lat. 66 (CLA 66) has the inscription *Orate pro me Dominico Presbitero Scriptore* ("Pray for me, Dominic the priest and writer") in large script at the end of Exodus. Paris, BnF, lat. 9382 (CLA 577) contains the Vulgate text of the Prophets copied at Echternach by several hands in insular script: folio 45v ends with a verse by Vergilius (Fergil) at the end of Jeremiah:

> *Adiuro te per uiuentem deum caeli clementem ut orare pro me digneris omnipotentem quicumque haec ueridici legeris famina uatis falso qui fungor uergili nomine frustra ipse mihi reddat in alto qui nos secum per se duxit in astra.*
>
> ("I adjure you by the living merciful God of heaven that you deign to pray the Omnipotent One for me, you whoever will have read these words of the truth-uttering seer, who enjoy mistakenly the name of Vergilius to no effect, that He may reward me on high, Who us with Himself, through Himself has led us to the stars." (translation from Howlett 1998: 33–34)

The Valerianus Gospels (Munich, BSB, Clm 6224 [CLA 1249; VL 13]) end *ego Valerianus scripsi* ("I, Valerianus, wrote this") with an elaborate prayer for the scribe and for the reader to understand the text (see McGurk 1961: 70). Laurentius names himself in an acrostic in the Augsburg Gospels (CLA 1215). The late eighth-century Cutbercht Gospels (Vienna, ÖNB, lat. 1224 [CLA 1500]) have the colophon *Cutbercht scripsit ista IIII euangelia* ("Cutbercht wrote these four gospels").

Several biblical manuscripts contain notes about how they were corrected. The Echternach Gospels (Paris, BnF, lat. 9389 [CLA 578]) fol. 222v has a colophon which reads:

> *Proemendaui ut potui secundum codicem de bibliotheca Eugipi praespiteri quem ferunt fuisse s(an)c(t)i Hieronimi indictione VI p(ost) con(sulatum) Bassilii u(iri) c(larissimi) anno septimo decimo*
>
> ("I corrected as I could, following the manuscript from the library of Eugippius the priest which they say belonged to St Jerome, in the sixth indiction the seventeenth year after the consulate of Basil.") (Wallenwein 2017: 294–95)

This refers to a copy of the Vulgate Gospels, linked to Jerome, which had come to the monastery of Eugippius and was used to correct the text in 558. Bishop Victor of Capua corrected his New Testament manuscript, Codex Fuldensis (CLA 1196), around 546. A now-palimpsested Old Latin text, the Würzburg Pentateuch (Würzburg, UB, M. p. th. 2° 64 [CLA 1620; VL 103]) contains the indication *contuli*, noting that it had been checked (Wallenwein 2017: 300 and Plate III), while the corrector of the Ashburnham Pentateuch noted *Contuli ut potui* "I have checked as far as I could" (Wallenwein 2017: 299 and her plate XIV).

Paratextual Material in Gospel Books

Fifty gospel books or fragments of gospel books copied before 800 have survived from Italy, while forty-one gospel books and fragments survive from Anglo-Saxon England (McGurk 1961). In addition to the biblical text, many contain prefatory materials. Jerome's *Preface to the Gospels*, a dedicatory letter to Pope Damasus, is found in most copies of the Vulgate Gospels (McGurk 1961: 114–17). It is often identified by its opening words, *Nouum opus*, and accompanied by *Plures fuisse*, the preface to Jerome's commentary on Matthew. Some codices with Northumbrian connections have a Latin translation of Eusebius of Caesarea's *Letter to Carpianus*, beginning *Ammonius quidam* (De Bruyne 2015). Prologues to the individual gospels are rarely present in Old Latin tradition, although the "anti-Marcionite" prologues were composed in the middle of the fourth century. From the fifth century the Eusebian sections of the gospel text, referred to in Jerome's *Preface*, were identified in the margins of the text (Houghton 2016: 200–2). The earliest instance is the half-uncial gospel book in St. Gall (Stiftsbibliothek 1395; see below), and such marginalia are common in sixth-century manuscripts[5] and Insular gospel books.[6] They are also found in several Frankish manuscripts.[7]

The creation of sets of chapter titles (*capitula*) is already attested in the third century: one series for the Gospels predates Cyprian, while Donatists created their own sets for the other books of the New Testament. In manuscripts, they are introduced by a variety of terms including *breues, breuiarium, tituli, elenchus, breues causae, capitulatio,* and *capitula lectionum*. Thirteen types for each Gospel survive, half deriving from old Latin versions (Houghton 2011; De Bruyne 2014).

[5] E.g., Fulda, Bonifatianus 1; Cambridge, Corpus Christi College 286; the Burchard Gospels; the Ancona Gospels; London, BL, Harley 1775; Verona 6; Milan, Ambr., C 39 inf.

[6] Wearmouth-Jarrow fragments in Durham A.II.17 and Utrecht 32; Gospel fragments in Avranches (BM, 48), Munich (BSB, Clm 29270[2]), Brussels (II 436), Namur, Prague, and St. Omer (BM, 257); Cambridge, Corpus Christi College 197B; St. Petersburg Gospels; Durham A.II.16; Oxford, Lincoln College, 92; Paris, BnF, lat. 281. Eusebian sections are also included in the Codex Amiatinus.

[7] St. Petersburg, NLR, O.v.I 2; New York, Morgan Library, Glazier G 58; Paris, BnF, lat. 256 and 17226; the Gundohinus Gospels.

THE EARLIEST GOSPELS

The earliest surviving manuscript of the Latin Gospels is the Codex Bobiensis, in Turin (CLA 465; VL 1) of which only Mark and Matthew survive (Cipolla 1913; Parker 1991). It has a square format, with text copied in uncial in fourteen long lines. The scribe uses a unique set of abbreviations for the *nomina sacra* (Traube 1907: 138–42). The gospel book in Vercelli (CLA 467; VL 3) may date before 371. It has the Gospels in the order Matthew–John–Luke–Mark. It was copied in uncial in two columns of twenty-four lines, with red ink for the first three lines of each Gospel (Gasquet 1914; D'Aiuto et al. 2000: 137–40). St. Gall Stiftsbibliothek 1394 (CLA 978; VL 16) contains most of a fifth-century Old Latin set of gospels copied in two columns of twenty-four lines in uncial. The volume is thought to have originated at Rome (Gamper et al. 2012). The Codex Corbeiensis (Paris, BnF, latin 17225 [CLA 666; VL 8]) is a large square-format fifth-century gospel book written on excellent white parchment in two columns of twenty-four lines in an expert early uncial hand, with an enlarged letter at the start of each column and the first line of chapters in red. Milan, Ambrosiana, O.210 sup. (CLA 360; VL 21) is written in beautiful calligraphic uncial in two columns of twenty-six lines, containing a fragment of Luke from the end of the fifth century.

There are a small number of luxury volumes copied in silver ink on purple parchment, containing an Old Latin gospel text. These include Codex Brixianus (CLA 281; VL 10); the fifth-century Codex Palatinus in two columns of twenty lines (CLA 437; VL 2), which may be of African origin (Vogels 1926; Radiciotti 2005); Codex Vindobonensis now in Naples, written at the end of the fifth century in a square format with fourteen long lines to a page (CLA 399; VL 17; D'Aiuto et al. 2000: 140–41); Codex Sarzanensis, fragments of the gospels in two columns of sixteen lines (CLA 436; VL 22); Codex Veronensis (CLA 481; VL 4), written in silver in two columns of eighteen lines with the first page of each gospel copied in gold. In addition to these gospel books, the Old Latin Psalter in Paris, BnF, lat. 11947 (CLA 616; VL 303) is copied in silver on purple parchment.

The earliest manuscript of the Latin Vulgate Gospels is a two-column, twenty-four-line, half-uncial fifth-century manuscript in St. Gall (Stiftsbibliothek 1395; CLA 984; Turner 1931). It is a small and unassuming book, with no decoration apart from simple colophons in uncial set off with a drawing of a leaf. Sections begin with a larger letter projecting into the margin. Autun, BM, 21 and Paris, BnF, nouv. acq. lat. 1628 ff. 5–14 is a palimpsested fifth-century Vulgate Gospel text in two columns of twenty-two to twenty-four lines (CLA 722; Royet 1922–23). Oxford, Bodleian Library, Auct. D.II.14 (CLA 230) is an Italian Gospel Book which had reached Anglo-Saxon England by the seventh century, copied in two columns of twenty-seven lines by one scribe in seventh-century uncial. There are enlarged initials and the invocation *Criste fave votis* ("Christ favour our prayers") at the start of the Gospels, an indication of the poor orthography found throughout. The opening lines and first word of each chapter are copied in red, and the main scribe added liturgical notes which were amplified by a second annotator with lessons for Advent, Christmas, Lent, and saints' feasts.

Several late antique Greek Latin bilingual manuscripts have survived (see chap. 11). The most notable are the Codex Bezae (CLA 140; VL 5), with the Gospels and Acts, the letters of Paul in the fifth-century Codex Claromontanus (Paris, BnF, grec 107; VL 75), the Psalters in Paris, BnF, Coislin 186 (VL 333) and Verona, Biblioteca Capitolare, I (VL 300), and the sixth-century copy of Acts from Sicily (VL 50) which was later used by Bede (Radiciotti 2005). Gothic-Latin bilinguals are the now-lost Codex Gissensis of Luke (VL 36) and Codex Carolinus of Romans in Wolfenbuettel (VL 79).

INSULAR GOSPEL BOOKS

Irish Latin tradition is treated in greater depth in chapter 10 (see also chap. 31), while Alexander has contributed a book-length study of the decoration of insular manuscripts (1978). The earliest insular gospel book is the Old Latin Codex Usserianus Primus (Dublin Trinity College 55; CLA 271; VL 14), copied in one column of twenty-two lines in insular half uncial. It is generally dated to the early seventh century, though Dumville has suggested a fifth-century date (1999: 39). Other early insular gospels include the Book of Durrow (Dublin, Trinity College 57); the Durham, Lindisfarne, and Echternach Gospels; the now-incomplete Cambridge Kk.1.24; British Library, Royal MS 1 B VII; the fragment Oxford, Lincoln College 92; the fragment of Luke, Freiburg 702; Gotha, Mbr. 1.18; the fragment Avranches, BM, 48; the Maaseik Gospels; the fragment Munich, BSB, Clm 29270(2); and the fragment St. Omer, BM, 257. Large and decorated initials or monograms, followed by display capitals, are found at the start of each gospel and Jerome's letter to Damasus. Less elaborate initials introduce other prologues and gospel prefaces and chapter lists. The first lines of text and first pages are often written in a different script, while a symbol page may augment or replace evangelist portraits. This elaboration of script and decoration marks a change from the gospel books of the fifth and sixth century.

An important group of Insular biblical manuscripts were copied in uncial at Wearmouth Jarrow: Durham A.II.17 part 2; the leaves attached to Utrecht 32; the "St. Cuthbert Gospel" of John; the Codex Amiatinus; the leaves from a second Wearmouth Jarrow pandect; the leaf from a Psalter in Cambridge. Uncial was also used for the luxury Stockholm Codex Aureus (VL 15), written in two columns of twenty-four to twenty-six lines on alternating leaves of purple and white parchment, with the Eusebian apparatus (Gameson 2001). Further uncial manuscripts include Gospel fragments in Munich (CLA 1335, 1336) and Avranches (CLA 730); a copy of Acts in Oxford, Bodleian, Selden Supra 30 (CLA 257); a Psalter leaf in Basle, UB, N.1.2 (CLA 850); the Vespasian Psalter; the Gospels in BnF, lat. 281 + 298; and Chartres, BM, 52, a leaf from the Gospel of John (CLA 747). The Freiburg Luke fragment, the Trier, Cuthbert, Leipzig, and Bigotianus Gospels all use two different scripts. In Durham A.II.17, certain passages are copied in much larger letters (Verey et al. 1980), a feature also seen in the Hereford Gospels and St. Gallen 51 (VL 48; see McGurk 1961: 118–19).

The size of insular Gospel Books varies considerably. The two leaves in Oxford, Lincoln College 92 had a written space estimated at 295 × 230 mm, indicating that they come from a volume larger than the Lindisfarne Gospels (which measure 235 × 190 mm) and are closer in size to the Stockholm Codex Aureus (280 × 245 mm). In contrast, the St. Cuthbert Gospel measures just 138 × 92 mm. The later tradition of Irish pocket gospel books has been treated by McGurk (1956).

OLD TESTAMENT MANUSCRIPTS

The earliest surviving Latin Old Testament manuscripts date from the fifth century and are now palimpsest: Naples, BNC, lat. 1, contains fragments from Genesis, Samuel, and Kings; VL 101); St. Gall 912 has Jeremiah in fifteen long lines (CLA 971; VL 180); Würzburg, UB, M.p.th.64 contains the Prophets (VL 177); Judges and Job occur in Vatican, BAV, Vat. lat 5763 and Wolfenbüttel, Weiss. 64, copied in the fifth century in a large bold uncial in eighteen long lines with an enlarged letter at the start of each page (Falluomini 1999). A set of leaves from a fifth-century manuscript with an Old Latin text of the Prophets is now in various German libraries (CLA 1174; VL 175): forty-six folios have survived, measuring around 280 × 260 mm in three columns of twenty-three lines (Lehmann 1912; Dold 1923). There are red and black colophons, with red being used for the opening lines and for the prophet's name. The manuscript has substantial glosses, written in the margins and also between the columns in a cursive script. These quote Greek on ten occasions, explain references to Christ and the persons of the Trinity, and even cite Origen on Micah 4:8. Although the glosses suggest that this manuscript was used for study, it also contains liturgical notes which serve as a reminder that the two categories could overlap. Vatican City, BAV, Vat. lat. 3281 is a deluxe manuscript of the Prophets in square format (300 × 300mm) written in twelve long lines with a thick pen (CLA 14). Another early copy of the Prophets survives as the lower text in a St. Gall palimpsest (St. Gall 193 + 567; CLA 916). The text was copied in twenty-one long lines in half uncial script (Dold 1917). Two fragments in Verona contain an Old Latin text of Proverbs and Wisdom in twenty-six long lines of sixth-century uncial (CLA 473; VL 167) and thirty-two long lines of slightly earlier half uncial in a square format (CLA 480; VL 168).

SCRIPT AND LAYOUT

Most biblical manuscripts were copied in uncial: seventy-five of these survive from before 600 CE, and ninety from 600–800 CE. Twelve were copied in half uncial before

600 CE, with nine in the following two centuries. Lowe described the script of sixty-two biblical manuscripts copied after 600 as majuscule (twenty-two are Anglo-Saxon) and ninety-seven as minuscule (see also Petitmengin 1985: 97, McGurk 1994: 3–8). Insular gospel books were originally copied in insular majuscule, though the Echternach and Maaseick Gospels are copied in a minuscule, and Durham A.II.17 often uses minuscule for the final lines of each page. Insular minuscule is used in the Gospel fragments in Prague (CLA 1567) and in St. Omer (CLA 826) and in the late eighth-century Colmar Pauline Epistles (CLA 750), the Werden Heptateuch (Barker-Benfield 1991), and the leaves of CLA 1339: all of these were written in Anglo-Saxon foundations on the continent.

Three manuscripts have the biblical text copied in three columns: the Darmstadt Prophets (VL 175), the Lyons Heptateuch (VL 100, and a leaf from the Gospel of Matthew in Munich (BSB, Clm 29270/1; CLA Addenda 1843; VL 45) copied in fifth-century uncial in three columns of seventeen lines. In the best manuscripts, the script was written between two ruled lines. Examples of this are Vatican City, BAV, Reg. lat. 9 of the Prophets (CLA 100), the Cividale Gospels (CLA 285), the Sarezzano Gospels (CLA 436; VL 22), the Lyons and St. Germain Psalters, Codex Veronensis of the Gospels, the Avranches Gospel fragment, and the Book of Kells. Not all manuscripts were of high quality, and Lowe (1934–71) described several manuscripts as written in "not very expert uncial."[8] The earliest uncial manuscripts have large letters at the start of each page, a common feature of all early Latin manuscripts. Uncial and half-uncial manuscripts use an enlarged letter projecting into the margin at the start of a new section. As noted above, the layout changed in Insular gospel books, where the gospels begin with a greatly enlarged letter or monogram, and the letters following enlarged capitals taper in size to form a diminuendo. The biblical text may end with a colophon in red and black, while the first words of sections are often copied in red ink in New Testament manuscripts.[9] In the early eighth-century Merovingian gospel book Paris, BnF, lat. 256 (CLA 524), the use of red is abandoned after the tenth chapter of Luke's Gospel.

ILLUSTRATIONS

The earliest manuscript illustrations in a Latin Bible[10] are found in the Quedlinburg Itala (VL 116), which perhaps originally contained two hundred illustrations for the Book of Kings. There are four scenes to a page in rectangular panels, and they have been painted over brief Latin instructions to the artist about what he was to depict. One, for example, read: "Make the tomb [by which] Saul and his servant stand and two men,

---

[8] E.g., CLA 51, 66, 230, 985, 1108.
[9] E.g., Paris, BnF, lat. 17226; Munich, BSB, Clm 6436; the Ancona Gospels; Vatican City, BAV, Vat. Lat. 7223; Cambridge, Corpus Christi College 286. For the Old Testament, see Orleans, BM, 19.
[10] See also chap. 31.

jumping over pits, speak to him and [announce that the asses have been found]" (Levin 1985). Cambridge, Corpus Christi College 286 is a gospel book dating to the end of the sixth century which has a page at the start of the Gospel according to Luke showing the evangelist seated holding his book below an arcade containing his symbol, with twelve small scenes from the Gospel on either side (see fig. 31.2). The Ashburnham Pentateuch (Paris, BnF, nouv. acq. lat. 2334) has eighteen surviving large miniatures, perhaps from a set of sixty-nine, depicting scenes from Genesis and Exodus, many with captions. The Valerianus Gospels (Munich, BSB, Clm 6224; VL 13) have small images of the evangelist symbols between the gospels: John's eagle is on top of the opening initial I, with a jeweled cross surmounted by a bust of Christ. The Gundohinus Gospels, a copy of a sixth-century original, end with a full-page illustration of Christ in majesty and pages with each of the evangelists, shown standing. The Carolingian gospels in Munich, BSB, Clm 23631, made for a bishop of Augsburg, have copies of earlier illustrations set in a cross. These show Joseph, the Adoration of the Magi and Massacre of the Innocents, Christ's infancy, and his appearances to the Apostles: Thomas, Christ at the lake of Tiberius, and the meal at Emmaus. The concordances of Gospel passages known as canon tables are often surrounded by architectural arcades sometimes containing images of the apostles (Nordenfalk 1938). Early canon tables are found in gospel books now in Brescia (CLA 281), Bergamo (CLA 1673), Vat. lat. 3806 (CLA 1766), and Harley 1775 (CLA 197).

The richest illustrations are found in Insular gospel books, several of which include an evangelist's portrait facing a blank page. Durham A.II.10 and further leaves from this insular half uncial book (CLA 147) have the enlarged monogram at the beginning of the Gospel of Mark made up of ribbon interlace terminating in animal heads, and there is a decorated colophon at the end of this gospel. In the Book of Durrow, each Gospel is preceded by a full page with the evangelist symbol in a decorated border and by a carpet page; there is also a page with all four Evangelist symbols. Carpet pages, which incorporate cross motifs, are also found in the Lindisfarne Gospels (see fig. 31.5), Lichfield Gospels, Augsburg Gospels (fol. 126v), Turin Gospels, St. Gall 51, and the Book of Kells, and there are also full-page evangelist symbols in the Echternach Gospels and Cambridge, Corpus Christi College, 197B. Durham A.II.17 (CLA 150) lacks evangelist portraits but contains a full page crucifixion miniature. In addition to the carpet pages, St. Gall 51 (CLA 901) has full-page illustrations of each of the four Evangelists, the Crucifixion, and the Last Judgement. The Lichfield Gospels (CLA 159), which may have been copied in Wales (Dumville 1999: 123), have two surviving Evangelist portraits and a page with all four Evangelist symbols. The Stockholm Codex Aureus (CLA 1642; VL 15) has two surviving Evangelist portraits; there is one in the Maaseick Gospels (CLA 1558) along with medallions at the top of each arch of the canon tables containing busts of the apostles. The Trier Gospels (CLA 1364), probably from Echternach, has a page with the tetramorph as well as evangelist portraits and a full-page illustration showing two named angels with title tablet for the Gospel of Matthew (Netzer 1994). The Codex Amiatinus (CLA 299) has full-page depictions of Ezra and the Tabernacle (see fig. 31.7), and diagrams of the divisions of Scripture. At the start of the New Testament is a full page illustration showing Christ in majesty between two angels in a central circle, surrounded by the Evangelists and their symbols (Chazelle 2019).

Single-Volume Bibles

The mid sixth-century Codex Fuldensis (also known as the "Victor Codex," CLA 1196) contains the New Testament, with the four Gospels replaced by a single gospel harmony but preceded by canon tables. It has a long, thin format, with the text in a single column of thirty-five lines, and was corrected by Bishop Victor of Capua in 546 (Petitmengin 1985: 107–10; Fischer 1963: 57–66). It later belonged to St. Boniface, who added glosses to the Epistle of James (Aris and Broszinski 1996).

Cassiodorus describes two pandects at Vivarium, the Codex Grandior of 760 folia and a volume written in smaller script of 636 folia (Mynors 1937: 37, 40; Fischer 1962). A poem describes a single volume Bible copied for John, Bishop of Saragossa, in 619, which has not survived (Vollmer 1905: 238–39). The Codex Amiatinus, copied at Wearmouth Jarrow before 716, comprises 1030 folia in two columns of forty-four lines (Marsden 1995; Chazelle 2019). It has canon tables. Each book starts with an enlarged letter, which is strikingly outsize in Matthew. Chapters start in red. The León palimpsest (CLA 1636; VL 67) is written on the remains of a complete seventh-century Bible copied in two columns of 71–76 lines in half uncial script, with some marginal annotations, originally some 322 folia (Ganz 2015). Paris, BnF, nouv. acq. lat. 1063 (CLA 679) is a small manuscript of the New Testament, copied in Merovingian cursive script at Corbie in the last third of the seventh century, which belonged to the cathedral of Beauvais. A fragment of Kings in Ghent (CLA 1827) may be a part of a companion Old Testament volume. There are liturgical annotations (Ganz 2016).

Liturgical Readings and Glosses

Many biblical manuscripts have marginal entries which indicate passages which were read during the liturgy. Such entries are found in Greek in the Codex Bezae. Italian volumes with this feature include: Milan C.39 inf. (CLA 313); the Cividale Gospels (CLA 285; see De Bruyne 1913a); the Ancona Gospels; the Spalato Gospels (CLA 1669); the Valerianus Gospels (CLA 1249; VL 13; see Gamber 1962 and Radiciotti 1993); the Burchard Gospels (CLA 1423; see Lenker 1997: 394–96); Würzburg, UB, M.p.th.q. 1a (CLA 1429); Paris BnF, lat. 17225 (CLA 666); Codex Vercellensis (VL 3; see Gasquet 1914: xvi–xix). These entries are often later than the copying of the manuscript.

Lists of readings for Naples are found in the Lindisfarne Gospels (CLA 187) and British Library, Royal MS I B VII (CLA 213) which also has marginal entries indicated by a cross (Morin 1891). Other insular lists are recorded by Ursula Lenker (1997) from Oxford, Bodleian, Auct. D.II.14 (Ganz 2001) and Durham A.II.17. Cambridge, University Library, Kk.I.24 and the Burchard Gospels have lists of Roman readings (Lenker 1997: 404–6; Morin 1911). Marginal notes recording Gallican lections are found in the following manuscripts: Würzburg, UB, M.p.th.q. 1a; Lyons, BM, 403; Trier, Dombib., 134; Paris, BnF, lat. 256; Paris, BnF, nouv. acq. lat. 1063. List of Pauline readings occur in: Codex Fuldensis; Codex Claromontanus; Vatican City, BAV, Vat. lat. 5755 (fol. 308); Orleans, BM, 19 (ff. 31–32); the Paris fragments (CLA 800); Munich, BSB, Clm 6229 (CLA 1251). The Codex Amiatinus also has Epistle readings (Marsden 1995: 189–90; Lenker 1997: 392–93).

The remarkable Old Latin version of the Heptateuch from the Lyons Cathedral Library (CLA 771; VL 100) reveals how this manuscript was used by that community over some two hundred years (Robert 1900, 1881). The text was copied in the sixth century, in three columns of twenty-seven lines on a page measuring 300 × 242 mm and has been carefully corrected to make it a Vulgate text. The first two lines of a book and first lines of each chapter are copied in red. In the seventh and eighth centuries this manuscript received marginal notes to identify biblical readings, such as *incipit* and *finit* (ff. 19r, 20v) or more specific directions such as *Legenda in uigiliis epiphanie* ("to be read on the eve of the Epiphany," fol. 94v) or *Licco nummini tempore illo egressi filii Israhel* ("Lection from Numbers (?); at that time when the children of Israel had gone out," fol. 107r). In addition to these marginal indications of when particular passages were to be read publicly, there is also a small number of marginal notes which respond to the biblical text (e.g., *hoc iudicium durum est*, "this judgment is harsh," on fol. 39v; *mortus est aron*, "Aaron died," on fol. 108r; *de balac*, "Concerning Balak," on fol. 109v). There are also notes about passages such as the iron bed of King Og of Basan and the Ten Commandments. Three lections from the First Epistle of Peter have been added beside the text on fol. 21v, while private prayers have been copied into the margins of fol. 52r.

A small number of surviving Bible manuscripts have extensive glosses. The earliest are the fifth-century glosses in the three-column manuscript of the Prophets (CLA 1174; VL 175), edited by Dold (1923: 167–93). St. Petersburg, NLR, F.v.I.3 is an Insular copy of Job with interlinear commentary from Philippus (CLA 1599; see Marsden 1995: 256–61). Folio 93 of Turin F.IV.24, was a single leaf, now destroyed, with the Epistle of Peter with Old Irish glosses (CLA 457); similarly Würzburg, UB, M.p.th.f. 12 is a copy of the Pauline Epistles with Latin and Old Irish glosses (CLA 1403). Both are edited by Stokes and Strachan (1901: I.494–714). Würzburg, UB, M.p.th.f. 61 is a glossed Gospel of Matthew (CLA 1415), with some extracts added on slips of parchment (Schepps 1897). A copy of the Pauline Epistles in Trinity College, Cambridge has extracts from the commentary of Pelagius (CLA 133; de Paor 2016). Seventh-century scratched drypoint Latin glosses drawing on Jerome, Ambrose, and Gregory are found in Luke's Gospel in Codex Usserianus Primus (Ó Néill 1998). The Gospels in Autun, BM, 3 (CLA 716) have twenty short commentaries, chiefly to Matthew, inserted in the text (Nees 1987: 248–50). The contemporary marginalia on the books of Chronicles in the fragmentary back flyleaves of Milan, Ambrosiana, D.84.inf. (CLA 333) do not seem to have been investigated. A leaf of Ezekiel in Zurich, Staatsarchiv (CLA 1008) has the biblical text in a central column with glosses from Gregory's Homilies on Ezekiel in columns on either side: this layout, which probably derives from glossed classical school authors, was used in the ninth century at Wissembourg and Fulda.

CAROLINGIAN MANUSCRIPTS

Charlemagne wanted gospel books, psalters, and mass books copied carefully by mature scribes. On Christmas Day 801, Alcuin presented Charlemagne with a single-volume complete Bible, and the scriptoria of Tours copied similar pandects for more than half a century, together with Tours Gospel books. Other Carolingian scriptoria, at Metz, St. Riquier, St. Germain, Konstanz, and Bobbio also produced single-volume pandects, and small-format volumes were carefully copied for Theodulf, but multivolume Bibles were also widely copied (Fischer 1957, 1965). Bishop Hunbert of Würzburg, Bishop Arn of Salzburg, and Abbot Hartmut of St. Gall all commissioned complete Bibles in several volumes. Gospel and Epistle lectionaries contained the readings for the Mass in the order of the liturgical year (Frere 1934, 1935). The Stuttgart, Amiens, and Utrecht Psalters all have illustrations for every psalm, while the Trier and Valenciennes Apocalypse manuscripts have many full page illustrations. A large number of Carolingian Gospel Books have full-page evangelist portraits (Koehler and Mütherich 1930–2013).

BIBLIOGRAPHY

Alexander, J. J. 1978. *A Survey of Manuscripts Illuminated in the British Isles. Vol. 1: Insular Manuscripts, 6th-9th Century.* London: Harvey Miller.

Andrieu, M. 1948. *Les "Ordines Romani" du haut Moyen Âge II.* Leuven: Spicilegium Sacrum Lovaniense.

Aris, M. -A., and H. Broszinski, eds. 1996. *Die Glossen zum Jakobusbrief aus dem Victor-Codex (Bonifatianus 1) in der Hessischen Landesbibliothek zu Fulda.* Fulda: Hessische Landesbibliothek.

Barker-Benfield, Bruce C. 1991. "The Werden Heptateuch." *Anglo-Saxon England* 20: 43–64.

Berger, Samuel. 1893. *Histoire de la Vulgate pendant les premiers siècles du moyen âge.* Nancy: Berger-Levrault.

Bogaert, Pierre-Maurice. 1988. "La Bible latine des origines au moyen age. Aperçu historique, état des questions." *Revue théologique de Louvain* 19: 137–59, 276–314.

Bogaert, Pierre-Maurice. 2003. "Aux origines de la fixation du Canon: Scriptoria, listes et titres. Le Vaticanus et la Stichométrie de Mommsen." In *The Biblical Canons*, edited by J.-M. Auwers and H. J. de Jonge, 153–76. BETL 163. Leuven: Leuven University Press.

Chazelle, Celia. 2006. "Christ and the Vision of God: The Biblical Diagrams of the Codex Amiatinus." In *The Mind's Eye: Art and Theological Argument in the Middle Ages*, edited by J. Hamburger and A.-M. Bouché, 84–111. Princeton: Princeton University Press.

Chazelle, Celia 2019. *The Codex Amiatinus and Its "Sister" Bibles: Scripture, Liturgy and Art in the Milieu of the Venerable Bede.* Leiden: Brill.

Cipolla, C. 1913. *Il codice evangelico k della Bibliotheca Universitaria Nazionale di Torino.* Turin: Molfese.

D'Aiuto, F., G. Morello, and A. M. Piazzoni, eds. 2000. *I Vangeli dei Popoli.* Vatican: Rinovamento nello Spirito Santo.

De Bruyne, Donatien 1913a. "Les notes liturgiques du Codex Forojuliensis," *Revue bénédictine* 30: 203–18.

De Bruyne, Donatien 1913b. "Gaudiosus, un vieux libraire romain." *Revue bénédictine* 30: 343–45.

De Bruyne, Donatien. 2014. *Summaries, Divisions and Rubrics of the Latin Bible.* Repr., Studia Traditionis Theologiae 18. Turnhout: Brepols.

De Bruyne, Donatien, 2015. *Prefaces of the Latin Bible.* Repr., Studia Traditionis Theologiae 19. Turnhout: Brepols.

De Paor, John Liam. 2016. *The Earliest Irish Glosses on the Pauline Epistles: An Edition of the Texts and Glosses of Vulgate Manuscript E as found in Cambridge B.10.5.* AGLB 41. Freiburg: Herder.

Dold, Alban. 1917. *Prophetentexte in Vulgata Übersetzung nach dem ältesten Handschriften Übersetzung der St Galler Palimpseste no 193 und no 567.* Beuron: Kunstschule der Erzabtei.

Dold, Alban. 1923. *Konstanzer altlateinische Propheten- und Evangelienbruchstücke mit Glossen.* Texte und Arbeiten 7–9. Beuron: Kunstschule der Erzabtei.

Dumville, D. N. 1999. *A Palaeographer's Review: The Insular System of Scripts in the Early Middle Ages.* Osaka: Kansai University.

Dyer, J. 2012. "The Bible in the Medieval Liturgy." In *New Cambridge History of the Bible: Vol. 2. From 600 to 1450,* edited by Richard Marsden and E. Ann Matter, 659–79. Cambridge: Cambridge University Press.

Falluomini, Carla. 1999. *Der sogenannte Codex Carolinus von Wolfenbüttel. (Codex Guelferbytanus 64 Weissenburgensis). Mit besonderer Berücksichtigung der gotisch-lateinischen Blätter (255, 256, 277, 280).* Wolfenbütteler Mittelalter-Studien. Wiesbaden: Harrassowitz.

Fischer, Bonifatius. 1957. *Die Alkuin Bibeln.* AGLB 1. Freiburg: Herder.

Fischer, Bonifatius. 1962. "Codex Amiatinus und Cassiodor." *Biblische Zeitschrift* 6: 57–79.

Fischer, Bonifatius. 1963. "Bibelausgaben des frühen Mittelalters." In *La Bibbia nell'alto medioevo,* edited by Ezio Franceschini, 519–600. Spoleto: CISAM.

Fischer, Bonifatius. 1965. *Bibeltext und Bibelreform unter Karl den Grossen.* Düsseldorf: Schwann.

Frere, W. H. 1934. *Studies in Early Roman Liturgy. II. The Roman Lectionary.* London: Oxford University Press.

Frere, W. H. 1935. *Studies in Early Roman Liturgy. III. The Roman Epistle Lectionary.* London: Oxford University Press.

Gallagher, Edmon L., and John D. Meade. 2017. *The Biblical Canon Lists from Early Christianity: Texts and Analysis.* Oxford: Oxford University Press.

Gamber, Klaus. 1962. "Die ältesten abendländischen Evangelien-Perikopenliste." *Münchener Theologische Zeitschrift* 13: 181–201.

Gameson, Richard, ed. 1994a. *The Early Medieval Bible. Its Production, Decoration and Use.* Cambridge: Cambridge University Press.

Gameson, Richard. 1994b. "The Royal I B vii Gospels and English Book Production in the Seventh and Eighth Centuries." In *The Early Medieval Bible. Its Production, Decoration and Use,* edited by Richard Gameson, 24–52. Cambridge: Cambridge University Press.

Gameson, Richard. 2001. *The Codex Aureus: An Eighth-Century Gospel Book*. Copenhagen: Rosenkilde and Bagger.

Gamper, Rudolf, P. Lenz, A. Nievergelt, P. Erhart, E. Schulz-Flügel, eds. 2012. *Die Vetus Latina-Fragmente aus dem Kloster St. Gallen. Faksimile, Edition, Kommentar*. Zürich: Urs Graf.

Ganz, David. 2001. "The Annotations in Oxford, Bodleian Library Auct D. II 14." In *Belief and Culture in the Middle Ages*, edited by R. Gameson and H. Leyser, 35–44. Oxford: Oxford University Press.

Ganz, David. 2015. "La bible palimpseste de Leon." In *Comment le Livre s'est fait livre. La fabrication des manuscrits bibliques (IVᵉ-XVᵉ siècle): Bilan, resultats, perspectives de recherche*, edited by C. Ruzzier and X. Hermand, 51–58. Turnhout: Brepols.

Ganz, David. 2016. "A Merovingian New Testament Manuscript and Its Liturgical Notes: Paris BNF Nouv. Acq. Lat. 1063." *Revue bénédictine* 126: 122–37.

Gasquet, Aidan. 1914. *Codex Vercellensis*. CBL 3. Rome: Pustet.

Houghton, H. A. G. 2011. "Chapter Divisions, Capitula Lists and the Old Latin Version of John." *Revue bénédictine* 121: 316–56.

Houghton, H. A. G. 2016. *The Latin New Testament: A Guide to Its History, Texts, and Manuscripts*. Oxford: Oxford University Press.

Howlett, David. 1998. "Insular Acrostics, Celtic Latin Colophons." *Cambrian Medieval Celtic Studies* 35: 27–44.

Jeffrey, P. 2013. "The Early Liturgy at St Peter's and the Roman liturgical year." In *Old St Peters, Rome*, edited by R. D. McKitterick, J. Osborne, C. M. Richardson, and J. Story, 157–76. Cambridge: Cambridge University Press.

Koehler, W., and Mütherich, F. 1930–2013. *Die Karolingischen Miniaturen* I–VIII. Berlin: Cassirer.

Lehmann, P. 1912. *Die Konstanz-Weingartener Propheten-Fragmente in phototypischer Reproduktion*. Leiden: Sijthoff.

Lenker, Ursula. 1997. *Die westsächische Evangelienversion und die Perikopenordnungen im angelsächischen England*. Munich: Fink.

Levin, Inabelle. 1985. *The Quedlinburg Itala*. Leiden: Brill.

Lowe, Elias Avery. 1934–71. *Codices Latini Antiquiores. A Palaeographical Guide to Latin Manuscripts Prior to the Ninth Century*. 11 vols. and Suppl. Oxford: Clarendon Press.

Marsden, Richard. 1995. *The Text of the Old Testament in Anglo-Saxon England*. Cambridge Studies in Anglo-Saxon England 15. Cambridge: Cambridge University Press.

McGurk, Patrick. 1956. "The Irish Pocket Gospel Book." *Sacris Erudiri* 8, no. 2: 249–69.

McGurk, Patrick. 1961. *Latin Gospel Books from AD 400 to AD 800*. Paris: Érasme.

McGurk, Patrick. 1994. "The Oldest Manuscripts of the Latin Bible." In *The Early Medieval Bible. Its Production, Decoration and Use*, edited by Richard Gameson, 1–23. Cambridge: Cambridge University Press.

Mommsen, Theodor. 1886. "Zur lateinischen Stichometrie." *Hermes* 21: 142–56.

Mommsen, Theodor. 1890. "Zur lateinischen Stichometrie." *Hermes* 25: 636–38.

Morin, Germain. 1891. "La liturgie de Naples au temps de Saint Gregoire d'après deux Évangeliaires du septième siècle." *Revue bénédictine* 8: 481–93, 529–37.

Morin, Germain. 1911. "Liturgie et basiliques de Rome au milieu du VIIᵉ siècle d'après les listes d'Évangiles de Würzburg." *Revue bénédictine* 28: 328–30.

Mynors, R. 1937. *Cassiodorus, Institutiones*. Oxford: Clarendon Press.

Nees, Lawrence. 1987. *The Gundohinus Gospels*. Cambridge MA: Medieval Academy of America.

Netzer, Nancy. 1994. *Cultural Interplay in the Eighth Century: The Trier Gospels and the Making of a Scriptorium at Echternach*. Cambridge: Cambridge University Press.

Newton, Francis L., Francis L. Newton Jr., and Christopher R. J. Scheirer. 2013. "Domiciling the Evangelists in Anglo-Saxon England: A Fresh Reading of Aldred's Colophon in the "Lindisfarne" Gospels." *Anglo-Saxon England* 41: 101–44.

Nordenfalk, Carl. 1938. *Die spätantiken Kanonentafeln*. Göteborg: Isacsons.

Ó Néill, P. 1998. "The Earliest Drypoint Glosses in Codex Usserianus Primus." In *"A miracle of learning": Studies in Manuscripts and Irish Learning. Essays in Honour of William O'Sullivan*, edited by T. Barnard, D. Ó. Cróinín, and K. Simms, 1–28. Aldershot: Ashgate.

Parker, D. C. 1991. "Unequally Yoked: The Present State of the Codex Bobbiensis." *Journal of Theological Studies ns* 42: 581–88.

Petitmengin, Pierre, 1985. "Les plus anciens manuscrits de la Bible latine." In *Le monde latin antique et la Bible*, edited by Jacques Fontaine and Charles Pietri, 89–123. BTT 2. Paris: Beauchesne.

Radiciotti, Paolo. 1993. "Problemi di datazione di codici in onciale Par. Lat. 10593, CLM 6224, Par. Lat. 10318." *Archivio della Società romana di storia patria* 116: 53–64

Radiciotti, Paolo. 2005. "Le Sacre Scritture nel Mondo Tardoantico Grecolatino." In *Forme e Modelli della Tradizione Manoscritta della Bibbia*, edited by P. Cherubini, 33–66. Vatican: Scuola Vaticana.

Robert, Ulysse. 1881. *Pentateuchi versio Latina antiquissima e codice Lugdunensi*. Paris: Firmin-Didot.

Robert, Ulysse. 1900. *Heptateuchi partis posterioris versio Latina antiquissima e codice Lugdunense*. Lyon: A. Rey.

Rouse, Richard H., and Charles McNelis. 2001. "North African Literary Activity: A Cyprian Fragment, the Stichometric Lists and a Donatist Compendium." *Revue d'Histoire des Textes* 30: 189–238.

Royet, A. 1922–23. "Un manuscrit palimpseste de la Vulgate hieronymienne des évangiles." *Revue Biblique* 31: 518–51; 32: 39–58, 213–37, 372–82.

Schepps, Georg. 1887. *Die ältesten Evangelienhandschriften der Würzburger Universitätsbibliothek*. Würzburg: A. Stuber.

Stenzel, M. 1953. "Die Konstanzer und St. Galler Fragmente zum altlateinischen Dodekapropheton." *Sacris Erudiri* 5: 27–85.

Stokes, W., and J. Strachan, eds. 1901. *Thesaurus Palaeohibernicus: A Collection of Old-Irish Glosses, Scholia, Prose and Verse*. 3 vols. Cambridge: Cambridge University Press.

Traube, Ludwig. 1907. *Nomina Sacra. Versuch einer Geschichte der Christlichen Kürzung*. Munich: C. H. Beck.

Turner, C. H. 1931. *The Oldest Manuscript of the Vulgate Gospels*. Oxford: Clarendon Press.

Verey, Christopher D., T. J. Brown, and E. Coatsworth. 1980. *The Durham Gospels Together with Fragments of a Gospel Book in Uncial*. Copenhagen: Rosenkilde & Bagger.

Vogels, H. J. 1926. *Evangelium Palatinum*. Münster: Aschendorff.

Vollmer, Friedrich. 1905. *Fl. Merobaudis Reliquiae. Blossii Aemilii Dracontii Carmina. Eugenii Toletani Episcopi Carmina Et Epistulae*. MGH 14. Leipzig: Harrassowitz.

von Dobschütz, Ernst. 1912. *Das Decretum Gelasianum de libris recipiendis et non recipiendis in kritischem Text*. Leipzig: Hinrichs.

Wallenwein, Kirsten. 2017. *Corpus Subscriptionum. Verzeichnis der Beglaubigungen von spätantiken und frühmittelalterlichen Textabschriften saec. IV-VIII)*. Stuttgart: Hiersemann.

CHAPTER 9

THE USE OF THE LATIN BIBLE IN THE EARLY CHURCH

PAUL MATTEI

INUENTIO: EXEGETICAL METHODS

IT is worth noting first of all that the form of the biblical text is likely to have an influence on its interpretation: both the Old Latin and the Vulgate may each provide readings which stimulate confusion. To take a single example, Proverbs 8:22 and 25 in the Septuagint (and therefore the Old Latin) seem to favor, against Nicene orthodoxy, a subordinationist assimilation between creation and generation with regard to Wisdom, which is the Son (κύριος ἔκτισέν με ἀρχὴν ὁδῶν αὐτοῦ . . . πρὸ δὲ πάντων βουνῶν γεννᾷ με, "the Lord *created* me the beginning of his ways . . . before all the hills he *begot* me"). Jerome's version, based on Hebrew, renders the same question void (Vulgate: *Dominus* possedit *me initium viarum suarum . . . ante colles ego* parturiebar, "the Lord *possessed* me, the beginning of his ways . . . before the hills I *was born*"). In this context, one might also set the plea that the same Jerome had made for the *Hebraica ueritas*, even though it is permissible to wonder exactly what "the version based on Hebrew" meant for him, bearing in mind the illusory character of a slogan which, all things being equal, has an anti-Jewish coloring (see further chap. 4).

In the fourth and fifth centuries, some biblical books appealed more than others to the commentators. The Latin world appears to be distinguished by a threefold interest, namely, in Paul, in Job, and in Revelation. Marius Victorinus (in Rome, under the Emperor Constantius), the anonymous Ambrosiaster (also in Rome, in the time of Pope Damasus), Jerome, and Pelagius wrote on all or part of the Pauline corpus. Augustine gave particular attention to Romans and Galatians, as did Julian of Eclanum, while Hilary of Poitiers had written an *Expositio epistulae ad Timotheum* (for Julian, see Simonetti 1985: 248). The attraction of the Apostle is down to his interest in the question of the connection between the two Testaments, between the Law and the Gospel: to put it another way, this addresses the problems of the manner and means of salvation, or the problem of grace. This also calls to mind *Epistulae* 74, 75, and 78 of Ambrose in the Maurist edition, which—perhaps by the intention of the author—form a group within his correspondence, directly addressing the Epistle to the Galatians. Job is the focus of a lost commentary by Hilary of Poitiers, an anonymous Arian, Pelagius, and Julian of Eclanum, and also Ambrose's treatise *De interpellatione Iob et Dauid*. Was this choice prescribed by the misfortunes of the century? Or was it the pervasiveness of the figure of the "righteous sufferer," described, from a stoicizing perspective (cf. Seneca, *De prouidentia* 2), as a valiant soldier whom God confronts with adversity in order to harden him for battle (as early as in Tertullian, *De patientia* 14.2–7 and Cyprian, *De bono patientiae* 18, inspired by Tertullian)? The Latin West left the oldest commentaries on Revelation, beginning with Victorinus of Poetovio in the 280s. A rich lineage stems from that of the fifth-century Donatist Tyconius, in Africa and in Spain, going as far as Beatus of Liébana, after 750 (Gryson 1997). Conversely, the East reserved judgment on the canonicity itself of a book which promoted millennarianism, as seen in the efforts of Eusebius of Caesarea in the early fourth century to challenge its attribution to John the Apostle;[1] the first Greek commentaries date from the sixth century. Finally, the exegetical sermons of the time were mainly concerned, it seems, with the Old Testament (Gregory of Elvira, in Spain, Ambrose, and the preachers of Northern Italy). This fact is undoubtedly related to the general ignorance of the faithful with regard to the Jewish Bible.

The principal distinction to be made is between literal and "allegorical" exegesis. To unlock the literal meaning of a text involves two different activities: to establish the content of the text (through a philological and grammatical investigation) and then to examine the underlying event (through a historical investigation). As for allegorical exegesis, contemporary scholars freely distinguish typology (the value of a character or an action in the Old Testament as a type or figure "of Christ and the Church") from an "anthropological" hermeneutics (the value of a character or an action in the Old Testament as a symbol which holds a significance regarding the soul and its faculties). To consider this in the abstract, the early Christian interpretation of the Song of Songs provides a good example of these layers. In the literal sense, the book is a collection of love poems; in the allegorical sense it contains on one hand the prefiguring of Christ's love for his Bride, the Church (and likewise the rabbis saw in it an image of God's affection for Israel), and on the other hand, an account of the marriage of the soul and the Word. The case of the Song of Songs shows how typological exegesis and anthropological exegesis are articulated: the marriage of the soul and the Word only find their realization in the love of Christ and the Church, and both will experience an eschatological blossoming.

Typology has been a tradition in Christianity since the New Testament. Perhaps the historical Jesus already had recourse to it to explain his mission, and a similar usage

---

[1] *Historia Ecclesiastica* 3.24.18, 3.25.2, esp. 3.39.6, and 7.25.6–27, where the historian allows himself to share the doubts of Dionysius of Alexandria (mid-third century).

is found with regard to the "Master of Justice" in Qumran (cf. Simonetti 1985: 12). Anthropological exegesis comes from Philo of Alexandria, himself an inheritor of the "naturalistic" explanations that Greek philosophers from the sixth century BCE offered for the "pagan" gods and myths. This entered orthodox Christianity with Origen. Ultimately, the distinction between literal interpretation and allegory is rooted in the manner in which patristic scholars understood inspiration. The author of Scripture, right up to its details, was God: accordingly, for the Fathers, its inspiration was equivalent to revelation. Nevertheless, this did not eclipse the human writers who lived in a particular place and time and used a specific language, *realia* which provide the material for literal exegesis.

TRENDS IN INTERPRETATION

In order to expound the Bible, Tertullian enlists the grammatical and rhetorical principles that held sway in the schools for the *explanatio* of classical texts. Following on from Irenaeus, he practices typology for the same reasons as his forerunner: to show, especially against Marcion, the connection of the two Testaments and the value of the Old Testament. Even so, he is wary of the allegorical symbolism beloved of the gnostics, which in his eyes is arbitrary. The heir of Tertullian in this practice, who also uses in part the *Testimonia* of Cyprian, is Lactantius, under the Emperor Constantine, who provides a typological *compendium* in Book 4 of his *Diuinae Institutiones* (Bowen and Garnsey 2004). Incidentally, a temporal shift should be noted: before Victorinus of Poetovio, there was no Latin writing dedicated to the explanation of a specific biblical book in itself, nothing which corresponded to the immense work of an Origen. The commentary on the Song of Songs by Reticius of Autun, written before 334 and known to Jerome, undoubtedly bore no comparison with what Origen had produced on the same book (cf. Doignon 1993).

The Fourth and Fifth Centuries

"Classical" Latin exegesis does not offer a uniform profile in terms of its methods: literalists rub shoulders with allegorists. Contrary to popular opinion, Arian literature is no more literalist in its approach than Catholic. Among the literalists, three names dominate: Marius Victorinus, the Ambrosiaster, and Pelagius. Victorinus has recourse to the techniques which he taught for a long time in the schools, as a professor of rhetoric and dialectic. Although he does not spurn a synthesis, when necessary, he applies himself to the analytical identification of Paul's thought. The Ambrosiaster occasionally emphasizes that the text on which he comments on is "clear": such literalism nevertheless does not avoid typology, as at Galatians 4:21–31 where Abraham's bigamy is interpreted as a figure of the two covenants.

The culmination of literalism is found in Julian of Eclanum. He was in close contact with Theodore of Mopsuestia, master of Antiochene exegesis: driven from the West after 418, Julian took refuge for a time with Theodore and translated the latter's commentary on the Psalms into Latin. His own commentary on Job uses Polychronius of Apamea, the brother of Theodore. While Julian may mock Origen's or Jerome's allegorizing, this is not without sometimes accepting typology or prophecy regarding the person of Christ (*in Christum*), at least in small doses and duly restricted, yet to a greater extent than is seen in Diodore of Tarsus or Theodore.

Allegorists are more numerous, and many also opt for traditional, figurative allegory. Origen and Philo are the guiding lights from the fourth century onward. The direct or indirect influence of Origen, combined with that of Didymus the Blind, precedes the translations made by Jerome and Rufinus. This is seen in Gregory of Elvira (d. 392) and his interpretation of the Song of Songs or of Noah's Ark (Schulz-Flügel 1994). Similarly, Ap(p)onius (in Rome at the beginning of the fifth century?) reads in the Song of Songs the adventures of Christ's love for the Church, as in the writings attributed to "Hippolytus," yet he also knows and draws on the commentary of Origen, in Rufinus's translation: consequently, he also reflects the other interpretative gambit of the Alexandrian, namely, the Song of Songs as dialogue between the Word and the soul. All these are outclassed by Hilary and Ambrose.

Hilary of Poitiers

Exegetical writings:

- Before exile: Commentary on the Gospel of Matthew (*In Matthaeum*).
- After exile: Commentary on the Psalms (*Tractatus in Psalmos*; Hilary did not comment on the whole psalter, or at least the whole of his commentary has not been preserved); *Tractatus mysteriorum*.
- At an unknown time, Hilary also composed *Tractatus in Iob* and *Expositio epistulae ad Timotheum*, although only fragments remain of these two works.

The episcopal career of Hilary was divided into two by his exile in Phrygia because of his adherence to Nicaea (356–60). Exile put Hilary in direct contact with Greek Christian thought, which was crucial in the development of his ideas on Trinitarian dogma. It had no less weight with regard to his hermeneutics (Doignon 1985). The *In Matthaeum* is already marked by an allegorical approach broadly typical of Origenism. His exposition of the Psalms, however, through its perception in the biblical book of a "deeper meaning" (*altius intellegere*), is far more deeply imbued with allegory, reliant (as far as it is possible to judge) on the now-lost commentary of Origen. The *Tractatus mysteriorum* is a companion work which presents the characters of the Old Testament from a figurative perspective.

Ambrose of Milan

Exegetical writings:[2]

- *Exaemeron* ("On the Six Days of Creation")
- *De Paradiso* ("On Paradise")
- *De Cain et Abel* ("On Cain and Abel")
- *De Noe* ("On Noah")
- *De Abraham II libri* ("On Abraham")
- *De Isaac et anima* ("On Isaac and the Soul")
- *De bono mortis* ("On Death as a Good")
- *De fuga saeculi* ("On Flight from the World", in part on the "towns of refuge" in Numbers 35:11)
- *De Iacob et uita beata* ("On Jacob and the Blessed Life")
- *De Ioseph* ("On Joseph")
- *De Helia et ieiunio* ("On Elijah and Fasting")
- *De Nabuthae historia* ("On the Story of Naboth")
- *De Tobia* ("On Tobit")
- *De interpellatione Iob et Dauid* ("On the Prayer of Job and David")
- *De apologia prophetae Dauid* ("On the Apology of the Prophet David"; an *Apologia Dauid altera* which follows this book in certain manuscripts of the eleventh century or later, is often considered pseudonymous)
- *Enarrationes in XII Psalmos Dauidicos* (Exegesis of Psalms 1, 35–40, 43 [unfinished], 45, 47, 48, and 61 [LXX])
- *Expositio Psalmi* CXVIII (Commentary on Psalm 118 [LXX])
- *Expositio Euangelii secundum Lucam* (Commentary on Luke)
- Only a few fragments remain of a Commentary on Isaiah (*Expositio Isaiae Prophetae*), quoted by Augustine.

There are four main characteristics of Ambrose's exegesis, which reinforce each other. First comes the *Sitz im Leben* of its origin in preaching, as seen in the homilies on the Gospel of Luke. The presentation of the "lives" of the patriarchs and other Old Testament characters is often no more than a pretext to develop moral or spiritual precepts unrelated to each individual. Second are his sources. Forced, as he says, to "teach before learning" (*De officiis ministrorum* 1.1.4), Ambrose enrolled himself in the school of his Greek predecessors, from whom he transcribed entire pages. In matters of "philosophy," he draws, for the most part, from the well of

---

[2] The following list provides no dates but instead follows the order of the biblical canon. The chronology of Ambrose's works is heavily debated: in addition, it should not be forgotten that, as Ambrose's exegetical treaties stemmed from his preaching, it is necessary to distinguish between the time of their original delivery and their publication.

(neo-)Platonism; in his exegesis, he relies on the various "allegorists" (proponents of typological allegory as well as of "symbolic" allegory): works attributed to Hippolytus of Rome, Philo (at the beginning of his career), Origen (later). Hence, despite the variety of sources (and even where Ambrose does not reproduce any detectable source), there is a pronounced spiritual warmth throughout. Third comes method. For Ambrose, Scripture explains Scripture, and Bible verses shed light on each other. This is the source of the disconcerting, almost poetic, virtuosity of Ambrosian exegesis, characterized by its freedom, its play on verbal parallels, and its predilection for lexical analogies. Fourth, and finally, is Ambrose's perspective. His spiritual warmth is nourished by a lively Christocentrism: in all the Scriptures, Ambrose, like Origen before him, perceives the voice of the Word. It is surprising that the Bishop of Milan, unlike Origen, never wrote a commentary on the Song of Songs, yet this book, which he never ceases quoting, is present in the background of all his exegetical activity. It is the Bridegroom (the Word) who speaks throughout the Bible, secretly in the Old Testament and openly in the New, attracting the souls to whom he speaks and giving them, in turns by his presence and his self-concealment, a desire for him. This, too, is the mission of the preacher, whose role is to share with his listeners the words of the Bridegroom, having first disposed himself in the silence of prayer and study to listen to the Master in order all the better to inspire, like a mystagogue, the community of which he is the pastor (cf. Nauroy 1985).

In sum, whatever the preferences of each author may be, and despite the dominance of allegory through the influence of Origen, Latin writers appear to observe a balance between literalism and allegory in their exegetical writings. To what extent this is also true of Augustine is the next stage of the investigation.

ATTEMPTS AT FORMALIZATION

It is in the writings of John Cassian, which are not, strictly speaking, exegetical, that the theory of the senses of Scripture is first presented as such in Latin tradition. This theory comprises four senses: the literal and historical; the allegorical or typological; the moral or tropological; and the anagogical. Cassian "dilates" the tripartite division which Origen had propounded into a fourfold theory which went on to enjoy considerable success (Simonetti 1985: 358–59). This is set out in his *Collationes patrum* 14.8, where he illustrates his proposal according to the various meanings of the noun Jerusalem: historically, the city of the Jews; allegorically, the Church of Christ; anagogically, the celestial City of God, mother of us all (cf. Galatians 4:26); tropologically, the human soul, which in this identification is often rebuked or praised by the Lord. This doctrine, either unchanged or with adaptations, is found right up to the writings of the Venerable Bede (even though he does not always abide by its strictures; cf. Vuillaume 2003) and from there is adopted by medieval writers.

Augustine, *De doctrina christiana*

Augustine's treatise *De doctrina christiana* ("On Christian Teaching") played such a central role in the development of theoretical reflection on exegetical practice that it deserves special examination (Green 1996; Bochet 1997; Arnold and Bright 1995). Its four books were written in two distinct stages. It appears that in 396–97 Augustine wrote the first two books and the third up to the quotation of Luke 13:21 at 3.25.36. In 426, while he was composing the *Retractationes*, he found the unfinished manuscript, finished Book 3, and added Book 4.[3] Despite this unusual gestation, there is no perceptible difference between the two parts, no differences in style or thought. The only questions are why Augustine's work was interrupted and whether the earlier portion circulated on its own, which need not detain us here (cf. Steinhauser 1995). The treatise may be summarized as follows:

Prologue

- Purpose of the work: to define the rules for interpreting the "signs" (*signa*) contained in Holy Scripture, and to show how to explain to others the discoveries that may be made by an interpretation along these lines.
- Responses to possible criticisms of this purpose.

Book 1

- Necessary distinctions: between *modus inueniendi* ("manner of discovery") and *modus proferendi* ("manner of expression"); *res* and *signa* ("object" and "signs"); *frui* and *uti* ("to enjoy" and "to use").
- Before examining the *signa* that make up Scripture, establish what are the *res* that these *signa* represent, and especially their hierarchy.
- This hierarchy is made by the distinction between worldly things which it is appropriate "to use" (*uti*) in order to achieve the end (i.e., God), and those it is necessary "to enjoy" (*frui*) through a charity that extends not only to God but also, in him, to one's neighbor, every human or good angel who, like us, whoever they may be, is called to be loved by God and to love him.
- The fundamental criterion of biblical hermeneutics is therefore charity, for the purpose of Scripture is to guide humans toward their true end.

Book 2

- Prerequisites: a general definition of *signa* (distinguishing between (1) proper signs and figurative [i.e. allegorical] signs, and (2) unrecognized signs and ambiguous signs); the obscurity of Scripture, and the finality of this obscurity.

---

[3] It is worth remembering that the *Retractationes* involved Augustine's critical review of all his earlier works in the light of the orthodoxy which he believed he had achieved.

- Unrecognized signs: proper signs, and how to acquire knowledge of them (e.g., how to discriminate between existing Latin translations and how to learn biblical languages); figurative signs, and how to acquire knowledge of them (by recourse to secular studies).
- Digression: the degree of utility of secular studies.
- Conclusion: the good use of the aforesaid studies.

Book 3

- Ambiguous signs: proper signs (dubious punctuation; ambiguous pronunciation; unclear syntax), and how to elucidate them (by resorting to context; not priding oneself on excessive purism in places where current usage removes all ambivalence); figurative signs, and how not to be mistaken (do not take a figurative expression for a proper expression and vice versa); a rule: everything that, taken in the literal sense, cannot be related to faith or charity is to be taken figuratively;[4] a review of the *regulae* put forward by Tyconius.

Book 4

- The purpose of the work: no longer discovery but expression (it is not about teaching precepts of rhetoric but about teaching the function of the Christian orator: *bona docere et mala dedocere*).
- The orator will find models in Scripture which combine eloquence and wisdom (i.e., the art of speaking well about the good).
- Christian eloquence respects "the three duties of the orator: to teach, to please and to persuade" (*tria officia oratoris: docere, delectare, mouere*); however, Cicero brought together under *docere* small subjects treated in a simple style, under *delectare* medium subjects in a moderate style, and under *mouere* great subjects in the sublime style. Now, for the Christian orator, whose object is salvation, there are only great subjects; even so, the orator will know how to vary the *officia* and, with them, the styles. Examples of this are taken from Scripture and Latin Christian authors (Cyprian; Ambrose).
- It is essential that the Christian speaker conforms their life to their words, and must pray before preaching or dictating.
- General conclusion: the length of the work; thanksgiving.

This analysis tries to bring out the coherence of the plan followed by Augustine, but it does not capture the care and the subtlety of his long developments and their meandering profusion. All of Augustine is in this, of whom too often it has been

---

[4] Cf. 3.15.23: *Seruabitur ergo in locutionibus figuratis regula huiusmodi, ut tamdiu uersetur diligenti consideratione quod legitur, donec ad regnum caritatis interpretatio perducatur.*

claimed that "his composition was unskilled" (Marrou 1958: 61).[5] Here there is firmness of thought and rigor in the overview, along with suppleness and finesse in pages which sometimes seem *extra ordinem*, yet never forget the heart of the matter (the original topic).

Among the overriding themes that stand out, the rest of this discussion examines the question posed by a hermeneutics based on semantics. This is the central question of Books 2 and 3, where its treatment is contingent on the developments of Book 1. In considering the standards of literal and allegorical exegesis, *De doctrina christiana* translates into theory the balance between the two preserved by Augustine in practice (as in the treatment of the main characters of the Old Testament in Books 12 and 22 of *Contra Faustum*). Semantics and hermeneutics are linked: it is according to a categorization of signs (semantics) that Augustine organizes the statement of his rules of interpretation (hermeneutics).

In terms of semantics, Augustine presents a series of definitions and distinctions:

- Of signs in general: "A sign is something which, in addition to the impression it produces on the senses, causes something else to come to the mind from it" (2.1.1).
- Of *signa naturalia* and *signa data*: the "natural sign" is produced "without a will or any desire of signifying" (*sine uoluntate atque ullo appetitu significandi*, 2.1.2); for example, smoke signals fire. The "given sign" expresses what a subject wishes to be understood (2.3.2): it is not a "conventional" but an "intentional" sign.
- Of words and writing: among the "given signs", the linguistic sign (the word) is superior, a sign "whose sole role is to signify." While other signs only signify in addition to what is already there (1.2.2), the word explains every other form of sign (while the converse is not true, 2.3.4). Writing is a sign of words (2.4.5).
- Of *signa propria* and *signa figurata*. The distinction between the two is explained at 2.10.15. The type of the "figurative sign" is metaphor, which is not a misleading sign as it does not have the intention to deceive. Augustine gives a broad definition of the "figurative sign," which could include Christian allegory.

In these definitions and distinctions, where is Augustine's original contribution to be located? The thought of *De doctrina* is found elsewhere in Augustine, in particular in the analysis in Book 1 of the *Confessiones* on the childhood acquisition of language and the impetus behind this, namely, the need to manifest one's will. It is not right to credit Augustine with an originality on which he does not pride himself: his reading and his experience as a teacher of rhetoric are enough to provide him with the essentials of his material. The Bishop of Hippo adopts standard material and systematizes it, but from the perspective of exegesis. The use he makes of the *Liber regularum* composed one generation earlier by Tyconius is of particular note (cf. Vercruysse 2004): in a way that may

---

[5] "[Il] compose mal": Marrou specifies further "that is to say, differently from us" ("c'est-à-dire autrement que nous" [1958: 75; cf. the table of contents on 617]).

not be entirely faithful to the thought of his predecessor, Augustine sees in these rules the methodological principles of allegorical exegesis.

As for hermeneutics, Augustine defines the *res* in Book 1 before defining the rules governing the *signa* in Books 2 and 3. It is as if the interpreter had no other goal than to give *signs* an interpretation that corresponded to *things* which were already known. Is there a "hermeneutic circle" in Augustine? The general resolution to this problem may be sketched with recourse to the notion, borrowed from Ricœur (who is also responsible for the image of "hermeneutic circle"; cf. Bochet 1997: 438–49), of "precomprehension": this serves as a basis and hypothesis for interpretation. More precisely, the problem must be resolved within the global logic of Augustinian thought and respecting its bent: faith and charity are at its head, and the explanation of Scripture ensures their development.

Excursus: Augustine's Exegetical Activity

The following list only includes Augustine's specifically exegetical writings: the rest of his output should not be overlooked (cf. Bochet 2004; La Bonnardière 1986).

General

- *De doctrina christiana* ("On Christian Teaching": for the date of composition, see above)

On the Old Testament

- *De Genesi aduersus Manichaeos* ("On Genesis against the Manichees"; Thagaste, 389)
- *De Genesi ad litteram liber imperfectus* ("On the Literal Interpretation of Genesis," unfinished; 395)
- *De Genesi ad litteram libri XII* ("On the Literal Interpretation of Genesis"; twelve books, 401–15)
- *Locutionum in Heptateuchum libri VII* and *Quaestionum in Heptateuchum libri VII* ("Expressions in the Heptateuch" and "Questions on the Heptateuch"; seven books each)
- *Adnotationes in Iob* ("Notes on Job")
- *De VIII quaestionibus ex Veteri Testamento* ("Eight Questions from the Old Testament")

On the New Testament

- *De sermone domini in monte* ("On the Sermon on the Mount"; 391–92)
- *Expositio LXXXIV propositionum ex epistola ad Romanos*; *Expositio epistolae ad Galatas*; *Epistolae ad Romanos inchoata expositio* (Commentaries on Romans and Galatians)

- *Quaestiones euangeliorum* ("Questions on the Gospels"; around 400)
- *De consensu euangelistarum* ("On the Agreement of the Evangelists"; around 400)

Preaching

- Various sermons
- *Enarrationes in Psalmos* (Sermons on the Psalms preached or dictated throughout his episcopate)
- *Tractatus in euangelium Iohannis* (124 Sermons on John, whose date is controversial [400–420])
- *Tractatus in epistolam Iohannis ad Parthos* (ten sermons on 1 John, preached from 413 to 418).

DISPOSITIO. GIVING AN ACCOUNT OF WHAT HAS BEEN UNDERSTOOD

The two main types of biblical exposition are commentaries and exegetical sermons, which are treated in separate sections.

Commentaries

Jerome's commentaries are a model *par excellence* of commentaries in the strict sense (Jay 1985). As one would expect, he is sensitive to the philological aspects. This gives rise to his hermeneutical "canon," which features the following general characteristics: (1) the balancing of the claims of philology and allegory; (2) the critical discussion of each passage studied, with a comparison between the Hebrew text and the Greek versions (especially the Septuagint); and (3) the exposition based first on the historical interpretation and then allegory (the latter most often taken from Origen or Didymus). "In his commentaries on the prophets, Jerome . . . usually starts from a double translation of the lemma, from Hebrew and from Greek, to bring out its literal meaning and to identify one or more spiritual interpretations. The realization of this simple scheme can obviously take various forms according to the difficulty of the text expounded or the richness of the interpretations which it allows" (Jay 1998: 39).

The appeal of the commentary for Jerome recalls, as we have seen in the case of other writers, the standard principles of the explanation of the classics in the schools. In particular, the *explanatio* has a very "myopic" nature: following a very brief introduction, which locates the (human) author of the biblical book and establishes the significance of the ideas which tacitly govern interpretation, it then reduces these to dust through its detailed attention to each verse. These methods are also found in his commentary on Matthew (the only exegetical work from Jerome's mature period devoted to the New Testament). However, the homilies on Mark and on the Psalms, preached before the monks in Bethlehem, emphasize the "spiritual" aspect.

Excursus: Jerome's Exegetical Output

Jerome's original work of biblical commentary comprises two principal groups of very different sizes:

- *Commentaries on Paul*, composed at Bethlehem in 386 in the order: Philemon, Galatians, Ephesians, Titus.
- *Commentaries on the Prophets*. From 374, Jerome was interested in Obadiah. From 393, while he was translating from Hebrew, he expounded the twelve Minor Prophets: Nahum, Micah, Habakkuk, Zephaniah, and Haggai, then Jonah and Obadiah, finally (in 406) Zechariah, Malachi, Hosea, Joel, and Amos. Then come the four Major Prophets: Daniel (407), Isaiah (408–10), Ezekiel (411–14), Jeremiah (interrupted by Jerome's death in 419).

To these may be added:

- *Commentary on Ecclesiastes* (Rome, then Bethlehem; 380s)
- *Hebrew Questions on Genesis* (Bethlehem, ca. 392)
- *Commentary on Matthew* (Bethlehem, 398; brief and literal).
- *Commentarioli in Psalmos* (Bethlehem, ca. 390). Short scholia on the Psalms before the revision of the Gallican Psalter and the translation *iuxta Hebraeos*.
- *Homilies on Mark* (Bethlehem)
- *Homilies on the Psalms* (Bethlehem)

Jerome's translations from Greek focused on the works of Origen, whom he venerated long before vilifying him, and Eusebius of Caesarea.

- Origen: *Homilies on the Prophets* (fourteen on Jeremiah, fourteen on Ezekiel, in Constantinople in 381; nine on Isaiah, in Bethlehem in 392); *Homilies on the Song of Songs* (two, in Rome, 383); *Homilies on the Gospel of Luke* (thirty-nine in Bethlehem in 390).
- Eusebius: *Chronicon* (not exegetical); the *Onomastica* (*Liber locorum*, *Liber nominum*), a collection of interpretations of scriptural names (in 390).

The result of this activity is a massive and diversified "scientific" apparatus. Through translating or revising the Bible, translating the Greek Fathers, and composing an enviable number of his own commentaries (above all, the enormous prophetic corpus), Jerome armed the Latins with an apparatus that finally brought them up to the level of the Greeks (see also Canellis 2017). This served to nourish all subsequent scholarship, as seen in the particular use of the onomastic tools such as the *Liber interpretationum nominum Hebraicorum* ("Book of the interpretations of Hebrew names") in the Middle Ages.

Sermons

Preaching in the patristic period was, in essence, interpreting the biblical text. This is shown in the words *tractatus* and *tractare*, meaning "exegetical sermon" and "to compose an exegetical sermon." These were often organized into collections of homilies explaining an entire biblical book, and the collections were intended as such by their author. This is seen in Augustine's sermon cycles mentioned above: the *Enarrationes in Psalmos*, the *Tractatus in Iohannem*, and the *Tractatus in Epistolam Iohannis*. Ambrose's practice was to revise and expand the text of his homilies, transcribed in shorthand by stenographers as they were delivered. These were reworked, sometimes completed, and assembled into longer works through the addition of transitions and more or less elliptical links. While this is principally the case for his exegetical works, among which the commentary on Luke is chief, it also applies at least in part to some of his moral and dogmatic treatises. Alongside sermons, the genre of *Quaestiones* is also deserving of mention. This type of collection also existed in Greek, consisting of written answers to problems posed by individual biblical passages. Several works of this nature have been noted above among the writings of Jerome and Augustine.

Is there a difference in approach between the two types of *dispositio*? Might there be more scholarly technicality in a commentary, reserved for the reading of scholars, than in a sermon, addressed to the people or, at least, a gathering? Jerome's practice of emphasizing spiritual aspects in his homilies lends credence to this view. But, albeit outside the context of the Bible and in full knowledge of how to accommodate his audience, Augustine rejects "double standards" (cf. *De dono perseuerantiae* 22.57). It should not be forgotten that commentaries and sermons are both, in fact, aimed at the same principal goal, which is spiritual. This specifically *mystical* direction is also attested toward the end of the period under consideration in the vast commentary endeavors of Gregory the Great on Job, Ezekiel, and so on (Leclercq 1990; see also chap. 12). These, too, offer a good example of the reworking of exegesis initially presented in an oral context.

THE MENTAL UNIVERSE: THE BIBLE EVERYWHERE

Beyond the processes of *inuentio* and *dispositio*, we can only trace the outlines of the vast continent constituted by the Bible in the mental universe of Latin Christianity in antiquity.

The Bible in Councils and Controversies

It was expected that Scripture would be used at least to provide a confirmation in support of the decisions made by synods, whether these were doctrinal or disciplinary. With regard to controversies, the role of the Bible in the struggles with Arianism provides an important case in point. The task was to find the "right faith" in Scripture. This was a challenge for the adherents of Nicaea, as multiple passages appeared at first sight to present a headache in terms of reconciling them with the orthodoxy whose victory was being sought. A sample of these, far from exhaustive, would include: the Old Testament theophanies, which since the early apologists (themselves influenced by Philo) had been seen as appearances of the *Logos*, with the Father alone remaining absolutely transcendent; Proverbs 8:22–25 (see above); Matthew 24:36 and parallels (the Son knows neither the day nor the hour); John 14:28 ("the Father is greater than I"); and 1 Corinthians 15:28 ("the Son will be subjected to the one who put all things in subjection under him"). The answer was in the development of simple, all-encompassing principles. Accordingly, Hilary of Poitiers promoted the idea of eternal *natiuitas*, which proclaimed both identity and difference between the Father and the Son, in harmony with the concept of *birth* in the flesh. Ambrose offered an "exegetical key," especially in the *De fide*, of explaining subordinationist verses by the doctrine of the two natures of Jesus, equal to the Father in his divinity, inferior to him in his humanity. Another response was to interpret Scripture by Scripture. In this way, "The Father and I are one" (John 10:30) could be combined with "I am in the Father and the Father is in me" (John 14:11) in order to move beyond generic unity in favor of numerical unity (uniqueness), without destroying the distinction.

Two further observations should be made. The first is that to describe the Bible as a "source" is ambiguous, as it involves simultaneously finding doctrine in Scripture and also making explicit what in Scripture remains hidden (or at least ambivalent). This is a kind of "hermeneutical circle," to adopt in a different sense a concept already used above. Second, up to the fourth century, there is no theology that is not biblical. It is only gradually that patristic argument emerges in order to beef up doctrine. This evolution is not only seen in Latin tradition: it may also be observed among the Greeks, in theological treatises and the acts of councils which are buttressed by lists of authorities. For instance, against the "enemies of grace," Augustine invokes not only Cyprian and Ambrose but also, in a slightly more "accommodating" manner, the two Gregorys and Chrysostom from the Greek side.

Poetry: The Bible in the Literary Aesthetics of Latin Christians

To understand the mission that Latin poetry assigns itself regarding biblical subjects, it is important not to forget the scorn poured on biblical phraseology by the educated who were accustomed to the splendor of classical works. The grammatical ruggedness of the sacred text in the Old Latin versions and the bizarreness of its imaginative world posed a stumbling block which caused both Jerome (cf. *Epistula* 22.20) and Augustine (*Confessiones* 3.5.9) to fall in their youth. Undoubtedly, it was to ward off the temptation to denigrate this that both of them, even after they had overcome their initial disgust, did not cease from their attempts to find in Scripture the use of poetic techniques comparable to those in classical authors (in Jerome's case; see his Prologue to the Book of Job in Hebrew [Canellis 2017]) or the presence of rhetorical models in conformity with those of ancient education (in the case of Augustine; *De doctrina christiana* 4.41.148–49). It was this same challenge, among others, that provided inspiration for biblical poetry (Charlet 1985).

The rewriting of the Bible is the goal of centos and paraphrases. The most striking example of the former is that of the noblewoman Faltonia Proba, who, around 360, undertook the rewriting of various biblical episodes exclusively in the form of extracts from Vergilian hexameters. Among the authors of paraphrase, Juvencus and Arator stand out (Green 2006). The former, a Spanish priest at the end of Constantine's rule, composed four books and two prologues on the Gospels with a total of 3,219 hexameters. Two centuries later, Arator, a high-ranking civil servant under the Ostrogoths, became a subdeacon of the Roman Church and wrote two books on the Acts of the Apostles (1,076 and 1,250 hexameters each; see Bureau and Deproost 2018). These two poets were read assiduously in the Middle Ages.

Poetry inspired by the Bible seeks to celebrate God by its offering of beauty. It mediates, or internalizes, the Word through the glory of verse and rhythm. This double purpose, both aesthetic and spiritual, is accompanied by an apologetic concern to clothe the Bible in a garment worthy of its importance. Arator is a prime example of this. His epic poetry praises the wonders of God and teaches truth, in contrast to the lies of classical versifiers, while serving to indicate his affiliation to a cultural heritage that goes beyond Christianity. Arator's truth is orthodoxy: his Christology, Nicene and Chalcedonian, seeks to prove its conformity in everything to the faith of the Roman Church, such that it results in an exaltation of Peter and his successors, as the poem becomes an encomium of that Church and its leader. Indeed, the author himself arranged for a public reading (*recitatio*) of his epic, lasting four days, before Pope Vigilius and the clergy and people of Rome in 544 at the church of St Peter *Ad Vincula*. (Although there is no biblical paraphrase among the works he wrote, the lyric, epic, and didactic poetry of the fourth-century Prudentius reveals the same both literary and spiritual aim.)

An Inner World Bathed in the Bible

Given the scale of the problems they raise, it is not possible to do more than list the issues raised by five further areas in which the Bible was used in the Latin world. With regard to activity, it offered models for personal conduct. This was not simply that of martyrdom in the pre-Constantinian era, when the influence of Maccabean literature, canonical or apocryphal, may be underlined. It also contributed to everyday ethics: in the third century, Cyprian's morality reflects not only the Roman and Stoic characteristic of *grauitas* but also the hallmarks of Wisdom literature (Proverbs, Ecclesiasticus; also Tobit). With regard to representation, the Bible played a role in liturgy, Christian art, and epigraphy (see the relevant chapters in Fontaine and Pietri 1985). There was a gradual development of a collection of liturgical readings for worship, whether Eucharistic or not: initially, the choice was that of the celebrant, which later gave way to lectionaries with a greater or lesser degree of prescription. The creation of a euchological style, too, is dependent in part on biblical material (see further chap. 29). An inventory of the scenes depicted in early Christian sculpture (e.g., on sarcophagi) and paintings (e.g., in the catacombs) would reveal the major role of the Bible. This corpus is in large part funerary, but not exclusively so: the mosaics on the triumphal arch of Santa Maria Maggiore, going back to the papacy of Xystus III (432–44), include a depiction of the hospitality of Abraham. Inscriptions preserve a variety of biblical verses, some customary and others less so, varying according to region and purpose. Finally, the linguistic impact of the Bible is seen in the way in which developments in the Latin language may be traced to scriptural usage (see further chap. 28). Over the course of the twentieth century, in particular, proposals to identify a "Christian Latin" excited considerable debate and, at times, polemic (Deléani 1997).

To examine the way in which biblical commentary polarized culture and contributed to its Christian reorientation, it is necessary to return to Augustine's *De doctrina christiana*. In the final chapters of Book 2, Scripture is made the foundation of culture, in terms of both its point of departure and its horizon. All arts and disciplines are not simply deployed in the service of the faith, or judged by the yardstick of their usefulness for the Christian (or, better, reassessed in the light of the cross). There is something more: no longer, it seems, are they accepted except from the perspective of biblical interpretation. This is particularly true of the natural sciences (e.g., geology or zoology): Augustine only calls for the multiplication of textbooks or collections on the model of Jerome's *Onomastica*, to serve as assemblies of *mirabilia*. Such a perspective appears utilitarian, with a clear danger of impoverishment or even sterilization if it were carried out undiminished across each domain of knowledge. Nevertheless, it would influence the Middle Ages, providing the *ratio studiorum* for Cassiodorus in his Vivarium, and the source of the encyclopedism of Isidore of Seville. The primary importance of the *De doctrina christiana*, as noted above, is its attempt at a synthesis. In second place, however, is its importance as a conception of a culture in which the Divine Word holds pride of place, and in which its interpretation becomes the responsibility underpinning all intellectual activity.

Augustine also offers the clearest example of recourse to the Bible as a mode of personal expression. The familiarity that the Fathers acquired from Scripture has already been mentioned with regard to Ambrose's virtuosic "Bible-speak." Yet it goes even deeper, as seen especially throughout the *Confessions*. Marrou rightly diagnosed it as follows:

> As a churchman, St. Augustine absorbed the Bible in the same way that, in his youth, he had learned to absorb Cicero and Vergil. His style is shot through with it, just as it remains imbued with classical formulae, no matter what effort he makes. Moreover,

this biblical character is often something he deliberately desires, or seeks: it has been observed how quotations and imitations multiply on his most elaborate pages, those on which the author seeks to express a particularly intense religious emotion. Gladly he effaces himself, so that his own word, the human word, is silent and gives way to the inspired word, the Word of God. (Marrou 1969: 57).

The Word cast on the four winds paradoxically becomes the tool of the most intimate and the most subjective introspection and verbalization.

CONCLUSION

What originality is there in the Latin approach to the Bible? Its methods and literary genres come from Greek, every phenomenon in Latin which involves the Bible has a corresponding Greek precursor, to a greater or lesser extent. And yet, unless I am mistaken, there is one exception. There is no exact equivalent among the Greeks of *De doctrina christiana*, both in its establishing of a formal practice (which is neither the scope nor target of Origen's *De principiis*) and in its outlining of a program of cultural reorientation. As for the spiritual significance of the use of the Bible, it is clear that, here too, the Latins join the Greeks, and for good reason. Here, indeed, lies the heart of the patristic endeavor: to build a wisdom *in Christo,* a flavorsome meditation on the Word, capable of irrigating the whole of culture. It is not only of the Word that Scripture speaks, it is he who speaks in it, and it is he whose face is sought incessantly by private reading, just as it is shared through preaching and writing. The centrality of the Song of Songs to so many authors, whether potential or actual, is revealing: it is about hearing, and making heard everywhere, the voice of the Beloved.

BIBLIOGRAPHY

Arnold, Duane W. H., and Pamela Bright, eds. 1995. *De doctrina christiana. A Classic of Western Culture.* Notre Dame: University of Notre Dame.

Bochet, Isabelle. 2004. *Le firmament de l'Écriture. L'herméneutique augustinienne.* Collection des études augustiniennes; Série Antiquité 172. Paris: Institut d'études augustiniennes.

Bochet, Isabelle, et al., eds. 1997. *Augustin. De doctrina christiana.* Bibliothèque augustinienne 11.2. Paris: Institut d'études augustiniennes.

Bowen, Anthony, and Peter Garnsey, trans. 2004. *Lactantius: Divine Institutes.* Liverpool: Liverpool University Press.

Bureau, Bruno, and Paul-Augustin Deproost. 2018. *Arator. Histoire apostolique.* Paris: Budé.

Canellis, Aline, et al. 2017. *Jérôme, Préfaces aux livres de la Bible. Introduction, traduction et notes.* SC 592. Paris: Cerf.

Charlet, Jean-Louis. 1985. "L'inspiration et la forme bibliques dans la poésie latine, du IIIᵉ au VIᵉ siècle." In *Le monde latin antique et la Bible,* edited by Jacques Fontaine and Charles Pietri, 613–45. BTT 2. Paris: Beauchesne.

Deléani, Simone. 1997. "Le latin des Pères, un domaine encore mal exploré." In *Les Pères au XXe siècle. Histoire-Littérature-Théologie*. Paris: Cerf, 251–64.

Di Berardino, Angelo. 2010. *Nuovo dizionario patristico e di antichità cristiane*. 2nd ed. Genoa: Marietti.

Doignon, Jean 1985. "Les premiers commentateurs latins de l'Écriture et l'œuvre exégétique d'Hilaire de Poitiers." In *Le monde latin antique et la Bible*, edited by Jacques Fontaine and Charles Pietri, 509–22. BTT 2. Paris: Beauchesne.

Doignon, Jean 1993. "Réticius d'Autun." In *Handbuch der lateinischen Literatur der Antike 5* (French translation), edited by Reinhart Herzog and Peter Lebrecht Schmidt, 474–75. Paris: Brepols.

Fontaine, Jacques, and Charles Pietri, eds. 1985. *Le monde latin antique et la Bible*. BTT 2. Paris: Beauchesne.

Green, Roger P. H. 1996. *Augustine: De doctrina christiana*. Oxford: Oxford University Press.

Green, Roger P. H. 2006. *Latin Epics of the New Testament: Juvencus, Sedulius, Arator*. Oxford: Oxford University Press.

Gryson, Roger. 1997. "Les commentaires patristiques latins sur l'Apocalypse." *Revue théologique de Louvain* 28: 305–37, 484–502.

Jay, Pierre. 1985. "Jérôme et la pratique de l'exégèse." *Le monde latin antique et la Bible*, edited by Jacques Fontaine and Charles Pietri, 523–42. BTT 2. Paris: Beauchesne.

Jay, Pierre. 1998. *Jérôme, lecteur de l'Écriture. La Vulgate*. Supplément aux cahiers Évangile 104. Paris: Cerf.

La Bonnardière, Anne-Marie. 1986. *Saint Augustin et la Bible*. BTT 3. Paris: Beauchesne.

Leclercq, Jean. 1990. *L'amour des lettres et le désir de Dieu. Initiation aux auteurs monastiques du Moyen Âge*. 3rd ed. Paris: Cerf.

Marrou, Henri-Irenée. 1958. *Saint Augustin et la fin de la culture antique*. 2nd ed. Paris: De Boccard.

Marrou, Henri-Irenée. 1969. *Saint Augustin et l'augustinisme*. 7th ed. Paris: Le Seuil.

Mattei, Paul. 2017. "La Bible dans la littérature latine chrétienne IIe-VIIIe siècle." In *Lectures de la Bible. Ier-XVe siècle*, edited by Laurence Mellerin, 239–92. Paris: Cerf.

Nauroy, G. 1985. "L'Écriture dans la pastorale d'Ambroise de Milan." In *Le monde latin antique et la Bible*, edited by Jacques Fontaine and Charles Pietri, 371–408. BTT 2. Paris: Beauchesne.

Quasten, Johannes. 1950–53. *Patrology*. 3 vols. Westminster, MD: Newman.

Quasten, Johannes, and Angelo Di Berardino. *Patrology, Vol. 4. The Golden Age of Latin Patristic Literature. From the Council of Nicea to the Council of Chalcedon*. 3 vols. Westminster, MD: Christian Classics.

Schulz-Flügel, Eva, ed. 1994. *Gregorius Eliberritanus, Epithalamium sive explanatio in Canticis canticorum*. AGLB 26. Freiburg: Herder.

Simonetti, Manlio. 1985. *Lettera e/o allegoria. Un contributo alla storia dell'esegesi patristica*. Rome: Institutum Patristicum Augustinianum.

Simonetti, Manlio. 2001. *Biblical Interpretation in the Early Church: An Historical Introduction to Patristic Exegesis*. Edinburgh: T&T Clark.

Steinhauser, Kenneth B. 1995. "Codex Leningradensis Q.v.I.3.: Some Unresolved Problems." In *De doctrina christiana. A Classic of Western Culture*, edited by Duane W. H. Arnold and Pamela Bright, 33–43. Notre Dame: University of Notre Dame.

Vercruysse, Jean-Marc, ed. 2004. *Tyconius: Liber regularum*. SC 488. Paris: Cerf.

Vuillaume, Christophe, ed. 2003. *Bède: Le Tabernacle*. SC 475. Paris: Cerf.

CHAPTER 10

....

THE BIBLE IN
INSULAR TRADITION

....

MARTIN MCNAMARA

THE BACKGROUND

....

CHRISTIANITY came to Ireland in the fifth century with St. Patrick (432 CE) and probably earlier. Soon afterward, monasteries and monastic schools flourished, with an emphasis on grammar and Bible study which attracted students from across the water. In early pre-Norman times (before 1200 CE), Ireland was intimately connected with Iona, Northumbria (Lindisfarne), and Anglo-Saxon England. Monks from Iona, under Aidan (succeeded by Finan and Colman), successfully evangelized Northumbria from 635 CE onward. They brought with them the Celtic celebration of Easter, differing from that of Rome and the Continent, which entered Northumbria with the marriage of King Oswy to the Roman-observant Queen Eanflæd. Debate and divisions rose on the matter leading to the Synod of Streaneshalc/Whitby in 664 CE. When the king sided with the Roman party, Colman and Irish monks, together with thirty Anglo-Saxons withdrew to Iona.[1] From there, they set out in 668 CE to found a new community on the island of Inishboffin of the Irish Mayo Coast. Misunderstandings had them part ways peacefully and the Anglo-Saxon monks formed a new community on the mainland at a place a place known as Mag n-Eó ("plain of the yew trees"). This community continued there until the ninth century, when Alcuin was in correspondence with it, and later. Streaneshalc/Whitby did not mark a break in contact between Ireland and Northumbria or their mutual influence (Stancliffe 2017; Hughes 1971). Bede, who died in 735, recounts that in the days of Bishops Finan and Colman many of nobility and lower ranks of the English went to Ireland either for divine studies or monastic life.[2] He made

....

[1] See Bede, *Historia Ecclesiastica* III.25–26.
[2] *Historia Ecclesiastica* III.27.

many positive references to the presence of Irish monks and scholars in Northumbria and England (Edwards 1983; McCann 2015). Picard (2005) showed that Bede made use of Irish sources both for his history and his exegesis.

The contact in the textual and exegetical field between Ireland and Northumbria, in particular the twin monasteries of Wearmouth-Jarrow founded in 672 and 681, is seen in a number of surviving documents. The fragments of Matthew and Mark in Durham Cathedral Library (A.II.10, ff. 2–5, 338–39; C.III.13, ff. 192–95; C.III.20, ff. 1–2; VL 19A) come from a gospel book copied in the middle of the seventh century (ca. 650), probably in Northumbria but representing Irish tradition. From a slightly later period we have the *Glossa Psalmorum* of the Vatican Codex Palatinus Latinus 68, copied in the early or mid-eighth century either in Ireland or Northumbria by the Northumbrian scribe who signed himself *Edilberict filius Berictfridi*, with early Northumbrian and Old Irish glosses. Contemporary with this are the Latin glosses on the Pauline Epistles in Cambridge, Trinity College, B.10.5. This manuscript was probably written in an Anglo-Irish center in Northumbria (the Irish symptoms are prominent) in the first half of the eighth century. Irish (Celtic) influence may still be detected as late as the eleventh and twelfth centuries in one of two Durham manuscripts (A.IV.28; Gryson 2001: 31–32, 189–92) with Bede's commentary on Revelation, in which the biblical text has been replaced by one very similar to that of the Book of Armagh (Dublin, Trinity College MS 52; VL 61).

A central feature of Irish exegesis of the Psalms is its dependence on Antiochene tradition, with a non-Christological emphasis. Such exegesis, however, was not restricted to Ireland: it was also at home in Northumbria, as is clear from the case of Edilberict, and from there passed to the European continent where it influenced the so-called Psalter of Charlemagne (Paris, BnF, lat. 13159: see McNamara 2000: 143–64). The present text of the *Glossa Psalmorum* most probably came from Northumbria. The pseudo-Bedan *Argumenta,* though probably compiled in Ireland, reached Anglo-Saxon England as early as the ninth century and enjoyed considerable popularity. The clearest evidence of Antiochene influence in Anglo-Saxon England is in the interpretation of the Psalms by King Alfred of Wessex (871–99), in particular in his Anglo-Saxon paraphrase of the first fifty psalms (Ó Néill 2002: 73–77).

IRISH BIBLICAL MANUSCRIPTS

There is no complete Bible from Ireland predating the Norman period, although the ninth-century Book of Armagh contains the entire Latin New Testament, as well as some Old Irish texts relating to St. Patrick. From the thirteenth or fourteenth century comes one complete Irish Latin Bible (London, Lambeth Palace Library, MS 534; James 1932; 64–66; Hawkes 1958; McNamara 2020). This is a portable *Biblia*, which was probably intended for use, on occasions at least, as a lectionary for the Epistles and Gospels during the celebration of Mass. The text of the Bible is Vulgate, with a prologue to each book and division of the text into chapters. Revelation, which has numerous annotations, is preceded by the prologue of Gilbert which introduces the *Glossa*. Matthew is also heavily annotated. The Psalms display the text of the Gallican Psalter, which is given no title. Another full Bible (*Biblia*) in Lambeth Palace Library (MS Sion L40.2/L4, thirteenth century) is described in the Catalogue as "written in England or possibly Ireland" (Ker 1969: 267–68). On fol. 376v there are six quatrains of Irish, the first five recording the names of the books of the Bible (O'Sullivan 1964). However, eleven English saints are listed at the end of the manuscript in a thirteenth-century hand: the absence of Irish names seems to favor an English origin. In the *Biblia* itself, the books of the Bible are in an unusual order, and the quatrains in Irish, also in a thirteenth-century hand, seem to be intended as an effort to rectify the order of the books. In any event, they serve to indicate Irish involvement with the Bible in the thirteenth century.

The only surviving Old Testament text from Ireland (apart from the psalter) is two fragments of a glossed text of Ezekiel written in Irish minuscule about 800 (Zurich, Staatsarchiv, W3.19, XII). The glosses are from an epitome of Gregory's *Homilies on Ezekiel*. The fragments shed new light on Irish learning of the period: the gloss does not consist of separate comments on individual texts, as was the custom. Instead, it is continuous, of the sort that led ultimately to the *Glossa Ordinaria* (Gorman 2004; Holtz 1984). Evidence for the existence and use of Irish Old Testament biblical texts is seen in the Irish ecclesiastical law code, the *Collectio Canonum Hibernensis*. This has about a thousand exact or close biblical quotations, almost two-thirds of which are from the Old Testament. Among Irish vernacular texts, the *Saltair na Rann* ("The Psalter of Quatrains") follows the Old Testament from Genesis through the reigns of David and Solomon to the period of the prophets Elijah and Elisha. A related poem by the late tenth-century Airbertach mac Coisse on twenty-two kings of Israel draws on the Books of Chronicles (MacEoin 1966: 112). Scholars have noted that the early history of Ireland as recounted in sources going back at least to the seventh and eighth centuries fits squarely into a narrative framework derived from the central events of Genesis and Exodus. Early Irish pseudo-history as presented in the work *Lebar Gabála Érenn* ("Book of the Taking of Ireland") draws heavily on Genesis 1–11, whose opening words are cited both in the Old Latin form, *in principio fecit*, and the Vulgate *in principio creauit*.

The existence of biblical manuscripts written in Ireland in the eighth and ninth centuries is shown in the oldest catalogue of the library of the Abbey of St. Gall (St. Gall, Stiftsbibliothek 728). This was begun around the year 850, and on page four gives a list of thirty "books in Irish script" (*libri scottice scripti*). These appear to have been manuscripts written in Ireland and brought to this abbey in Switzerland. Nine are texts of the Bible: two from the Old Testament (Genesis, Ezekiel), one of the Gospel of John, two copies of the Acts of the Apostles, one of the Catholic Epistles, and three of Revelation (Duft 1954: 40–41). This library is still in the possession of ninth-century codices in Irish script, including a bilingual Greek-Latin copy of the gospels (discussed below).

Irish texts are also preserved in liturgical codices with biblical readings. The Stowe Missal, probably from the early ninth century, contains just two brief biblical texts, an epistle and gospel relating to the Eucharist (1 Corinthians 11:26–32 and John 6:51–57; Warner 1915). The Corpus Missal is one of three late Irish missals, the others being the Drummond and the Rosslyn Missals (Warren 1879). Most scholars have followed Gwynn in dating it in the decade 1120–30, suggesting that it preserves a form of liturgy used in Ireland in the early eleventh century (Gwynn 1992: 20, 1964: 68; O'Donoghue 2011: 89; Holland 2001: 301). The Corpus Missal has one hundred and twenty biblical texts in all, thirty-two from fifteen books of the Old Testament, with Proverbs, Wisdom, and Ecclesiasticus given under the designation *Libri Sapientiae* (Warren 1879: 14). For Palm Sunday the Corpus Missal has the lengthy Passion narrative from Matthew 26–27, with the typically Irish interpolation at Matthew 27:49, *alius autem accepit lanceam: pupungit latus eius et continuo exiit aqua et sanguis* ("but another took a spear: he pierced his side and straightaway came out water and blood"). We may presume that the other biblical texts of this Corpus Missal are also of the Irish tradition. The Rosslyn Missal also has these biblical lections: although only the opening and closing words are presented in the edition, the collation in an appendix suggests that it features Irish readings, although not the interpolation at Matthew 27:49 (Lawlor 1899: 97–110). The Drummond Missal (Forbes 1882) has very few Masses, but eighty-four biblical lections.[3]

PSALTER TEXTS AND MANUSCRIPTS

For the Latin Psalms in Ireland, ten texts or portions of texts are preserved of the Gallican Psalter found in the Vulgate (*Gallicanum*) alongside three full manuscripts and two sets of fragments of Jerome's version from the Hebrew (*Hebraicum*; see further chap. 5). Table 10.1 lists these witnesses and each is discussed here in detail (see further McNamara 2015a: 143–209, 2000: 19–164).

The *Cathach* is fragmentary, containing the text of Psalms 30:10–105:14 (LXX), and titles for each psalm (Lawlor 1916; see fig. 31.1). It has a good early Vulgate biblical text, identical to the Gallican text of the Double Psalter of St.-Ouen. A feature of the *Cathach* is the presence of the asterisk and obelus as critical signs. In the *Cathach* a number of the obeli mark words absent not from Jerome's *Hebraicum* but from the specifically Irish version of the *Hebraicum*. These suggest that the *Cathach* was copied from a double psalter of the Rouen type, without the glosses. The psalm titles in the *Cathach* (*Tituli Psalmorum*) have close affiliations with the *Glosa Psalmorum ex traditione Seniorum*, compiled in southern France about 600 CE (McNamara 2000: 302–52). One feature of these *tituli* is the formula *Legendus ad* ("to be read at"), followed by some text from a specified biblical book. These words seem to serve the same linking purpose as

---

[3] These are distributed as follows: Proverbs 1; Wisdom 5; Ecclesiasticus 19; 2 Maccabees 2; Matthew 15; Mark 3; Luke 9; John 10; Acts 5; Romans 1; 1 Corinthians 1; 2 Corinthians 3; Philippians 1; 2 Timothy 1; Hebrews 7; and Revelation 2.

Table 10.1 Irish Manuscripts of the Psalter before 1200

Gallicanum Text

The *Cathach* of St. Columba	6th–7th century	Dublin, Royal Irish Academy, s.n.
Wax Tablets of Springmount Bog	7th century	National Museum of Ireland
The Faddan More Fragments	ca. 800	National Museum of Ireland
Cotton Vitellius F. XII	ca. 920?	London, BL
Double Psalter of Saint-Ouen	10th century	Rouen, BM, 24
Sister Copy of Saint-Ouen Double Psalter (fragments)	10th century	Dublin, Trinity College, MS 1337
Southampton Psalter	Late 10th or early 11th century	Cambridge, St. John's College, C 9
Vat. Lat. 12910	11th century	Vatican City, BAV
Cotton Galba A.V	12th century	London, BL
The 'Psalter of Caimín'	11th–12th century	University College Dublin, Franciscan MS A.1
The Psalter of Cormac	1150–1250	London, BL, Add. MS 36929

Hebraicum Text

Double Psalter of St.-Ouen	10th century	Rouen, BM, 24
Sister Copy of St.-Ouen Double Psalter (fragments)	10th century	Dublin, Trinity College, MS 1337
Fragments of an Irish *Hebraicum* Psalter	ca. 1000	Paris, BnF, fr. 2452, ff. 75–84
The Edinburgh Psalter	ca. 1025	Edinburgh, University Library, MS 56
The Psalter of Ricemarch	post 1055	Dublin, Trinity College, MS 50

the later Irish formulae *haeret* ("it goes with") or *coniungitur ad* ("is connected with"), providing evidence of exegetical activity in the sixth-century Irish Church (McNamara 2022: 106–12, 2000: 315–24).

The Springmount Bog Tablets (Dublin, National Museum of Ireland, S.A. 1914.2; seventh century; Sheehy 2000; McNamara 2000: 31–34) were found in a bog in County Antrim, and were purchased by the National Museum in 1914. They consist of a book of six wooden "leaves" inlaid with wax on both sides of each (except for the two outer ones, which have no wax on the outside). The six tablets when found were bound together as a book by a thong of leather stitching. A certain amount of the writing is damaged. They contain Psalms 30–32 (LXX). The text is Gallican with some variant readings due to the influence of the Old Latin, and others apparently from careless transcription or from the fact that the copyist depended on his memory. The tablets probably came from an ancient monastery, where they may have been used in primary instruction, to initiate the pupil into the art of reading and writing. The scribe was probably the schoolmaster, and the purpose of the tablets can explain the inaccuracies of transcription.

The fragmentary psalter text of Faddan More was discovered in 2006 (Read 2011). The legible fragments represent the remnants of an entire psalter, which in Irish tradition was divided through illumination into three equal groups, known as the Three Fifties. Its biblical text is Vulgate (*Gallicanum*) but with an abundance of Old Latin readings, not ascribable to any single known recension.

Two manuscripts held in the British Library, Cotton Vitellius F. XII and Cotton Galba A.V., have been described (McNamara 2000: 151–56) but are yet to be fully collated. The decoration of the Codex Vitellius is similar in style to the cross of Muiredach at Monasterboice, probably erected for the abbot who died in 923 CE: an Irish text once at the end of this psalter wishes God's blessing on Muiredach, scholar and abbot (O'Sullivan 1966). Although these were once thought to be the same Muiredach (Henry 1960), Duncan (2005: 18, 44). maintained that this identification is untenable.

The Double Psalter of Saint-Ouen, of which fragments of a contemporary sister manuscript also survive, contains a full text of both the *Gallicanum* and the *Hebraicum*. Both the text and the system of obeli in the *Gallicanum* are identical to those in the *Cathach* (De Coninck 2012: xi), indicating the early existence of the specifically Irish recension of the *Hebraicum*, by the sixth century at the latest. Both biblical texts in this manuscript have been fully collated (Abbey of St. Jerome 1953; De Sainte-Marie 1954; see also McNamara 2015a: 176–82). Duncan (2005) offers a palaeographical and codicological comparison of this manuscript with four other psalters, three contemporary and one earlier. A detailed introduction to the Double Psalter of Saint-Ouen is found in De Coninck (2012), with special attention to the glosses on Psalm 1:1–16:11a, Psalm 39, and other glosses of a historical nature.

The Southampton Psalter has been critically edited by Ó Néill (2002), who regards it as of Hiberno-Latin origin. The manuscript was copied in the late tenth or early eleventh century. It contains a later form of the *Gallicanum*: the greatest proportion of its variants agrees with the eleventh-century Irish text in Vatican City, BAV, Vat. lat. 12910. The Southampton Psalter is heavily glossed throughout, with two distinct strata of glosses: the first depends overwhelmingly on the *Glosa Psalmorum ex traditione seniorum* (see above); the second reflects a historically oriented type of exegesis very close to that of the manuscript Vatican City, BAV, Palatinus Lat. 68. These glosses are not the creation of the scribe but were entered from an earlier text. The editor regards the Irish-language glosses as Old Irish, dating them, and with them the body of Latin glosses, to the mid-ninth century.

The so-called Psalter of Caimín is a fragment of Psalm 118 (LXX), apparently from a large glossed psalter written at Clonmacnoise in the eleventh or twelfth century (McNamara 2015a: 182–98). The glosses are drawn from a Latin epitome of Julian of Eclanum's translation of the *Commentary on the Psalms* by Theodore of Mopsuestia and from the eighth-century Irish commentary in Vatican, BAV, Palatinus lat. 68 (see above), or an earlier form of it. The *Hebraicum* text is entered in an abbreviated form on the upper margins above the *Gallicanum* in these fragments.

The Psalter of Cormac was written by a scribe who signed himself *Cormacus* (Cormac) in the colophon. Both script and illumination are Irish, and the manuscript was probably copied in Ireland (on the dating see James 1907: 259–60; McNamara 2015a: 165–76; Howlett 1995). The text is the *Gallicanum*, given in the Three Fifties, followed by the Canticles and Psalm 151, without any indication that the latter is apocryphal (see chap. 7). The precise affiliation of the biblical text remains to be determined, one of many questions relating to this, probably the latest Irish Psalter, which also seems to have Cistercian connections.

The Paris fragments of a psalter were identified in 1971 as portions of the *Hebraicum* in Irish script. In the catalogue of Avril and Stirnemann (1987: 10), it is dated to the ninth century and assigned a Welsh origin. Duncan (2005: 37–40), however, places the manuscript in a later tenth-century Gaelic context; the present writer collated it in 2009 and, unaware of Duncan's study, assigned it a post-900 date by reason of the frequency of the *for*-sign (f with a stroke above it; McNamara 2015a: 157–65, 199–209). The fragments carry the specifically Irish recension of the *Hebraicum,* and, despite their late date, probably an earlier textual form of the recension than those already known.

The Edinburgh Psalter (Edinburgh, University Library, MS 56; about 1025; see Finlayson 1962; McNamara 2000: 74–76) is a pocket *Hebraicum* psalter written in Irish minuscule and with Irish decoration. It contains ten original quires mostly of fourteen leaves, together with a quire of two leaves supplied in the fifteenth or sixteenth century. Fol. 50r has English eleventh-century decoration of the "Winchester" style. In Irish fashion the psalms are divided into the Three Fifties, each beginning with a special page of decoration. A prayer has been supplied in a gothic hand at the end of the first Fifty (fol. 49). The text of the lost beginning (Psalm 1:1–2) and end (Psalms 148:14–150:6) were supplied in the fifteenth or sixteenth century from a *Hebraicum* text of a different tradition. The text of Psalms 101:1, 3 and 120:2–128:5 is also lost but has not been supplied. The work seems to have been unbound in separate quires for a considerable time. Where the text of the *Hebraicum* coincides with that of the *Gallicanum* words are often represented only by initials or simply omitted.

The Psalter of Ricemarch (Dublin, Trinity College, MS 50; after 1055; see Lawlor 1914; De Sainte-Marie 1954: xli; McNamara 2000: 76–77; Lawlor 1914) was copied and decorated in Wales by Ricemarch and his brother John, sons of Sulien. Sulien, a Welshman, came to Ireland in 1045 CE to study and be trained as a scribe and illuminator, remaining there about ten years before returning and imparting his newly acquired knowledge to his two sons, among others. The psalter, in Irish fashion, is divided into the Three Fifties, but is without canticles or collects, in keeping with its *Hebraicum* text. It belongs to the later Irish *Hebraicum* family, invariably following the text form found in K (Karlsruhe, BLB, Cod. Aug. perg. 38). It is uncertain whether Sulien's sons copied this text from an original their father brought with him from Ireland or from a manuscript being used in Wales.

GOSPEL BOOKS

From 1850 onward, a group of five related manuscripts was identified as having a Celtic/ Irish text of the Latin gospels (see Westcott 1863). Comprising the Book of Armagh, the Egerton Gospels, the Lichfield Gospels, the Book of Kells, and the Rushworth Gospels, this group was known as DELQR from the sigla assigned to these manuscripts in the Oxford Vulgate (Wordsworth and White, 1889–98). Intense study has been devoted to the Hiberno-Latin gospel tradition and the characteristics of its text (see McNamara 1990 and 2015a: 289–306; Houghton 2016: 72–77).

There are twenty-eight surviving gospel manuscripts or fragments which were written in Ireland or by Irish scribes abroad, together with some eleven manuscripts written abroad but related to Irish tradition (McNamara 2015b: 92–98). These documents date from the seventh to the twelfth centuries. The oldest are Codex Usserianus (Dublin, Trinity College, MS 55; VL 14) and the Durham fragments of Matthew and Mark (VL 19A; see above), which both have an Old Latin text, and the Book of Durrow (Dublin, Trinity College, MS 57), which is a true Vulgate text. The remainder consists of a mixture of Vulgate and Old Latin, made up in various ways: some simply display occasional Old Latin readings in Vulgate texts; others have a strong concentration of Old Latin readings in certain sections; yet others feature unadulterated blocks of Old Latin which pass imperceptibly into a Vulgate text (see chap. 1). The nature and origin of the Irish mixed texts remain a matter of interest. In several manuscripts, it appears that the text arose from the correction of an Old Latin version toward the Vulgate, while others may be essentially Vulgate texts with additions distinctive of Irish tradition, most notably the addition at Matthew 27:49 (mentioned above) and other Irish interpolations (Houghton 2016: 159–60, 166–67). A recent study of Matthew in the "Garland of Howth" (Dublin, Trinity College, MS 56; VL 28) reveals the depth of Old Latin forms in this mixed-text manuscript: some very ancient forms are not attested in surviving Old Latin texts but correspond to known Greek readings (Houghton 2019). The systematic examination of Irish Latin gospel texts is now ongoing, with the creation of modern electronic transcriptions preceding a full collation.[4]

OTHER NEW TESTAMENT BOOKS

After the psalter, the second principal area of study in the early Irish schools was the Pauline Epistles. Here again, Irish tradition is linked with that of Northumbria, as seen in the key text: a set of Latin glosses on the Pauline Epistles in Cambridge, Trinity College, B. 10. 5, which is linked to two other glossed texts of Paul. The Cambridge gloss

---

[4] See McNamara 2015a and the website at <http://www.insulargospels.net/>.

was most probably copied in an Anglo-Irish center in Northumbria (the Irish symptoms are prominent) in the first half of the eighth century. Of a total of approximately 1,500 items, attributed or anonymous, around 600 come from Pelagius (Bishop 1964: 70; De Paor 2016). The contemporary gloss in the text, earlier than any comparable material, and to a large extent *sui generis*, has many parallels with material of apparently Irish provenance, such as St. Gall 73, Sedulius Scottus, and the Latin and Latin-Irish glosses in Würzburg M. p. th. f. 12 (Bishop 1964: 73). Although serious objections have been raised in more recent years about the Irish origin of St. Gall 73, one view favoring origin in Southern France about 600 CE, it is, however, cited in an Old Irish text (see McNamara 2015a: 43–46).

The Würzburg gloss was copied in Ireland in the eighth century. It has a Latin text of the Pauline Epistles, including Hebrews, and is heavily glossed, both interlinearly and in the margins as far as Hebrews 7:9. The manuscript was intended as a school text. The glosses are excerpts from Origen (in the translation of Rufinus), "Hilary" (i.e. Ambrosiaster), Jerome, Augustine, Cassiodorus, Gregory the Great, Isidore, and above all else Pelagius, from whose commentary alone 1311 glosses are taken (Kenney 1966: 635–36; Frede and Stanjek 1996–97). De Paor (2016: v) believes that the Würzburg gloss is dependent on the Cambridge manuscript, while a Freising manuscript (Munich, BSB, Clm 6235, ff. 1–31) used the Würzburg gloss as a source.

Two Irish Latin commentaries on the Catholic Epistles survive from the seventh century: one, anonymous, is from the middle of the century; the other, under the name of "Hilarius," is slightly later (McNally 1973). These are the earliest-known commentaries on the Catholic Epistles, predating Bede, who apparently used and commented on the "Hilarius" text (Picard 2005). As noted above, three Irish manuscripts of Revelation are listed in the ninth-century St. Gall Library catalogue. This may be taken as an indication of early Irish readership of this book, and possibly of glosses or commentaries on it. There is a detailed commentary on the work in the (probably Irish) "Reference Bible," *De enigmatibus*. This is closely related to another found in Cambridge, University Library, Dd.X.16 and in a compilation of Theodulf of Orleans (Paris, BnF, lat. 15679). Gryson believes that all these depend on a Hiberno-Latin (presumably Irish) commentary from the first half of the eighth century (Gryson 2011: 64–68).

IRISH SCRIBES AND SCHOLARS ON THE EUROPEAN CONTINENT

There were numerous Irish monks on the European continent in the eighth and ninth centuries. Their Irish heritage is often seen in the epithet *Scottus*, while in one case this was combined with the name *Eriugena* ("born in Ireland"). The Irish were viewed by their contemporaries in two different ways, one positive (*Iromanie*) and one negative (*Irophobie*). The positive view is seen in the writings of the ninth-century scholar

Sedulius Scottus, born and educated in Ireland but who became a leading light on the continent. He compared his compatriots to the biblical Magi: coming out of the West instead of the East, they brought the gift of wisdom in place of the biblical gold, frank-incense, and myrrh (Contreni 1986: 86). Bischoff (1954) identified a corpus of anony-mous biblical exegetical texts from the years 650 to 800 which he regards as of Irish origin or Irish related. While some of those seem clearly of Irish origin (for instance, the commentaries on the Psalms and probably those on Revelation) the corpus as a whole still requires further exploration.

By the mid-ninth century a new approach to biblical exegesis was coming to the fore, in part aided by the work of Irish grammarians (see chap. 12). One was Clemens Scottus at the court of Charlemagne, while shortly afterward another Irish grammarian, Muirethach, was either a teacher or colleague of the early Carolingian exegete Haimo of Auxerre, and seems to have influenced his exegesis, particularly of the Pauline Epistles. The two most famous Irish scholars were Sedulius Scottus and John Scottus Eriugena. The latter was renowned for his command of Greek and his commentary on the Gospel according to John, also writing glosses on the Bible in Latin and in Old Irish (Contreni and Ó Néill 1997; see also chap. 12). The former wrote lengthy commentaries on Matthew and the Pauline Epistles and was also well-versed in Greek, having copied a manuscript of the Greek psalter which still survives (Paris, Bibliothèque de l'Arsenal 8407): in the colophon after Psalm 151 he writes in Greek capitals: ΣΗΔΥΛΙΟΣ ΣΚΟΤΤΟΣ ΕΓΩ ΕΓΡΑΨΑ ("I, Sedulius Scottus, wrote this"; McNamara 2000: 62–64). A very learned letter is extant in Latin on the translation of the psalter from Greek, written by a *Scottus* residing in the territory of Milan, which may be by Sedulius Scottus or one of his dis-ciples (McNamara 2000: 64–66). The three interlinear bilingual manuscripts from the second half of the ninth century also attest to Irish scholarship on the Greek Bible (see McNamara 2000: 58–61; chap. 11).

Bibliography

Abbey of St. Jerome. 1953. *Biblia Sacra iuxta Latinam Vulgatam Versionem: Liber Psalmorum ex recensione Sancti Hieronymi*. Rome: Vatican Polyglot Press.

Avril, François, and Patricia Danz Stirnemann. 1987. *Manuscrits enluminés d'origine insulaire, VIIᵉ–XXᵉ siècle*. Paris: Bibliothèque Nationale.

Bischoff, Bernhard 1954. "Wendepunkte in der Geschichte der lateinischen Exegese im Frühmittelalter." *Sacris Erudiri* 6: 189–281.

Bishop, T. A. M. 1964. "Pelagius in Trinity B. 10. 5." *Transactions of the Cambridge Bibliographical Society* 4, no. 1: 70–76.

Contreni, John J. 1986. "The Irish Contribution to the European Classroom." In *Proceedings of the Seventh International Congress of Celtic Studies*, edited by D. Ellis Evans, John G. Griffiths, and E. M. Jope, 79–90. Oxford: D. E. Evans.

Contreni, John J., and Pádraig P. Ó Néill, eds. 1997. *Glossae Divinae Historiae. The Biblical Glosses of John Scottus Eriugena*. Florence: SISMEL, Galluzzo.

De Coninck, Luc. 2012. *Expositiones Psalmorum duae sicut in codice Rothomagensi 24 asservantur*. CCCM 256. Turnhout: Brepols.

De Paor, John Liam. 2016. *The Earliest Irish Glosses on the Pauline Epistles. An Edition of the Text and Glosses of Vulgate Manuscript E, as found in Cambridge B.10.5*. AGLB 41. Freiburg: Herder 2016.

De Sainte-Marie, Henri 1954. *Sancti Hieronymi Psalterium iuxta Hebraeos*. CBL 11. Vatican: Libreria Vaticana.

Duft, Johannes, and Peter Meyer, eds. 1954. *The Irish Miniatures in the Abbey Library of St. Gall*. Berne: Olten.

Duncan, Elizabeth. 2005. "Contextualising 'The Rouen Psalter': Palaeography, Codicology, and Form." *Journal of Celtic Studies* 5: 17–60.

Edwards, Thomas Charles. 1983. "Bede, the Irish and the Britons." *Celtica* 15: 42–52.

Finlayson, C. P. 1962. *Celtic Psalter: Edinburgh University Library ms. 56*. Umbrae Codicum Occidentalium 7. Amsterdam: North Holland.

Forbes, G. H., ed. 1882. *Missale Drummondiense: The Ancient Irish Missal, in the Possession of the Baroness Willloughby de Eresby, Drummond Castle, Perthshire*. Burntisland: Pitsligo.

Frede, H. J., and H. Stanjek, eds, 1996–1997. *Sedulii Scotti Collectaneum in Apostolum. I. In Epistolam ad Romanos II. In Epistolas ad Corinthios usque ad Hebraeos*. AGLB 31–32. Freiburg: Herder.

Gorman, Michael M. 2004. "*La plus ancienne édition commentée*. The Ezechiel Fragment in Irish Minuscule, now in Zurich (CLA 7.1008)." *Revue bénédictine* 114: 276–88.

Gross-Diaz, Theresa. 1996. *The Psalms Commentary of Gilbert of Poitiers: From Lectio Divina to Lecture Room*. Leiden: Brill.

Gryson, Roger, ed. 2001. *Bedae Presbyteri Expositio Apocalypseos*. CCSL 121A. Turnhout: Brepols.

Gryson, Roger, ed. 2011. *Tyconii Afri Expositio Apocalypseos. Accedunt eiusdem expositionis a quodam retractatae fragmenta Taurinensia*. CCSL 107A. Turnhout: Brepols.

Gwynn, Aubrey. 1992. *The Irish Church in the Eleventh and Twelfth Centuries*. Edited by Gerard O'Brien. Dublin: Four Courts.

Gwynn, Aubrey. 1964. "The Irish Missal of Corpus Christi College Oxford." In *Studies in Church History 1*, edited by C. W. Dugmore and Charles Duggan, 47–68. London: Thomas Nelson.

Hawkes, William. 1958. "The Liturgy in Dublin, 1200–1500: Manuscript Sources." *Repertorium Novum. Dublin Diocesan Historical Record* 2, no. 1: 33–67.

Henry, Françoise. 1960. "Remarks on the Decoration of Three Irish Psalters." *Proceedings of the Royal Irish Academy* 61C: 23–40.

Holland, Martin. 2001. "The Dating of the Corpus Christi Missal." *Peritia* 15: 280–301.

Holtz, Louis. 1984. "Les manuscrits latins glosés et à commentaire de l'antiquité à l'époque Carolingienne." In *Il libro e il testo*, edited by C. Questa and R. Raffaeli, 139–67. Urbino: Università degli studi di Urbino.

Houghton, H. A. G. 2016. *The Latin New Testament. A Guide to Its Early History, Texts, and Manuscripts*. Oxford: Oxford University Press.

Houghton, H. A. G. 2019. "The Garland of Howth (Vetus Latina 28): A Neglected Old Latin Witness in Matthew." in *The Future of New Testament Textual Scholarship. From H.C. Hoskier to Editio Critica Maior and Beyond*, edited by Garrick V. Allen, 247–63. WUNT I.417. Tübingen: Mohr Siebeck.

Houghton, H. A. G. 2020. "The Latin Text of John in the Saint Gall Bilingual Gospels (Codex Sangallensis 48)." In *At One Remove: The Text of the New Testament in Early Translations and Quotations*, edited by H. A. G. Houghton and Peter Montoro, 149–71. T&S 3.24. Piscataway: Gorgias.

Howlett, David. 1995. "The Polyphonic Colophon to Cormac's Psalter." *Peritia* 9: 81–91.

Hughes, Kathleen, 1971. "Evidence for Contacts between the Churches of the Irish and the English from the Synod of Whitby to the Viking Ages." In *England before the Conquest: Studies in Primary Sources Presented to Dorothy Whitelock*, edited by Peter Clemoes and Kathleen Hughes, 49–67. Cambridge: Cambridge University Press.

James, M. R. 1907. *Catalogue of Additions to the Manuscripts in the British Museum in the Years MDCCCC–MDCCCCV*. London: British Museum.

James, M. R. 1932. *A Descriptive Catalogue of Manuscripts in the Library of Lambeth Palace; the Mediaeval Manuscripts*. Cambridge: Cambridge University Press.

Kenney, James F. 1966. *The Sources for the Early History of Ireland: An Introduction and Guide. Volume 1: Ecclesiastical*. New York: Octagon.

Ker, N. R. 1969. *Medieval Manuscripts in British Libraries*, vol. I. London: Oxford University Press.

Lawlor, H. J., ed. 1899. *The Rosslyn Missal. An Irish Manuscript in the Advocates' Library Edinburgh*. London: Henry Bradshaw Society.

Lawlor, H. J., ed. 1914. *The Psalter and Martyrology of Ricemarch*. London: Henry Bradshaw Society.

Lawlor, H. J. 1916. "The Cathach of St. Columba." *Proceedings of the Royal Irish Academy* 33 C: 241–443.

Lowe, Elias Avery, ed. 1972. *Codices Latini Antiquiores. 2. Great Britain and Ireland*. 2nd ed. Oxford: Clarendon Press.

Macalister, R. A. Stewart. 1938. *Lebor Gabála Érenn. The Book of the Taking of Ireland. Part I*. Dublin: Irish Texts Society.

MacEoin, Gearóid, ed. 1966. "A Poem by Airbertach Mac Cosse." *Ériu* 20: 112–39.

McCann, Sarah. 2015. "*Plures de Scottorum regione*: Bede, Ireland, and the Irish." *Eolas. The Journal of the American Society of Irish Medieval Studies* 8: 20–38.

McNally, Robert E. 1973. *Scriptores Hiberniae Minores*. Pars I. CCSL 108B. Turnhout: Brepols.

McNamara, Martin. 1990. *Studies on the Text of Early Irish Latin Gospels (A.D. 600–1200)*. Steenbrugge-Dordrecht: Kluwer.

McNamara, Martin. 2000. *The Psalms in the Early Irish Church*. Sheffield: Sheffield Academic.

McNamara, Martin. 2015a. *The Bible and the Apocrypha in the Early Irish Church A.D. 600–1200. Collected Essays*. Instrumenta Patristica et Mediaevalia 66. Turnhout: Brepols.

McNamara, Martin. 2015b. "Irish Gospel Texts Publication Project." *Proceedings of the Irish Biblical Association* 38: 85–98.

McNamara, Martin. 2020. "13th-14th-Century Entire Latin Bible: Lambeth Palace Library MS 534. A Preliminary Study." *Proceedings of the Irish Biblical Association* 43.

McNamara, Martin (with the assistance of Michael T. Martin). 2022. *The Bible in the Early Irish Church (A.D. 550 to 850)*. Commentaria 13. Leiden: Brill.

O'Donoghue, Neil Xavier. 2011. *The Eucharist in Pre-Norman Ireland*. Notre Dame: University of Notre Dame.

Ó Néill, Pádraig. 2002. "Irish Transmission of Late Antique Learning: the Case of Theodore of Mopsuestia's Commentary on the Psalms." In *Ireland and Europe in the Early Middle Ages: Texts and Transmission*, edited by Proinséas Ní Chatháin and Michael Richter, 68–77. Dublin: Four Courts.

Ó Néill, Pádraig, ed. 2012. *Psalterium Suthantoniense*. CCCM 240. Turnhout: Brepols.

Orschel, Vera. 2001. "Mag nEó na Sacsan: An English Colony in Ireland in the Seventh and Eighth Centuries." *Peritia* 15: 81–107.

O'Sullivan, Anne. 1964. "Leabhair an Bhíobla. Mnemonic Verses on the Canonical Order of the Books of the Bible." *An Sagart* 7.3–4: 34–35.

O'Sullivan, Anne 1966. "The Colophon of the Cotton Psalter (Vitellius F. XI)." *Journal of the Royal Society of Antiquaries of Ireland* 96: 179–180.

Picard, Jean-Michel 2005. "Bède et ses sources irlandaises." In *Bède le Vénérable: entre tradition et posterité*, edited by Stephane Lebecq, Michel Perrin, and Olivier Szerwiniack, 43–62. Villeneuve d'Ascq: Centre de Recherche sur l'Histoire de l'Europe du Nord-Ouest.

Read, Anthony 2011. *The Faddan More Psalter. Discovery, Conservation and Investigation*. Dublin: National Museum of Ireland.

Sheehy, Maurice 2000. "Wax Tablets from Springmount Bog." In *The Psalms in the Early Irish Church*, edited by Martin McNamara, 116–19. Sheffield: Sheffield Academic.

Stancliffe, Clare 2017. "The Irish Tradition in Northumbria after the Synod of Whitby." In *The Lindisfarne Gospels: New Perspectives*, edited by Richard Gameson, 19–42. Leiden: Brill.

Warner, George F. (1915). *The Stowe Missal*. London: Henry Bradshaw Society. First published 1906. Repr, in 1 vol., 1989.

Warren, Frederick Edward. 1879. *The Manuscript Irish Missal belonging to the President and Fellows of Corpus Christi College, Oxford*. London: Henry Bradshaw Society.

Westcott, B. F. 1863. "Vulgate." In *Dictionary of the Bible: Comprising Its Antiquities, Biography, and Natural History*, edited by William Smith ed., 1688–1718. 3 vols. London: John Murray.

Wordsworth, John, and Henry Julian White, eds. 1889–98. *Nouum Testamentum Domini nostri Iesu Christi latine secundum editionem sancti Hieronymi. I. Quattuor Euangelia*. Oxford: Clarendon Press.

CHAPTER 11

LATIN IN MULTILINGUAL BIBLICAL MANUSCRIPTS

H. A. G. HOUGHTON

THE PURPOSE AND TYPOLOGY OF BILINGUAL MANUSCRIPTS

MANUSCRIPTS of the Bible that include text in more than one language bear witness to a specific set of circumstances at the time of their production or later use. Some bilingual manuscripts were originally conceived as such, with a layout to facilitate comparison between the two languages. Other manuscripts became multilingual at a later stage, when users added material to assist with the demands of another linguistic context. Multilingual manuscripts normally transmit a writing seen as particularly authoritative, and thus worthy of study in an original or more prestigious language with which users are not familiar: as such, it is not surprising that many such manuscripts surviving from Late Antiquity and the early Medieval period contain biblical text. Numerous combinations of languages are found, including an extensive tradition of early Greek–Coptic bilinguals as well as fragments of Origen's scholarly edition of the Old Testament in six parallel columns (the Hexapla), but the present survey is confined to biblical manuscripts which include a text in Latin.[1]

Bilingual manuscripts are found in several formats. In the oldest surviving biblical examples, the two languages are written on facing pages, with the source or less familiar language normally on the left-hand page (*verso*) and the translation on the right (*recto*). An effort is normally made to divide the text into phrases

---

[1] For more on multilingual printed Bibles, such as Erasmus's New Testament or the Complutensian Polyglot, see chap. 18; on vernacular bilinguals, chap. 21.

or sense-lines, in order to permit easy comparison between the two versions, although in some cases the parallelism may only be approximate. When a division is made into shorter sense-units, or later manuscripts are written in more compressed scripts, the different languages may be written in two columns on the same page. Most of these continue to arrange the texts in the same way as on facing pages, but in some cases, one language may occupy the two inner columns either side of the central gutter and the other may be written on the outer column of each page. Interlinear bilingual manuscripts may be seen as a development of the technique of glossing, with the translation written above the source text. Their format is less practical than columnar bilinguals, in which there is broad correspondence between the sense-units: with an interlinear text, a choice has to be made between disrupting the syntax of one language—which may result in nonsense—or losing the one-to-one word mapping between the two versions.

It is not always simple to identify or classify manuscripts as bilingual. The addition of occasional glosses in another language could be deemed to result in a bilingual document, but these are often sparsely distributed and are not the same as a continuous translation.[2] Some writings may switch between languages (e.g., quotations in their original form, or the use of technical terms) without two versions of the same text being present. Manuscripts that contain a text in one language and a translation of it elsewhere do not fulfil the same purpose as those in which the two versions can be viewed simultaneously.[3] Certain single-language documents may have originated as bilinguals, through the separate copying of the translation into a new document. There are also instances in which one language may be written in the script of another: in contrast to the phonetic transliteration of Greek in many psalters, the Book of Armagh (VL 61) includes the text of the Lord's Prayer and occasional other Latin words in Greek characters (Houghton 2016: 76). None of the instances described in this paragraph will be treated as bilingual for the purpose of the present chapter.

The relationship between the texts of the different languages in a bilingual manuscript is a perennial question, involving the analysis of scribal competence, editorial activity, and textual transmission. Was one form adjusted to match the other, and if so, did such change happen only in one direction? If a translation was produced as part of the creation of the document, an exact match between the two languages would be expected, although the translator's familiarity with other versions and alternative readings can never be entirely ruled out. Many bilingual manuscripts were created

---

[2] Sometimes alternative readings are added in the same language as the main text, which may be explanations, corrections, or text-critical observations (e.g., the Echternach Gospels). For more on glosses in early Latin manuscripts, see chap. 8 and chap. 10 and, on glossing technique and terminology, Moran and Whitman 2022.

[3] One example of this is the seventeenth-century Milan, Ambrosiana, D. 25. inf, where extracts from a Greek catena on Luke are followed by an apparently autograph Latin translation.

by bringing together two texts of separate origin: occasional differences are therefore likely between the source of the translation and the original-language text in the manuscript. Depending on their linguistic ability, a copyist or editor could have tried to bring the texts into a closer relation during the production of the codex. Alterations might have been introduced by later readers, which were incorporated into subsequent copies (as in the descendants of Codex Claromontanus described below): some of these may have been based on the other text in the manuscript; others could derive from external sources, particularly if the document was only being used for one of its languages. Users of bilingual codices were rarely equally proficient in both languages. Although it might be expected that priority would be given to the original language, and the translation adjusted on this basis, it is not beyond the bounds of possibility that a reader with sufficient expertise might try to improve the text of the original language on the basis of the translation.[4] The direction of influence could also have depended on the relative prestige of the versions: in a context where a Latin text was taken as standard, it may have been acceptable to adjust a reading in the Greek (Lorenz 2020: 181–83). In studying bilingual documents, therefore, careful attention should be paid to both texts, and modern assumptions about priority and the direction of influence may need to be set aside.

Several lists of bilingual manuscripts (including biblical codices) are available, following different criteria (Parker 1992: 52–65; Metzger 1984; Radiciotti 1998; Dickey 2015). Drawing on these and other sources, table 11.1 presents thirty-two bilingual Latin New Testament manuscripts, whereas table 11.2 contains forty-seven Latin bilingual psalters (which normally also include the biblical Odes, or Canticles).[5] The entries are in roughly chronological order; the language given first is that of the far left-hand column or the main line of text, and a dagger indicates that the Greek is transliterated.

The *Liber Commonei* (VL 111) in table 11.2 is an exception, included here because of its liturgical purpose. It contains two series of lections, the first from the Minor Prophets (with the majuscule Greek text in the left column) and the second the Old Testament readings for the Easter Vigil in a form preceding the reforms of Gregory the Great (with a transliterated Greek text in the right column). This appears to be the only surviving Latin bilingual manuscript featuring Old Testament books outside the Psalms.[6]

---

[4] A famous example of the reconstruction of a source text in the history of the New Testament is Erasmus's retranslation from Latin of passages of Revelation which were missing from the catena manuscript he used.

[5] Although often included in lists of bilinguals, Dickey 2019 shows that the Pauline glossary in Papyrus 99 is based on a commentary rather than a New Testament manuscript. Parker (1992: 59) notes that the bilingual element in Lectionary 925 is restricted to a few transliterated Greek headings. On the Odes, see chap. 7.

[6] Paris, BnF, gr. 18 is a thirteenth-century copy of parts of the Old Testament with extensive Latin glosses added later.

Table 11.1 Latin Multilingual New Testament Manuscripts

Manuscript	Sigla[a]	Languages and format	Date (century)	Origin	Contents
Codex Bezae: Cambridge, UL, Nn.II.41	GA 05, D, VL 5	Greek–Latin (facing pages)	V	Berytus?	Gospels, Acts, 3 John
Codex Claromontanus: Paris, BnF, grec 107	GA 06, VL 75	Greek–Latin (facing pages)	V	South Italy/ Sardinia?	Pauline Epistles
Florence, BML, PSI XIII 1306	GA 0230, VL 85	Greek–Latin (facing pages)	V–VI	Italy? Found in Antinoopolis	Ephesians (frag.)
Codex Carolinus: Wolfenbüttel, HAB, Weiss. 64	VL 79, gue, w	Gothic–Latin (two columns)	VI in.	North Italy	Romans (frag., palimp.)
Fragmentum Gissense: Giessen UB, 651/20	VL 36	Gothic–Latin (facing pages)	VI	Italy; found in Egypt	Luke (frag., destroyed)
Laudian Acts: Oxford, Bodleian, MS Laud gr. 35	GA 08, E, VL 50	Latin–Greek (two columns)	VI–VII	Sardinia	Acts
Lindisfarne Gospels: London, BL, Cotton Nero D.IV	Y	Latin–Old English (interlinear)	VIII in.	Northumbria	Gospels
Mondsee Fragments: Vienna, ÖNB, Cod. 3093*		Latin–Old High German (facing pages)	VIII–IX	Mondsee	Matthew (frag.)
Rushworth/MacRegol Gospels: Oxford, Bodleian, MS Auct. D.2.19	R	Latin–Old English (interlinear)	IX in.	Ireland/ Northumbria	Gospels
Codex Sangallensis (Tatian): St Gall, Stiftsbibliothek, Cod. Sang. 56		Latin–Old High German (two columns)	ca. 830	Fulda	Gospel harmony
Codex Augiensis: Cambridge, Trinity College, B.17.1	GA 010, F, VL 78	Latin–Greek (two columns; Latin outer)	IX	Reichenau	Pauline Epistles
Codex Sangallensis (gospels): St. Gall, Stiftsbibliothek, Cod. Sang. 48	GA 037, Δ, VL 27	Greek–Latin (interlinear)	IX med.	Bobbio? St. Gall?	Gospels
Codex Boernerianus: Dresden, Sächsische Landesbibliothek, A.145b	GA 012, G, VL 77	Greek–Latin (interlinear)	IX med.	Bobbio? St. Gall?	Pauline Epistles
Codex Sangermanensis: St. Petersburg, NLR, F.v.XX	GA 0319, D[abs1], VL 76	Greek–Latin (two columns)	IX/X	Corbie? Fulda?	Pauline Epistles
Sigüenza, Chapter Library, 150		Latin–Arabic	ca. 900	Spain?	Galatians (frag.)

(continued)

Table 11.1 Continued

Manuscript	Sigla[a]	Languages and format	Date (century)	Origin	Contents
Codex Waldeccensis: Mengeringhausen and Marburg	GA 0320, D[abs2], VL 83	Greek–Latin (facing pages)	X ex.	Fulda	Pauline Epistles (frag., lost)
St. Gall, Stiftsbibliothek, Cod. Sang. 18 etc.	GA 0130	Latin–Greek (two columns: Latin outer?)	ca. 1000	St. Gall	Mark, Luke (frag., palimp.)
Venice, BNM, Gr. Z. 11	GA 460	Greek–Latin–Arabic (three columns)	XII	Sicily	Acts and Epistles
Florence, BML, Conv. Soppr. 150	GA 620	Greek–Latin (two columns)	XII		Epistles and Revelation
Paris, BnF, gr. 54	GA 16	Greek–Latin (two columns)	XIII 2/2	Constantinople?	Gospels
Vatican, BAV, Barberini gr. 541	GA 165	Greek–Latin (two columns)	1291/2	Rhegina/ Calabria	Gospels
Vatican, BAV, Vat. gr. 1136	GA 866b + 1918	Latin–Greek (two columns)	XIII/XIV		Paul, Revelation (frag.)
Vatican, BAV, Ottob. gr. 258	GA 628	Latin–Greek (two columns; Latin outer)	XIV		Acts, Epistles, Revelation
Vatican, BAV, Ottob. gr. 298	GA 629	Latin–Greek (two columns)	XIV		Acts and Epistles
Vatican, BAV, Urb. gr. 4	GA 1269	Greek–Latin (interlinear)	XIV ex.		Gospels
Oxford, Bodleian, Lyell 95	GA 2883, g[abs]	Greek–Latin (two columns)	XV 1/2	Milan	Matthew
Leiden, Univ., B.P. Gr. 74	GA 79	Latin–Greek (two columns)	XV		Gospels
Vatican, BAV, Vat. gr. 359	GA 130	Latin–Greek (two columns)	XV		Gospels
London, BL, Add. 24114	GA 694	Greek–Latin (two columns)	XV		Gospels
Paris, BnF, gr. 55	GA 17	Greek–Latin (two columns)	XV 2/2		Gospels
Paris, BnF, syr. 17 (Zotenberg 44)		Syriac–Latin	1521	Rome	Gospels[b]
Vatican, BAV, Reg. gr. 70	GA L1289	Greek–Latin–Greek† (three columns)	1544		Lectionary (frag.)

[a] GA refers to Gregory-Aland; VL to the Vetus Latina numbering; alphabetical sigla tend to be those of earlier editions.

[b] This may be a copy of a printed book: the first few pages of each gospel are written in two columns with the Latin Vulgate alongside the Syriac Peshitta (Hermann Zotenberg, *Manuscrits orientaux. Catalogues des manuscrits syriaques et sabéens de la Bibliotheèque nationale* [Paris: Imprimerie nationale, 1874], 15).

Table 11.2 Latin Bilingual Psalter Manuscripts to the Thirteenth Century

Manuscript	Sigla	Languages and format	Date (century)	Origin
Verona Psalter: Verona, Bib. cap., 1	GA L1347, VL 300, Rahlfs R	Greek†–Latin (facing pages)	VI–VII	North Italy
Coislin Psalter: Paris, BnF, Coislin. 186	VL 333, Rahlfs 188	Latin–Greek (facing pages)	VII	Rome?
Vespasian Psalter: London, BL, Cotton Vespasian A.I	VL 372	Latin–Old English (interlinear)	VIII	Canterbury
Lincoln Psalter: New York, Pierpont Morgan Library, M. 776	VL 459	Latin–Old English (interlinear)	VIII 2/2	England
Liber Commonei: Oxford, Bodleian, Auct. F.4.32	VL 111	Greek–Latin and Latin–Greek† (two columns)	ca. 817	Wales
Psalter of Sedulius Scottus: Paris, Arsenal, MS 8407	VL 250 (Rahlfs 1129)	Latin–Greek (facing pages: Odes only)	IX med.	Liège
Basle Psalter: Basle, UB, A.VII.3	VL 334, Rahlfs 156	Greek–Latin (interlinear)	IX med.	Bobbio? St. Gall?
Symeon Psalter: Berlin, Staatsbibliothek, Hamilton 552	VL 408, Rahlfs 1040	Greek†–Latin (facing page)	IX 2/2	Milan
St. Gall, Stiftsbibliothek, Cod. Sang. 17, 133–342	GA L1349, VL 335, Rahlfs 1053	Latin–Greek (two columns)	IX ex.	St. Gall
Vatican, BAV, Reg. lat. 1595, 50–67	VL 342, Rahlfs 1169	Greek†–Latin (interlinear)	IX–X	
St. Gall, Stiftsbibliothek, Cod. Sang. 1395 II, 336–361 (frag.)	VL 336, Rahlfs 1054	Latin–Greek† (facing pages)	IX–X	(Caroline minuscule)
Murbach Psalter: Gotha, Forschungsbibl., Membr. I.17	VL 338, Rahlfs 27	Greek–Latin (interlinear)	IX–X	Murbach?
Würzburg, Seminarbibl., Membr. o. 1	Rahlfs 1225	Greek–Latin (interlinear)	IX–X	(Insular script)
Bernkastel-Kues, Cusanusstift, Cusa 9 (frag.)	VL 340, Rahlfs 1043	Greek†–Latin–Greek (three columns)	X in.	Germany
Psalterium Salomonis III: Bamberg, Staatsbibliothek, Msc. Bibl. 44	VL 311, Rahlfs 1037	Latin–Latin–Latin–Greek† (four columns)	909	St. Gall
Junius Psalter: Oxford, Bodleian, Junius 27	VL 375	Latin–Old English (interlinear)	X 1/2	Winchester
Regius Psalter: London, BL, Royal 2.B.V	VL 377	Latin–Old English (interlinear)	X med.	Winchester?

(continued)

Table 11.2 Continued

Manuscript	Sigla	Languages and format	Date (century)	Origin
Bernkastel-Kues, Cusanusstift, Cusa 10	VL 341, Rahlfs 1044	Greek–Latin (facing pages)	X 2/2	Fulda?
Bosworth Psalter: London, BL, Add. MS 37517	VL 383	Latin–Old English (interlinear)	X 2/2	Canterbury
Salisbury Psalter: Salisbury, Cathedral, Ms. 150	VL 382	Latin–Old English (interlinear)	ca. 975	England
Psalter of Theophano: Trier, Stadtbibl., 7/9	VL 337, Rahlfs 1206	Latin–Greek (interlinear)	X ex.	
Cologne, Dombibl., 8	VL 314, Rahlfs 1077	Latin–Latin–Latin–Greek† (four columns)	X–XI	
Essen, Münsterschatz, s.n.	VL 315, Rahlfs 1049	Latin–Latin–Latin–Greek† (four columns)	X–XI	
Cambridge Psalter: Cambridge, UL, Ff.1.23	VL 376	Latin–Old English (alternate lines)	ca. 1000	Kent
Lambeth Psalter: London, Lambeth Palace, 427	VL 380	Latin–Old English (interlinear)	ca. 1025	England
Paris Psalter: Paris, BnF, lat. 8824	VL 308	Latin–Old English (two columns; Psalms only)	XI 1/2	Canterbury?
Naples, BN, gr. 20	Rahlfs 1222	Greek with marginal Arabic and Latin	XI	
Bamberg, Staatsarchiv, A 246 no. 20; Coburg, Staatsarchiv, Fragm. 2; Freiburg, Univ. 629 (frag.)	VL 458	Latin–Latin–Latin–Greek† (four columns; frag.)	XI	Banz
Vitellius Psalter: London, BL, Cotton Vitellius E. XVIII	VL 373	Latin–Old English (interlinear)	XI med.	Winchester
Cambridge, Pembroke College 312, Harlem, Sonderhausen (frag.)	VL 477	Latin–Old English (interlinear)	XI med.	England
Stowe Psalter: London, BL, Stowe 2	VL 379	Latin–Old English (interlinear)	XI 2/2	Winchester
Arundel Psalter: London, BL, Arundel 60	VL 381	Latin–Old English (interlinear)	XI 2/2	Winchester
Tiberius Psalter: London, BL, Cotton Tiberius C. VI	VL 377	Latin–Old English (interlinear)	XI ex.	Winchester
Odo of Cambrai's Psalter: Paris, BnF, nouv. acq. lat. 2195	VL 312, Rahlfs 1143	Latin–Latin–Latin–Greek† (four columns)	ca. 1105	Tournai
Graz, Universitätsbibl. 86	VL 462	Latin–Latin–Latin–Greek† (four columns)	XII 1/2	
London, BL, Harley 5786	Rahlfs 174	Greek–Latin–Arabic (three columns)	1130–53	Sicily

Table 11.2 Continued

Manuscript	Sigla	Languages and format	Date (century)	Origin
Valenciennes, BM, 14	VL 313, Rahlfs 1210	Latin–Latin–Latin–Greek† (four columns)	1145–53	Saint-Amand
Monte Cassino, Archivio della Badia, 467 BB	VL 310, Rahlfs 1916	Latin–Latin–Latin–Greek†–Latin (five columns)	XII	
Eadwine Psalter: Cambridge, Trinity College, R.17.1	VL 319	Latin–Anglo-Norman (interlinear); Latin–Old English (interlinear)	XII med.	Canterbury
Admont, Stiftsbibliothek, 42	VL 461	Latin–Latin–Latin–Greek† (four columns)	XII	Admont
Paris, BnF, lat. 15198	VL 329, Rahlfs 1745	Latin–Latin–Greek† (three columns)	XII ex.	
Norfolk, Holkham Hall, MS 22	Rahlfs 1062	Greek–Latin (?) (two columns)	XII ex.	Germany
Cambridge, Corpus Christi College, 468	VL 409, Rahlfs 1553	Latin–Greek† (two columns)	XIII 1/2	France?
Paris, BnF, suppl. gr. 188	Rahlfs 1747	Greek†–Latin (interlinear)	XIII 1/2	Paris?
London, BL, Add. MS 47674	Rahlfs 1062	Greek–Latin (two columns)	ca. 1220	Paris
Vatican, BAV, Vat. gr. 1070	VL 455, Rahlfs 1787	Greek–Latin (two columns)	1291	South Italy
Oxford, Bodleian, Canon gr. 63	Rahlfs 1711	Greek–Latin (two columns)	XIII ex.	
Paris, BnF, gr. 24	Rahlfs 162	Greek–Latin (interlinear)	XIII ex.	

[a] See especially Alfred Rahlfs, *Verzeichnis der griechischen Handschriften des Alten Testaments* (Berlin: Weidmann, 1914) ; Roger Gryson, *Altlateinische Handschriften/Manuscrits Vieux Latins.* 2. Mss 300–485 (VL 1/2B). (Freiburg: Herder, 2004).

Note. Radiciotti 1998: 114 lists eighteen Greek–Latin Psalters from the fourteenth to the sixteenth century (including VL 456/Rahlfs 1575); see also Rahlfs 151, 224, 277, 290, 1573, 1643, 1672, 1724, 1782, 1784, and 1899.

Multilingual Manuscripts in Context

Multilingual Latin biblical manuscripts comprise Greek–Latin bilinguals, Latin–Gothic bilinguals, and some early vernacular bilinguals (e.g. Old English, Old High German). There are also some rare trilingual manuscripts with Greek, Latin, and Arabic.

Early Greek–Latin Bilinguals

The first Latin translations of the Bible were made in an oral setting (see chap. 1). Taking into account their linguistic characteristics, the ancient practice of composing literary works by dictation, and the cost of manuscript production, it is almost inconceivable that the Latin Bible originated as a written bilingual document. By the late fourth century, however, and possibly earlier (see Metzger 1984: 333–34), a bilingual format had become established in which a Greek biblical text is presented to the left of a Latin version. The use of sense-lines in order to permit easy comparison between the two languages means that a relatively high proportion of each page remains blank, resulting in a larger number of folios and a correspondingly higher production cost. The establishment of Latin as the language of Christian theology in the West and the doctrinal controversies of this period provide an obvious context for the creation and use of these substantial volumes.

A parchment fragment found in Egypt of just four lines from the Epistle to the Ephesians, with Greek on one side and Latin on the other, has been claimed as the oldest Greek–Latin biblical manuscript known to survive, possibly from the fourth century (VL 85; GA 0230: see Radiciotti 1999: 155–57; Dahl 1979). A detailed recent study, however, has revised its dating to the fifth or sixth century (Fressura 2016). The quality of the script, the Latin written in neat rustic capitals, as well as the use of parchment indicate that this document was created for formal use. Although earlier editors proposed a two-column format, the length of the surviving sense-lines suggests that the languages were written on facing pages (Fressura 2016: 83–86).

Codex Claromontanus (VL 75; GA 06), from the middle of the fifth century, contains all fourteen Pauline Epistles with Greek and Latin on facing pages. This too is a luxury production: the margins are wide, and red ink is used for the opening lines of each book and for biblical quotations, which are also indented. The text is organized in relatively short sense-lines, although it has been suggested that the manuscript was copied from a bilingual exemplar written in even shorter lines (Dahl 1979: 93). The copyist seems equally at home in both languages, although paratextual details such as the use of running titles and the form of the *explicit* indicate that Latin was the principal text. No fewer than nine correctors worked on the manuscript: while the Greek corrections tend toward the standard Byzantine text, most of the Latin alterations differ from the Vulgate. The exception is a series of twenty-five corrections in Romans 3–9 indicated by the letters "*ro*" in the margin: this presumably designates a Roman edition, and almost all provide the Vulgate reading.[7]

The most famous Greek–Latin biblical bilingual is Codex Bezae (VL 5; GA 05). The format is very similar to Codex Claromontanus, with the same indications that Latin was the principal language. Parker (1992: 270–78) suggests that Codex Bezae was produced in Berytus around the year 400. The manuscript contains the four gospels in the Old Latin order, before several missing quires which ended with the Johannine Epistles: the final page of 3 John is preserved in Latin. This is followed by the Acts of the Apostles, which breaks off around the end of chapter 22. The sense lines of Codex Bezae

---

[7] Frede (1964: 27) observes that this is the earliest connection of the Vulgate version of the Pauline Epistles with Rome.

are generally longer than those of Codex Claromontanus. Parker demonstrates that, in the Gospels, the copyist was responsible for combining shorter sense-lines from the exemplar and made several mistakes in matching the Greek with the Latin (1992: 76–80). In Acts, on the other hand, Codex Bezae appears to maintain the lineation of the manuscript from which it was copied, with punctuation which implies that smaller units had already been combined: this makes Codex Bezae at least a third-generation bilingual (Parker 1992: 80–82). No fewer than eighteen corrector hands have been identified in Codex Bezae: some worked on both columns, while others focused on a single language (Parker 1992: 48–49). The manuscript was in Lyons in the ninth century, where pages were added to replace some that had been lost. In the sixteenth century, it was acquired by Theodore Beza, from whom it took its present name.

Codex Bezae is renowned for its biblical text. In Acts, it provides the principal evidence for the so-called Western text, a version longer than the standard form. In the Gospels, the Greek text of Codex Bezae often provides the only parallel for readings widely attested in Latin tradition, and the possibility of Latin influence on the Greek text of Codex Bezae continues to be discussed (e.g. Lorenz 2020). This is the oldest surviving Greek witness to the longer ending of Mark and the *Pericope Adulterae*, and is the sole tradent of the "Cambridge pericope" after Luke 6:4, an additional saying of Jesus about working on the Sabbath. Despite their similarities, differences between the columns indicate that the Latin and the Greek texts were independent in origin (Parker 1992: 194ff.; see also Lorenz 2022). Many of the apparent discrepancies in the Latin text may be explained as translational variants or changes in word order, and both columns harmonize to parallel passages elsewhere in the Gospels.

Radiciotti (2005: 57) connects the next set of Greek–Latin bilinguals with an influx of Byzantine dignitaries into Italy in the seventh century, which also had an impact on book production. The Laudian Acts (VL 50; GA 08), which only contains the Acts of the Apostles, is written in two very narrow columns, mostly consisting of one to three words per line. It was copied in Sardinia at the end of the sixth century, but subsequently used by Bede in Northumbria: numerous biblical citations in his commentary on Acts agree only with the Latin column of this manuscript. The Latin text is an Old Latin form which has been adapted in order to correspond to the Greek column. Unlike the earlier bilinguals, the Latin appears on the left and there are indications of the priority of the Greek, which is the sole language of the subscriptions and alone has *nomina sacra*. The displacement of some Greek text by longer lines of Latin, especially toward the end of the manuscript, indicates that it was copied from a bilingual exemplar.

The Verona Psalter (VL 300), copied around the same time as the Laudian Acts, is a facing-page bilingual. The Greek on the *verso* is written phonetically in Roman letters, suggesting that it may have been used for liturgical reading or language study: there are numerous errors in the Greek word division, and a later editor has corrected the transliteration conventions. The Latin text is an Old Latin form attested in the fourth century (see chap. 5). An incomplete seventh-century psalter now in Paris may have been copied in a Greek monastery in Rome (Radiciotti 1999: 163–64, 2005: 56–57). The widespread use of the Gallican Psalter, translated from the Septuagint, explains why a Greek rather than Hebrew text is found in bilingual psalters.

Latin–Gothic Bilinguals

Very few manuscripts remain of the Gothic translation of the Bible produced by Wulfilas in the middle of the fourth century. Wulfilas used a Greek source, close to the Byzantine tradition, although certain readings shared only between Latin and Gothic suggest that he may also have had recourse to a Latin version (Houghton 2016: 52; Falluomini 2015: 80–82). Gothic was used alongside Latin in North Italy, where Theoderic the Great had his court in Ravenna at the beginning of the sixth century, providing a context for the creation of bilingual manuscripts. Two fragments of Latin–Gothic biblical codices survive. Codex Carolinus (VL 79) includes four palimpsest pages from an early sixth-century manuscript of the Epistle to the Romans. The texts are in two narrow columns, with Gothic on the left. Parallelism between the texts is enhanced by the use of indentation for longer phrases. The Fragmentum Gissense (VL 36), a single bifolium from a slightly later copy of Luke, has each language on a separate page, with longer lines. Again, the Gothic is on the left. The presence of Eusebian canon numbers in the margin of the Latin indicates that its text is affiliated with the Vulgate, although there are also some Old Latin readings.

Two other Latin New Testament manuscripts have been connected with Gothic. Codex Brixianus (VL 10), a purple gospel book copied in north Italy in the sixth century, has an almost identical format to Codex Argenteus, the most substantial Gothic gospel manuscript. The first quire, which was bound in at a later date, includes a Latin preface to a Gothic translation of the Bible: it explains that readings (or glosses) which agree with Greek are indicated by *GR* and those which match Latin by *LA*, although this practice is not attested in surviving manuscripts (Falluomini 2015: 105–7, 178–80). Although its text is close to the Vulgate, Codex Brixianus features several readings which are only otherwise present in Gothic, and it is generally agreed that it was copied from a bilingual exemplar: the same proposal has been made for some fifth-century palimpsest fragments of Matthew (VL 43; Falluomini 2015: 101–4).

The First Vernacular Bilinguals

The creation of a full interlinear translation is a natural development from glosses, which are found in Insular manuscripts from the seventh century (see chap. 10). The earliest surviving English biblical text is the Old English gloss added to the Vespasian Psalter a century after it was copied: the scribe who copied the interlinear version is known to have been active in Canterbury in the second quarter of the ninth century (see fig. 31.4). This book was in regular liturgical use for many years, as is shown by the addition of replacement pages with both Latin and Old English texts in the eleventh century: numerous psalters in this format were created in England between the tenth and twelfth centuries (table 12.2; see further Toswell 2014: ch. 4). Only the eleventh-century Paris Psalter has an Old English text in a separate column.

Interlinear Old English versions were added to two Insular gospel books in the north of England. The continuous gloss in the Lindisfarne Gospels was inserted by a priest called Aldred around the year 970. A few years later, the same happened to the Rushworth/MacRegol Gospels, originally produced in Ireland around the beginning of the ninth century. Two copyists were responsible for the gloss: Farman, who wrote in Mercian, and Owun, who supplied an existing Northumbrian gloss (as shown by source readings which differ from the Latin in the manuscript). Although it should be emphasized that the vernacular text in these manuscripts remains a word-for-word gloss rather than a fluent and grammatically correct Old English version, these documents are of great linguistic significance.

Complete Old High German biblical translations from the early ninth century also provide the first evidence of this vernacular language. The Mondsee fragments feature Latin and Old High German texts of a number of Christian texts, including the Gospel according to Matthew, on facing pages with Latin on the left and Old High German on the right. Codex Sangallensis 56 is a bilingual gospel harmony copied in Fulda around the year 830 that has two columns on each page with the same disposition of languages.

Later Greek–Latin New Testament Bilinguals

Ongoing interest in Greek–Latin bilingual manuscripts, and perhaps also the scarcity of such documents, is shown by two copies of Codex Claromontanus.[8] Codex Sangermanensis (VL 76; GA 0319) was produced in the ninth century by scribes whose understanding of Greek was limited, possibly in Fulda.[9] They combined the facing pages into two columns and incorporated most of the corrections, but sometimes misinterpreted the alterations: deleted letters were copied with lines through them rather than being removed, similar characters were misread, and replacements were treated as additions. The second copy, Codex Waldeccensis (VL 83; GA 0320), was made a century later. This preserves the original facing-page layout, but the length of each column is doubled because each page combines two from the exemplar. The few pages which have been preserved suggest that these copyists were more successful than their predecessors in interpreting the Greek corrections.

Also connected with Codex Claromontanus are two other Greek–Latin bilinguals of the Pauline Epistles from the end of the ninth century. Shared lacunae in Codex Augiensis (VL 78; GA 010) and Codex Boernerianus (VL 77; GA 012) show that they derive from the same Greek exemplar, but they treat the Latin in very different ways.[10]

---

[8] In addition, Frede (1964: 46–47) describes a transliterated passage of Ephesians in a ninth-century compilation manuscript which appears to have been transcribed from Codex Claromontanus.

[9] Berschin (1987: 129) observes that bilingual copies of Luke and John, the Psalms, and the Pauline Epistles are listed in the Fulda library catalogue produced around 830, but other authorities prefer Corbie as its origin.

[10] Frede believed that the archetype of Codex Boernerianus was very similar to that of Codex Claromontanus (1964: 51–52).

Codex Augiensis is the earliest biblical manuscript with the Latin on the outside of each page and the Greek on the inner column. The text is not divided into sense-lines, but the copyist tries to match Greek words which are split across a line with similar breaks in the Latin: a number of erasures and errors in line division indicate that this layout was being created during production. The Latin text is broadly Vulgate; in addition, there are a few Latin glosses added above the Greek, some of which match readings which are only otherwise found in Codex Boernerianus. However, it remains unclear whether their exemplar was itself a bilingual codex, or whether these occasional overlaps in Latin are coincidental.

Codex Boernerianus is one of a group of three contemporary Greek–Latin in-terlinear bilinguals associated with the monastery of St. Gall. The other two are a gospel book in St. Gall (VL 27; GA 037) and a psalter in Basle (VL 334). These appear to have formed a project by a team of Irish monks on the European continent to create a bilingual tool for biblical study. The presence of monks interested in Greek (*fratres ellinici*) at the monastery of St. Gall toward the end of the ninth century is attested in a letter of Notker the Stammerer (see further Kaczynski 1988). The current consensus is that these three manuscripts were created elsewhere, possibly in Columbanus's monastery in Bobbio, and brought to St. Gall by a Bishop Mark and his nephew Moengal, also known as Marcellus; later on, around the year 880, Notker himself produced a bilingual copy of the Catholic Epistles, although this no longer survives (Berschin 1987: 145–48).

All three codices consist of a main line of Greek, written in a Western majuscule hand, with a continuous word-for-word gloss above it. Features of the interlinear text show that, at least in certain books, the translation was created while the manuscript was being written (Houghton 2020). Some of the glosses appear to have been pro-vided ad hoc by the copyist; others were added later, while certain Greek words still lacked a Latin equivalent. Reference was also made to at least one Latin biblical man-uscript, as seen in "translations" that do not correspond to the text below, comments that a phrase is lacking in Greek, and lines left blank in order to provide a portion of text that was missing from the Greek exemplar (e.g., Matthew 4:23 and John 7:53–8:11; Romans 1:1b–5a and 1 Corinthians 3:8–16a). In each manuscript, there are occasions when more than one Latin form is provided in the interlinear version, either a syn-onym or a grammatical alternative which more closely matches the Greek. In addi-tion, there are several linguistic comments, often highly abbreviated, concerning the number, gender, or tense of a particular Greek term. The margins also contain a series of letters, apparently to draw attention to particular linguistic features or glosses to be supplied, and theological observations (Houghton 2020: 156–60). These show that these bilingual codices were used over a period of time both for language study and for theological purposes. A slightly later bilingual gospel book, produced at St. Gall itself was left unfinished with hardly any of the Latin column written, and reused as a palimpsest (Cod. Sang. 18 etc.).

Bilingual Psalters in the Middle Ages

The remarkable number of Greek–Latin bilingual psalters preserved from the ninth century onward (see table 12.2) attest to the important role which they played. Berschin (1987: 20–25) notes that Greek texts were already embedded in Western liturgy, and as the biblical book used most frequently in the monastic office, the Psalms served as an ideal text for language learning. The impetus seems to have come from Irish scholars in Europe such as Sedulius Scottus, although in the psalter which he himself copied (VL 250) a full translation is only provided for the biblical Odes. The interlinear model found in the Basle Psalter is matched by several psalters from the following decades, although other formats were also employed. Fragments from an early tenth-century psalter which later belonged to Nicholas of Cusa (VL 340) clearly demonstrate the use of the Psalms in learning Greek. It is written in three narrow columns: on the left is a phonetic Latin transliteration of the Greek, which appears in its own alphabet on the right. Between the two comes the Latin translation. The parallels between the Latin and Greek texts are exaggerated by the omission of most of the definite articles from the Greek columns. Although older manuscripts tend to use Greek characters, transliterated forms (which are attested as early as the Verona Psalter) became more popular, and were also used liturgically (Berschin 1987: 39). Both practices are attested in the two sections of the remarkable *Liber Commonei* (described above), which indicates the use of Greek at this time in the Easter liturgy.

A particularly influential scholarly tool, created in St. Gall in 909 for its abbot, Bishop Salomon III, was the *psalterium quadruplex*. This took the three principal versions of the Latin Psalter (Gallican, Roman, and *Iuxta Hebraeos*), which had already been brought together in Latin triple psalters, and added a fourth column on the far right consisting of a transliteration of the Greek. Several of the subsequent examples of this format (e.g., in Cologne and Essen) are direct copies of Salomon's Psalter (VL 311), now held in Bamberg (Berschin 1987: 148–49). One twelfth-century psalter in Monte Cassino (VL 310) went even further, adding a fifth column of Latin which contained a new translation based on Hebrew. An interesting exception to the typology of medieval bilingual psalters is the so-called Psalter of Theophano (VL 337). Copied in Trier at the end of the tenth century, the main text is in Latin, with an interlinear version in Greek. It has been suggested that it was intended for Greek exiles to learn Latin, although no direct connection has been proven to the empress after whom it is named (the Byzantine wife of Emperor Otto II) and it was commissioned by Archbishop Egbert (Berschin 1987: 192).

Multilingualism in the High Middle Ages

Under the Normans in the twelfth century, Sicily was a cultural center bringing together Norman, Arabic, and Byzantine traditions, with official documents being produced in the languages of these three communities, and a translation culture focusing on philosophical and scientific texts (Berschin 1987: 231–32). This multilingualism is reflected in two tri-lingual biblical manuscripts copied there, a psalter written in the year 1153 and a slightly later New Testament codex of the Acts and Epistles (GA 460). Each has three relatively narrow columns to a page, in the order Greek, Latin, and Arabic. The texts were assembled from existing traditions, and the paratextual material is supplied independently in each language. The order in which the columns were copied appears to vary, although the Latin was always added last (O'Hogan 2022: 170–72; Schulthess et al. 2018: §8).

Arabic notes in the margin of the psalter indicate that it was used during worship ac-cording to the Latin Rite. The same three languages are found in an eleventh-century psalter in Naples, although the Arabic and Latin translations were added in the outer and lower margins sometime after the initial production with the Greek text alone. The sole surviving Latin–Arabic biblical bilingual, a leaf from Galatians, was copied in Spain around the year 900 in the context of the Mozarabic community (De Bruyne and Tisserant 1910). The Arabic was written first, with the Latin column abbreviated in order to fill the available space.

Greek–Latin biblical manuscripts from the twelfth to the fifteenth century reflect the changing political situation of the Byzantine Empire and its relationship to the Western Church. Many of these documents are incomplete: either circumstances changed or the challenge of keeping the two languages in step was too great. Few have been studied in depth, with the exception of one deluxe gospel book (GA 16). Maxwell (2014) has suggested that this codex was commissioned by Emperor Michael VIII Palaeologus as a gift for Pope Gregory X at the time of the brief Union of the Greek and Latin Churches promoted at the second Council of Lyons in 1274, but it was abandoned after the emperor's death in 1282. In addition to a fine cycle of miniatures, the text is written in four colors which distinguish between narrative sections (bright red), quotations from the Old Testament and the discourse of the disciples (blue), other direct speech (black), and the words of Jesus (crimson). As is often the case in later bilingual codices, the Latin column is significantly narrower because of the greater compression of its script: in addition to this, a series of minims is frequently inserted on the Latin side in order to maintain the align-ment of the texts. Multiple hands worked on the Latin text, although large sections remain blank: sometimes it is an accommodation of the Vulgate to the Greek column, but in a few places a fresh translation has been attempted. Although this and similar documents may have been created for political purposes, like the earlier bilinguals they provide a window onto the context of their conception and intended use, the linguistic capabilities of their producers, and the ways in which they were subsequently employed and preserved.

BIBLIOGRAPHY

Berschin, Walter. 1987. *Greek Letters and the Latin Middle Ages: From Jerome to Nicholas of Cusa* (Rev. and expanded version of *Griechisch-lateinisches Mittelalter: Von Hieronymus zu Nikolaus von Kues* [1980]). Translated by Jerold C. Frakes. Washington, DC: Catholic University of America.

Dahl, Nils Alstrup. 1979. "0230 (=PSI 1306) and the Fourth-Century Greek-Latin Edition of the Letters of Paul." In *Text and Interpretation, Studies in the New Testament Presented to Matthew Black*, edited by E. Best and R. McLachlan Wilson, 79–98. Cambridge: Cambridge University Press.

De Bruyne, Donatien, and Eugène Tisserant. 1910. "Une feuille arabo-latine de l'épître aux Galates." *Revue Biblique* 7, no. 3: 321–43.

Dickey, Eleanor. 2015. "Columnar Translation: An Ancient Interpretive Tool That the Romans Gave the Greeks." *Classical Quarterly* 65, no. 2: 807–21.

Dickey, Eleanor 2019. "A Re-examination of New Testament Papyrus P99 (Vetus Latina AN glo Paul)." *New Testament Studies* 65: 103–21.

Falluomini, Carla. 2015. *The Gothic Version of the Gospels and Pauline Epistles. Cultural Background, Transmission and Character*. ANTF 46. Berlin: De Gruyter.

Frede, Hermann J. 1964. *Altlateinische Paulus-Handschriften*. AGLB 4. Freiburg: Herder.

Fressura, Marco. 2016. "PSI XIII 1306: Note codicologiche e paleografiche." In *Spazio scritto e spazio non scritto nel libro papiraceo*, edited by Natascia Pellé, 77–128. Edaphos 2. Lecce: Pensa.

Houghton, H. A. G. 2016. *The Latin New Testament. A Guide to Its Early History, Texts, and Manuscripts*. Oxford: Oxford University Press.

Houghton, H. A. G. 2020. "The Latin Text of John in the Saint Gall Bilingual Gospels (Codex Sangallensis 48)." In *At One Remove: The Text of the New Testament in Early Translations and Quotations*, edited by H. A. G. Houghton and Peter Montoro, 149–71. T&S 3.24. Piscataway: Gorgias.

Kaczynski, Bernice M. 1988. *Greek in the Carolingian Age. The St. Gall Manuscripts*. Cambridge, MA: Medieval Academy of America.

Lorenz, Peter E. 2020. "An Examination of Six Objections to the Theory of Latin Influence on the Greek Text of Codex Bezae." In *At One Remove: The Text of the New Testament in Early Translations and Quotations*, edited by H. A. G. Houghton and Peter Montoro, 173–87. T&S 3.24. Piscataway: Gorgias.

Lorenz, Peter E. 2022. *A History of Codex Bezae's Text in the Gospel of Mark*. ANTF 53. Berlin: De Gruyter.

Maxwell, Kathleen. 2014. *Between Constantinople and Rome: An Illuminated Byzantine Gospel Book (Paris gr. 54) and the Union of Churches*. Burlington: Ashgate.

Metzger, Bruce M. 1984. "Bilingualism and Polylingualism in Antiquity: With a Check-List of New Testament MSS Written in More than One Language." In *The New Testament Age: Essays in Honor of Bo Reicke*, edited by William C. Weinrich, 327–34. Macon: Mercer University Press.

Moran, Pádraic, and John Whitman. 2022. "Glossing and Reading in Western Europe and East Asia: A Comparative Case Study." *Speculum* 97 no. 1: 112–39.

O'Hogan, Cillian. 2022. "The Harley Trilingual Psalter, a Witness to Multilingualism at the Court Scriptorium of Roger II of Sicily." In *Medieval Multilingual Manuscripts: Case Studies from Ireland to Japan*, edited by Michael Clarke and Máire Ní Mhaonaigh, 162–82. Berlin: De Gruyter.

Parker, D. C. 1992. *Codex Bezae: An Early Christian Manuscript and Its Text*. Cambridge: Cambridge University Press.

Radiciotti, Paolo. 1998. "Manoscritti digrafici grecolatini e latinogreci nell'Alto Medioevo." *Römische Historische Mitteilungen* 40: 49–118.

Radiciotti, Paolo. 1999. "Manoscritti digrafici grecolatini e latinogreci nella tarda antichità." In *Da Ercolano all'Egitto. Ricerche varie di papirologia*, edited by Mario Capasso, 153–85. Papyrologica Lupiensia 7 1998. Galatina: Congedo.

Radiciotti, Paolo. 2005. "Le Sacre Scritture nel mondo tardoantico grecolatino." In *Forme e modelli della tradizione manoscritta della Bibbia*, edited by Paolo Cherubini, 33–60. Vatican City: Scuola Vaticana.

Schulthess, Sara, with Anastasia Chasapi, and Martial Sankar. 2018. *A Trilingual Manuscript of the New Testament in Digital Research* [Online]. Accessed June 2021 at <https://humarec. org/webbook/book/>.

Toswell, Mary Jane. 2014. *The Anglo-Saxon Psalter*. Medieval Church Studies 10. Turnhout: Brepols.

CHAPTER 12

THE BIBLE IN THE CAROLINGIAN AGE

SHARI BOODTS

ACHIEVEMENTS AND MOTIVATION

THE Carolingian empire, ruled by Charlemagne (from 768 to 814) and his immediate successors, has left us many spectacular Bibles, a qualifier that holds true whether we are referring to the technical and artistic qualities of the physical manuscripts or to the intellectual achievements revealed by their text.[1] The Moutier-Grandval Bible (London, BL, Add. MS 10546) (fig. 31.6) combines several of the characteristics of ninth-century luxury bibles.[2] This is a single-volume Bible, or pandect, of impressive dimensions: 449 folios measuring 495 × 380 mm. Up to twenty scribal hands have been identified, indicating the scale of production at the scriptorium of Tours, where this book was produced, probably between 830 and 850 (McKitterick 1994: 71–72). The scribes used Caroline minuscule, an innovative script that was much more readable than the un-wieldy uncial and semiuncial Merovingian scripts in use before. The text is that of the Vulgate, which would gradually become dominant during the Carolingian period. While a clear example of some of the novelties introduced by Carolingian scribes and scholars, the Moutier-Grandval Bible also demonstrates the debt to tradition that was an intrinsic part of Carolingian culture, in its four full-page illustrations, which echo the style of classical art.

The achievements of Carolingian scholars in the field of biblical studies are just as impressive as those in manuscript production. One striking example is the

---

[1] For general introductions to the field of Carolingian biblical studies, see Chevalier-Royet 2006; Houghton 2016; Contreni 1983; Chazelle and Van Name Edwards 2003.

[2] Full digitization at <https://www.bl.uk/manuscripts/Viewer.aspx?ref=add_ms_10546_f001r>.

Saint-Germain Bible (Paris, BnF, lat. 11937).[3] This manuscript is a pandect as well, but smaller in size, counting 179 folios measuring 280 × 220 mm. The pages are densely covered with writing and contain numerous marginal annotations. These are text-critical notes recording variant readings in the biblical text, including some from the Hebrew Bible. The Saint-Germain Bible is one of the bibles of Theodulf of Orleans, a document of some of the most advanced scholarship the Carolingians produced on the text of the Bible (Candiard and Chevalier 2012: 34). Although the comparison with Hebrew is a unique feature in Carolingian biblical scholarship, it shows both the lengths to which ninth-century scholars went in their quest for clar-ification of the biblical text and the boundaries that continued to hold them back (see also chap. 22).

   If these two manuscripts serve as illustrations of the broad spectrum of Carolingian Bible production, they also hint at the motivation that pushed the Carolingians to these achievements. Starting with Pepin in 751, the Carolingian kings replaced the Merovingians as rulers of the Franks. With Charlemagne, the Frankish realm expanded to encompass most of Western continental Europe. This vast and heterogeneous domain presented a number of challenges. Charlemagne designated the centralization of religious rites and the reform of education as the key to the consolidation of his empire and therefore a clear priority (Chazelle and Van Name Edwards 2003: 3–4). He exhibited a genuine concern for the establishment of the correct text of the Bible (Bogaert 2012: 80). Several sources detail Charlemagne's wishes regarding the proper instruction in and execution of religious rites, the most important of which are the *Epistola de litteris colendis* to Baugulf of Fulda (784/ 785), the *Admonitio Generalis* (789), and the *Libri Carolini* (before 794).[4] The nov-elty of the Carolingian legislation lies not so much in its originality but in the fact that it was clearly formulated and consistently applied (Contreni 1983: 75). With the rulers' emphasis on the education of both the clergy and the laity as the driving force, Carolingian scholars produced both the primary sources (i.e., manuscripts of the Bible) and an impressive amount of secondary materials to elucidate the Bible (i.e., exegetical commentaries, compilations of patristic writings on the Bible, and guidebooks and miscellaneous manuscripts setting out a program of biblical studies) (see among others Brunhölzl 1975; Contreni 1995, 1996; Kaczynski 1995; McKitterick 1977, 1989: 135–210; Phelan 2006). In the remainder of this chapter, we explore the activities of the Carolingians regarding the Bible in three domains: the revision and correction of the text of the Bible, the production of bible manuscripts, and the task of biblical exegesis.

---

[3] Full digitization at <https://gallica.bnf.fr/ark:/12148/btv1b8490069j>.

[4] Edited, respectively, in Edmund E. Stengel, ed., *Urkundenbuch des Klosters Fulda I* (Marburg: N.G. Elwert, 1958), 246–54; *MGH, Leges II, Capitularia regum Francorum I* (Hannover: Hahn, 1883), 52–62; and *MGH, Leges IV, Concilia II, Suppl. I* (Hannover: Hahn, 1998), 303–22.

REVISION OF THE BIBLE TEXT
UNDER CHARLEMAGNE

As far as we know, Charlemagne never ordered a systematic revision of the biblical text in order to have a single version imposed over others, yet his concern for the correct text of the Bible to be used in the liturgy constituted a clear call to the enterprise of biblical revision (Chevalier-Royet 2006). The nature of this revision consisted mainly of grammatical and orthographical corrections and, by more audacious revisers, alterations to the number and order of the biblical books and recordings of variant readings gleaned from comparison between different text versions (Contreni 1983: 77–78). Though Charlemagne's call was answered by two men in particular, Alcuin of York and Theodulf of Orleans, there is evidence of revisions to the bible text in several manuscripts not associated with these two (Fischer 1985: 101–202).

Alcuin of York and the Text of the Tours Bibles

Alcuin of York (ca. 735–804) was an Anglo-Saxon scholar who came to the Carolingian court around 782 to serve as a personal adviser and tutor to Charlemagne and his family. In 796, he became abbot at Tours. His work on the Bible probably commenced around the time of this appointment. Alcuin's revision of the biblical text does not stray outside the realm of classic medieval textual scholarship: he corrected bad grammar, eliminated errors and barbarisms introduced by incompetent scribes, and adapted the orthography. Initially, this was not particularly successful, with the early results of his revision being inferior to the text offered by other Carolingian Bibles (Ganz 2012: 330). Alcuin systematically preferred Jerome's translation over the *Vetus Latina* versions. Despite his relatively conservative attitude, overall, some four thousand readings across the whole Bible have been attributed to Alcuin's revision (Houghton 2016: 84).

The very first manuscripts containing the results of Alcuin's activity have not survived, but we know from the dedicatory poems written by Alcuin that he presented a Bible to Charlemagne on the occasion of his coronation in 800 and another one at Christmas 801 (Ganz 2012: 330, see also Fischer 1985: 254–69). Several manuscripts are extant today that can be dated and located to the Tours scriptorium during his abbacy: Tours, BM, 10; Monza, Bibl. Cap., g-1/1; Paris, BnF, lat. 8847; St. Gall, Stiftsbibliothek, 75 (Lobrichon 2004, 215–16; Fischer 1985: 256). The sources employed by Alcuin to establish his biblical text remain a subject of debate, but they appear to have originated largely in the North of France. Connections can be made with the Bible of Maurdramnus of Corbie (Amiens, BM, 6, 7, 9, 11, 12), the Harley Gospels (London, BL, Harley 2788) and the Codex Fuldensis (Fulda, Hochschul- und Landesbibliothek, Codex Bonifatianus 1) (Chevalier-Royet 2006: 14; Houghton 2016: 84).

Alcuin's emended text formed the basis for the Bibles produced in great numbers by the scriptorium of Tours. The standard version of a Tours Bible included the Hieronymian prefaces and used the *Versio Gallicana* of the Psalter, two choices with far-reaching consequences, as both would eventually become the standard (Ganz 2012: 332). The order of the biblical books introduced by Alcuin would be followed in nearly all the Bibles produced at Tours, the exceptions being Bibles of which the quires were bound together at a later stage (Fischer 1985: 275). Nevertheless, some nuances have been offered regarding the purpose, immediate impact, and uniformity of Alcuin's text. Fischer (1985: 322–24) states that by the end of his life, an Alcuinian text of the Bible was established at Tours and continued to be used by his successors, with the exception of a revision of the Gospels, Acts, and Pauline Epistles during the abbacy of Adalhard (834–43). He notes that the Tours Bibles served first as a means to correct, rather than replace local biblical versions (Fischer 1985: 402–3). Lobrichon (2004: 218–19) also warns against overestimating the *immediate* impact of Alcuin's work, noting that other Bible versions continued to circulate at the height of the Tours production. Houghton (2016: 84) is skeptical about the existence of a uniform Alcuinian text as the basis of all products of the Tours scriptorium. He notes, specifically with regard to the number of Old Latin readings, differences in the "textual complexion" between the Tours Bibles. Overall, Alcuin's work on the bible text derives its importance not so much from the intrinsic merit of his revisions and emendations but from the impact his text had on the later Middle Ages.

Theodulf of Orleans

Like Alcuin, Theodulf (ca. 750/760–821) was a key member of the Carolingian court and a close confidant of Charlemagne. He was of Visigothic descent but took refuge in Southern France, in the Septimanie region. In 789, he was appointed Bishop of Orleans and abbot of several monasteries, including the Benedictine abbey of Fleury (Fenner 2012). He is the author of the *Opus Caroli regis contra synodum*, or *Libri Carolini* (Chazelle 1993). Theodulf's work on the biblical text ran largely concurrently with the activities of Alcuin. However, the nature of their work and how they approached the challenges posed by the biblical text were quite different. Theodulf's revision can be termed "textual criticism" in the modern sense of the word. His goal appears to have been to reconstruct Jerome's version as closely as possible, the *Hebraica ueritas* in Latin. Today, six Bibles are extant in which Theodulf had a hand (along with a few fragments).[5]

1. Stuttgart, Württembergische Landesbibl., HB. II 16. This is the oldest surviving example of Theodulf's text, but it is incomplete.

---

[5] For fragments of a ninth-century Theodulf Bible from the collegiate church of St. Ursus in Solothurn, see <http://www.e–codices.unifr.ch/en/list/one/sl/0003>.

2. London, BL, Add. MS 24142 or *Codex Hubertianus*, a heavily corrected manuscript originally produced in Tours. Like extant Spanish pandects from the time, it has three columns to a page.

3. Le Puy, Trésor de la Cathédrale, s.n. or Codex Aniciensis.[6] This is a complete Bible, the dedication, Psalms and Gospels copied on purple parchment and passages of note and titles drawn in gold. Produced under Theodulf's direction around 800.

4. Paris, BnF, lat. 9380, also known as the Mesmes Bible. This is a complete Bible, which belonged to the cathedral of Orleans and could be Theodulf's personal copy (van Liere 2014: 35).

5. Paris, BnF, lat. 11937, with provenance Saint-Germain-des-Prés, is a copy of a Theodulf Bible, containing today only part of the Old Testament.

6. Copenhagen, Royal Library, NKS 1, consisting of parts from a manuscript that used to belong to the cathedral treasure of Carcassonne, was lost in the seventeenth century and subsequently rediscovered.

Only the manuscripts of Le Puy and Orleans contain the complete Theodulf Bible with the dedicatory texts and the appendices, which consist of Isidore of Seville's *Chronographia*, Eucherius of Lyons's *De nominibus hebraicis*, Melito's *Clavis*, and the pseudo-Augustinian *Speculum* or *Liber de diuinis scripturis* (Chevalier-Royet 2011: 181). These tools for the reader, attesting to Theodulf's pedagogical interest (Contreni 1983: 79), are supplementary texts that contextualize biblical chronology, explain rare or difficult words, and provide a starting point for exegesis. Compared to the Tours Bibles, Theodulf's Bibles are more modest affairs. The script is a tiny Caroline minuscule and the page size is smaller. Overall, the Bibles seem more immediately suitable for use in a scholarly context than in a liturgical setting.

The text of the six Theodulf Bibles reveals progressive stages of an ongoing critical evaluation and correction of the biblical text. This is manifested in marginal annotations, numerous corrections, and erasures. The marginal annotations reveal that Theodulf made careful parallel comparisons with different versions of the Latin Bible. We find variant readings marked with *alii* ("other" versions), *spanus* (Spanish Bible versions), *albinus* (Alcuin's version), *ii* (accords between the texts of the Spanish and Alcuinian versions), and *hebraeus* (the Hebrew text). Theodulf's marginal annotations grow more numerous in the later Bibles (Candiard and Chevalier-Royet 2012). The relations between the different witnesses suggest that Theodulf kept an unbound exemplar in the scriptorium to which he added corrections and adjustments and that individual books were revised in between the production of complete Bibles (Fischer 1985: 135–47).

Theodulf also applied his critical attitude to the Bible as a whole. He introduced the book of Baruch, while choosing not to include a number of apocryphal books: 3 and 4 Ezra (which are included in the Bible of Maurdramnus of Corbie and a number of bible

---

[6] This is the only one of these six bibles not currently available in a full online digitization, and is not to be confused with Paris, BnF, lat. 4, another complete Bible with provenance Le Puy and known by the name Codex Aniciensis.

manuscripts from Northern France), 3 Corinthians (commonly found in Italian Bibles at the time), and the widely disseminated Epistle to the Laodiceans (see further chap. 7). The order of the books is that set out by Isidore of Seville and includes the Priscillian apparatus to the Pauline Epistles typical of the tradition of which the Codex Cavensis is the best representative (Houghton 2016: 85). Theodulf's Spanish heritage is present in his Bible version and also in the exemplars he used as sources, but he went beyond that, to Bibles of Italian origin (Contreni 1983: 75–76; Bogaert 2012: 84).

Theodulf's bible revision, while more advanced than Alcuin's from our modern perspective, did not have as great an impact as Alcuin's text. The six Theodulf Bibles form a closed group in the textual transmission of the Latin Bible. Chevalier-Royet (2007: 253) explains the success of Alcuin's text versus that of Theodulf by observing that Alcuin answered an urgent need: Carolingian exegetes required a clear, uniform, accessible text as a framework within which to place the patristic heritage they were organizing, for which a correct and reliable bible text was necessary. While Theodulf's text was evidently a work in progress, with multiple variants between which readers needed to choose, Alcuin's Bible addressed the needs of the time.

THE PRODUCTION OF BIBLE MANUSCRIPTS IN THE CAROLINGIAN AGE

The ninth century witnessed a steep rise in manuscript production, alongside and because of technical innovations and new practices that increased scribal efficiency.[7] The pivotal role of the Carolingian court in educational and religious reform provided a strong impetus to the creation of more books to support these ambitious programs. Furthermore, the recent conquest of what would become the Carolingian empire and the need to consolidate the Carolingian dynasty stimulated the creation of luxury manuscripts, suitable for the exchange of gifts and for the glorification of the court. Bible manuscripts were at the center of this dynamic.[8]

The Earliest Carolingian Bibles

One of the most profound and lasting innovations of the Carolingian period is the Caroline minuscule script. This script is believed to have been developed at Corbie, in response to the difficulties presented by the diversity of minuscule scripts in

---

[7] See Bischoff 2014, 2004, 1998. For bible manuscripts in particular, see Fischer 1985: 163–216.

[8] For information on the use of Carolingian Bibles in critical editions, see the lists of sigla in Houghton 2016: 283–96. Stegmüller's *Repertorium Biblicum Medii Aevi* remains a fundamental systematic overview: an open-access electronic version is available at <http://www.repbib.uni-trier.de/cgi-bin/rebiIndex.tcl>.

Merovingian Gaul. The script was created in the 770s, under abbot Maurdramnus, who was in office from 772 to 781. The Maurdramnus minuscule is the earliest datable example of Caroline minuscule and is "an excellent and superbly balanced script" (Ganz 1990: 12). The Maurdramnus Bible was originally divided into ten to thirteen codices, of which five survive in Amiens, BM, 6 (Pentateuch), 7 (Joshua, Judges, Ruth), 9 (Daniel, Minor Prophets), 11 (1–2 Maccabees) and 12 (Wisdom books) and fragments of a sixth in Paris, BnF, lat. 13174 (Bogaert 2012: 81). The impact of Caroline minuscule was tremendous. Because it was easy to read and reproduce, it quickly became widely used and thereby allowed for the free circulation of manuscripts (Ganz 1995), the foundation for a national program of bible studies and use of the Bible in educational reform (Chazelle and Van Name Edwards 2003: 3–4).

The second major technical development of the Carolingian age is the large-scale production of single-volume Bibles, or pandects. While pandects are attested before the ninth century, this was the time when they became commonplace. The earliest evidence we have of a pandect Bible is from the sixth-century scriptorium of Vivarium, where Cassiodorus (ca. 485–ca. 585) lived in the final years of his life. At Vivarium, a pandect Bible, the Codex Grandior, was produced. This manuscript was taken from Italy to the monastery of Wearmouth–Jarrow in Northumbria by abbot Ceolfrid (in office 689–716) around the year 678. There it served as a model for three pandect Bibles. Only fragments are conserved of two, but the third is extant, the Codex Amiatinus (Florence, BML, Amiatino 1; Chazelle 2019, Hawkes and Boulton 2019, Fischer 1985: 9–35). The first properly Carolingian pandect we know of is the Bible of Angilram, named after the Bishop of Metz and court chaplain of Charlemagne, who died in 791. Only the second part of that Bible survived, from Proverbs up to Revelation 12:13, in Metz, BM, 7. In 1944, that part, too, was destroyed, though photographs survive. The text of the Bible of Angilram appears to be independent from Alcuin's version, though it was corrected at a later stage using a Tours Bible (Chevalier-Royet 2011: 171). The idea of producing a Bible in one or two volumes quickly caught on, as only a little later, the Tours scriptorium and other abbeys in Northern France started producing pandects as well (Fischer 1985: 161–62).

The Tours Scriptorium

Over the course of the first half of the ninth century, under four successive abbots, Alcuin (796–804), Fridugisus (807–34), Adalhard (834–43), and Vivian (843–51), the scriptorium at Saint-Martin-de-Tours was the most important center for the production of bible manuscripts in the Carolingian empire (Ganz 1994). The number of extant Tours Bibles is impressive. For the period between 796 and approximately 850, Fischer counts more than forty Bibles, mostly fragmentary, and more than twenty gospel books, preserved in whole or in part (1985: 254–69; see also Ganz 1990: 61–62). Based on these numbers, it is estimated that the Tours scriptorium produced an average of two pandect Bibles and a gospel book every year for the entire first half of the ninth century. In order to sustain such a massive enterprise, the Tours abbey required significant resources and personnel (Fischer 1985: 271–72, n.182). Up to twenty copyists could work on un-bound quires simultaneously, sometimes using different exemplars for the same book (see Ganz 2012: 333 for lists of scribal hands). Each text was scrupulously compared with its original after copying and markings such as *req* for *requisitum est* (or the Tironian equivalent) were used to indicate that a check was complete (Houghton 2016: 82).

The Tours Bibles have a uniform and distinctive form and layout, which was estab-lished under Alcuin's abbacy. They are pandects written on large sheets of parchment, measuring 47–54 cm in height and 35–39 cm in width. A Tours pandect consists of be-tween 350 and 450 folios, usually written in two columns of ca. fifty lines (Houghton 2016: 82). The margins are generous, with the text block measuring ca. 38 cm in height and 26 cm in width. The script is of course the Caroline minuscule, used in different sizes to indicate the hierarchical structure of the text. These typical characteristics remained remarkably stable throughout the five decades the scriptorium performed at its peak, though some codices stand out, mostly because of their lavish decorations. Tours Bibles were produced on commission as gifts but also served for communal reading or as templates for the production of further Bibles (van Liere 2014: 35; see also Germann 2010; Kessler 1977; and Rand 1929, 1931, 1934).

The most important Tours Bibles (when it comes to their text critical value) are grouped together in the Stuttgart Vulgate under the siglum Φ, which derives from Alcuin's nickname *Flaccus*:

  - London, BL, Add. MS 10546, the Moutier-Grandval Bible (Tours, ca. 830–34)
  - Paris, BnF, lat. 8847 (Tours, ca. 800)
  - Monza, Biblioteca Capitolare, g-1/1 (Tours, ca. 800)
  - St. Gall, Stiftsbibliothek, 75 (Tours, ca. 802)
  - Bamberg, Staatliche Bibliothek, Msc. Bibl. 1 (formerly A.I.5) (Tours, ca. 834–37)
  - Rome, Bibl. Vallicelliana, B.6, the Codex Vallicellianus (Rheims, mid-ninth century)
  - Zurich, Zentralbibliothek, Car. C. 1 (ca. 820–25)

The first five were copied at Tours, the sixth was produced slightly later, around 850, in Rheims (Houghton 2016: 262–64; Lobrichon 2004: 214). The Codex Vallicellianus is a symptom of the changing times: the production of Tours Bibles petered out dramatically after the death of Vivian in 851, due to the Viking raids that destroyed the abbey in 852, and the locus of manu-script production shifted from Tours to Rheims. For the period after the middle of the ninth century, only three pandect Bibles and seven gospel books from Tours are preserved.

Manuscripts Associated with Charlemagne's Court

Many of the Bibles associated with Charlemagne, his immediate family and his successors stand out as hallmarks of luxury and artistry. These codices were produced at Charlemagne's Court school or made at important scriptoria to be given as gifts to the royal family. The most important collection of Carolingian royal manuscripts is the so-called Ada Group. It consists of ten gospel books, most likely copied in Aachen between 781 and 814. The name of the whole derives from the two-part Ada Gospels, also known as the Trier Golden Gospels, (Trier, Stadtbibliothek, 22; see Embach 2010) which were made for Charlemagne's sister and subsequently offered by her to the abbey of St. Maximinus of Trier. Other members of this group are the Dagulf Psalter (Vienna, ÖNB, lat. 1861), which Charlemagne had made to give to Pope Hadrian I in the final years of the eighth century and contains the *uersio gallicana* of the Psalter in accordance with Charlemagne's liturgical reforms; the Gospels of Charlemagne (Paris, BnF, nouv. acq. lat. 1203), the first to testify to Charlemagne's liturgical reforms; the Gospels of Saint-Denis (Paris, BnF, lat. 9387); the Gospels of Saint-Médard de Soissons (Paris, BnF, lat. 8850),which were produced before 827 and presented by Louis the Pious to the church of Saint-Médard de Soissons; the Godescalc Gospels (Paris, BnF, lat. 1203); the Harley Golden Gospels (London, BL, Harley 2788); the Abbeville Gospels (Abbeville, BM 4); the Ingolstadt Gospels (Munich, BSB, Clm 27270); and the Lorsch Gospels (Alba Iulia, Batthyaneum, s.n. and Vatican City, BAV, Pal. lat. 50). The group has many features of luxury manuscripts, with full-page illustrations containing portraits of the evangelists, writing in gold ink, purple parchment leaves, and carved ivory covers in a style that is reminiscent of late-antique practices. The Ada group represents the stylistic characteristics of Charlemagne's Court school illuminations, which was very influential in establishing the Carolingian style of illumination, a revival of Roman classicism, fused with Insular motifs and Byzantine styles (Chevalier-Royet 2011: 169–71).

Alongside the Ada Group, a second cluster of four royal gospel books produced between 795 and 810 revolves around the so-called Coronation Gospels or Vienna Golden Gospels (Vienna, Hofburg, Schatzkammer Inv. XIII 18). Legend has it the Coronation Gospels were discovered in Charlemagne's tomb when it was opened two hundred years after his death (Houghton 2016: 81). It is unclear precisely which models were used for these royal bible manuscripts, whether a new version was created specifically for use at court or whether the copyists used available sources. The text of the Ada Group is a Vulgate version, but one that appears to evolve through the different members of the group. Neither Alcuin nor Theodulf appears to have used it for their own revisions, but we do find contemporary traces in Bibles at Trier, Metz, and Rheims (Chevalier-Royet 2011: 169–71).

The production of royal manuscripts continued under Charlemagne's successors. Two examples from the reign of Charles the Bald are Paris, BnF, lat. 1, the "first" Bible of Charles the Bald which was produced at Tours under Vivian (Dutton and Kessler 1997), and the magnificent Bible of St. Paul Outside the Walls (Rome, Abbazia di S. Paolo fuori le Mura, s.n.), which was offered by Charles the Bald to Pope John VIII in 875 on the occasion of his coronation as emperor (Diebold 1994).

CAROLINGIAN BIBLE COMMENTARIES

Commentaries on Scripture were one of the main forms of intellectual output during the Carolingian period.[9] A rough yet evocative count states that only seventy surviving Latin biblical commentaries were composed between 500 and 750, while no fewer than two hundred and twenty were produced by fifty-one identifiable authors between 750 and 1000 (Contreni 2012: 525–31). Some of the Carolingian commentaries circulated widely and found resonance in later centuries as well, as is evident from the 1,850 extant manuscripts Chazelle and Van Name Edwards counted in their preliminary survey of 130 Carolingian exegetical treatises (2003: 2). However, few of these commentaries were widely disseminated. There was a preference for certain biblical books, which were much discussed. On the importance of the Pauline Epistles, Heil states that "no other group of scriptural texts found so many interpreters in the few decades between 800 and 860, in either homiletic selections or comprehensive commentaries" (2003: 75–76).

The focus on exegesis in the eighth and ninth century did not limit itself to the creation of new bible commentaries. It also resulted in a great interest in earlier exegetical endeavors. The exegetical works of the Fathers of the early Church (also including numerous anonymous works wrongly attributed to patristic authorities) were copied abundantly and arranged and excerpted in numerous anthologies (Chazelle and Van Name Edwards 2003: 5). This deference to the authority of the Church Fathers led to the scholarly dismissal of Carolingian commentators as second-rate compilers (with the exception, perhaps, of Paschasius Radbertus and John Scottus: see Contreni 1983: 74). This attitude has been abandoned in recent research (Chambert-Protat et al. 2017). In fact, it is predominantly via the Carolingians' engagement with the patristic heritage that we can discern the development of their exegesis through the eighth and ninth century (see Berndt and Fédou 2013, in particular the chapters by Dahan and Shimahara).

Three stages have been identified in the development of Carolingian exegesis (Chazelle and Van Name Edwards 2003: 10–13). First, at the turn of the ninth century, anthologies were produced that focused on a single author, along with the first Carolingian commentaries. This generation is represented by Peter of Pisa/Petrus Grammaticus (744–99) (Gorman 2007: 276–98), Wigbod (Gorman 2002: 1–29, 200–36; Passi 2002), Josephus Scottus (d. 791–804), and Alcuin's own commentaries, which include *Quaestiones in Genesim* and treatises on the Psalms, Ecclesiastes, the Gospel of John, and several Pauline Epistles. In this earliest stage, the works of the Church Fathers were being read and organized. The quotations reveal that the Carolingian

---

[9] As such, the field is extensive: the spectrum of research is shown by Chambert-Protat et al. (2018); Shimahara (2009); Leonardi and Orlandi (2005); and Heil (1998). Still relevant are the major works on medieval exegesis, de Lubac (1959–63) and Smalley (1983) (with an update for the period 1984–2013 in Ocker and Madigan 2015), and on medieval literature in general, Brunhölzl (1975). Unfortunately, much of the rich corpus of Carolingian bible commentaries remains unedited or accessible only in outdated editions.

authors were not yet completely at ease with the source materials: they employ a relatively limited range of sources and struggle with questions of authorship. Second, in the first half of the ninth century, the reforms of Charlemagne and his son, Louis the Pious, began to pay off. There was a wider availability of books and significant progress had been made in the realm of education in general and biblical studies in particular (Contreni 1995). The most prominent commentators in this second stage are Claudius of Turin (d. 827), Hrabanus Maurus (d. 856), and Angelomus of Luxeuil (d. 855). These authors demonstrate "a greater variety of sources, were more likely to identify them accurately, more skilfully balanced one against another, and presented a more critical attitude toward their teachings" (Chazelle and Van Name Edwards 2003: 11). This period saw the elaboration of compilation commentaries founded on patristic writings (see Chambert-Protat et al. 2017). Efforts were also made to comment on biblical books that had heretofore been neglected, such as Kings, Esther, Judith, and so on. The third stage, around the middle of the ninth century, was marked by the assimilation of the patristic heritage as collected and organized in the two previous stages. The involvement of the authors in the commentaries increased, their selections of patristic material became more condensed and to the point, and the selection of quotations no longer reflected their original context but rather the preoccupations of Carolingian intellectual life. The main representatives of this phase are Walafrid Strabo (d. 849) (Albarello 2003), Haimo of Auxerre (d. ca. 865–75), Paschasius Radbertus (d. 865), and John Scottus (d. ca. 877).

Prominent Carolingian Exegetes

Hrabanus Maurus

Hrabanus Maurus (ca. 780–856) is the author of more than thirty exegetical works, commentaries, and sermon collections (on the latter, see Etaix 1984). He was a pupil of Alcuin and became Abbot of Fulda and eventually Archbishop of Mainz, his native city. Several of his commentaries were dedicated to senior members at court, including Louis the Pious and his wife Judith. Hrabanus's commentaries, although not anthologies in the strictest sense of the term, incorporate numerous, often verbatim, quotations from the Church Fathers. Among others, he wrote a commentary on Paul around 836–40, at the demand of his pupil Lupus of Ferrières, and a commentary on Matthew.[10] A particular influence on this commentary was the Augustinian compilation on Paul created by the Venerable Bede in the previous century. He not only quoted at length from Bede's selection of Augustine but also copied Bede's habit of including abbreviated references to the source works in the margins of his commentary (see Boucaud 2013: 322–26, Heil 1998, and especially Cantelli 2006). Hrabanus was the first to comment on the books of Deuteronomy, Judith, Esther, Wisdom, and Chronicles. His work on the

---

[10] The commentary on Paul appears in PL 111: 1273–1616 (Romans) and PL 112: 9–834 (1 Corinthians–Hebrews), while the commentary on Matthew was edited in 2000 (CCCM 174–174A).

historical books of the Bible would form the basis for the *Glossa ordinaria* (van Liere 2014:148–49; see chap. 14).

Claudius of Turin

Claudius of Turin (ca. 780–ca. 830) worked at the court of Louis the Pious, where he lectured on the Bible. Several of his commentaries were also written at the request of Louis the Pious, who made him Bishop of Turin around 816. Claudius wrote commentaries on the Octateuch (although he was unable to finish the project), Matthew, and the Pauline corpus. His commentary on 1 and 2 Corinthians, sent into circulation around 820, sparked controversy, although he was not formally condemned for heresy. Gorman describes him as the first in the Carolingian period to "break free from what might be called the catena mentality" (1997: 318–19). Rather than interpreting a scriptural passage by linking together excerpts that deal with that passage, Claudius placed greater emphasis on the original interpretation of Scripture through a personal reflection on patristic exegesis. Claudius, like Hrabanus Maurus, was influenced by Bede's exegetical commentaries and adopted the same habit of adding references to his sources in the margins of his commentaries (Gorman 1997: 312). Much of his exegetical work remains unedited, although the commentaries on Matthew and Paul at least were disseminated widely during the ninth century (however, see Boucaud 2013 and Boulhol 2002).

Florus of Lyons

If Claudius of Turin was the first to include his own voice in his commentaries, Florus of Lyons is the master of the patristic compilation commentary. He lived from ca. 785 to 861–62 and became deacon of the church of Lyons around 827. He was widely acknowledged as one of the greatest scholars of his time and famed for his knowledge of Scripture and the Church Fathers. His greatest accomplishments in the field of exegesis are the *Collectio ex dictis XII Patrum* and the *Expositio Epistolarum beati Pauli apostoli ex operibus sancti Augustini* (see Chambert-Protat et al. 2017). The former is a commentary on the Pauline corpus consisting of 1,081 excerpts from the works of twelve patristic writers, including the great names, such as Jerome and Gregory the Great, but also lesser known authors such as Ephrem the Syrian and Avitus of Vienne. Florus's *magnum opus*, however, is his *Expositio*, a compilation of more than 4,000 excerpts from the works of Augustine, organized to form a line-by-line commentary on Paul's Epistles. The work is very valuable for editions of Augustine's works, as the *Expositio*'s original manuscript witness, partially in Florus's own hand (Lyons, BM, 484), and several more direct copies from the ninth century are extant. Florus's compilations represent the apex of the Carolingian effort to centralize and organize the patristic heritage.[11] Florus was not the only one to create so-called patristic compilation commentaries. Another interesting example from the first half of the ninth century is the Romans commentary wrongly attributed to Charlemagne's court chaplain Helisachar of

---

[11] The *Collectio* is edited in CCCM 193–193A–193B (2002, 2006, 2007). The first volume of the long-awaited edition of the *Expositio* appeared as CCCM 220B in 2011. The second volume is in preparation.

Saint-Riquier (Paris, BnF, lat. 11574), consisting of 841 fragments from a range of patristic authors (Fransen 2001).

John Scottus

John Scottus Eriugena (ca. 815–ca. 877) was an Irish scholar who came to the Carolingian court around 845. A Neoplatonist philosopher and theologian, he was particularly well versed in Greek for the time and became the leader of the Palace school under Charles the Bald. He, like Claudius of Turin, faced accusations of heresy. Though not considered his most important works today, John Scottus wrote a commentary on the Greek text of the Gospel according to John (Jeauneau 1972) and he produced a series of glosses on the Bible (Contreni and Ó Néill 1997). According to Contreni and Ó Néill (1997), John Scottus stands out as the sole Carolingian exegete to have truly made use of Theodulf's biblical edition in the redaction of his *Glossae Diuinae Historiae*, though this assessment is nuanced by Chevalier-Royet (2007: 253).

Haimo of Auxerre

Haimo of Auxerre (fl. 840–70) is something of an odd one out in this collection of Carolingian exegetes. Whereas much is known about the others' lives, their political connections, and their intellectual networks, Haimo presents more of a mystery. He was a monk and a key figure in the school of Auxerre, which was an important center for biblical studies under Charles the Bald (Iogna-Prat et al. 1991). He wrote commentaries on a great many biblical books, including Genesis and the entire Pauline corpus, and he may have intended to complete a commentary on the whole Bible.[12] Although his immediate context is largely unknown, his later reception is extensive and complicated. His are perhaps the most widespread of the Carolingian commentaries, with a vast and complicated manuscript tradition that reveals their use in the context of the schools, the liturgy, and as a source in later exegetical works. Today, some 180 manuscripts of his Pauline commentary survive, with 146 of his commentary on Revelation. His Pauline commentary was quoted by humanist scholars Lorenzo Valla and Erasmus and he was an important source for the *Glossa ordinaria*. As perhaps the most successful of the Carolingian exegetes, he has received considerable scholarly attention (see further Shimahara 2007: 9–20).

Other Forms of Exegesis

In addition to biblical commentary, which could comprise original Carolingian analysis, the compilation of patristic fragments, or something in between, other forms of explanation or elucidation of the biblical text also made an appearance in the

---

[12] Genesis is edited in CCCM 135 (2005), while for the Pauline commentaries, see PL 117: 361–938 and Levy 2009.

Carolingian era. A few examples are bilingual editions, in particular of the Psalter (Ganz 2012: 336); sermons, whether original Carolingian creations such as the homiliary of Smaragdus of Saint-Mihiel (Barré 1962; Amos 1989) or compilations of patristic sermons like Paul the Deacon's patristic homiliary (Grégoire 1980); and, finally, glossed Bibles, in particular, at this early stage, the glossed Psalter. The oldest surviving example of a glossed Psalter where the ruling in advance shows the intent to include both the text and the gloss arranged on the page is a manuscript produced in Fulda, ca. 800 (Frankfurt am Main, Stadt- und Universitätsbibl., Barth 32; see Ganz 2012: 335; Bogaert 2012: 87).

THE CAROLINGIAN LEGACY

The program of reform instigated by Charlemagne and carried on by his successors was a success. From the years 770–80 onward, the effect of the central role played by the Carolingian court in establishing schools, promoting the creation and circulation of manuscripts, and drawing attention to the importance of biblical studies is unmistakable. Taken up by the leading intellectuals of the ninth century, the project of bible production, revision, and commentary has ensured the Carolingians' lasting impact on the transmission of the Latin Bible, both in terms of the physical transmission of the Bible and in terms of the text that was being copied and studied. Nevertheless, we must beware of speaking in superlatives and neglecting to nuance the accomplishments of the Carolingians. The uniformity and standardization of the material form of the bible codex was realized much sooner than that of the biblical text, and there was an arc of development during the Carolingian period itself. Still, by the middle of the ninth century, several standards were established that would cast a long shadow.

The format of the physical bible manuscript popularized in the Carolingian period—a single volume, two columns to a page, a clear presentation of the hierarchy of the text, use of Caroline minuscule script—became an enduring standard. The practice of copying an entire Bible in a single volume had its effects on the establishment of the biblical canon. When copying a Bible in a single volume, the number and order of the books are a much more immediate concern than when copying a Bible in ten or so volumes (Bogaert 2012: 72). From around 850 onward, Jerome's translation became the common text of the Bible, in part due to the wide diffusion of the bibles of Tours. This does not mean that complete uniformity was achieved, merely that Jerome's translation was inexorably moving toward becoming the Vulgate. For the Psalter, the Gallican version prevailed, against Theodulf of Orleans's preference for the *Iuxta Hebraeos* (Fischer 1985: 407–11). Different texts continued to be used in different scriptoria, particularly in grand abbeys with rich libraries, such as Corbie and Saint-Germain.

The importance accorded to the reading and study of the Bible as the key to a true Christian life (Shimahara 2009: 6) sparked a great number of biblical commentaries. However, here too we must not overestimate their importance. As Contreni puts it, "while these commentaries are important, they are only the tip of the iceberg. Their diffusion in Carolingian times was relatively limited. . . . The commentaries reflect the conditions of Carolingian biblical study but were not the mainstays of it" (1983: 93–94). The Carolingian commentaries hardly replaced, then or in later times, the powerfully authoritative exegetical writings of the Church Fathers (Ganz 2012: 325). However, the Carolingians did play a crucial role in putting together a corpus and establishing a methodology for the study of the Church Fathers. The prologues and marginal annotations in the commentaries display the Carolingian authors' integrity (Contreni 1983: 82–83). The Carolingians were keenly aware of their responsibility in accurately presenting the thoughts of the Church Fathers and their proper teachings. It is a sense of responsibility that seems characteristic of all their dealings with the Latin Bible.

BIBLIOGRAPHY

Albarello, Carlo. 2003. "Walafrid Strabo commente l'Exode: tradition textuelle et grammaire exégétique." *Recherches augustiniennes* 33: 179–207.

Amos, Thomas L. 1989. "Preaching and the Sermon in the Carolingian World." In De ore Domini: *Preacher and Word in the Middle Ages*, edited by Thomas L. Amos, Eugene A. Green, and Beverly Mayne Kienzle, 41–60. Kalamazoo: Medieval Institute.

Barré, Henri. 1962. *Les Homéliaires carolingiens de l'école d'Auxerre: Authenticité—Inventaire—Tableaux comparatifs*. Vatican City: BAV.

Berndt, Rainer, and Michel Fédou, eds. 2013. *Les réceptions des Pères de l'Église au Moyen Âge. Le devenir de la tradition ecclésiale*. Münster: Aschendorff.

Bischoff, Bernhard. 1998–2014. *Katalog der festländischen Handschriften des neunten Jahrhunderts*. 3 vols. Wiesbaden: Harrassowitz.

Bogaert, Pierre-Maurice. 2012. "The Latin Bible, *c.* 600 to *c.* 900." In *New Cambridge History of the Bible: Vol. 2. From 600 to 1450*, edited by Richard Marsden and E. Ann Matter, 69–92. Cambridge: Cambridge University Press.

Boucaud, Pierre. 2013. "*Corpus Paulinum.* L'exégèse grecque et latine des Épîtres au premier millénaire." *Revue de l'histoire des réligions* 230, no. 3: 299–332.

Boulhol, Pascal. 2002. *Claude de Turin: Un évêque iconoclaste dans l'Occident carolingien. Etude suivie de l'édition du "Commentaire sur Josue."* Paris: Institut d'études augustiniennes.

Brunhölzl, Franz. 1975. *Geschichte der lateinischen Literatur des Mittelalters. Erster Band: Von Cassiodor bis zum Ausklang der karolingischen Erneuerung*. Munich: Wilhelm Fink.

Candiard, Adrien, and Caroline Chevalier-Royet.2012. "Critique textuelle et recours à l'hébreu à l'époque carolingienne. Le cas exceptionnel d'une Bible de Theodulf. Bible de Saint-Germain, ms. Paris, BnF lat, 11937." In *Études d'exégèse médiévale offertes à Gilbert Dahan par ses élèves*, edited by Annie Noblesse-Rocher, 13–34. Turnhout: Brepols.

Cantelli, Silvia B. 2006. *Hrabani Mauri Opera Exegetica: Repertorium Fontium. Rabano Mauro Esegeta. Le Fonti. I Commentari.* 3 vols. Turnhout: Brepols.

Chambert-Protat, Pierre, Franz Dolveck, and Camille Gerzaguet, eds. 2017. *Les Douze Compilations Pauliniennes de Florus de Lyon. Un carrefour des traditions patristiques au IXe siècle*. Rome: École Française de Rome.

Chazelle, Celia. 1993. "Images, Scripture, the Church, and the *Libri Carolini.*" *Proceedings of the PMR Conference* 16, no. 17: 53–76.

Chazelle, Celia. 2019. *The Codex Amiatinus and Its "Sister" Bibles: Scripture, Liturgy, and Art in the Milieu of the Venerable Bede*. Leiden: Brill.

Chazelle, Celia, and Burton Van Name Edwards, eds. 2003. *The Study of the Bible in the Carolingian Era*. Turnhout: Brepols.

Chevalier-Royet, Caroline. 2006. "Les révisions bibliques carolingiennes." *Temas Medievales* 14: 7–30.

Chevalier-Royet, Caroline. 2007. "Les révisions bibliques de Theodulf d'Orléans et la question de leur utilisation par l'exégèse carolingienne." In *Études d'exégèse carolingienne: Autour d'Haymon d'Auxerre*, edited by Sumi Shimahara, 237–56. Turnhout: Brepols.

Chevalier-Royet, Caroline. 2011. "Lectures des Livres des Rois à l'époque Carolingienne." PhD diss., Université Paris-Sorbonne.

Contreni, John J. 1983. "Carolingian Biblical Studies." In *Carolingian Essays*, edited by Uta-Renate Blumenthal, 71–98. Washington, DC: Catholic University of America.

Contreni, John J. 1995. "The Carolingian Renaissance: Education and Literary Culture." In *The New Cambridge Medieval History, vol. II, c. 700–c. 900*, edited by Rosamond McKitterick, 709–57. Cambridge: Cambridge University Press.

Contreni, John J. 1996. "Carolingian Biblical Culture." In *Iohannes Scottus Eriugena: The Bible and Hermeneutics*, edited by Gerd Van Riel, Carlos Steel, and James McEvoy, 1–23. Leuven: Leuven University.

Contreni, John J. 2012. "The patristic legacy to c. 1000." In *New Cambridge History of the Bible: Vol. 2. From 600 to 1450*, edited by Richard Marsden and E. Ann Matter, 505–35. Cambridge: Cambridge University Press.

Contreni, John J., and Pádraig P. Ó Néill, eds. 1997. *Glossae divinae historiae. The Biblical Glosses of John Scottus Eriugena*. Florence: SISMEL, Galluzzo.

de Lubac, Henri. 1959–63. *Exégèse médiévale: Les quatre sens de l'Écriture*. Paris: Aubier. (English translation 1998.)

Diebold, William J. 1994. "The Ruler Portrait of Charles the Bald in the S. Paolo Bible." *The Art Bulletin* 76, no. 1: 6–18.

Embach, Michael. 2010. *Des Ada-Evangeliar (StB Hs 22). Die karolingische Bilderhandschrift*. Kostbarkeiten der Stadtbibliothek Trier 2. Trier: Paulinus.

Étaix, Raymond. 1984. "L'Homéliaire composé par Raban Maur pour l'empereur Lothaire," *Recherches augustiniennes* 19: 211–40.

Fenner, Chris. 2012. "Theodulf: Theologian at Charlemagne's Court, Poet, and Bishop of Orleans." *The Hymn* 63, no. 1: 13–20.

Fischer, Bonifatius. 1985. *Lateinische Bibelhandschriften im frühen Mittelalter*. AGLB 11. Freiburg: Herder.

Fransen, Pierre-Irenée. 2001. "Le dossier patristique d'Hélisachar: Le manuscrit Paris, BnF, lat, 11574 et l'une de ses sources," *Revue bénédictine* 111: 464–82.

Gameson, Richard, ed. 1994. *The Early Medieval Bible: Its Production, Decoration, and Use*. Cambridge: Cambridge University Press.

Ganz, David. 1990. *Corbie in the Carolingian Renaissance*. Sigmaringen: Jan Thorbecke.

Ganz, David. 1994. "Mass Production of Early Medieval Manuscripts: The Carolingian Bibles from Tours." In *The Early Medieval Bible: Its Production, Decoration, and Use*, edited by Richard Gameson, 53–62. Cambridge: Cambridge University Press.

Ganz, David. 1995. "Book Production in the Carolingian Empire and the Spread of Caroline Minuscule." In *The New Cambridge Medieval History, vol. II, c. 700–c. 900*, edited by Rosamond McKitterick, 786–808. Cambridge: Cambridge University Press.

Ganz, David. 2012. "Carolingian Bibles." In *New Cambridge History of the Bible: Vol. 2. From 600 to 1450*, edited by Richard Marsden and E. Ann Matter, 325–33. Cambridge: Cambridge University Press.

Germann, Martin. 2010. "Sankt Martin in Tours und eine seiner monumentalen Bibeln des 9. Jahrhunderts: Wie haben die Hersteller deren harmonische Proportionen bestimmt? Untersucht am Pandekt Ms. C1 der Zentralbibliothek Zürich." *Basler Zeitschrift für Geschichte und Altertumskunde* 110: 7–20.

Gorman, Michael M. 1997. "Claudius of Turin and Biblical Studies under Louis the Pious." *Speculum* 72, no. 2: 279–329.

Gorman, Michael M. 2002. *Biblical Commentaries from the Early Middle Ages*. Florence: SISMEL, Galluzzo.

Gorman, Michael M. 2007. *The Study of the Bible in the Early Middle Ages*. Florence: SISMEL, Galluzzo.

Grégoire, Réginald. 1980. *Homéliaires liturgiques médiévaux. Analyse de manuscrits*. Spoleto: CISAM.

Hawkes, Jane, and Meg Boulton, eds. 2019. *All Roads Lead to Rome: The Creation, Context and Transmission of the Codex Amiatinus*. Turnhout: Brepols.

Heil, Johannes. 1998. *Kompilation oder Konstruktion? Die Juden in den Pauluskommentaren des 9. Jahrhunderts*. Hannover: Hahn.

Heil, Johannes. 2003. "Labourers in the Lord's Quarry: Carolingian Exegetes, Patristic Authority, and Theological Innovation, a Case Study in the Representation of Jews in Commentaries on Paul." In *The Study of the Bible in the Carolingian Era*, edited by Celia Chazelle and Burton Van Name Edwards, 75–96. Turnhout: Brepols.

Houghton, H. A. G. 2016. *The Latin New Testament: A Guide to Its Early History, Text, and Manuscripts*. Oxford: Oxford University Press.

Iogna-Prat, Dominique. 1991. "L'œuvre d'Haymon d'Auxerre: état de la question." In *L'école carolingienne d'Auxerre: de Murethach à Remi 830-908*, edited by Dominique Iogna-Prat, Colette Jeudy, and Guy Lobrichon, 157–79. Paris: Beauchesne.

Jeauneau, Édouard, ed. 1972. *Jean Scot, Commentaire sur l'évangile de Jean. Introduction, texte critique, traduction, notes et index*. Paris: Cerf.

Kaczynski, Bernice M. 1995. "Edition, Translation, and Exegesis: The Carolingians and the Bible." In *"The Gentle Voices of Teachers": Aspects of Learning in the Carolingian Age*, edited by Richard E. Sullivan, 171–85. Columbus: Ohio State University.

Kessler, Herbert L. 1977. *The Illustrated Bibles from Tours*. Princeton: Princeton University.

Dutton, Paul E. and Kessler, Herbert L. 1997. *The Poetry and Paintings of the First Bible of Charles the Bald*. Ann Arbor: University of Michigan.

Leonardi, Claudio, and Giovanni Orlandi, eds. 2005. *Biblical Studies in the Early Middle Ages*. Florence: SISMEL, Galluzzo.

Levy, Ian C. 2009. "Trinity and Christology in Haimo of Auxerre's Pauline Commentaries." In *The Multiple Meaning of Scripture. The Role of Exegesis in Early-Christian and Medieval Culture*, edited by Ineke Van't Spijker, 101–23. Leiden: Brill.

Lobrichon, Guy. 2004. "Le texte des bibles alcuiniennes." In *Alcuin, de York à Tours. Ecriture, pouvoir et réseaux dans l'Europe du haut Moyen Âge*, edited by Philippe Depreux and Bruno Judic, 209–19. Rennes-Tours: Presses Universitaires.

McKitterick, Rosamond. 1977. *The Frankish Church and the Carolingian Reforms, 789-895*. London: Royal Historical Society.

McKitterick, Rosamond. 1989. *The Carolingians and the Written Word*. Cambridge: Cambridge University Press.

McKitterick, Rosamond. 1994. "Carolingian Bible Production: The Tours Anomaly." In *The Early Medieval Bible: Its Production, Decoration, and Use*, edited by Richard Gameson, 63–77. Cambridge: Cambridge University Press.

McKitterick, Rosamond, ed. 1995. *The New Cambridge Medieval History, vol. II, c. 700–c. 900*. Cambridge: Cambridge University Press.

Ocker, Christopher, and Kevin Madigan. 2015. "After Beryl Smalley: Thirty Years of Medieval Exegesis 1984–2013." *Journal of Bible Reception* 2, no. 1: 87–130.

Passi, Sara. 2002. "Il commentario inedito ai Vangeli, attribuito a Wigbod." *Studi Medievali* 43: 59–156.

Phelan, Owen M. 2006. "The Carolingian Renewal and Christian Formation in Ninth-Century Bavaria." In *Texts and Identities in the Early Middle Ages*, edited by Richard Corradini, Rob Meens, Christina U. Pössel, and Philip Shaw, 389–400. Vienna: Österreichische Akademie der Wissenschaften.

Rand, Edward K. 1929. *A Survey of the Manuscripts of Tours*. Cambridge, Mass.: Medieval Academy of America.

Rand, Edward K. 1931. "A Preliminary Study of Alcuin's Bible." *Harvard Theological Review* 24: 323–96.

Rand, Edward K. 1934. *The Earliest Book of Tours with Supplementary Descriptions of Other Manuscripts of Tours*. Cambridge, Mass.: Medieval Academy of America.

Shimahara, Sumi, ed. 2007. *Études d'exégèse carolingienne: autour d'Haymon d'Auxerre*. Turnhout: Brepols.

Shimahara, Sumi. 2009. "L'exégèse de la Bible à l'époque carolingienne." In *Herméneutique du texte d'histoire: orientation, interprétation et questions nouvelles*, edited by Shoichi Sato, 5–14. Nagoya: Graduate School of Letters.

Smalley, Beryl. 1983. *The Study of the Bible in the Middle Ages*. 3rd ed. Oxford: Basil Blackwell (1st ed. 1941).

van Liere, Frans 2014. *An Introduction to the Medieval Bible*. Cambridge: Cambridge University Press.

CHAPTER 13

THE PRODUCTION OF MEDIEVAL BIBLES

GUY LOBRICHON

THE Latin Bible is one of the most obvious markers of Western cultural heritage. In the twelfth century, it flourished in all the churches, schools, universities, and even private homes, and it provided the base for translation into vernacular languages in kingdoms where this was encouraged. Despite its diminution in countries affected by the reforms of the sixteenth century, it never disappeared and continued to dominate in Catholic Europe, increased by the status of Latin as a learned language, without losing any of its prestige. Until recently, three outdated assertions have impeded scholarly understanding of the Christian Middle Ages: first, that the illiteracy of the medieval clergy deprived them of any desire even to read the Scriptures; second, that the laity were forbidden from owning and reading the unmediated text of the Bible (see Gow 2013); third, following this, that laypeople were only allowed to read carefully redacted paraphrases. The present chapter offers a brief outline of developments regarding the Bible in the West from the eleventh to the fifteenth centuries, in order to understand how communities—however they may be defined—were able to increase the total of their differences without in any way disavowing the Book, which contained the code of their common Christianity.

CONTENTS AND ORGANIZATION

Pandects, containing the entire Bible in a single volume of large dimensions, and smaller books devoted to separate parts of Scripture, coexisted for a long time. The former were rare before those created in Tours in the first half of the ninth century (Ganz 2015: 51): they remained confined to treasuries or royal or princely chapels until about the year 1000. Apart from books containing individual biblical writings, collections were made for liturgical use, study, or public display or for a community

or an ecclesiastical or lay patron. Specialists distinguish several types of biblical manuscript for liturgical use, including psalters. Gospel books, sometimes known as
Evangeliaries (*Evangelia*, *Tetraevangelia* or *Evangelaria*), contain the full text of the canonical gospels along with canon tables, prefaces, and introductions; from the seventh
to the tenth or eleventh centuries, a list of gospel readings according to the cycle of
the liturgical year was sometimes appended, known as the *Capitulare evangeliorum*.
The *Epistolarium* contained only the passages from the Epistles which were read at
Mass:[1] the *Evangelistarium*, or Book of Pericopes (sometimes, confusingly, also called
an Evangeliary) did the same for the Gospels (Crivello 2017a: 114). Later gospel books
were commissioned by individuals rather than serving a liturgical function (such as
the twelfth-century Harvard, Houghton Library, Riant 20; see Light 1988: 21–23). All
these manuscripts were prestigious, if not sacred. They were copied on high-quality
parchment right up to the fifteenth century, when the widespread availability of paper
permitted a reduction in production costs. A scribe could be engaged from a range
of professional copyists, lay or religious, men or women, in scriptoria or well-reputed
workshops. The writing of a text as large as the Old and New Testaments required about
a year of work for a competent scribe. Large workshops therefore employed several
artisans for this task, who divided the work between them under the direction of an experienced coordinator.

   How was the impeccable transmission of the biblical text assured? From the manuscript used as a source (the exemplar or antigraph) to its copy (or apograph), errors
could be introduced both by the head of the workshop and by the copyists. A rigorous
division of labor was therefore required. The coordinator verified the order of the biblical books, which had to conform to the liturgical practices of the church or monastery, and possibly even regional ecclesiastical usage. The quires of the exemplar were
separated into *libelli*, and one or more were given to each copyist along with gatherings
of blank parchment. The process of copying brought together a reader, who read the
exemplar out loud, a *notarius* who transcribed the text, a *rubricator* who wrote titles
and subtitles, and finally a reviser or corrector, who needed to be aware of any updates
in the choice of vocabulary. The book was generally decorated in a final phase: painters
were engaged for the frontispieces, cycles of images, which may be based on the books
of Genesis, Kings, Job, or the Psalter, and decorated letters and initials, whether or not
these were historiated. The choice of format involved several variables, relating to the
size of the manuscript, the text, and the decoration. Copying in long lines or two or three
columns was in part due to the type of script adopted, but from the ninth century a page
with two columns predominates in continental Europe. The selection of the exemplar
(or exemplars) was not necessarily easy (Shepard 2012: 393), although the type of text
to follow was relatively straightforward: from the ninth century, the version known as
the Vulgate as revised by the team of Alcuin outranked its competitors (the Bibles of
Theodulf and, for the Gospels, the "Lothar text" produced at Aix-la-Chapelle/Aachen),

---

[1] A luxury example is that of Padua Cathedral (Padua, Biblioteca Capitolare, MS E 2), illustrated in
1259 by Giovanni di Gaibana.

yet well into the thirteenth century, in particular regions, the text of some books or groups of books could be drawn from older versions. Moreover, it was common knowledge that the Books of Kings were the most corrupt of all the Latin Bibles (Linde 2012: 33, 117, 121). The head of the workshop could decide to follow a single-source manuscript conforming to the received tradition of the Latin text in that region, but when the task was the creation of a Bible of symbolic importance, it seems that recourse was made to two or more copies.

The choice of the exemplar determined the quality and authority of its copy. It is extremely rare that one can compare local exemplars to ancient witnesses before the eleventh century: the tendency is rather to mixed compilations. In the church of Rome itself, around 1050, those responsible for the first "Atlantic" Bibles sought to bring together two external exemplars, held by two abbeys not far from the papal city: Codex Amiatinus, of Northumbrian origin from around 715, and Codex Cavensis, of Hispanic origin from around 850, remain points of reference even today (Lobrichon 2000). At the beginning of the twelfth century, Stephen Harding, the Abbot of Cîteaux, had no particular concern to search for manuscripts of great antiquity but restricted himself to Carolingian exemplars. One hundred years later in Bohemia, the compiler of Codex Gigas (Stockholm, KB, Ms. A 148; VL 51; 1207–25) relied on an Anglo-Saxon gospel text from the eighth century, while taking the Acts of the Apostles and the Apocalypse from a manuscript of the *Vetus Latina*. In the third quarter of the twelfth century, the compiler of the Bible of St. Hugh of Lincoln (Oxford, Bodleian, Auct. E inf. 1 and 2) decided to provide two translations for the books of Job, Judith, and the Psalms one after the other, the first according to the Septuagint and the second according to the Hebrew text. When the monks of St. Gall began to copy "quadruple" psalters (Gallican, Roman, "Hebrew," and "Greek"), they made luxury books for the rich prelates of the empire who, even at the beginning of the eleventh century, were still accustomed to celebrating with the Greeks (Berschin 2005: 203–13). In Sicily, a triple psalter was made, in Greek, Latin, and Arabic for Queen Margaret (London, BL, Harley MS 5786, before 1153; see chap. 11). The instability of the biblical text remained part of its nature until the triumph of the printing press: even so, it is important to recognize that the evidence copyists worked from permitted textual forms (Fravventura 2017: cliii).

The text followed by the scribes and the sequence of biblical books bear witness to their fidelity to Christian tradition. Over time, the content of Scripture had been reorganized, without ever compromising the integrity of the whole. In the Old Testament, the position of the prophetic books varied (either directly following the Octateuch or not), often for liturgical reasons; there were also displacements in the New Testament, involving the grouping of Acts, the Epistles (where the sequence Philippians–Thessalonians–Colossians was changed to Philippians–Colossians–Thessalonians), and Revelation. The division of books or sections could be indicated by rubricated headings. What status should be given to Lamentations, the Prayer of Jeremiah (Lamentations 5), and the Book of Baruch? In Codex Gigas, they are run together as a single unit, whereas the Paris Bibles give each its own identity. Other prayers were often treated separately (e.g., the *Oratio Salomonis*, *Oratio Manasse*, and *Oratio Abacuc*). Similarly, Nehemiah (2 Ezra) is sometimes independent from 1 Ezra and sometimes not, although certain epilogues to the books of Job and Daniel bear witness to unusual traditions that survive here and there in the manuscripts (e.g., the Bible of Hugh du Puiset: Durham Cathedral Library, MS A.II.1).

It was also necessary to select the paratexts, whose main function was to frame and close each book and to guide readers toward a proper appreciation of each textual unit. These could include the canons of Eusebius, which mark the concordances between the Gospels (included in luxury manuscripts until the end of the twelfth century), stichometric indications of length, prefaces, divisions into chapters (*capitula* or *tituli*) with varying numeration and titles, and the rubrics in the Song of Songs. The Roman reformers from 1050–75 granted a canonical status to the prologues attributed to Jerome, although this was insufficient: other series of prologues and *argumenta* were preferred in different regions. Should apocryphal texts such as 3 Ezra (1 Esdras) and Psalm 151 be included or not?[2] One of the "Atlantic Bibles," from around 1080, incorporates texts from Isidore of Seville's *Allegoriae* (Vatican City, BAV, Barb. lat. 587). The compiler of Codex Gigas added at the end of 2 Maccabees extracts from Flavius Josephus's *Antiquitates Iudaicae* and *De Bello Iudaico*, as well as the *Etymologiae* of Isidore of Seville and some medical texts. In addition to these biblical paratexts, other additions to manuscripts include lists of relics, covenants, oaths, and charters, which benefit from the sacredness added by their context and solemnly confirm the goods and social ties of owners of the Bible in question.

FROM ATLANTIC BIBLES TO PARIS BIBLES

The physical form of Bibles varied for a long time, but signals of dissatisfaction accumulated during the eleventh century. They came from scattered groups of monks, canons, and laypeople, who all called for a reorganization of practices with reference to teaching the Bible, in particular the New Testament. It was then that new types of Bibles appeared. It is often said that there was a break in continuity which affected both production and decoration: this is frequently connected with the effects of the devastation caused by Normans, Hungarians, and Saracens (e.g., Crivello 2017b: 146). The change, however, may be more confidently recognized in the form of new experiments resulting from the introduction of ideas from Constantinople into Ottonian Germany, such as the New Testament illustration cycles that took root in Ottonian manuscripts from around 960. These are seen at Corvey, at Trier under Archbishop Egbert, at Cologne, at Mainz under Archbishop Willigise (975–1011), at Hildesheim under Bishop Bernward (993–1022), and in Lotharingia. However, these workshops did not produce

---

[2] 3 Ezra, generally avoided, appears in a number of thirteenth-century Italian Bibles, the Bible of Charles V, and the Bible of Robert de Bylling (see below); Psalm 151 is found in certain bibles of English origin and some Atlantic Bibles from Geneva (Togni 2001: 370–73; see also chap. 7).

many Bibles. It seems that between 920 and 1050, fewer Bibles were copied, and instead liturgical books, gospel lectionaries, psalters, and prayerbooks, often of considerable luxury, were made to order by imperial command for favored abbeys and cathedrals or for their palatial chapels.[3] Many others were commissioned by the wives of princes for the churches of their countries of origin, as in the case of the wives of Duke Władysław Herman (1079–1102): Judith of Bohemia (d. 1086) was the patron of the *Codex aureus Gnesnensis* (Kraków, Bibl. Czartoryskich 1207; Gniezno, Bibl. Kapitulna 1a), while her successor, Judith-Marie, sister of Henry IV, had Kraków, Bibl. Kapitulna 209 copied in Regensburg in 1101/02 for the cathedral of Kraków (Mews 2002: 89). In Bavaria, at Regensburg, Freising, and Tegernsee, in the island of Reichenau and in St. Gall, Carolingian models continued to fascinate. Ninth-century exemplars were attractive in Anglo-Saxon England, Normandy, the Loire Valley, and Burgundy: thus, those responsible for the Harley Psalter reproduced the Utrecht Psalter (see chap. 31), while the Bible of Cluny (around 1010) clearly depends on a model copied in 850–70 at the Abbey of Saint-Germain d'Auxerre.

Gradually, indicators of practice from southern regions, including Rome, slowly began to spread, especially in France. Around 1020, a Bible produced in the Benedictine abbey of Saint-Vaast (Arras, BM, 559) attests to a new freedom. Fresh expectations and changes in taste soon turned the history of biblical production upside down. The multiplication of liturgical services (masses), the transformation of collective rites over the course of Christianization, and ecclesiastical reforms (in particular, for Easter, baptismal ceremonies, cults of patron saints, and the expansion of monastic and canonical rites), and the dissemination of individual practices (such as the addition of prayers in personal psalters) allowed the customization of certain books such as the gospel book of Queen Margaret of Scotland (copied in England in the second quarter of the eleventh century) or the one Countess Matilda of Tuscany gave to the Abbey of San Benedetto in Polirone at its foundation (Carmassi 2016).

The Experiment of "Atlantic" Bibles (Bibbie atlantiche)

The rapid conversion of the West to the idea of a global Christianity during the eleventh century led ecclesiastical elites along new paths. These rallied around the Roman project

---

[3] For example, the Ottonian gospel book of the Sainte-Chapelle (Paris, BnF, lat. 8851, end of the tenth century); the Liuthar Gospels for Otto III (Aachen, Domschatzkammer, G 25); the Gospels of Otto III (Munich, BSB, Clm 4453); the Book of Pericopes of Henry II (Munich, BSB, Clm 4452, datable to 1007–12); Vatican City, BAV, Barb. Lat. 711, from around 1000; the Gospels of Bishop Bernward de Hildesheim (Hildesheim, Domschatz, Hs. 18); the gospels commissioned by Henry II from the *scriptorium* of St Emmeram in Ratisbon for Montecassino (Vatican City, BAV, Ottob. Lat. 74); the Hillinus Gospels (Cologne, Dombibliothek 12, copied 1010–40 in Seeon); the *Codex aureus* of Speyer for Conrad II and Gisela (Escorial, Vitrinas 17); Codex Caesareus, a gospel book for Henry III (Uppsala, Universitetsbibliothek, C93); and the mid-eleventh-century psalter of Vatican City, BAV, Ross. 184, created in Tegernsee.

of ecclesiastical reform, also known as the "Gregorian reform." Launched in the 1050s, this endeavor promoted a new perception of Christianity, which was Roman, episcopal, and universalist. In Rome and its surrounding area, from the 1050s, monumental Bibles were produced, which were given the name "Atlantic Bibles" because of their gigantic size. These substantial Bibles of four hundred to five hundred sheets, with an average size of 65 × 35 cm, and a minimum thickness of 10 cm, were designed for display in the choir of a church.[4] An effort was made to standardize the layout, the script (a Caroline minuscule easily read throughout the West), the text (testifying to several revisions), and the iconography. They have been preserved precisely because of their symbolic character. Against all odds, their earliest patrons were imperial protagonists, a fact that throws into disorder the maps imposed by traditional historiography. Their number includes two leading prelates, the Bishops of Geneva and Sion, as well as two antagonists who symbolize in themselves the struggle between the empire and the Roman party: while King Henry IV raised one armed hand against Pope Gregory VII and with the other gave a Roman Bible of the "Atlantic" type to the Abbey of Hirsau in 1074, Countess Mathilda of Tuscany, an ally of the Pope, gave a similar Bible to the Abbey of Polirone (now preserved in Mantua). Subsequently, a Bishop of Troia provided some twenty-nine copies to the churches of his diocese between 1107 and 1137. The true destination of these giant volumes is not always clear. One of the most famous (Vatican City, BAV, Pal. Lat. 3, 4 and 5, from the third quarter of the eleventh century) seems to have been intended either for a double monastery or for an unspecific reader, as an inscription at the beginning of the Psalter states, "Read in peace, dearest brother or sister" (*Lege in pace frater karissime atque soror*).

Those behind the concept of the Atlantic Bibles, from the second half of the eleventh century, wanted to return to the pandect, to a well-founded text, and to the Hieronymian order of books (characterized in particular by the insertion of the books of the Prophets after the four books of Kings), adapted to liturgical use. They therefore wanted a book of reliable orthodoxy, intended for public reading in the choir of a church or in the refectory. They made the biblical text more presentable, even producing a new edition of certain books. They favored a modular structure constituted by series of biblical books in codicological sets, permitting a division of labor between several copyists and better control of the sequence of writings (Ruzzier 2015: 164; Maniaci 2000: 47–60). They also devoted attention to the layout (*mise en page*) and illustration. One of their goals was to weaken the links of local churches to their rulers, at the same time that these kingdoms entered a cycle of consolidation, while they also sought to express a desire for universal conformity. However, the initiative of the "Atlantic Bibles" came up against the wall of the churches, which were for the most part fixed in their traditional loyalties. These Bibles therefore only experienced limited success outside Italy; beyond the Alps, the workshops only retained the format and the first initial letter of Genesis. They did

---

[4] These manuscripts are grouped into categories based on their height and width: small (less than 32 cm); medium small (32–49 cm); medium large (49–67 cm); large (more than 67 cm). On Atlantic Bibles, see the works of Togni and Unfer Verre.

not accept the revisions to the text. Even in southern Italy, they resisted the "Atlantic" style, persisting in the use of Beneventan script (e.g., Berlin, SB, Hamilton 3). However, the model did make an impression. It was readopted for the production of liturgical, patristic, and canonical books.[5] It was in England and, especially, South Germany and Bohemia that the copying of giant Bibles was maintained in the second half of the twelfth century, often for the renewal of liturgical books, as was the case at the Abbey of Wessobrunn (Munich, BSB, Clm 22005–6), the Cistercian foundation at Kaisheim (Munich, BSB, Clm 28164–68), and Augsburg Cathedral (Munich, BSB, Clm 3901): each of these appears to be an independent production.

The Bible and Religious Orders

The new religious orders of the Carthusians, Cistercians, and Premonstratensians did not want to impose a homogeneous Bible in their houses. When he had his famous Bible copied (Dijon, BM, 12–15), Stephen Harding, the Abbot of Cîteaux, opted for an order of books borrowed from the Hebrew canon, but he did not think of codifying either this sequence or a common text. The failure of the Romans to impose the "Atlantic" Bibles was offset by another initiative, that of the *Glossa ordinaria* (see chap. 14). The Gloss was an interpretative tool which leveled the field of the biblical revolution of the twelfth century. It was only slightly later, in the second quarter of the twelfth century, that the production of Bibles tended to a conservative uniformity, in the case of both the (giant) choir Bibles and smaller productions. This is seen in their layout, in the choice and development of the prefaces to each biblical book, and in textual matters. Broad geographical areas maintained certain characteristic features of decoration and script, such as the Bible of San Isidoro de León from 1162 (Suarez Gonzalez 1997). As the "Roman" style opened up, however, the borders softened. The influence of Constantinople spread through Sicily and Venice in the latter half of the twelfth century (Crivello 2017b: 162–63), although this only affected the form and color of the illustrations and had no effect on the content. During this time, monks and canons of all orders protected the variety of their Bibles. The Cistercians themselves, grouped according to the daughter abbeys of Cîteaux, created bibles necessary for their new foundations as far as that of Alcobaça (Portugal), with no concern in their copies to imitate those of the mother abbey.

The Bible at the Pinnacle: Paris in the Thirteenth Century

In France, the workshops of Paris dominated from the last decades of the twelfth century, when the city was effectively chosen to be the capital of the kingdom. This was

---

[5] For instance, the commentary of Haimo of Auxerre on the Pauline Epistles was copied in this format at St. Cecilia in Trastevere in Rome in 1067 (Oxford, Bodleian, Add. D. 104); on the large-scale copy of Augustine's *Enarrationes in Psalmos* produced at Salerno, see Chirivì 2014.

the origin of two highly successful works, the Gloss and the *Historia scholastica* of the Parisian Peter Comestor (Pierre le Mangeur). The popularity of exegesis and the entry of the Bible into the syllabus of all the higher schools and, from there, the universities and *studia* created in the thirteenth century, sounded a call to take a greater interest in the quality of the text and the design of Bibles which were better adapted to these new markets and for secular as well as ecclesiastical elites. From the 1230s, a pattern spread which originated in Paris, due to a standardization of the practice of copying workshops, in particular the use of *pecia* (Ruzzier 2014, 2022; see chap. 16). The "modular structure," typical of the area in which Atlantic Bibles were produced, disappeared during the thirteenth century. The Parisian workshops only observed these divisions in four positions: before the Psalter, between the Psalter and Proverbs, between the Old and the New Testament, and finally between Revelation and the *Interpretation of Hebrew Names*.

The characteristics of Paris Bibles are well known: a small format (less than 38 cm in size), a regular layout with two columns, no division of words (including between quires), a fixed order of books, a new division of the books into chapters (the *capitulatio*, almost identical to that which has become standard since the sixteenth century), and a largely stable series of prologues.[6] Table 13.1 presents these. At the same time, the lists of summaries practically

Table 13.1 Order of Books and Prologues in English Bibles and Paris Bibles

"Perfect" Parisian Order	Prologues and *Argumenta* of 11th–12th-century English Bibles	Prologues and *Argumenta* of 13th-century Paris Bibles
	284	284: *Frater Ambrosius*
Pentateuch Genesis–Deuteronomy	285	285: *Desiderii*
Joshua	311	311: *Tandem finito*
Judges	314	
Ruth		
1 Samuel–2 Kings	323	323: *Viginti et duas*
1 Chronicles	328	328: *Si septuaginta*
2 Chronicles + Prayer of Manasses	327	327: *Quomodo grecorum*
1 Ezra-Nehemiah/2 Ezra	330	330: *Utrum difficilius*
Tobit	332	332: *Mirari*
Judith	335	335: *Apud hebreos*
Esther	341+343	341: *Librum Esther* +343: *Rursum*
Job	344	344: *Cogor* 357: *Si aut fiscellam*

[6] For the list of sixty-four prologues identified by Ker and Branner, see Bogaert 2015.

Table 13.1 Continued

"Perfect" Parisian Order	Prologues and *Argumenta* of 11th–12th-century English Bibles	Prologues and *Argumenta* of 13th-century Paris Bibles
Psalms (Gallican Psalter)		
Proverbs	457	457: *Iungat epistola*
Ecclesiastes		462: *Memini me*
Song of Songs		
Wisdom	468	468: *Liber sapientiae*
Ecclesiasticus	*Multorum nobis*	*Multorum nobis*
Isaiah	482	482: *Nemo cum prophetas*
Jeremiah	487	487: *Hieremias prophetam*
Lamentations + Prayer of Jeremiah	*Post interpretacionem elementorum*	
Baruch	491	491: *Liber iste*
Ezekiel	492	492: *Ezechiel propheta*
Daniel	494	494: *Danielem prophetam*
Minor Prophets	500	500: *Non idem ordo*
Hosea		507: *Temporibus*
Joel	510	511: *Sanctus Ioel* 510: *Ioel filius Phatuel*
Amos	512	512: *Amos propheta* 513: *Hic Amos propheta*
Obadiah	516	517: *Hebrei*
Jonah	522	524: *Sanctum Ionam* 521: *Ionas Columba*
Micah	525	526: *Temporibus Ioathe*
Nahum	527	528: *Nahum prophetam*
Habakkuk	529	531: *Quatuor prophetae*
Zephaniah	532	534: *Tradunt Hebrei*
Haggai	535	538: *Ieremias propheta*
Zechariah	540	539: *In anno secondo*
Malachi	544	543: *Deus per Moysen*
1–2 Maccabees	551	547: *Cum sim promptus* 553: *Memini me* 551: *Maccabeorum libri*
Matthew	595	590: *Matheus ex iudeis* 589: *Matheus cum primo*
Mark	607	607: *Marcus evangelista*
Luke	620	620: *Lucas syrus*

(continued)

Table 13.1 Continued

"Perfect" Parisian Order	Prologues and *Argumenta* of 11th–12th-century English Bibles	Prologues and *Argumenta* of 13th-century Paris Bibles
John	624	624: *Hic est Iohannes*
Romans	669	677: *Romani sunt*
1 Corinthians	685	685: *Corinthii sunt*
2 Corinthians	699/700	699/700: *Post actam*
Galatians	707	707: *Galathae sunt*
Ephesians	715	715: *Ephesi sunt*
Philippians	728	728: *Philippenses sunt*
Colossians	736	736: *Colossenses et hi*
1 Thessalonians	747	747: *Thessalonicenses sunt*
2 Thessalonians	752	752: *Ad Thessalonicenses*
1 Timothy	765	765: *Timotheum instruit*
2 Timothy	772	772: *Item Timotheo*
Titus	780	780: *Titum commonefacit*
Philemon	783/784	783: *Philemoni familiaris*
Hebrews	793/794	793/794:
Acts of the Apostles	640	793: *Lucas natione syrus*
Catholic Epistles	809	809: *Non ita ordo*
James	807	
1–2 Peter		
1–3 John		
Jude		
Revelation	834	839: *Omnes qui pie volunt*

Note. The number of the prologue is that in *RBMA (Repertorium biblicum medii aevi)* (Stegmüller 1950–80).

disappeared, and instead the *Interpretation of Hebrew Names* was inserted, often along with indications of liturgical lections. Illustration followed a set of possible models but remained confined to the initials of each book and sometimes prologues (Ruzzier 2015; Gameson 2013: 77–78; Lobrichon 2004; Light 1988). In certain workshops connected with the masters of the University of Paris, an effort was made to correct the text, as proposed by the various "correctories" of Dominican and Franciscan origin, but without a noticeable effect on workshops outside Paris (Linde 2012; Dahan 2004; see also chap. 16).

Bibles in this mold have been named "Paris Bible" or "University text," but these appellations are doubly awkward. No obligatory model was imposed on all Parisian workshops, and their association with the university came only from the copyists' proximity to these institutions and their potential clientele of masters and students. The new scheme was introduced into large church Bibles, but booksellers, to suit the new market, reduced the size of Bibles to make them portable (less than 20 cm in height). This new Latin Bible was designed to facilitate the overview of the text, its comprehension, and its consultation (Parkes 1976: 133; Petrucci 2005). It spread quickly through the channels of the new religious orders, in particular Franciscans and Dominicans. It seems that in the Dominican convents of Italy, copies were made on the spot which reproduced several features of this so-called Parisian type (Light 2016). The Order of Preachers in particular sought to provide their priests with practical volumes, intended not only for the preparation of public sermons but also for liturgical life. Their Bibles are therefore very frequently decorated with tools for preaching: "distinctions" (alphabetical guides to the meaning of biblical terms), lists of *exempla*, an index of themes, along with aids for the daily office such as lists of biblical lections for the days of the year and feasts. Independently of the mendicant orders, the first complete copies of the "Bible of the thirteenth century" in Old French, around 1250, were adjusted to the Parisian model. In southern Italy, copyists in the service of Manfred, King of Sicily from 1258 to 1266, procrastinated, but those of his successor Conradin took the plunge and arranged the biblical books according to the decision of the Parisian masters.[7]

BIBLE PICTURE BOOKS

At the same time as the developments described above, another revolution was taking shape, that of the Bible in pictures. This ancient tradition, maintained in the Byzantine Empire for specific books of the Bible (Genesis, Joshua), had extended as far as England. Until the end of the twelfth century, no one in the West had thought of illustrating the entire Bible. The phenomenon of the transposition and reuse of narrative forms was revitalized first in the initial pages of psalters for noble patrons in the North. This tradition of aristocratic psalters was gradually transformed at the end of the eleventh century. First came the psalters of prominent women, such as Christina of Markyate (Hildesheim, St. Godehard), Eleanor of Aquitaine (The Hague, KB, 76 F 13), Ingeburg (Chantilly, Musée Condé 9), and Christina (Copenhagen, KB, GKS 1606 4°). These were followed by royal psalters, such as those of the Kings of Denmark that were copied and decorated in England between 1193 and 1201 (Copenhagen, KB, Thott 143 2°). From the 1120s, an image cycle of the Life of Christ was integrated, which was then further

---

[7] The "Manfred Bibles" include Vatican City, BAV, Vat. lat. 36; London, BL, Add. 31830; Palermo, BN, Ms. I.C.13; Turin, BNU, Ms. E.IV.14; Paris, BnF, lat. 40; Paris, BnF, lat. 10428; Paris, BnF, lat. 217; Bourges, BM 5; the "William Foyle Bible," sold at Christie's on July 11, 2000. Bibles of Conradin (d. 1268) include Baltimore, Walters Art Gallery, W.152; Vatican City, BAV, Pal. lat. 13; Paris, St.-Geneviève, 14; Paris, BnF, lat. 8114; Oxford, Bodleian, Can. bib. lat. 59. See further Soffientino 2020; Ruzzier 2015: 163; Manzari 2018; and Toubert 1977, 1979.

developed in Flanders during the twelfth century. At the Abbey of Saint Bertin, a psalter was illustrated with typological scenes from the Old Testament, the Life of Christ and the deeds of the saints (The Hague, KB, 76 F 5; see Carlvant 2012). These may have been typical in such books from the twelfth and first half of the thirteenth century, but, because they were easily dismembered, only fragments remain (Morgan 1982: 68–72). Apart from the quality of their paintings, these were relatively restricted in scope. Everything changed with the first Bibles in pictures.

The Pamplona Bibles

Curiously, it was not in the public space of the great monarchies that an important innovation appeared. The first experiments were conducted on two royal books in Navarre in the last years of the twelfth century. The first was painted in Pamplona in 1195–97 by order of the chancellor of a small Spanish kingdom, for his patron, who was none other than King Sancho VII of Navarre (Amiens, BM, 108). This book had a twin copied a few years later on the order of King Sancho, perhaps for his wife (Augsburg, UB, I.2.4°.15; see Bucher 1970; Raff 1987; and Hilg 2007). They both cover a selection of biblical episodes, depicted in outline, which is sometimes enhanced with color. The coordinator of the book copied captions above or below the image; these short texts identify the subject thanks to quotations from the Spanish Vulgate form, supplemented by a few words drawing the attention of the reader to an allegorical explanation (see Scheller 1995; Terrier Aliferis 2016). Each of these books thus contains, in pictures, an account of the Bible and of Christian history from creation to the end of time. Nevertheless, the distinctive order betrays the influence of some Bibles of French origin—not those of León—and the *Historia scholastica*. For example, Job occurs between Judges and 1 Samuel, while Daniel is joined with Judith.

The Bibles Moralisées and Their Successors

The two Navarre Bibles were too modest in appearance to appeal to kings. However, the idea of a large Bible in pictures could have passed from Navarre to Paris, courtesy of Queen Blanche of Castile, because it was in the years 1220–30 that the exceptional artistic edifice arose of the *Bible moralisée* (a name assigned in the fifteenth century). The design of this Bible was entrusted to masters whose orthodoxy was certain, and who would exclude any theological bold statement and oversee the work of painters in workshops, which were perhaps those of the independent booksellers who served universities. The first generation of *Bibles moralisées*, produced in four installments between 1220 and 1240, took the form of an abbreviated Bible, set out in groups of eight medallions on each page, each of which was illustrated and supplemented by a short text, following the Parisian order of books (Lowden 2000; Hediger 2005; Christe and Brugger 2003). This was completely original and unprecedented, even though it derived from experiments by artists and designers in Paris from the end of the twelfth century and during the reign of Philippe Auguste. Historically, it was short-lived, since, of the fifteen copies from 1225 to around the middle of the fifteenth century, eight bring together text and images. All are of the highest artistic level, reserved for members and allies of the French royal family (Lobrichon 2005).

The first *Bible moralisée* inspired the creation of other Bibles in pictures. The most sumptuous, of disputed origin, was produced in the north of France around 1244–55. This is the Morgan Picture Book, also known as the "Maciejewski Bible" (New York, Morgan Library, M.638), painted by an artist fully aware of Parisian initiatives and who knew the cycle devoted to the patriarch Joseph in the *Bible moralisée* now divided between Oxford, Paris, and London. These initiatives of great luxury gave rise to several much more modest books, although it is not possible to identify a relationship of direct dependence. Three may be mentioned here: the "Bibbia Bassetti" of 1250–75 (Trento, Biblioteca Comunale, 2868; see Liotta 2012); the "Paduan Bible Picture Book" (Rovigo, Accademia dei Concordi, Ms. 212; London, BL, Add. MS 15277); in England, the Holkham Bible Picture Book (London, BL, Add. MS 47682; see fig. 31.12), worthy of comparison with the pictorial encyclopedia *Omne bonum* (London, BL, Royal 6 E VI).

A NEW OFFERING

During the thirteenth century, Western societies awoke to different priorities. Theology became less scriptural, and more engaged in logic and dogmatic formulae which led to a system. The triumph of the Parisian model of the Bible seemed to be complete, yet it suffered severe erosion during its exportation.

Princely Bibles and Court Bibles

During this period production of Latin Bibles became scattered, with a loss of quality. In Paris itself, it faded away, with a few small and beautiful exceptions, such as the so-called Bible of Charles V (Paris, Arsenal, 590), decorated in the workshop of Master Honoré at the beginning of the fourteenth century, or that copied by Robert de Bylling and illustrated by Jean Pucelle in 1327 which was in royal hands until Louis XI (Paris, BnF, lat. 11935). Other centers took over, without being able to dominate the market. The workshops of southern Italy produced sumptuous books for the heirs of the emperor Frederick II, but none of them could ever compete with the *Bibles moralisées*.

The Angevin kings of Naples took part in the harvest of *Bibles moralisées*. King Robert I (1278–1343) had a Bible copied in Naples (Paris, BnF, fr. 9561; see Besseyre and Christe 2011) whose decoration is related to a contemporary production now in Leuven (Katholieke Universiteit, Maurits Sabbebibliotheek, MS 1; see Magrini 2005; Perriccioli Saggese 2013). Robert promoted a strong intellectual and university life in his capital, where highly skilled workshops produced at least seven (possibly nine) luxury Bibles in the first two thirds of the fourteenth century. These craftsmen followed the Parisian order of books but did not hesitate to integrate the apocryphal letter to the Laodiceans in at least two of these Bibles and to mix rarer prologues with those of the normative series (e.g., London, BL, Add. MS 47672; Vatican City, BAV, Vat. lat. 14430). Naples thus established itself as a major center, disdainful of current methods in university workshops. Other isolated centers managed to produce copies of very good quality, such as the Teramo Bible (Vatican City, BAV, Vat. lat. 10220; see Massolo 2018). Clergy viewed these luxurious productions from a distance, without renouncing them as ceremonial books. In 1362, the monk Matteo di Planisio, then Abbot General of the Order of Celestines, had a splendid Bible crafted in Naples (Vatican City, BAV, Vat. lat. 3550). It seems, however, that the popes, cardinals, and prelates of Avignon preferred glossed Bibles to complete Bibles without glosses.[8] All such deluxe books manifested their patrons' desire for self-esteem. They are symbolic proof of earthly power, which clearly exceeds the requirements of private devotional and public liturgy.

Workshops in capital cities placed themselves at the service of great patrons of the thirteenth, fourteenth, and fifteenth centuries, from Jeanne de Navarre (see Finch 2012) to the wonders of the Bibles of the Dukes of Ferrara and the more restrained books of Jean de Foix, Bishop of Comminges (1466–1501).[9] Henceforth, the Holy Scriptures were enthroned in all the princely libraries and those of the urban elites. However, workshops producing Latin Bibles faced strong competition from the 1310s. Copies of the *Bible historiale* in French soon supplanted Bibles in Latin in many aristocratic or merchant houses. This work, designed by the Flemish canon Guiart des Moulins from 1292 to 1295, revised in 1297 and again around 1312, initially had no other ambition than to offer a translation of the *Historia scholastica* by Peter Comestor. Despite this, between 1310 and 1360, anonymous adapters removed the original text and replaced the summaries by Guiart with direct translations from Latin, sometimes glossed, often literal and of good stylistic quality. The French version of the *Bible historiale*, conveyed in six successive editions of which more than 120 manuscripts are known, almost all luxury productions, soon inspired translations into Dutch and German (*Historienbibeln*). These fulfilled the

---

[8] Two exceptions are the Bibles of Clement VII: London, BL, Add. MS 47672 (created at Naples in 1330 but requisitioned for the pontifical library) and Paris, BnF, lat. 18. See also the strange five-volume Bible of Benedict XIII (Paris, BnF, lat. 61, 87, 91, 139 and 255), written in large script for the personal use of the aging Pope.

[9] Bible of Niccolo III of Este (1383–1441): Vatican City, BAV, Barb, lat. 613 (completed in 1434); Bible of Borso d'Este (1413–71): Modena, Biblioteca Estense Universitaria, V.G. 12–13 (Lat. 422–23), copied and illuminated from 1455 to 1461; Bible for Jean de Foix: Paris, BnF, nouv. acq. lat. 3192 (ca. 1490–1500; Toulouse).

requirements of audiences who were less comfortable with Latin. From then on, the production of Latin Bibles shifted to the ecclesiastical market. Even though clergy may have provided a constant demand, the abundance of stock made in the thirteenth century and a reduction in the creation of new parishes limited any hopes for increased sales. Devotees of picture Bibles did not disappear, which explains how the model of the Pamplona Bibles was taken up again in Prague in the second quarter of the fourteenth century, when a canon who was lawyer to the Duke of Bohemia and his son, the Emperor Charles IV, commissioned a Bible, which bears his name, the "Velislaus Bible" (Prague, Národní knihovna, MS XXIII; see Panušková 2018). In fact, booksellers saw the continued growth of a cultivated readership and, in parallel, a demand for tools of Christian pedagogy. They duly turned to the production of other books devoted to the Bible.

Toward Parabiblical Works

The stimulation for this change of horizon in the fourteenth century came from circles that previously had been largely invisible, especially the chaplains who offered spiritual direction to guilds of laypeople and the urban elite. Their prescription was for less demanding reading, possibly in the vernacular, with "speaking Bibles" reduced to a pictorial scheme which itself presented the keys to Christian interpretation. Bibles of this new type would place the life of Jesus back at the heart of the visual scheme and put it into perspective through quotations from the Old Testament.

The *Speculum humanae salvationis* ("Mirror of human salvation") comes from the beginning of the fourteenth century, possibly from a Dominican monastery in Alsace (perhaps Strasbourg in 1324). Its origin and date have been the subject of debate following the discovery of a primitive version apparently from Italy or Provence. This work was organized in a didactic rather than chronological manner, with forty-two chapters predominantly Mariological in tone. Its diffusion was remarkable, with more than 380 surviving manuscripts, especially in Germany, Flanders, England, and France.[10] The composition of the *Speculum humanae salvationis* is very straightforward. Each page is divided into two columns, which have text at the top and bottom and an image in the middle. An opening of two pages therefore has four images, which are not narrative but doctrinal, framed by text. From left to right, a drawing of the life of Christ (from the Annunciation to the Coronation of the Virgin), is followed by three figures from either the Old or sometimes the New Testament. Thus the scene of the meal where Mary Magdalene anoints the feet of Jesus (Luke 7:36–50) is amplified by the figures of the Penance of Manasseh (2 Chronicles 33:11–13), the Prodigal Son (Luke 15:18–21) and

[10] Early examples include Rome, Biblioteca dell'Accademia Nazionale dei Lincei e Corsiniana, 55.K.2, copied in Avignon around 1330 (see Frugoni and Manzari 2006) and a Latin–German bilingual produced between 1325 and 1330 (Kremsmünster, Stiftsbibliothek 243).

David's Penance (2 Samuel 12). The reader thus learned to juggle the stories of the two Testaments, which the earliest manuscripts of the *Speculum* combined with diagrams of world history from the creation of Adam and Eve to the first church of the Apostles (Neumüller 1997: 31–32; Frugoni and Manzari 2006).

At the same time, in Southern Germany and Austria, other educators invented a scheme that, by its brevity and its characteristic assembly of images and captions, was even more effective: the success of these books called the "Bible of the Poor" (*Biblia pauperum, Armenbibel*) never ceases to amaze. They brought to perfection the doctrinal statement centered on a typological demonstration. A normal *Biblia pauperum* is relatively large (50 cm tall on average), but with only nine to twenty-one folia (eighteen to forty-two pages). These comprise, in principle, between thirty-four and forty-one pictures. Three principal families of *Biblia pauperum* have been identified by Schmidt (1959), coming from Austria, Weimar, and Bavaria (Lobrichon 1986). The genealogy of this work is not easy to set out, but the series of episodes from the Life of Christ and its parallels with typological scenes from the Old Testament immediately call to mind the cycles introduced in psalters in the twelfth century, in particular what remains of the Psalter of Henry the Lion from 1168 to 1169 (London, BL, Lansdowne MS 381/1). Each illustration is organized around a central image depicting an episode from the life of Christ and the Virgin Mary, from the Annunciation to the Coronation of Mary; the central image itself is surrounded by four prophets from the Old Testament which each cites a verse of their own prophecy, while on each side an Old Testament scene flanks the whole. Versicles and responses from liturgical antiphons are copied in the upper and lower margins and biblical readings (*lectiones*, lections) in the left and right margins. In the earliest copies, these are in Latin; later ones are in German or in both Latin and German.

Over time, copyists experimented with simpler visual formulae. From the second quarter of the fourteenth century, the central image was highlighted in a circular medallion surrounded by four medallions of smaller diameter, while the Bible readings were reduced in length. Another formula used in Upper Bavaria in the second half of the fourteenth century (Munich, BSB, Cgm 20) has the page in two sections: the Old Testament at the top and the New at the bottom. The link between the illustrated page, liturgical life, and private devotion is clear: it provides an appropriate response to the expectations of laypeople, in particular members of guilds. Certain guilds owned *Biblia pauperum*, and at least one example was copied by a lay member.[11] It is curious that no copy of the *Biblia pauperum* is found outside southern Germany and Austria before the fifteenth century. The furthest to the West may have been made around 1395–1400 for Margaret of Cleves (1375–1411), wife of Duke Albert of Bavaria and Holland (London, BL, Kings MS 5). In the fifteenth century, however, the model won contemporary support: it was applied to illustrated gospel books (e.g., Bamberg, Staatsbibliothek Msc. Theol. 41), to "Concordances of the Old and New Testaments" (e.g., Mainz, Stadtbibliothek I.219), and

---

[11] Dated 1448, and previously at Moritzburg in Saxony (*Katalog der deutschsprachigen illustrierten Handschriften des Mittelalters* 2, no. 4: 280–81, n. 16.0.10).

to biblical extracts without images.[12] Very quickly reproduced by the processes of xylography and printing, this model leaves the domain of the book and is exhibited on the walls of certain churches and even in tapestries from the beginning of the sixteenth century (Saulnier-Pernuit 1993).

CONCLUSION

The diversity of Latin Bibles over time in the West and the multiplicity of their forms should be sufficient to eradicate the myth of a strict control and hold maintained by the Church of Rome on the production and circulation of the Scriptures. This historical survey has revealed five major forms in turn: the liturgical Bible, the glossed Bible, the portable Bible, the luxury Bible, and the picture Bible. Each experienced varying fortunes, but all fulfilled their role of transmission. However, numerous gray areas remain which cannot be investigated in a brief account. Too little is known about the actual state of bookcases and libraries in parishes and in the guilds of medieval towns; rarely are insights provided about what nuns and beguines would read. One might hope that an immense mass of medieval Bibles would have been preserved to excite curiosity and meet the expectations of historians. The reality is that a considerable proportion of the Bibles in use in cathedrals, abbeys, and convents have disappeared. Librarians who were aware of the value of large luxury Bibles will have acted to preserve them, but the scant evidence that has been transmitted to us about the use of these sumptuous books leaves many doubts regarding the functions they served: were they considered convenient and useful objects, proofs of status, precious and inalienable goods, symbols of power, or allegories of proximity to celestial powers? The problem lies, of course, in the judgment of the humanists who wanted to break down the walls of Latinity and return to the original languages of the Bible (i.e., Hebrew and Greek). No technological innovation was as groundbreaking as the thunderous start of printing from the 1450s. The flow of Latin Bibles printed between 1452 and 1500 is astonishing, and the flood was so great that Latin biblical manuscripts, considered obsolete, were put in the cupboard or pillaged, and only surviving fragments have been carried on the tide. Nevertheless, recent work on the books of the clergy show that some parishes of Germany were much better equipped before the advent of printing than has been repeatedly claimed since the sixteenth century (Wranovix 2017). Although in the course of some thirty years, handwritten Bibles became historical artifacts and the objects of scholarly study, we are still far from mapping this archipelago that had been submerged by the reforms of the sixteenth century. It is time to recall it to memory.

---

[12] Numerous manuscripts which are not described as *Biblia pauperum* have their typical incipit, e.g., Kassel, Landesbibliothek, 2° Ms. theol. 39; Cologne, Stadtarchiv W 318; the *Biblia figurata* of Lüneburg, Ratsbücherei, Theol. 2° 82.

Acknowledgments

I warmly thank Hugh Houghton for his English rendering of this chapter and Bruno Lobrichon (Ottawa) for his judicious checking.

Bibliography

Berschin, Walter. 2005. *Mittellateinische Studien*. Vol. 1. Heidelberg: Mattes.

Besseyre, Marianne, and Yves Christe. 2011. *Biblia moralizada de Nápoles*. Barcelona: M. Moleiro.

Bogaert, Pierre-Maurice. 2015. "Les Préfaces des bibles latines. Essai de typologie et application à Job." In *Comment le Livre s'est fait livre. La fabrication des manuscrits bibliques (IVᵉ-XVᵉ siècle): Bilan, résultats, perspectives de recherche*, edited by Chiara Ruzzier and Xavier Hermand, 145–54. Bibliologia 40. Turnhout: Brepols.

Bucher, François. 1970. *The Pamplona Bibles*. New Haven: Yale University Press.

Carlvant, Kerstin. 2012. *Manuscript Painting in Thirteenth-Century Flanders: Bruges, Ghent and the Circle of the Counts*. Studies in Medieval and Early Renaissance Art History 63. London: Harvey Miller.

Carmassi, Patrizia. 2016. "Libri al tempo di Matilde: l'evangeliario New York, Pierpont Morgan Library, MS M 492." In *Lucca e Matilda di Canossa tra storia e mito*, edited by Raffaele Savigni, 29–40. Lucca: Pacini Fazzi.

Chirivì, Alessandra 2014. "Ancora sui manoscritti del Museo Diocesano di Salerno: Le *Enarrationes in Psalmos* di sant'Agostino." *Rivista di storia della miniatura* 18: 17–30.

Christe, Yves, and Laurence Brugger. 2003. "Une Bible moralisée méconnue: La Bible napolitaine de Paris (BnF, ms fr. 9561, fol 1r-112v)." *Arte cristiana* 91: 237–51.

Cremascoli, Giuseppe, and Francesco Santi, eds. 2004. *La Bibbia del XIII secolo. Storia del testo, storia dell'esegesi*. Millennio Medievale 49. Florence: SISMEL, Galluzzo.

Crivello, Fabrizio. 2017a. "Bibbie dalla tarda Antichità ai Carolingi." In *Bibbia. Immagini e scrittura nella Biblioteca Apostolica Vaticana*, edited by Ambrogio Piazzoni and Francesca Manzari, 114–39. Vatican City: BAV.

Crivello, Fabrizio. 2017b. "Bibbie ottoniane." In *Bibbia. Immagini e scrittura nella Biblioteca Apostolica Vaticana*, edited by Ambrogio Piazzoni and Francesca Manzari, 146–59. Vatican City: BAV.

Dahan, Gilbert. 2004. "*Sorbonne II*. Un correctoire biblique de la seconde moitié du XIIIᵉ siècle." In *La Bibbia del XIII secolo. Storia del testo, storia dell'esegesi*, edited by Giuseppe Cremascoli and Francesco Santi, 113–53. Millennio Medievale 49. Florence: SISMEL, Galluzzo.

Finch, Julia A. 2012. "Bibles en images: Visual Narrative and Translation in New York Public Library Spencer MS 22 and Related Manuscripts." PhD diss., University of Pittsburgh.

Fravventura, Vera, ed. 2017. *Alcuini Enchiridion in Psalmos. Edizione critica*. Florence: SISMEL, Galluzzo.

Frugoni, Chiara, and Francesca Manzari. 2006. *Immagini di san Francesco in uno Speculum humanae saluationis del Trecento. Roma, Biblioteca dell'Accademia Nazionale dei Lincei e Corsiniana 55.K.2*. Padua: Francescane.

Furlan, Italo. 2004. "Venezia, Constantinopoli, Palestina. Aspetti e circolazione della pittura 'crociata.'" *Saggi e Memorie di storia dell'arte* 28: 15–32.

Gameson, Richard. 2013. "Durham's Paris Bible and the Use of Communal Bibles in a Benedictine Cathedral Priory in the Later Middle Ages." In *Form and Function in the Late Medieval Bible*, edited by Eyal Poleg and Laura Light, 67–104. Leiden: Brill.

Ganz, David. 2015. "La bible palimpseste de Leon." In *Comment le Livre s'est fait livre. La fabrication des manuscrits bibliques (IVe-XVe siècle): Bilan, résultats, perspectives de recherche*, edited by Chiara Ruzzier and Xavier Hermand, 51–58. Bibliologia 40. Turnhout: Brepols.

Gow, Andrew. 2013. "Une histoire de *Geschichtsklitterungen* protestantes. Les bibles médiévales." *Church History and Religious Culture* 93: 171–88.

Hediger, C., ed. 2005. *Tout le temps du veneour est sanz oyseuseté. Mélanges offerts à Yves Christe pour son 65e anniversaire.* Turnhout. Brepols.

Hilg, Hardo. 2007. "Cod. I.2.4° 15." In *Lateinische mittelalterliche Handschriften in Quarto der Universitätsbibliothek Augsburg. Vol. I.3*, 67–70. Wiesbaden: Harrassowitz.

Light, Laura. 1988. *The Bible in the Twelfth Century.* Cambridge: Harvard College Library.

Light, Laura. 2016. "What was a Bible for? Liturgical texts in thirteenth-century Franciscan and Dominican Bibles." *Lusitania sacra* 34: 165–82.

Linde, Cornelia. 2012. *How to Correct the Sacra Scriptura? Textual Criticism of the Latin Bible between the Twelfth and Fifteenth Century.* Oxford: Society for the Study of Medieval Languages and Literature.

Liotta, Filippo. 2012. "Barnaba Morano." *Dizionario Biografico degli Italiani* 76. Online.

Lobrichon, Guy. 1986. "La Bible des pauvres du Vatican, Palat. Lat. 871." *Mélanges de l'École Française de Rome. Moyen Âge* 98 : 295–327 (=Lobrichon 2003: 211–238).

Lobrichon, Guy. 2000. "Riforma ecclesiastica e testo della Bibbia." In *Le Bibbie atlantiche. Il libro delle Scritture tra monumentalità e rappresentazione*, edited by Marilena Maniaci and Giulia Orofino, 15–26. Milan: Centro Tibaldi. (= Lobrichon 2003: 94–108).

Lobrichon, Guy. 2003. *La Bible au Moyen Âge.* Paris : Picard.

Lobrichon, Guy. 2004. "Les éditions de la Bible latine dans les universités du XIIIe siècle." In *La Bibbia del XIII secolo. Storia del testo, storia dell'esegesi*, edited by Giuseppe Cremascoli and Francesco Santi, 15–34. Millennio Medievale 49. Florence: SISMEL, Galluzzo.

Lobrichon, Guy. 2005. "Le bibbie ad immagini, secoli XII-XV." In *Forme e modelli della tradizione manoscritta della Bibbia*, edited by Paolo Cherubini, 423–57. Vatican City: Scuola Vaticana.

Lowden, John. 2000. *The Making of the "Bibles Moralisées."* University Park: Pennsylvania State University Press.

Magrini, Sabina. 2005. "La Bibbia di Matheus de Planisio (Vat. Lat. 3550, I-III): Documenti e modelli per lo studio della produzione scritturale in età angioina." *Codices Manuscripti* 50–51: 1–16.

Maniaci, Marilena. 2000. "La struttura delle Bibbie atlantiche." In *Le Bibbie atlantiche. Il libro delle Scritture tra monumentalità e rappresentazione*, edited by Marilena Maniaci and Giulia Orofino, 47–60. Milan: Centro Tibaldi.

Maniaci, Marilena, and Giulia Orofino, eds. 2000. *Le Bibbie atlantiche. Il libro delle Scritture tra monumentalità e rappresentazione.* Milan: Centro Tibaldi.

Manzari, Francesca 2018. "La Bibbia in Italia tra XIII e XIV secolo." In *Bibbia. Immagini e scrittura nella Biblioteca Apostolica Vaticana*, edited by Ambrogio Piazzoni and Francesca Manzari, 218–19. Vatican City: BAV.

Massolo, Lola. 2018. "Bibbia teramana." In *Bibbia. Immagini e scrittura nella Biblioteca Apostolica Vaticana*, edited by Ambrogio Piazzoni and Francesca Manzari, 249–51. Vatican City: BAV.

Mews, Constant J. 2002. "Manuscripts in Polish Libraries Copied before 1200 and the Expansion of Latin Christendom in the Eleventh and Twelfth Centuries." *Scriptorium* 56 no. 1: 80–118.

Morgan, Nigel. 1982. *Early Gothic Manuscripts, I, 1190–1250*. London: Harvey Miller.

Neumüller, Willibrord. 1997. *Speculum humanae salvationis. Codex Cremifanensis 243 des Benediktinerstiftes Kremsmünster*. Glanzlichter der Buchkunst 7. Graz: Akademische Druck-u. Verlaganstalt.

Panušková, Lenka. 2018. *The Velislav Bible, Finest Picture-Bible of the Late Middle Ages. Biblia Depicta as Devotional, Mnemonic and Study Tool*. Amsterdam: Amsterdam University Press.

Parkes, Malcolm B. 1976. "The Influence of the Concepts of *Ordinatio* and *Compilatio* in the Development of the Book." In *Medieval Learning and Literature. Essays Presented to R. W. Hunt*, edited by J.J.G. Alexander and Margaret Gibson, 115–41. Oxford: Clarendon Press.

Perriccioli Saggese, Alessandra. 2013. "Cristoforo Orimina," *Dizionario biografico degli Italiani* 79 [Online].

Petrucci, Armando. 2005. "Leggere nel Medioevo." In *La lettura spirituale*, edited by Luci Coco, 7–25. Milan: Sylvestre Bonnard.

Piazzoni, Ambrogio, and Francesca Manzari, eds. 2017. *Bibbia. Immagini e scrittura nella Biblioteca Apostolica Vaticana*. Vatican City: BAV.

Raff, Thomas. 1987. "Kat. Nr. 8, Bilderbibel, Cod. I.2.4° 15." In *Universitätsbibliothek Augsburg: Wertvolle Handschriften und Einbände aus der ehemaligen Oettingen-Wallersteinschen Bibliothek*, edited by Rudolf Frankenberger and Paul Berthold Rupp, 51–53. Wiesbaden: Reichert.

Ruzzier, Chiara. 2014. "Quelques observations sur la fabrication des bibles au XIIIᵉ siècle et le système de la pecia." *Revue bénédictine* 124, no. 1: 151–89.

Ruzzier, Chiara. 2015. "Continuité et rupture dans la production des bibles au XIIIᵉ siècle." *Comment le Livre s'est fait livre. La fabrication des manuscrits bibliques (IVᵉ-XVᵉ siècle): Bilan, résultats, perspectives de recherche*, edited by Chiara Ruzzier and Xavier Hermand, 155–68. Bibliologia 40. Turnhout: Brepols.

Ruzzier, Chiara. 2022. *Entre Université et ordres mendiants. La production des bibles portatives latines au XIIIᵉ siècle*. Manuscripta Biblica 8. Berlin-Boston: De Gruyter.

Ruzzier, Chiara, and Xavier Hermand, eds. 2015. *Comment le Livre s'est fait livre. La fabrication des manuscrits bibliques (IVᵉ-XVᵉ siècle): Bilan, résultats, perspectives de recherche*. Bibliologia 40. Turnhout: Brepols.

Saulnier-Pernuit, Lydwine 1993. *Les Trois Couronnements. Tapisserie du Trésor de la Cathédrale de Sens*. Tours: Mame.

Scheller, Robert W. 1995. *Exemplum. Model-Book Drawings and the Practice of Artistic Transmission in the Middle Ages (ca. 900-ca. 1400)*. Translated by Michael Hoyle. Amsterdam: University Press.

Schmidt, Gerhard. 1959. *Die Armenbibeln des XIV. Jahrhunderts*. Graz, Germany: Bohlau.

Shepard, Dorothy 2012. "Romanesque display Bibles." In *New Cambridge History of the Bible: Vol. 2. From 600 to 1450*, edited by Richard Marsden and E. Ann Matter, 392–403. Cambridge: Cambridge University Press.

Smith, Kathryn A. 2001. "Bibles." in *Leaves of Gold. Manuscript Illumination from Philadelphia Collections*, edited by James R. Tanis and Jennifer A. Thompson, 21–43. Philadelphia: Philadelphia Museum of Art.

Soffientino, Francesca. 2020. *La committenza di Manfredi. Fonti e opere*. Rome: Viella.

Stegmüller, Friedrich. 1950–80. *Repertorium biblicum medii aevi*. 11 vols. Madrid: CSIC.

Suarez Gonzalez, Ana I. 1997. *Los Codices III.1, III.2, III.3, IV y V (Biblia, Liber capituli, Misal)*. León: Real Colegiata de León.

Terrier Aliferis, Laurence. 2016. "The Models of the Illuminators in the Early Gothic Period." In *The Use of Models in Medieval Book Painting*, edited by Monika E. Müller, 29–56. Cambridge: Cambridge Scholars.

Togni, Nadia. 2001. "La Bibbia atlantica di Ginevra: analisi di un testimone della Vulgata all' epoca della Riforma gregoriana." Unpublished PhD diss., University of Cassino.

Togni, Nadia 2015. "Italian Giant Bibles: The Circulation and Use of the Book at the Time of the Ecclesiastical Reform in the Eleventh and Twelfth Centuries." In *Writing in Europe, 500–1450. Texts and Contexts*, edited by Aidan Conti, Orietta Da Rold, and Philip Shaw, 59–82. Woodbridge: D. S. Brewer.

Togni, Nadia, ed. 2016. *Les Bibles atlantiques. Le manuscrit biblique à l'époque de la réforme de l'Église du XI*^{e} *siècle*. Florence: SISMEL.

Toubert, Hélène. 1977. "Trois nouvelles bibles du Maître de la Bible de Manfred et de son atelier." *Mélanges de l'École française de Rome. Moyen-Âge, Temps modernes* 89, no. 2: 777–810.

Toubert, Hélène. 1979. "Autour de la Bible de Conradin: trois nouveaux manuscrits enluminés." *Mélanges de l'École française de Rome. Moyen-Âge, Temps modernes* 91, no. 2: 729–84.

Unfer Verre, Gaia Elisabetta. 2014. "Problemi di minatura romana nell'età della Riforma: l'Evangeliario Piana 3.210 di Cesena." In *Il codice miniato in Europe: libri per la chiesa, per la città, per la corte*, edited by Giordana Mariani Canova and Alessandra Periccioli Saggese, 93–103. Padua: Il Poligrafo.

Wranovix, Matthew 2017. *Priests and Their Books in Late Medieval Eichstätt*. Lanham: Lexington.

CHAPTER 14

···

GLOSSED BIBLES

···

ALEXANDER ANDRÉE

WITH few exceptions, medieval teaching, in sacred as well as secular learning, began with authority. There was always a text in the classroom that the master took as point of departure for his lectures.[1] In this case, the authority was the Bible. From the Old and New Testaments, the medieval teacher derived key theological concepts: the doctrines of the Trinity, of Creation, of the Fall, of the Incarnation, of the Church, of the Last Judgement, and so on. Since the Bible did not always yield its truths immediately, however, medieval biblical teaching largely consisted of the master explaining how to tease out the theological truths from the sacred page. Hence medieval theologians referred to themselves as "masters of the sacred page"—*magistri sacrae paginae*—whose task it was to subject the biblical text to scrutiny. To help them in this effort, they had at their disposal a most powerful interpretative tool. Since ancient times, a three- or fourfold hermeneutic—or method of interpretation—had been employed to unlock the secrets of the sacred Scriptures. Adhering to the theories developed by Augustine that, in the Bible, words could be signs for other realities (see chap. 9), the masters maintained that the Bible could be read at different levels, according to different senses.

The most obvious reading of the text was according to its letter. This yielded its **literal** or historical sense: God did in fact create the world in six days, Abraham really did climb Mount Moriah to sacrifice his only son at God's command, and Moses really did part the Red Sea to allow the Hebrew people to escape the pursuing Egyptians. But the same facts could also be interpreted as signs standing for a deeper truth. In the case of events recounted in the Old Testament, they were read as looking forward to the coming

---

[1] The term "classroom" is used for simplicity's sake. The twelfth-century counterparts of our classrooms were normally not more than a space, a nook, a corner, in the cloister; students either stood or sat on the ground listening to the master's lecture, perhaps with some straw to warm them on a cold winter day. The master would have either sat on a stool or stood behind a lectern where the text that served as the basis of his lecture was positioned for easy access.

of Christ, understood as the Messiah promised in the Hebrew Scriptures. Alternatively, they could be taken as **symbols** of various points of doctrine or sacraments such as baptism, holy orders, and the Eucharist. For example, in addition to the historical event it portrayed, the narrative of Abraham and Isaac was thus also a symbol for a higher truth, namely, Christ's sacrifice on the cross, while the crossing of the Red Sea was seen as foreshadowing the sacrament of baptism. In the **anagogical** sense, the text was understood to refer to a higher reality, pointing to things of eschatological importance such as the end and purpose of the human journey on earth, the heavenly Jerusalem. Finally, a **tropological** or **moral** explanation could be extracted from the events, with an application to the reader's behavior in this life and, thus, with relevance for the salvation of their immortal soul. By this method, almost everything in the Old Testament could be given a Christological or an ecclesiological interpretation and thus provide the material for necessary theological extrapolations.

Scriptural commentators were not free to interpret each subject according to their own fancy. Instead, they were required to take into account previous and established interpretations, particularly those of the Fathers of the Church, the writers of the first Christian centuries who had devoted their lives to the scrutiny of the Scriptures and who had developed the first coherent interpretation of the Scriptures as a whole: Ambrose, Augustine, Jerome, Gregory the Great, and the Venerable Bede. Their authority was regarded as more fundamental in accordance with their closeness in time to Jesus and his apostles. Based on patristic authority, commentaries continued to be written through the early medieval centuries, culminating in the sumptuous scholarship of the Carolingian renaissance (see chap. 12).

By the twelfth century, changes in society, especially the rise of the cathedral schools and the professional clerical class they educated, prompted a rationalized curriculum. Ease of access to the sources and stringency in knowledge acquisition were valued over rumination and contemplation, which had been the hallmarks of the monastic approach to the Scriptures. Building their teaching on previous patristic commentary, sometimes washed through Carolingian conduits, the twelfth-century cathedral school masters sorted and digested their source material and delivered it in the schoolrooms. Their teaching yielded commentaries on the books of the Bible and on secular authors in the form of reports from the masters' classes. The masters referred to this practice of orally expounding authorities as "glossing," the written text eventually and potentially resulting from it, a "gloss."

At this point, the difference between a commentary and a gloss should be mentioned. Scholars have sometimes suggested that in order to qualify for the designation "gloss," the text must be formatted as surrounding and interweaving the text it aims to expound. This may be seen in many commentaries on classical authors from the eleventh and twelfth centuries, as well as in the distinctive layout of the biblical *Glossa ordinaria* (Clanchy and Smith 2010: 17–18), to which we will return below. Contrary to this assumption, however, is William of Conches's opinion in his *Glosae super Platonem* that a so-called commentary (*commentum*) is a collection of many things held together in the mind by study or teaching, which only pursues the sense (*solam sententiam exequens*) of the text being studied. The *glosa* does this too, but it also seeks to provide further clarity about the text. Hence everything is found in the gloss that one would find in a commentary but also more: on the one hand, an explanation of the text (*expositio litterae*); on the other, the evidence of the continuity of ideas displayed by the text as a whole (*continuatio litterae*):

> *Commentum dicitur plurium studio uel doctrina in mente habitorum in unum collectio. Et quamuis secundum hanc diffinitionem commentum possit dici quislibet liber, tamen non hodie uocamus commentum nisi alterius libri expositorium. Quod differt a glosa. Commentum enim, solam sententiam exequens, de continuatione uel expositione literae nichil agit. Glosa uero omnia illa exequitur. Vnde dicitur glosa, id est lingua. Ita enim aperte debet exponere ac si lingua doctoris uideatur docere.*[2]

> ("A collection of many things held together in the mind by study or teaching is called commentary [*commentum*]. And although according to this definition any book could be called a *commentum*, nevertheless, today we do not call it a *commentum* unless it expounds another book. This differs from the gloss. For the *commentum* only pursues the meaning and is not at all concerned with the context of the exposition of the letter. But the gloss pursues all these things. Hence it is called gloss [i.e., tongue]. For so openly ought it to expound, as if it seemed to teach by a master's tongue.")

The etymological connotation should not be overstated, but the fact remains that the meaning of the Greek word *glossa* is "tongue," and that the connection between works labeled as such and the classroom is crucial. This link is an essential feature of the genre, which has nothing to do with a particular format or manuscript *mise-en-page*. On the contrary, a *glosa* may very well refer to a continuously written commentary (as could the similar terms *glosula* and indeed, though less frequently, *commentarius* or *commentarium*, *commentum*, *expositio*, *explanatio*, and other related terms; see Häring 1982: 176) and was used for the kind of classroom-issuing and authority-based commentary that was the hallmark of the twelfth century. The practice of glossing, to be sure, was not something original to the twelfth century, but as with so many other forms of intellectual activity, it certainly gained speed at this time and became, as it were, best practice in lecture rooms.

Although a multitude of biblical commentaries have been preserved from the eleventh and twelfth centuries, we shall focus here in particular on those that issued from the school of Laon and the teaching of Master Anselm, since they came to play an extraordinary role in the later development of biblical teaching and theology. First I review the teaching of the Laon school as evidenced by contemporary sources, proceeding to analyze the surviving results of that teaching, the continuous Laon-glosses or

---

[2] Édouard Jeauneau, ed., *Guilelmi de Conchis Glosae super Platonem* (CCCM 203) (Turnhout: Brepols, 2006), 19. All translations are my own.

commentaries. I then investigate how these commentaries were mined for material in the creation of the quintessential Laon product, the biblical *Glossa*, eventually designated "*ordinaria*."

THE CONTINUOUS LAON-GLOSSES

Students flocked from near and far to hear Master Anselm teach in the first decades of the twelfth century: there is evidence of students coming in scores to Laon from England, Italy, the Empire (Germany), and, of course, various parts of the Frankish kingdom (Giraud 2010). Most famously, Anselm attracted the attention of Peter Abelard who, by his own testimony, went to Laon in 1112 to study *diuinitas* with Anselm. It is primarily from Abelard's testimony, his autobiographical letter known as the *Historia calamitatum* ("The History of my Misfortunes") that we are informed of the teaching methods of the Laon school. Although we should take what Abelard says with a pinch of salt, uttered as it is with strong bias, his reports of the teaching methods appear innocuous enough to be believed more or less prima facie.

Two related but distinct methods of teaching are mentioned in Abelard's account. The first is the *lectio*, a term the author mentions rather offhandedly, saying: *Paulatim uero me iam rarius et rarius ad lectiones eius accedente* ("Gradually, however, as I turned up more and more rarely to his lectures").[3] In the *lectio* ("lecture"), the master explained a book of the Bible, line by line, providing comments and parallels to other biblical books, explaining words and concepts, and employing the fourfold method of interpretation to extract doctrinal truths. In this process, great weight was placed on the earlier interpretations of the Fathers and later authorities. Often the lectures consisted of the master's digest and reorganization of these authorities, sorted after the biblical text ("the lemma") being commented on.

The other method was the *collatio sententiarum*, mentioned by Abelard later in the same passage: *Accidit autem quadam die, ut post aliquas sententiarum collationes nos scolares inuicem iocaremur* ("so it happened one day, after the comparison of some teachings, that we students were joking together").[4] This activity involved two or more students debating a question that had arisen from the lecture, which the presiding master finally harmonized or "determined." The process yielded the master's "sentence," a magisterial pronouncement on a point of theological doctrine. Collections of these were eventually gathered and distributed for further usage in the schools, thereby paving the way for the most famous such collection, the *Libri quatuor sententiarum*

---

[3] Alexander Andrée, ed., *Peter Abelard, Historia calamitatum. Edited from Troyes, Médiathèque du Grand Troyes, MS 802* (Toronto Medieval Latin Texts 32) (Toronto: Pontifical Institute of Mediaeval Studies, 2015), 35.

[4] Ibid., 35.

of Peter Lombard and, eventually, the *Summae* of the thirteenth century and beyond (Giraud 2010).

The lectures on sacred Scripture are what concern us here. In these, the master reviewed the biblical text with his students, read it out aloud, and then provided commentary and explanation of passages as required. This commentary was not limited to matters of exegesis or theology but could also range from points of geography and grammar to history and ethnography depending on the master's interests, the text, and the subject matter. This, at least, is what may be gleaned from the manuscripts preserving the commentaries that have survived from Laon. The masters' comments, originally delivered from mouth to ear, were eventually written down, yielding a "gloss." From Abelard's account of his days at Laon, we know that the master's teaching was recorded by his students. Abelard describes the effect of his first lectures on the Book of Ezekiel on his fellow students:

> *Omnibus tamen, qui affuerunt, in tantum lectio illa grata extitit, ut eam singulari preconio extollerent et me secundum hunc nostre lectionis tenorem ad glosandum compellerent. Quo quidem audito hii, qui non interfuerant, ceperunt ad secundam et terciam lectionem certatim concurrere, et omnes pariter de transcribendis glosis, quas prima die inceperam in ipso earum initio, plurimum solliciti esse.*[5]

> ("To all who were present my lecture appeared so pleasing that they praised it with one mouth and forced me to gloss it [*ad glosandum*] according to the tenor of this lecture. When those who had not been present heard this, they began to come in droves to the second and third lecture, and all were very eager to transcribe the glosses [*de transcribendis glosis*] which I had begun in the very beginning on the first day.")

These primitive reports, probably made on wax tablets or *schedulae*, scrap pieces of parchment, were eventually written up in a fair copy, connected and contextualized. We do not know whether or not this took place under the master's oversight. The result is what has been preserved: continuously written, lemmatic commentaries, at several removes from the master's lecture and the notes taken at that point. Some of these commentaries are little more than brief notes; others are more complex texts, obviously revised and updated with material from other sources. But whether they are preserved as nothing but short notes or have been altered to include longer theological discussions, the structure of the commentaries ought to represent, at least roughly, the outline of the master's original lecture.

Several such commentaries on a variety of biblical books survive from Laon and are connected in various ways with Anselm and his school. Associated with Anselm's name are one commentary on the Psalms, three on the Songs of Songs, four on the Gospel of

---

[5] Ibid., 36–37.

Matthew, one on the Gospel of John, and two on Revelation (Andrée 2017: 17–24). A full internal comparison of these texts still remains to be made, but from preliminary soundings it appears that the three commentaries on the Song of Songs are in some way connected (Giraud 2009; Leclercq 1949), as are the commentaries on Matthew (Andrée 2015). The Laon commentary on John, the *Glosae super Iohannem* or *Verbum substantiale*, is the only one of these texts that has been critically edited and was recently restored to Anselm of Laon himself (Andrée 2014). The distinctive features displayed by this commentary may help us to identify further material from Anselm and the Laon school.

The Laon glosses all have some characteristics in common. First of all, they are all lemmatic—that is, the exposition moves sequentially through the Bible text, quoting from the text in the process, sometimes just a word, sometimes a short sentence. This lemma then forms the basis of the following explanation. Here is an example from Anselm's commentary on the Gospel of John, the *Glosae super Iohannem*:

> ET VERBVM ERAT APVD DEVM. *Quasi filius subsistit in patre in unitate essentiae et personali diuisione. Alii inter homines subito apparuisse dicunt Dei filium, Iohannes apud Deum semper fuisse dicit:* ET VERBVM ERAT APVD DEVM, *id est filius apud patrem. Alii uerum hominem, Iohannes ipsum uerum Deum confirmat:* ET DEVS ERAT VERBVM, *id est ipse filius erat Deus. Alii hominem eum apud homines temporaliter conuersatum, Iohannes in principio apud Deum manentem ostendit:* HOC ERAT IN PRINCIPIO APVD DEVM.[6]

> ("AND THE WORD WAS WITH GOD. As if the Son subsists in the Father in unity of essence and individual separation. Some among men say that God's Son appeared suddenly, John says that he was always with God: AND THE WORD WAS WITH GOD, that is the Son with the Father. Others say that he is true man, John confirms that he is true God: AND THE WORD WAS GOD, that is the Son was God. Yet others say that he dwelled with men in time, John shows that he was with God in the beginning: THE WORD WAS WITH GOD IN THE BEGINNING.")

The other commentaries follow the same pattern of exegesis but are of differing length and depth. The three commentaries on the Song of Songs, called, respectively, *In hoc libro* (Paris, BnF, lat. 14801, ff. 1r–33v), *Salomon rex* (Paris, BnF, lat. 568, ff. 1r–64v), and *Enarrationes in Cantica* (PL 162), are a case in point. Although the extent and detail of the exposition varies, as well as the precise wording, there is a core of common ground to be discovered in the texts' exegesis, and they are obviously related; if not as parent and offspring, they at least share a common storehouse of exegesis from which each

---

[6] Alexander Andrée, ed., *Anselmi Laudunensis Glosae super Iohannem* (CCCM 267) (Turnhout: Brepols, 2014), 7.

commentary draws, as may be gleaned from the following sample from the exposition of Song of Songs 1:1:

In hoc libro (fol. 2r)

OSCVLETVR ME dico et non figurato osculo, sicut fecit per Heliseum prophetam, sed OSCVLO ORIS SVO, id est per uisitationem sui presentis. Per Heliseum enim Deus osculatus est genus humanum figurate. Qui Heliseus misit puerum suum et baculum suum ad suscitandum quemdam mortuum. Quem cum per baculum non posset suscitare, uel per puerum, ipsemet Heliseus uenit et membratim equauit se illi mortuo, ita quod os eius, scilicet mortui et cetera membra similiter fuerunt adequata, et *sic* per inspirationem mortuum suscitauit.

Salomon rex (ff. 3r–3v)

OSCVLETVR ME OSCVLO ORIS SVO. Hec uox est amicarum de nouo siue de ueteri testamento cum quodam timore et humilitate dicentium non "osculare," quod posset dicere sponsa, sed OSCVLETVR, id est tangat me OSCVLO ORIS SVO, id est dulcedine presentiae suae. Quod est dicere: non osculetur me figuratiuo osculo, ut olim fecit per Eliseum, qui misit seruum suum atque baculum ad resuscitandum filium Sunamitis. Qui cum a seruo resuscitari non posset, uenit ipse Eliseus et posuit os suum super os eius et pectus suum super pectus eius et cetera membra membris pueri coequauit et *sic* puerum Sunamitis resuscitauit. Eodem modo Dominus Iesus misit seruos suos, id est patriarchas et prophetas, ad resuscitandum genus humanum, quod dicitur filius Sunamitis, id est captiuae, id est filius primi parentis, qui pro peccato suo eiectus est de paradyso.

Enarrationes in Cantica (PL 162: 1189D)

OSCVLETVR ME . . . Deus ipse sicut praenuntiatus est per patriarchas et per prophetas, ipse *idem* iam OSCVLETVR ME, id est iam delectet me osculo, id est praesentia, ORIS SVI, id est Filii sui, qui dicitur os Patris sicut et Verbum, quia per ipsum Pater mundo manifestatur.

In hoc libro (fol. 2r)

LET HIM KISS ME, I say, and not with a figurative kiss, as he did through the prophet Elisha, but WITH THE KISS OF HIS MOUTH, that is through the appearance of his presence. For through Elisha God kissed mankind in a figurative manner. This Elisha sent his boy and his staff to resurrect a certain dead person. When he could not be revived through the staff, or by the boy, Elisha himself came and levelled himself limb by limb with the dead, in such a way that his mouth and other limbs were similarly levelled with those of the dead, and thus through inspiration he resurrected the dead man.

Salomon rex (ff. 3r–3v)

LET HIM KISS ME WITH THE KISS OF HIS MOUTH. This is the voice of the female friends from the Old and New Testaments saying with fear and humility not "to kiss," which the bride could say, but LET HIM KISS ME, that is he touches me WITH THE KISS OF HIS MOUTH, that is by the sweetness of his presence. That is to say: he does not kiss me with a figurative kiss, such that he did once through Elisha, who sent his servant and staff to resurrect the son of the Shulamite woman. When he was not able to be revived by the servant, Elisha himself came and placed his mouth over his mouth and his breast over his chest and levelled his other limbs over the boy's limbs and thus resurrected the boy of the Shulamite woman. In the same way the Lord Jesus sent his servants, that is the patriarchs and prophets, in order to resurrect mankind, which is called the son of the Shulamite woman, that is of a captive, that is the son of the first parent, who because of his sin was cast out from Paradise.

Enarrationes in Cantica (PL 162: 1189D)

LET HIM KISS ME . . . God himself as announced by the prophets and by the patriarchs, LET HIM himself KISS ME now, that is let him now delight me WITH THE KISS, that is by his presence, OF HIS MOUTH, that is of his Son, who is called the mouth of the Father just as the Word, because through him the Father is announced to the world.

The central theme in all three texts is the kiss with which the bridegroom kisses the bride in the Song of Songs and how this is to be understood on an allegorical level. The two most closely related commentaries, *In hoc libro* and *Salomon rex*, share the reference to Elisha in 2 Kings 4:34, where the prophet raises the son of a Shulamite woman from the dead not with a proper kiss but by holding his face, breast, and the rest of his body close to that of the boy in a "figurative" kiss. The bridegroom's kiss, that is Christ's kiss, is not at all like this, but it is a proper kiss that is the sweetness of his presence. The latter point is shared by all three commentaries. *Salomon rex* and *Enarrationes* also share the point about the servant sent by Elisha not being able to resurrect the boy: this is a figure for the prophets and patriarchs of the Old Testament, who fail to save the human race from sin, which only Christ can do. The exact relationship between these texts may never be entirely established, because of the different ways the texts originated and the different stages at which they are removed from the original lecture and from each other: the commentaries either originate in the same lecture, but from notes taken down by different reporters, or stem from notes taken at different lectures, perhaps by different masters. But the result is too close not to have a common origin.

As for their contents, the Laon commentaries all build on previous exegesis. They make extensive, and sometimes complex, use of earlier commentary tradition, testifying to the ease with which the masters navigated the source material preparing the lectures from which they issued. All traditional levels of interpretation are represented: the historical/literal, the allegorical, the tropological or moral, and the anagogical. Rarely is the specific approach spelled out: it is either passed over in silence or referred to as *historice* or *mystice*, the latter comprising all three nonliteral modes of analysis. In their exposition, the Laon masters were guided by the sources they employed, but as they very rarely mentioned the sources they were using, they were at liberty to forego whatever sense and interpretation had been prescribed by their predecessors. Compiling his work on the Gospel of John, for example, Anselm went first to his two most recent sources, Alcuin's commentary on John, and Heiric of Auxerre's gospel homilies; much of Anselm's text relies on these two works, although he sometimes substantially rewrote them. Through Alcuin and Heiric, Anselm also had access to their sources, the most important of which were Bede and Gregory, both of whom were heavily inspired by Augustine, whose *Tractatus in Iohannis euangelium* colored all subsequent Johannine exegesis. However, Anselm went beyond his immediate predecessors and also used their sources directly, adding his own comments, thoughts, and transitions (Andrée 2014).

Though the Laon commentaries differ in composition, common to all is that they are in some way propaedeutic to the Gloss, being involved in the creation of the corresponding books of the *Glossa*, later to become known as the *ordinaria*. The master's organized extracts—shorter, more succinct than the originals from which they were taken—were subsequently further arranged in manuscripts, presumably by students, together with the Bible text, thus yielding one of the more distinctive literary creations of the Middle Ages, the biblical Gloss. Two of the Matthew commentaries, *Cum post ascensionem* (Alençon, BM, 26, ff. 91r–190v), and *Nomen libri* (Valenciennes, BM, 14, ff. 160r–169r), were mined for material which was used to create the Gloss on Matthew

(Andrée 2015). The Gloss on John was compiled from Anselm's *Glosae super Iohannem* together with John Scottus Eriugena's rare commentary on John (Andrée 2011). Similarly, the Laon commentaries on the Song of Songs were used for the corresponding book of the Gloss.[7]

The extracts culled from the Laon commentaries were worked into the margins and in between the lines of manuscripts in which a central column of biblical text had been copied on each page. This distinctive format came to be a great success in the twelfth-century schools, with the biblical text written in a central column of each page, flanked and interwoven by marginal and interlinear glosses. The shorter interlinear glosses served either as a dictionary, an *aide-mémoire*, for the master explaining the text, or to provide him with quick access to concise theological opinions. The marginal glosses contain the digest of patristic opinion mentioned above, giving the most salient points of interpretation of the associated passages of the biblical text. In order to know which gloss referred to which word or words of the biblical text, the interlinear glosses were written immediately above the word or words they aimed to explain, and the marginal glosses were either written parallel to the text or were preceded by the first few words of the lemma to which they belonged. Sometimes, if it was not obvious, the relationship was emphasized by scribes or readers adding letters, tie-marks, or even lines connecting the gloss with its text. The reader thus had simultaneous access to three levels of text, an aspect of the Gloss that cannot be underestimated and that made it into a wonderfully usable tool for teaching the Bible.

THE *GLOSSA* "*ORDINARIA*"—THE GLOSS ON THE BIBLE

Arranged in the format of the Gloss,[8] the Laon teaching bore ripe fruit once it had been transplanted to the fertile soil of Paris, whose cathedral school had assumed the role of primary educational institution in the *sacra pagina* after Anselm's death in 1117. Here it was used by masters such as Gilbert of Poitiers and Peter Lombard, and by the latter's students Peter Comestor and Stephen Langton. The received narrative is that Gilbert of Poitiers expanded the Gloss on the Psalms and the Pauline Epistles into what was to become known as the *Media glosatura*, to separate it from Anselm's earlier, smaller gloss on these books, the *Parua glosatura*. Peter Lombard then used both of these glosses to create his own magisterial commentary, the *Magna glosatura* (Smalley 1983). Recent research has revealed that the story is not as clear-cut as this, and that the scenario may be partly different (Ekman 2019; Clark 2017). The Gloss stood at the basis of all these

[7] Mary Dove, ed., *Glossa ordinaria in canticum canticorum* (CCCM 170) (Turnhout: Brepols, 2007).

[8] For the printed edition, see *Biblia latina cum glossa ordinaria. Facsimile reprint of the editio princeps: Adolph Rusch of Strassburg 1480/81* (Turnhout: Brepols, 1992).

teachers' work, to be sure, and not only for the Psalms and Pauline Epistles. In fact, according to the new perspective, Peter Lombard used the Gloss both as a point of departure for all his biblical teaching, including the *Sentences*, and as a foil in debate with which he hammered out his theological teachings. Indeed, by the second half of the twelfth century, the Gloss had become so ubiquitous in the masters' lectures that Robert of Melun, himself teaching at the school on the Mont Sainte-Geneviève, criticized those who used it for giving as much authority to the glosses as to the text they were supposed to expound.[9] This description fits remarkably well with the practices of Peter Comestor who taught in Paris in the 1150s and 1160s. Curiously, the Gloss never seems to have served to curry favor for famous masters such as Peter Abelard and Hugh of Saint Victor, who belonged to a generation that only just saw the introduction of the Gloss in the schools before they died.

Although the distinctive format of the glossed books of the Bible remained essentially the same, the layout went through important refinements throughout the twelfth century. Scholars have identified three stages of development of the gloss format: simple, transitional, and complex (Smith 2009; de Hamel 1984). The earliest manuscripts of the Gloss come from Laon (Stirnemann 1994; for an exception, see Petke 1995). They were obviously manuscripts both issuing from teaching, as described above, and designed to be used in teaching. The earliest manuscripts are often quite small and irregularly inscribed. The page was ruled for a central column of biblical text, which was first written out, from beginning to end. The glosses were then supplied, the longer ones in the margins, on individual ad hoc ruling, and the shorter ones between the lines, often on top of the word or words they were connected to, and preceded by a paraph sign. Because of the uneven amount of commentary to the biblical text—some passages elicited ample interest, others hardly any—this rather unplanned writing process resulted in some pages being overcrowded with text and others seeing just a few glosses with much blank space in between them. This first stage of development, Smith's "simple format" (Smith 2009: 94–105), practiced mainly by nonprofessional scribes— who were students and, possibly, masters working outside of an established scriptorium (the French cathedrals did not have designated and well-equipped writing rooms)— lasted up to around the 1130s, when the Gloss had become a success and a tool to which teachers of the Scriptures and theology at least had to refer.

Around the second quarter of the twelfth century, when the Gloss reached Paris, home of professional scribes, the format started to undergo important changes with increasing degrees of complexity. Fueled by a desire to economize the layout of the page, there was first experimentation with the ruling and how much parchment could be spared by allowing the width of the central column to vary according to the amount of glossing a page would be expected to hold. In the original format, some pages would be completely full of marginal glosses, extending to the upper and lower margins as well

---

[9] R. M. Martin, ed., *Œuvres de Robert de Melun: vol. 3. Sententiae* (Leuven: Spicilegium sacrum Lovaniense, 1952).

as the ones flanking the Bible text column; others would contain only one, two, or three glosses, which created large amounts of empty space. Adjusting the width of the central column partially addressed this anomalous state of affairs, in that it allowed for a narrower central column when glosses were plentiful, and one that was wider (sometimes extending almost the entire width of the page) when they were few. Smith refers to this format as "transitional," since it was soon to be replaced by what she calls the "complex" format (Smith 2009: 105–20). By the middle of the century, professional scribes in Paris and possibly elsewhere came up with a format and method that would economize the way of copying the glossed books of the Bible. Instead of first copying the biblical text in a central column of varying width throughout the gatherings that would make up the codex and then filling out the glosses, marginal and interlinear, as they would appear in the exemplar from which they were copying, scribes would now plan the layout of each page individually. This involved ruling the page according to a standard pattern for both Bible text and glosses but copying the latter in letters of larger script on every second line. The width of the central column could be varied as desired, even in one single page, and the glosses copied as required in the margins, between the lines and sometimes even, if they were plentiful, in place of the biblical text. In the complex format, no page looks exactly like another.

Two more or less distinct elements make up the contents of most glossed books of the Bible. First there is the prefatory material, or *prothemata*, which is followed by the glossed biblical text. The *prothemata* were designed to introduce the text and, in applicable cases, its author. Taken over from the *accessus* of the lemmatic commentaries and expanded with new material, these introductory glosses often cover a wide variety of topics and formats (for the genre, see Minnis 1998 and Quain 1945), ranging from discussions of the circumstances of composition, the place of the text in the canon of biblical books, to the literary and historical aspects of the work. Not surprisingly, perhaps, it is among the prefaces that one sees the most variation. Earlier versions of certain glossed books, such as Matthew, display a variety of prefaces before a standard is set in manuscripts produced by the middle of the century. The Gospels are normally preceded by the so-called Monarchian prologues, understood in the Middle Ages to have been written by Jerome, sometimes copied, like the biblical text, in a central column in the middle of the page and surrounded by the other prefaces as marginal glosses. Later in the century, Peter Lombard wrote his own set of prefaces for the Gospels, with which his student Peter Comestor prefaced his lectures on the Gloss on these books (Clark 2014a).

The glossed text makes up the bulk of the manuscripts. Although there is less variation among the choice of marginal and interlinear glosses than among prefaces, the text of the glosses is not always consistent. Sometimes a marginal gloss that in one manuscript is written continuously is divided into two distinct glosses in another copy. A gloss that in one manuscript is found in the margin has in another been written between the lines of the biblical text. There seems thus to be no overarching principle of function of the position of the glosses on the page: convenience and relative length are the deciding factors. Glosses may be skipped from one manuscript to another, but scribal or reader awareness of this gives rise to the notion among medieval users of the Gloss as making up one individual yet unified and cohesive body of literature. For example, a reader of a copy of glossed Lamentations added a note, remarking: *hic deficit glossa hystorice* idem *et allegorice* ("Here is missing a gloss on the historical and allegorical understanding").[10] Reflecting the development from oral teaching to written books, some glossed books exist in multiple recensions or versions. Indeed, it seems common to most books that a revision of the original Laon version(s) was undertaken sometime before the mid-twelfth century, and that it was this revision that henceforth became the daily bread of masters and scholars.[11]

Scholars have studied the format of the glossed books more than their practical use. However, since only so much may be gleaned merely from looking at the manuscripts themselves, it is the scrutiny of those teachers who made use of the Gloss that will inform readers about its purpose, function, and use. Peter Lombard was one of the first masters to use the biblical Gloss in the classroom. He may have been preceded by Gilbert of Poitiers, but the evidence is scant (Gross-Diaz 1996). Also Zachary of Besançon appears to be one of the first masters to have used the Gloss as a teaching tool, making it the basis of his own Gospel harmony, the *Unum ex quatuor*.[12] However, Zachary's precise relationship to the Gloss remains to be established.

If Peter Lombard and, perhaps, Gilbert of Poitiers, introduced the Gloss in the twelfth-century schoolroom, it was Peter Comestor, the former's student, who utilized the Gloss to its full potential. Through Comestor's lectures, readers learn as much as is possible about its use but also about its limitations. Comestor lectures as much on the Gloss as on the biblical text it is supposed to explain. He begins by quoting from the gospel lemma and, sometimes using information found in the appurtenant glosses, sometimes heading to other sources, or making use of his seemingly limitless storehouse of knowledge, he explains it to his students. He then either parses the glosses whose contents he has already employed or refers his students to them by citing their opening word or words. In this process he often reorganizes the glosses grammatically and contextually, exhorting his audience in what order to read the glosses. His signal to read a gloss is either simply *glosa* or *interlinearis*, or *modo lege illam <glosam>, post hanc illam <glosam>, aliam glosam habes, habes glosam modicam, glosa notat*, depending on the situation, or when attention is directed to parts of glosses, *dimitte glosam hic, resume glosam ubi dimisisti, resume residuum glose quod primo dimisisti*, and *modo sume residuum alterius glose quod secundo dimisisti* ("now read this gloss," "after that gloss," "you have another gloss," "you have a small gloss," "the gloss remarks," and "leave this

---

[10] Alexander Andrée, ed., *Gilbertus Universalis: Glossa ordinaria in Lamentationes Ieremie prophete. Prothemata et Liber I* (Studia Latina Stockholmiensia 52) (Stockholm: Almqvist & Wiksell International, 2005), 104.

[11] Ibid.; also Jenny Kostoff-Käärd, ed., "The 'Glossa Ordinaria' on Ecclesiastes: A Critical Edition with Introduction" (Unpublished PhD diss., University of Toronto, 2015).

[12] Jacques-Paul Migne, ed., *Zachariae Chrysopolitani in unum ex quatuor sive de Concordia evangelistarum Libri quatuor* (PL 186) (Paris: Garnier, 1854).

gloss here," "resume the gloss that you had left," "resume the rest of the gloss that you skipped over earlier," etc.).[13]

Comestor therefore uses the Gloss much like a textbook for the study of the Bible, but he employs it not only to teach the Bible and theology but also for instruction in grammar, rhetoric, and dialectic, alongside the arts of the *quadrivium*. For Comestor, the Gloss becomes the channel for an entire world of knowledge that is integral and associated. The Bible and its Gloss bring all branches of knowledge—of human and divine things—together. But he also is aware of their deficiencies and does his utmost to explain and structure them for his students. A result of his work using the Gloss in the classroom, reconsidering its place in biblical teaching, was his master work, the *Historia scholastica*, a systematic review of the biblical narrative from Creation to the Death, Resurrection, and Ascension of Christ in historic sequence.[14] Here the Gloss is much more subtly employed than in the lectures, though much of the contents of the narrative and the discussions arising from it is to be found in the Gloss (Clark 2015).

Scholars have pondered the use of the glossed books of the Bible, reaching the consensus that what was first designed to be used in the classrooms eventually became a library book. This process was already in place around the middle of the twelfth century. The change in format is adduced as evidence for this development (Smith 2009: 104, 109–14). Earlier volumes, smaller and easier to carry around, and displaying a format that was reasonably clear and easy to navigate, were particularly suitable for a master to bring with him to the classroom. On the other hand, as soon as the complex format won the day, with its intricate layout and often larger page size, the Gloss ceased to be brought into the classrooms but functioned instead as a reference tool, used by preachers and theologians who wanted quickly to find a reference to the received interpretation of a given biblical passage. With recent research into Comestor's lectures on the glossed Gospels, however, this narrative stands in need of a slight revision. Indeed, the Gloss was originally conceived and employed as a tool for the masters to use in their teaching of the *sacra pagina*, and teachers such as Lombard or Comestor used it to pull authoritative opinions to adorn their own lectures, or as fuel for debate, or as the objects themselves of further lectures. It is clear that Comestor in his lectures on the glossed gospels used a copy containing the text as found in the stabilized, "ordinary," form, extant from around the mid-twelfth century and normally copied in the complex layout. Comestor's use thus disqualifies the suggestion that the Gloss became a library book concurrent with the development of its format (Andrée 2019). Indeed, further evidence from later in the twelfth and early thirteenth century, from the lectures of Stephen Langton, Hugh of Saint-Cher, and others, seems to corroborate this claim: the Gloss continued to be used for lectures well into the thirteenth century. At the same time, the books were of course there in the libraries and book rooms to be consulted by anyone who so wished.

---

[13] Peter Comestor, *Glosae in euangelium Matthei glosatum*. Paris, BnF, lat. 620, ff. 1–85, and Troyes, Médiathèque du Grand Troyes, 1024, ff. 1–87v.

[14] Peter Comestor, *Historia scholastica*. Vienna, ÖNB, lat. 363.

There is evidence that the Gloss formed part of an educational scheme that reached beyond biblical studies and theology. Gilbert the Universal used Lamentations to teach Ciceronian rhetoric, and compiled a gloss on that biblical book for this purpose, which was later incorporated into the Glossa "ordinaria." Comestor's lectures on the glossed gospels teach not only theology, perhaps not even primarily theology, but a wide variety of related fields, ranging from etymology and grammar through geography and history to exegesis and theology. If any term would be appropriate to use of Comestor's teaching, it would be philology, with Comestor indulging in the art of a *Realphilolog*.

To summarize, the origin of the Gloss is to be sought in the oral lectures of Anselm and other masters of the *sacra pagina*, its purpose first to gather their teaching in a convenient format and then to act as tools or aids to further teaching of the sacred page, beyond the lecture rooms of the Laon school. As such, it achieved unprecedented success compared with previous biblical commentaries, and its influence reached far beyond the lecture halls of northern France. From the latter half of the twelfth century, copies of the Gloss are to be found in libraries across the European continent. There are indications that it spread fast: the very earliest datable copy of any book of the Gloss, on Lamentations, was copied in Bamberg in 1131 by the subdeacon Siegfried (Petke 1995). The term *ordinaria*, which is never to be seen in the earlier manuscripts, may arise from the ubiquity of the Gloss in contemporary teaching: it was the text that masters were supposed to use if they were teaching the Bible and theology at this time.

BIBLIOGRAPHY

Andrée, Alexander. 2008. "The *Glossa ordinaria* on the Gospel of John: A Preliminary Survey of the Manuscripts with a Presentation of the Text and its Sources." *Revue bénédictine* 118: 109–34, 289–333.

Andrée, Alexander. 2011. "Anselm of Laon Unveiled: the *Glosae super Iohannem* and the Origins of the *Glossa ordinaria* on the Bible." *Mediaeval Studies* 73: 217–60.

Andrée, Alexander, ed. 2014. *Anselmi Laudunensis Glosae super Iohannem*. CCCM 267. Turnhout: Brepols.

Andrée, Alexander. 2015. "Le *Pater* (Matth. 6, 9–13 et Luc, 11, 2–4) dans l'exégèse de l'école de Laon: La *Glossa ordinaria* et autres commentaires." In *Le "Notre Père" au XIIe siècle. Lectures et usages*, edited by Francesco Siri, 29–74. Turnhout: Brepols.

Andrée, Alexander. 2016. "Peter Comestor's Lectures on the *Glossa 'ordinaria'* on the Gospel of John: the Bible and Theology in the Twelfth-Century Classroom." *Traditio* 71: 1–34.

Andrée, Alexander. 2017. "'Diuersa sed non aduersa': Anselm of Laon, Twelfth–Century Biblical Hermeneutics, and the Difference a Letter Makes." In *From Learning to Love: Schools, Law, and Pastoral Care in the Middle Ages. Essays in Honour of Joseph W. Goering*, edited by Tristan Sharp, with Isabelle Cochelin, Greti Dinkova-Bruun, Abigail Firey, and Giulio Silano, 3–28. Toronto: Pontifical Institute of Mediaeval Studies.

Andrée, Alexander. 2019. "The Master in the Margins: Peter Comestor, the 'Buildwas Books', and Teaching Theology in Twelfth-Century Paris." *Scriptorium* 73: 35–64.

Bain, Emmanuel 2013. "Le travail du maître dans le commentaire sur l'évangile de Matthieu." In *Pierre le Mangeur ou Pierre de Troyes, maître du XIIe siècle*, edited by Gilbert Dahan, 89–123. Bibliothèque d'histoire culturelle du Moyen Âge 12. Turnhout: Brepols.

Ballentyne, Adrian. 1986. "A Reassessment of the Exposition of the Gospel According to St Matthew in Manuscript Alençon 26." *Recherches de théologie et philosophie médiévales* 56: 19–57.

Brady, Ignatius. 1966. "Peter Manducator and the Oral Teachings of Peter Lombard." *Antonianum* 41: 454–90.

Clanchy, Michael, and Lesley Smith. 2010. "Abelard's Description of the School of Laon: What Might It Tell Us about Early Scholastic Teaching?" *Nottingham Medieval Studies* 54: 1–34.

Clark, Mark J. 2014a. "Peter Comestor's *Historia Genesis* and the Biblical Gloss." *Medioevo. Rivista di Storia della Filosofia Medievale* 39: 135–72.

Clark, Mark J. 2014b. "The Biblical *Gloss*, the Search for Peter Lombard's Glossed Bible, and the School of Paris." *Mediaeval Studies* 76: 57–113.

Clark, Mark J. 2015. *The Making of the Historia scholastica, 1150–1200*. Studies and Texts 198, Mediaeval Law and Theology 7. Toronto: Pontifical Institute of Mediaeval Studies.

Clark, Mark J. 2017. "Peter Lombard, Stephen Langton, and The School of Paris: the Making of the Twelfth-Century Scholastic Biblical Tradition.," *Traditio* 72: 171–274.

Copeland, Rita. 2012. "Gloss and Commentary." In *The Oxford Handbook of Medieval Latin Literature*, edited by Ralph Hexter and David Townsend, 171–91. Oxford: Oxford University Press.

Dahan, Gilbert. 2013. "Les exégèses de Pierre le Mangeur." In *Pierre le Mangeur ou Pierre de Troyes, maître du XIIᵉ siècle*, edited by Gilbert Dahan, 49–87. Bibliothèque d'histoire culturelle du Moyen Âge 12. Turnhout: Brepols.

Ekman, Annika. 2019. "Anselm of Laon, the *Glossa Ordinaria*, and the Tangled Web of Twelfth-Century Psalms-Exegesis." Unpublished PhD diss., University of Toronto.

Giraud, Cédric. 2009. "*Lectiones magistri Anselmi*: Les commentaires d'Anselme de Laon sur le Cantique des cantiques." In *The Multiple Meaning of Scripture: The Role of Exegesis in Early-Christian and Medieval Culture*, edited by Ineke van't Spijker, 177–201. Leiden: Brill.

Giraud, Cédric. 2010. *Per verba magistri: Anselme de Laon et son école au XIIᵉ siècle*. Bibliothèque d'histoire culturelle du Moyen Âge 8. Turnhout: Brepols.

Gross-Diaz, Theresa. 1996. *The Psalms Commentary of Gilbert of Poitiers: From* lectio divina *to the Lecture Room*. Brill's Studies in Intellectual History 68. Leiden: Brill.

Hamel, Christopher de. 1984. *Glossed Books of the Bible and the Origins of the Paris Booktrade*. Woodbridge: Brewer.

Häring, Nikolaus. 1982. "Commentary and Hermeneutics." In *Renaissance and Renewal in the Twelfth Century*, edited by Robert L. Benson and Giles Constable, 173–200. Cambridge, MA: Harvard University.

Leclercq, Jean. 1949. "Le commentaire du Cantique des cantiques attribué à Anselme de Laon." *Recherches de Théologie et Philosophie Médiévales* 16: 29–39.

Minnis, Alastair. 1998. *Medieval Theory of Authorship: Literary Attitudes in the Late Middle Ages*. 2nd ed. Philadelphia: University of Pennsylvania Press.

O'Hagan, Peter. 2017. "The Gloss, Peter Lombard, and Stephen Langton on Romans." Unpublished PhD diss., University of Toronto.

Petke, Wolfgang. 1995. "Eine frühe Handschrift der Glossa ordinaria und das Skriptorium des Augustiner-Chorherrenstifts Riechenberg bei Goslar." In *Papstgeschichte und Landesgeschichte: Festschrift für Hermann Jakobs zum 65.Geburtstag*, edited by J. Dahlhaus and A. Kohnle, 255–96. Cologne: Bohlau.

Quain, Edwin A. 1945. "The Medieval *Accessus ad auctores*." *Traditio* 3: 215–64.

Sharp, Alice Hutton. 2015. "*In principio*: The Origins of the *Glossa ordinaria* on Genesis 1–3." Unpublished PhD diss., University of Toronto.

Smalley, Beryl. 1983. *The Study of the Bible in the Middle Ages*. 3rd ed. Oxford: Oxford University Press.

Smith, Lesley. 2009. *The Glossa Ordinaria: The Making of a Medieval Bible Commentary*. Leiden: Brill.

Stirnemann, Patricia. 1994. "Où ont été fabriqués les livres de la glose ordinaire dans la première moitié du XIIe siècle?" In *Le XIIe siècle. Mutations et renouveau en France dans la première moitié du XIIe siècle*, edited by F. Gasparri, 257–301. Paris: Cahier du Leopard d'or.

CHAPTER 15

....

LATIN GOSPEL HARMONIES

....

ULRICH B. SCHMID

HISTORY OF RESEARCH

....

FROM the perspective of the history of research, the Latin gospel harmony tradition falls largely into two categories (see further Petersen 1994). On the one hand, we have a multitude of mostly unpublished Latin harmony manuscripts which carry a thoroughly Vulgate textual cloak. The oldest of these is the mid-sixth century Codex Fuldensis (Fulda, Hochschul- und Landesbibliothek, Codex Bonifatianus 1).[1] On the other hand, we can infer that there once must have been a much earlier version of a Latin harmony which was closer to its ultimate source, namely, Tatian's Diatessaron (ca. 170–80 CE), and hence is thought to have been extant as an Old Latin gospel harmony.

As scholarship was mostly interested in the late second-century Tatianic gospel text, the focus has been on extracting the Old Latin harmony from the extant harmony tradition in the West. The thoroughly Vulgate gospel harmony tradition was, for the most part, considered of less value for this purpose and has accordingly received little attention on its own. Instead, late medieval vernacular gospel harmonies (Middle Dutch, Middle High German, and Middle Italian) from the thirteenth to the fifteenth centuries were considered more promising ways of accessing an otherwise-lost Old Latin harmony. This is also true of the only notable study into the extant Latin gospel harmony tradition from the first half of the twentieth century (Vogels 1919). Vogels was almost

---

[1] High-resolution color images are now available on the library website <https://fuldig.hs-fulda.de/viewer/image/PPN325289808/1/>. Although a full transcription has been published (Ernst Ranke, ed., *Codex Fuldensis. Novum Testamentum latine interprete Hieronymo ex manuscripto Victoris Capuani* [Marburg: Elwert, 1868]), its errors are such that the edition is unusable, although the *Prolegomena* as well as the *Apparatus Diplomaticus* and *Apparatus Criticus* remain excellent pieces of scholarship worth consulting.

exclusively interested in the Old Latin element he thought he could extract from the basically Vulgate harmonies he was examining.

The method of Vogels and other scholars working on late medieval vernacular harmonies was to compare the oldest item (Codex Fuldensis) with the younger texts in order to find older elements in them that could not have been mediated through Fuldensis. These older elements were then considered to be remnants of the Old Latin harmony. A group of three Latin manuscripts and one bilingual Latin and Old High German harmony from the ninth century were examined by Rathofer with regard to their relationship to Fuldensis (Rathofer 1971, 1972, 1973). He not only found out that at least one of the later harmonies must have been directly copied from Fuldensis—something Vogels had denied—but that the entire methodology that had been used in this type of Diatessaronic scholarship was seriously flawed. On the one hand, the method was not precise enough to spot the influence of local Vulgate gospel texts on the copying of harmony manuscripts, as Rathofer was able to demonstrate for the text local to the monastery of Fulda in the ninth century. On the other hand, the method was overscrupulous in that it managed to elevate printing errors in modern editions of harmony manuscripts to Diatessaronic status (Schmid 2004a).

Petersen described the effect of Rathofer's findings as "a knife through the heart of the 'Methode der Diatessaronforschung'" (1994: 304). Schmid took up work on the Latin Gospel Harmony tradition from here, endeavoring to classify the part of the tradition that derived from Codex Fuldensis (Schmid 2004b, 2004c, 2005, 2013, 2019). This was comparatively straightforward, once it had been recognized that paratextual elements such as chapter divisions and macrotextual features such as differing harmonistic sequences are much more diagnostic than individual readings on the microtextual level. As a result, there is now a solid basic understanding of the developments from Codex Fuldensis through two ninth-century harmony manuscripts (one in St. Gall, one in Rheims; Sa and Re in the present study) into a rich and diverse tradition that included commentaries by Zacharias Chrysopolitanus and Peter the Chanter, editions of glossed harmonies, and further reworkings, such as those by Peter Comestor and the anonymous editor of the "Munich harmony" in the twelfth to fourteenth centuries (MA and MD in the present study; Schmid 2005: 57–193).

Beyond this large body of "Fuldensis-type" and "Fuldensis-type influenced" Latin gospel harmony tradition there are other late medieval Latin gospel harmonies, most of which have been less studied and remain unedited. Among these is a unique harmony manuscript of the fifteenth century from the Staatsbibliothek in Berlin (Th in the present study), and a harmony attributed to Hermann Zoest (or Hermannus de Soest) also from the fifteenth century. The latter text is available in at least two Munich manuscripts (BSB Clm 721 and 5599) and one in Würzburg (UB, M.ch.q.87). Two more Latin harmonies that were conceived according to the principles and examples outlined by Augustine's *De consensu euangelistarum* have received some scholarly attention. First is the *Concordia quattuor evangelistarum* which was produced in the middle of the twelfth century by Clement, Prior of Llanthony on the Welsh border. Although the Latin text has not been edited, it was translated into English and is related to the Lollard Bible (Smith 1985). It has been clearly established that Clement based his work on Augustine and was independent of the Fuldensis tradition (Smith 2014; Schmid 2005: 178–80). Second, Jean Gerson, the former chancellor of the University of Paris, published his *Monotessaron* in 1420, another gospel harmony inspired by Augustine with no detectable influence from the Fuldensis tradition (De Lang 1991).

As already indicated, research into Latin gospel harmony tradition has yielded good results when features of the paratext and harmonistic sequence are taken into account. What is lacking, however, are more studies of the textual developments of Latin gospel harmony tradition, as well as potential influences from harmonies on other genres, such as Old Latin gospel manuscripts (e.g., Codex Vercellensis, VL 3) or poetic texts (e.g., Sedulius's *Carmen paschale*). We know that Codex Fuldensis contains a good early Vulgate text very similar to the text of Codex Amiatinus (Fischer 1963: 552), but we are less familiar with the text of later harmony manuscripts. Moreover, there is also not much published material concerning the marginal and interlinear glosses that are found in glossed harmony manuscripts from the twelfth century. To fill that void, in part, the latter part of this chapter presents the textual evidence from one pericope of the Gospel according to John as found within the Latin gospel harmony tradition in order to provide an idea of the type of textual developments that took place over the course of time.

The Text of John 2:1–11 in the Latin Gospel Harmony Tradition

This section presents the text of John 2:1–11 in a variety of Latin harmony manuscripts. The text is split into lemmata, followed by a critical apparatus and commentary. This is followed by a discussion of the findings.

Presentation

The lemma gives the text of the sixth-century Codex Fuldensis (F). The distinction between F* (the first hand) and F^c (the corrector) has been made on the basis of Ranke's edition. The apparatus comprises the following manuscripts:

F: Codex Fuldensis (Fulda, Hochschul- und Landesbibliothek, Cod. Bonif. 1, 547 CE)
Sa: Codex Sangallensis (St. Gall, Stiftsbibliothek, Cod. Sang. 56, ninth century)
Ka: Codex Cassellanus (Kassel, Universitäts- und Landesbibliothek, 2° Ms. theol. 31, ninth century)
MC: Munich, BSB, Clm 23346 (ninth century)
Re: Rheims, BM, 46 (ninth century)

Ph: Berlin, Staatsbibliothek, Phillipps 1707 (thirteenth century)
Ma: Paris, Bibliothèque Mazarine 292 (thirteenth century)
L1:   Leipzig, UB, 192 (thirteenth century)
L2:   Leipzig, UB, 193 (thirteenth century)
MA: Munich, BSB, Clm 23977 (fourteenth century)
MD: Munich, BSB, Clm 10025 (fourteenth century)
MB: Munich, BSB, Clm 7946 (fourteenth century)
Th: Berlin, Staatsbibliothek, theol. lat. fol. 7 (fifteenth century)
Za: lemma of Zacharias Chrysopolitanus, *In unum ex quatuor II*, cap. 45 (PL 186: 17–168) (twelfth century)

This list includes three manuscripts giving deviating harmony arrangements: the "Munich harmony" is constituted by MA and MD, while Th belongs neither to the Fuldensis family nor to the "Munich harmony". Except for MA and MD, which are taken from Vogels (1919), the witnesses have been collated from microfilm or digital images available online.

The following spelling regularizations have been employed:

- The variant spellings of the diphthong *ae* (either *ae*, *æ*, *e-caudata*, or simple *e*), the different presentations of the aspiration in *hydriae* (either *hy-* or *ẏ-*), and the different presentations of the cardinal number six (either *sex* or *vi*) have not been recorded.
- The use of the semivowel *u* in front of another vowel has been kept. In consequence, the text of Zacharias Chrysopolitanus as published in PL 186 has been adapted to this rule.
- *Nomina sacra* have been resolved and standardized to *Iesus* and *mater*; other abbreviations have also been resolved.

Throughout, the variant readings of the Latin gospel harmony tradition are compared only to other Latin witnesses (either gospel manuscripts or patristic texts). Not all known Latin readings from the editions have been included, but only those that offer parallels for the readings found in the harmony witnesses. For the Vulgate text, the edition and the sigla of the Oxford Vulgate (W-W) have been used. Where a reading mentioned below is the dominant Vulgate reading (given by more than 50 percent of the manuscripts), it is referred to as the "Vulgate reading" and individual witnesses are not listed. Where one of the readings is attested in more than five Vulgate manuscripts, it is labeled "alternative Vulgate reading," and only the number of Vulgate manuscripts containing it is given. In all other cases, the manuscripts are cited individually, prefixed with Vg. Old Latin manuscripts are given according to the *Vetus Latina* edition, in which the patristic data have also been checked.[2]

---

[2] Manuscripts have been cited from the online edition at <http://www.iohannes.com/vetuslatina/edition/index.html>.

The Evidence

2:1a et die tertio

2:1b nuptiae factae sunt in chanam galileae.

2:1c et erat mater iesu ibi.

2:1a die tertio F Sa Ka MC Re Ph (die tercio) L1 L2: in die tercio Ma: die tercia MA
MD Th (die 3a): ~ tercia die MB: om. Za

2:1b nuptiae factae sunt F Ph Ma L1 MA MD Th: ~ factae sunt nuptiae MB L2 Za |
chanam F: canan Sa: chana Ka MC Re Ph MB Ma L1 L2 MA MD Th: cana Za

No other gospel manuscripts can be adduced for the reading *in die tertio*. Although
die tertia is an alternative Vulgate reading (W-W cite seven Vulgate manuscripts) also
found in VL (3) 6 8 (9A) 10 15 27 29 30 35, *die tertio* is the standard Vulgate text. The
reading *tertia die* is only attested for VL 2 4 13 (47); the spelling difference *tercia* is found
in Vg W and VL 6. It is interesting to note that the later harmony manuscripts give a
great variety of readings in this case. While three of them (Ph L1 L2) side with the text of
F, the three harmony manuscripts (MA MD Th) which differ considerably in sequence
from F give the alternative Vulgate reading. The two readings from Ma and MB are only
rarely attested. The omission of *die tertio*, as in Za, is also found in the textual tradition of Arnobius, *Expositiunculae in Euangelium Iohannis* 2 (CSEL 31: 271.15, v.l.). In a
few other patristic writings we find the substitution *in illo tempore*, usually in title or
lemma texts (Bede, *Homeliarum euangelii* 1.14 [CCSL 122: 95, v.l.]; Maximus, *Homiliae*
2 [PL 57: 917A]). Augustine, *Tractatus in Euangelium Iohannis* 8.6.12 (CCSL 36: 95) has
altera die, while two Vulgate manuscripts (Vg D Y) read *die altero*. The omission (and
substitution) of *die tertio* seems to be a feature predominantly related to commentaries.
There are no other witnesses for the reversed word order *factae sunt nuptiae* in 2:1b (MB
L2 Za). The reading *chanam* in F could be taken as an accusative, but this would make
hardly any sense in context: as the place name is given in some Latin gospel manuscripts
as *chana* (Vg Z, cf. Sa above and F + Sa in John 21:2), but in others as *chanaan* (VL 8 15),
channan (VL 30 48), *cannan* (VL 47) or *canan* (Vg C X), this could simply be a scribal
change from -*n* to -*m*.

2:2 uocatus est autem ibi et iesus et discipuli eius ad nuptias.

2:2 ibi et iesus F Sa Ka^c MC^c: ~ et iesus ibi Ka* MC* Re Ma L1 L2: et iesus MB MA MD
Za: iesus Ph Th

The Oxford Vulgate gives no information about the varying position of *ibi*, but only its presence (Vulgate reading; fourteen manuscripts) or absence (also a Vulgate reading; fourteen
manuscripts and the rest of the Old Latin tradition). The omission of *et* is paralleled in Vg D
E J and VL 10 11 11A 13 15 22 29 30 32 35 48. In this case we find a variant reading within the old
harmony manuscripts concerning word order: the three ninth-century manuscripts, Ka*,
MC*, and Re, are joined by three younger manuscripts (Ma L1 L2). Unfortunately, there is

no information in the editions to allow comparison. It is interesting to note that Ka* and MC* have been corrected in exactly the same way.

2:3a et deficiente uino.
2:3b dicit mater iesu ad eum.
2:3c uinum non habent.

2:3b dicit F Sa Ka MC Re MB Ma L1 L2 Th Za: dixit Ph MA MD | iesu F rell: eius Th

Only one other witness (VL 2) offers a parallel for the reading *dixit*, but this is as part of a rearranged text: *mater autem Iesum dixit ad eum*. The fragmentary VL 22 is the sole other example of *eius* instead of *iesu*.

2:4a et dicit ei iesus:
2:4b quid tibi et mihi est mulier.
2:4c nondum uenit hora mea.

2:4a et dicit F Sa Ka MC Re MB Ma L1^mg L2 Th Za: et dixit Ph MA: dicit L1 MD
2:4b tibi et mihi F Sa: ~ mihi et tibi Ka MC Re Ph MB Ma L1 L2 MA MD Th Za | est F Sa Ka MC Re MB L1 L2 MA MD Th Za: om. Ph Ma
2:4c nondum F rell: nundum Ma

The omission of *et* is found in VL 3 9A 48 (and possibly 22) and *dixit* for *dicit* appears in VL 4 13 (and possibly in 22; VL 2 reads *et respondens Iesus dixit*). These readings are found in younger harmony manuscripts. In this case, the two manuscripts of the "Munich Harmony" (MA, MD) deviate from each other. The marginal addition of *et* in L1 was probably written by the scribe, and so could be the immediate correction of a simple oversight. As in the preceding verse, Ph and MA have the perfect tense *dixit* for the present tense *dicit*. The word order *mihi et tibi* in 2:4b is the dominant Vulgate reading, also given by all Old Latin manuscripts; the inversion *tibi et mihi* of F and Sa is an alternative Vulgate reading (W-W give seven Vulgate manuscripts). The omission of *est* is found in Vg Z* and VL 2 10 13 27 35. Among all the harmony manuscripts, F and Sa are the only ones with the reversed word order. In 2:4c, *nundum* is also found in Vg G (=VL 7).

2:5a Dicit mater eius ministris.[3]
2:5b quodcumque dixerit uobis, facite.

2:5a dicit F rell: dixit MA
2:5b quodcumque F Sa MC Re MB Ma L1 L2 MA MD Th: quodcunque Ka Za: quaecumque Ph | dixerit F rell: dicerit Th | facite F rell: seruate et facite MA

---

[3] Grein erroneously prints *ministres* for Ka (Christian W. M. Grein, *Die Quellen des Heliand. Nebst einem Anhang: Tatians Evangelienharmonie herausgegeben nach dem Codex Cassellanus* [Kassel: Theodor Kay, 1869]).

The reading *dixit* in 2:5a is given by VL 10 13, albeit followed by *autem*: the perfect tense appears to be characteristic of MA (cf. 2:3b, 2:4a). *Quodcunque* is a younger form and is present in Vulgate editions (e.g., the Sixtine Vulgate). For *quaecumque* instead of *quodcumque, dicerit,* and *seruate et facite,* no parallels could be found. Again, younger harmony manuscripts give deviating readings. The readings *quaecumque* and *seruate et facite* are probably influenced by the Vulgate text of Matthew 23:3: *omnia ergo quaecumque dixerint uobis seruate et facite.*

2:6a erant autem ibi lapideae hydriae sex positae.
2:6b secundum purificationem iudaeorum.
2:6c capientes singulae metretas binas uel ternas.

2:6a lapideae hydriae F rell: ~ hydriae lapideae Ph
2:6b secundum F rell: iuxta(m) L2
2:6c singulae F rell: singulas L2 | metretas F rell: metretas suas MB*

The reversed word order in 2:6a is also found in VL 2 (3) 4 8 (9A) 10 11 13 22 27 29 30 47. Again, one of the younger harmony manuscripts (Ph) deviates from the Vulgate consensus. The substitution of *secundum* with *iuxta(m)* is found nowhere else. The reading *singulas* appears in VL 9A 11* 15 (Vg D Y read *singuli*). No other witness can be adduced for the addition of *suas* after *metretas.*

2:7a dicit eis iesus
2:7b implete hydrias aqua.
2:7c Et impleuerunt eas usque ad summum.

2:7a dicit F Sa MC Re Ka Ph MB Ma (L1 qicit!) L2 Th Za: dixit MA MD | eis F Ph MB L1 L2 MA MD Th Za: ei Ma
2:7c impleuerunt F rell: implerunt Sa | summum F^c rell: + dicit eis iesus implete hydrias aqua. Et impleuerunt eas usque ad summum F* (dittography, corrected by Victor)

The reading *dixit* is also found in VL 2 10 13. The nonsense reading *qicit* in L1 is due to the fact that the later ornamental capital D was mistakenly executed as Q. The reading *ei* instead of *eis* is also found in Vg H, yet it hardly makes sense. While it could be explained as a harmonization to 2:4, through Mary's role in 2:5a, it is more likely to be an accidental omission of the final letter. Again, the "Munich Harmony" manuscripts (MA, MD) unite in giving the perfect tense *dixit.* No other Latin parallels can be presented for the contracted form *implerunt* (Sa) or the lengthy dittography in F.

2:8a Et dicit eis iesus.
2:8b haurite nunc et ferte architriclino
2:8c et tulerunt.

2:8a dicit F Sa Ka MC Re Ph MB Ma L1 L2 Th Za: dixit MA MD
2:8b haurite Fc Sa Ka MC Re: aurite F* | architriclino F^c Sa Ka MC Re: archetriclino F*

Again, the perfect tense *dixit* (also in VL 10 13) is present in the "Munich Harmony" manuscripts (MA, MD) The nonaspirated *aurite* (F*) is an alternative Vulgate reading (W-W give eleven manuscripts), also found in VL 4 10 13 15* 29 35 47 48. The reading *archetriclino* (F*) occurs in Vg A D EP O Y and in VL 2.

2:9a ut autem gustauit architriclinus. aquam uinum factam.
2:9b et non sciebat unde esset.
2:9c ministri autem sciebant qui haurierant aquam.
2:9d Uocat sponsum archetriclinus.

2:9a architriclinus F^c rell: archetriclinus F* | gustauit architriclinus F Ph MB L1 L2 MD
   Th Za: gustaret architriclinus MA: ~ architriclinus gustauit Ma | uinum factam F Sa
   Ka MC Re Ph MB Ma L1* L2 MA Za: ~ factam uinum MD: uinum factum L1^c Th
2:9c haurierant F Sa (aurierant Re*): hauserunt MC*: hauserant Ka MC^c Re^c Ph MB
   Ma L1 L2 MA MD Th Za
2:9d archetriclinus F: architriclinus rell

In 2:9a, *archetriclinus* (F*) is an alternative Vulgate reading (W-W list seven manuscripts) also found in VL 2. No other witness for *gustaret* or the inverted word order (*architriclinus gustauit*) can be adduced, although VL 47 omits *gustauit*. The reading *uinum factum* is found in Vg E X* Y and in VL 2 3 4 8* 10 11A 13 15 27^c 30 33 47; *uinum factam* is the dominant Vulgate reading, whereas there is no parallel for the reversed word order *factam uinum*. The competing past tenses *(h)aurierant* and *(h)auserant* seem to be competing Vulgate readings: W-W opted for *hauserant*, yet more Vulgate (and all VL) manuscripts read *haurierant*. It is interesting to see that *hauserant* has been preferred by the correctors of the older harmony manuscripts MC^c (possibly contemporary with the first hand) and Re^c (clearly a later correction), by another ninth-century manuscript (Ka) and by all the younger manuscripts. In 2:9d, the reading *archetriclinus* in F, which again seems to be an alternative Vulgate reading, has not been subjected to correction.

2:10a et dicit ei.
2:10b Omnis homo primum bonum uinum ponit.
2:10c et cum inebriati fuerint. tunc id quod deterius est.
2:10d tu seruasti bonum uinum usque adhuc.

2:10b uinum F rell: om. Th
2:10c tunc F rell: om. MB
2:10d tu F Ka MC Re* L1: tu autem Sa Re^c Ph MB Ma L2 MA MD Th Za | bonum
   uinum F Ka MC Re Ph MB Ma L1 MA MD Th: ~ uinum bonum L2 Za | adhuc F
   Ka MC Re Ph MB Ma L1 L2 Th Za: huc MA MD

No other witnesses are recorded for the omission of *uinum*, perhaps through homoeoteleuton with *bonum*. The omission of *tunc* is found in VL 2 3 11 11A 13 33 (and possibly 22). The evidence for and against *autem* (or *uero*) is evenly balanced. Old Latin manuscripts, with the exception of VL 6 7 32 33 47 48, tend to give *autem* (or *uero*), as does a slight majority of Vulgate manuscripts (W-W cite fifteen), whereas twelve Vulgate manuscripts mentioned in W-W lack *autem* (or *uero*). The inverted word order *uinum bonum* is also found in Vg EP T and VL 9A 29. No other witnesses for the reading *huc* are recorded in the editions, yet two manuscripts of Hermann Zoest's Harmony also give this reading: again, the manuscripts of the "Munich Harmony" (MA, MD) unite in a rarely attested reading.

2:11a Hoc fecit initium signorum iesus
2:11b in chana galileae.
2:11c et manifestauit gloriam suam.

2:11c manifestauit F rell: manifestabit Ph | suam F Sa MC Ka Re L1 L2 Za: + et crediderunt in eum discipuli eius Ph Ma MA MD Th: ~ et crediderunt discipuli eius in eum MB

The reading *manifestabit* is also found in Vg T, yet the interchange of *b* and *u* (or vice versa) is common in manuscripts; taken as a real future tense, it would, of course, be a mistake. The absence of the final clause of verse 11 (*et crediderunt in eum discipuli eius*) and its correction in MB is a most interesting feature, which will be discussed below. No other witnesses omitting this clause are recorded. The reversed word order as given by MB is also found in VL 47.

Discussion

The first observation from this comparison is that the older manuscripts are remarkably close to each other: in verses 3, 6, and 11 they display no differences at all. When these manuscripts disagree, the deviation is usually a prominent Vulgate reading (cf. 2, 4b, 9c, 10d); this holds true even for the seemingly slight differences, such as in 8b, 9a, 9d. The sole exceptions are 1b (also a slight difference) and 7c. On the basis of 2, 4b, 9c (and, perhaps, 1b), Sa seems to be closer to F than Ka MC Re; Sa departs from F at 7c (with no other parallel) and 10d (competing Vulgate reading). On the other hand, Ka MC Re depart from each other only at 5b (Ka alone) and 9c (before correction).

Regarding the younger manuscripts, the "Munich Harmony" witnesses MA and MD are clearly outliers: they agree in rare readings at 3b, 7a, 8a, 10d (cf. 1a, 2). Three of these involve the perfect tense *dixit* in place of *dicit*, and in two instances where MA and MD depart from each other, a tendency toward the perfect tense can again be observed

(4a, 5a). The remaining three differences between MA and MD involve rare readings for which no other witnesses were found (5b, 9a [*gustaret architriclinus*], 9a [*factam uinum*]). A second observation is that Th, whose harmony arrangement differs from both Fuldensis and the "Munich Harmony," is barely distinct from the others in its text (see 3b, 5b, 10b). This is because there are considerable textual discrepancies between the manuscripts which display the Fuldensis sequence: Ph (cf. 3b, 4a, 4b, 6a, 11c); MB (cf. 1a, 1b, 6c, 10b, 11c); Ma (cf. 4b, 4c, 7a, 9a); L2 (cf. 1b, 6b, 6c, 10d). It is interesting to note that, among the younger manuscripts, L1 has the most agreements with F. Where L1 departs from F, it usually gives a competing Vulgate reading (cf. 2, 4b, 9c), or is corrected to a competing Vulgate reading (cf. 9a) or to F (cf. 4a). Readings 2, 4b, and 9c indicate that L1 is closely related to the ninth-century manuscripts Ka MC Re.

It is true that some of the rare readings displayed by the younger harmony manuscripts have Old Latin support, several of which are paralleled in VL 13 (1a: *tertia die*; 4a: *et dixit*; 4b: om. *est*; 5a: *dixit*; 6a: ~ *hydriae lapideae*; 7a: *dixit*; 8a: *dixit*; 10c: om. *tunc*). However, only four of these appear in the same manuscript (the instances of *dixit* in MA), and there are numerous unusual readings in VL 13 which are not found in any of the harmony manuscripts. This implies that the unusual readings given by younger harmony manuscripts, some of which are also found in Old Latin manuscripts, are, in fact, readings that belonged to the later stages of the Vulgate transmission rather than indications of Old Latin influence.

The omission of the final clause of John 2:11 from the Wedding at Cana in all the older harmony manuscripts, as well as L1, L2, and Za, is striking. In these witnesses, the clause is found within the story of the Miraculous Draught of Fish (Luke 5:1–11), between Luke 5:10 and 5:11. All the younger manuscripts belonging to the Fuldensis group (Ph MB Ma), which have the clause in its "normal" position in John 2:11 and repeat the clause in this second, Lukan, context. In order to assess this puzzling feature, it is important to know that within the Fuldensis family the Wedding at Cana (John 2:1–11) appears after the Sermon on the Mount (Matthew 5–7 par.), whereas the Miraculous Draught of Fish (Luke 5:1–11) is found among the stories of the Calling of the Disciples (John 1:35–51; Matthew 4:18–25; Matthew 9:9 + Luke 5:28), before the Sermon on the Mount. The displacement of John 2:11d to Luke 5:1–11 and its omission from the Wedding at Cana certainly belonged to the archetype of the Fuldensis family, as this arrangement is already present in Codex Fuldensis. The addition of John 2:11d to its original context in the Wedding at Cana, while retaining it within the context of the Miraculous Draught of Fish, as found in younger manuscripts of the Fuldensis family (Ph, MB, Ma), must be a subsequent redactional element. One or more users of the Fuldensis harmony supplied the missing final clause to the Johannine story, resulting in double occurrences of John 2:11d in this later branch. Direct evidence to support this is seen in the extensive twelfth-century glosses in Re, which include the addition of *et crediderunt in eum discipuli eius* at the end of the line ending *gloriam suam* (John 2:11c).

Glosses in Gospel Harmony Manuscripts

Glosses form an important part of the later manuscript tradition of gospel harmonies, and for that reason it is appropriate to provide an example of these for the passage under consideration. The seven glosses in one of the Leipzig manuscripts (L2) are therefore presented here (for other glossed harmony manuscripts, see Schmid 2005). They occur in between the lines or in the margin of folios 48r–49r, where John 2:1–11 is written (see further chap. 14).

i. On fol. 48r, the comment *Io solus* is written above *tertio* indicating that this is a story found only in the Gospel of John.

ii. In the next line *zelus* appears above *in chana* and *transmigrationis* above *galilee*. The same enigmatic interpretation is found in Zacharias (PL 186: 167C), ascribed to Alcuin: *in cana galilaeae, id est, in zelo transmigrationis fiunt nuptiae* ("in Cana of Galilee, that is to say, in the zeal of/for transformation the wedding took place"). *The Glossa ordinaria* (1046D) ascribes this comment to Augustine.

iii. On fol. 48v are two comments related to the lemmata *qui(d) michi et tibi* and *nondum et cetera*. Both comments are virtually identical with comments made by Peter Comestor, as shown in table 15.1:

Table 15.1 Glosses on John 2:4

Leipzig 193	Peter Comestor (PL 198: 1559B)
quasi	et est sensus
petis fieri miraculum	uis fieri miraculum
sed ad hoc agendum	sed ad hoc agendum
quid habeo tecum commune	quid habeo tecum commune
... quasi	quasi diceret
hoc non fatiam	ex natura tibi communi
ex natura tibi communi	non ago hoc,
sed hoc quod in hora passionis	sed in hora passionis
quae nondum uenit	quae nondum uenit
ex communi mihi et tibi	ex communi natura tibi et mihi
natura patiar	patiar

The difference between *petis* (Leipzig 193) and *uis* (Comestor) may, again, be accounted for by the intermediary of Zacharias (PL 186: 167D): *miraculum quod petis*.

iv. Above the line *uenit hora mea* is the comment: *non fata tibi sed a me disposita. sed uotis non necessitatis in qua morenturum* (?) ("not [the hour] of fate as for you, but [the hour] at my disposal; [the hour] in which I shall die is [set according] to my wish, not out of necessity"). This may be compared with Peter Comestor and Zacharias:

> *nec est credendum, secundum geneaticos, hoc dixisse dominum, qui putant unumquemque horam suam mortis habere ineuitabilem, secundum horam constellationis, in qua natus est, sed uocauit horam suam, id est a se dispositam. uoluntate enim mortuus est, non necessitate* (Comestor, PL 198: 1559BC) ("it is not to be believed that the Lord had said this in the manner of the astrologers, who suppose everybody has their predetermined hour of death following from the constellation of stars at their hour of birth; rather he called it his hour, that is to say [the hour] at his disposal").
>
> *hora passionis, non necessitatis scilicet hora, ut haeretici calumniantur, sed uoluntatis ... non enim auctor temporum, fato temporis regitur* (Zacharias, PL 186, 168A) ("the hour of [his] passion, not an hour out [set] of necessity, as the heretics slander, but out of free will ... because the creator of time[s] is not to be ruled by the fate of time.")

These two comments explain the marginal gloss in the Leipzig manuscript: his hour (i.e. the hour of his death), is not to be perceived according to human fate, but it is at his disposal because he is about to undergo death voluntarily and not out of necessity. Moreover, every catchword found in the gloss can be paralleled from the two sources mentioned.

v. Above *architriclino* appears the gloss *primati inter conuiua(nte)s* (?). This gloss may be compared with Peter Comestor (PL 198: 1559C): *et tulerunt aquam uino facto architriclino, id est primati inter conuiuantes in triclino* ("and they brought the water that became wine to the 'architriclinus' [head-waiter], that is to say, to the first among those dining in the 'triclinus' [banqueting room]").

vi. Above *(aquam uinum) factam* is the gloss *uel factum*, either referring to an alternative reading also found in Vulgate and Old Latin manuscripts, or simply a grammatical observation reflecting the gender of *uinum*.

vii. Above *omnis homo* is the gloss *carnaliter haereticus* ("a heretic in the flesh").

Summary

Several important conclusions may be drawn from this examination of John 2:1–11 in Latin gospel harmony tradition. First, it considerably broadens the perspective toward an ongoing history of the Latin harmony tradition flowing from Codex Fuldensis. This text was not only transmitted and read but subjected to extensive exegetical and hermeneutical glossing in the twelfth and thirteenth centuries. Some manuscripts of this era were designed to accommodate both a harmony text of the Fuldensis family and additional material such as synoptic parallels, smaller and larger exegetical

comments, marginal glosses, and interlinear insertions. This should come as no surprise, for the twelfth century was famous for its efforts to produce harmonizing gospel
commentaries, such as the *Historia Evangelica* of Peter Comestor (d. 1178), *In unum
ex quatuor* by Zacharias Chrysopolitanus (ca. 1150) and the *(Glossae) Super unum ex
quatuor* of Peter the Chanter (d. 1197).

The heavily glossed manuscripts not only display the same type of gospel harmony,
but they also generally refer to the same traditions. Although the evidence discussed
in this chapter is only a small sample, it is striking that virtually every comment could
be paralleled from the works of Peter Comestor or Zacharias Chrysopolitanus, and
often from the two sources simultaneously. Sometimes direct dependence seems to
be the only explanation for the verbatim agreement. Further analysis reveals that
this exegetical tradition ties in with the traditions condensed in the twelfth-century
Glossa ordinaria, an exegetical tool used for several centuries in theological education
throughout Europe (Schmid 2005). Leipzig 193 therefore serves as a perfect illustration of the twelfth-century exegetical efforts centered around and devoted to the harmony tradition. Since the harmony text used is a fairly good reproduction of the Codex
Fuldensis model, two important links can be established. The first bridges the gap between medieval comments and glosses on the separate gospels and the commentaries
on gospel harmonies. The second connects the later harmony tradition from the
twelfth/thirteenth centuries onward to the older medieval harmony tradition, known
through Codex Fuldensis and its ninth-century descendants, by means of the arrangement of their text. Perhaps it is not just by coincidence that those texts flourished in
the thirteenth century especially in Latin and from the fourteenth century onward in
vernacular languages as well. It is worth pointing out that there are more twelfth- and
thirteenth-centuries harmony manuscripts that were designed to include an apparatus
of interlinear and marginal glosses (including London BL, Royal MSS 2 D XXV; 3 B VIII;
3 B XV; 4 A IV; Oxford, Bodleian, MS Auct. D. 1. 8, and Laon, BM, 100). These serve to
illustrate the popularity of the genre of glossed Latin harmony manuscripts throughout
the thirteenth century.

A Hypothesis on the Latin Sources of Vernacular Harmonies

The model of the glossed harmony genre may also be employed to examine vernacular
harmonies, such as the Middle Dutch Liège manuscript, the Middle Italian Venetian
manuscript, and the Middle English Pepysian manuscript, which must have taken
onboard this type of material. Diatessaronic research has often suggested that biblical
readings in the vernacular harmonies which could not be found in Codex Fuldensis
point to an Old Latin Harmony and, ultimately, to an earlier stage of the harmony
tradition closer to the Diatessaron. There are, however, two major obstacles to this

hypothesis. First of all, its champions could not present physical evidence in the form of a manuscript of their postulated Old Latin type. This is hardly surprising: all the Latin harmonies currently known and examined have been shown either to be descendants of Codex Fuldensis or at least to display a Vulgate text. The evidence for an Old Latin harmony tradition independent of Codex Fuldensis is almost entirely derived from vernacular harmonies or Latin texts of a different genre such as medieval *Vitae* (Lives of the Saints). The second major obstacle is the fact that there is no consistent pattern of agreements in non-Fuldensis readings among the vernacular harmonies. Sometimes such readings are found in all of these harmonies, but often only two of them agree while the rest give the usual reading. To explain these inconsistent patterns of agreement, Diatessaronic scholarship usually refers to the concept of "vulgatization," the partial adaptation of the supposed Old Latin harmony to the Vulgate. This implies that individual vernacular harmonies (and other Latin texts that used it as a source) derived from differing versions of the Old Latin harmony. The problem is that this creates a complicated and completely hidden textual transmission of the Old Latin harmony. In other words, the vernacular harmonies' dependence on an Old Latin harmony can only be maintained if a constant remodeling of that text by various processes of "vulgatization" is assumed. Although not entirely inconceivable, this complex hypothesis relies on a parallel Old Latin harmony tradition of which not a single piece of direct physical evidence has survived among all known Latin harmony manuscripts.

Leipzig 193 offers an alternative hypothesis for the vernacular harmonies, suggesting that these do not depend upon an Old Latin harmony but derive from descendants of Codex Fuldensis which have been augmented by various episodes of glossing. From the twelfth century onward, we find not only such commentaries associated with the Fuldensis harmony tradition but also Fuldensis-type harmony manuscripts incorporating the same sort of collected exegetical information. Moreover, these manuscripts also contain an extensive gloss apparatus of synoptic parallels. Anyone working on a vernacular version of a gospel harmony in subsequent centuries could have used these glossed manuscripts for translation purposes. There was no need to collect all the information *de nouo*, or even consult the separate gospels in order to check parallel passages, for this task had already been done on the basis of a harmony text that ultimately goes back to Codex Fuldensis.

These glossed Latin harmony manuscripts presented above provide an attractive new genre which may have been responsible for the genesis of the vernacular harmonies. The main characteristic of this genre is the combination of a Fuldensis-type harmony text (not an Old Latin harmony text) with medieval exegetical glosses and parallel gospel passages. In these manuscripts the various parts are brought together physically on the same page and transparently arranged by means of apparatus systems: the layout was designed so that commentaries and glosses were not confused with the gospel (harmony) text. The conflation of the two is found only in the vernacular harmonies, where the task of translating and explaining seems (at least in part) to have been performed simultaneously.

Bibliography

Burger, Christoph, August A. den Hollander, and Ulrich B. Schmid, eds. 2004. *Evangelienharmonien des Mittelalters*. Assen: Royal Van Gorcum.

De Lang, Mareike H. 1991. "Jean Gerson's Harmony of the Gospels (1420)." *Nederlands archief voor kerkgeschiedenis/Dutch Review of Church History* 71: 37–49.

Fischer, Bonifatius. 1963. "Bibelausgaben des frühen Mittelalters." In *La Bibbia nell'alto Medioevo*, edited by E. Franceschini et al., 519–600. Settimane di studio del CISAM 10. Spoleto: Presso la Sede del Centro. Repr., *Lateinische Bibelhandschriften im frühen Mittelalter*. AGLB 11. Freiburg: Herder, 1985.

Petersen, William L. 1994. *Tatian's Diatessaron. Its Creation, Dissemination, Significance, and History in Scholarship*. Supplements to Vigiliae Christianae 25. Leiden: Brill.

Rathofer, J. 1971. "Zur Heimatfrage des althochdeutschen Tatian. Das Votum der Handschriften." *Annali Instituto Universitario Orientale, sezione germanica* 14: 7–104.

Rathofer, J. 1972. "'Tatian' und Fulda. Die St. Galler Handschrift und der Victor-Codex." In *Zeiten und Formen in Sprache und Dichtung. Festschrift für Fritz Tschirch zum 70. Geburtstag*, edited by K.-H. Schirmer and B. Sowinski, 337–56. Cologne: Böhlau.

Rathofer, J. 1973. "Die Einwirkung des Fuldischen Evangelientextes auf den althochdeutschen 'Tatian'. Abkehr von der Methode der Diatessaronforschung." In *Literatur und Sprache im europäischen Mittelalter. Festschrift für Karl Langosch zum 70. Geburtstag*, edited by Alf Önnerfors et al., 256–308. Darmstadt: Wissenschaftliche Buchgesellschaft.

Schmid, Ulrich B. 2003. "In Search of Tatian's Diatessaron in the West." *Vigiliae Christianae* 57: 176–99.

Schmid, Ulrich B. 2004a. "Genealogy by Chance! On the Significance of Accidental Variation (Parallelism)." In *Studies in Stemmatology, Vol. 2*, edited by P. van Reenen, A. den Hollander, and M. van Mulken, 127–43. Amsterdam: John Benjamins.

Schmid, Ulrich B. 2004b. "Evangelienharmonien des Mittelalters. Forschungsgeschichtliche und systematische Aspekte." In *Evangelienharmonien des Mittelalters*, edited by Christoph Burger, August A. den Hollander, and Ulrich B. Schmid, 1–17. Assen: Royal Van Gorcum.

Schmid, Ulrich B. 2004c. "Lateinische Evangelienharmonien. Die Konturen der abendländischen Harmonietradition." In *Evangelienharmonien des Mittelalters*, edited by Christoph Burger, August A. den Hollander, and Ulrich B. Schmid, 18–39. Assen: Royal Van Gorcum.

Schmid, Ulrich B. 2005. *Unum ex Quattuor. Eine Geschichte der lateinischen Tatianüberlieferung*. AGLB 37. Freiburg: Herder.

Schmid, Ulrich B. 2013. "Tatian's Diatessaron." In *The Text of the New Testament in Contemporary Research: Essays on the Status Quaestionis*, edited by Michael W. Holmes and Bart D. Ehrman, 115–42. 2nd ed. Leiden: Brill.

Schmid, Ulrich B. 2019. "Before and After: Some Notes on the Pre- and Post-History of Codex Fuldensis." In *The Gospel of Tatian: Exploring the Nature and Text of the Diatessaron*, edited by Matthew R. Crawford and Nicholas J. Zola, 171–90. The Reception of Jesus in the First Three Centuries 3. London: T&T Clark.

Smith, Paul. 1985. "An Edition of Parts I-V of the Wycliffite Translation of Clement of Llanthony's Gospel Harmony Unum Ex Quattuor, Known as Oon of Foure." PhD diss., University of Southampton.

Smith, Paul. 2014. "Clement of Llanthony's Gospel Harmony and Augustine's 'De Consensu Evangelistarum.'" *Church History and Religious Culture* 94: 175–96.

Vogels, Heinrich Joseph. 1919. *Beiträge zur Geschichte des Diatessaron im Abendland.* Neutestamentliche Abhandlungen 8.1. Münster: Aschendorff.

Wordsworth, John, and White, Henry Julian et al., eds. 1889–1954. *Nouum Testamentum Domini nostri Iesu Christi latine secundum editionem sancti Hieronymi.* 3 vols. Oxford: Clarendon Press.

CHAPTER 16

....

PARIS BIBLES AND SCHOLARSHIP

....

GILBERT DAHAN

TEACHING THE BIBLE

....

IN a letter to a friend, the Premonstratensian Philip of Harvengt (d. 1183) congratulated his correspondent for having gone, "driven by his love of science," to Paris, which he identified by the biblical name of Qiryat-Sefer, "City of the Book," and whose importance in the study of the Bible he emphasized as follows:

> Happy that city in which so many manuscripts are leafed through, whose astounding mysteries are clarified by the gift of the outpouring Spirit, a city in which the zeal of readers and the knowledge of texts are such that it deserves to be called Cariath Sepher, the City of Books.

This was written at the end of the twelfth century, before the prodigious expansion of the city in the thirteenth century. During the whole of the twelfth century, there was a remarkable increase in schools, often episcopal, throughout Western Europe, whether in Laon, Rheims, Chartres or Poitiers in France, York or Canterbury in England, Cremona or Ravenna in Italy, and Trier or Cologne in Germany (Riché 1979; Lesne 1940). It seems, however, that the Parisian schools had a dominant role, especially in the teaching of the Bible: following the school of Saint-Victor, which renewed the exegetical approach, and that of Sainte-Geneviève, it was the episcopal school that inspired the praise of Philip of Harvengt. This prominence is exemplified by a succession of prestigious teachers who are sometimes referred to as representatives of a "biblical-moral school," notably Peter Comestor, Peter the Chanter (Petrus Cantor), and Stephen Langton.

At the highest level of the school, the teaching of the Bible occupied first place (Grabmann 1911: 2.467–636; Smalley 1983: 196–263). Without being codified, as later it would be at the university, it took a specific form: commentaries covered large parts of the Bible, they tended to consist of brief notes, they often used the *Glossa ordinaria*, written in Laon and Auxerre at the beginning of the century (see chap. 14), and, above all, they gave an increasingly large role to the technique of question-and-answer (Dahan 2013a). Inquiries about the actual content of the biblical texts studied were first integrated into the teacher's lesson; these questions were brief, attempting to elucidate difficulties of all kinds (semantic, narrative, historical, doctrinal). Later, they became more complex and formed the subject of a special afternoon session following the continuous explanation of the text, as seen in the case of Robert of Melun or Simon of Tournai (Martin 1932: xxiv–xlvi). In this, doctrinal content was privileged. The role played by Peter Comestor's *Historia scholastica* should also be noted: this is a presentation of the narrative content of the Bible, placed in its historical context and accompanied by a summary of the exegetical tradition (Dahan 2013b). This was soon adopted as a textbook in schools (the title means "Biblical Narrative for Students") and was the subject of lessons, the texts of some of which have been preserved in commentaries by Stephen Langton and Hugh of Saint-Cher (Clark 2005).

The most important development took place in the thirteenth century, with the creation of the university and of the mendicant orders, mainly the Franciscans and the Dominicans. The principal importance here of the latter is in their setting up of educational establishments, the *studia*; while the Dominicans immediately emphasized the importance of study, the Franciscans also quickly created their own framework. The higher educational institutions of both orders, *studia generalia*, both allocated a major place in their programs to the study of the Bible (Centro di studi 1978; Mulchahey 1998). Moreover, they were sometimes connected to the universities (especially in Paris), with some of the masters of the *studia* holding chairs at the university, along with forms of teaching which were common to both.

At universities (first in Paris and Oxford, and later in others), the curriculum of the faculty of theology centered on two texts: the *Sentences* of Peter Lombard, which had a role as a theological textbook, and the Bible (Denifle 1894). Teaching was provided on two levels: a more elementary form, delivered by bachelors, which went through a series of books in two years; the bachelor was said to "read" the text *cursorie*, focusing on its narrative development and the main points of doctrine, with the major part being occupied by literal explanation although not exclusively so. More detailed teaching was entrusted to the master (Glorieux 1968). Such lessons were structured in three parts:

1. the *divisio textus*, the segmentation of the text to be expounded, first through the division of the whole book under consideration and then a series of subdivisions up to the level of the verse or an even smaller unit. These *divisiones* were extremely important: some commentaries, such as those of the Franciscan Peter John Olivi (d. 1297) on the Minor Prophets, are in fact developments of *divisiones*. The task was not to provide the "plan" of the book but rather to highlight its articulations, based on hermeneutical choices (which explains why these *divisiones* are often different from one another). This method also has a pedagogical impact, insofar as the commentator must situate each part of the text within the overall predefined

arrangement; another advantage is that the schematic approach involved in this technique totally avoids paraphrase and obliges the teacher to take an analytical approach (Dahan 2010);

2. the *expositio textus*, the explanation of the text, lemma by lemma or word by word, which endeavors to solve quickly all problems linked to a literal approach (as in the approach of the schools, mentioned above: semantics, narrative, historical context, and doctrine);

3. the *questiones* or *dubia*: the end of each lesson was devoted to questions, especially of a doctrinal nature, posed by the commented text. In particular, these involved contradictions with other passages of Scripture or those raised by certain exegetes (fairly often based on the affirmations of the *Glossa*); such questions were also termed *dubia*, "doubts." Even though they share a similar basic scheme, they are simpler in form than the "scholastic" question, which developed through the exercises of the same faculty of theology (disputed questions, or quodlibetical questions): a difficulty regarding a lemma of the text is highlighted in the form of a question; straightaway, an alternative opinion is put forward; finally the master provides their own responses and, above all, resolves the problem posed by the differing opinion.

This tripartite scheme, in fact, only appears rarely in commentaries written after the classes: it is sometimes present, for example, in Bonaventure, but not in Thomas Aquinas (who integrates the *questiones* into the *expositio textus*). It is interesting to note that the complete form is illustrated by authors who were not masters at the university, such as Nicholas of Gorran (d. 1295), a Dominican who was active in Saint-Jacques (Paris) in the last third of the thirteenth century.

Paris Bibles

The development of biblical studies at the university and in the *studia* of the mendicant orders resulted in a great demand for copies of the Bible. To meet this demand, Parisian booksellers increased production, applying a quasi-industrial technique to the manufacture of their books, based on a sort of assembly line, the so-called technique of *pecia*: a book serving as a model *(exemplar)* is divided into its constituent quires (*pecia* = "piece"), each of which is reproduced by a team of copyists (Murano 2005). Although the normal sign of books produced by *pecia* is an indication of the wages owed to the copyist, these do not appear in Paris Bibles even though it is clear that this process was used. The rapid production seems to have been carried out in an unscientific way: around 1266, Roger Bacon counted among the deadly sins of theology these Bibles made without care by "illiterate and married" booksellers.[1]

---

[1] Roger Bacon, *Opus minus*, ed. J. S. Brewer (London: Longman et al. 1859), 333. See also Light 2001; Rouse and Rouse 2000.

In reality, scholars reacted very quickly: at the convent of Saint-Jacques (Paris), Hugh of Saint-Cher led a team that developed a *correctorium*, a set of text-critical notes on the biblical text (Denifle 1888; Dahan 1997). It seems that at the same time another group of Dominicans took the initiative of fixing a text, in an approach that was initially recognised by the order but later condemned.[2] In any case, the Dominicans never ceased to be active in this field of textual criticism: a rather sumptuous Bible was copied at Saint-Jacques, probably around 1250 (Paris, BnF, lat. 16719–22), but within a decade (and possibly less) its text was corrected and accompanied by a *correctorium* written in the margin. These notes were collected to form the material of another Dominican *correctorium*, *Sorbonne I*, probably written around 1270 (Paris, BnF, lat. 15554, fol. 1–146). The same Dominicans produced a more complete *correctorium*, which is a masterpiece of textual criticism, *Sorbonne II* (Paris, BnF, lat. 15554, fol. 147–253; see Dahan 2004).

The Franciscans engaged in comparable work: the *correctorium* of William de la Mare is also a remarkable monument of textual criticism (Vatican City, BAV, Vat. lat. 3644). While these works are based on direct study of the sources, Gerard de Huy's somewhat later *correctorium* merely brings together the notes from the previous collections but contains an extremely interesting preface (Vatican City, BAV, Vat. lat. 4240; ed. Denifle 1888: 298–310), which includes an inventory of Greek translations of the Old Testament. These works of textual criticism on the Vulgate seem to go further than those attempted in the sixteenth century and even those of the nineteenth-century philologists. They are founded on an impressive body of documentation: Latin texts of the Vulgate (with a distinction between pre-Charlemagne manuscripts, those from the post-Carolingian period, and recent or "very recent" [*novissimi*] Bibles, the latter from the thirteenth century); texts now called *Vetus Latina*, which they designated *Septuaginta* (as found in the Fathers before Jerome and in specific manuscripts); and Greek and Hebrew originals (for Greek, see Dahan 1998; for Hebrew, see chap. 22). Their method was rigorous, not unlike recent manuals of textual criticism, with a classification of errors into additions, omissions, and alterations (with subdivisions within each category). Some of these *correctoria* were used in the sixteenth century for the establishment of the Vulgate decided at the Council of Trent (1546), finalized by Clement VIII (see chap. 19).

What is the text of these Bibles from the thirteenth century, especially those from Paris, studied and criticized by the correctors? Some modern scholars have spoken of a "Paris text." This does not exist: Bibles copied in the thirteenth century contain quite different texts, although all are examples of the Latin Vulgate which had gradually established itself in the West. The decisive moment was Charlemagne's decision to impose a uniform text throughout his empire; he entrusted the creation of this text to Alcuin, who proceeded to establish it by comparing Latin manuscripts of various origins (see chap. 12). The result was a series of Bibles copied in Tours in particular, which would serve as a model (Berger 1893: 185–242; Fischer 1957; Ganshof 1974). It should be noted

---

[2] Cf. B. M. Reichert, ed., *Acta capitulorum generalium ordinis praedicatorum*, vol. 1 (Paris/Stuttgart/Rome: In domo generalitia, 1898), 9 (1236) and 82 (1256).

that, at the same time as Alcuin, another scholar, Theodulf of Orleans, also provided an "edition" of the Latin Bible based on different foundations, since for the Old Testament it relied on a comparison with Hebrew. His activity is visible in several manuscripts: for example, Paris, BnF, lat. 11937 has, transcribed in its margins, a more literal translation of certain problematic passages (Delisle 1879; Power 1924). Unfortunately, Theodulf's fall from favor did not help the dissemination of his text, and it was the Alcuinian recension that dominated up to and including the Clementine Vulgate.

In the twelfth century, there were isolated attempts at revision comparable to those of Theodulf. In particular, a Bible was established at Cîteaux under the direction of Stephen Harding (Dijon, BM 12–15; Zaluska 1989: 63–111), who called on Jews to translate the problematic passages of the Old Testament for him. Nicholas Maniacoria produced some scholarly work in Rome around 1140, particularly on the Psalms (Peri 1977). Yet such endeavors were not followed up; for example, the Cistercian Bibles do not take into account Stephen Harding's recension (Cauwe 1993). It is therefore a text of Alcuinian origin that dominates, with all the accidents associated with manuscript transmission, and in particular the integration, depending on the region, of various textual traditions, often with the influence of texts known through the liturgy (Berger 1893; Glunz 1933; Loewe 1969; Dahan 1999: 161–238). It was these various texts that the Parisian booksellers of the thirteenth century copied and distributed; careful study of the biblical manuscripts therefore prohibits talk of a "Paris text."

On the other hand, the external appearance of the Bibles seems to have been homogenized (Martin 1889–90). The most important is certainly the adoption of a "modern" capitulation (chapter numbers), which is roughly the one we have today. It dates from the beginning of the thirteenth century and seems to be the work of Stephen Langton (d'Esneval 1978). It replaces the old divisions, which were often shorter than our current chapters: for example, in the book of Joshua, which currently has 24 chapters, the old divisions give 33, 110, and 11 chapters (De Bruyne 1914). The new capitulation was gradually adopted during the first half of the thirteenth century; many Bibles were prepared according to an older system, with the new chapter numbers added in the margins later. However, the development of biblical tools, notably concordances (see below), seems not only to have accelerated the adoption of modern capitulation but also to have imposed a system of internal marking within chapters by a division into seven virtual sections, indicated by the letters *a* to *g*. Thus, in the latter half of this century, and especially in the fourteenth century, precise references are multiplied. For instance, William de la Mare identifies the lemmas in his *correctorium* of Zephaniah as *i.a* [1:1]; *item c.* [1:14]; *ii.a* [2:2]; *item f.* [2:14]; *iii.a* [3:2]; *item e* [3:14] (Vatican City, BAV, Vat. lat. 3466, fol. 110r).

Apart from these chapter numbers, other elements became standardized in thirteenth-century Bibles, which are referred to as "paratexts." Among these, the prologues or "arguments" of the biblical books were fixed (see chap. 13, esp. table 13.1). Some had been in use for a long time, especially those by Jerome; in other cases, texts by Hrabanus Maurus were adopted. Another element present in almost all thirteenth-century Bibles is the list of *Interpretationes nominum Hebraicorum*, a lexicon giving sometimes multiple meanings for the names of persons that appear in Hebrew (or Greek) in the Bible. It seems that Jerome was the first to have produced such a tool in Latin; lists inspired by him were elaborated in the Middle Ages, but one particular list came to the fore in the thirteenth century and appears in almost all Bibles, beginning *Aaz apprehendens* ("Ahaz <means> he who seizes"; see Dahan 1996). The provision of summaries (also known as *tituli* or *capitula*), descriptive lists of the contents of each book by chapter, was an ancient practice which continued to be observed in some but not all thirteenth-century Bibles. Earlier forms were gradually adapted or replaced by those that followed standard capitulation. An example is seen in Paris, BnF, lat. 15475, where the summaries precede the biblical text (and are much less carefully presented); in several cases, they are copied immediately before the text of a book, in keeping with the earliest examples.

TOOLS FOR SCHOLARSHIP

The thirteenth century was the period during which work on the Bible became scientific, and it seems that Paris also played a determining role in this respect. This may be seen very clearly in the approach of the authors of the *correctoria*, but other tools were developed at that time which supported a scientific approach to the Bible. First of these were concordances, which were notably compiled in Paris (Mangenot 1926; Rouse and Rouse 1974a, 1984). The oldest is the work of a team of Dominicans (probably led by Hugh of Saint-Cher), before 1239, in Saint-Jacques. (Twenty-two manuscripts of this type are listed in Rouse and Rouse 1974a.) The work is remarkable, but the design is unsatisfactory: only the headword is given, without context, along with the scriptural reference according to the new capitulation and the seven subdivisions of each chapter. For example, the following entry is given for *Abel* (Paris, BnF, lat. 16279; modern verse references have been added in square brackets):

Gen. iiii.a.b.c.	[Genesis 4:2–9]
Iud. xi.f.	[Judges 11:33]
Tercio Reg. xv.f.	[1 Kings 15:20]
Math. xxiii.g.	[Matthew 23:35]
Luc. xi.g.	[Luke 11: 51]
Heb. xi.a., xii.d.	[Hebrews 11:4; 12:24]

A second concordance was also made at Saint-Jacques, by a team of English Dominicans between 1250 and 1270. In this, the complete verse in which the headword appears is given for each reference: its defect is thus the opposite of that of Hugh's concordance. Again, the entry for *Abel* serves as an example (Paris, BnF, lat. 514; Rouse and Rouse 1974a list sixteen manuscripts of this type):

Gen. iiii.a. *Fuit abel pastor ouuium et chaym agricola* [Genesis 4:2]

Iudic. xi.f. *Iepte percussit ab aroer usque abel que est in uineis consita* [Judges 11:33]

I Reg. vi.f. *usque ad abel magnum super quem posuerunt archam domini* [1 Samuel 6:18]

Heb. xi.a. *Fide plurimam hostiam abel quam chaym obtulit deo* [Hebrews 11:4].

The third concordance, made between 1270 and 1280, achieves a balance: the head-word is given with a reduced context but which allows the place of the quotation to be identified without difficulty (Paris, BnF, lat. 15252; more than eighty manuscripts are known of this type):

Ge. iiii.a. *pastor ouium*	[Genesis 4:2]
Mt. xxiii.d. *a sanguine abel iusti*	[Matthew 23:35]
Luc. xi.g. *a sanguine abel usque ad san<guinem>*	[Luke 11:51]
Heb. xi.a. *plurimam hostiam abel*	[Hebrews 11:4]
xii.f. *melius loquentem quam abel*	[Hebrews 12:24]

This is very close to the modern concordance. Medieval concordances were printed in the sixteenth and seventeenth centuries under the name of Hugh of Saint-Cher (Albaric 2004) and continued to be printed until the nineteenth century, when new concordances appeared.

The purpose of another scholarly tool, the collections of *distinctiones*, remains an open question. These are dictionaries of the meanings of words in the Bible, especially spiritual ones, arranged alphabetically: each word is followed by a list of verses in which it is found (Rouse and Rouse 1974b; Bataillon 1982). The first collection was the *Summa Abel* of Peter the Chanter (d. 1197). The following example of the *distinctio "abyssus"* ("abyss") shows how this tool works (Paris, BnF, lat. 455):[3]

Abyssus dicitur

— quandoque malus homo. Unde: *Congregans sicut in utre aquas maris ponens in thesauris abyssos* [Psalm 32:7 (LXX)];

— quandoque Scriptura. Unde: *Abyssus abyssum inuocat* [Psalm 41:8 (LXX)];

— quandoque profunditas iudiciorum Dei. Unde: *Dei aby<ssus> iu<dicia tua>* [Psalm 35:7 (LXX)];

— quandoque profunditas vitiorum. Unde: *De abyssis terre iterum redu<xisti>* [Psalm 70:20 (LXX)];

— quandoque profunditas cordis hominis. Unde: *Profundum est cor hominis et inscrutabile et quis cognoscet illud?* [Jeremiah 17:9].

The presentation is schematic (for some entries, there is a division into positive and neg-ative meanings); each meaning is illustrated by a biblical verse, indicated by text rather

---

[3] See now S. A. Barney, ed., *Petri Cantoris Distinctiones Abel* (Turnhout: Brepols, 2020), 8.

than chapter reference. Subsequently, various collections were compiled in the thirteenth and fourteenth centuries, including three written in Paris, the *Alphabeticum* of Peter of Capua (d. 1242) and the works of the Dominicans Nicholas of Byard (ca. 1250) and Nicholas of Gorran (d. ca. 1295). This tool was intended for the preacher, in order to find material for a sermon, rather than for the exegete. Some commentaries from the thirteenth century onward include *distinctiones* (see chap. 17), but it seems that in most cases these were composed by the exegetes themselves, who did not rely on such collections.

Tools were also developed in the twelfth and thirteenth centuries to assist spiritual exegesis (Dahan 1999: 325–50); the following chapter explains the importance of the exegesis of realities *(res)*, and there are specialized lists which present the meanings of animals (bestiaries), plants (herbals), stones (lapidaries), or numbers. Although most of them are of monastic origin, it is worth mentioning the tools used by exegetes. Among the lapidaries (Pannier 1882; Studer and Evans 1924), the best known is that of Marbod of Rennes (d. 1123);[4] exegetes used this for the list of the twelve stones of the high priest's breastplate (Exodus 28:17–20) and for the twelve stones of Revelation 21:10–20. A number of bestiaries were composed in the twelfth and thirteenth centuries (McCulloch 1960; Bianchiotto 1980), including those of Hugh of Fouilloy (d. 1174) and Peter of Beauvais (before 1206). The meaning of numbers, based on Wisdom 11:20, was developed into theories by writers such as Eucherius of Lyons and Isidore of Seville.[5] Among later texts on arithmology, chapter 14 of *De Scripturis* by Hugh of Saint-Victor is worthy of particular note.[6] One might also consider the extent to which the encyclopedias that flourished in the thirteenth century might also be numbered among tools for biblical study, since, apart from their objective description of realities, they included expansions on their spiritual meaning (Dahan 2009a: 103–33).

In the field of literal exegesis, lexicons must be mentioned. The two fundamental dictionaries, constantly used by exegetes, were the *Elementarium* of Papias (ca. 1060) and the *Derivationes* of Uguccio (ca. 1140–1210). Later, these were joined by the *Catholicon* by John of Genoa (1286), while the *Summa* of William Brito deals with the "difficult words" of the Bible (Berger 1879; Daly and Daly 1975; Weijers 1991).

PARISIAN MASTERS

As shown in the letter of Philip of Harvengt quoted at the beginning of this chapter, from the second half of the twelfth century onward Paris attracted all those who were

---

[4] M. E. Herrera, ed. and Spanish trans., *Marbodus Redonensis. Liber lapidum* (Paris: Belles-Lettres, 2006).

[5] Eucherius, *Formulae spiritualis intelligentiae*, ch. 11 (PL 50: 769–72); Isidore (?), *Liber numerorum* (PL 83: 179–200).

[6] PL 175: 22–23; see also Dahan 2009a: 135–60; Lange 1979.

interested in the study of the Bible, either as teachers or as students. The birth of the university and the development of the *studia* of the mendicant orders only served to reinforce this. Almost all the exegetes of the latter part of the Middle Ages could thus be included in this chapter, but the present section will only mention the principal ones, which appear to have a significant connection with Paris (Glorieux 1933–34). Monastic exegesis provides a good point of departure, since certain abbeys based in Paris welcomed exegetes. This was the case at the beginning of the twelfth century in the priory of Saint-Eloi (in the Cité), home of Rainaud who wrote commentaries on the Pentateuch (preceded by a substantial preface), Joshua, Ruth, and Isaiah (Dahan 2009a: 321–50).

The development of the Paris schools during the course of the twelfth century has already been highlighted. In many cases, it was the prestige of a master who attracted listeners. The most famous example is that of Peter Abelard (1079–1142), who taught at the Montagne Sainte-Geneviève on several occasions. His exegetical work, which has been little studied, includes commentaries on the Hexameron and the Epistle to the Romans; the prologue to his *Sic et non* contains methodological considerations of interest to exegesis; in the *Problemata Heloissae*, he answers forty-two questions from Heloise on biblical passages.[7] Several of Abelard's students left biblical commentaries. Apart from the Cambridge commentaries on the Pauline epistles (named after the location of the manuscript in which they are transmitted [Trinity College, B.1.39]; see Landgraf 1937–45), the work of Robert of Melun (d. 1167) is worth mentioning: the introduction to his *Sentences* contains important considerations on hermeneutics and the *questiones* of his lectures have been preserved (Martin 1932–52). From the point of view of the history of exegesis, the school of Saint-Victor played a major role (Berndt 2009; Poirel 2010). In his theoretical works (*Didascalicon, De Scripturis et scriptoribus sacris*), Hugh of Saint-Victor lays down the rules for interpreting the Bible, both on the literal level and on that of spiritual exegesis, insisting on the need to study the letter of the text with its multiple implications. His commentaries on the Hexateuch follow this direction, while those on Ecclesiastes and Lamentations contain a significant amount of spiritual exegesis (PL 175; Dahan 2011a). Andrew of Saint-Victor is one of the few commentators of the Middle Ages to devote himself exclusively to literal exegesis (Berndt 1991). He commented on almost all of the Old Testament, and his exegesis of the passages of Isaiah considered to be an announcement of the coming of Christ (in particular Isaiah 7:14) provoked sharp criticism, beginning with his contemporary Richard of Saint-Victor (*De Emmanuele, PL* 196: 601–66). The latter is the author of a collection of spiritual interpretations (*Allegoriae*), but neither does he neglect the literal meaning (cf. Châtillon 1988).

In the second half of the twelfth century, the episcopal school experienced a prodigious expansion and was exemplified by the masters mentioned above. The aim of these scholars was to comment on the whole of Scripture. The results may be seen in

---

[7] PL 178; see also Dahan 2016: 219–32; Peppermüller 1972; Luscombe 1969.

Peter Comestor's *Historia scholastica*, and the series of commentaries by Peter the Chanter (Baldwin 1970) and Stephen Langton (some of which have come down to us in several recensions; see Lacombe et al. 1930; Bataillon et al. 2010); Peter Comestor also wrote a commentary on the Gospels (Dahan 2011b, 2013b). The teaching of these masters marks a step in the evolution of Western exegesis, which is reflected in the balance achieved between literal and spiritual exegesis, the important role played by question-and-answer technique, the recourse to techniques used in the study of secular texts, and the frequent use of the *Glossa ordinaria*. To these names may be added that of Peter of Poitiers (ca. 1130–1205), the successor of Peter Comestor and chancellor of the schools in 1192. He composed a summary of sacred history up to Christ with a large place for genealogical diagrams (*Arbor historiae biblicae*), an *Allegoriae super tabernaculum Moysi*, and a commentary on the Psalms in the form of *distinctiones* (Moore 1936, 1938). Another significant figure was Praepositinus of Cremona (ca. 1150–ca. 1210), who taught in Paris from 1191 to 1194 and from 1203 to 1210, was chancellor from 1206 to 1209, and wrote a commentary on the Psalms (Lacombe 1927).[8]

The first secular masters at the university still conformed to the exegesis of the schools, and thus ensured the transition between this and university exegesis. John Halgrin of Abbeville (d. 1237) is one such example; his career was mostly ecclesiastical, but, after having taught in his own school, he was regent in theology around 1216. From his pen come commentaries on Genesis to 1 Kings, the Psalms, and the Song of Songs.[9] Thomas of Chobham (d. ca. 1235) was a master in 1212–13 (and perhaps until 1229); the introduction to his preaching manual contains a prologue with a wealth of hermeneutical reflection (see further chap. 17). Philip the Chancellor (d. 1236) is important for his role in the beginnings of the University of Paris (which he opposed, causing the great strike of 1229). Although he left no commentaries, his Sermons on the Psalms provide material for preachers, emphasizing their role in edification (Dahan and Rillon-Marne 2017). The exact dates of Nicholas of Tournai, a master around 1230 and author of quite a few commentaries (Genesis, Exodus, Judith, Psalms, Luke) are unknown. Odo of Châteauroux (d. 1273) was a master from 1230 and chancellor from 1238 to 1244. He is known for his introductions (*Introitus*) to many biblical books, and was also the author of *Distinctiones* on the Psalms, although none of his commentaries have been preserved. William of Auvergne (ca. 1180–1249), Bishop of Paris in 1228, managed the affairs of the university although it is not known whether he taught. His commentaries on Proverbs and Ecclesiastes, like those of Hugh of Saint-Cher, confirm the transition to university exegesis (Morenzoni and Tilliette 2005). The exegetical production of one of the principal masters of the second half of the thirteenth century, Henry of Ghent (d. 1293, regent from 1276 to 1292), is not abundant. A commentary on Genesis is attributed to him,

---

[8] Among the manuscripts of the Psalm commentary, see BnF lat. 454, ff. 73–136v; lat. 14417, ff. 242–308.

[9] Only the last of these has been printed, in PL 206: 22–862.

but it is his theological works that contain hermeneutical considerations of great interest (Macken 1972, 1994; Smalley 1953). Pierre d'Ailly (1350–1420), a master in 1381, was chancellor in 1389. He composed two *principia*, several works on the Psalms (*Verbum abbreviatum, Meditationes super Psalmos poenitentiales*) and various treatises (On the Gospel Canticles, on the Lord's Prayer), but he is most interesting for his defense of the Vulgate, *Epistola ad novos Hebreos*, whose tone is anti-Jewish and which only knows works relating to Jerome's translation by hearsay (Salimbene 1887–89; Dahan 2007). Jean Gerson (1363–1429), a master in 1392, succeeded Pierre d'Ailly as chancellor in 1395; his scriptural work is not abundant, although a commentary on the Song of Songs and some introductory texts survive.

In the case of the Dominicans, the *studium generale* of Paris (Saint-Jacques) was organized as early as 1229; it was recognized by the university and therefore provided it with one, and later two, chairs of theology. Many students and masters of the Order passed through Paris. The first Dominican master was Roland of Cremona (d. 1259), but he taught in Paris for only a short time (1229–30), before going to Toulouse and Bologna. He composed a very interesting commentary on Job (Paris, BnF, lat. 405; see Dondaine 1941). The imprint of Hugh of Saint-Cher (d. 1263) on biblical studies is considerable. At the head of several teams at Saint-Jacques, he was responsible for the first concordance of the Bible, a *correctorium*, and, above all, a commentary on the whole of Scripture, the *Postille*, which used the work of the masters of the "biblical-moral school" but introduced all the subsequent advances in exegesis, thus providing an intermediate stage between the exegesis of the schools and university exegesis (Bataillon et al. 2004). Guerric of Saint-Quentin (d. 1245), a master at Saint-Jacques from 1233 to 1242, wrote numerous commentaries which remain unpublished (on the Wisdom books, Ezekiel, Pauline Epistles, Revelation, principally in Paris, BnF, lat. 15604). Before teaching in Cologne, Albert the Great (1206–80) was regent at Saint-Jacques between 1242 and 1248; his biblical commentaries do not seem to date from his sojourn in Paris (Vaccari 1932; Meyer and Zimmerman 1980). His pupil Thomas Aquinas (1225–74) himself taught in Paris in 1256–59 and 1269–72. Apart from his biblical *principia*, his commentaries on Isaiah, Jeremiah, Matthew, and John come from his Parisian teaching (Arias Reyero 1971; Torrell 2015; Roszak and Vijgen 2015). Peter of Tarentaise (d. 1276), a master from 1259 to 1264 and from 1269 to 1272, who would become Pope Innocent V, expounded the Pauline Epistles with a striking number of questions (Laurent 1947). William of Alton (d. 1265) succeeded Thomas Aquinas. Of the many biblical commentaries attributed to him, only those on Ecclesiastes, Wisdom, Isaiah, Jeremiah, Lamentations, Ezekiel, and John can be securely assigned (Bellamah 2011). The commentaries on the Song of Songs and Wisdom by John of Varzy (d. 1278) are interesting. Nicholas of Gorran (d. ca. 1295) was not a master but taught in the Paris *studium*; he commented on almost the entire Bible, although some attributions are not certain (Dahan 2013c). Meister Eckhart (ca. 1260–1327) certainly contributed to the exegesis of the Bible with his commentaries on Genesis, Exodus, Wisdom, and John, but his teaching does not seem to originate in Paris.

Even more than the Dominicans, most of the Franciscan masters passed through Paris. Again, only those whose presence was significant are mentioned here, thus excluding authors such as Roger Bacon, Peter John Olivi, and Ramon Llull. The Paris *studium generale* of the order had been in operation since 1230, located in the convent of the Cordeliers. The integration of Alexander of Hales (ca. 1175–1245), a master at the university before 1229, into the Order of Friars Minor gave the Franciscans a chair in theology. The prologue to his theological *summa* contains important reflections on the Bible (see chap. 17). In addition to commentaries on the Gospels, others are attributed to him of dubious authenticity (Pelster 1921). His pupil and successor, John of La Rochelle (d. 1245), taught from 1238; he is credited with quite a few commentaries (Daniel, Matthew, Mark, Luke, Pauline Epistles, and Revelation, as well as others not preserved) as well as *principia*. William of Meliton (d. 1257) taught in Paris and then at Cambridge; he too left many commentaries (Pentateuch, Ecclesiastes, Wisdom, Ecclesiasticus, Song of Songs, Job, Minor Prophets, Mark, Romans, and Catholic Epistles). Bonaventure (John of Fidenza, 1221–74) studied in Paris: he obtained a bachelor's degree in biblical studies and a licentiate in theology but was not able to teach until later (1257); his biblical commentaries (Luke, Ecclesiastes, Wisdom, and John) and his *collationes* on John, the Ten Commandments, and the Hexameron belonged fully to university exegesis and were very influential (Bougerol 1988; Karris 2002). John Peckham (a. 1235–92) studied in Paris and was a master there from 1269 to 1271, before returning to England. He left commentaries on Lamentations (published among the works of Bonaventure), Luke, John, and Hebrews (with others, now lost), as well as a treatise on the interpretation of numbers and a thematic collection of scriptural citations (*Collectarium sacrae Bibliae*). Alexander of Alexandria (d. 1314) began his studies in Paris and taught there in 1307–8; he wrote *Postilla* on Job (?), Isaiah, John, and Romans. Nicholas of Lyra (a.1274–1349) was one of the major exegetes of the Middle Ages, whose influence continued until the eighteenth century; a master in 1308, he taught until 1311 and then devoted himself to the writing of his *Postilla*, which covers the whole of the Bible and includes a literal section and a spiritual section (*moraliter*). Although he was not particularly innovative in his hermeneutical thinking, he renewed exegesis through his notable use of Hebrew, the *Targum* (Aramaic translation), rabbinic texts, and Jewish commentaries including that of Rashi (see chap. 22; Krey and Smith 2000; Dahan 2009b, 2011c). Peter Aureoli (d. 1322) trained in Paris before teaching in Bologna, Toulouse, and then Paris (1316–20). He was responsible for a *principium* and a kind of summary of the literal interpretation of Scripture (*Compendium litteralis sensus*), as well as a commentary on Isaiah.

The other religious orders produced fewer Parisian masters devoted to the study of Scripture. Two hermits of Saint Augustine, an order approved in 1256 and whose Parisian house was founded around 1260, should nevertheless be mentioned. Giles of Rome (ca. 1245–1316), a disciple of Thomas Aquinas, taught in Paris from 1285 to 1291. He left treatises on the Hexameron, on Noah's Ark, and on Psalm 44 (LXX) and commentaries on the Song of Songs, Ecclesiastes, and Romans. Augustinus Triumphus of Ancona (1243–1328) was a master in Paris in 1303–4 and 1314–16; he left commentaries on Matthew, and both the Pauline and the Catholic Epistles.

CONCLUSION

Paris thus had a major place in the study of the Bible in the twelfth and thirteenth centuries. The development of schools and then of the university attracted many foreign students, while the mendicant orders built their most prestigious *studia generalia* there. This success led to a proliferation of Bibles: without corresponding to a precise model regarding their form or, especially, regarding their text, the Paris Bibles definitively fixed the biblical canon of the West and imposed a set of paratexts. Substantial work was carried out on the biblical text, with the text-critical contribution of the *correctoria*. The university promoted a didactic approach that would henceforth be that of scholarly commentaries, even if a certain flexibility was observed in practice. The arrival of other European universities put an end to the monopoly of Paris in the study of the Bible, but at the end of the Middle Ages this city could still claim to be a Qiryat-Sefer.

BIBLIOGRAPHY

Albaric, M. 2004. "Hugues de Saint-Cher et les concordances bibliques latines (xiiie-xviiie siècles." In *Hugues de Saint-Cher († 1263), bibliste et théologien*, edited by L.-J. Bataillon, Gilbert Dahan, and P.-M. Gy, 467–79. Turnhout: Brepols.

Arias Reyero, M. 1971. *Thomas von Aquin als Exeget*. Einsiedeln: Johannes.

Baldwin, John W. 1970. *Masters, Princes and Merchants. The Social Views of Peter the Chanter and hic Circle*. Princeton: Princeton University Press.

Bataillon, L.-J. 1982. "Intermédiaires entre les traités de morale pratique et les sermons: les *distinctiones* bibliques alphabétiques." In *Les genres littéraires dans les sources théologiques et philosophiques*, 213–26. Leuven: Brepols.

Bataillon, L.-J., N. Bériou, Gilbert Dahan, and R. Quinto, eds. 2010. *Étienne Langton, prédicateur, bibliste, théologien*. Turnhout: Brepols.

Bataillon, L.-J., Gilbert Dahan, and P.-M. Gy, eds. 2004. *Hugues de Saint-Cher († 1263), bibliste et théologien*. Turnhout: Brepols.

Bellamah, T. 2011. *The Biblical Interpretation of William of Alton*. Oxford: Oxford University Press.

Berger, Samuel. 1879. *De glossariis et compendiis exegeticis quibusdam medii aevi*. Paris: Berger-Levrault and Fischbacher.

Berger, Samuel. 1893. *Histoire de la Vulgate latine pendant les premiers siècles du Moyen Âge*. Paris: Berger-Levrault.

Berndt, Rainer. 1991. *André de Saint-Victor († 1175), exégète et théologien*. Turnhout: Brepols.

Berndt, Rainer, ed. 2009. *Bibel und Exegese in der Abtei Saint-Victor zu Paris*. Münster: Aschendorff.

Bianciotto, G. 1980. *Bestiaires du Moyen Âge*. Paris: Stock.

Bougerol, J. G. 1988. *Introduction à saint Bonaventure*. Paris: Vrin. English translation 1963, Paterson NJ: St. Anthony Guild.

Branner, Robert. 1977. *Manuscript Painting in Paris during the Reign of Saint Louis. A Study of Styles*. Berkeley: University of California Press.

Cauwe, M. 1993. "La Bible d'Étienne Harding. Principes de critique textuelle mis en œuvre aux livres de Samuel." *Revue bénédictine* 103: 414–44.

Centro di studi sulla spiritualità medievale. 1978. *Le scuole degli ordini mendicanti (sec. XIII-XIV)*. Todi: Accademia Tudertina.

Châtillon, J. 1988. "Richard de Saint-Victor." In *Dictionnaire de Spiritualité, vol. 13*, 593–654. Paris: Beauchesne.

Clark, M. 2005. "The Commentaries on Peter Comestor's *Historia scholastica . . .*," *Sacris erudiri* 45: 301–446.

Dahan, Gilbert. 1996. "Lexiques hébreu-latin? Les recueils d'interprétations des noms hébraïques." In *Les manuscrits des lexiques et glossaires, de l'Antiquité à la fin du moyen âge*, edited by J. Hamesse, 481–526. Louvain-la-Neuve: FIDEM.

Dahan, Gilbert. 1997. "La critique textuelle dans les correctoires de la Bible du XIIIe siècle." In *Langages et philosophie. Hommage à Jean Jolivet*, edited by A. de Libera, A. Elamrani-Jamal, and A. Galonnier, 365–92. Paris: Vrin.

Dahan, Gilbert. 1998. "La connaissance du grec dans les correctoires de la Bible du XIIIe siècle." In *Du copiste au collectionneur. Mélanges d'histoire des textes et des bibliothèques en l'honneur d'André Vernet*, edited by J.-F. Genest and D. Nebbiai-Dalla-Guarda, 89–109. Turnhout: Brepols.

Dahan, Gilbert. 1999. *L'exégèse chrétienne de la Bible en Occident médiéval (XIIe-XIVe s.)*. Paris: Cerf.

Dahan, Gilbert. 2004. "*Sorbonne II*. Un correctoire biblique de la seconde moitié du XIIIe siècle." In *La Bibbia del XIII secolo. Storia del testo, storia dell'esegesi*, edited by G. Cremascoli and F. Santi, 113–53. Florence: SISMEL.

Dahan, Gilbert. 2007. "Critique et défense de la Vulgate au XIVe siècle." In *Exégèse et critique des textes sacrés*, edited by D. Delmaire and G. Gobillot, 119–36. Paris: Geuthner.

Dahan, Gilbert. 2009a. *Lire la Bible au moyen âge. Essais d'herméneutique médiévale*. Geneva: Droz.

Dahan, Gilbert. 2009b. *Nicolas de Lyre, franciscain du XIVe siècle, exégète et théologien*. Troyes: Médiathèque de l'Agglomération Troyenne.

Dahan, Gilbert. 2010. "Le schématisme dans l'exégèse médiévale." In *Qu'est-ce que nommer? L'image légendée entre monde monastique et pensée scolastique*, edited by C. Heck, 31–40. Turnhout: Brepols.

Dahan, Gilbert. 2011a. "Quelques notes sur l'herméneutique et l'exégèse de Hugues de Saint-Victor." In *Ugo di Vittore. Atti del XLVII Convegno storico*, 113–34. Spoleto: CISAM.

Dahan, Gilbert. 2011b. *Pierre de Troyes, dit Pierre le Mangeur*. Troyes: Médiathèque du Grand Troyes.

Dahan, Gilbert, ed. 2011c. *Nicolas de Lyre, franciscain du XIVe siècle, exégète et théologien*. Paris: Études augustiniennes.

Dahan, Gilbert. 2013a. "L'enseignement de l'Écriture, des écoles à l'Université." In *Les débuts de l'enseignement universitaire à Paris (1200-1245 environ)*, edited by J. Verger and O. Weijers, 255–73. Turnhout: Brepols.

Dahan, Gilbert, ed. 2013b. *Pierre le Mangeur ou Pierre de Troyes, maître du XIIe siècle*. Turnhout: Brepols.

Dahan, Gilbert. 2013c. "Nicolas de Gorran sur l'échelle de Jacob (Genèse 28, 10-22): instantané d'un exégète au travail." In *Portraits de maîtres offerts à Olga Weijers*, edited by C. Angotti, M. Brinzei, and M. Teeuwen, 361–71. Porto: FIDEM.

Dahan, Gilbert. 2016. *Études d'exégèse médiévale. Ancien Testament*. Strasbourg: Presses Universitaires.

Dahan, Gilbert, and A.-Z. Rillon-Marne, eds. 2017. *Philippe le Chancelier, prédicateur, théologien et poète parisien du début du XIIIᵉ siècle*. Turnhout: Brepols.

Daly, L. W., and B. A. Daly. 1975. *Summa Britonis sive Guilelmi Britonis expositiones vocabulorum Biblie*. 2 vols. Padua: Antenore.

De Bruyne, Donatien. 1914. *Sommaires, Divisions et Rubriques de la Bible latine*. Namur: Godenne. Repr., *Summaries, Divisions and Rubrics of the Latin Bible*. Turnhout: Brepols, 2014.

Delisle, L. 1879. "Les Bibles de Théodulfe." *Bibliothèque de l'École des Chartes* 40: 5–47.

Denifle, H. 1888. "Die Handschriften der Bible-Correctorien des 13. Jahrhunderts." *Archiv für Literatur- und Kirchengeschichte des Mittelalters* 4: 264–311, 471–607.

Denifle, H. 1894. "Quel livre servait de base dans l'enseignement des maîtres en théologie dans l'Université de Paris?" *Revue thomiste* 2: 149–61.

d'Esneval, A. 1978. "La division de la Vulgate latine en chapitres dans l'édition parisienne du XIIIᵉ siècle." *Revue des sciences philosophiques et théologiques* 62: 559–68.

Dondaine, A. 1941. "Un commentaire scripturaire de Roland de Crémone, le livre de Job." *Archivum fratrum praedicatorum* 11: 109–37.

Féret, Pierre 1894–97. *La faculté de théologie de Paris et ses docteurs les plus célèbres*. 4 vols. Paris: A. Picard.

Fischer, Bonifatius. 1957. *Die Alkuin-Bibel*. AGLB 1. Freiburg-im-Breisgau: Herder.

Ganshof, F. L. 1974. "Charlemagne et la révision du texte latin de la Bible." *Bulletin de l'Institut historique belge de Rome* 44: 271–84.

Glorieux, Palémon. 1933–34. *Répertoire des maîtres en théologie de Paris au XIIIᵉ siècle*. 2 vols. Paris: Vrin.

Glorieux, Palémon. 1968. "L'enseignement au moyen âge. Techniques et méthodes en usage à la faculté de théologie de Paris au XIIIᵉ siècle." *Archives d'histoire doctrinale et littéraire du moyen âge* 35: 68–186.

Glunz, H. H. 1933. *History of the Vulgate in England from Alcuin to Roger Bacon*. Cambridge: Cambridge University Press.

Grabmann, Martin 1911. *Die Geschichte der scholastischen Methode*. 2 vols. Freiburg im Breisgau: Herder.

Karris, R. J. 2002. "St. Bonaventure as Biblical Interpreter: His Methods, Wit and Wisdom." *Franciscan Studies* 60: 159–208.

Krey, P., and L. Smith, eds. 2000. *Nicholas of Lyra. The Senses of Scripture*. Leiden: Brill.

Lacombe, G. 1927. *La vie et les œuvres de Prévostin*. Paris: Vrin.

Lacombe, G., B. Smalley, and A. L. Gregory. 1930. "Studies on the Commentaries of Cardinal Stephen Langton." *Archives d'histoire doctrinale et littéraire du moyen âge* 5: 5–266.

Landgraf, A. ed. 1937–45. *Commentarius Cantabrigiensis in epistolas Paul e schola Petri Abaelardi*. 4 vols. Notre Dame: University of Notre Dame.

Lange, H. 1979. *Les données mathématiques des traités du XIIᵉ siècle sur la symbolique des nombres*. Copenhagen: Institut du moyen âge grec et latin.

Laurent, M. H. 1947. *Le bienheureux Innocent V (Pierre de Tarentaise) et son temps*. Vatican City: BAV.

Lesne, E. 1940. *Histoire de la propriété ecclésiastique en France*: Vol. V. *Les écoles*. Lille: Facultés catholiques.

Light, Laura 2001. "Roger Bacon and the origin of the Paris Bible," *Revue bénédictine* 111: 483–507.

Loewe, R. 1969. "The Medieval History of the Latin Vulgate." In *The Cambridge History of the Bible. Vol. 2*, edited by G. W. H. Lampe, 102–54. Cambridge: Cambridge University Press.

Luscombe, D. E. 1969. *The School of Peter Abelard*. Cambridge: Cambridge University Press.

Macken, Raymond, ed. 1972. *La "lectura ordinaria super sacram Scripturam" attribuée à Henri de Gand*. Leuven: Éditions universitaires.

Macken, Raymond. 1994. *Essays on Henry of Ghent*. Leuven: Medieval Philosophers of the Former Low Countries.

Mangenot, E. 1926. "Concordance de la Bible." In *Dictionnaire de la Bible*, vol. 2, col. 892–905. Paris: Letouzey & Ané.

Martin, J. P. P. 1889–90. "Le texte parisien de la Vulgate latine." *Le Muséon* 8: 444–66; 9: 55–70, 301–16.

Martin, Raymond. M. 1932–52. *Œuvres de Robert de Melun*. 4 vols. Leuven: Spicilegium sacrum Lovaniense.

McCulloch, F. 1960. *Medieval Latin and French Bestiaries*. Chapel Hill: University of North Carolina.

Meyer, G., and A. Zimmermann, eds. 1980. *Albertus Magnus, Doctor universalis, 1280–1980*. Mainz: M. Grünewald.

Moore, P. S. 1936. *The Works of Peter of Poitiers, Master in Theology and Chancellor of Paris*. Notre Dame: University of Notre Dame.

Moore, P. S., and J. A. Corbett, eds. 1938. *Peter of Poitiers: Allegoriae*. Notre Dame: University of Notre Dame.

Morenzoni, F., and J.-Y. Tilliette, eds. 2005. *Autour de Guillaume d'Auvergne († 1249)*. Turnhout: Brepols.

Mulchahey, M. Michèle, 1998. *"First the bow is bent in study . . ." Dominican Education before 1350*. Toronto: Pontifical Institute of Medieval Studies

Murano, G. 2005. *Opere diffuse per "exemplar" e pecia*. Turnhout: Brepols.

Pannier, L. 1882. *Les lapidaires français du moyen âge*. Paris: F. Vieweg.

Pelster, F. 1921. "Exegetische Schriften des Alexander von Hales." *Biblica* 2: 453–57.

Peppermüller, R. 1972. *Abaelards Auslegung des Römerbrief*. Münster: Aschendorff.

Peri, V. 1977. "*Correctores immo corruptores*. Un saggio di critica testuale nella Roma del XII secolo." *Italia medioevale e umanistica* 20: 19–125.

Poirel, D. 2010. *L'école de Saint-Victor de Paris. Influence et rayonnement du moyen âge à l'époque moderne*. Turnhout: Brepols.

Power, E. 1924. "Corrections from the Hebrew in the Theodulfian MSS of the Vulgate." *Biblica* 5: 233–58.

Riché, Pierre. 1979. *Écoles et enseignement dans le Haut Moyen Âge*. Paris: Aubier.

Riché, Pierre, and Guy Lobrichon, eds. 1984. *Le Moyen Âge et la Bible*. BTT 4. Paris: Beauchesne.

Roszak, P., and J. Vijgen, eds. 2015. *Reading Sacred Scripture with Thomas Aquinas. Hermeneutical Tools, Theological Questions and New Perspectives*. Turnhout: Brepols.

Rouse, Richard H., and Mary A. Rouse. 1974a. "The Verbal Concordance to the Scriptures." *Archivum fratrum praedicatorum* 44: 5–30.

Rouse, Richard H., and Mary A. Rouse. 1974b. "Biblical distinctions in the XIIth century." *Archives d'histoire doctrinale et littéraire du moyen âge* 41: 27–37.

Rouse, Richard H., and Mary A. Rouse. 1984. "La concordance verbale des Écritures." In *Le Moyen Âge et la Bible*, edited by Pierre Riché and Guy Lobrichon, 115–22. BTT 4. Paris: Beauchesne.

Rouse, Richard H., and Mary A. Rouse. 2000. "*Illiterati et uxorati*." *Manuscripts and their Makers. Commercial Book Producers in Medieval Paris*. Turnhout: Brepols.

Salimbene, L. 1887–89. "Une page inédite de l'histoire de la Vulgate." *Revue des sciences ecclésiastiques* 56: 483–95; 60: 23–37, 97–108, 257–67, 369–82, and 519–30.

Smalley, Beryl. 1953. "A commentary on the Hexaemeron by Henry of Ghent." *Recherches de théologie ancienne et médiévale* 20: 60–101.

Smalley, Beryl. 1983. *The Study of the Bible in the Middle Ages*. 3rd ed. Oxford: Basil Blackwell.

Studer, P., and J. Evans, 1924. *Anglo-Norman Lapidaries*. Paris: Champion.

Torrell, J.-P. 2015. *Initiation a saint Thomas d'Aquin*. New ed. Paris: Cerf.

Vaccari, Alberto. 1932. "S. Alberto Magno e l'esegesi medievale." *Biblica* 13: 257–72, 369–84.

Verger, Jacques, and Olga Weijers, eds. 2013. *Les débuts de l'enseignement universitaire à Paris (1200-1245 environ)*. Turnhout: Brepols.

Weijers, Olga. 1991. *Dictionnaires et répertoires au moyen âge*. Turnhout: Brepols.

Zaluska, Y. 1989. *L'enluminure et le Scriptorium de Cîteaux*. Cîteaux: Abbaye de Cîteaux.

....

CHAPTER 17

THE EXEGESIS OF THE LATIN BIBLE IN THE MIDDLE AGES

....

GILBERT DAHAN

THE study of the Bible in the Middle Ages led to a genuine biblical exegesis, whose major characteristic is that it achieved a harmonious balance between a confessional approach (since the text of Scripture was received as the very word of God) and a scientific approach, which did not leave to one side any problematic areas, from textual criticism to divergent theological statements.[1] The present chapter traces the major features of this exegesis, by enumerating the main sources of hermeneutical reflection, by defining the major principles of this exegesis, by describing the major literary genres of exegetical production, and by analyzing some of the procedures employed. The focus here is on Western Christian exegesis, the reference text being, of course, the Vulgate. Among general studies dealing with medieval exegesis (e.g., Lampe 1969; Riché and Lobrichon 1984; Cremascoli and Leonardi 1996), it is worth mentioning the works of Ceslas Spicq (1944), both historical and attentive to the methods applied, Beryl Smalley (1983), focusing on history but very sensitive to the progress of literal exegesis, and Henri de Lubac (1959–64), of great richness but starting from a set of presuppositions. More recent approaches have sought to describe the methods of exegesis and to define the hermeneutical options (Evans 1984, 1985; Dahan 1999).

SOURCES FOR HERMENEUTICS
....

Throughout the Middle Ages (i.e., the long period from the sixth and seventh centuries to the fifteenth century), reflection on the exegesis of the Bible underwent a development.

---

[1] The distinction between these two approaches stems from Paul Ricoeur, "Herméneutique. Les finalités de l'exégèse biblique," in *La Bible en philosophie*, ed. D. Bourg and A. Lion (Paris: Cerf, 1993), 27–51.

The culmination of this was seen in university teaching and the *studia* of the mendicant orders in the thirteenth century (see chap. 16). There are multiple locations in which this hermeneutical practice may be observed, which will be treated separately.

Treatises

Specific treatises devoted to hermeneutics had a variety of aims. Two patristic texts were particularly influential: Augustine's *De doctrina christiana* (see chap. 9) and Cassiodorus's *Institutiones*. Among the oldest medieval treatises, the importance of *De schematibus et tropis* by Bede (673–735) must be underlined.[2] This precise analysis of figures of speech and thought in the Bible presents definitions from classical rhetoric, while all the examples are biblical quotations. It should be recalled that in the preface to his commentary on the Psalms,[3] Cassiodorus had emphasized the usefulness of rhetorical analysis, and Bede's treatise seems to be a response to this. In the twelfth century, hermeneutical treatises were multiplied, pride of place going to those of Hugh of Saint-Victor (d. 1141). His *Didascalicon* is an introduction to the literal reading of Scripture.[4] Hugh insists on the necessity of understanding the letter in its many aspects: vocabulary and grammar (*littera*), historical context (*sensus*), and doctrinal meaning (*sententia*), before moving on to spiritual exegesis. The same requirement is set out in another treatise, *De scripturis et scriptoribus sacris*, in which he also establishes the rules of spiritual exegesis.[5] Peter the Chanter (d. 1197), one of the masters of the Paris "biblical-moral school," wrote *De tropis loquendi*, a study of figures of speech combined with an important reflection on the contradictions of Scripture (cf. Valente 1997). From the thirteenth century onward, hermeneutical reflection took place in *principia* and theological works (see below). An important treatise from the beginning of the fourteenth century, *De expositione sacre Scripture*, consists of two parts: a precise study of biblical language, and an analysis of the meaning of the "realities" mentioned in the Bible.[6] It thus brings together the study of the letter, on the one hand, and of the spiritual meaning on the other. A little later, John Wycliffe's treatise *De veritate sacrae Scripturae* made a significant contribution to hermeneutic reflections, with its consideration of the senses of Scripture, their Christological essence, and the role of the Church (see Levy 2016b).

Among these treatises, a special place must be given to the *Artes praedicandi*, preaching manuals that flourished in the twelfth and thirteenth centuries. They all contain important reflections on the exegesis of the Bible. The *Quo ordine sermo*

---

[2] *Bedae Venerabilis Opera didascalica*, ed. C.B. Kendall (CCSL 123A) (Turnhout: Brepols, 1975), 142–71.

[3] *Expositio Psalmorum*, ed. M. Adriaen (CCSL 97) (Turnhout: Brepols, 1958), 2–25.

[4] *Hugonis de Sancto Victore Didascalicon de studio legendi*, ed. C. H. Buttimer (Washington, DC: Catholic University Press, 1939). Repr., New York: Columbia University Press, 1991) (English trans. J. Taylor).

[5] PL 175: 9–28.

[6] Paris, BnF, lat. 614, ff. 1–69; Oxford, Bodleian, Canon misc. 95, ff. 1–80. See further Dahan 2016b.

fieri debeat of Guibert de Nogent (1053–ca. 1130) sets out the four senses of Scripture discussed below.[7] Guibert's preference is for tropology (spiritual exegesis applied to the movements of the soul, which is sometimes equated with the moral sense), and he sets out its rules. The prologue of the *Summa de arte praedicandi* by Thomas of Chobham (d. ca. 1235) constitutes a manual of exegesis.[8] After defining the four senses, he reproduces the seven rules of Tyconius as expounded by Augustine. William of Auvergne was the author of a small preaching manual and also of *De faciebus mundi*, which contains an excursus on the *similitudo*, an "image" or "metaphor" (Paris, BnF, lat. 15965, ff. 143–56; see Dahan 2005). John of La Rochelle (ca. 1195–1245) wrote a *Processus negociandi themata sermonis* ("On the Arrangement of Themes in Sermons"), which contains a list of the seven "realities" that give rise to spiritual interpretation inspired by Hugh of Saint-Victor (see Cantini 1951). Other *Artes praedicandi* contain further hermeneutical reflections, for example, Richard of Thetford's *De dilatatione sermonis*, Pseudo-Bonaventure's *Ars concionandi*, and Robert of Basevorn's *Forma praedicandi* (see Dahan 1999: 398–401; Charland 1936).

Prefaces and Prologues

The prefaces or prologues of commentaries are another place where exegetes provide exegetical considerations. Prologues take various forms, not all of which contain hermeneutical reflections. The prologue to the Pentateuch by the Benedictine Rainaud of Saint-Eloi is a particularly interesting example (Dahan 1987). Drawing on a treatise that was not widely transmitted, the *Instituta regularia divinae legis* by Junilius (d. 548–49), he sets out the principles of exegesis and proposes a list of five senses: *historia* (literal sense), *mores* (moral sense), *prophetia*, *typus* (typology), *allegoria*. The prologues of Andrew of Saint-Victor (d. 1175), one of the few authors to devote himself solely to literal exegesis, contain few hermeneutical reflections, although his prologue to the sapiential books does provide a development of the notion of parable.[9] Several prologues to Stephen Langton's commentary on the Pentateuch offer reflections on exegesis, emphasizing the four senses: these came to be normative in his time, presumably as a result of his influence (Smalley 1931; Quinto 1989; Bataillon et al 2010). The *Principium super totam Bibliam* of Dominic Grima, which preceded his commentary on the Pentateuch, provides some interesting elements without proposing a theory of exegesis (Paris, BnF, lat. 365, ff. 2–5). The *Postilla* of Nicholas of Lyra is preceded by three prologues, two for the literal *postilla* and one for the moral one.[10] Although it may appear

[7] Ed. R. B. C. Huygens (CCCM 127) (Turnhout: Brepols, 1993), 47–63.

[8] Ed. F. Morenzoni (CCCM 82) (Turnhout: Brepols, 1988), 3–17; French trans. Dahan 2009; see also Morenzoni 1995.

[9] *Expositiones in libros Salomonis*, ed. R. Berndt (CCCM 53B) (Turnhout: Brepols, 1991), 3–5; see further Berndt 1991.

[10] *Biblia sacra cum Glossa ordinaria . . . cum postilla Nicolai Lyrani* (Antwerp: J. Meursius, 1634), t. I (without pagination); PL 113: 25–36. See Levy 2016a; Dahan 2011: 99–124.

that Nicholas was behind in comparison with the progress made in his time, these texts are very rich: he gives the four senses their classical expression (with the use of the distich of Augustine of Dacia) and insists on the importance of the literal sense, better understood thanks to the use of Hebrew.

Principia

With the developments in teaching in the thirteenth century (see chap. 16), a genre of its own was to energize hermeneutical reflection: the *principia*, or introductions to the lessons of biblical bachelors or masters (Spatz 1992; Sulavik 2004; Prügl 2004). These inaugural lectures were codified and usually consisted of two parts: a commendation *(Recommandatio)* of Scripture, and a division *(Divisio)* of the biblical books. Both are of considerable interest, for their statement of hermeneutical possibilities and for their analysis of the books. The main authors of the thirteenth century left these introductions, which always start from a biblical verse (technically called a "theme"), whose division permitted them to set out their hermeneutical choices. Mention should be made of the two *principia* of John of La Rochelle (on Revelation 10:10–11 and Baruch 4:1),[11] that of Albert the Great (on Ecclesiasticus 24:33),[12] that of the Dominican Peter of Scala (d. 1295),[13] the five *principia* of Peter John Olivi (on Psalm 45:11 [LXX], Revelation 5:1, Ezekiel 1:1 and 10:2, Revelation 4:8),[14] that of the Dominican Armand de Bellevue (on Genesis 1:1; Paris BnF, lat. 2584, ff. 39–40), and a *Divisio sacre Scripture* by the Franciscan Peter Aureoli (Paris, BnF, lat. 14796, ff. 1–11). Thomas Aquinas left two *principia* from his biblical teaching as a bachelor (on Baruch 4:1 and Psalm 103:13 [LXX]). Nicholas of Gorran was the author of a *principium* on Baruch 4:1, which, exceptionally, contains seven questions (Paris, BnF, lat. 14416, ff. 1–3). Henry of Ghent is credited with an introduction to Scripture, the theme of which is also Baruch 4:1.[15]

Commentaries

Commentaries on individual biblical passages often provided an opportunity to set out general ideas on exegesis. This was the case for the two pericopes that truly provided the foundation of Christian exegesis: Luke 24:13–27, where Jesus explains to the pilgrims of Emmaus that his coming was announced in all the Scriptures (see, for example,

---

[11] F. Delorme, "Deux leçons d'ouverture . . .," *La France franciscaine* 16 (1933): 345–60.
[12] Edited by A. Fries, in *Studia Albertina. Festschrift B. Geyer* (Münster: Aschendorff, 1952), 128–47.
[13] Edited by A. Sulavik in *Angelicum* 79 (2002): 87–126.
[14] D. Flood and G. Gal, eds., *Peter of John Olivi on the Bible* (St. Bonaventure: Franciscan Institute, 1997), 17–151; French trans. Of fourth *principium*, Dahan 2009a: 81–116. See also Schlageter 2016.
[15] *Lectura ordinaria super sacram Scripturam*, ed. R. Macken (Leuven: Éditions Universitaires, 1980), 5–38; see Dahan 2016c.

the commentaries of Bonaventure and Nicholas of Gorran), and Galatians 4:22–26, which establishes the use of allegory (see the commentaries of Peter Lombard, Stephen Langton, Thomas Aquinas, and Peter of Tarentaise, and, further, Freytag 1975 and Dahan 2008). The beginning of Ezekiel, with its vision of the four living creatures and the wheel (1:15–18), was also a text that opened up hermeneutical considerations, following the use made of it by Gregory the Great. The same is true of Revelation 5:1, with the book written on both sides and sealed with seven seals.

Theological Writings

To these biblically-oriented writings it is necessary to add theological works, which often contain reflections on Scripture and its hermeneutics. This is the case in the commentaries on the *Sentences* by Peter Lombard, who began his work with a passage from Augustine's *De doctrina christiana* on realities and signs (*de rebus et de signis* = I *Sent.*, dist. 1): when commenting on this passage, some authors engage in reflections on biblical exegesis (e.g., Bonaventure). Lombard's *Sentences*, together with the Bible, were the object of teaching in the theological faculties: bachelors and masters also gave an introductory lesson, parallel to the biblical *principia*, in which they defined the nature of theology and, in particular, how it differed from biblical exegesis. Important reflections on biblical hermeneutics are provided in this way by a significant number of cases. The passages in which the "mode" of theology is studied, defined as "scientific" and opposed to other modes, including the poetic mode present in Scripture, are fascinating. This intense reflection leads to the conception of theology as science, "discourse *on* God," different from the study of the "discourse *of* God" that is biblical exegesis. Such reflections are, of course, of considerable importance in the quest for a medieval hermeneutic. They are to be found in almost all commentators on the *Sentences*, among them Thomas Aquinas (Oliva 2006).

The theological *summae* of the thirteenth century also contain elements of interest to biblical hermeneutics, as is the case for the great *Summa* of Alexander of Hales.[16] Similarly, the *Summa Theologica* of Thomas Aquinas begins with considerations of "sacred doctrine" (Ia, q. 1), which concern both theological science and the study of Holy Scripture, especially in the articles dealing with metaphor and multiple meanings (art. 9 and 10; see Dahan 2015; Prügl 2016b). The *Summa of Ordinary Questions* of Henry of Ghent may be put in the same category.[17] In articles 6 to 19, he studies the nature of theology, with considerations on the author and authority of Scripture (arts. 9 and 10), and on the mode of transmission of this science (arts. 13–17). There are various other theological works that deal with problems of hermeneutics, such as question 6 of Thomas

---

[16] *Summa theologica*, ed. P. P. Collegii S. Bonaventurae (Florence: Quaracchi Fratri Editori, 1924), vol. 1, 1–13; see Prügl 2016a.

[17] *Summa Quaestionum ordinariarum* (Paris: J. Badius, 1520) (Repr., St. Bonaventure: Franciscan Institute, 1953; partial French trans. Dahan 2009a: 117–42).

Aquinas's *Quodlibet* VII on the meanings of Sacred Scripture.[18] However, it is not possible to list them all here.

FUNDAMENTAL PRINCIPLES

Through theoretical reflections but also through the work of commentators, a number of principles can be identified as the basis of medieval exegesis. The first is the divine origin of the Scriptures, an affirmation that was constantly repeated (Dahan 1999: 37–45). This received an elaborated form in the thirteenth century with the study of the efficient cause, both in the prologues of commentaries and in the *principia* and other more theoretical works. The system of the "four Aristotelian causes" was adopted in the thirteenth century as the major form of the prologues: its analysis identifies the efficient cause (the author), the material cause (the subject), the formal cause (the style or mode), and the final cause (the goal) of the books studied. A distinction was made in this period between the principal efficient cause and the secondary efficient cause (Minnis 1988). The secondary cause was seen to be the author under whose name the book is transmitted (the Prophets, the Apostle Paul, Moses for the Pentateuch, David for the Psalms, etc.), but the principal cause was the Holy Spirit or, if preferred, the divine inspiration through which the Prophets or Apostles spoke. The notion of inspiration was the subject of many reflections, notably in relation to 2 Timothy 3:16 or 2 Peter 1:19–21, but also other verses of the Old and New Testaments (such as Psalm 44:2 [LXX]).

The divine inspiration of Scripture has as its consequence the absolute truth of the message it transmits as well as its transcendent character. It cannot be limited by the narrowness of the human mind or by the contingencies of transmission. It is true that the message is addressed to humanity and must be brought within its reach: this is the role of the Prophets, the Apostles and other "secondary" authors of Scripture, but these are human beings who can only use the instruments at their disposal, namely, human language. Both Jewish and Christian interpreters constantly repeat the same principle: "The words of the Law are in the language of humans," according to the rabbinic adage, expressed also by Augustine as "God speaks by means of a human in the manner of humans," and by Andrew of Saint-Victor as "In speaking of God, Scripture uses our language."[19] Peter John Olivi made a lovely affirmation that God addresses humans in Scripture just as a mother babbles to her baby in infantile words.[20] This concept explains what is without doubt the major characteristic of medieval exegesis, the fact that it unites confessional and scientific exegesis.

---

[18] *Opera omnia* (Leonine ed.), vol. XXV/1, ed. R. A. Gauthier (Paris: Vrin/Rome: Ed. di San Tommaso, 1996), 27–32 (French trans. Dahan 2009a: 61–79).

[19] Babylonian Talmud, tract. *Yevamot*, fol. 71r; *De ciuitate Dei* 17.6.2; *Expositio super Ysaiam* 52:5 (CCCM 53C) (cf. Berndt 1991: 243).

[20] *Commentary on Genesis 2:19–20*, ed. D. Flood (St. Bonaventure: Franciscan Institute, 2007), 123.

In fact, even though the divine Word is transcendent, the fact that it is in human language carries the implication that it must be studied with all the means provided by scholarly endeavor, including textual criticism, since its copying by human agents means that the biblical text is subject to all the accidents which may afflict written transmission. Moreover, this Word, whose truth is permanent, is captured at certain moments of human history, and bears the trace of the context in which it was put into writing. Two approaches are therefore necessary for the exegete: the study of the historical context (which is found, for example, in one of the most common medieval manuals, the *Historia scholastica* of Peter Comestor), and its application to the contemporary world, since Scripture speaks to each generation. While the latter approach is most characteristic of preaching, it is also constant in exegesis, especially in tropological developments. In Christian exegesis, the passage from the transcendence of the divine Word to the immanence of human society is, of course, facilitated by the mediating role of Christ who, as has been said, explained to humans the meaning of the Scriptures but also made it possible, by his very humanity, to grasp the divine truth. This fundamental theme is developed by Peter John Olivi in his *principium De Christo medio Scripturae* ("On Christ, the centre of Scripture").[21]

One of the consequences of the transcendent character of the divine message is that its elucidation cannot be anything less than infinite: humans have to keep on peeling back its layers in order to try to understand it. This idea, affirmed by both Jewish and Christian authors (see Banon 1987; Bori 1987), leads to another major feature of medieval exegesis, the notion of progress. Henry of Ghent provides the clearest explanation of this: just as Jesus taught the Apostles while leaving many things to be explained, so they passed on their knowledge to the doctors, leaving them to complete this teaching; these doctors are the Fathers of the Church, but also all the medieval masters who succeeded them in the explanation of Scripture: each generation thus enriches its knowledge in the knowledge that the next generation will have to go further.[22] The notion of progress is fundamental in medieval thought and finds its fulfilment in the exegesis of the Bible. But this is a progress that is anchored in tradition, and here again medieval exegesis harmoniously brings together two requirements that sometimes seem to be opposed: fidelity to tradition—in that the Church Fathers remain a major source of inspiration—and the need for progress, as it is necessary to go further than the Church Fathers and further even than the previous generation (Dahan 2013).

Another consequence of the transcendent character of the divine message and its infinite interpretation is the multiplicity of the senses of Scripture. While rabbinic tradition speaks of the "seventy faces of Scripture" (the number seventy representing the notion of infinity), Christian tradition codified the multiplicity of meanings. Until the twelfth century, a list of three senses dominated: literal, allegorical, and tropological. But from this time onward, four senses of Scripture played an increasingly important role in

---

[21] D. Flood and G. Gal, eds., *Peter of John Olivi on the Bible* (St. Bonaventure, Franciscan Institute: 1997), 127–38 (French trans. Dahan 2009a).

[22] *Summa quaest. ord.* VIII, q. 6 (fol. 69r of the edition cited in note 17) (trans. Dahan 2009a: 137–38).

the reflections of exegetes and eventually became normative in the thirteenth century. They are often illustrated by the example of Jerusalem, which according to the literal sense designates the earthly city, according to allegory is a figure of the Church militant, according to the tropological sense refers to the human soul, and according to the anagogical sense is the glorious city of the end of time.[23] The twelfth century had reached a deeper definition of the literal sense, especially in the school of Saint-Victor, by defining three aspects: *littera* in the strict sense, with the study of vocabulary, grammar, and rhetorical devices; *sensus*, with the study of the historical and sociological context (e.g., the history of the Hebrews in the light of surrounding civilizations and the history of the first Christian communities in the background of their Jewish environment); and *sententia*, with the study of the lessons in terms of doctrine or theology to be learned from the text under consideration.[24]

This more complex approach to the literal sense made it possible to rebalance it in relation to the spiritual sense, which also comprises three aspects: *allegoria*, allegorical exegesis (typological when applying figures to Christ and his enemies; ecclesiastical when it concerns the Church militant); *tropologia*, sometimes assimilated to a moral interpretation but in reality going further, by applying the texts of Scripture to the history of the soul—even as far as what we would term a "psychoanalytical approach" in the case of Guibert of Nogent; and *anagogia*, an interpretation that proceeds toward the end of history, whether eschatology itself or realities that persist after the end of history (the opposing medieval terms being *in via*, "in the way" of the present life, and *in patria*, "in the homeland," where all the promises will be fulfilled).

The contrast between these two ternary schemes seems important: literal study is not devalued in favor of spiritual exegesis, but each of the two aspects covers complex realities, as can be seen in the exegesis of the thirteenth century which gives a major place to the letter (Dahan 2009b: 199–224). Moreover, this opposition brings us to the very foundation of Christian exegesis, the opposition between letter and spirit, well defined by St. Paul. Some major works (which are responsible for modern definitions of medieval exegesis) have overestimated the importance of the "four senses": apart from numerous theoretical affirmations made in the thirteenth and fourteenth centuries, it does not seem that the "four senses" are the most frequently employed approach in medieval exegesis. Very few commentaries are constructed according to this scheme, and the construction of those that are appears artificial. What dominates, and what undoubtedly constitutes the very essence of Christian exegesis (especially medieval exegesis), is the Pauline opposition between letter and spirit, based on what has been called the "hermeneutical leap" of the passage from the literal to the spiritual sense (Dahan 2009b: 225–47). Yet it seems that this too can itself be questioned, at least as an approach to be employed, as is shown particularly in the exegesis of the prophetic books. The reading of the question in Thomas Aquinas's Quodlibet VII shows what is at stake: what

---

[23] For example, Guibert of Nogent, *Quo ordine*, 53; see chap. 9 for the origin of this fourfold division and example in John Cassian.

[24] Cf. Hugh of Saint-Victor, *Didascalicon* VI, 8.

matters is not so much the master's answer, which could only consecrate the four senses which had been standardized fifty years earlier, as the serious objections to these and the answers to the objections.

The aim of this section has thus been to highlight the complexity and richness of medieval hermeneutics, in their harmonizing of the transcendence of the divine Word and the immanence of the message destined for man, of tradition and progress, of a confessional approach and scientific study. Even today, this creative tension retains its strength and relevance for those who try to understand the sacred books of the Old and New Testaments.

LITERARY FORMS

Three phases can be distinguished in the history of medieval exegesis: monastic exegesis, school exegesis, and university exegesis. A particular type of commentary corresponds to each of these phases, but it is not appropriate to separate them completely because, in a certain way, monastic exegesis continued until the end of the Middle Ages, just as school exegesis was still practiced in the fourteenth and fifteenth centuries (and even beyond).[25]

In the first phase, work on the Bible was carried out mainly in monasteries (Leclercq 1990; Dahan and Noblesse-Rocher 2014). This was both collective (during the *collatio*) and individual: Peter of Celle provides a praise of the study undertaken by the monk in his cell (Leclercq 1946: 233–34). The term *lectio* refers to such studies: they involved reading and explanation of the texts, but also internalization: medieval authors described it as "rumination." A major part of this exegesis was therefore of a tropological nature, with the teachings of Scripture being applied and adapted to the monks' condition. For example, God's exhortation to Abraham to leave his country, his family, and his father's house (Genesis 12:1) is understood as an invitation to abandon worldly life and to devote oneself to a monastic life. Monastic tropology is a characteristic of this form of exegesis (e.g., in the writings of William of Flay, Bernard of Clairvaux, Guerric of Igny, and Isaac of Stella) even if some (such as Guibert of Nogent) sought to apply it more generally to the individual soul.

As it did not generally belong to an organized teaching framework, monastic commentary employed free forms. During the early Middle Ages, it often took the form of an "anthology," largely composed of extracts from earlier authors, especially the Church Fathers. The commentaries of Hrabanus Maurus, which were in very wide circulation, illustrate this type, even though his work of adaptation is not to be overlooked. There are also more personal commentaries, such as those of Paschasius Radbertus. With the

---

[25] A general introduction to the overall picture is provided in Dahan 2000; for the practices of the schools and university, see also chap.16.

birth of new orders (the Premonstratensians, the Cistercians) and the renewal of the Order of St Benedict, monastic exegesis flourished and evolved in the twelfth century, but the importance of the spiritual (especially tropological) approach continued to be its main characteristic. It should also be noted that commentaries in the form of homilies (sermons that follow the sequence of the biblical text) are frequent in monastic exegesis (e.g., Bernard of Clairvaux and Gilbert of Hoyland on the Song of Songs).

During the eleventh century, as a result of the increasing urbanization of Western society, urban schools developed and flourished in a remarkable way. The Bible was taught at a higher level, which required a certain organization. Commentary adapted to these requirements, particularly in light of the constraints of teaching time, and became more compact and brief. The basic form was that of the "gloss," a brief commentary of a literal or spiritual nature, and (as observed in chapter 16) the use of question-and-answer technique increased considerably. The separation between the levels of meaning (identified by marginal headings such as *litteraliter* and *mystice*) should also be noted. Another feature encountered fairly often is an application to preaching: brief indications in the margins once again indicate themes to the reader that could be the subject of sermons. Such education is clearly for future clergy, and that the need for quality preaching was emphasized throughout the twelfth century. For example, in Stephen Langton's commentary on Exodus (Paris, BnF, lat. 355), the following marginal indications are found: *De tribus peccatis* ("On the three sins") on Exodus 1:11 (fol. 50r); *Contra prelatos* ("Against the prelates") on Exodus 1:16–17 (fol. 50v); *Allegorice, sermo in passione Domini* ("Allegorically, a sermon on the Lord's Passion") on Exodus 10:29 (fol. 54v), and so on.

The *Glossa ordinaria* (as it would later be termed), developed in Laon, Auxerre, and perhaps Paris in the first third of the twelfth century, played an important part in this exegesis (see further chap. 14, as well as Smalley 1981, 1983; de Hamel 1984; Gibson 1992). Replacing earlier attempts ("outdated glosses," according to Beryl Smalley), the collection initiated by Anselm and Ralph of Laon, then by Gilbert the Universal, quickly established itself as the basic textbook for the study of the Bible. The biblical text is surrounded by the "marginal gloss," drawn from passages of the Fathers and authors of the early Middle Ages: these are sometimes identified by an abbreviation, such as *Aug.* for Augustine or *Ier.* for Jerome. A brief "interlinear gloss" accompanies certain words of the biblical text, which may be literal as well as spiritual; although the latter may have been written by the authors of the collection, the editorial activity in assembling the marginal gloss should not be underestimated. For the two most frequently expounded books, the Psalms and the Pauline Epistles, the *Glossa ordinaria* was completed by the so-called *Media glossatura*, by Gilbert of Poitiers, and the *Magna glossatura* of Peter Lombard. In fact, Gilbert's gloss was not as successful as that of Laon, whereas Peter Lombard's gloss was constantly used for these writings from the end of the twelfth century onward and even became the subject of metacommentaries (such as those of Stephen Langton).

Again, in chapter 16, it has already been noted how, with the birth of the universities and the mendicant orders, a codified teaching of Scripture was established which gave rise to organized commentaries. Although the tripartite schema (*divisio, expositio, quaestiones*) was more of a theoretical ideal, not always found in the commentaries that have been preserved, these different elements fed into Scriptural exegesis despite greater freedom in the way in which the works were structured. What is clear is the role of the *divisio textus*, the importance given to the literal meaning (in all its complexity, including its theological deployment), the frequent separation of the levels of meaning, and the treatment of difficulties by means of *quaestiones* (or *dubia*).

The Procedures

Whether they belong to monastic, scholastic, or academic exegesis, all commentaries deploy common procedures, which will be presented here very briefly. Once again, a balance is generally maintained between the literal and the spiritual sense, even though the latter dominates in monastic production. Several procedures may be listed in terms of literal exegesis: textual criticism (discussed in chapters 16 and 22), research into semantics (in particular through the use of dictionaries such as the *Elementarium* of Papias, the *Derivationes* of Uguccio, and the *Catholicon* of John of Genoa), rhetorical analysis (advocated by Cassiodorus and facilitated by a number of treatises), the study of historical context (institutions, events), and the deployment of philosophical and doctrinal information. It should be emphasized that, from the thirteenth century, exegesis made space for Greek writers (in particular Aristotle) and Arabic ones (including the Jew Maimonides), who had recently been translated or retranslated. This is the case, for example, in the commentaries of Albert the Great, Thomas Aquinas, Bonaventure, Denis the Carthusian, and many others.

A remarkable point, present both in the prologues of commentaries and those of several theological works, is the analysis of the *modi* ("modes"). It seems that reflection on this topic was driven by the desire to establish theology as a science (Chenu 1969; Dahan 1999: 416–26). Certainly, such analysis appears as early as the twelfth century in the prologues that follow the scheme of the *accessus*, under the heading *modus agendi* which, in principle, involve defining the "style" of the work studied. In the thirteenth century, the analysis of the *modi* first concerns theological language, which an effort was made to define as "scientific," thus contrasting it with the language of biblical books, which could be narrative, legislative, prophetic, or poetic. From the middle of this century, such analysis was often applied systematically to the biblical books. The *principium* of Peter Aureoli (d. 1322) contains a typology of *modi* which serves as a basis for his classification of the biblical books (Paris, BnF, lat. 14796, ff. 1–11): political and legislative (Pentateuch), historical and narrative (Joshua, Judges, Kings, etc.), "hymnodic" or poetic, dialectical and based on dispute (Job, Ecclesiastes), ethical (Proverbs, Wisdom, Ecclesiasticus), prophetic, "testimonial" (Gospels), and epistolary.

A series of specific procedures are the basis of spiritual exegesis, although they are not exclusive to it. The first of these is concordant verses (Gilson 1955: 156–59; Dahan 1999: 350–58): This procedure serves as a basis for contemporary explanations (especially on the levels of semantics and history), but it was also a foundation of medieval exegesis. It is not limited to correspondences between the Old and New Testaments. First come verbal concordances, scriptural words which, through exegetical tradition, have been charged with content which may be recalled by the listener simply as they are heard, such as the word "deer" in Psalm 41 (LXX). The parallelism between two verses containing the same word thus makes it possible to establish an exegesis. Then there are thematic concordances, two verses which share the same theme and therefore shed light on each other. For example, Stephen Langton expounds Genesis 12:1 with the help of Luke 2:49 (when Jesus remains in the Temple and is separated from his parents). Finally, structural concordances can be found, especially in the explanations of texts read in the liturgy: Anthony of Padua gives remarkable examples of this procedure (Dahan 1996a).

Distinctio is a systematization of verbal concordances. Already present in the monastic exegesis of the twelfth century and in the exegesis of the schools, it played an important role in university exegesis, in which it received a specific form. It involved providing, in connection with a word encountered in the text, verses that contained this word and were likely to shed light on it. In the thirteenth century, *distinctio* had a schematic form; it appeared within the commentary or was given in the margin (or at the foot of the page). The complexity of certain *distinctiones* led writers to distinguish between positive and negative meanings, as in the collection of Peter of Capua (post-1219; see Dahan 2010). Despite the existence of collections of *distinctiones* from the second half of the twelfth century onward (the *Summa Abel* of Peter the Chanter, the *Summa "Quot modis"* of Alan of Lille), it seems that exegetes of the thirteenth century compiled their own *distinctiones*: the collections that flourished at this time were intended rather for preachers, making use of the contributions from exegetes. It should be noted that several commentaries from the end of the twelfth and beginning of the thirteenth centuries are composed solely of *distinctiones*, notably those on the Psalms by Peter of Poitiers, Michael of Corbeil, Odo of Châteauroux, and Philip the Chancellor.

Another procedure particularly characteristic of medieval exegesis is the *interpretatio* ("translation") of proper names in Scripture, whether Hebrew or Greek. Tools developed precisely for this were at the disposal of commentators (Dahan 1996b): while Jerome's collection may have been difficult to consult, from the early Middle Ages onward attempts were made to adapt it, leading at the beginning of the thirteenth century to the list beginning *Aaz apprehendens* found in most Bibles. Rigorously alphabetical, this brings together all the translations of proper names (Szerwiniack 1994). Also present in monastic exegesis, which draws on other lists, *interpretatio* is one of the procedures that establish spiritual exegesis: the name given to a person or a place is considered to correspond to its essence or its role, and more generally, beyond the historical character, to a form of teaching. This is frequently the basis of the tropological exegesis of Guibert of Nogent or William of Flay; it is also often found in the thirteenth century, notably in Bonaventure.

The importance of the meaning of realities *(res)* in spiritual exegesis should also be noted: for medieval thinkers, words signified as much as realities did (Brinkmann 1980). The distinction started, as has already been noted, with Augustine's consideration of *verba* and *res*, "words" and "realities." Drawing on the reflections of the writers of the Middle Ages, this schema can be completed by setting out three categories: realities, realities that are also signs, and signs (including words). The study of the meaning of *res* was one of the bases of medieval exegesis. Lists were elaborated of these significant realities, notably in the *De Scripturis* of Hugh of Saint-Victor, the *Sentences* of Robert of Melun, the *Allegoriae* of Peter of Poitiers, and in the manual of preaching of John of La Rochelle. Chapter 16 has described the development of other tools, including bestiaries, lapidaries, herbaria, and treatises on arithmology: encyclopedias, too, responded to the same demand (Dahan 1999: 325–50).

This set of procedures (concordant verses, *distinctiones*, *interpretationes*, the meaning of *res*) may appear to relate more specifically to spiritual exegesis, but once again it should be noted that the separation between spiritual and literal exegesis is not always clear-cut. For example, *distinctiones* often led to moral teaching, which is not the domain of spiritual exegesis. In addition, correspondence between the verses of the Old and New Testament also seems to call into question this duality, at least in a confessional approach to exegesis.

Summary

The considerations presented above highlight the richness and complexity of medieval exegesis. It is wrong to compartmentalize it into fixed schemes, such as that of the "four senses" of Scripture. Although the opposition between letter and spirit seems to be the most widely invoked, both in monastic and academic exegesis, it is often difficult to separate the two. It also seems that, far from sticking to a "fundamentalist" type of interpretation of the Old Testament, medieval exegetes prefigured the "mythical" analysis familiar from recent studies of the history of religions or anthropology. In particular, their approach to the Genesis narratives enabled them to find fundamental teachings describing the evolution of humanity and underlining basic human behavior (as in the story of Cain and Abel, or David and Bathsheba; see Dahan 2015b). In this way, the role of tropological exegesis should be better recognized in contemporary scholarship. Indeed, perhaps this is the most lasting contribution of medieval exegesis, notwithstanding the considerable progress it also brought to the literal approach.

Bibliography

Banon, D. 1987. *La lecture infinie. Les voies de l'interprétation midrachique*. Paris: Seuil.

Bataillon, L.-J., N. Bériou, G. Dahan, and R. Quinto, eds. 2010. *Étienne Langton, prédicateur, bibliste, théologien*. Turnhout: Brepols.

Berndt, Rainer. 1991. *André de Saint-Victor (d. 1175), exégète et théologien*. Turnhout: Brepols.

Bori, P. C. 1987. *L'interpretazione infinita. L'ermeneutica cristiana antica e le sue trasformazioni.* Bologna: Il Mulino.

Brinkmann, Hennig. 1980. *Mittelalterliche Hermeneutik.* Darmstadt: Wissenschaftliche Buchgesellschaft.

Cantini, G. 1951. "*Processus negociandi themata sermonum* di Giovanni della Rochelle, o.f.m." *Antonianum* 26: 247–70.

Chazelle, Celia, and Burton Van Name Edwards, eds. 2003. *The Study of the Bible in the Carolingian Era.* Turnhout: Brepols.

Chenu, M. D. 1969. *La théologie comme science au XIIIᵉ siècle.* 3rd ed. Paris: Vrin.

Cremascoli, Giuseppe, and Claudio Leonardi. 1996. *La Bibbia nel Medio Evo.* Bologna: Dehoniane.

Dahan, Gilbert. 1987. "Une introduction à l'étude de l'Ecriture au XIIᵉ siècle: le Prologue du Commentaire du Pentateuque de Rainaud de Saint-Éloi." *Recherches de théologie ancienne et médiévale* 54: 27–51. Repr., Dahan, *Lire la Bible au moyen âge. Essais d'herméneutique médiévale,* 321–50. Geneva: Droz, 2009.

Dahan, Gilbert. 1996a. "Saint Antoine et l'exégèse de son temps." In *Congresso internacional Pensamento e Testemunho. 8° Centenario do Nascimento de Santo Antonio,* edited by M. C. Pacheco, 147–77. *Actas.* Braga: Universidade Catolica Portuguesa.

Dahan, Gilbert. 1996b. "Lexiques hébreu-latin? Les recueils d'interprétations des noms hébraïques." In *Les manuscrits des lexiques et glossaires, de l'Antiquité à la fin du moyen âge,* edited by J. Hamesse, 481–526. Louvain-la-Neuve: FIDEM.

Dahan, Gilbert. 1999. *L'exégèse chrétienne de la Bible en Occident médiéval (XIIᵉ–XIVᵉ s.).* Paris: Cerf.

Dahan, Gilbert. 2000. "Genres, forms and various methods in Christian exegesis of the Middle Ages." In *Hebrew Bible / Old Testament: The History of Its Interpretation:* Vol. I/2. *The Middle Ages,* edited by M. Saebo, 196–236. Göttingen: Vandenhoeck & Ruprecht.

Dahan, Gilbert. 2005. "L'exégèse de la Bible chez Guillaume d'Auvergne," in *Autour de Guillaume d'Auvergne (d. 1249),* edited by F. Morenzoni and J.-Y. Tilliette, 236–70. Turnhout: Brepols.

Dahan, Gilbert. 2008. "Thomas d'Aquin, lecteur de Galates. Exégèse et herméneutique." In *Thomas d'Aquin, Commentaire de l'épître aux Galates,* edited by J.-E. Stroobant de Saint-Eloy, xxxi–xxxiii. Paris: Cerf.

Dahan, Gilbert. 2009a. *Interpréter la Bible au moyen âge. Cinq écrits du XIIIᵉ siècle sur l'exégèse de la Bible traduits en français.* Paris: Parole et silence.

Dahan, Gilbert. 2009b. *Lire la Bible au moyen âge. Essais d'herméneutique médiévale.* Geneva: Droz.

Dahan, Gilbert. 2010. "Le schématisme dans l'exégèse médiévale." In *Qu'est-ce que nommer? L'image légendée entre monde monastique et pensée scolastique,* edited by C. Heck, 31–40. Turnhout: Brepols.

Dahan, Gilbert. ed. 2011. *Nicolas de Lyre, franciscain du XIVᵉ siècle, exégète et théologien.* Paris: Études augustiniennes.

Dahan, Gilbert. 2013. "Tradition patristique, autorité et progrès dans l'exégèse médiévale." In *Les réceptions des Pères de l'Église au Moyen Âge. Le devenir de la tradition ecclésiale,* edited by R. Berndt and M. Fédou, 349–68. Archa Verbi Subsidia 10. Münster: Aschendorff.

Dahan, Gilbert. 2015. "Thomas Aquinas: Exegesis and Hermeneutics." In *Reading Sacred Scripture with Thomas Aquinas. Hermeneutical Tools, Theological Questions and New Perspectives,* edited by P. Roszak and J. Vijgen, 45–70. Turnhout: Brepols.

Dahan, Gilbert. 2015b. "Mythe et histoire dans l'exégèse médiévale de la Genèse. Quelques notes préliminaires." *Revue des sciences philosophiques et théologiques* 99: 97–120.

Dahan, Gilbert. 2016a. *Études d'exégèse médiévale. Ancien Testament*. Strasbourg: Presses Universitaires.

Dahan, Gilbert. 2016b. "Les genres grammaticaux dans un traité d'herméneutique de la fin du XIIᵉ siècle, le *De expositione sacrae Scripturae*." In *La rigueur et la passion. Mélanges en l'honneur de Pascale Bourgain*, edited by C. Giraud and D. Poirel, 347–57. Turnhout: Brepols.

Dahan, Gilbert. 2016c. "Henri de Gand. L'*introductio generalis ad sacram Scripturam*." In *Handbuch der Bibelhermeneutik von Origenes bis zur Gegenwart*, edited by Oda Wischmeyer and Michaela Durst, 207–19. Berlin: De Gruyter.

Dahan, Gilbert, and Annie Noblesse-Rocher, eds. 2014. *L'exégèse monastique au moyen âge (xiᵉ–xivᵉ s.)*. Paris: Études augustiniennes.

de Hamel, Christopher F. R. 1984. *Glossed Books of the Bible and the Origins of the Paris Book Trade*. Woodbridge: D. S. Brewer.

Emery, Kent, and Mark Jordan, eds. 1992. *Ad litteram: Authoritative Texts and their Medieval Readers*. Notre Dame: University of Notre Dame.

Evans, Gillian R. 1984. *The Language and Logic of the Bible. The Earlier Middle Ages*. Cambridge: Cambridge University Press.

Evans, Gillian R. 1985. *The Language and Logic of the Bible. The Road to Reformation*. Cambridge: Cambridge University Press.

Freytag, H. 1975. "*Quae sunt per allegoriam dicta . . . .*" In *Verbum et Signum. Festschrift F. Ohly*, edited by Hans Fromm, Wolfgang Harms, and Uwe Ruberg, 1. 27–43. Munich: Fink.

Gameson, Richard, ed. 1994. *The Early Medieval Bible*. Cambridge: Cambridge University Press.

Gibson, Margaret T. 1992. "The Place of the *Glossa ordinaria* in Medieval Exegesis." In *Ad litteram: Authoritative Texts and their Medieval Readers*, edited by K. Emery and M. D. Jordan, 5–27. Notre Dame: University of Notre Dame.

Gibson, Margaret T. 1993. *Artes and the Bible in the Medieval West*. Aldershot: Variorum.

Gilson, E. 1955. "De quelques raisonnements scripturaires au Moyen Âge." In *Les idées et les lettres*, 155–69. Paris: Vrin.

Lampe, G. W. H., ed. 1969. *The Cambridge History of the Bible: Vol. 2. The West from the Fathers to the Reformation*. Cambridge: Cambridge University Press.

Leclercq, Jean. 1946. *La spiritualité de Pierre de Celle*. Paris: Vrin.

Leclercq, Jean. 1990. *Initiation aux auteurs monastiques du moyen âge. L'amour des lettres et le désir de Dieu*. 3rd ed. Paris: Cerf.

Lerner, Robert E., ed. 1996. *Neue Richtungen in der hoch- und spätmittelalterlichen Bibelexegese*. Munich: Oldenbourg.

Levy, I. C. 2016a. "Nicholas of Lyra. The Biblical Prologues." In *Handbuch der Bibelhermeneutik von Origenes bis zur Gegenwart*, edited by Oda Wischmeyer and Michaela Durst, 239–53. Berlin: De Gruyter.

Levy, I. C. 2016b. "John Wyclif. The Hermeneutics." In *Handbuch der Bibelhermeneutik von Origenes bis zur Gegenwart*, edited by Oda Wischmeyer and Michaela Durst, 255–70. Berlin: De Gruyter.

Lobrichon, Guy. 2003. *La Bible au Moyen Âge*. Paris: Picard.

Lourdaux, W., and D. Verhelst, eds. 1979. *The Bible and Medieval Culture*. Leuven: University Press.

Lubac, Henri de. 1959–64. *Exégèse médiévale. Les quatre sens de l'Écriture*. 4 vols. Paris: Aubier.

Marsden, Richard, and E. Ann Matter, eds. 2018. *New Cambridge History of the Bible: Vol. 2. From 600 to 1450*. Cambridge: Cambridge University Press.

Minnis, A. J. 1988. *Medieval Theory of Authorship. Scholastic Literary Attitudes in the Later Middle Ages*. Aldershot: Wildwood House.

Morenzoni, F. 1995. *Des écoles aux paroisses. Thomas de Chobham et la promotion de la prédication au début du xiiie siècle*. Paris: Études augustiniennes.

Ocker, Christopher. 2002. *Biblical Poetics before Humanism and Reformation*. Cambridge: Cambridge University Press.

Oliva, A. 2006. *Les débuts de l'enseignement de Thomas d'Aquin et sa conception de la "Sacra doctrina."* Paris: Vrin.

Prügl, T. 2004. "Medieval Biblical *Principia* as Reflections on the Nature of Theology." *Archa Verbi Subsidia* 1: 253–75.

Prügl, T. 2016a. "*Summa Halensis*. Tractatus introductorius, q. 1: De doctrina theologiae." In *Handbuch der Bibelhermeneutik von Origenes bis zur Gegenwart*, edited by Oda Wischmeyer and Michaela Durst, 161–76. Berlin: De Gruyter.

Prügl, T. 2016b. "Thomas von Aquin. Summa theologiae I, 1, 9–10." In *Handbuch der Bibelhermeneutik von Origenes bis zur Gegenwart*, edited by Oda Wischmeyer and Michaela Durst, 191–206. Berlin: De Gruyter.

Quinto, R. 1989. "Stefano Langton e i quattro sensi della Scrittura." *Medioevo* 15: 67–109.

Riché, Pierre, and Guy Lobrichon, eds. 1984. *Le Moyen Âge et la Bible*. BTT 4. Paris: Beauchesne.

Rost, Hans. 1939. *Die Bibel im Mittelalter. Beiträge zur Geschichte und Bibliographie der Bibel*. Augsburg: Seitz.

Santiago-Otero, Horacio, and Klaus Reinhardt. 2001. *La Biblia en la peninsula ibérica durante la edad medio (s. xii–xv): el texto y su interpretacion*. Coimbra: Arquivo da Universidade de Coimbra.

Schlageter, J. K. 2016. "Petrus Johannis Olivi. Hermeneutik der Heiligen Schrift." In *Handbuch der Bibelhermeneutik von Origenes bis zur Gegenwart*, edited by Oda Wischmeyer and Michaela Durst, 221–38. Berlin: De Gruyter..

Smalley, Beryl. 1931. "Stephen Langton and the Four Senses of Scripture," *Speculum* 6: 60–76.

Smalley, Beryl. 1981. *Studies in Medieval Thought and Learning*. London: Hambledon.

Smalley, Beryl. 1983. *The Study of the Bible in the Middle Ages*. 3rd ed. Oxford: Basil Blackwell.

Spatz, N. 1992. "Principia: A study and edition of inception speeches delivered before the faculty of theology at the University of Paris, ca. 1180–1286." Unpublished PhD diss., Cornell University.

Spicq, Ceslas. 1944. *Esquisse d'une histoire de l'exégèse latine au moyen âge*. Paris: Vrin.

Stegmüller, Friedrich, and Klaus Reinhardt, eds. 1950–80. *Repertorium biblicum medii aevi*. 11 vols. Madrid: CSIC.

Sulavik, A. 2004. "*Principia* and *Introitus* in Thirteenth-Century Biblical Exegesis with related texts." In *La Bibbia del XIII secolo. Storia del testo, storia dell'esegesi*, edited by G. Cremascoli and F. Santi, 251–303. Florence: SISMEL.

Szerwiniack, O. 1994. "Des recueils d'interprétations de noms hébreux chez les Irlandais et le Wisigoth Théodulf." *Scriptorium* 48: 187–258.

Valente, L. 1997. *Phantasia contrarietatis. Contraddizioni scritturali, discorso teologico e arti del linguaggio nel* De tropis loquendi *di Pietro Cantore*. Florence: Leo S. Olschki.

Vernet, André, and Anne-Marie Genevois. 1989. *La Bible au moyen âge. Bibliographie*. Paris: CNRS.

Wischmeyer, Oda, and Michaela Durst, eds. 2016. *Handbuch der Bibelhermeneutik von Origenes bis zur Gegenwart*. Berlin: De Gruyter.

CHAPTER 18

THE LATIN BIBLE IN THE RENAISSANCE AND EARLY PRINT CULTURE

PAUL NEEDHAM

THE GUTENBERG BIBLE

IN the spring of 1452, a scribe in Mainz began to transcribe onto fine sheets of vellum the text of what was planned as an unusually large and luxurious copy of the Vulgate (Washington, DC, Library of Congress, MS 8). This scribe had the habit of recording at the end of each book its date of completion, showing that the creation of this Bible took some fifteen months, ending in July 1453. Soon after, again in Mainz, a second scribe copied a Vulgate on high-quality paper in a cursive book hand, destined for use by the Brethren of the Common Life in Butzbach (Giessen, University Library, MS 653). Notes on the flyleaf provide a breakdown of the production costs and indicate that the work was finished on September 19, 1454. At the same time as these scribal commissions, a Mainz workshop was creating a third Bible, using a radically different technique. At least four workers stood at wooden frames, looking at different sections of a source manuscript and pulling from more than two hundred boxes small metal solids with reverse images of letters, to be locked up into sets of double columns of forty-two lines. These were then stamped over with a viscous, oil-based ink and printed one page at a time onto sheets of paper and vellum under a strong screw-driven press. After many months, from stacks of printed pages, one full copy after another could be assembled of essentially identical Vulgate Bibles.

This anonymous production was what we now call the Gutenberg Bible. It was probably completed sometime in 1455. Between 160 and 180 copies were produced, consisting of 643 leaves of Royal folio size (40 × 28 cm), intended to be bound in two volumes: the first from Genesis through to the Psalms, the second of the Wisdom books, Prophets, Maccabees, and the New Testament. Around one-quarter of the output was on vellum for sale at a higher price, the remainder on paper (Needham 1985a). The buyers received only the gathered sheets, containing the black text laid out on pages with carefully planned white spaces. Rubricators would be hired to enter in these spaces, in red (and often blue) ink, the titles of the books and prologues, their beginning initials, chapter initials, and chapter numbers. In the Psalms, blank spaces were left before each verse for the rubricator to supply well over two thousand "versal" letters. Two supplementary sheets were provided by the publisher prescribing the exact wording of each title, carefully laid out according to the shape of the white space provided (Powitz 2012). Although most of the rubricators followed this printed guide, this extensive hand-finishing means that no two of the roughly fifty surviving copies of the Gutenberg Bible look alike. A number were very expensively illuminated, with painting or gilding of the larger initials. The vellum copy at the Berlin State Library, decorated by a shop in Leipzig or Prague, stands among the most beautiful illuminated Bibles of the fifteenth century.

The text of the Gutenberg Bible has a close relationship to the thirteenth-century Paris Bibles (see chap. 13 and chap. 16). In a classic study, Heinrich Schneider compared the text of Paris Bibles with the Gutenberg Bible across eighty-one selected chapters between Genesis and Job (Schneider 1954; Powitz 2009). Within this sample, close to 250 "Paris" readings appear in the Gutenberg Bible, indicating that Gutenberg's exemplar did not predate the thirteenth century. At the same time, there are numerous places in this sample when the Gutenberg Bible matches older Vulgate witnesses, which are sufficiently frequent to establish that Gutenberg's direct source was not a Paris Bible. Schneider's summaries indicate that Paris Bible readings in the Gutenberg Bible are considerably more frequent in the Pentateuch than in the subsequent collated chapters: it could be that the compositors for these three units were working from different exemplars, the first of which had a denser layer of Paris Bible readings. On a broader scale, the Gutenberg Bible follows the Paris Bible order of books and chapter divisions, although it should be noted that many fifteenth-century Vulgate manuscripts do not follow this sequence, while others include additional writings. The Gutenberg Bible contains IV Ezra, found in a minority of Vulgate Bibles from the late twelfth century onward, but its structural position shows that it was interpolated from a different source at a late stage of printing; it had not been part of the original plan (Needham 1985b; see also chap. 7). Similarly, the Gutenberg Bible omits twenty-two Paris prologues and adds thirteen from outside that group. The largest group of omissions, of all prologues to the Minor Prophets apart from Jerome's brief introduction, almost certainly reflects a late printing shop decision rather than their absence from the exemplar: they appear to have been cut so that the text of the Minor Prophets would end neatly on the last line of the last page of the final quire of its composition unit.

In short, in the fifteenth century there was no recognized template for "the" Vulgate Bible, unlike that reflected in the large group of Paris Bibles two centuries earlier. Every Bible was, so to speak, individual. This is illustrated by comparing the Gutenberg Bible with its two contemporaries from Mainz mentioned above. Each is textually independent, despite having been made in the same city within a narrow time frame. The Gutenberg Bible contains IV Ezra, the other two lack it; the Butzbach Bible, unusually, omits Baruch. The Butzbach Bible omits sixteen Paris prologues, and adds nineteen from elsewhere, in a wholly different pattern to the prologues of the Gutenberg Bible. The Library of Congress Giant Bible has all the Paris prologues but adds forty-eight more, including thirteen accompanying the Psalms (where there are none in Paris Bibles). In both the Gutenberg Bible and Giant Bible, the Prayer of Manasseh is printed as a distinct text with an explanatory *titulus*; the Butzbach Bible lacks it. The differences between these three Bibles show that Jerome's remark that the Latin Bible had as many texts as there were copies remained true a thousand years later.[1] The Gutenberg Bible was, in fact, the first Bible to contradict the adage. Whatever the quality of its text, this was essentially identical in its 180 copies. Readers hundreds of miles apart might turn to any given page and see, for better or for worse, the same text, and even the same typographical errors.

DEVELOPMENTS IN PRINTED BIBLES IN THE FIFTEENTH CENTURY

The printed-book trade in Europe spread slowly through the 1460s and then increased in pace in subsequent decades. North of the Alps, the prominent printing towns were Strasbourg, Lyons, Nuremberg, and Basle; south of the Alps, Venice was preeminent. By the end of the fifteenth century, eighty-one editions of the Latin Bible had been printed, along with fourteen giant editions in which the text was surrounded by one of the three standard commentaries (discussed below). These subsequent editions closely followed the text of the Gutenberg Bible, with relatively minor textual revision. As one printed Bible was based on the text of another, the Gutenberg text continued into the sixteenth century and, eventually, the Sixto-Clementine Vulgate of 1592 and later (Quentin 1922; Needham 1986a, 1986b, 1987).

The most influential channel of descent from the Gutenberg Bible flowed from Mainz to Rome to Venice to Basle. The 1462 Mainz Bible of Gutenberg's former associates, Johann Fust and Peter Schoeffer, is an elegant Royal folio, with a larger print run than the Gutenberg Bible, and more than half the copies printed on vellum. It was set from a copy of the Gutenberg Bible to which a number of emendations had been made, probably at the Benedictine convent of Mainz (Needham 2006). A copy of this widely distributed Bible was used in Rome by the printers Conrad Sweynheym and Arnald Pannartz to set their Royal folio edition of 1471, edited by the humanist Giovanni Andrea Bussi. It presents the text in Roman type, set in long lines rather than double columns. Bussi seems to have done little if any textual editing, but he excluded IV Ezra and added some twenty book prologues common to the Paris Bible but not included in the Gutenberg Bible, including those for the Minor Prophets. This 1471 Rome Bible was the exemplar

---

[1] *Prologue to Joshua*; see also his *Prologue to the Gospels* (Stuttgart Vulgate 2007: 285, 1515).

for a Chancery folio Bible printed by Franz Renner in Venice in 1475. The Renner edition embodies a considerable amount of anonymous editorial work. Besides significant textual emendations, there are more than two dozen additional prologues, almost all of which can be traced in Italian Vulgate manuscripts of the fifteenth century; IV Ezra was restored from a printed edition descended from the Gutenberg Bible. This "Renner shape" of text and structure was broadcast widely, both to later Venice editions and, via the 1479 Basle edition of Johann Amerbach, to northern European printing towns.[2]

By the 1490s, the Gutenberg Bible and all other early editions would have looked old-fashioned. The only other edition to employ formal square Gothic type was Bamberg 1461, produced from Gutenberg's own type. Early experiments with Roman type likewise did not take hold, being used in only two editions, Rome 1471, and Strasbourg 1473. The appropriate type for the Bible, as for most other nonclassical Latin printing, was Gothic rotunda; not until the 1520s did Roman type for Bibles become widespread, especially under the influence of Paris shops. The size of pages also decreased. The first fourteen Bibles printed, up to 1474, were all Royal folios (40 × 28 cm), appropriate for reading from lecterns in services or refectory. After these, Chancery folio Bibles in a single volume became the common format (30 × 21 cm), with no Royal folio editions printed after 1480. In the 1490s, even smaller and more portable formats, quarto (21 × 14.5 cm) and octavo (16 × 11 cm), became popular. From the mid-1470s, Bibles began to be published with printed titles, chapter numbers, and headlines, requiring little or no additional work by rubricators to make them usable; a few left spaces for woodcut initials for book and chapter beginnings, but the printed guide letters were often taken by users as sufficient in themselves.

A fuller apparatus of auxiliary material was also added in the last quarter of the fifteenth century (Needham 1999; Saenger 1999). Sweynheym and Pannartz included the thirteenth-century *Interpretations of Hebrew Names* in their 1471 edition, as did Renner in 1475 (but from a different source). Nine lectern Bible editions printed between 1474 and 1480 included the ancient Eusebian apparatus of gospel parallels, which then disappeared again until it was revived in the influential quarto Bible published by Lucantonio Giunta in Venice 1511. The reference system developed by the Paris Dominicans in the middle of the thirteenth century, subdividing chapters into sections lettered A to G (for shorter chapters, A to D), although originally notional, began to be printed in the margin: the first instance of this was the 1477 Basle Royal folio Bible, for the New Testament. The system was extended to the entire Bible in two 1491 editions, produced in Basle and Freiburg. This became standard until Robert Estienne's divisions in the second half of the sixteenth century. Gospel Registers, a table of contents for each of the Gospels based on the chapters of the Paris Bible, were developed in Basle in 1479. They were adopted in other Basle editions, with the addition of the other New Testament books in 1487 but did not become part of broader tradition. In contrast, a

---

[2] The Stuttgart Vulgate, in noting all variants from the Clementine Vulgate, implicitly documents the text of the Gutenberg Bible: most of the Clementine variants descend from the Gutenberg text, modified in places by the 1462 Mainz or 1475 Venice editors.

series of summaries called *Casus summarii* (abbreviated C.S.) was developed by an anonymous Ulm editor for Johann Zainer's Royal folio Bible of 1480. Prefixed to each chapter, they were advertised by Zainer as being helpful for unlearned clerics (*ad simplicium sacerdotum utilitatem*). These were later taken up by Venetian publishers, and continued to feature into the sixteenth century. Many editions included one of several traditional verse mnemonics for the order of the biblical books. More extensive was the mnemonic arbitrarily known as the *Summarium Biblicum*, beginning *Sex prohibet peccant*: its 212 hexameter lines provide keywords for each chapter following the sequence and divisions of the Paris Bible. This was first printed in a 1494 Venice edition, and thenceforth became common (Dolezalová 2013). In many later Bibles, it was joined with the *Tabula*, an alphabetical subject index to the Bible compiled in 1490 by a Venetian Franciscan, Gabriele Bruno, to form part of a "quadruplex repertorium" of helps advertised on title pages.

Bibles and Commentaries

As in other genres, the first decades of printing supplied not new texts but rather a multitude of copies of works that had long been part of Europe's religious, literary, and intellectual heritage. Through printing, three immense Bible commentaries of earlier centuries gained a renewed readership that extended far beyond the fifteenth century. These were the *Glossa ordinaria*, the mid-thirteenth commentary of the Paris Dominicans attributed to Hugh of Saint-Cher, and the *Postilla litteralis* (1331) and *Postilla moralis* (1339) of the Franciscan Nicholas of Lyra (see chap. 14 and chap. 17). The *Postilla litteralis* was first printed in Rome by Sweynheym and Pannartz, in five Royal folio volumes, in 1471–72. The edition followed the traditional manuscript layout, with the biblical lemmata set without differentiation from the commentary: the work would have been nearly unusable until a rubricator had meticulously distinguished the lemmata by a red underline. A Strasbourg edition of 1472 set the text in the same manner, adding substantial supplements: the critical *Additiones* of the converted Jew Paul of Burgos, Bishop of Cartagena; the "Replies" to Paul by the Saxon Franciscan Thomas Doering; and a commentary on many traditional prologues by a thirteenth-century Paris Franciscan, William Brito. Four more editions were produced up to 1488, copying either the Rome or the Strasbourg model, along with a dozen partial editions. Those printed after 1480 clarified the text by marking off the biblical lemmata with parentheses or brackets, or by setting them in larger type. Starting with the Venice edition of 1481, printers presented the full *Postilla litteralis* and its supplements in a new form, as a commentary in small type surrounding the full text of the Bible in larger type. Nine such editions (Venice, Nuremberg, Strasbourg, Lyons) were issued before the end of the fifteenth century. Lyra's *Postilla moralis* was printed three times (Cologne, Strasbourg, Mantua) as a self-standing folio edition. There were also nine editions from 1490 to 1519 of what may have been a publisher's invention: smaller-format books containing the gospel and epistle readings for Lent and Easter, surrounded by Lyra's combined *Postilla litteralis* and *moralis* for just those readings.

The *Glossa ordinaria* was published in 1480 by a consortium of printers: Adolf Rusch in Strasbourg, Johann Amerbach in Basel, and Anton Koberger in Nuremberg. It was presented in four massive Imperial folio volumes (leaf dimensions of about 48 × 35 cm), and must have been widely and successfully distributed, for it survives in nearly four hundred copies. Considerable effort would have gone into collecting exemplars for the compositors to work from, for the *Glossa* was formed and transmitted as individual biblical books or groups, not as a unified collection. The Rusch-Amerbach-Koberger project thus created a new form of book, a full Bible with *Glossa*, and gave life to a group of texts that had been dormant for two centuries (Gumbert 1999). In 1492, the Venice printer Paganinus de Paganinis received a ten-year privilege for printing at considerable expense a Bible surrounded by the *Glossa* and the *Postilla litteralis* of Lyra, as well as Brito's prologue commentaries. This 1495 publication employed a complex system of small reference letters to match the Bible text with the two commentaries. A Basle edition was completed in 1498, adding the supplements of Paul of Burgos and Thomas Doering, as well as Lyra's *Postilla moralis*. In terms of types set, this was the largest printing job of the fifteenth century, roughly six times the extent of the Latin Bible alone. Ten more editions of this massive reference Bible were printed from 1502 to 1634, taking both the *Glossa* and Nicholas of Lyra well into the seventeenth century.

The third of the major medieval commentaries, attributed to Hugh of Saint-Cher, was even longer than the other two combined. Hugh's commentaries were copied with the same layout as those of Nicholas of Lyra, with the biblical lemmata demarcated from the commentary by rubrication. A Basle 1482 edition of Hugh's commentary on the Gospels, and two editions of his commentary on the Psalter (Venice 1496; Nuremberg 1498) followed this layout, setting the lemmata in larger type. Three years after the Basle edition of the reference Bible with the *Glossa* and Nicholas of Lyra, Koberger commissioned a complement: a Bible surrounded by the commentary of Hugh of Saint Cher. This appeared in seven volumes, reaching completion in November 1502: it established the pattern for all later editions of this commentary, from a Basle reprint of 1504 to a Venice printing in 1754. Koberger even considered publishing a kind of super-Bible that would surround the Vulgate with all three commentaries, the *Glossa*, Nicholas of Lyra, and Hugh, but this went beyond the practical possibilities of typography at the time.

The New Market

By the end of the fifteenth century, the eighty-two plain text editions of the Latin Bible and thirteen editions with commentary had resulted in tens of thousands of copies, of which well over nine thousand survive today. Such an output in just forty-five years would have overwhelmed Europe's existing store of manuscript Bibles. Venice editions were sold more widely across Europe than those of any other printing town, and they survive today in larger numbers. Evidence for the size of print runs is only rarely preserved. A notarial contract for a 1478 Venice Latin Bible specifies that the printer would complete 930 copies: one hundred of these are extant. A letter of Anton Koberger, the most active investor in Latin Bible publishing, records that sixteen hundred copies had been printed of his giant edition of the Bible with the commentary of Hugh of Saint-Cher: about 240 copies remain, most of which are partial sets. The success of the portable Bibles in octavo format is indicated by their numbers. Johann Froben in Basle printed two editions, 1491 and 1495, each of which survives in some 280 copies. A slightly larger octavo Bible printed by Paganinus in Venice in 1497 survives in some 160 copies. It is probable that all three editions originally ran to well over a thousand copies. The distribution of printed editions varied markedly by region. Relatively few printed Bibles were sold in the Iberian Peninsula; most of these came from Venetian shops, which had the most far-reaching trade network. French churches and convents also seem to have been slow to acquire printed Bibles. Only one Latin Bible was printed in Paris (1476), of which a number of copies were sold in England. The other printed Bibles in early French ownership were mostly editions from Lyons and Venice.

The Sixteenth Century

In the first three decades of the sixteenth century, a considerable number of printed Latin Bibles continued to adhere to the structure of the Basle, Lyons, and Venice editions of the 1490s, buttressing the text with a large apparatus of prologues, indexes, mnemonics, marginal cross references, and chapter summaries (Gordon and Cameron 2016). Still more supplementary material was added in this period, mostly set in small type in the margins. A Basle edition of 1509 provided marginal references to Gratian's *Digest* of Canon Law, which were expanded in the 1511 quarto Venice Bible published by Lucantonio Giunta. The latter introduced a further layer of marginalia, with indications of variant readings. These typically consisted of no more than a single word or even a variant spelling, prefixed by *Alias* ("Others"). They have been seen as an editorial milestone in the textual criticism of the Vulgate, but this may be overstated. Corrections to the Gutenberg Bible text had been incorporated silently in both the Mainz 1462 edition and the Venice 1475 edition. The variant readings in Giunta's edition derive from the *correctoria* of the mid-thirteenth century (see further chap. 16), but unlike the *correctoria* they do not indicate a preferred reading. Such a tradition of noting variants can also be found in Italian Vulgate manuscripts, and it is likely that Giunta's editor, the Dominican Albertus Castellanus, was aware of this tradition (van Lopik 2020). Both the canon law references and the textual variants were copied into many subsequent editions, for publishers did not want to seem to offer less than their competitors: a 1516 Lyons Bible printed by Jacques Sacon for the Koberger firm included notes extracted from the historical writings of Josephus, which became part of subsequent Lyons editions.

There were, however, distinctive changes in this period. The major centers of Bible production shifted. Bibles in smaller formats became considerably more popular. Editions of partial Bibles proliferated. Overall, the market for Latin Bibles expanded significantly. In the forty-five years of fifteenth-century printing, just over a hundred biblical editions were produced, while the first forty-five years of the sixteenth century saw well over 550 editions. The largest part of the increase was in partial Bibles, most notably the New Testament by itself. In the fifteenth century, there had only been a single separate edition of the Latin New Testament, a quarto printed in Louvain in 1478. Between 1501 and 1545, Paris became a prominent and even the dominant center of Bible production. Some twenty-four full Bibles and more than 160 partial Bibles were issued by Paris publishers within this period, outnumbering those of Lyons, which was responsible for about half of all full Bibles. In contrast, the role played by Venice diminished, with only five editions being produced. The focus of the Koberger firm shifted from Nuremberg to Lyons, where it stored an extensive set of illustration woodblocks to be used in one Bible printing after another. Many of the partial Bibles were published for school use, with Proverbs being particularly favored. In the 1490s, two small quarto editions were printed in Paris, consisting of the New Testament Epistles and the "Salomonic" books, while three editions of the Pauline Letters were produced in Deventer and Zwolle. The number of school editions increased considerably in the early sixteenth century, particularly in Augsburg, Leipzig, and Wittenberg. They were normally set with widely spaced lines for the interlinear glossing of individual words.

Single-volume Bibles in octavo format became a widespread normal publication form. At least forty-eight such editions were produced before 1545, aimed at buyers who wanted easily portable volumes. These typically had the same contents and two-column layout as folio editions, achieving economy of size by the use of smaller type. From the early 1520s, New Testaments and other partial Bibles were also commonly printed as octavos, but in single columns with no significant reduction in the typeface. Partial Bibles in miniature formats, most commonly sextodecimo (16mo; about 11 × 7 cm), were a Paris innovation of the early 1520s that quickly found a receptive market. Books of this size could be not only carried but almost fully hidden in the hand. The innovator was Pierre Vidoue, who in 1521 published a New Testament in an even smaller format, "long" 24mo (about 10 × 5.5 cm), producing copies with narrow leaves and very short lines. The next year, the printer Simon de Colines began printing Bible parts in the less narrow 16mo format, which soon dominated the market. These are strikingly handsome, using a specially designed Roman type. Up to the early 1540s, Colines's shop produced more than seventy partial Bible editions, which could be acquired separately or assembled as complete Bibles according to the wishes of individual buyers. This model was copied by other Paris presses, as well as those in Antwerp and Lyons. More than 170 16mo editions of Bible texts are recorded before the Council of Trent, a figure which must be conservative.

The Impact of Philology

The stream of Latin Bible production was soon thrown into turmoil by a new factor: the philological study of the Latin text and of its Hebrew and Greek sources. It is a strange coincidence that the book that introduced this turn of events was brought to print by Desiderius Erasmus, a decade before he worked on his Greek–Latin New Testament (see below). The text he edited was the *Annotationes* on the New Testament of the Roman humanist Lorenzo Valla (d. 1457), a closely argued series of notes based on Valla's comparison of the Latin text with the Greek. Most of Valla's writings had been enthusiastically reproduced by printers, particularly his *Elegantiae latinae linguae*, but the *Annotationes* had disappeared after his death. A first recension survives in just two manuscripts, while Valla's extensive revision is found only in the manuscript that Erasmus chanced upon in the summer of 1504 in the library of Park Abbey, outside Louvain (it is now in the Royal Library, Brussels). Erasmus transcribed the text but made a multitude of small changes, partly to sweeten Valla's caustic style, and had the work printed the following year by Badius Ascensius in Paris. In Valla's *Annotationes*, Erasmus encountered a model of engagement with the biblical text for which he had prepared himself through the intensive study of Greek. In the autumn of 1507, he wrote to Aldus Manutius expressing his surprise that Aldus had not yet printed a Greek New Testament (and possibly hinting at himself as a suitable editor for such a project). Although Aldus had apparently considered the idea of printing a trilingual Bible (Hebrew–Greek–Latin) in the late 1490s, no serious steps had been taken toward this, and a Greek edition only appeared in 1518.

The Complutensian Polyglot and Polyglot Psalters

A much more ambitious and expensive project of applying philology to the study of the Bible was formulated by the powerful Spanish cleric Francisco Jiménez de Cisneros, Archbishop of Toledo, sometime Regent of Spain, grand inquisitor, and cardinal. In the first decade of the sixteenth century, Cisneros gathered a group of scholars, including learned Jewish converts, at Alcalá de Henares near Madrid, to prepare a massive edition of the Bible that would place the Latin text alongside its Hebrew and Greek sources. At the press between 1513 and 1517, this Bible, the Complutensian Polyglot (Complutum being the name of the original Roman settlement at Alcalá) also included the early Aramaic ("Chaldean") version of the Pentateuch known as the Targum Onkelos (Martín Abad 1999; Carbajosa 2014). Cisneros originally planned to print the targums for the other books of the Hebrew Bible, and gathered Aramaic manuscripts for the purpose but finally decided to leave them out. The printer, Arnaldo Guillén de Brocar, was recruited to Alcalá from Logroño. Cisneros made heavy investments in creating the necessary types: besides the expected Roman and Rotunda fonts, new Hebrew and Greek fonts in multiple sizes were engraved and cast for the project. The New Testament volume was completed first, its colophon date being January 10, 1514, followed by a dictionary-grammar volume for Hebrew and Aramaic in March and May 1515, and then by the Old Testament in four volumes. In the Pentateuch volume, the Complutensian Polyglot fits onto each page the Hebrew, Latin, and Greek in parallel columns, with an interlinear literal Latin translation in the Greek column. The Targum Onkelos was printed at the foot of the page, alongside its own literal Latin version. To keep the Hebrew, Latin, and Greek columns aligned, the compositors used typographic line fillers in the Latin and Greek columns, shaped as wedges and the letter o, and added extra spacing between words where necessary.

The manuscripts available at Alcalá included two important tenth-century Vulgate Bibles in Visigothic script, referred to in the scholarly literature as Codex Complutensis 1 and 2. It has been stated repeatedly that these were used in establishing the Vulgate text of the Polyglot, but this rests on a misunderstanding. There are few if any indications that readings from these ancient sources were brought into the Polyglot's Latin columns, which largely present the common text of the printed editions descending from the 1475 Venice edition. Within this text are some inauthentic readings which made their first appearance in the Gutenberg Bible, indicating that, for the Latin columns, the compositors copied a printed Vulgate edition from the late fifteenth or early sixteenth century.

The Polyglot volumes were completed on July 10, 1517, and four months later Cardinal Cisneros died. The copies were not issued for three years. In March 1520, informed of the posthumous delays, Pope Leo X called for the edition to go on sale, noting that six hundred or more copies had been printed. In the interim, other scholarly projects had come on the market, superseding significant portions of the Alcalá project. Erasmus's Greek–Latin New Testament was completed in Basle in February 1516. Bishop Agostino Giustiniani's Genoa Psalter, an "eightfold" polyglot including Arabic and Aramaic texts, was finished in November 1516: only a quarter of its two thousand copies were sold, showing how this luxurious edition had misjudged the potential market. This psalter was only the second text printed with Arabic type: it was preceded by a 1514 Book of Hours produced by the Gregorii firm of Venice for use by Christians in Syria. Erasmus's 1516 nine-volume edition of the works of Jerome included, as a separate appendix to volume VIII, a *Quadruplex Psalterium* edited by Konrad Pellikan, with parallel columns of Greek, Hebrew, the Gallican Latin version, and the Latin version *iuxta Hebraeos*. Both this and Giustiniani's Psalter were dedicated to Pope Leo X.

A little earlier, Jacques Lefèvre d'Étaples had edited a *Quincuplex Psalterium*, printed by Estienne in 1509 (and reprinted with revisions in 1513). This presented five Latin versions of the Psalms: the familiar Gallican Psalter of the Vulgate Bible; Jerome's revision *iuxta Hebraeos*; the Roman Psalter in liturgical usage; an "Old" (*Vetus*) Psalter, extracted from the lemmata in Augustine's *Enarrationes in Psalmos*; and a "Reconciled" (*Conciliatum*) Psalter constructed by Lefèvre himself. This took into account the multiple differences between the older versions but varied little from the Gallican Psalter: all changes were signaled by asterisks. For the Roman and *iuxta Hebraeos* texts Lefèvre used at least one early triple psalter manuscript, loaned to him by either the Celestines or Carthusians of Paris. The interlinear translation of the Septuagint in the

Complutensian Polyglot eventually provided a sixth Latin Psalm version. The whole translation was published as a self-standing Old Testament in Basle in 1526, although the printer Cratander made no acknowledgement of his source. A seventh psalter, of considerable influence, was the 1515 Venice *Psalterium ex Hebraeo* translated by the Augustinian hermit Felix of Prato. Felix was a converted Jew who was the chief editor of Daniel Bomberg's *Biblia rabbinica*, an edition of the Hebrew Bible with the traditional Jewish commentaries, which appeared in Venice in 1517 (Hobbs 2018; Grendler 2008). Felix worked under the patronage of Leo X, who granted a ten-year privilege to his psalter: copies were owned by both Erasmus and Martin Luther, and it was reprinted in Hagenau and Basle in the 1520s.

Desiderius Erasmus

Of the Bible editions that appeared while the Complutensian sheets were in storage, the most influential by far was Erasmus's 1516 Greek New Testament, printed in parallel columns with his Latin translation (Wallraff 2016). When he first traveled to Basle in the late summer of 1514 to meet with the publisher Johann Froben, Erasmus brought with him a mass of notes and papers for a wide range of scholarly publications. His plan was not so much for a Greek–Latin New Testament, as for a substantial commentary on the Vulgate: the *Annotationes* which form the second part of the 1516 volume. Similarly, a Greek New Testament would have been a radical departure for Froben, who had published an entirely conventional folio Vulgate in Rotunda type with the traditional apparatus only two months before Erasmus's arrival. Soon after reaching Basle, Erasmus decided to join a Greek text to his New Testament *Annotationes* and wrote to Johannes Reuchlin asking to borrow a Greek New Testament manuscript (Andrist 2018). The choice to add a Latin translation was not made until the summer of 1515: in his prologue, matching those of Jerome, Erasmus states several times that this was not by his own wish but at the urging of unnamed friends. In the next decades, Erasmus's Latin version, printed separately, gained an enormous readership, extending far beyond the circle of scholars who wanted to encounter and study the Greek text. Thierry Martens of Louvain printed an octavo edition in 1519, the first of the sixteenth-century editions of the New Testament by itself. More than sixty more octavo editions of Erasmus's version followed in the next twenty-five years, from publishers in many cities, in contrast with just thirty-five octavo editions of the Vulgate New Testament.

   Before long, however, Erasmus's bilingual edition became the subject of bitter theological controversy and accusations of heterodoxy. In 1520, it was attacked by two antagonists, Edward Lee, a future Archbishop of York, and Diego Lopez de Zuniga (latinized as Stunica), one of the editors of the Complutensian Polyglot. The most serious criticism was that Erasmus had omitted the Johannine Comma (1 John 5:7–8), an early Latin interpolation intended to lend canonical authority to the doctrine of the Trinity (see McDonald 2016). Erasmus explained that he had omitted the clause as it was not in his Greek sources, but this explanation was seen as inadequate, disingenuous, and doctrinally suspect. The Complutensian Polyglot did include the Trinitarian clause, silently supplying a translation into Greek to avoid leaving a lacuna in that column. Erasmus correctly suspected that the Complutensian Greek sources lacked the clause, and challenged Stunica to reply on this point, but no response was forthcoming. However, while Erasmus was in Louvain in 1521, an English friend brought him a Greek New Testament manuscript that contained the Johannine Comma. This manuscript (now at Trinity College, Dublin) was of recent making, probably written in Oxford close in time to Erasmus's 1516 first edition. Erasmus would have seen that it was new, written on fresh, bright, glazed paper. On its basis, he included the Comma in the third edition of his Greek–Latin New Testament (1522), but the accompanying *Annotationes* make it clear that he suspected the clause to be no more than a translation from the Vulgate Latin. Robert Estienne's editions of the Greek New Testament likewise accepted the text as supplied in the manuscript shown to Erasmus and so it continued to appear in Greek New Testaments well into the eighteenth century.

Translations from Hebrew

Latin translations of the Old Testament were considerably less controversial than Erasmus's New Testament. Besides the translations in the Complutensian Polyglot, Giustiniani's Genoa Psalter, and Felix of Prato's Psalter, Latin versions of the Hebrew Proverbs were published by an obscure English Hebraist, Robert Shirwood (Antwerp, 1523) and by Philip Melanchthon (Hagenau, 1525, with many reprints). A widely influential new translation of the Hebrew Bible was made by the Dominican Santi Pagnini, an exact contemporary of Giustiniani (Dahan 2018; Grendler 2008). Pagnini, a native of Lucca, lived in the convent of San Marco in Florence under Savonarola in the 1490s, taught in Rome in the late 1510s, and moved to Lyons in the 1520s. While in Rome, he worked on an elaborate Hebrew–Aramaic-Greek Psalter that included both Jewish and Christian commentaries. Its printing was financed by Leo X, but stopped, far short of completion, at the pope's death in late 1523: only two copies survive of the sheets that had already been printed. Pagnini's translation of the Old Testament from Hebrew was published as part of a full Bible in Lyons in 1528, under papal privilege and with financial support from the Giunta firm in Florence. Its size is intermediate (about 25 × 17 cm): it uses larger Median paper than a normal quarto. The paper itself is of poor quality, and the pages are rather crowded. Pagnini, a learned humanist, kept his Latin version as close as practicable to the Hebrew words and word order, making it a valuable reference tool for students. The books of the Old Testament were printed in Vulgate order, each headed with a statement that Pagnini was its translator. The deuterocanonical books of the Septuagint follow in a separate section, with a Vulgate text which was revised by Pagnini. The New Testament is Erasmus's version, with occasional modifications. An innovation of the Pagnini Bible was the numbering of subsections of chapters, often closer to paragraph than verse numbering. The appended index of Hebrew and Greek names, however, is keyed to the older A–G chapter divisions even though these are not printed in the Bible.

A second influential translation of the Hebrew Bible was published six years later in Basle (1534–35). This was a two-volume Hebrew–Latin Old Testament, in a version by Sebastian Münster, a former Franciscan turned Lutheran who besides being a Hebrew scholar had a second, overlapping scholarly career as cosmographer and geographer (Shuali 2018). The Münster Old Testament is a stately and handsome tall folio. It presents the books in the order of the Hebrew Bible, not the Vulgate. Daniel and Esther include only the Hebrew (and Aramaic) chapters, omitting the Septuagint addenda, and the deuterocanonical books are not present. At the end of each chapter, Münster added notes largely drawn from the major rabbinic commentaries. Münster's translation itself was reprinted in Zurich in 1539, as the chief component of a full Bible which added the deuterocanonical books from the interlinear Latin version in the Greek column of the Complutensian Polyglot and the New Testament in Erasmus's version. This was the first full Latin Bible consisting solely of "modern" translations.

Robert Estienne and Gobelinus Laridius

Although the first decades of the sixteenth century saw a proliferation of new Latin biblical versions, only two figures undertook significant critical investigation of the Vulgate text itself. One was Robert Estienne, one of the great scholar-printers of the century. The other, Gobelinus Laridius, was an obscure Carthusian whose name is buried within his own edition, and whose textual investigations went unnoticed in his time, being brought to light only in the twentieth century.

The preface to the first of Estienne's three large-format Bibles (1528) states that he began his research in 1524, when he collated the readings of two ancient Bibles at the convent of Saint-Germain-des-Prés in Paris (an easy walk from his shop) and another at Saint-Denis. He also consulted the Complutensian Polyglot and a variety of other printed Bibles, compiling a notebook of variants which he compared to a thirteenth-century *correctorium*. In the printed text of the Vulgate Old Testament, Estienne used a wedge-shaped obelus to mark words and passages not present in the Hebrew, and an asterisk for passages omitting words from the Hebrew. In the preface to his next edition, of 1532, Estienne gave a more lengthy explanation of his labors and methods. In addition to numerous small corrections, he made the obelus and asterisk more conspicuous by putting the marks both within the main text and in the margins where they would be easily spotted. Both these editions present the books in the order of the earlier printed editions and retain most of the Old Testament prologues. The traditional prologues to the Gospels were replaced by the relevant brief chapters of Jerome's *De uiris illustribus*, which also supplied prologues for Paul, James, Peter, and Jude, while those before Acts and Revelation were omitted. Estienne constructed a new and very clear index of names, replacing the traditional *Interpretationes nominum Hebraicorum*. Both editions are beautifully designed and produced, but with differing layouts. The

1528 edition is a folio on Super-Median paper (about 36 × 25 cm), printed in double columns of sixty-one lines. The 1532 edition is a folio on Royal paper (about 41 × 28 cm), printed in fifty-four long lines per page: this provided ample room for notes in smaller type in both margins. The preface of Estienne's Royal 1540 Vulgate Bible, a typographic masterpiece, acknowledged that the editorial markings of his preceding editions had created controversy. Having consulted the theology faculty of Paris, he provided a list of all the manuscripts and printed editions he had used. These included five manuscripts at Saint-Germain-des-Prés, two at Saint-Denis, and the Sorbonne's thirteenth-century *correctorium*, as well as the Complutensian Polyglot, a Basle edition "in minute types" (presumably Froben's 1495 octavo), and the 1462 Mainz Bible of Johann Fust and Peter Schoeffer. Several of these sources are cited in the apparatus of the Oxford, Roman, and Stuttgart Vulgates, placing Estienne's 1540 Vulgate at the head of a line of scholarly printed editions; his 1528 and 1532 editions are reported in the apparatus of the Roman Vulgate, where their readings often point toward the Sixtine and Clementine Vulgates.

The editorial work of Laridius (also known as Gobelinus Speck), a Carthusian who was elected prior of the Mainz Charterhouse in 1523, is embodied in a folio Vulgate printed in Cologne in 1530 (Vaccari 1958; Quentin 1922). This is a book of old-fashioned appearance, printed in Rotunda rather than Roman type. The anonymous preface, which makes no mention of Gobelinus's religious credentials, praises his revision of the Old Testament, saying that he had consulted no fewer than fifteen manuscripts in Latin and Hebrew (although no details of these are provided), and explains his editorial method. Words and passages found in Vulgate manuscripts but not the original languages are printed in smaller Roman type; those supported neither by the sources nor by ancient Vulgate manuscripts are omitted, either silently or with a marginal note. Although this practice is continued in the New Testament, it is not clear whether these revisions were by Gobelinus, who is credited only for work on the Old Testament.[3]

The contrast in presentation between Estienne's editions and that of Gobelinus is evident in Proverbs, whose text in the Paris Bible and many earlier witnesses contains numerous interpolations translated from the Septuagint. Most of these had already been marked in the *correctoria* as lacking a Hebrew basis, but the Gutenberg Bible and its descendants did not expunge them. Giunta's 1511 edition printed about one-third of these without annotation, while the others are marked with an *Alias* note in the margin (see above). Estienne includes all of them, but with notes that they are found neither in Hebrew nor in in ancient Vulgate witnesses. Gobelinus's text puts the first of the interpolations in Roman type, but then omits the remainder without note. As Gobelinus's edition escaped the notice of later sixteenth-century editors, the Sixtine and Clementine Vulgates retain all but two of the interpolations. It was only in the early twentieth century that the textual significance of this 1530 Bible of unremarkable appearance was noticed. Henri Quentin, the first editor of the Roman Vulgate, observed that

---

[3] The Johannine Comma is printed without demarcation: a Greek text for this clause would have been present in the Complutensian Polyglot and, from 1522 onward, Erasmus's New Testament.

Gobelinus had in many places modified the Vulgate text of his day in favor of readings attested in some of the most ancient witnesses. This edition thus anticipates many of the editorial decisions in modern Vulgates: its readings are regularly noted in the apparatus of the Roman Vulgate, even though it represents a scholarly path not taken by others for several centuries.

Indices of Proscribed Books

In the early 1540s, in the eyes of the theology faculties of Catholic universities, no edition of the Vulgate Bible was to be positively recommended, but there were many to be condemned. In Paris, Robert Estienne came under the greatest scrutiny, but he had been protected since obtaining the king's warrant in 1539. On the death of François I early in 1547, open attempts to censure Estienne led him to move his printing enterprise from Paris to Geneva. According to Estienne's own account, he had been under attack by Paris theologians since 1522. The theology faculty appears to have been divided, since Estienne's editions all bear royal privileges that depended on approbation by the university; a feature of his 1540 edition, as noted above, was his consultation with the faculty on how to present the variants. The first printed index of books censured by the Paris theologians was published in August 1544. It gave no attention to Latin Bibles, although it did feature the Paraphrases of the New Testament by Erasmus, which the faculty had condemned in 1527 (De Bujanda 1985).

After the Paris index appeared, the theology faculty at Louvain wrote to their French counterparts to express their surprise that Estienne's Bibles had been omitted. They published their own index in the summer of 1546, with Latin Bibles at the top of the list (De Bujanda 1986). Twenty-five editions were specified, including Estienne's 1532 and 1540 editions, along with many "others of the same kind." The preface refers to editions whose biblical text was corrupted, and those such as Estienne's, whose high-quality text was embedded within prefaces, notes, and indexes whose orthodoxy had not been verified. The Louvain index does not include the Bible of Gobelinus Laridius, but it does interdict a Cologne Bible of the previous year published by Peter Quentell. This 1529 edition contains a large number of notes referring to the Hebrew text, contributed by Petrus Ubelius: most of these notes are no more than suggested alternative translations of specific words, and it is hard to imagine that this edition would truly have been heterodox. In fact, the problem with Latin Bibles in the eyes of Catholic defenders of the faith reflected the situation of Bible publishing from Gutenberg onward. No edition had ever been created under ecclesiastical authority, with the only possible exceptions being the polyglot projects supported by Leo X. Essentially, all decisions to print Latin Bibles, as was true of hundreds of other titles of all kinds, were commercial, not ecclesiastical.

In 1547, the first Latin Bible acceptable to the Louvain theologians was published under imperial privilege, edited by John Henten (see chap. 19). His preface specifically noted Estienne's editions, which he characterized as being excellent in their text but damaged by the paratextual insertions. Henten's edition, however, is almost entirely a reprint of the 1540 Estienne edition, retaining its obeli and asterisks but not the marginal references. Although more than thirty additional manuscripts consulted by Henten are listed, there is little evidence that these significantly influenced his text. The only major innovation was a new subject index, as Estienne's own index would have been doctrinally suspect. Proof of the Louvain edition's textual heritage is its treatment of the Prayer of Manasseh, printed after 2 Chronicles. In 1540, Estienne announced that he had found the Greek text of this prayer in a codex at the Augustinian convent of Saint-Victor in Paris.[4] Accordingly, he revised the Latin text according to the Greek, printing them side by side. Estienne's Latin version appeared not only in Henten's edition but also in the Clementine Vulgate and hundreds of later editions (Schneider 1960). The original Latin version was not reedited until the Stuttgart Vulgate of 1969. As with other examples cited in this chapter, this curious case shows how formative and long-lasting were the effects of the first century of the printing of Latin Bibles.

BIBLIOGRAPHY

Andrist, Patrick. 2018. "Érasme 1514–1516 et les étapes de la préparation du texte biblique et les prologues grecs du Novum Instrumentum: le témoignage des manuscrits." In *La Bible de 1500 à 1535*, edited by Gilbert Dahan and Annie Noblesse-Rocher, 135–95. Turnhout: Brepols.

Bedouelle, Guy. 2008. "Attacks on the Biblical Humanism of Jacques Lefèvre d'Etaples." In *Biblical Humanism and Scholasticism in the Age of Erasmus*, edited by Erika Rummel, 117–41. Leiden: Brill.

Carbajosa, Ignacio, and Andrés García Serrano, eds. 2014. *Una Biblia a varias voces: Estudio textual de la Biblia políglota Complutense*. Madrid: Ediciones Universidad San Dámaso.

Dahan, Gilbert. 2018. "La Bible de Santi Pagnini (1528)." In *La Bible de 1500 à 1535*, edited by Gilbert Dahan and Annie Noblesse-Rocher, 261–81. Turnhout: Brepols.

Dahan, Gilbert, and Annie Noblesse-Rocher, eds. 2018. *La Bible de 1500 à 1535*. Turnhout: Brepols.

De Bujanda, J. M., Francis M. Higman, and James K. Farge, eds. 1985. *Index des Livres Interdits, I: Index de l'Université de Paris 1544, 1545, 1547, 1549, 1551, 1556*. Geneva: Droz.

De Bujanda, J. M., and Léon-E. Halkin, eds. 1986. *Index des Livres Interdits, II: Index de l'Université de Louvain 1546, 1550, 1558*. Geneva: Droz.

Doležalová, Lucie. 2013. "The Summarium Biblicum: A Biblical Tool both Popular and Obscure." In *Form and Function in the Late Medieval Bible*, edited by Eyal Poleg and Laura Light, 163–84. Leiden: Brill.

Gordon, Bruce, and Euan Cameron. 2016. "Latin Bibles in the Early Modern Period." In *New Cambridge History of the Bible: Vol. 3. From 1450 to 1750*, edited by Euan Cameron, 187–216. Cambridge: Cambridge University Press.

Grendler, Paul F. 2008. "Italian Biblical Humanism and the Papacy, 1515–1535." In *Biblical Humanism and Scholasticism in the Age of Erasmus*, edited by Erika Rummel, 227–76. Leiden: Brill.

---

[4] Schneider (1960) suggests, following Volz, that this manuscript is Paris, BnF, suppl. gr. 188, a thirteenth-century psalter which contains this prayer on fol. 147v.

Gumbert, J. P. 1999. "The Layout of the Bible Gloss in Manuscript and Early Print." In *The Bible as Book: The First Printed Editions*, edited by Paul Saenger and Kimberley Van Kampen, 7–13. London: The British Library & Oak Knoll Press.

Hobbs, Gerald. 2018. "The Two Polyglot Psalters of 1516." In *La Bible de 1500 à 1535*, edited by Gilbert Dahan and Annie Noblesse-Rocher, 97–116. Turnhout: Brepols.

Light, Laura. 1994. "French Bibles c.1200–30: A New Look at the Origin of the Paris Bible." In *The Early Medieval Bible: Its Production, Decoration and Use*, edited by Richard Gameson, 155–76. Cambridge: Cambridge University Press.

Light, Laura. 2012. "The Thirteenth Century and the Paris Bible." In *New Cambridge History of the Bible: Vol. 2. From 600 to 1450*, edited by Richard Marsden and E. Ann Matter, 380–91. Cambridge: Cambridge University Press.

Martín Abad, Julián. 1999. "The Printing Press in Alcalá de Henares: the Complutensian Polyglot Bible." In *The Bible as Book: The First Printed Editions*, edited by Paul Saenger and Kimberley Van Kampen, 101–15. London: The British Library & Oak Knoll Press.

McDonald, Grantley. 2016. *Biblical Criticism in Early Modern Europe: Erasmus, the Johannine Comma and Trinitarian Debate*. Cambridge: Cambridge University Press.

Needham, Paul. 1985a. "The Paper Supply of the Gutenberg Bible." *Papers of the Bibliographical Society of America* 79: 303–74.

Needham, Paul. 1985b. "Division of Copy in the Gutenberg Bible: Three Glosses on the Ink Evidence." *Papers of the Bibliographical Society of America* 79: 411–26.

Needham, Paul. 1986a. "The Cambridge Proof Sheets of Mentelin's Latin Bible." *Transactions of the Cambridge Bibliographical Society* 9: 1–35.

Needham, Paul. 1986b. "A Gutenberg Bible Used as Printer's Copy by Heinrich Eggestein in Strassburg, ca, 1469." *Transactions of the Cambridge Bibliographical Society* 9: 36–75.

Needham, Paul. 1987. "The Text of the Gutenberg Bible." In *Trasmissione dei Testi a Stampa nel Periodo Moderno* II, edited by Giovanni Crapulli, 43–84. Rome: Ateneo.

Needham, Paul. 1999. "The Changing Shape of the Vulgate Bible in Fifteenth-Century Printing Shops." In *The Bible as Book: The First Printed Editions*, edited by Paul Saenger and Kimberley Van Kampen, 53–70. London: The British Library & Oak Knoll Press.

Needham, Paul. 2006. "The 1462 Bible of Johann Fust and Peter Schøffer (GW 4204): A Survey of Its Variants." *Gutenberg-Jahrbuch* 81: 19–49.

Powitz, Gerhardt 2009. "Der Text der Gutenberg–Bibel im Spiegel seiner zeitgenössischen Rezeption." *Gutenberg-Jahrbuch* 84: 29–70.

Powitz, Gerhardt. 2012. "Die Tabula rubricarum der Gutenberg–Bibel." *Gutenberg-Jahrbuch* 87: 31–52.

Quentin, Henri. 1922. *Mémoire sur l'établissment du texte de la Vulgate. I. Octateuque*. Rome: Desclée.

Rummel, Erika, ed. 2008. *Biblical Humanism and Scholasticism in the Age of Erasmus*. Leiden: Brill.

Saenger, Paul 1999. "The Impact of the Early Printed Page on the Reading of the Bible." In *The Bible as Book: The First Printed Editions*, edited by Paul Saenger and Kimberley Van Kampen, 21–51. London: The British Library & Oak Knoll Press.

Schneider, Heinrich. 1954. *Der Text der Gutenbergbibel, zu ihrem 500jährigen Jubiläum untersucht*. Bonn: Peter Hanstein.

Schneider, Heinrich. 1960. "Der Vulgata-Text der Oratio Manasse: Eine Rezension des Robertus Stephanus." *Biblische Zeitschrift* 4: 277–82.

Shuali, Eran. 2018. "La Bible hébraïque de Sébastien Münster (1534–1535)." In *La Bible de 1500 à 1535*, edited by Gilbert Dahan and Annie Noblesse-Rocher, 283–98. Turnhout: Brepols.

Vaccari, Alberto. 1958. "Chi fu Gobelino Laridio, Ottimo Editore della Volgata nel Cinquecento?" In *Scritti di Erudizione e di Filologia, Volume Secondo*, 439–47. Rome: Storia e Letteratura. (First published in 1925.)

van Lopik, Teunis. 2020. "On the Earliest Printed Editions of the Vulgate with a Text-Critical Apparatus." In *At One Remove: The Text of the New Testament in Early Translations and Quotations*, edited by H. A. G. Houghton and Peter Montoro, 211–37. Piscataway: Gorgias.

Wallraff, Martin, Kaspar von Greyerz, and Silvana Seidel Menchi, eds. 2016. *Basel 1516: Erasmus' Edition of the New Testament*. Tübingen: Mohr Siebeck.

....

CHAPTER 19

THE COUNCIL OF TRENT AND THE SIXTO-CLEMENTINE VULGATE

....

ANTONIO GERACE

THE VULGATE IN THE SIXTEENTH CENTURY
....

> Only from the beginning of the sixteenth century was it [the word Vulgate] used to designate the commonly encountered content of Latin Bibles, which had been more or less stable since the first printing (at Mainz, c. 1450) and even before.
>
> (Bogaert 2012: 69)

BECAUSE of its role in Western Christianity over many centuries, the "commonly encountered content of Latin Bibles" had attained prestige; however, because of that same long history, this was countered by the presence of scribal mistakes. Errors in the many hundreds of copies stemmed from a variety of reasons: these included mistakes in transcription as a result of poor knowledge of Latin or carelessness, and sometimes deliberate interventions in order to amend the language of the text or even to change its meaning. In other words, the history of the Vulgate provides proof of its authority as well as proof of its unreliability, which led to the medieval masters, who were mainly based in Paris, making attempts to amend the biblical text during the course of the thirteenth century, providing the so-called *correctoria* (see chap. 16).

Further emendations were undertaken in the fifteenth and sixteenth centuries. Lorenzo Valla (1407–57) was one of several early modern scholars who ventured to emend the Vulgate while calling into question its reliability (Rex 2016). In 1516, the influential Dutch humanist Erasmus of Rotterdam (1466–1536) made his first translation of the New Testament from a few Greek codices (Metzger and Ehrman 2005: 143–45). The Italian biblical scholar Santi Pagnini (1470–1541) contributed a translation of the Old

Testament directly from Hebrew to Latin in 1527, while Robert Estienne himself drew upon both Greek and Hebrew sources in his 1528, 1532, and 1540 editions of the Bible (see chap. 18). Eventually, the Spanish orientalist Benito Arias Montano (1527–98) "regarded the Vulgate a philological absurdity" (Rekers 1972; 49; see also Voet and Voet-Grisolle 1980–83: I, 280–315; Wilkinson 2007: 67–75).

In addition to the *ad fontes* approach of the humanists, who criticized the "barbarian" Latin of the Bible, another challenge to the Vulgate was posed by the Reformation, which brought with it new vernacular translations and even "Protestant" Latin editions (Gordon 2017; see chap. 21). These various scriptural versions were soon made widely available thanks to the invention of the printing press. This led directly to a proportionate increase in the number of typographical mistakes and deliberate corrections, causing huge discrepancies among printed Bibles (Rongy 1927/28: 22) in addition to their differences from manuscript sources.

Traditionalist theologians strongly disapproved of the humanists' criticism of the Vulgate, and continued firmly to maintain the authoritative character of the Vulgate in the Western Church. The University of Louvain was one of the most notable institutions where such scholars endeavored to minimize the impact of the humanists' perspective on the Latin Bible while maintaining the importance of studying Greek and Hebrew, in addition to Latin, in order to gain a deeper understanding of the Scriptures. In essence, this university reemphasized the fundamental reliability of the Vulgate as the solid foundation of the Catholic faith. Among the most important Louvain theologians, mention should be made of Jacobus Latomus (1475–1544), the Franciscan Frans Titelmans (1502–37) who was an opponent of Erasmus's work (Sartori 2008: 215–23), and John Driedo (1480–1535; see Gielis 2008). In particular, Driedo's views on the Vulgate—and Bible versions in general—were gathered in his *De ecclesiasticis scripturis et dogmatibus* (1533), which inspired the Council Fathers during the Fourth Session (François and Gerace 2018).

Following Luther's claim of *sola Scriptura* ("Scripture alone"), Roman Catholicism felt the need of a means of reclaiming the Scriptures. Soon after the end of the Third Session of the Council of Trent, on February 4, 1546, at which the *Decretum de Symbolo Fidei* ("Decree touching the Symbol of Faith") was issued, the General Congregation started preparing the Fourth Session on Scripture and Traditions. At the end of this session, two decrees were issued, the first was the *Decretum de Canonicis Scripturis* ("Decree concerning the Canonical Scriptures") and the second was the *Decretum de Editione et Usu Sacrorum Librorum* ("Decree concerning the Edition and the Use of the Sacred Books"). The latter is also known by its first word as the *Insuper* ("Moreover") decree, and records the declaration by the Fourth Session of the Vulgate as the "authentic" version of the Sacred Scriptures for Catholics. This was a milestone in the history of the Latin Bible, leading to decades of text-critical study in order to produce the official version of the Scriptures for the Roman Church. Its result was the Sixto-Clementine Vulgate of 1592, which held this position until the adoption of the *Nova Vulgata* in the Apostolic Constitution *Scripturarum Thesaurus* issued on April 25, 1979 (see chap. 25).

TRIDENTINE DISCUSSIONS AND DECREES ON SCRIPTURE

The discussions leading to the Fourth Session of the Council of Trent were opened on February 8, 1546. The first point was the reception of the canon of Scripture, although an additional issue was underlined: abuses related to the use of the Bible. On March 1, the Council Fathers started analyzing these abuses. To do so, they were divided into three groups of cardinals, called *classes*, led respectively by the three Papal legates, Giovanni Maria Ciocchi del Monte (1532–77; the future Pope Julius III), Marcello Cervini (1501–55; the future Pope Marcellus II), and Reginald Pole (1500–58). Only the records of Cervini's group are available, but through them it is possible to have an idea of the challenges that the cardinals had to face before the issue of the *Insuper* decree.

The first abuse to have been identified was the presence of editions of the Bible that did not "conform" or were even "corrupted."[1] In order to solve this problem, Cervini's *classis* considered the humanistic *ad fontes* approach: to emend the Latin Old Testament, reference to the Hebrew text was deemed necessary, although Greek sources were the basis for the correction of the Latin New Testament. The Council Fathers did, indeed, ask for both the creation of a committee of experts in the three biblical languages and the collection of all the possible ancient Latin sources, "not because we doubt the translation of St Jerome and other doctors and saints, but in order that the emendation of corrupted and distorted places may be improved" by the comparison of many examples.[2] It was precisely because the authority of the Vulgate had been questioned, as well as the number of editions in circulation of the Scriptures in Hebrew, Greek, Latin, or in the vernaculars (cf. François 2018; Engammare 2008), that the Tridentine Fathers had to decide which edition would be the definitive Bible for the Roman Catholic Church.

The second abuse was the distorted interpretation of the Scriptures, which could be fixed only by determining "which sense is Catholic and which is not."[3] Third, Cervini's group pointed out the need for strict control over printing and selling the Bible, with the aim of avoiding the circulation of "unfaithful" editions. Marginal notes in Bible editions could be accepted, but only if previously approved by censors (CT V: 22, 28–31). The question arose whether vernacular translations of the Scriptures should also be provided (Agten and François 2018). The fourth abuse was related to the preaching of the Scriptures, focusing on who (*qui*) could preach, where (*in quo loco*), what (*quae*), how (*quomodo*), and how often (*quotiens*) (CT V: 23, 1–49).

---

[1] *Non omnes textus sunt conformes, immo plures sunt corrupti* (Concilium Tridentinum [CT] V: 22, 12).

[2] *Quantum ad translationem, habeantur et colligantur tot antiqui translatores, aliter dicti interpretes, quot haberi potuerunt, non quod dubitemus de translatione B. Hieronymi et aliorum doctorum ac sanctorum, sed ut emendatio ipsa circa loca corrupta et depravata melius fieri possit* (CT V: 22, 18–21).

[3] *Ideo determinetur, quis scripturae sensus sit catholicus et quis non* (CT V: 22, 22–24).

On March 17, 1546, the General Congregation discussed the four abuses related to the use of the Bible, in a slightly different order to those of Cervini's *classis*. The solution to the first one (the presence of many editions of the Bible) was "to have only one edition, namely, the ancient and common one, which all would use as authentic" in the Catholic Church.[4] This declaration shows the practicality of the solution: the expression "ancient and common" (*vetus et vulgata*) is—implicitly—in clear opposition to other versions of the Scriptures, whether they be new or less widespread. Among the former, the Congregation had in mind those produced since the development of the printing press, while the latter could include ancient editions such as Old Latin versions or the Septuagint itself. In fact, the Septuagint was also deemed by the Congregation to be authoritative, as a "pure and true translation" sometimes used by the Apostles, and other editions were accepted "insofar as they assist with understanding the authentic one."[5] The purpose was therefore to provide uniformity within the Catholic Church by establishing one Bible text as official, not only for preaching and liturgy but also as a reference source for exegesis. However, as the Council Fathers went on to point out, manuscripts of the "ancient and common edition" incorporated a variety of errors: the solution to this (now defined as the second abuse) was a careful emendation of the Latin text, with the intention of having also both a Greek and a Hebrew edition of the Sacred Scriptures (CT V: 29, 14–21).

The third abuse was the idiosyncratic interpretation of the Bible. The obvious solution was to follow only the sense of the Scriptures as given by the Church and the consensus of the Church Fathers (CT V: 29, 22–31). The fourth abuse was the publication of Bible editions without the formal permission of the Church, including those with paratextual elements such as marginal annotations or explanations which could combine (*miscere*) interpretations accepted by the Church with others that were not. The remedy was therefore to make the "ancient and common edition" uniform throughout the Catholic world through strict control over printing and selling the Bible (CT V: 30, 5–9).

On March 23, the three *classes* of cardinals and bishops gathered again for further discussions. Eventually, the Bishop of Fano, Pietro Bertani (1501–58), brought the meeting to a close, maintaining that the *Vulgata* was ancient (*antiqua*), and was always (*semper*) the version of the Bible used by the Church since Jerome and its author was the Holy Spirit.[6] The Vulgate was therefore received as "authentic," but it was again underlined that this did not mean that the "other" versions were to be rejected.

[4] *Remedium est, habere unicam tantum editionem, veterem sc. et vulgatam, qua omnes utantur pro authentica in publicis lectionibus, disputationibus, expositionibus et praedicationibus* (CT V: 29, 7–11).

[5] *[N]on detrahendo tamen auctoritati purae et verae interpretationis septuaginta interpretum, qua nonnumquam usi sunt apostoli, neque reiiciendo alias editiones, quatenus authenticae illius intelligentiam iuvant* (CT V: 29, 11–13).

[6] In fact, in his Third Diary of the Council, Bishop Angelo Massarelli (1510–66) noted that during the *classis* of March 23, Bertani maintained that the Church always used the Vulgate, and—anachronistically—even Christ and his disciples used it (*hac vulgata hoc modo semper usa est ecclesia, immo Christus ipse et discipuli ea usi sunt*, CT I: 527, 41–42). This was probably a confusion with the Septuagint.

Nonetheless, the Vulgate was considered superior to these, even though it was acknowledged that there was value in certain other versions, even among those produced by heretics. In any case, it was precisely the multitude of versions of the Bible which necessitated the determination of a single text to be used as "authentic." Bertani then pointed out the presence of *mendae* ("mistakes") within the text of the Vulgate, underlining that this problem could not be solved by the Council but, instead, was the concern of the Pontiff, who alone had the resources to provide for the emendation of the Vulgate (CT V: 37).

On April 3, 1546, the General Congregation reconvened to discuss the abuses and to define the last details of the decree. The Council Fathers expressed their views and eventually voted on specific questions by indicating *placet* ("approve") or *non placet* ("reject"). The first involved the possibility of printing books anonymously (CT V: 65, 25): no member assented to this except the Bishop of Worcester, Richard Pate (d. 1565). Concerning the possibility of having more than one edition of the Scriptures available on the market, as suggested by Reginald Pole (for whom the abuse was the consideration of any edition as "authentic" rather than the existence of other Bible editions), the Council Fathers were asked whether the decree should mention these and whether versions by heretics should be expressly rejected. In both cases, the members preferred to avoid any reference in the decree to editions other than the Vulgate (CT V: 65).

The question that led to the most discussion was the possibility of having the Vulgate available in different languages. Three options were placed before the Council Fathers. The first was to make the Bible available in any language (*in uno quoque idiomate*). This was the proposal of the Prince-Bishop of Trent, Cardinal Christopher Madruzzo (1512–78), who had asked the Fathers not to consider it to be an abuse to translate the Scriptures "into a mother language" (*in maternam linguam*; CT I: 37, 42). The second was to make it available in three languages, Hebrew, Greek, and Latin, as proposed by Girolamo Seripando (1493–1563), in line with the General Congregation's statement of March 17. The third was to accept only the Latin Vulgate, put forward by the Bishop of Jaén, Cardinal Pedro Pacheco Ladrón de Guevara (1488–1560). The last, most traditional, option eventually won the majority vote. In any case, the solution of the question regarding the authenticity of the Vulgate was difficult: if the Council unanimously wanted a single edition to be regarded as authentic, the choice of the Vulgate was not at all simple. Some members affirmed that "no Bible exists in Hebrew or in Latin which would be included under the name of a common edition (Vulgate)" which might lead to ridicule outside Catholicism; to this, however, other cardinals replied that the decree was intended for the Latin Church only.[7]

On April 5, the General Congregation discussed other abuses in the use of the Scriptures. First, Catholics were ignorant of the Bible's teachings, with some paying excessive attention to "profane literature" (CT V: 73–74). The remedy to this was

---

[7] *Addiderunt nonnulli, nullam esse neque apud Hebreos neque apud Latinos biblia, que sub nomine vulgate editionis comprehenderetur, et propterea facile fieri, ut esteri nostrum hunc decretum irriderunt. Non defuerunt qui dicerent, hoc decretum propter Latinos tantum fieri* (CT I: 44, 9–12).

the institution of Scripture classes wherever possible, such as schools, monasteries, convents, and cathedrals. In order for uneducated children and adults to have access to the Scriptures, the General Congregation asked for the publication of the Catechism either in Latin or in the vernacular, with the "authentic" Vulgate to be used as the source for biblical quotations. (The Catechism was duly published in 1566.) The next abuse concerned preaching, and the failure of many bishops and priests to observe their mandate to evangelize. The remedy was to ensure not only that bishops and priests themselves preach but also that they exercise a strict control over preachers who do not belong to the parish or the cathedral church, such as friars (CT V: 73–74). Third came the use of the Scriptures for divination and other "diabolical enchantments" (CT V: 75, 35–45), which was clearly illegal. The discussions continued over the next two days.

On April 8, both decrees were issued. The *Decretum de Canonicis Scripturis* set out the list of canonical books (CT V: 91, 15–27) which included the deuterocanonical ones rejected by Protestants, while the *Decretum de Editione et Usu Sacrorum Librorum* (the *Insuper* decree) declared the Vulgate the standard edition and called for the revision of its text:

> the old well known Latin Vulgate edition which has been tested in the Church by long use over so many centuries should be kept as the authentic text in public readings, debates, sermons and explanations; and no one is to dare or presume on any pretext to reject it ... the Council decrees and determines that thereafter the sacred Scriptures, particularly this ancient Vulgate edition, shall be printed after a thorough revision.[8]

From this point onward, the Vulgate was therefore regarded as the official version of the Catholic Church.

The correct interpretation of the adjective "authentic" (*authentica*) in the *Insuper* decree was the source of much debate during the sixteenth and seventeenth centuries (Brodrick 1928: I, 298). It continues to spark debate in modern scholarship (see chap. 26; and Letis 2002), with the question resting on whether such authenticity is solely "juridical" or also "critical" (Emmi 1953: 110). The discussions leading to the *Insuper* decree clarify that the Council mandated a single edition among others to be regarded as authoritative (cf. Allgeier 1940, 1948; Vosté 1947; Muñoz Iglesias 1946: 138). The Vulgate was considered *juridically* authentic, with normative power "to confirm dogmas, and restore morals in the Church" (Tanner and Alberigo 1990: 664–65). Such juridical authenticity had been acquired by its usage over many centuries, not by the critical accuracy of the text itself (Rongy 1927/28: 27; Muñoz Iglesias 1946: 143–44; Bellarmine in Le Bachelet 1911a: 112–13). It is worth noting that "authentic" has a specific juridical

---

[8] *Haec ipsa vetus et vulgata editio, quae longo tot saeculorum usu in ipsa Ecclesia probata est, in publicis lectionibus, disputationibus, praedicationibus et expositionibus pro authentica habeatur, ut nemo illam reiicere quovis praetextu audeat vel praesumat . . . decernit et statuit, ut posthac Sacra Scriptura, potissimum vero haec ipsa vetus et vulgata editio, quam emendatissime imprimatur* (translation from Tanner and Alberigo 1990: 664–65).

connotation: for instance, a few years after the *Insuper* decree, the Italian jurist Emilio Ferretti (1489–1552) states that "authentic" (*authenticum*) means "original" (*originale*), and therefore cannot be mistaken for "reproduction" (*exemplum*).[9] The Dutch jurist Antonius Matthaeus III (1635–1710) is even clearer than Ferretti, proclaiming that "What is authentic is the model (*exemplar*), not the reproduction (*exemplum*), although they are often confused with each other, and it is the model because many reproductions can be repeatedly produced from it."[10] Paraphrasing Ferretti and Matthaeus, we might say that the Council only viewed Jerome's original unaltered and uncorrupted translation as being juridically "authentic" (Gerace 2020: 223). As Muñoz Iglesias emphasizes, the Council could only consider the "critical" authenticity of the Vulgate *indirectly*, as the Vulgate did not contain dogmatic or moral errors; it could not be considered *directly* because it did contain scribal errors (Muñoz Iglesias 1946: 144). Eventually, the Vulgate was declared to be "authentic" only in comparison with the other Latin editions: the same approbation was not required for the Hebrew and Greek versions, as they were the sources, as explained by Robert Bellarmine (1542–1621).[11] This was partially confirmed during the General Congregation of March 17, 1546, when the Septuagint was regarded as "pure and true translation" (see above).

THE VULGATE AFTER THE COUNCIL
OF TRENT

Only one year after the promulgation of the *Insuper* decree, in November 1547, the University of Louvain responded to the Council's request for a new edition, in the form of the so-called *Vulgata Lovaniensis*. This was edited by John Henten (1499–1566), under the supervision of two Louvain theologians, Ruard Tapper (1480–1559) and Peter de Corte (1491–1567). The swift publication of this work can be explained by its complete reliance on Robert Estienne's 1540 edition, despite the fact that this work was listed in the *Index librorum prohibitorum* (1546) by the Louvain theologians (see chap. 18; and François et al 2020: 235). Henten followed Trent's decree to the letter and prudently opted for an edition based only on Latin sources: twenty-six manuscripts and one incunabulum (listed in Gerace 2020: 226). In this way, he could simultaneously follow the Council Fathers'

---

[9] *Authenticum est, quod originale alias appellatur . . . Distinguit multis in locis ius authenticum ab exemplo* (Aemilius Feretus, *In titulum de pactis, transactionibus, probationibus, fide instrumentorum, testibus, testamentis.* [Lyons: Bonhomme, 1553], 374).

[10] *Authenticum id exemplar, non exemplum, quanquam saepe confundantur, et exemplar idcirco, quod possint multa exempla ex eo iterum deduci* (Antonius Matthaeus, *De probationibus, de testibus, de fide instrumentorum et recognitione chirographi tractatus.* [Leyden: Lopez, 1686], 214–15).

[11] Robert Bellarmine, *De editione Latina Vulgata, quo sensu a Concilio Tridentino definitum sit, ut pro authentica habeatur* (1589–91); see Gerace 2020: 222. Bellarmine's work was first published in 1748 (see van Boxel 2006: 268, n. 75).

official instructions for an emended edition on the basis of the Latin Vulgate as the only "authentic" version of the Scriptures, while, on the other hand, indirectly making use of Greek and Hebrew sources by consulting Estienne's text-critical work in which those "original" biblical materials were in fact used (François et al. 2020: 236).

Henten's Vulgate was soon considered a work of reference, as is attested by its positive reception: after the *editio princeps* was printed in Louvain, it was widely reprinted in places such as Antwerp, Lyons, and Frankfurt-am-Main.[12] It should be noted that this Louvain Vulgate continued to be printed during the period when the Plantin Press in Antwerp was publishing the Polyglot *Biblia Regia* (1568–73). According to Hamilton, the latter "was regarded in many circles as an actual criticism of the Vulgate, and such a view was strengthened by the inclusion of Pagnini's translation of the Old Testament and Arias Montano's of the New" (2016: 147). The Spanish orientalist would have preferred to provide the Plantin Polyglot only with Pagnini's Latin translation, but in 1568 Philip II asked Arias Montano to include also the Vulgate, taken from the Complutensian Polyglot, precisely because of its authority in the Catholic Church (Cañas Reillo 2020: 216–17). In this way, the market had a choice between a more Trent-oriented Vulgate and a more humanist-minded Latin Bible. Henten's decision only to use Latin sources meant his Vulgate was warmly received in Rome, as testified by a private letter that Seripando sent to Cardinal Marco Antonio da Mula ("Amulio"), in June 1561 (Gerace 2016: 204, 2019: 43).

Amulio's commendation of Henten's Vulgate in 1561 followed the establishment that year of the first of five Roman Committees for the emendation of the Vulgate by Pius IV. This was composed of Amulio himself, Giovanni Gerolamo Morone (1509–80), Gianbernardino Scotti (1478–1568), and Vitellozzo Vitelli (1531–68).[13] However, a task of this kind was not easy, and other committees were subsequently established. In 1566, the second Committee was instituted by Pius V, with Jérôme Souchier (1508–71), Guglielmo Sirleto (1514–85), Cristoforo Madruzzo (1512–78), and Antonio Carafa (1538–91) among its members. While they were at work in Rome, the Louvain Faculty of Theology requested the revision of Henten's work by a young but talented scholar, Francis Lucas "of Bruges" (1548/49–1619).[14] Following Henten, and not to interfere with the work of the Roman Committee, Lucas opted for a simple republication of Henten's Vulgate, using the same accepted text, but he also undertook a comparison of the Latin with the Hebrew and Greek "originals." In the preface to the new *Vulgata Lovaniensis*, printed in 1574 by Plantin, Lucas stated that instead of changing the readings (*lectiones*), he chose to make notes in the margin where he disagreed with Henten.[15] This reflects

---

[12] Johannes Hentenius, ed., *Biblia. Ad vetustissima exemplaria nunc recens castigata . . .* (Louvain: Bartholomeus Gravius, 1547). The Universal Short Title Catalogue (USTC; https://www.ustc.ac.uk/ lists reprints in Antwerp in 1559, 1563, 1565, 1567, 1569, and 1570, in Lyons in 1569 and 1573, and in Frankfurt-am-Main in 1571: see Gerace 2020: 228.

[13] On the five Roman Committees, see Gerace 2020; Wicks 2008; Andreu 1987; Quentin 1922; and Höpfl 1913.

[14] On Lucas and his text-critical work on the Vulgate, see Gerace 2016, 2019: 50–74.

[15] Franciscus Lucas Brugensis, ed., *Biblia Sacra. Quid in hac editione Theologis Lovaniensibus praestitum sit, paulo post indicatur* (Antwerp: Christopher Plantin, 1574).

another of Lucas's projects, the *Notationes in Sacra Biblia*, a text-critical work that he claimed would show all the possible *lectiones* handed down during the centuries in the many biblical languages (Hebrew, Aramaic, Greek, and Latin for the Old Testament, and Greek, Syriac, and Latin for the New Testament).[16] In 1583, at Lucas's request, Plantin published his Vulgate accompanied by the *Notationes* in an appendix.[17]

Meanwhile, in 1578, at the suggestion of Cardinal Felice Peretti (1521–90), Gregory XIII had established a committee for the emendation of the Septuagint, under the supervision of Cardinal Carafa. The Vatican Septuagint edition was published in 1587 in Greek, and in 1588 in Latin (Andreu 1987: 82–84), after Peretti's elevation to the papacy as Pope Sixtus V (De Saint-Marie 1987: 61). Sixtus appointed committees for the emendation of the Hebrew Old Testament, under the supervision of Cardinal Marco Antonio Colonna, and for the emendation of the Greek New Testament, under the supervision of Robert Bellarmine (García-Moreno 1987: 54), in line with the proposals that the General Congregation had made on March 17, 1546 (see above). Moreover, Sixtus established the third Roman Committee on the Vulgate in 1586: this too was presided over by Cardinal Carafa and composed of five biblical scholars: Flaminio de' Nobili (Flaminius Nobilius, ca. 1532–90), Antonio Agelli (1532–1608), Lelio Landi (d. 1609), Bartholomé Valverde, and Pietro Morino (b. 1531).

Further evidence of the close relations between Louvain and Rome during these years can be found in the copy of Lucas's 1583 Vulgate that the third Committee used as its reference text for the emendation of the Vulgate, now known as Codex Carafianus (Vatican, BAV, Vat. lat. 12959–60). Carafa often appealed to the oldest known copy of the Latin Vulgate, Codex Amiatinus, to emend the parts of the Louvain edition with which he disagreed, together with other important manuscripts.[18] In 1588, the Committee presented its emended Vulgate to the Pope, who apparently "ordered [Carafa] out of the room with harsh words" (Brodrick 1928: I. 279; also Letis 2002: 17). The reason for Sixtus V's response has been attributed to the fact that the changes made were numerous (about ten thousand) but generally concerned style and more superficial details, and the Pope wanted to avoid publishing a text so drastically different from what was familiar to the faithful (De Saint-Marie 1987: 63–64; Andreu 1987: 86).

From November 1588 to November 1589, Sixtus worked together with Francisco de Toledo and Angelo Rocca on another Vulgate based on the Louvain text of 1583 (Andreu 1987: 87). In the Bull *Aeternus ille*, issued on March 1, 1590 (although it has been questioned whether it was formally promulgated) Sixtus declared his own *Vulgata Sixtina* as

---

[16] Franciscus Lucas Brugensis, *Notationes in sacra Biblia, quibus variantia discrepantibus exemplaribus loca, summo studio discutiuntur* (Antwerp: Christopher Plantin, 1580).

[17] Here I have the occasion to amend an earlier error (in Gerace 2016: 203). Two editions of the Louvain Vulgate were issued in 1583: it was not the former (entitled *Biblia sacra: quid in hac editione a Theologis Lovanienibus prestitum sit, paulo post indicatur*) but the latter (*Biblia Sacra, quid in hac editione a theologis Lovaniensibus praestitum sit, eorum praefatio indicat*) which had the *Notationes* in the appendix. I thank Gauvain Maffeo for this correction.

[18] On the codices used for the emendation, see Wicks 2008: 634; De Saint-Marie 1987: 62–63; Quentin 1922: 173–80; Höpfl 1913: 114. On the Third Committee, see Amann 1912: 28–44.

"authentic," and it was printed soon after (Balboni 1987).[19] The edition encountered much criticism in the few months before the death of the Pope on August 27, 1590 (De Saint-Marie 1987: 64–67). On September 5, 1590, the Congregation of Cardinals ordered the withdrawal of the *Sixtina* from the market: by 1594, almost all copies had been destroyed.[20]

The edition of the Vulgate required a further two years and two committees to be realized. Gregory XIV established the fourth Committee on the Vulgate on February 7, 1591, composed of four cardinals: Marco Antonio Colonna (1523–97), William Allen (1532–94), Federico Borromeo (1564–1631), and Agostino Valier (1531–1606). Later, the Pope invited additional members, thereby establishing the fifth and final Committee (Quentin 1922: 147–208; Andreu 1987: 68–97). On November 9, 1592, the Sixto-Clementine Vulgate was issued. Its designation reflected the official position that it was a simple emendation of the *Sixtina* (Le Bachelet 1911: 457–87; Amann 1912: 96; Gerace 2020: 234). According to Metzger and Ehrman (2005: 109), it featured just under five thousand alterations. In contrast to the Louvain Vulgate, the Sixto-Clementine edition included in an appendix the Prayer of Manasses, 3 Ezra, and 4 Ezra, specifying that these books were not part of the Tridentine canon but had been added since many Church Fathers made reference to them and they were present in manuscripts and printed Latin Bibles (see chap. 7). In this way, the Pontiff stressed the importance of tradition for the Roman Catholic Church—in clear contrast to Luther's *sola Scriptura*—by accepting noncanonical books which had been regarded as authoritative in earlier Christian tradition. At last, the request of the Council Fathers in 1546 had been fulfilled: the Roman Catholic Church had an official text of the Bible which could be used worldwide.

It has been questioned whether the Sixto-Clementine Vulgate should indeed be considered the "authentic" edition of the Vulgate, since it makes no formal claim to authenticity in its preface (Wicks 2008: 636). However, such a claim was hardly necessary, as the Council had clearly established the Vulgate's authority from a "juridical" point of view by referring to its doctrinal use "in public readings, debates, sermons, and explanations" in the *Insuper* decree (see above). Furthermore, the *Praefatio ad Lectorem* ("Preface to the Reader") in the Sixto-Clementine edition refers specifically to the Council of Trent, which "by a most weighty decree declared only the ancient and common edition, which had been approved by long use in the Church over many centuries, to be authentic" (*solam veterem ac vulgatam, quae longo tot saeculorum usu in Ecclesia probata fuerat, gravissimo Decreto authenticam declaravit*). From a "critical" perspective, the Sixto-Clementine must be considered the authentic version, since Clement VIII affirms "in perpetual memory" that his edition was "restored and purified of faults as accurately as

---

[19] The Jesuit Ferdinand Alber (1548–1617) maintained in 1609 that it was certain that the Bull was not promulgated, as Bellarmine also attested (see Amann 1912: 118); other positions are described in Andreu 1987: 91–92.

[20] See Balboni (1987: 110–16), who reproduces Baumgarten's list of forty surviving copies and adds further examples preserved in Genoa, Bologna, and Naples, without being aware of those preserved in Brescia, Messina, Modena, Monreale, Palermo, Perugia, and Trent (listed in the USTC). The full list of copies preserved in Italy is available on the Italian Online Public Access Catalogue https://opac.sbn.it/bid/RMLE005409.

possible" (*restitutus et quam accuratissime mendis expurgatus*; see Gerace 2019: 65, n. 64). This means that this Vulgate was considered to be faithful to Jerome's translation. As its text was thus in conformity with the original, it was seen as necessary to conserve it in precisely the same form, leading to what Jean-Pierre Delville called the "petrification" of the Vulgate (2008: 80; see also Gerace 2016: 224 and 2020: 234–36).

In order to ensure that no changes were made to the text of the Latin Bible, Clement VIII established a tight control over printing and selling the Vulgate—as suggested on March 1, 1546 by Cervini's *classis* to counter the third abuse—by imposing a ten-year ban, which meant that only the Vatican Press had the right to print and sell the Sixto-Clementine edition.[21] Only after this decade-long monopoly could the Vulgate be printed and sold elsewhere, and only then after having received a copy to use as a reference text directly from the Vatican, and on the condition that nothing would be changed within it.[22] Following the 1592 edition, the Vatican Press again published the Sixto-Clementine Vulgate in 1593 and 1598. Neither was free from typographical errors: the 1598 edition provides an *index corrigendorum*, following Clement VIII's *Ad perpetuam rei memoriam*, indicating the mistakes in the three editions (1592, 1593, and 1598) due to "the negligence of the workers."[23] The Sixto-Clementine Vulgate then remained the official Bible for the Catholic Church for almost four hundred years.

ACKNOWLEDGMENTS

I would like to thank Eliza Halling for checking the English of this chapter.

BIBLIOGRAPHY

Agten, Els, and Wim François. 2018. "The Council of Trent and Vernacular Bible Reading: What Happened in the Build-Up to and during the Fourth Session?" In *The Council of Trent: Reform and Controversy in Europe and beyond (1545-1700), 1: Between Trent, Rome and Wittenberg*, edited by Wim François and Violet Soen, 101–30. Göttingen: Vandenhoeck & Ruprecht.

Allgeier, Arthur. 1940. "Authentisch auf dem Konzil von Trient. Eine Wort- und Begriffsgeschichtliche Untersuchung." *Historische Jahrbuch* 60: 142–58.

Allgeier, Arthur. 1948. "*Haec vetus et vulgata editio*. Neue wort- und begriffsgeschichtliche Beiträge zur Bibel auf dem Tridentinum." *Biblica* 29: 353–90.

Amann, Fridolin. 1912. *Die Vulgata Sixtina von 1590: Eine quellenmässige Darstellung ihrer Geschichte, mit neuem Quellenmaterial aus dem Venezianischen Staatsarchiv*. Freiburg: Herder.

---

[21] The same ban was set out by Sixtus V in the Bull *Aeternus Ille*.

[22] In 1597, the Pope gave permission to the Plantin Press to print and sell the Sixto-Clementine edition on the basis of an exemplar from 1593: the first copies of the Antwerp Sixto-Clementine Vulgate were issued in 1599 (see Gerace, 2019: 64–67, 2016). The only other publishing house to print this edition before the end of the Vatican monopoly was the Venetian Giunta, which issued the Vulgate in 1600.

[23] *negligentia operarum*: see *Biblia sacra vulgatae editionis, Sixti V p.m. iussu recognita atque edita* (Rome: Stamperia Apostolica Vaticana, 1598).

Andreu, Francesco. 1987. "Il teatino Antonio Agellio e la Volgata Sistina." In *La Bibbia "Vulgata" dalle origini ai nostri giorni. Atti del simposio internazionale in onore di Sisto V. Grottamare, 29–31 agosto 1985*, edited by Tarcisio Stramare, 68–97. Vatican City: BAV.

Balboni, Dante 1987. "L'edizione a stampa della 'Vulgata' di Sisto V." In *La Bibbia "Vulgata" dalle origini ai nostri giorni. Atti del simposio internazionale in onore di Sisto V. Grottamare, 29–31 agosto 1985*, edited by Tarcisio Stramare, 107–17. Vatican City: BAV.

Baumgarten, Paul Maria. 1911. *Die Vulgata Sixtina von 1590 und ihre Einführungsbulle. Aktenstücke und Untersuchungen*. Münster: Aschendorff.

Bogaert, Pierre Maurice. 2012. "The Latin Bible, c. 600 to c. 900." In *New Cambridge History of the Bible: Vol. 2. From 600 to 1450*, edited by Richard Marsden and E. Ann Matter, 69–92. Cambridge: Cambridge University Press.

Brodrick, James. 1928. *The Life and Work of Blessed Robert Francis Cardinal Bellarmine*. 2 vols. London: Burns, Oates, and Washbourne.

Cañas Reíllo, José Manuel. 2020. "La Vulgata en las políglotas de Alcalá y de Amberes." In *La Vulgate au XVIᵉ siècle. Les travaux sur la traduction latine de la Bible.*, edited by Gilbert Dahan and Annie Noblesse-Rocher, 165–219. Turnhout: Brepols.

Concilium Tridentinum (CT). 1901–38. *Diariorum, Actorum, Epistularum, Tractatuum nova Collectio*. Freiburg im Breisgau: Societas Goerresiana.

Delville, Jean-Pierre. 2008. "L'évolution des Vulgates et la composition de nouvelles versions latines de la Bible au XVIᵉ siècle." In *Biblia: Les Bibles en latin au temps des Réformes*, edited by Marie-Christine Gomez-Géraud, 71–106. Paris: Presses de l'Université Paris-Sorbonne.

De Saint–Marie, Henri. 1987. "Sisto e la Volgata." In *La Bibbia "Vulgata" dalle origini ai nostri giorni. Atti del simposio internazionale in onore di Sisto V. Grottamare, 29–31 agosto 1985*, edited by Tarcisio Stramare, 61–67. Vatican City: BAV.

Emmi, Beniamino. 1953. "Il decreto tridentino sulla Volgata nei commenti della seconda polemica protestantico-cattolica." *Angelicum* 30: 107–30, 228–72.

Engammare, Max. 2008. "Un siècle de publication de la Bible en Europe: la langue des éditions des Textes sacrés (1455–1555)." *Histoire et Civilisation du Livre* 4: 47–91.

François, Wim. 2018. "Vernacular Bible Reading in Late Medieval and Early Modern Europe." *The Catholic Historical Review* 102: 23–56.

François, Wim, Benedict Fischer, Luke Murray, and Antonio Gerace, 2020. "The 'Golden Age' of Catholic Biblical Scholarship (1550–1650) and its Relation to Biblical Humanism." In *Renaissance-Humanismus: Bibel und Reformbewegungen des 15. und 16. Jahrhunderts und ihre Bedeutung für das Werden der Reformation*, edited by Herman Selderhuis, 217–74. Göttingen: Vandenhoeck & Ruprecht.

François, Wim, and Antonio Gerace. 2018. "Trent and the Latin Vulgate: A Louvain Project?" In *The Council of Trent: Reform and Controversy in Europe and Beyond (1545–1700), 1: Between Trent, Rome and Wittenberg*, edited by Wim François and Violet Soen, 131–74. Göttingen: Vandenhoeck & Ruprecht.

García-Moreno, Antonio. 1987. "Reflexiones en torno a la Sessión IV de Trento." In *La Bibbia "Vulgata" dalle origini ai nostri giorni. Atti del simposio internazionale in onore di Sisto V. Grottamare, 29–31 agosto 1985*, edited by Tarcisio Stramare, 40–60. Vatican City: BAV.

Gerace, Antonio. 2016. "Francis Lucas 'of Bruges' and Textual Criticism of the Vulgate before and after the Sixto-Clementine (1592)." *Journal of Early Modern Christianity* 3: 201–37.

Gerace, Antonio. 2019. *Biblical Scholarship in Louvain in the "Golden" Sixteenth Century*, Göttingen: Vandenhoeck & Ruprecht.

Gerace, Antonio. 2020. "1547–1592: Dalla *Vulgata Lovaniensis* alla Sisto-Clementina." In *La Vulgate au XVIᵉ siècle. Les travaux sur la traduction latine de la Bible*, edited by Gilbert Dahan and Annie Noblesse-Rocher, 221–38. Turnhout: Brepols.

Gielis, Marcel. 2008. "Louvain Theologians as Opponents of Erasmus and of Humanistic Theology," In *Biblical Humanism and Scholasticism in the Age of Erasmus*, edited by Erika Rummel, 197–214. Leiden: Brill.

Gordon, Bruce. 2017. "The Bible in the Reformation." *Archiv für Reformationsgeschichte* 108: 134–42.

Hamilton, Alastair. 2016. "In Search of the Most Perfect Text: The Early Modern Printed Polyglot Bibles from Alcalá (1510–1520) to Brian Walton (1654–1658)." In *New Cambridge History of the Bible: Vol. 3. From 1450 to 1750*, edited by Euan Cameron, 138–56. Cambridge: Cambridge University Press.

Höpfl, Hildebrand. 1913. *Beiträge zur Geschichte der Sixto-Klementinischen Vulgata*. Freiburg: Herder.

Le Bachelet, Xavier-Marie. 1911a. *Bellarmin et la Bible Sixto-Clémentine: étude et documents inédits*. Paris: Beauchesne.

Le Bachelet, Xavier-Marie. 1911b. *Bellarmin avant son cardinalat (1542–1598). Correspondance et documents*. Paris: Beauchesne.

Letis, Theodore P. 2002. "The Vulgata Latina as Sacred Text: What Did the Council of Trent Mean When It Claimed Jerome's Bible Was *Authentica*?" *Reformation* 7: 1–21.

Metzger, Bruce M., and Ehrman, Bart D. 2005. *The Text of the New Testament: Its Transmission, Corruption and Restoration*. 4th ed. Oxford: Oxford University Press.

Muñoz Iglesias, Salvador 1946. "El decreto tridentino sobre la Vulgata y su interpretación por los teólogos del siglo XVI." *Estudios Biblicos* 5: 137–69.

Quentin, Henri. 1922. *Mémoire sur l'établissement du texte de la Vulgate. Ière Partie. Octateuque*. Rome: Desclée; Paris: Gabalda.

Rekers, Bernard. 1972. *Benito Arias Montano (1527-1598)*. Leiden: Brill.

Rex, Richard. 2016. "Humanist Bible Controversies." In *New Cambridge History of the Bible: Vol. 3. From 1450 to 1750*, edited by Euan Cameron, 61–81. Cambridge: Cambridge University Press.

Rongy, Henri. 1927/28. "La Vulgate et le concile de Trent." *Revue ecclésiastique de Liège* 19: 19–31.

Sartori, Paolo. 2008. "Frans Titelmans, the Congregation of Montaigu, and Biblical Scholarship." In *Biblical Humanism and Scholasticism in the Age of Erasmus*, edited by Erika Rummel, 214–23. Leiden: Brill.

Stramare, Tarcisio, ed. 1987. *La Bibbia "Vulgata" dalle origini ai nostri giorni. Atti del simposio internazionale in onore di Sisto V. Grottamare, 29–31 agosto 1985*. Vatican City: BAV.

Tanner, Norman P., and Giuseppe Alberigo, eds. 1990. *Decrees of the Ecumenical Councils*. Washington: Georgetown University.

Van Boxel, Piet. 2006. "Robert Bellarmine, Christian Hebraist and Censor." In *History of Scholarship: A Selection of Papers from the Seminar on the History of Scholarship Held Annually at the Warburg Institute*, edited by Christopher Ligota and Jean-Louis Quantin, 251–75. Oxford: Oxford University Press.

Voet, Leon, and Jenny Voet-Grisolle. 1980–83. *The Plantin Press (1555-1589): A Bibliography of the Works Printed and Published by Christopher Plantin at Antwerp and Leiden*. 6 vols. Amsterdam: Van Hoeve.

Vosté, Jacques-Marie. 1947. "The Vulgate and the Council of Trent." *Catholic Biblical Quarterly* 9: 9–25.

Wicks, Jared. 2008. "Catholic Old Testament Interpretation in the Reformation and Early Confessional Eras." In *Hebrew Bible/Old Testament: Vol. 2. From the Renaissance to the Enlightenment*, edited by Magne Sæbø, 617–48. Göttingen: Vandenhoeck & Ruprecht.

Wilkinson, Robert J. 2007. *The Kabbalistic Scholars of the Antwerp Polyglot Bible*. Leiden: Brill.

CHAPTER 20

LATIN BIBLICAL SCHOLARSHIP IN THE HUMANIST AGE

WIM FRANÇOIS

BIBLICAL–HUMANIST SCHOLARSHIP IN SIXTEENTH-CENTURY CATHOLICISM

ALTHOUGH some had initial hesitations with regard to the biblical–humanist approach, numerous Catholic theologians engaged in text-critical study of the Bible (Hebrew, Greek, and especially Latin), which they made instrumental for the design of sound biblical commentaries, as well as Bible-based sermons. Their output equals or even surpasses that of their Protestant counterparts, even though there has been a tendency to overlook the results of this Golden Age of Catholic biblical scholarship. There is, nevertheless, a tradition of scholarship in textual criticism, biblical commentaries, and sermon books produced by early modern Catholic scholars, which will be the object of the first part of this chapter (see also Fischer et al. 2019; Wicks 2008; Gibert 2008; Bedouelle 1989).

In Italy, the Dominican friar Santi Pagnini (1470–1541) published a Latin Bible in 1528 with the support of Pope Leo X. His Latin translation of the Old Testament was directly based upon the Hebrew, while he largely used Erasmus's translation for the New Testament (Dahan 2018). Another Dominican, Thomas de Vio, called "Cajetan" (1469–1534) and a cardinal since 1517, was a notable precursor in Catholic biblical studies. Cajetan published an array of Bible commentaries, the first of which was the *Ientacula Novi Testamenti* (1525). His first aim in his commentaries was to give a new Latin translation of the Greek and Hebrew text, since he considered the Vulgate an imperfect rendering. He focused particularly upon the explanation of Scripture in its literal sense, taking into consideration the inspiration of the author, the context, and the interpretative tradition of patristic and medieval writers (especially Thomas Aquinas). In the spirit of the humanist approach, however, he did not fear to abandon traditional interpretations that were not sustained by a literal reading of the text, including allegorical approaches. Cajetan intended his fresh and daring approach to Scripture as the foundation of a genuine renewal of the Church and the education of the faithful to a real Christian life. His approach earned him the disapproval of his Dominican confrère Ambrosius Catharinus (Lancelot Politi), among others (O'Connor 2017).

Whereas Erasmus, Lefèvre, and even Cajetan were distrusted by an important block of theologians at the Faculty in Paris, other members of the same institution were less conservative. One of these was Jean de Gaigny or Gagny (d. 1549), who wrote several commentaries on New Testament books which were published in the 1540s and 1550s and frequently reprinted. Gaigny made use of the Greek as well as the Latin text, and from his commentary on the Psalms (1547), it may even be deduced that he (or his source) had a mastery of Hebrew. Even so, Gaigny's biblical work awaits proper scholarly research (Delville 2004: 352–57). In their private study, Catholic biblical scholars continued to consult and use the Bible in the original languages, notwithstanding the declaration of the Latin Vulgate as the "authentic" text of Scripture by the Council of Trent (see chap. 19). Indeed, the conciliar decrees provided significant impetus to the development of biblical studies in the Catholic Church across Europe, from the university milieux of Louvain and Douai in the northern borderlands with Bible-based Protestantism to the Jesuit Order in Spain and Catholic scholarly circles in Italy and France.

As a consequence of Trent's Fifth Session on June 17, 1546, the Emperor Charles founded a "royal" chair of Sacred Scripture that year in Louvain, as well as one of scholastic theology (François 2012: 247–62). Theology students in Louvain were keen to follow the language courses that were taught at the College of the Three Languages (*Collegium Trilingue*), established in 1517, notwithstanding the initial reserve of some professors in these early years (Papy 2018: 5–31). The most influential of Louvain's biblical scholars in this generation was Cornelius Jansen of Ghent (Jansenius the Elder, 1510–76), one of the theologians present at the Third Period of the Council of Trent who was later made the first Bishop of Ghent. As early as 1549, he published a gospel harmony, to which he added an influential commentary in 1571 which was reprinted across Europe for more than a century. In his biblical–humanist approach to the study of Scripture—to a large degree in common with his Protestant counterparts—Jansenius paid great attention to philological questions, relying upon the Greek and even Hebrew in order primarily to explain the literal sense of the text. For Jansen, word analysis was the way to discover the *scopus* of the Gospels, viz., the sense of the holy text as it was meant by the inspired writers. Jansen also took into consideration the context of each pericope and compared the versions in the various Gospels. He consulted the writings of the Church Fathers (mainly Chrysostom, Jerome, and Augustine), as well as the scholarship of his contemporaries, including Erasmus (Screech 1987, 1990) and even Protestant authors. Jansen had only a limited interest in the spiritual senses of Scripture, mentioning them simply as a tribute to tradition. He intended his work to have a pastoral application, for the use of parish priests in preaching. Jansen may thus be considered an exponent of genuine renewal within the Catholic Church following the Council of Trent (Gerace 2019: 129–49; Delville 2004: 474–87).

Another of Louvain's alumni was Andreas Masius (1514–73). On becoming a diplomat in the service of various German princes, he spent much time in Rome where he developed his knowledge of Oriental languages. He contributed to the Syriac part of Plantin's Polyglot Bible (1571–74) and wrote, as a Catholic layman, a commentary on the Book of Joshua (published 1574) which still has value in the present day, as it made use of an eighth-century manuscript of the Syro-Hexapla which is now lost. Masius, moreover, did not recoil from calling into question the authorship of the Pentateuch by Moses and the eponymous book of Joshua (François 2009; Van Roey 1978). In complete contrast was Thomas Stapleton (1535–98), an Elizabethan exile who taught controversialist theology and Scripture in Douai and, subsequently, in Louvain. He published a series of *Promptuaria* (1589–94), homiletic expositions intended to help fellow-clergymen in the preparation of their sermons, as well as *Antidota* (1595–98), academic commentaries on New Testament books meant as an antidote to the "venomous" commentaries of John Calvin and Theodore Beza. The commentaries of Stapleton show how the next generation of biblical scholars had taken their place in the Catholic Church: less rooted in genuine biblical–humanist scholarship, Stapleton characterized himself as a Molinist and defender of human free will in the process of salvation, against his Reformed adversaries and even his Catholic opponents who adhered to an anti-Pelagian Augustinian doctrine of grace. Stapleton's *Promptuaria* proved to be very popular in the first decades of the seventeenth century, especially in Germany, since they went through several reprints up until the eighteenth century (Gerace 2019: 160–75; Frymire 2010: 417–35).

In Italy, it was primarily the Dominican Order that continued the tradition of biblical studies (Füllenbach 2019). In addition to those mentioned above, the figure of Sixtus of Siena (1520–69) deserves further attention. His most important work is the *Bibliotheca sancta* (first printed 1566; several reprints until 1742). Divided into eight books, it contains the first distinction in early modern Catholicism between proto- and deutero-canonical writings, as well as consideration of biblical hermeneutics, commentaries on all books of the Old and New Testament, and discussions of controversialist theology. It makes manifold references to Hebrew and Greek. In this sense, the *Bibliotheca sancta* offers a kind of interim compendium of the totality of Catholic biblical studies, the first in its genre (Parente 2007: 207–13).

In France, the work of the Benedictine monk Gilbert Génébrard or Genebrardus (1535–97) should be mentioned. He was a specialist in Hebrew and rabbinic literature, who worked at the *Collège de France* from 1566 until 1591, after which he was appointed Archbishop of Aix-en-Provence. Génébrard wrote one of the finest commentaries on the Psalms, first published in 1577–78, along with one on the Prophet Joel (1563) and another on the Song of Songs (1570; repr. 1585). As in the case of Jean de Gaigny, these commentaries still await a thorough investigation (Kessler-Mesguich 1998: 357–73).

The first generation of Jesuits were generally enthusiastic about the contribution of rhetoric and linguistic studies to the explanation of Scripture, at the same time being more conservative about the blunt application of text-critical methods to the text of the

Vulgate. Among the many Jesuits who distinguished themselves in the field of biblical scholarship are the Spaniards Alfonso Salmerón (1515–85), Francisco de Toledo (1532–96), Benito Pereira (1535–1610), and Francisco de Ribera (1537–91) and the Portuguese Manuel de Sá (1530–96) (Reiser 2016: 76–79). Perhaps the most influential Jesuit biblical scholar of this generation was Juan Maldonado (1533–83). First active in Paris, he moved to Bourges, specifically Pont-à-Mousson, where he elaborated his biblical commentaries, for which he drew on his extensive knowledge of Greek, Hebrew, Aramaic, and Syriac. In addition to the Church Fathers and medieval masters, Maldonado demonstrably used Erasmus's *Annotationes* (Screech 1990: 351) and Protestant writers, with whom he entered into a controversy, especially when the doctrines of predestination, grace, and free will were at stake. His most popular biblical work was his *Commentarii in quatuor Evangelistas* ("Commentary on the Four Evangelists"), first published in 1596–97 and reprinted as late as the nineteenth century (Reventlow 2011: 201–9; Bedouelle 1989: 361–68).

Another very influential Jesuit is Robert Bellarmine (1542–1612). After joining the order in 1560, Bellarmine was sent to its study house in Louvain: in addition to his work on Thomas of Aquinas's *Summa*, he became immersed in the Bible-based approach practiced in the local theological milieu. In the biblical realm, Bellarmine is best known for his Hebrew grammar (1578) and for his *Explanatio in Psalmos* (1611). In the latter, Bellarmine frequently compares the Latin Vulgate with the Hebrew Bible and the Greek Septuagint, appealing to the Church Fathers in order to resolve problems raised by the existence of variant versions. The Fathers also play a crucial role in Bellarmine's Christological reading of the Psalms. Bellarmine's commentaries are never far away from the controversy with the Protestants, against whom he upholds the official teachings of the Church as well as the age and accuracy of the Septuagint, denouncing the superiority of the Masoretic text (Hobbs 2010; Wicks 2008: 646–48).

CATHOLIC BIBLICAL SCHOLARSHIP IN THE EARLY SEVENTEENTH CENTURY

With Bellarmine, we have arrived in the early seventeenth century, when Catholic biblical commentary reached its apogee. A delicate balance was maintained between text-critical approaches with interest in additional (Semitic) languages and textual traditions and due respect for the Vulgate and the doctrinal definitions of the Church. The two most influential Catholic Bible commentators of this era—measured by the amount of reprints of their works—were the Douai professor Guilielmus Estius (William Hessels van Est), and the Jesuit Cornelius a Lapide. Estius (1542–1613), a native of Holland, was educated at the University of Louvain, became professor in Douai and later President of the Royal Seminary there. His *Commentaries on All the Epistles of Paul and on the Canonical Letters*, published posthumously in two volumes in 1614 and 1616, proved to be very important (François 2014: 119–30). Cornelius a Lapide (1567–1637) published his commentary on the Epistles of Paul at the same time, in 1614, when teaching at the study house of his Order in Louvain. This interest in the Pauline Epistles was not a coincidence: their interpretation was at the core of the debates on predestination, grace, and free will which dominated controversy with Protestants as well as inner-Catholic debates (François 2012: 262–88). From 1616 until his death, A Lapide worked in Rome. As a result of his studies, commentaries on all the books of the Bible (with the exception of the Psalms and Job) were published (Fischer 2020; Murray 2019: 105–83; François 2017).

The methods used by Estius and A Lapide were quite similar. Although they had to accept that the Vulgate was the authoritative text of the Church, they nevertheless started their scrutiny of a biblical passage with a consideration of variant Latin text traditions, as well as the Greek "original" and Syriac versions, thus integrating the achievements of humanist text-critical scholarship. Their aim was to discover the historical-literal sense of the biblical passage under consideration, which they considered as the basis for the construction of a coherent theological reading. While Estius preserved a more rigid exegetical approach, he cherished an outspoken anti-Pelagian Augustino-Thomistic doctrine of predestination, grace, and free will. A Lapide, in contrast, held to Trent's mainstream theology, leaving more room for human cooperation with God's grace, and gave due consideration to the traditional spiritual senses of the text. This made his commentary far more suitable for homiletic purposes and pastoral exhortation. Cornelius a Lapide was by far the most successful Bible commentator of the Golden Age of Catholic biblical scholarship, and his commentaries were reprinted and used until well into the twentieth century.

Among the Jesuits, biblical scholarship was continued by Jacques Bonfrère (1573–1642), Giovanni Stefano Menochio (1575–1655), and Jacobus Tirinus (1580–1636), among others. In "Jansenist" circles in the North, biblical scholarship was held in high esteem and considered the core of theology and the renewal of the life of faith. Cornelius Jansen "of Ypres" (1585–1638), who lent his name to the movement—and should not be confused with the aforementioned Cornelius Jansen "of Ghent"—was professor in Louvain (1618) and held the royal chair of Sacred Scripture from 1630, before becoming Bishop of Ypres. His most important commentaries were published posthumously, especially his *Pentateuchus* (1641), as well as his *Tetrateuchus* or commentary on the four Gospels (1639), which were reprinted several times. They were popular in radical anti-Pelagian Augustinian or "Jansenist" milieux (François 2014: 130–35). Libertus Fromondus (1587–1653), a friend of Jansen and his successor as royal professor in Louvain, continued his work of commentary. His commentary on the Song of Songs appeared in 1653, bearing witness to an increased emphasis on mystical experiences and theology in Jansenist circles, whereas his commentary to the Acts of the Apostles (1654) was the most successful among his posthumous works (François 2014: 136–42; also Chédozeau 2007: 37–53).

The early seventeenth century also saw increased interest in more ancient biblical languages, such as the Syriac Old Testament, Arabic translations, and the so-called Samaritan Pentateuch and Targum. The integration of these texts in the Polyglot Bible of Paris (1628–45) was the work of Jean Morin (1591–1659), who was a professor at the *Collège de France*. Morin pointed to the correspondences between the Samaritan Targum and the Greek Septuagint, using these as an argument for the greater authenticity of the Septuagint (and the Vulgate!). Against the proponents of the *Hebraica Veritas*, both Catholics and Protestants, Morin argued that the Masoretic Hebrew text had been corrupted in the sixth century, citing his contemporary Louis Cappel's profound doubts about the ancient character of the vowel pointing (Hardy 2017: 249–74; Gibert 2008: 767–72).

Scholars such as Morin and, before him, Masius pointed to the coming era of historical-critical scholarship on the Bible. First, the Golden Age of Catholic biblical scholarship was concluded by Jean de la Haye (1593–1661), who published an encyclopedic *Biblia magna* in five volumes (1643) and a *Biblia maxima* in nineteen volumes (1660). In these, the Vulgate was compared with versions in various ancient languages, accompanied with elaborate historical knowledge, and provided with commentary from Jean de Gaigny, Guilielmus Estius, as well as the Jesuits Manuel de Sá, Giovanni Stefano Menochio, and Jacobus Tirinus, among others. He thus provided an overview of the characteristics of Catholic biblical scholarship over the previous century and a half.

PROTESTANT BIBLICAL SCHOLARSHIP IN THE HUMANIST AGE

Although they claimed to base their work primarily upon the Bible in Hebrew and Greek, the production of biblical commentaries by Protestants was essentially Latin (and occasionally vernacular), relying on and revising the scholarship of their biblical–humanist predecessors. In this sense, they resembled their Catholic counterparts, apart from the latter's greater regard for the Vulgate, and both traditions were familiar with each other's writings. As the sixteenth century progressed, the theological and ecclesiological framework of these commentaries frequently turned them into controversialist literature. One of the distinguishing features between the two groups was their position regarding allegory, from which Protestants (at least in theory) sought to distance themselves. The Protestant commentators' struggling with allegorical explanations remains one of the leitmotivs in various contemporary studies on early modern Protestant biblical scholarship (including McKim 2007; Reventlow 2011; Stanglin 2018: 113–51).

Fundamental to the development of the Protestant tradition of biblical scholarship was the output produced by Martin Luther, whose biblical commentaries were often based upon the courses he had taught in Wittenberg (Kolb 2016: 35–208; on Luther's text, see chap. 21). Luther's primary insight of *sola scriptura* or, rather, *prima scriptura* (Van den Belt 2016), had become connected to the humanist ideal of the importance of ancient languages to restore the "original" biblical text and to come as close as possible to God's Word. In Luther's view, the Bible's literal sense was also a spiritual one, since it speaks about justification from faith alone in God's grace and about the opposition between the Gospel and the Law. The message that emerges from biblical writings such as Romans, the Gospel according to John, or 1 Peter, provided a norm for the interpretation of other parts of the Bible (*analogia fidei*), and Luther argued that sections that still presented difficulties should be interpreted from other, more obvious, passages (*analogia scripturae*).

Luther's conviction of a single sense in Scripture meant that he distanced himself from the fourfold sense. He especially ridiculed allegory, since it obscured the clarity of the text. Even so, as a child of his time, he could not detach himself entirely from this and typological explanations, not least because Paul too used allegories and Luther also maintained that Christ was to be found in each part of Scripture. As already observed, all Reformers had to search for a balance in "combatting allegorical interpretations of the Old Testament, without losing its Christological significance" (Bray 1996: 172). In Luther's eyes, the practical-spiritual and moral relevance of Scripture for the life of faith was also important, an aspect that Protestants of all denominations would emphasize in the years to come. Mainstream Protestants were generally open in their exegesis to the writings of the Church Fathers, maintaining the principle that the older the testimony, the greater its credibility, while at the same time admitting that the Fathers had erred (especially in the decrees of Popes and Councils). In short, the authority of traditional interpretations of Scripture was decreasing considerably (Stanglin 2018: 122–32).

In Wittenberg, and other Lutheran universities, at least half of the professors of theology had a focus on Scripture, with biblical commentaries constituting an important part of their academic publications. Among the most influential and prolific authors, Philip Melanchthon (1497–1560) wrote biblical commentaries, including one on Paul's Letter to the Romans, in which he approached Scripture as Sacred Rhetoric, while using dialectics to develop the central topics or *loci* included in the book under discussion. Johannes Brenz (1499–1570) produced an important series of scriptural commentaries, whereas Matthias Flacius Illyricus (1520–75) authored an influential hermeneutical work, the *Clavis Scripturae sacrae* ("Key to Sacred Scripture," 1567), as well as a *Glossa compendiaria in Novum Testamentum* in 1570 (Kolb 2016: 239–73, and 302–94; Wengert 1997).

An important group of biblical–humanist scholars based in Strasbourg, Basle, Zurich, and Bern, later known as the "Upper Rhine School of Biblical Scholarship," actively contributed to the establishment of the Reformation. They developed a vivid interest in linguistic studies, with an emphasis on Hebrew, as well as rhetoric. Their focus on the Hebrew Bible was fundamental, as it led them to emphasize the unity of the Old and the New Testament and thus to seek passages where Christ was foreseen and predicted, resulting in typological (and occasionally allegorical) interpretations. They also strove to establish moral lessons from Scripture for the readers of their time. In this sense, their framework was still largely that of the medieval *quadriga* and of Erasmus. Among the prominent members of this school were Konrad Pellikan (1478–1556), whose *Commentaria Bibliorum* (1532–39) had a Latin text of the Old Testament emended on the basis of the Hebrew (discussed in chap. 21). Another exegete based in Basle was Johannes Oecolampadius (1482–1531), whose Isaiah commentary of 1525, accompanied by his own version of the Latin text, stands out among his numerous Bible commentaries.

In Zurich, the Reformation found expression in the biblical work of Ulrich Zwingli (1484–1531) and the *Prophezei*, the renowned group of biblical scholars who started their activities in June 1525 and gathered five times a week to study the text of the Bible. This resulted in the production of commentaries, and eventually a German (1531) as well as a Latin Bible translation (1543) in which Zwingli himself often defended the superior quality of the Septuagint over the Masoretic text. The Zurich Reformers were also keen to see typological references to Christ throughout the biblical text. Other important representatives of this "Upper Rhine School of Biblical Scholarship" are Martin Bucer (1491–1551), the Reformer of Strasbourg, whose commentary on the Psalms achieved some renown despite its long-windedness, as well as Wolfgang Musculus (1497–1563), Peter Martyr Vermigli (1499–1562), and Jerome Zanchi (1516–90) (Roussel and Hobbs 1989; Gordon 2016: 462–72; Opitz 2008: 407–28).

John Calvin (1509–64) was without any doubt the most skillful Bible commentator of the Protestant Reformation (Holder 2007; also Pitkin 2009; Steinmetz 2006). Rooted in the late medieval exegetical tradition, perfectly trained in biblical–humanist methods, and convinced of Scripture as the primary basis of the Reformed faith, Calvin commented, taught, and preached on nearly every book of the New Testament (with the exception of 2 and 3 John and Revelation), as well as about half of the Old Testament. This exegetical work also led him to include his own Latin translation in his commentaries, so that nearly a complete text of the Bible in Latin can be extracted from his books. Calvin's aim was to explain, in short and clear words (his famous *in perspicua brevitate*) the core of the biblical passage under consideration, and to come as close as possible to the *mens scriptoris*, the intention of the inspired writer. This required philological and grammatical analysis of the original text in Hebrew and Greek (which were accepted to have absolute priority above the Latin version), scrutiny of the immediate context of the passage, as well as the way in which it was embedded in the framework of the whole Bible, while also considering its historical context. Such an approach was deemed to lead the commentator to the discovery of the literal sense of the Bible.

This focus upon the literal sense, understood as the intention of the inspired writer, was a reaction against all kinds of Christological prophecies or allegorical interpretations that were not based upon a literal reading of Scripture or sustained by an understanding of the context. Calvin refused to see a reference to Christ in various passages that had traditionally been interpreted in this way, such as Genesis 3:15, most of the Psalms, and the book of Job. Even among the Reformers, Calvin was noted for his minimalistic attitude: "Christological and trinitarian themes were invoked only in the context of clearly prophetic and messianic passages" (Muller 2007: 30). Allegorical interpretations were only accepted if they were already attested within Scripture, usually in the evangelists or Paul, and played a greater role in Calvin's Old Testament sermons than in his commentaries. Calvin's adversaries, and not only those on the Catholic side, did not hesitate to rebuke him because of his "Judaizing explanations" of Scripture.

Notwithstanding his aversion to allegory, Calvin accepted that Christ is the *scopus* of the whole Bible, both in the Old and the New Testament, and the goal of the task of interpretation. By taking Christ as the completion of God's promises both to Adam and to Abraham, Calvin's "Covenant theology . . . gave the church a way of reading the Old Testament as a Christian book without lapsing into allegory, and it soon became the accepted framework for almost all Protestant biblical interpretation" (Bray 1996: 167; see also Muller 1990). Calvin considered reading, contemplating, interpreting, and commenting upon the Bible as a spiritual process, an encounter with the Spirit who convinces the reader of the truth of the message of Holy Writ (*testimonium internum Spiritus Sancti*), namely, Christ. Reading and interpreting the Bible was thus beneficial for the individual believer, and also yielded fruit for the practical and devotional life of the Church.

Theodore Beza (1519–1605) was Calvin's successor in Geneva and one of the founding fathers of Protestant orthodoxy. He published five major editions of the New Testament (1556/57, 1565, 1582, 1589, and 1598), containing the Latin Vulgate as well as his own Latin translation (see chap. 21). These texts were accompanied by *Annotationes*, philological and theological explanations of Scripture. From the second edition onward, Beza also provided a Greek text of the New Testament. His view of Scripture was in accordance with that of Calvin, in that he devoted considerable attention to languages, philological analysis, and the context. Beza, however, was much more prepared than Calvin to accept a Christological reading of the Old Testament. In line with the advancing confessionalization of all of Europe's churches, Beza also added doctrinal definition to biblical explanation, especially when it came to determining the main tenets of Reformed theology, namely, grace, free will, and predestination. This gave his writing a polemical aspect, leading Gordon and Cameron to observe that "Beza meant to build— brick by brick, word by word—a translation that embodied Calvinist teachings; it was unashamedly partisan" (Gordon and Cameron 2016: 209; also Gordon 2016: 474). Next only to that of Calvin, Beza's influence on Reformed tradition continued well into the seventeenth century.

PROTESTANT BIBLICAL SCHOLARSHIP AND THE "ERA OF HIGH ORTHODOXY"

Toward the end of the sixteenth century and throughout the seventeenth century, Protestant biblical scholars kept to the biblical–humanist hermeneutical principles of previous generations. These included an emphasis on the literal sense of Scripture, consideration of the broader context in which a passage is situated (*analogia scripturae*), interpretation from a position of faith established from the Bible (*analogia fidei*), focus on Christ as the center of Scripture—notwithstanding the thorny issue of typological and even allegorical explanations—as well as Scripture's practical value for Christian life. To this, seventeenth-century exegetes added a concern for the determination and defense of sound doctrine, rooted in the authentic text of Scripture.

This concern was equally present among Catholic as well as Protestant biblical scholars. It was preeminently manifest in the work of William Perkins (1558–1602), an English Puritan and one of the leading Reformed theologians and Bible interpreters of his time. In 1592, his exegetical work *Prophetica, sive de sacra et unica ratione concionandi tractatus* was published, also appearing in the vernacular as the *Arte of Prophecying*. Perkins numbered among those Reformed scholars who were inclined to accept a significant degree of typological and even allegorical scriptural explanation. Perkins saw such interpretation as included in the single, literal sense of Scripture, which was at the same time historical-grammatical and spiritual-typological, even though this did not prevent him from reacting against the fourfold sense of Scripture. In the spirit of Reformed scholasticism, Perkins further used syllogisms and distinctions to unfold the doctrinal content of biblical passages, using Ramism as a tool in biblical scholarship.[1] In this sense, he differed from Calvin and Beza, who were far more close to biblical–humanist scholarship with its emphasis on languages and textual criticism. Perkins also maintained a constant focus on the practical effect of Scripture on the life of the believer. His hermeneutical views found concrete expression in the commentaries he wrote on Galatians and Jude, as well as individual sections such as the Sermon on the Mount, Revelation 1–3, or Hebrew 11 (McKim 2007: 815–19; Stanglin 2018: 141–44).

Francis Turretin (1623–87), who achieved fame as the "paragon" of seventeenth-century Reformed orthodoxy in Geneva, also aligned himself with the Reformed tradition of biblical scholarship. The passages devoted to biblical hermeneutics in his famous *Institutio theologicae elencticae*, also known as the *Institutes* (published in three parts between 1679 and 1685), are of particular interest. In contrast to Perkins, Turretin was "less willing to allegorize beyond the specific instances in the New Testament" (Stanglin 2018: 146), and he was very dismissive of the allegories found in "uninspired" writers such as Origen. Turretin and like-minded theologians saw the importance of emphasizing verbal inspiration, the idea that every word of Scripture is given or dictated by God, for the determination of sound doctrine. This even extended to the formal aspects of the words in the inspired text: the Hebrew vowel points were considered to date back to no later than the time of Ezra and "the Great Synagogue," and were therefore to be esteemed as divinely inspired, and above criticism. In this regard, Turretin entered into debate with Louis Cappel (1585–1658), who argued for a late origin of the Hebrew vowel points, which he identified with the Masoretes of Tiberias and certainly no earlier than the fifth century CE. It was therefore appropriate for the study of the

---

[1] Pierre de la Ramée or Peter Ramus (1515–72) was a French humanist and philosopher and a convert to Protestantism. He developed a new method of systematizing knowledge, including religious knowledge, in opposition to Aristotelianism, but nevertheless making moderate use of the tools of logic while blending these with rhetoric. Ramus also had an eye for the practical applicability of knowledge to the life of humankind. He was killed during the St Bartholomew's Day massacre in August 1572, contributing to his fame among Protestant academics.

Bible to take into consideration other ancient versions of the Old Testament, namely, the Septuagint, the Samaritan Pentateuch, and other Semitic translations such as the Targums. This position brought Cappel objectively into line with Catholic scholars, especially Jean Morin (and Bellarmine before him), who shared this fascination for an array of ancient Bible versions while defending the preeminence of the Septuagint (and thus the Vulgate) over the Masoretic text. Turretin's strong opinions with regard to the divinely inspired Hebrew (Masoretic) text, including its vowel points, found expression in the Swiss *Consensus Formula* of 1675, although this was suspended in Geneva in 1706 (Hardy 2017: 308–34).

One representative of "Lutheran High Orthodoxy" and a proponent of a Bible-based theology was Abraham Calovius or Calov (1612–86). He even so claimed the divine inspiration of the Hebrew Bible, including the authenticity of the vowel points—against Morin, Cappel, and others—as a basic requirement for "proving the truth of theological statements" (Reventlow 2011: 228). Calovius published his *Biblia Veteris Testamenti illustrata* and his *Biblia Novi Testamenti illustrata* (four volumes, 1672–76; new edition, 1719), which offered a running commentary on the entire text of the Bible. In them, he provides philological analysis as well as a long series of possible explanations of a biblical verse, as given both by scholars who were in line with his own understanding and those who were at variance. Combined with these were forceful theological interpretations, as might be expected, as well as observations on the importance of the biblical text for the life of believers and the Church. The New Testament was introduced by an elaborate biblical chronology, combined with other "factual" knowledge of biblical times. Calovius reacted against the historical-critical approach favored by Hugo Grotius who, in his *Annotationes*, had departed from a confessional-theological reading of the Bible and instead accompanied his scientific method with a relativizing of the doctrinal differences between the confessions, opting for an irenic attitude (Reventlow 2011: 223–32; Jung 1999). Apart from Calovius, another influential Lutheran Bible commentator of the same century was Sebastian Schmidt (1617–96), the author of the *Collegium Biblicum* (1671).

Conclusion

Biblical scholarship in the humanist age developed into text-critical scholarship, which used knowledge of Greek, Hebrew, Syriac, and other languages to scrutinize manuscripts, ancient versions, and patristic evidence with the ultimate aim of coming as close as possible to the original text of Scripture. This text was subsequently expounded in Latin annotations and commentaries, and explained in vernacular sermons to the populace. The literal sense was considered of primary relevance, to which was added a theological reading that, with the advent of the Reformation and the development of confessionalization, received increasingly strident doctrinal emphases. The majority of commentaries also maintained an emphasis on the practical relevance of Scripture for the life of the Church. Whereas Catholics continued to accept, in principle, the traditional fourfold interpretative scheme (known as the *quadriga*), Protestants were generally critical of allegories not supported by Scripture itself, although most of them were prepared to accept a prophetic and typological reading within the literal sense of Scripture. Text-critical issues that had doctrinal consequences (one of the most famous examples being Erasmus's reservations regarding the Johannine Comma) were kept under check in a confessional era, only to resurface in the course of the seventeenth century. Doubts regarding the divine inspiration of the entire Bible (Hugo Grotius), or Moses's authorship of the Pentateuch (Richard Simon, and Andreas Masius before him), along with a more rigidly rational, undogmatic, and morally inspired approach to the Bible (Jean Leclerc), are only a few examples heralding a more fundamental shift toward the historical-critical scholarship of the coming centuries.

BIBLIOGRAPHY

Baroni, Victor. 1943. *La Contre-Réforme devant la Bible: la question biblique*. Lausanne: Éditions La Concorde. Repr., Geneva: Slatkine, 1986.

Bedouelle, Guy. 1989. "La Réforme catholique." In *Le temps des Réformes et la Bible*, edited by Guy Bedouelle and Bernard Roussel, 327–68. BTT 5. Paris: Beauchesne

Bray, Gerald. 1996. *Biblical Interpretation: Past and Present*. Leicester: Apollos/Inter-Varsity Press.

Cameron, Euan, ed. 2016. *New Cambridge History of the Bible: Vol. 3. From 1450 to 1750*. Cambridge: Cambridge University Press.

Chédozeau, Bernard. 2007. *Port-Royal et la Bible. Un siècle d'or de la Bible en France 1650–1708*. Paris: Nolin.

Crehan, Joseph. 1963. "The Bible in the Roman Catholic Church from Trent to the Present Day." In *The Cambridge History of the Bible: Vol. 3. The West from the Reformation to the Present Day*, edited by S. L. Greenslade, 199–237. Cambridge: Cambridge University Press.

Dahan, Gilbert. 2018. "La Bible de Santi Pagnini (1528)." In *La Bible de 1500 à 1535*, edited by Gilbert Dahan and Annie Noblesse-Rocher, 261–81. Turnhout: Brepols.

Delville, Jean-Pierre. 2004. *L'Europe de l'exégèse au XVIᵉ siècle. Interprétations de la parabole des ouvriers à la vigne (Matthieu 20,1-16)*. Leuven: Peeters.

Fischer, Benedict D. 2020. "The Impact of Erasmus on the 1614 Pauline Commentary of Cornelius a Lapide, S.J." In *Authority Revisited: Towards Thomas More and Erasmus in 1516*, edited by Wim François, Violet Soen, Anthony Dupont, and Andrea Aldo Robiglio, 371–411. Turnhout: Brepols.

Fischer, Benedict D., Wim François, Antonio Gerace, and Luke Murray. 2019. "The 'Golden Age' of Catholic Biblical Scholarship (1550–1650) and Its Relation to Biblical Humanism." In *Renaissance-Humanismus: Bibel und Reformbewegungen des 15. und 16. Jahrhunderts und ihre Bedeutung für das Werden der Reformation*, edited by J. Marius J. Lange van Ravenswaay and Herman Selderhuis, 217–74. Göttingen: Vandenhoeck & Ruprecht.

François, Wim. 2009. "Andreas Masius (1514–1573): Humanist, Exegete and Syriac Scholar." *Journal of Eastern Christian Studies* 61: 199–244.

François, Wim. 2012. "Augustine and the Golden Age of Biblical Scholarship in Louvain (1550–1650)." In *Shaping the Bible in the Reformation: Books, Scholars and their Readers in the Sixteenth Century*, edited by Bruce Gordon and Matthew McLean, 235–89. Leiden: Brill.

François, Wim. 2014. "Efficacious Grace and Predestination in the Bible Commentaries of Estius, Jansenius and Fromondus." In *Der Jansenismus–eine "katholische Häresie"? Das Ringen um Gnade, Rechtfertigung und die Autorität Augustins in der frühen Neuzeit*, edited by Dominik Burkard and Tanja Thanner, 117–43. Münster: Aschendorff.

François, Wim. 2017. "Grace, Free Will, and Predestination in the Biblical Commentaries of Cornelius a Lapide." *Annali di Storia dell'Esegesi* 34, no. 1: 175–97.

Frymire, John M. 2010. *The Primacy of the Postils: Catholics, Protestants, and the Dissemination of Ideas in Early Modern Germany*. Leiden: Brill.

Füllenbach, Elias H. 2019. "Bibel- und Hebräischstudien italienischer Dominikaner des 15. und 16. Jahrhunderts." In *Bibelstudium und Predigt im Dominikanerorden: Geschichte, Ideal, Praxis*, edited by Viliam Štefan Dóci and Thomas Prügl, 255–71. Rome: Angelicum.

Gerace, Antonio. 2019. *Biblical Scholarship in Louvain in the "Golden" Sixteenth Century*. Göttingen: Vandenhoeck & Ruprecht.

Gibert, Pierre. 2008. "The Catholic Counterpart and Response to the Protestant Orthodoxy." In *Hebrew Bible/Old Testament: The History of Its Interpretation: Vol. 2. From the Renaissance to the Enlightenment*, edited by Magne Sæbø, Michael Fishbane, and Jean Louis Ska, 758–73. Göttingen: Vandenhoeck & Ruprecht.

Gordon, Bruce. 2016. "The Bible in Reformed Thought, 1520–1750." In *New Cambridge History of the Bible: Vol. 3. From 1450 to 1750*, edited by Euan Cameron, 468–88. Cambridge: Cambridge University Press.

Gordon, Bruce, and Euan Cameron. 2016. "Latin Bibles in the Early Modern Period." In *New Cambridge History of the Bible: Vol. 3. From 1450 to 1750*, edited by Euan Cameron, 187–216. Cambridge: Cambridge University Press.

Hardy, Nicholas. 2017. *Criticism and Confession: The Bible in the Seventeenth-Century Republic of Letters*. Oxford: Oxford University Press.

Hobbs, Rowland. 2010. "Reading the Old Testament after Trent: Cardinal Robert Bellarmine and his Italian Predecessors on Psalm Four." *Reformation & Renaissance Review* 12: 207–34.

Holder, R. Ward 2007. *John Calvin and the Grounding of Interpretation: Calvin's First Commentaries*. Leiden: Brill.

Jung, Volker. 1999. *Das Ganze der Heiligen Schrift. Hermeneutik und Schriftauslegung bei Abraham Calov*. Stuttgart: Calwer.

Kessler-Mesguich, Sophie. 1998. "L'enseignement de l'hébreu et de l'araméen à Paris (1530–1560) d'après les œuvres grammaticales des lecteurs royaux." In *Les origines du Collège de France (1500–1560)*, edited by Marc Fumaroli, 357–74. Paris: Collège de France and Klincksieck.

Kessler-Mesguich, Sophie. 2013. *Les études hébraïques en France: de François Tissard à Richard Simon (1508-1680)*. Geneva: Droz.

Kolb, Robert. 2016. *Martin Luther and the Enduring Word of God: The Wittenberg School and Its Scripture-Centered Proclamation*. Grand Rapids: Baker Academic.

McKim, Donald K., ed. 2007. *Dictionary of Major Biblical Interpreters*. Downers Grove: InterVarsity Press.

Muller, Richard A. 1990. "The Hermeneutic of Promise and Fulfillment in Calvin's Exegesis of the Old Testament Prophecies of the Kingdom." In *The Bible in the Sixteenth Century*, edited by David C. Steinmetz, 68–82. Durham: Duke University Press.

Muller, Richard A. 2007. "Biblical Interpretation in the Sixteenth and Seventeenth Centuries." In *Dictionary of Major Biblical Interpreters*, edited by Donald K. McKim, 22–44. Downers Grove: InterVarsity Press.

Muller, Richard A., and John L. Thompson, eds 1996. *Biblical Interpretation in the Era of the Reformation: Essays Presented to David C. Steinmetz in Honor of His Sixtieth Birthday*. Grand Rapids: Eerdmans.

Murray, Luke. 2019. *Jesuit Biblical Studies after Trent: Franciscus Toletus & Cornelius A Lapide*. Göttingen: Vandenhoeck & Ruprecht.

O'Connor, Michael. 2017. *Cajetan's Biblical Commentaries: Motive and Method*. Leiden: Brill.

Opitz, Peter. 2008. "The Exegetical and Hermeneutical Work of John Oecolampadius, Huldrych Zwingli and John Calvin." In *Hebrew Bible/Old Testament: The History of Its Interpretation: Vol. 2. From the Renaissance to the Enlightenment*, edited by Magne Sæbø, Michael Fishbane, and Jean Louis Ska, 407–51. Göttingen: Vandenhoeck & Ruprecht.

Papy, Jan, ed. 2018. *The Leuven Collegium Trilingue 1517-1797: Erasmus, Humanist Educational Practice and the New Language Institute: Latin, Greek, Hebrew*. Leuven: Peeters.

Parente, Fausto. 2007. "Quelques contributions à propos de la biographie de Sixte de Sienne et de sa (prétendue) culture juive." In *Les juifs et l'Église romaine à l'époque moderne*, edited by Fausto Parente, 205–32. Paris: Honoré Champion.

Pascoe, Louis B. 1966. "The Council of Trent and Bible Study: Humanism and Scripture." *The Catholic Historical Review* 52: 18–38.

Pitkin, Barbara. 2009. "John Calvin and the Interpretation of the Bible." In *A History of Biblical Interpretation: Vol. 2. The Medieval through the Reformation Periods*, edited by Alan J. Hauser, and Duane F. Watson, 341–71. Grand Rapids: Eerdmans.

Puckett, David L. 2007. "Calvin, John *(1509-1564)*." In *Dictionary of Major Biblical Interpreters*, edited by Donald K. McKim, 287–94. Downers Grove: InterVarsity Press.

Reventlow, Henning Graf. 2011. *History of Biblical Interpretation: Vol. 3. Renaissance, Reformation, Humanism*, trans. James O. Duke. Leiden: Brill.

Reiser, Marius. 2016. "The History of Catholic Exegesis, 1600–1800." in *The Oxford Handbook of Early Modern Theology, 1600–1800*, edited by Ulrich L. Lehner, Richard A. Muller, and A. G. Roeber, 75–88. Oxford: Oxford University Press.

Roussel, Bernard, and R. Gerald Hobbs. 1989. "Strasbourg et 'l'école rhénane' d'exégèse." *Bulletin de la Société de l'histoire du protestantisme français* 135: 36–53.

Screech, Michael Andrew. 1987. "Erasmus and the Concordia of Cornelius Jansenius, Bishop of Ghent: Christian Folly and Catholic Orthodoxy." In *Colloque érasmien de Liège. Commémoration du 450ᵉ anniversaire de la mort d'Érasme*, edited by Jean-Pierre Massaut, 297–307. Paris: Les Belles Lettres.

Screech, Michael Andrew. 1990. "The Diffusion of Erasmus' Theology and New Testament Scholarship in Roman Circles despite the Tridentine Index." In *Théorie et pratique de l'exégèse. Actes du troisième colloque international sur l'histoire de l'exégèse biblique au XVIᵉ siècle*, edited by Irena Backus and Francis Higman, 343–53. Geneva: Droz.

Stanglin, Keith D. 2018. *The Letter and Spirit of Biblical Interpretation: From the Early Church to Modern Practice*. Grand Rapids: Baker Academic.

Steinmetz, David C., ed. 1990. *The Bible in the Sixteenth Century*. Durham: Duke University Press.

Steinmetz, David C. 2006. "John Calvin as an interpreter of the Bible." In *Calvin and the Bible*, edited by Donald K. McKim, 282–91. Cambridge: Cambridge University Press.

Van den Belt, Henk. 2016. "*Sola Scriptura*: An Inadequate Slogan for the Authority of Scripture." *Calvin Theological Journal* 51: 204–26.

Van Roey, Albert. 1978. "Les études syriaques d'Andreas Masius." *Orientalia Lovaniensia Periodica* 9: 141–58.

Wengert, Timothy J. 1997. "The Biblical Commentaries of Philip Melanchthon." In *Philip Melanchthon (1497-1560) and the Commentary*, edited by Timothy J. Wengert and M. Patrick Graham, 106–48. Sheffield: Academic Press.

Wicks, Jared. 2008. "Catholic Old Testament Interpretation in the Reformation and Early Confessional Eras." In *Hebrew Bible/Old Testament: The History of Its Interpretation: Vol. 2. From the Renaissance to the Enlightenment*, edited by Magne Sæbø, Michael Fishbane, and Jean Louis Ska, 617–48. Göttingen: Vandenhoeck & Ruprecht.

CHAPTER 21

PROTESTANT LATIN BIBLES

ANNIE NOBLESSE-ROCHER

ONE of the aims of the Protestant Reformation, from the 1520s onward, was the transmission of the Bible to all the faithful (Arnold 2017: 259; Heckel et al. 2017: 1–27). To this end, the Reformers gave priority to a huge translation enterprise to provide the Bible in the vernacular (see Chambers 1983). Indeed, by promoting the priesthood of all believers, the Reformers intended to encourage the reading of the Bible by all in the language they knew. This effort to popularize the text of Scripture is the common foundation on which the entire Protestant Reformation rests, despite its differing and diverse theological and ecclesiological aspirations (Vénard 1992: 15–221). However, in addition to their great project of translating the Bible into everyday language, Protestants did not abandon the use of the Latin Bible, either in the form of the common version, the so-called Vulgate, which the Council of Trent in 1546 was to recognize as the only authoritative one but was then to be revised in various ways or through new Latin translations (Dahan and Noblesse-Rocher 2020).

MAINTAINING *LATINITAS*

The first generation of Reformers was formed intellectually through the traditional religious orders or by nascent Humanism, and they thus retained the culture of Latinity (*latinitas*). For them, Latin remained the language of the literate and became the vernacular of a transconfessional *sodalitas* ("companionship"). The Zurich reformer Theodore Bibliander, for example, saw Latin as the unifying language of humanity, which had been subject to linguistic dispersion since Babel.[1] Nevertheless, through its

---

[1] Theodore Bibliander, *De Ratione communi omnium linguarum et literarum commentarius* [1548], ed. and English trans. by H. Amirav and H.-M. Kirn (Geneva: Droz, 2011), 104ff.

semantic precision and lexical richness, Latin prevented the epistemological confusion of disciplines (Eskhult 2012: 168).

The Latin language not only granted access to the great masters of Antiquity, but also carried a *pietas litterata* ("lettered piety"; Mesnard 1965: 298; Arnold 2009). The humanist Juan Luis Vivès considered in his *De disciplinis* that a lack of knowledge of Latin (as of other ancient languages) leads to a lack of understanding of the lessons transmitted by classical writers, and also to the impossibility of following in their footsteps.[2] This *pietas litterata* was promoted in the new educational project of the humanists involved in reform, as shown by the work of Johannes Sturm in Strasbourg. As a result, the study of the Latin language for educational purposes continued within the Reformation: the Latin Bible, as was the case in the Middle Ages, could serve to support such learning, as proposed in Paul Eber's *Biblia germanolatina* (see below). The Vulgate, from this perspective, was not a dead letter: revisions were undertaken with great respect for the traditional Bible. Thus, in anticipation of certain criticisms, the Zurich Bible (1543–44) maintains the validity of the Hieronymian version, arguing that the faulty versions in circulation probably do not go back to the famous translator.[3] Another stated goal was the scholarly study of the Latin Bible by educated people for exegetical purposes, in the private sphere. This scenario is reflected in the revision of the Vulgate attributed to Martin Luther in 1529 (see below).

THE REVISION OF THE VULGATE AND ITS METHODS

While the Vulgate retained a place of honor, its text was often considered corrupted (*corruptus*) and in need of correction (see also chap. 19). Vulgates edited by Protestants are therefore very often entitled *Biblia sacra emendata* ("Corrected Holy Bible").[4] However, the term *emendata* covers very different realities. Revisions varied depending on the context of production or, sometimes, the issues represented by the correction. If the Clementine Vulgate, which is the closest to the majority of medieval and modern Vulgates, is taken as a point of reference, it is possible to see some editions that leave the text almost untouched, while others provide transformations that range from

[2] Juan Luis Vivès, *De disciplinis* [1531], ed. and trans. T. Vigliano (Paris: Les Belles Lettres, 2013), 30–31 (*Ita ignoratis magnorum scriptorum linguis quid nobis praeciperent, qua eundum et quo suaderent, non intelleximus; veterum autorum cognitionem, qui graeca aut latina lingua monimenta ingeniorum suorum consignassent ac posteris tradidissent, ademit prorsus nobis ignoratio harum linguarum*).

[3] *Biblia sacrosancta Testamenti Veteris et Novi, e sacra Hebraeorum lingua Graecorumque fontibus, consultis simul orthodoxis interpretibus, religiosissime translata in sermonem latinum* (Zurich: Christophus Froschoverus, 1543–44), 13.

[4] Another similar appellation is *ad veritatem hebraicam restituta* ("restored to Hebrew accuracy"; e.g., Basle 1538).

the smallest corrections to a recasting that results in a thoroughly renewed text. The publisher Johann Schott, in Strasbourg, offers an example of minimal intervention. Although he rallied to the Reformation in 1520, he published a Vulgate in 1535 without marginal notes or revisions, but which set out the order of the books of the Hebrew Bible (which he said he had borrowed from David Kimhi): no doubt, this was in order to appeal to both a Protestant and a Catholic public, as the order is the same as that given by Jerome in his prologues.[5]

One type of revision consisted of marginal annotations of corrections to certain Vulgate terms following consultation of the Hebrew, leaving the text of Jerome untouched. The *Biblia* published in Basle in 1538 belongs to this category. In his preface, the publisher Hieronymus Froben referred to "the Parisian edition" (i.e., the Bible of Robert Estienne [Stephanus]), whose 1528 edition was often used as a point of reference by subsequent editors and widely praised. Even so, he states that this edition, introducing Hebrew idioms, should not be imitated: rather, he wished to offer a new complete version, especially of the Prophets, and the most thoroughgoing correction possible for the rest. In fact, his undertaking was much less daring and consisted mainly of integrating some very occasional revisions in the form of marginal notes (Dahan 2020). For example, at a variant in Genesis 3:15, a marginal note mentions that the Hebrew supports *ipsum* (*hu*, masculine in the Masoretic text) instead of *ipsa*, a very widespread reading, notably in *Biblia* published in Lyons in 1509 and 1515 as well as Estienne's 1528 edition (Dahan 2020). In Froben's 1538 *Biblia*, the names of the biblical books are given according to their Hebrew titles; Jerome's prefaces are retained, as in most of the Protestant Vulgates; for the New Testament, Erasmus's revision is given next to the *versio vulgata*, with him thus serving as an authenticated reviser.

A similar example is found in Andreas Osiander's *Biblia*.[6] This stands at the head of a line of Latin Bibles corrected by the Osiander family. In his preface, Andreas Osiander states that he had no manuscripts at his disposal and referred only to the Hebrew text. He corrected the meaning where necessary, but with caution not to offend his reader. Some grammatical forms seemed barbaric to him, but he did not hesitate to transcribe the Hebrew names with a certain freedom. The books from Genesis to Numbers are annotated in the margin, with reference to the Masoretic text, albeit decreasing in frequency. The first chapters of Genesis are heavily annotated. Osiander systematically indicated what the Masoretic text has for a particular Vulgate term that seems to him too far from the literal meaning. Thus for "heaven" (*caelum*) in Genesis 1:1, Osiander specifies that in Hebrew the term (*shamayim*) is always in the plural (*Hebrei celos ubique pluraliter enunciant*). Similarly, in Genesis 1:4b, Osiander noted in the margin that the Hebrew has "He divided between the light and the darkness" (*Hebrei Divisit*

---

[5] *Biblia veteris et Novi Testamenti, iuxta Vulgatam aeditionem, ad hebraicam veritatem candori pristino restituta* (Strasbourg: Johann Schott, 1535); for the order of the books, see page [8].

[6] Andreas Osiander, *Biblia sacra utriusque Testamenti, diligenter recognita, emendata, non paucis locis, quae corrupta erant, collatione hebraicorum voluminum restitutis* (Nuremberg: Fr. Peypus et Jo. Koberger, 1522); see further Quentin 1922: 100–101.

inter lucem et inter tenebras). In the episode of the conflict between Cain and Abel, at Genesis 4:8, the very common interpolation found in the Septuagint (which reads "let us go out into the field"), reflected in some Vulgates by *Egrediamur foras*, is rejected by Osiander: "Let us go out is not in the Hebrew" (*Egrediamur foras non est in hebreo*). Marginal annotations become less frequent after the twentieth chapter of Genesis, as Osiander did not have time to complete his revision in the turbulent context of the Nuremberg reformation.

Another more significant type of intervention consists of replacing terms in the text itself of the Vulgate with others conforming more closely to the Masoretic text, for a more literal sense. Martin Luther's *Pentateuchus*, published in Wittenberg in 1529, belongs to this type of revision.[7] Such corrections can sometimes take on significance that the reviser did not initially envisage, as is the case with Luther. He worked on the Pentateuch, the books of Joshua, Judges, and Kings, and on Erasmus's New Testament, with which he was dissatisfied. Initially, his intervention was simply to repair the negligence of the printers, but the Pentateuch, in particular, proved to be so "distorted" by this incompetence that it was necessary to compare it with the original Hebrew and "old Latin manuscripts" to reestablish the authenticity of the text.[8] This revision on the basis of Hebrew was so extensive that it resulted in a new Latin translation, although this would not achieve the predominance that his *Deutsche Bibel* did.

Luther's preface calls for caution, as the Vulgate still remained the authoritative text. His new Latin version was for private and scientific use, not for public reading in church. Although the Bible was translated into the vernacular at Wittenberg for the faithful, it was also necessary to have a scholarly version, a study Bible, for scholars trained in *latinitas*. In order to create this version, Luther used an impressive arsenal of tools: the Hebrew Psalter of Wolfgang Capito (Basle, 1516), the *Biblia* with concordance (Lyons, 1521), a copy of which has been preserved with the Reformer's extensive annotations, also found in the *Biblia* published in Basle in 1509, and Erasmus's *Novum Testamentum* (Basle, 1527). He also consulted Erasmus's *Annotationes* (1505) and Nicholas of Lyra's *Postilla* (Noblesse-Rocher 2011).

Luther's preferences may be demonstrated from the first chapter of Genesis: he often returns to the Masoretic text, but this is not systematic. In Genesis 1:2, he prefers *super abyssum* ("over the abyss"), whereas the Vulgate, following the Hebrew text, has *super faciem abyssi* ("over the face of the abyss"). The first day (*dies primus*, Genesis 1:5) is less faithful to Hebrew than the Vulgate's "day one" (*dies unus*). Luther restores certain words elided in the Vulgate, notably the verb "to be" when it is present in Hebrew (e.g., Genesis 1:8). He consistently translates *wa-yhi* (Vulgate *factum est*, "it was done") as *fiebat* ("it was being done"), thus restoring the incomplete aspect of the Hebrew verb. Luther reproduces a Hebraism in Genesis 1:11, putting *germinet gramen* ("shall make a seed

---

[7] Martin Luthers *Deutsche Bibel* [Text der Vulgata-Revision (1529)] Kritische Gesamtausgabe [WA DB] 5, *Pentateuchus, Liber Josue, Liber Iudicum, Libri Regum*, (ed. E. and E. Nestle (Weimar: Böhlau, 1914).

[8] Luther, *Pentateuchus*, 1–2.

sprout") to translate the Hebrew *tadshe* ("shall make sprout") and *deshe* ("seed, grass"), rather than the common Vulgate reading *terra germinet herbam virentem* ("the earth shall sprout green grass"). However, he did not keep the second Hebraism *mazria' zera'* ("producing seed").

This type of revision is even more developed in the *Biblia* edited in Zurich in 1543–44 by Konrad Pellikan, but conceived by Leo Jud and then Theodore Bibliander in the framework of the *Prophezei*. This was a daily meeting instituted by Reformers in the Rhineland (but which spread further afield, including London) in which the Bible was studied in Hebrew, Greek, and Latin and then translated into the vernacular, for pastors and educated laymen. In the Zurich Bible, the Hieronymian text partly disappears beneath a new text which, however, still does not claim to be such. Leo Jud, the main translator, according to the supposed author of the preface, Heinrich Bullinger, gave particular thought to the issues involved in Bible translation. He consulted several Hebrew copies, the Septuagint, and multiple Latin editions about difficult and ambiguous *loci*.[9] He observed Ciceronian Latin but nevertheless came back to terms established by "usage," preferring *evangelizare* to *laetum nuntium affere*, *benedicere* to *fortunare*, *benedictus* to *laudandus*, *fides* to *fiducia*. "Why propose a new version?" wondered the writer of the preface. Should its innovations be shocking to some, he referred the reader to the Vulgate: while considered to be a good version, it was not sufficiently faithful to the Hebrew and Greek. However, he did express a doubt: might the transmitted Vulgate not correspond exactly to that of Jerome? At the end came the statement of the *scopus* of the translator, no doubt to secure the approval of his reader: to know only Jesus and Jesus crucified.[10] Examples typical of this revision include: the addition in Genesis 1:5 of the name of God (*i*), omitted by the Vulgate; *expansio* is preferred to *firmamentum* (Vg), to preserve the double meaning of the term *raqia'* in Genesis 1:6. Yet there are also some exceptions to this fidelity to the Masoretic text: as in Luther's revision, which undoubtedly provided the inspiration, *supra abyssum* does not faithfully translate *'al peney tehom* in Genesis 1:2, whereas the Vulgate with *super faciem abyssi* does follow the Hebrew. The revisions are sufficiently numerous to raise the question of whether the Zurich text is still a modified Vulgate or constitutes a new translation.

LATIN AND VERNACULAR BIBLES

The Reformation favored the publication of bilingual Bibles, mostly for pedagogical purposes, in order to maintain the study of Latin through comparison with the vernacular language given opposite. The *Francolatina*, published in Geneva in 1568, gives the French translation of Pierre Olivetan, extensively corrected by Calvin (whose

---

[9] *Biblia sacrosancta Testamenti Veteris et Novi*, 10.
[10] Ibid., 17.

1567 edition was published in Geneva by Perrin). The Latin text was heavily reworked by him, adopting some of the choices of the Zurich Bible cited above (*expansio, appellavit, Deus*).

In the Holy Roman Empire, Paul Eber's *Biblia germanolatina* was dedicated to Alexander, Duke of Saxony.[11] Alexander was the fourth child of Augustus I, Elector of Saxony, and the leader of the evangelical league in the German Empire, but he died prematurely at the age of 11 in 1565. In his dedication, Eber states that he added to the Latin text of Bible the German translation by Martin Luther, without any changes and with the marginal notes and prefaces of the Reformer. This double Bible served as a Latin textbook for Duke Alexander, supporting continuous reading alongside a translation to help the duke progress in the language of Vergil. The prince was clearly still in the early stages of learning Latin! This double Bible is laid out in two columns in both the first edition of 1565 and the second of 1574, each consisting of ten volumes. The Latin text, provided according to a standard Vulgate version, is presented in the left-hand column, with the German on the right. Georg Major, a prominent figure in the academic circles of Wittenberg, was given the responsibility of providing the Latin text. The double texts of Genesis 1:1 and 1:4 are set out as follows:

In principio creavit Deus coelum et terram	Am Anfang schuff Gott Himel und Erden.
Terra autem erat inanis et vacua, et tenebrae	Und die Erde war wust und leer, und es war
Erant super faciem abyssi	finster auff der Tieffe
Et spiritus dei ferebatur super aquas	Und der Geist Gottes schwebet auff dem Wasser
Et vidit Deus lucem	Und Gott sahe das Licht
Quod esset bona,	gut war
Et divisit Deus lucem *a* tenebris	Da scheidet Gott das Liecht *vom* Finsternis

The most daring undertaking in the field of Protestant polyglots was, without doubt, Elias Hutter's *Biblia sacra*. Its three volumes provide the Hebrew, Aramaic, Greek, Latin, German (Lutheran version), and Saxon (Saxon German) versions, in an edition published in Hamburg in 1596 and then in Nuremberg in 1599.[12] It was the same publisher who issued a *Via sacra*, a Hebrew text of Genesis to Ruth, specifying for each Hebrew term its triliteral root in bold type, for educational purposes.[13] Augustin Calmet identified the first four languages of Hutter's *Biblia sacra*, including Latin, with the versions provided in the Antwerp Polyglot of 1568–72.[14] In other editions, the sixth

---

[11] Paul Eber, *Biblia germanolatina* (Wittenberg: Tobias Steinman, 1574); see Gehrt and Leppin 2014: 275–77.

[12] Elias Hutter, *Biblia sacra, hebraice, chaldaice, graece, latine, germanice, saxonice* (Nuremberg: Anon., 1599); see Redslob 1881.

[13] *Via sacra sive Biblia Sacra eleganti et maiuscula characterum forma* (Hamburg: Hutter, 1587); see van Staalduine-Sulman 2017: 162.

[14] Calmet 1730: 299. The Antwerp Polyglot was printed by Christoph Plantin under the patronage of King Philip II of Spain, who had entrusted the Dominican Benito Aria Montano with its scientific direction. This new polyglot was originally to replace the Complutensian Polyglot (see chap. 18), but

column could offer a Slavonic or French translation. The Antwerp Polyglot also served as a model for the Bible produced by David Wolder in four volumes in 1596.[15] This provides not just the current Vulgate version but also the translation of Santi Pagnini (see chap. 18), an indication of its reception in Protestant circles, along with the 1545 German translation by Martin Luther.

THE *BIBLIA* OF LUCAS OSIANDER

Lucas Osiander was the son of Andreas Osiander, the Nuremberg reformer and editor of the *Biblia* of 1523 mentioned earlier. Lucas Osiander's *Biblia* of 1599 is a Vulgate revised on the Hebrew for the Old Testament and on the Greek for the New.[16] Lucas says that he used Luther's German Bible alongside the Latin version. In his preface, he justified his undertaking on the basis that there was only one Bible circulating in the regions of Thuringia and Saxony, the *Biblia* published in 1544 in Leipzig: this was, in fact, the Vulgate revised by Robert Estienne in 1532 (Gilmont 2003: 245–50). Lucas also pointed out that Martin Luther's version, the Leipzig *Biblia*, and the Vulgate annotated by his own father Andreas in 1523, all largely overlap. Lucas Osiander's *Biblia* contains, among its paratexts, the prefaces by Martin Luther and Jerome to the Old Testament books, as well as Robert Estienne's *Summa*, with its astonishing destiny: this was a brief confession of faith which he published in 1532 (*Haec docent sacra librorum scripta*); it was translated, then widely distributed, and reached German and Lutheran revisers before being reinserted into Catholic publications at the end of the century (Gilmont 1995). In his own preface, Lucas states that the biblical text was based on Andreas Osiander's version. Differences between the two are indicated by smaller letters, with the following signification: a. something missing or implied; b. something redundant; c. (by a cross symbol) something more rigorously translated, especially in the Old Testament; d. finally, something which can be expressed more precisely than in his father's version.

Lucas adds annotations borrowed from the *Germanolatina* of Paul Eber (see above). For example, in Genesis 1:2, "The spirit of the Lord was carried over the waters" is the

---

it proved to be a much more ambitious undertaking, resulting in eight volumes, three of which were dedicated to critical and linguistic tools. The Old Testament was provided in Latin, Greek, Hebrew, and Judeo-Aramaic (the Targum of Onkelos and its Latin translation). The New Testament was given in Latin, Greek, and partially in Syriac (with Latin translation), as well as a transliteration of the Syriac into Hebrew characters. This Antwerp Polyglot used the revised *Biblia* of Santi Pagnini and the critical apparatus gave numerous references to the *Biblia* of Sebastian Münster (see below) and to the Talmud, which provoked hostile reactions in the Roman Catholic Church.

[15] David Wolder, *Biblia Sacra, graece, latine et germanice: in usum ecclesiarum germanicarum praesertim earum quae sunt in ditionibus Illustrissimorum Ducum Holsatiae* (Hamburg: Jacob Lucius, 1596).

[16] Lucas Osiander, *Biblia sacra Veteris et Novi Testamenti secundum Vulgatam versionem* (Leipzig: Tobias Steinman, 1599).

subject of two annotations. The first states, with regard to "was carried over the waters" (*ferebatur super aquis*): "in Hebrew: brooded on the waters" (*incubabat aquis*). Although this expression is present in the interlinear *Glossa* (and, before that, Jerome's *Hebrew Questions on Genesis*), Osiander probably draws on the commentary of Rashi on Genesis. The second annotation concerns "the spirit of the Lord" (*spiritus Domini*). The Hebrew term *ruah* means both "wind" and "spirit," but this annotation makes it clear that since the wind had not yet been created, *spiritus* (spirit, *ruah*) must here be understood in the sense of Holy Spirit ([*Spiritus*] *Ventus tunc nondum fuit, Ergo necesse est nomen spiritus hic significare Spiritum sanctum*). At Genesis 1:4 ("And God saw that the light was good"), good (*bona*) is explained: "that is, useful, beautiful, superior."[17]

New Latin Versions

Alongside these revisions of the Vulgate, Protestants undertook completely new Latin translations. The new translation by the Catholic Santi Pagnini (1528) had been well received, even by Protestant commentators (see above, and chap. 20). This did not discourage new initiatives: those of Sebastian Münster, Sebastian Castellio, and Immanuel Tremellius and Franciscus Junius will be presented in order, followed by that of Theodore Beza.

Sebastian Münster

In 1534 and 1535, Sebastian Münster published a new Latin translation of the Old Testament in two volumes in Basle under the title *Miqdash Adonai* ("Sanctuary of God"; cf. 1 Chronicles 22:19).[18] The translation was based on Hebrew, augmented by "annotations from the commentaries of the rabbis that clarify ambiguous words and obscurities' (Dahan 2017: 237–38). Münster here provides the first Protestant translation to be made from Hebrew. This translation, close to the Hebrew but attentive to the target text, was intended for exegesis. In his extensive preface, with no fewer than sixteen pages, Münster quotes his Jewish sources: Rabbi Solomon (Rashi), David Kimhi, Abraham Ibn Ezra, Rabbi Menahem (Recanati), the *Seder 'Olam*, Moses of Coucy, Moses of Girona (Nahmanides), among other authors and texts. He may have encountered some of these in the *Biblia rabbinica* produced by Daniel Bomberg in Venice in 1517 (with a new, expanded edition in 1524–25). Münster also quotes authors who are not in the Bomberg

---

[17] Ibid., [58].
[18] *En Tibi Lector Biblia Latina Planeque Nova Sebast. Munsteri tralatione, post omneis omnium hactenus ubivis gentium aeditiones evulgata, et quoad fieri potuit, hebraicae veritati conformata: aiectis insuper e rabinorum commentariis annotationibus* (Basle: Bebel, 1534); see Shuali 2018 and Dahan 2017.

Bible, using texts less familiar to Christians, such as Moses de Coucy's *Sefer mitsvot gadol* ("Great Book of Precepts"), published around 1480, which marked a milestone in the history of Christian Hebraists and in the history of exegesis (Dahan 2017: 242). Münster also alludes to the dispute over vowel indications, as some contemporary exegetes considered this vocalization to be late and unfaithful (see chap. 20; and Joosten 2018: 105–6).

Münster's Bible is presented in two columns, with the Masoretic text on the right and, on the left, the Vulgate text corrected according to the Hebrew. Two verses of the latter are offered as examples: *Terra autem erat informis et inanis . . . et spiritus Dei movebat se super faciem aquarum* (Genesis 1:2); *et distinxit deus inter lucem et inter tenebras* (Genesis 1:4). Münster's annotations are especially rich. On *informis* in Genesis 1:2, for instance, he writes:

> According to the Hebrew, *tohu wa-bohu* have almost the same meaning. Indeed, *tohu* is that which has neither form nor figure but is in a disposition ready to receive them. This is what Greeks call *hyle* [the word is given in Hebrew and then in Greek]. But others call it *homer ha-rishon*, "raw material". And by "earth" is understood the mixture of the four elements, which Moses of Girona [Nahmanides] calls *ha-colel*, "the whole". The Chaldean [= Aramaic] translator Onqelos translates as follows: "And the land was barren or desolate and empty."[19]

Sebastian Castellio

In 1551, the *Biblia* of Sebastian Castellio was published in Basle.[20] This new translation sparked off a lively controversy in Reformed circles in Geneva, particularly on the part of Theodore Beza who denounced it covertly in the preface to his own *Novum Testamentum* of 1556. Beza (and Erasmus) had a conception that differed from that of Castellio. For the former, Hebrew and Greek were sacred languages inspired by the Spirit; the translator's duty was therefore to respect their original spirit by restoring their syntax and idiomatic expressions in the translations. Beza criticized Castellio for sacrificing the authenticity of the Hebrew for the sake of Latin elegance (Backus 2012). For his part, Castellio defined his goal in three of his writings (Eskhult 2012: 179). This was a focus on the target language, in order to give a text which was *latinior* (i.e., more in conformity with the spirit of Latin), combining purity and faith, Latin elegance, and piety, according to the humanist ideal mentioned above. Castellio thus adopted a humanist approach to translation and Latin, seeking out all the resources and richness of the Latin lexicon, and all the possibilities of syntactic variations (Backus 2012: 189; see also chap. 28). His translation of Genesis 1:3–4, presented below, shows Castellio's use of

---

[19]   *En Tibi Lector Biblia Latina Planeque Nova*, 2.
[20]   *Biblia interprete Sabastiano Castalione una cum eiusdem annotationibus* (Basle: J. Parcus and J. Oporinus, 1551).

two characteristics of classical Latin, that of the linking relative (*quam*) and the infinitive proposition (*cum videret Deus esse bonam*). There is an example of the learned renewal of vocabulary (*secrevit*), and even the beginnings of interpretation (*jussit*). Castellio's version could, without doubt, also be used to learn classical Latin.

Castellio	Vulgate
Jussit Deus ut existet lux,	*Dixitque Deus fiat lux*
et extitit lux;	*et facta est lux*
quam cum videret Deus esse bonam,	*et vidit Deus lucem quod esset bona*
lucem secrevit a tenebris.	*et divisit lucem ac tenebras*

Immanuel Tremellius and Franciscus Junius

Immanuel Tremellius was born into a Jewish family in Ferrara, and then converted to Catholicism before joining the ranks of Protestant Reform (Austin 2007). He was a professor of Hebrew at the universities of Strasbourg, Cambridge, and Heidelberg, and later at Sedan, a Protestant academy (Eskhult 2012: 181–83). His expertise as a Hebraist enabled him to produce a new Latin version from Hebrew, to which were added the deuterocanonical books as translated by Franciscus Junius, and the Latin version of the New Testament by Theodore Beza.[21] Tremellius's translations can sometimes include an element of interpretation. In Genesis 1:2, the translation of *tohu-bohu* is rendered in a way that shows the problems raised by this Hebrew expression, the difficulty of designating such an unprecedented upheaval, by the use of *res* ("thing"): *Terra autem erat res informis et inanis in superficie abyssi: spiritus Dei incubabat superficiei aquarum* ("the earth was a formless and empty thing, and darkness was on the surface of the deep: and the spirit brooded on the surface of the waters"). Tremellius's use of *incubabat* ("brooded") is clearly dependent on Rashi's commentary on Genesis (see also the comment on Lucas Osiander). In Genesis 1:4, Tremellius translates the Hebrew definite article *ha* with the Latin demonstrative *haec* (*ha-or/hanc lucem*), which is a rare occurrence. Hebrew proper names are written as close to their pronunciation as possible, as shown by *Chavva* for Eve (e.g., Genesis 3:20). The other name of God in Genesis 2:4, the *Tetragrammaton*, is presented with the accepted vocalization of *Iehoua* ("Jehovah"). In Genesis 4:8, the Septuagint interpolation *Egrediamur foras* ("Let us go out") is, of course, absent. Tremellius follows the Hebrew without concession: he translates the verb *wa-yomer*, "he said," by *colloquebatur* ("he was speaking"), to resolve the difficulty of a verb that normally introduces a reply. This appears in one of the silences in this famous

---

[21] *Testamenti veteri Biblia sacra sive libri canonici priscae Judaeorum ecclesiae a Deo traditi latini recens ex hebraeo facti ab Immanuele Tremellio et Francisco Junio. Accesserunt libri qui vulgo dicuntur Apocryphi, latine redditi a Francisco Junio, quibus etiam adjuximus Novi Testamenti libros a Theodoro Beza ex graeco in latinum versos ac recens* (Hanover, 1596).

text, the abortive dialogue between Cain and Abel: by choosing an intransitive verb, Tremellius manages to render this as a nondialogue.

THE NOVUM TESTAMENTUM
OF THEODORE BEZA

In 1552, Robert Estienne asked Theodore Beza, professor of Greek at the Academy of Lausanne, to help with the edition of a Latin Bible in two volumes. The Old Testament was to be given in the 1528 version of Santi Pagnini, annotated by Vatable. The New Testament was to be a Latin translation with annotations for which Beza was responsible (Bedouelle and Roussel 1989: 431–39). At the end of 1556, the first edition of this new Latin version of the New Testament appeared, with two columns containing the standard text of the Vulgate and the translation of Beza opposite.[22] His annotations are given at the bottom of the page. In the prefatory letter, Beza situates himself in relation to Erasmus and his translation, and explains his hermeneutics and method. He does not reject the current version of the Vulgate, but for him there are "some marvellous secrets" (*mirifica quaedam arcana*) hidden in the words. Beza had a distinctive vision of his work as a translator: for him, the Holy Spirit had expressed itself in Greek, and therefore the Hebraisms present in the New Testament text needed to be maintained. For the establishment of his text, Beza relied on the collection of Greek texts of Robert and Henri Estienne, but he also used a manuscript he discovered, the Codex Bezae Cantabrigiensis (VL 5), along with another Old Latin bilingual, the Codex Claromontanus (VL 75; see chap. 11). Beza did not hesitate to correct Erasmian spellings, sometimes also conceding that the Vulgate could preserve a variant that should be retained. His activity, with its many editions, constantly evolved: Bernard Roussel noted, for instance, that the annotations of the 1582 edition take into account the Latin version of the Syriac New Testament by Immanuel Tremellius (Roussel 2007).

CONCLUSION

Despite their desire to promote the Bible in the vernacular, the Protestant Reformers remained no less attached to the Latin Bible. For them, it was the best way to preserve the vigor of the *latinitas* in which they had been trained, and even as a means of teaching Latin. But the primacy of the original texts, Hebrew and Greek, led them to undertake revisions of the Vulgate to greater or lesser extents. Although the first endeavors

---

[22] *Novum D. N. Jesu Christi Testamentum latine jam olim a vetere interprete nunc denuo a Theodoro Beza versum* (Geneva: Robert Estienne, 1556).

consisted mainly of marginal annotations giving the literal meaning of the Hebrew, as the years went by, the amount of revisions intensified, leading to significantly reworked versions such as the Zurich Bible. At the same time, Protestant Latin Bibles, in the philological movement of Humanism, presented layouts in the form of the polyglots inspired by great enterprises such as the Antwerp Polyglot. Alongside these revisions, new Latin translations were published that favored the target language (Castellio), or integrated the contributions of the great Jewish commentators. Protestant Latin Bibles responded to confessional, pedagogical, and philological issues of primary importance; they demonstrated the permanence in evangelical circles of the concern to preserve this traditional Bible, often in spite of professions of faith which advocated the sole importance of the vernacular.

BIBLIOGRAPHY

Arnold, M., ed. 2009. *Johannes Sturm (1507-1589): Rhetor, Pädagogue und Diplomat.* Tübingen: Mohr Siebeck.

Arnold, M. 2017. *Luther.* Paris: Fayard.

Austin, Kenneth. 2007. *From Judaism to Calvinism. The Life and Writings of Immanuel Tremellius, c. 1510-1580.* London: Routledge.

Backus, Irena. 2012. "Moses, Plato and Flavius Josephus. Castellio's Conceptions of Sacred and Profane in his Latin Versions of the Bible." In *Shaping the Bible in the Reformation; Books, Scholars and Their Readers in the Sixteenth Century*, edited by Bruce Gordon and Matthew McLean, 143–65. Library of the Written Word 20. Leiden: Brill.

Bedouelle, Guy, and Bernard Roussel, eds. 1989. *Le temps des Réformes et la Bible.* BTT 5. Paris: Beauchesne.

Calmet, Augustin. 1730. *Dictionnaire historique, critique, chronologique, géographique et littéral de la Bible. Tome 4: V–Z.* Paris: Emery-Saugrain-Pierre Martin.

Chambers, B. T. 1983. *Bibliography of French Bibles, t. 1, Fifteenth- and Sixteenth-Century French-Language Editions of the Scriptures.* Travaux d'Humanisme et Renaissance 192. Geneva: Droz.

Dahan, Gilbert. 2017. "Sebastian Münster, Extrait de la Préface de la Bible hébraïque." *Études théologiques et religieuses* 92: 237–48.

Dahan, Gilbert. 2020. "Les éditions de la Vulgate de 1500 à 1546." In *La Vulgate au XVIᵉ siècle*, edited by Gilbert Dahan and Annie Noblesse-Rocher, 13–52. Turnhout: Brepols.

Dahan, Gilbert, and Annie Noblesse-Rocher, eds. 2018a. *La Bible de 1500 à 1535.* Turnhout: Brepols.

Dahan, Gilbert, and Annie Noblesse-Rocher, eds. 2018b. *Les hébraïsants chrétiens en France au XVIᵉ siècle.* Geneva: Droz.

Dahan, Gilbert, and Annie Noblesse-Rocher, eds. 2020. *La Vulgate au XVIᵉ siècle.* Turnhout: Brepols.

Eskhult, Josef. 2012. "Latin Bible Translations in the Protestant Reformation. Historical Contexts, Philological Justification, and the Impact of Classical Rhetoric on the Conception of Translation Methods." In *Shaping the Bible in the Reformation; Books, Scholars and Their Readers in the Sixteenth Century*, edited by Bruce Gordon and Matthew McLean, 167–85. Library of the Written Word 20. Leiden: Brill.

Gehrt, D., and V. Leppin, eds. 2014. *Paul Eber (1511-1569), Humanist und Theologe der zweiten Generation der Wittenberger Reformation*. Leucora-Studien zur Geschichte der Reformation und der Lutherischen Orthodoxie 16. Leipzig: Evangelische Verlagsanstalt.

Gilmont, Jean-François. 1995. "Le *Sommaire des livres du vieil et nouveau testament* de Robert Estienne, ou l'étrange périple d'une confession de foi." *Revue de l'histoire des religions* 212, no. 2: 175–218.

Gilmont, Jean-François. 2003. *Le livre et ses secrets*. Geneva: Droz/Université catholique de Louvain.

Gomez-Géraud, Marie-Christine, ed. 2008. *Biblia. Les Bibles en latin au temps des Réformes*. Paris: Presses de l'Université Paris-Sorbonne.

Gordon, Bruce, and Matthew McLean, eds. 2012. *Shaping the Bible in the Reformation; Books, Scholars and Their Readers in the Sixteenth Century*. Library of the Written Word 20. Leiden: Brill.

Heckel, U., J. Kampmann, V. Leppin, and C. Schwöbel, eds. 2017. *Luther heute, Ausstrahlungen der Wittengerberger Reformation*. Tübingen: Mohr Siebeck.

Joosten, Jan. 2018. "Le débat sur la vocalisation massorétique de la Bible, d'Elie Levita à Louis Cappel." In *Les hébraïsants chrétiens en France au XVIᵉ siècle*, edited by Gilbert Dahan and Annie Noblesse-Rocher, 105–16. Geneva: Droz.

Mesnard, P. 1965. "La Pietas litterata de Jean Sturm et le développement à Strasbourg d'une pédagogie œcuménique." *Bulletin de la Société de l'Histoire du Protestantisme Français* 111: 281–302.

Noblesse-Rocher, Annie. 2011. " 'Ce bon Nicolas de Lyre'; quelques postures de Martin Luther à l'égard du Postillator." In *Nicolas de Lyre, franciscain du XIVᵉ siècle, exégète et théologien*, edited by Gilbert Dahan, 335–57. Paris: Institute d'études augustiniennes.

Quentin, Henri. 1922. *Mémoire sur l'établissement du texte de la Vulgate*. Rome: Desclée-Gabalda.

Redslob, M. 1881. "Hutter, Elias." *Allgemeine Deutsche Biographie* 13: 475–76.

Roussel, Bernard. 2007. "Le *Novum Testamentum* de Théodore de Bèze, l'édition, la traduction et l'annotation de l'épître de Jude." In *Théodore de Bèze (1519-1605). Actes du colloque de Genève (septembre 2005)*, edited by Irena Backus, 85–186. Geneva: Droz.

Shuali, E. 2018. "La bible hébraïque de Sébastien Münster." In *La Bible de 1500 à 1535* edited by Gilbert Dahan and Annie Noblesse-Rocher, 283–98. Turnhout: Brepols.

van Staalduine-Sulman, E. 2017. *Justifying Christian Aramaism: Editions and Latin Translations of the Targums from the Complutensian to the London Polyglot Bible (1517-1657)*. Leiden: Brill.

Vénard, M., ed. 1992. *Histoire du Christianisme*, t. VIII, *Le temps des confessions (1530-1620/30)*. Paris: Desclée.

CHAPTER 22

THE LATIN BIBLE AND JEWISH TRADITION

GILBERT DAHAN

ALTHOUGH Christian exegesis soon defined itself in opposition to Jewish exegesis, the relationship between the two remained constant throughout the Middle Ages and intensified in the sixteenth century. Christians realized that knowledge of Hebrew was indispensable for approaching the Old Testament as well as for understanding the rites and different customs that served as a backdrop to the New Testament. In this way, the use of Hebrew and Jewish traditions touches on the main areas of biblical study, from the establishment of the text to its exegesis. These different aspects are studied here, but first the chapter addresses the question of how Christians were able to access the texts of Jewish tradition.

ACCESS TO JEWISH TRADITIONS

The texts of Jewish tradition, including the Old Testament, are written in Hebrew (and Aramaic). The vast majority of people who studied the Bible in the Middle Ages did not know Hebrew, but the number of references to Jewish interpretations made in Christian commentaries is striking. Most of these mentions come from discussions with Jews: even if accounts of such encounters mainly concern polemical debates, peaceful exchanges around the biblical text were frequent (Dahan 1990). For example, Walter of Châtillon (d. 1201), in a treatise against Jews, related that he used to have a discussion on Sundays with a Jew from his circle.[1] In several cases, Jewish interpretations were provided by a privileged interlocutor, whom the Christian exegete designates as *Iudeus meus*, "my Jew" (i.e., my friend or my informant).

---

[1] *Tractatus contra Iudeos*, PL 209: 457.

Such exchanges multiplied in the twelfth century under the influence of the school of Saint-Victor: Hugh of Saint-Victor (d. 1141) required a good understanding of the letter of the text before embarking on spiritual interpretation, and the former included the understanding of grammar, vocabulary, and institutions (see further chap. 17). Christian exegetes were often at a loss in this respect and accordingly turned to Jews. This was not by chance: in Northern France, Jewish exegesis experienced significant growth (Geiger 1855; Touitou 1985). The successors of the French rabbi known as Rashi (Salomon of Troyes, 1040–1105) fulfilled his wish for predominantly literal exegesis (see Liber 1970; Banitt 1985; Dahan et al. 1997; Sirat 2006), and he also influenced Christian writers (Hailperin 1963). Before this, as continued to be the case in Rashi's own time, Jewish exegesis largely centered on *derash*, a nonliteral interpretation based on the stories of rabbinic literature (*midrashim*). This had the function of illustrating the biblical text, and it may be compared to parables (Gelles 1981; see further below).

With the masters of the Northern French school, in particular Joseph ben Simeon Qara (ca. 1060–ca. 1130), Samuel ben Meir of Ramerupt (ca. 1080–ca. 1174), Joseph Bekhor Shor of Orleans (twelfth century), Eliezer of Beaugency (twelfth century), and Jacob ben Meir of Ramerupt (ca. 1100–71), it was the *peshat* (literal interpretation) that came to the fore. This involved the study of vocabulary (French equivalents were often provided, designated by the term *la'azim*), of narrative, and of the sociological and historical context, matching the *desiderata* noted above of their contemporary Hugh of Saint-Victor. However, it should be noted that the main informants for the Christians were not the masters themselves but rather simple members of the faith community. While these were certainly literate, they were not always well informed of the progress of their learned co-religionists, which meant that they transmitted explanations from the *peshat* as well as from the *derash*, sometimes leading to perplexity for their Christian interlocutors who tended to take all the interpretations literally. Authors of the "biblical-moral school" continued to hold these exchanges, and a number of Jewish interpretations are found in their commentaries, notably in the *Historica scholastica* of Peter Comestor as well as in Peter the Chanter and Stephen Langton.

Knowledge of Hebrew

In the thirteenth century, there was something of a change in conditions, with the situation of Jews deteriorating in England, Germany, and France. Exchanges between Christians and Jews about the Bible continued, but it seems that the role of converts to Christianity became more important, and that these proselytes served as relays (Dahan 1990: 239–70); a striking example is that of Thibaud of Sézanne, who became a Dominican in Paris (Dahan and Nicolas 1999: 95–120). The most significant transformation, however, was the learning of Hebrew by Christians. Such teaching took place in an ad hoc manner from the second half of the twelfth century in England, as shown by the example of Herbert of Bosham along with Hebrew psalters annotated in Latin for the purpose of language learning (Smalley 1951; Loewe 1953; Dahan 1999b; Olszowy-Schlanger and Grondeux 2008). In the thirteenth century, this teaching was no longer limited to courses for individuals but was available to groups. Some Dominican *studia* in Spain (notably in Barcelona) developed a teaching of Hebrew (and Arabic) which enabled a certain Raymond Martini to know the language perfectly (Cortabarria Beitia 1970). At the same time, Roger Bacon and Ramon Llull continued to campaign for the learning of Greek, Arabic, and Hebrew; their efforts were crowned with success at the Council of Vienna in 1311–12, which decided to create chairs in the universities of Paris, Oxford, Bologna, and Salamanca and at the seat of the Papal Curia.[2] The outcome of these ventures varied, but there seems to have been some continuity in the fourteenth and fifteenth centuries (Rashdall 1936). Even outside this university teaching, it seems that the study of Hebrew developed in Germany and Italy during the fifteenth century (Walde 1916; Miletto 2018). This explains the role of a certain number of Hebraists who were to have a decisive influence on the following generation, such as Giannozzo Manetti or Johannes Reuchlin (Vanderjagt 2008; Kessler-Mesguich 2008).

The sixteenth century saw a remarkable progression in the study of Hebrew (and Greek and Arabic). Humanist movements encouraged this development, but the recourse to the original languages of Scripture appeared a necessity for those studying the Bible (Friedman 1983; Kessler-Mesguich 2013). The creation of chairs of Hebrew in various institutions of higher learning (the *Collegium Trilingue* in Louvain, the *Collège Royal* in Paris) gave concrete expression to these aspirations. The printing press also made a considerable contribution to the rise of Hebrew studies, with the publication of alphabets, methods, and finally texts (Schwarzfuchs 2004, 2008; Torrens 2018). Among the Hebrew grammars, that of Johannes Reuchlin had a very notable influence.[3] Preceded by a more modest essay by Konrad Pellikan (Strasbourg, 1504), it was followed by grammars by François Tissard (Paris, 1508), Agazio Guidacerio (Paris, 1529?), and others (see Kukenheim 1951; Kessler-Mesguich 2013). The teaching of biblical languages was seen as indispensable in Reformed circles, and throughout the sixteenth century Hebrew classes were created for adults (in Zurich, Strasbourg, etc.) or in secondary schools (as in Lausanne, Geneva, La Rochelle, Nîmes, Sedan; see Bourchenin 1882). It should also be noted that exchanges between Christians and Jews continued, and that certain Jewish scholars made an important contribution to Hebrew studies, the best-known being the grammarian and philologist Elie Levita (1469–1549; see Weil 1963). In this way, what had seemed throughout the Middle Ages to be reserved for a specialized elite, working on polemics or biblical criticism, began to reach much wider areas.

---

[2] *Conciliorum Œcumenicorum Decreta*, ed. J. Alberigo et al. (Bologna: Istituto per le scienze, 1973), 379; see also Altaner 1933.

[3] *De rudimentis hebraicis* (Pforzheim: Thomas Anshelm, 1506); see Morgenstern 2018.

Translations

Another form of access to texts of Jewish tradition was through translations, almost always in Latin. In the sixteenth century, such translations multiplied, including, for example, medieval Jewish commentaries by David Kimhi, Abraham Ibn 'Ezra, and others.
The Kabbalistic tradition also had a significant influence on a number of Christian
authors, such as Giovanni Pico della Mirandola, Johannes Reuchlin, Guillaume Postel,
Guy Le Fèvre de la Boderie, and many others (Secret 1964a, 1964b).

In the Middle Ages, such translations were rarer. Fragments were translated in
the polemical writings of the Jewish convert Peter Alphonsus.[4] Peter the Venerable
transmitted some passages of ancient rabbinic literature, also in a polemical work.[5]
The discovery of the existence of nonbiblical Jewish texts, however, seems to have
shaken the Western Christian world: in 1239, a Jewish convert possibly of Karaite origin, Nicholas Donin, drew the attention of Pope Gregory IX to the importance of rabbinic literature among the Jews. The Pope ordered the seizure of such books and an
investigation of their contents. His directive was only applied in France, where Jewish
books were seized and a trial held of the literature in Paris with the participation of
all university authorities: the result was the burning of all the copies that had been
confiscated (Dahan and Nicolas 1999; Chazan 1988; Dahan 2017a: 41–63). In the context of this trial, however, extracts were translated, perhaps with the collaboration of
Thibaud of Sézanne: these *Extractiones de Talmud* are preserved in a single manuscript
(Paris, BnF, lat. 16558; see Cecini and Vernet i Pons 2017; Merchavia 1970). Although
the translations were faithful and rigorous, the extracts were taken out of context and
categorized according to polemical choices: the authority of the Talmud, the sages
and teachers; blasphemies against the humanity of Christ; errors; incantations; and so
on. In any case, this made an initial corpus available to the Christian West, including
passages from Talmudic literature, Jewish liturgy, and commentaries by Rashi (Dahan
1978, 1992; Hasselhoff 2017). For at least one generation, it was the main source of knowledge of these texts.

Not long after, however, another attitude emerged, also marked by a public dispute:
held in Barcelona in the year 1263, the participants were Pablo Christia and the Jewish
scholar Nahmanides (Moses ben Nahman, 1194–1270), a leading Bible commentator
and author (Chazan 1977; Dahan 1990: 356–59). As a result of this controversy, the need
to read Jewish texts in their original language became apparent. Accordingly, the po-
lemicist Raymond Martini assembled numerous translations that he himself had made
from Hebrew (and Arabic): published in Paris in 1651 and in Leipzig in 1687, his *Pugio
fidei* was to have a permanent influence on Christians concerned with Judaism.[6] At the

---

[4] *Petrus Alfonsi. Dialogue against the Jews*, Eng. trans. I. M. Resnick (Washington, DC: Catholic
University of America, 2006). See also Merchavia 1970: 93–127.

[5] *Adversus Iudeorum inveteratam duritiem*, ed. Y. Friedman (Turnhout: Brepols, 1985), xvi–xvii.

[6] *Ramon Marti's Pugio fidei. Studies and Texts*, ed. G. Hasselhoff and A. Fidora (Santa Colomer de
Queralt: Obrador Edèndum, 2017).

beginning of the fourteenth century, the Franciscan Nicholas of Lyra, who constantly used the Targum, rabbinic literature, and Rashi in his commentary on the Bible (the *Postilla*), established a typology of Jewish texts that should be known and used in response to Jewish arguments.[7]

In parallel, the translations of Maimonides' works should also be mentioned. That of his *Guide for the Perplexed* (*Dux perplexorum seu neutrorum*) was probably made in Paris around 1240: despite numerous imperfections, it was used by Christian authors from the second half of the thirteenth century onward (Albert the Great, Thomas Aquinas, Thomas of York, Thomas Docking, Dominic Grima, etc.; see Dahan 1990: 314–22; Hasselhoff 2004). Meister Eckhart frequently quoted *Rabbi Moyses* in his commentary on Exodus.

THE ESTABLISHMENT OF THE VULGATE TEXT

One area in which knowledge of Hebrew was required was in textual criticism, both in the Middle Ages and in the sixteenth century (see chap. 16). After some resistance, the Latin version of Jerome was adopted by the Christian West, generally speaking, from the seventh century onward. Yet it was Charlemagne who was first to impose it on his empire, after asking his director of studies Alcuin to proceed with the establishment of a reliable text: this he did, but only by collating the Latin manuscripts between themselves. At the same time as Alcuin, another scholar, Theodulf, was revising the Latin text of the Bible but with recourse to Hebrew for the Old Testament (see chap. 12). It is probable that this work was done with the help of Jews or converts, including perhaps the author of some commentaries attributed to Jerome. The manuscripts that attest this work include in their margin a literal translation from the Hebrew for passages that raise questions (e.g. Paris, BnF, lat. 11937).

The next most eloquent example is the Bible of Stephen Harding, the third Abbot of Cîteaux (Dijon, BM, 12–15). After the construction of the abbey church, he wanted it to have a good Bible and so borrowed Latin manuscripts from neighboring monasteries. On realizing that there were differences between them, especially the presence of interpolations, he decided to compare them with the Hebrew of the Old Testament. For this purpose, he called together several learned Jews in 1109, who translated the problematic verses word for word; Harding then proceeded to correct his text, erasing the passages missing from the Hebrew (Kaufmann 1889; Zaluska 1989: 63–111). A little later, Nicholas Maniacoria (d. 1145) revised the Latin text of the Bible, resulting in a collection of observations on the whole of Scripture, the *Suffraganeus biblicus*, and two works on the Psalms. He learned Hebrew and Greek, but for the

---

[7] *Utrum ex sacris scripturis receptis a Iudeis possit efficaciter probari Salvatorem nostrum fuisse Deum et hominem* (Paris, BnF, latin 3644); see Dahan 1998: 95–97.

Hebrew he turned for assistance to Jews: one scholar, whom he described as a "very subtle investigator," may have been the great exegete Abraham Ibn 'Ezra (1092–1167; see Peri 1977).

With the birth of the university and the *studia* of the mendicant orders, the production of Bibles underwent a great expansion, resulting in texts of mediocre quality which were soon the subject of critical notes in the *correctoria* (see chap. 16). The authors of these notes not only compared Latin Bibles with each other but also had recourse to Hebrew, Aramaic, and Greek texts. Their work testifies to a genuine knowledge of these languages (Dahan 1992b); perhaps they consulted Jews or, in any case, converts, as shown by the example of Thibaud of Sézanne, a possible translator of the *Extractiones de Talmud* but also a collaborator in the *correctorium* that accompanies the Bible of Saint-Jacques, in which his name is found several times. However, from the next generation onwards, with the Franciscan William de la Mare and the *Sorbonne I* and *Sorbonne II correctoria*, it seems that the authors of these remarks were Hebraizing Christians. Recourse to Hebrew was very frequent for the Old Testament: apart from interpolations or omissions, there are numerous transcriptions of Hebrew, grammatical remarks, and details about the vocabulary. The correctors refer to the Hebrew (*Hebreus*) or to the Hebrew manuscripts (*hebrei [codices]*); their text is a priori the Masoretic text, but it remains possible that, in a few rare cases, some witnesses to non-Masoretic texts remain. This work continued in the fourteenth and fifteenth centuries.

In the sixteenth century there was a major expansion. With the birth of printing, the production of Bibles multiplied considerably; even though the first printed Bibles are, in all respects, medieval Bibles, including the fluctuations in their text, attempts at improvement were soon made. Highlights include the Venice edition of 1511, that of Osiander, those of Nüremberg and Cologne (both 1530), and above all those of Robert Estienne (Paris: 1528, 1532, 1545, 1546; Geneva: 1555, 1557), Jean Benoît (Paris, 1541) and John Henten (Louvain, 1547; see Dahan and Noblesse-Rocher 2020). In all cases, the editors state in their prefaces that they have used the Hebrew text. The most important date is that of the Council of Trent, which decided in its session of April 8, 1546, that the official text of the Bible was the translation of Jerome: prior to this, no such decision had been made by ecclesiastical authorities, as Charlemagne's was political. Its request for scholarly work of correction led to the Latin Bible published under the authority of Clement VIII in 1592 after the failed edition of Sixtus V (see chap. 19). The teams of scholars involved in its constitution used the *correctoria* of the thirteenth century (particularly that of William de la Mare) and often compared the Latin texts with the (Masoretic) Hebrew. The *Notationes in sacra Biblia* (Antwerp, 1580) by Francis Lucas give an idea of this work, which continued even after the publication of the Sixto-Clementine Vulgate. Such activity was facilitated by several major publications: the Complutensian Polyglot Bible (see chap. 18), Daniel Bomberg's editions of the *Biblia Rabbinica* (Hebrew text with medieval Jewish commentaries; see Schwarzbach 2018) and the Antwerp Polyglot (1568–72; see chap. 21).

CHRISTIAN USE OF JEWISH EXEGESIS

The two foundational texts of Christian exegesis affirm positions from the outset that seem to be opposed to those of Jewish exegesis. In the account of the Journey to Emmaus (Luke 24:27), Jesus explains that all the Scriptures concern him—thus establishing the principle of a Christological interpretation. In Galatians 4:21–27, Paul sees Hagar as a figure of the present Jerusalem (the Synagogue) and Sarah as a figure of the Jerusalem above (the Church)—thus laying the foundation for allegorical interpretation. Jewish exegesis applied prophecy to a coming Messiah and, at first, used a different system of allegory. Nevertheless, Jews were considered custodians or transmitters of the Old Testament. Christian authors tended to see the end of Judaism as the time of Jesus: in this way, Jews could also contribute to explaining practices reported in the Gospels and other New Testament texts. Moreover, it seems that the very process of traditional rabbinic exegesis, based in part on the deciphering of foundational narratives and on a structural analysis through the comparison of anecdotes intended to shed light on biblical texts (*haggadot, midrashim*), forms a constitutive element of all traditional exegesis: Christian recourse to pagan myths in the twelfth century and to Jewish *midrashim* from the thirteenth century onward responds to this need.

Jewish interpretations are designated in two ways in medieval exegesis: *Hebrei dicunt* ("Hebrews say") introduces a positively received literal interpretation based on grammar, semantics, or history, while *Iudei fabulantur* ("Jews tell stories") introduces a midrashic type of interpretation (often considered literal), rejected a priori (Dahan 1999a: 359–87). The substantial body of interpretations introduced by *Iudei fabulantur* prohibits speaking of a clear and simple rejection. The category of *fabula* corresponds to that of "myth," and it has been said that this approach is an integral part of exegesis (Dahan 2009a). Throughout the Middle Ages, Jewish interpretations of each category are mentioned in Christian commentaries. Certain authors were reproached for "Judaizing," the most significant being that of Andrew of Saint-Victor, one of the few to practice purely literal exegesis.[8] Nevertheless, references to Jewish exegesis did not provoke general condemnation: on the contrary, at the beginning of the fourteenth century Nicholas of Lyra drew up a list of authoritative Jewish texts for use in polemic, but which he used himself to enrich his commentary. It was only with Johannes Förster in the sixteenth century that recourse to Jewish interpretations was seen as reprehensible in itself.

It should be noted that Jewish interpretations cited by Christian exegetes are not always firsthand: a good number go back to Jerome (and other Fathers), especially his *Quaestiones in Genesim* and commentaries on the Prophets. Similarly, in Carolingian times works pseudonymously attributed to Jerome had a similar role.[9] Yet there was no shortage of "new"

---

[8] See also the anonymous commentary *Secundum Salomonem. A 13th Century Latin Commentary on the Song of Songs*, ed. S. Kamin and A. Saltman (Ramat-Gan: Bar-Ilan University, 1989).

[9] *Pseudo-Jerome. Quaestiones on the Book of Samuel,* ed. A. Saltman (Leiden: Brill, 1975); see also Saltman 1973.

interpretations, originating from direct consultation with Jews and then, in the case of some authors, from reading Jewish commentaries: knowledge of Hebrew and the increase in translations meant that such interpretations were multiplied in the sixteenth century.

The Carolingian Period

Jewish interpretations were not frequent in the eighth and ninth centuries (Blumenkranz 1960, 1963), despite its developments in biblical exegesis, especially in Auxerre and Fulda. At the latter monastery, Hrabanus Maurus (ca. 780–856) composed a commentary on multiple biblical books in the form of an anthology, which was widely circulated. Most of the Jewish interpretations he cites, especially on Genesis, can be traced back to Jerome, but there is also a "modern-day Hebrew," who could be Pseudo-Jerome, author of the Hebrew Questions on the Books of Kings. Angelomus of Luxeuil also refers several times to "Hebrews," as does Paschasius Radbertus. Mention should also be made of Agobard of Lyons, whose work is not exegetical but polemical.

The Twelfth Century

The emphasis on literal interpretation in the influential Parisian school of Saint-Victor means that it is unsurprising to find mentions of Jewish interpretations, supposed to shed light on the letter of the text, in Hugh, Andrew, and even Richard of Saint-Victor (van Zwieten 1987; Berndt 1989, 1991). Parisian exegetes independently also consulted Jews and introduced some of their explanations into their commentaries: the proximity of the Jewish settlements and the schools facilitated these exchanges. In the second half of the century, masters from the moral-biblical school continued this tradition: the *Historia scholastica* of Peter Comestor (originally from Troyes, where the school of Rashi flourished) fairly frequently quotes the opinions of Jews on biblical narratives (Berndt 1994; Geiger 2013). Similar quotations are not lacking from Peter the Chanter, who did not always seem to be well disposed to Jews (Dahan 1985a). Similarly, Stephen Langton cited multiple Jewish interpretations (either "new" or from Jerome) but did not shy away from polemical attacks (Dahan 1985b). Even outside the schools of Paris, exegetes had recourse to Jewish exegesis more or less frequently, through earlier writers (notably in the *Glossa ordinaria* and Rupert of Deutz) or through direct contact with Jews (Alexander Neckham). It should be remembered that Herbert of Bosham was a Hebraist, who may have been inspired by Abraham Ibn 'Ezra (Loewe 1953: 63).

The Thirteenth Century

Mentions of Jewish interpretations are always present in biblical commentaries of the thirteenth century, sometimes in a surprising way. For example, in Albert the Great's commentaries on the Prophets (Isaiah, Minor Prophets), he cites a certain number of Jewish "fables" in order to condemn them: as he considers them to be "daydreams" or "lies," why does he mention them at all? His practice appears to indicate the usefulness of these midrashic passages for exegesis which, even more than in previous centuries, claimed to be "rational" and scientific but could not fail to include "mythical" elements even while condemning them (Dahan 2019). Such material is especially present in relation to prophetic texts. Although Jewish commentaries were quoted to illuminate a historical context, the original content of their exegesis is often recalled: they interpret Messianic prophecies in the light of the historical context of the prophet, or postpone their fulfillment to Messianic times to come (Dahan 2009b). This obviously contradicts the Christological character of Christian exegesis, yet one may wonder whether there were more points in common than is generally believed: several Christian exegetes of the sixteenth century cited Jewish explanations of Messianic prophecies and observed that they shed light on the way in which they could be applied to Jesus Christ. In any case, all commentaries on Old Testament books cite Jewish interpretations (Dahan 1997).

There is a perceptible development during this century. It seems that the Latin translation of the *Extractiones de Talmud* was more widespread than is suggested by the single manuscript in which it is preserved (see above), and that many Christian authors used the material it provides, especially the passages taken from Rashi's commentary. Exchanges with Jews also continued and provided Christian exegetes with elements from Jewish exegesis. In the final decades, with progress in Hebrew teaching and, in particular, the translations of Raymond Martini, more substantial material was made available to Christians.

The Fourteenth and Fifteenth Centuries

In the early fourteenth century, Nicholas of Lyra provides a major turning point (Krey and Smith 2000; Dahan 2011). Although some scholars have underestimated his skills, he was a Hebraist with at least a "passive" knowledge (i.e., able to read and understand Hebrew texts). His *Postilla* on the Old Testament constantly quotes texts from Jewish tradition (Hailperin 1963: 137–264; Bunte 1994; Smith 2008). The most visible is his use of Rashi: the abbreviation *Ra. Sa.* (for *Rabbi Salomon*) can be found on every page. He also used the Targum quite often, which he refers to as the *glossa* of the Jews. (This is entirely apt if one remembers that the Targum is not a simple Aramaic translation of the Bible but includes elements of explanation or updating: it was often used by Jewish commentators for the initial interpretation of difficult passages.)

Nicholas also produced a significant number of midrashic interpretations, which came from the great collections of Jewish tradition (the *Midrash rabba*, the Babylonian Talmud). It is not known how he became familiar with these texts: the hypothesis that he was of Jewish origin is the fruit of ancient scholars' imagination and has no factual basis. He was probably in contact with Jewish teachers in his native Normandy before the expulsion of the Jews in 1306. Nicholas collected his notes on the Hebrew text in a *Tractatus de differentia littere hebraice et nostre translationis* ("Tractate on the Difference of the Hebrew Text and our Translation"): in this he compares Jerome's translation of certain passages with the Masoretic text, which he scrupulously retranslates. Here and there he uses the remarks of Jewish commentators, notably Rashi (Dahan 2007). His commentary was the subject of criticism (*Additiones*), by Paul of Burgos (or of Santa-Maria), a converted Jew (1353–1435). It was not Nicholas's use of Jewish sources that was the object of this criticism but rather that the author of the *Postilla* did not go far enough or did not assimilate certain Jewish interpretations well enough (apart from divergences on translation or purely theological questions). These remarks themselves attracted responses (*Replicae*) from the Franciscan Matthias Döring (ca. 1390–1469), who entitled his treatise in defense of Nicholas of Lyra as *Correctorium corrupturii* ("Correction of what has been Corrupted"; Reinhardt 2011). Other authors of the fourteenth and fifteenth centuries had recourse to Hebrew and Jewish interpretations, often at second hand and especially through using Nicholas of Lyra. It was in Italy, and later in Germany, that interest in Hebrew and Jewish texts developed in the second half of the fifteenth century, the main lines of which can be traced from their outworking in the sixteenth century.

The Sixteenth Century

Pico della Mirandola and Reuchlin played a decisive role in the development of Hebrew studies. Even though their interest was mainly in the doctrines of Jewish mysticism (Kabbalah), they stimulated an infatuation with Hebrew throughout the West. Reuchlin provided the first textbook, which was constantly used in the following generation before Christian Hebraists became familiar with David Kimhi's grammar, and produced grammars in their turn. The attention to ancient languages characteristic of humanism, especially the languages of the Bible, only accentuated this movement. The return to *sola scriptura* and the desire for new translations (both Latin and vernacular) in Reformed circles and also among Catholics contributed to the development of Greek and Hebrew studies. The printing and translation of texts by Jewish commentators and of the biblical texts themselves provided Christian exegetes with material, of which some made considerable use.

Characteristic of sixteenth-century exegesis is the use of Jewish commentaries by Catholics (Thomas Cajetan, Jean Cinqarbres, Gilbert Génébrard, Jean Mercier, Benito Arias Montano, etc.) and Reformed exegetes (Konrad Pellikan, Wolfgang Capito, Martin Bucer, Philip Melanchthon, Sebastian Münster, Ulrich Zwingli, John Oecolampadius, etc.; see also chap. 20). Their aim was not to justify the position of the Jewish exegetes but rather, based on their linguistic knowledge and the faithfulness of the textual transmission, to read them in order better to understand Old Testament texts, including the prophecies announcing the coming of the Messiah. In this respect, the preface provided by Sebastian Münster to his Latin translation of the Old Testament is very revealing and unambiguous with relation to his Christian commitments.[10]

This use of Jewish authors provoked criticism. First of all, the work of Johannes Reuchlin was violently attacked by the Dominican (Jewish convert) Johannes Pfefferkorn, and he defended himself in a treatise "against the slanderers of Cologne."[11] In Reformed circles, following Luther's negative attitude toward rabbinic texts, the Wittenberg masters condemned the use of Jewish authors. Johannes Förster wrote a New Hebrew Dictionary, from which he excluded the commentaries of the rabbis and Christian scholars "who foolishly imitated them."[12] However, his dictionary shows a total misunderstanding of the structure and function of Hebrew, and it attracted severe and justified criticism from Johannes Isaac, a professor in Cologne.[13] In fact, the approach to Jewish texts in Wittenberg is often contrasted with that in Basle, more broadly called the "Rhenish school." Almost all the masters of Strasbourg, Basle, and Zürich resorted often to Jewish interpretations (Noblesse-Rocher 2010). The same is true of Catholic exegetes, including Hebraists such as the professors at the *Collège Royal*: those without Hebrew had recourse to Jewish texts by using Nicholas of Lyra, by reading translations, or by taking advantage of the work of the Hebraists.

Throughout the Middle Ages and in the sixteenth century, exchanges with Jews or the reading of texts from the rabbinic tradition and Jewish commentators on the Bible were constant in Christian exegesis. This contribution was not restricted to the study of the letter of Scripture, as was often the case in the twelfth century: above and beyond grammatical information and their description of institutions, Jewish authors stimulated an in-depth approach to the Bible, even if this was often through polemic. For the history of the Vulgate, the importance of recourse to the Masoretic text, to the Targum and, at least in the sixteenth century, to rabbinic interpretations which permitted textual options, must not be forgotten.

Bibliography

Altaner, Berthold. 1933. "Raymundus Lullus und der Sprachkanon (can. 11) des Konzils von Vienne (1312)." *Historisches Jahrbuch* 53: 190–219.

Banitt, M. 1985. *Rashi, Interpreter of the Biblical Letter*. Tel Aviv: University.

Bedouelle, Guy, and Bernard Roussel, eds. 1989. *Le temps des Réformes et la Bible*. BTT 5. Paris: Beauchesne.

---

[10] *Miqdash Adonay . . . Hebraica Biblia* (Basle: Bebel, 1534): French translation of excerpts, Dahan 2017b; see also chap. 21 and Shuali 2018.

[11] *Defensio Ioannis Reuchlin* (Tübingen: Thomas Badensis, 1513); see Overfield 1971.

[12] *Dictionarium hebraicum novum non ex rabinorum commentis nec nostratium doctorum stulta imitatione descriptum, sed ex ipsis thesauris sacrorum Bibliorum et eorundem accurata locorum collatione depromptum, cum phrasibus scripturae Veteris et Novi Testamenti diligenter annotatis* (Basle: Froben, 1557)

[13] *Hegionot. Meditationes hebraicae in artem grammaticam* (Cologne: Jacob Soter, 1558); see Friedman 1983: 165–76.

Berndt, Rainer. 1989. "Les interprétations juives dans le commentaire de l'Heptateuque d'André de Saint-Victor." *Recherches augustiniennes* 24: 199–240.

Berndt, Rainer. 1991. "La pratique exégétique d'André de Saint-Victor. Tradition victorine et influence rabbinique." In *L'abbaye parisienne de Saint-Victor au moyen âge*, edited by J. Longère, 271–90. Paris: Brepols.

Berndt, Rainer. 1994. "Pierre le Mangeur et André de Saint-Victor. Contribution à l'étude de leurs sources." *Recherches de théologie ancienne et médiévale* 61: 88–114.

Blumenkranz, Bernhard. 1960. *Juifs et chrétiens dans le monde occidental, 430-1096*. Paris: Mouton. Repr., Paris: Peeters, 2006.

Blumenkranz, Bernhard. 1963. *Les auteurs chrétiens latins du moyen âge sur les juifs et le judaïsme*. Paris: Mouton. Repr., Paris: Peeters, 2007.

Bourchenin, D. 1882. *Étude sur les Académies protestantes en France au XVIe et XVIIe s.* Paris: Grassart.

Bunte, W. 1994. *Rabbinische Traditionen bei Nikolaus von Lyra*. Frankfurt: Peter Lang.

Cecini, U., and E. Vernet i Pons, eds. 2017. *Studies on the Latin Talmud*. Bellaterra: Universitat Autonoma de Barcelona.

Chazan, Robert. 1977. "The Barcelona 'Disputation' of 1263: Christian Missionizing and Jewish Response." *Speculum* 52: 824–42.

Chazan, Robert. 1988. "The Condemnation of the Talmud reconsidered (1239-1248)." *Proceedings of the American Academy for Jewish Research* 55: 11–30.

Cortabarria Beitia, A. 1970. "L'étude des langues au Moyen Âge chez les dominicains. Espagne, Orient, Raymond Martin." *Mélanges de l'Institut dominicain d'études orientales* 10: 189–248.

Dahan, Gilbert. 1978. "Rashi sujet de la controverse de 1240." *Archives juives* 14: 43–54.

Dahan, Gilbert. 1985a. "Les interprétations juives dans les commentaires du Pentateuque de Pierre le Chantre." In *The Bible in the Medieval World. Essays in Memory of Beryl Smalley*, edited by D. Wood and D. Ward, 131–55. Oxford: Basil Blackwell.

Dahan, Gilbert. 1985b. "Exégèse et polémique dans les commentaires de la Genèse d'Étienne Langton." In *Les Juifs au regard de l'histoire. Mélanges B. Blumenkranz*, edited by G. Dahan, 129–40. Paris: Picard.

Dahan, Gilbert. 1990. *Les intellectuels chrétiens et les juifs au moyen âge*. Paris: Cerf.

Dahan, Gilbert. 1992a. "Un dossier latin de textes de Rashi autour de la controverse de 1240." *Revue des études juives* 141: 321–36.

Dahan, Gilbert. 1992b. "La connaissance de l'hébreu dans les correctoires de la Bible du XIIIe siècle. Notes préliminaires." *Revue théologique de Louvain* 23: 178–90.

Dahan, Gilbert. 1997. "La connaissance de l'exégèse juive par les chrétiens, du XIIe au XIVe siècle." In *Rashi et la culture juive en France du Nord au moyen âge*, edited by Gilbert Dahan, Gérard Nahon, and Élie Nicolas, 343–59. Louvain: Peeters.

Dahan, Gilbert 1998. *The Christian Polemic against the Jews in the Middle Ages*. Engl. trans. J. Gladding. Notre Dame: University of Notre Dame.

Dahan, Gilbert. 1999a. *L'exégèse chrétienne de la Bible en Occident médiéval (XIIe-XIVe s.)*. Paris: Cerf.

Dahan, Gilbert. 1999b. "Deux psautiers hébraïques glosés en latin." *Revue des études juives* 158: 61–87.

Dahan, Gilbert. 2007. "Critique et défense de la Vulgate au XIVe siècle." In *Exégèse et critique des textes sacrés*, edited by D. Delmaire and G. Gobillot, 119–36. Paris: Geuthner.

Dahan, Gilbert. 2009a. "*Fabula* between *mythos* and *aggada*. Concerning Christian Exegesis in the Middle Ages." In *Scriptural Exegesis: The Shapes of Culture and the Religious Imagination*.

Essays in Honour of Michael Fishbane, edited by D. A. Green and S. L. Lieber, 268–80. Oxford: Oxford University Press.

Dahan, Gilbert. 2009b. "L'utilisation de l'exégèse juive dans la lecture des livres prophétiques au XIIIe siècle." In *Lire la Bible au moyen âge. Essais d'herméneutique médiévale*, 365–91. Geneva: Droz.

Dahan, Gilbert, ed. 2011. *Nicolas de Lyre, franciscain du XIVe siècle, exégète et théologien*. Paris: Études augustiniennes.

Dahan, Gilbert. 2017a. *Les juifs en France médiévale. Dix études*. Paris: Cerf.

Dahan, Gilbert. 2017b. "Sebastian Münster, Extrait de la Préface de la Bible hébraïque." *Études théologiques et religieuses* 92: 237–48.

Dahan, Gilbert. 2019. "L'utilisation de l'exégèse juive chez les exégètes chrétiens, XIIe-début du XIVe siècle." In *Judaïsme et christianisme au Moyen Âge*, edited by M.-A. Vannier, 29–50. Turnhout: Brepols.

Dahan, Gilbert, and Élie Nicolas, eds. 1999. *Le Brûlement du Talmud à Paris, 1242-1244*. Paris: Cerf.

Dahan, Gilbert, and Annie Noblesse-Rocher, eds. 2018a. *La Bible de 1500 à 1535*. Turnhout: Brepols.

Dahan, Gilbert, and Annie Noblesse-Rocher, eds 2018b. *Les hébraïsants chrétiens en France au XVIe siècle*. Geneva: Droz.

Dahan, Gilbert, and Annie Noblesse-Rocher, eds. 2020. *La Vulgate au XVIe siècle*. Turnhout: Brepols.

Friedman, Jerome. 1983. *The Most Ancient Testimony. Sixteenth Century Christian-Hebraica in the Age of the Renaissance*. Athens: Ohio University Press.

Geiger, Abraham. 1855. *Parschandatha: Die nordfranzösische Exegetenschule des 11. und 12. Jahrhunderts*. Leipzig: Schnauss.

Geiger, Ari. 2013. "*Historia Judaica*: Petrus Comestor and his Jewish Sources." in *Pierre le Mangeur ou Pierre de Troyes, maître du XIIe siècle*, edited by Gilbert Dahan, 125–45. Turnhout: Brepols.

Gelles, B. J. 1981. *Peshat and Derash in the Exegesis of Rashi*. Leiden: Brill.

Gordon, Bruce, and Matthew McLean, eds. 2002. *Shaping the Bible in the Reformation. Books, Scholars and their Readers*. Leiden: Brill.

Hailperin, Herman. 1963. *Rashi and the Christian Scholars*. Pittsburgh: University of Pittsburgh.

Hasselhoff, G. 2004. *Dicit Rabbi Moyses. Studien zum Bild von Moses Maimonides im lateinischen Westen vom 13. bis zum 15. Jahrhundert*. Würzburg: Königshausen & Neumann.

Hasselhoff, G. 2017. "Rashi's Glosses on Isaiah in BnF Ms. latin 16558." In *Studies on the Latin Talmud*, edited by U. Cecini, and E. Vernet i Pons, 111–28. Bellaterra: Universitat Autonoma de Barcelona.

Kaufmann, D. 1889. "Les juifs et la Bible de l'abbé Étienne de Cîteaux." *Revue des études juives* 18: 131–33.

Kessler-Mesguich, Sophie. 2008. "Early Christian Hebraists." In *Hebrew Bible/Old Testament: The History of Its Interpretation: Vol. 2. From the Renaissance to the Enlightenment*, edited by Magne Sæbø, Michael Fishbane, and Jean Louis Ska, 254–75. Göttingen: Vandenhoeck & Ruprecht.

Kessler-Mesguich, Sophie. 2013. *Les études hébraïques en France, de François Tissard à Richard Simon (1508-1680)*. Geneva: Droz.

Krey, P., and L. Smith, eds. 2000. *Nicholas of Lyra. The Senses of Scripture*. Leiden: Brill.

Kukenheim, Louis. 1951. *Contributions à l'histoire de la grammaire grecque, latine et hébraïque à l'époque de la Renaissance*. Leiden: Brill.

Liber, M. 1970. *Rashi*. Engl. trans.; New York: Hermon Press.

Loewe, R. 1953. "Herbert of Bosham's Commentary on Jerome's Hebrew Psalter." *Biblica* 34: 44–77, 159–92, 275–98.

Merchavia, Chen. 1970. *The Church versus Talmudic and Midrashic Literature*. Jerusalem: Bialik Institute. [In Hebrew]

Miletto, G. 2018. "L'apport des hébraïsants italiens Agazio Guidacerio et Agostino Giustiniani aux études hébraïques en France." In *La Bible de 1500 à 1535*, edited by Gilbert Dahan and Annie Noblesse-Rocher, 69–86. Turnhout: Brepols.

Morgenstern, M. 2018, "Reuchlin et les hébraïsants chrétiens en France au XVIe siècle." In *La Bible de 1500 à 1535*, edited by Gilbert Dahan and Annie Noblesse-Rocher, 47–68. Turnhout: Brepols.

Muller, Richard A., and John L. Thompson, eds. 1996. *Biblical Interpretation in the Era of the Reformation*. Grand Rapids: Eerdmans.

Noblesse-Rocher, Annie. 2010. "L'école rhénane d'exégèse et ses sources juives." In *La Théologie: Vol. 3. Anthologie, Renaissance et réformes*, edited by B. Lauret, N. Lemaître, and M. Lienhard, 84–97. Paris: Cerf.

Olszowy-Schlanger, J., and A. Grondeux, eds. 2008. *Dictionnaire hébreu-latin-français de la Bible hébraïque de l'abbaye de Ramsey (XIIIe s.)*. Turnhout: Brepols.

Overfield, J. H. 1971. "A New Look at the Reuchlin Affair." *Studies in Medieval and Renaissance History* 8: 165–207.

Peri, V. 1977. "*Correctores immo corruptores*. Un saggio di critica testuale nella Roma del XII secolo." *Italia medioevale e umanistica* 20: 19–125.

Rashdall, Hastings. 1936. *The Universities of Europe in the Middle Ages*. Ed. F. M. Powicke and A. B. Emden. 3 vols. Oxford: Oxford University Press. Repr., 1997.

Reinhardt, K. 2011. "Les controverses autour de la Postille au XVe siècle." In *Nicolas de Lyre, Franciscain*, edited by Gilbert Dahan, 269–79. Paris: Études augustiniennes.

Saltman, A. 1973. "Raban Maurus and the Pseudo-Hieronymian Quaestiones . . ." *Harvard Theological Review* 66: 43–75.

Schwarzbach, B. E. 2018. "Les Bibles 'rabbiniques' de l'imprimeur Daniel Bomberg, 1517 et 1524-1525." In *La Bible de 1500 à 1535*, edited by Gilbert Dahan and Annie Noblesse-Rocher, 197–224. Turnhout: Brepols.

Schwarzfuchs, L. 2004. *Le livre hébreu à Paris au XVIe siècle*. Paris: Bibliothèque nationale.

Schwarzfuchs, L. 2008. *L'hébreu dans le livre lyonnais au XVIe siècle*. Paris: Ecole normale supérieure.

Secret, François. 1964a. *Les kabbalistes chrétiens de la Renaissance*. Paris: Dunod.

Secret, François. 1964b. *Le Zôhar chez les kabbalistes chrétiens de la Renaissance*. Paris: Mouton.

Shuali, E. 2018. "La bible hébraïque de Sébastien Münster." In *La Bible de 1500 à 1535*, edited by Gilbert Dahan and Annie Noblesse-Rocher, 283–98. Turnhout: Brepols.

Sirat, René-Samuel, ed. 2006. *Héritages de Rachi*. Paris: Éditions de l'éclat.

Smalley, Beryl. 1951. "A Commentary of Herbert of Bosham on the Hebraica." *Recherches de théologie ancienne et médiévale* 18: 29–65.

Smith, L. 2008. "Nicholas of Lyra and Old Testament Interpretation." In *From the Renaissance to the Enlightenment*, edited by Magne Sæbø, Michael Fishbane, and Jean Louis Ska, 49–63. Göttingen: Vandenhoeck & Ruprecht.

Steinmetz, David C. ed. 1990. *The Bible in the Sixteenth Century*. Durham: Duke University Press.

Torrens, A. 2018. "Les imprimeurs d'hébreu et l'hébraïsme en France au premier xvIᵉ siècle." In *La Bible de 1500 à 1535*, edited by Gilbert Dahan and Annie Noblesse-Rocher, 89–103. Turnhout: Brepols.

Touitou, E. 1985. "Quelques aspects de l'exégèse biblique juive en France médiévale." *Archives juives* 21: 35–39.

Vanderjagt, A. 2008. "*Ad fontes!* The Early Humanist Concern for the *Hebraica Veritas*." In *Hebrew Bible/Old Testament: The History of Its Interpretation: Vol. 2. From the Renaissance to the Enlightenment*, edited by Magne Sæbø, Michael Fishbane, and Jean Louis Ska, 154–89. Göttingen: Vandenhoeck & Ruprecht.

van Zwieten, J. W. M. 1987. "Jewish Exegesis within Christian Bounds." *Bijdragen* 48: 327–35.

Walde, Bernhard. 1916. *Christliche Hebraisten Deutschlands am Ausgang des Mittelalters.* Münster: Aschendorff.

Weil, G. E. 1963. *Elie Levita, humaniste et massorète 1469-1549.* Leiden: Brill.

Zaluska, Y. 1989. *L'enluminure et le Scriptorium de Cîteaux.* Cîteaux: Abbaye de Cîteaux.

CHAPTER 23

MODERN SCHOLARSHIP ON THE LATIN BIBLE

THOMAS JOHANN BAUER

The Beginnings of Critical Research in the Seventeenth and Eighteenth Centuries

PARALLEL to work on the Sixto-Clementine edition of the Vulgate, efforts to produce an edition of the older Latin text of the Bible had also begun in the sixteenth century. Flaminio de' Nobili (ca. 1532–90), who was the first to present a critical edition of the Old Latin translation, was also a member of the third Roman committee on the Vulgate (see chap. 19). His edition of the Old Testament was based on the Greek edition of the Septuagint published in 1587 under the direction of Antonio Carafa.[1] The majority of the Latin text follows citations in the Church Fathers, and an apparatus provides information about the origin of the material. For the numerous passages for which no witnesses were available, Nobili prepared his own translation from the Septuagint.

The first publication of Old Latin manuscript witnesses appeared in Rome in 1688 in the edition by Giuseppe Maria Tomasi (1649–1713) of old tables of contents of the Scriptures.[2] Plans for a better edition of the Old Latin text of the Bible, based on quotations and manuscripts, were made by the French Benedictine Jean Martianay (1647–1717) of the Congregation of St. Maur. For his edition of Jerome's writings, he and his confrere Antoine Pouget (1650–1709) published the *Divina Bibliotheca* (i.e., the text

---

[1] Flaminius Nobilius (ed.), *Vetus Testamentum secundum LXX Latine redditum et ex auctoritate Sixti V. pont. max. editum* (Rome: Ferrarius, 1588); see further Stummer 1928: 181; Corssen 1900: 3.

[2] Giuseppe Maria Caro [Tomasi] (ed.), *Sacrorum Bibliorum iuxta editionem seu LXX interpretum seu B. Hieronymi veteres tituli siue capitula sectiones et stichometriae.* (2 vols.) (Rome: Corbelletti, 1688).

of the Vulgate) as the first volume in 1693.[3] Among the manuscripts they consulted were witnesses to the Old Latin translation, of which Martianay published the text of two manuscripts from Corbie in 1695 as separate collations for the Gospel of Matthew (VL 9) and the Epistle of James (VL 66).

The French Benedictine Pierre Sabatier (1682–1742), also of the Congregation of St. Maur, took up Martianay's work. He succeeded in producing a satisfactory scholarly edition of the Old Latin translation, which provided reliable information, verse by verse, about the material known to survive and the attestation of the text. However, he died before his work was published in Rheims. Printing was completed in 1749, although all three volumes give the year 1743 on the title page.[4] Volumes 1 and 2 cover the books of the Old Testament, volume 3 the New Testament. A general preface at the beginning of the first volume, with additions at the beginning of the third, provides information about the history of the Old Latin translation, its attestation in manuscripts and quotations, and the principles of the edition. In addition to tables of contents, there is a separate preface at the beginning of individual writings or groups. Each page of the edition has two columns, the inner column offering the text of the Roman Vulgate (i.e., the Sixto-Clementine edition) and the outer the Old Latin text parallel to it. The outer margin of the page indicates the witnesses for the Old Latin, the inner margin biblical parallels. In the lower part of each page, a critical apparatus offers variants in manuscripts and quotations as well as supplementary information on individual Old Latin readings or on the Greek text. In passages for which no Old Latin translation is attested, both columns are used for the Vulgate. In the case of the Psalter, Jerome's translation from the Hebrew is printed in a third column between the Vulgate and the Old Latin text.

At the same time as Pierre Sabatier, Giuseppe Bianchini (1704–64), an Italian Oratorian, produced an edition of the Old Latin translation of the Gospels. His two-volume edition, which provides the text of four Old Latin manuscripts (VL 3, 4, 8 [9 in Matthew], 10) on a single opening for comparison, was published in Rome in 1749.[5] One of his sources was Martianay's collation of the Corbie manuscript of Matthew (VL 9), which he adopted unaltered. Bianchini is clearly less comprehensive than Sabatier, and the differing layout of their editions reflects opposing views on the beginnings of the Latin Bible: Sabatier, like Nobili, wanted to recreate a single translation that stood at the beginning of the Latin Bible, while Bianchini saw its origin in several independent translations.

[3] Johannes Martianay (ed.), *Sancti Eusebii Hieronymi Stridonensis Presbyteri Divina Bibliotheca.* (Paris: Roulland, 1693).

[4] Petrus Sabatier (ed.), *Bibliorum Sacrorum Latinae versiones antiquae, seu Vetus Italica, et ceterae quaecunque in Codicibus Mss. & antiquorum libris reperiri potuerunt: Quae cum Vulgata Latina, & cum Textu Graeco comparantur* . . . (3 vols.) (Rheims: Florentain, 1743[–1749]), 2nd unaltered ed., Paris 1751). See further Houghton 2016: 113–15; Cimosa 2008: 157f.; Metzger 1977: 319; Stummer 1928: 30–33; Corssen 1900: 3f.

[5] Josephus Blanchinus (ed.), *Evangeliarium quadruplex Latinae versionis antiquae seu veteris Italicae. Nunc primum in lucem editum ex codicibus manuscriptis* . . . (2 vols.) (Rome: Rubeis, 1749). See Houghton 2016: 136; Metzger 1977: 319f.

RESEARCH ON THE LATIN BIBLE IN THE NINETEENTH CENTURY

After Sabatier and Bianchini, research on the Old Latin Bible came to a stand-still for almost a century, before resuming with studies of its beginnings and early history.

The Old Latin Translation

Nicholas Wiseman (1802–65), later Cardinal Archbishop of Westminster, attempted to prove that there was in fact only one initial Latin translation, justifying the view that the beginnings of the Latin Bible were in North Africa (1832).[6] His assumption of a single translation was later contradicted by Leo Ziegler (1842–1918), a Protestant theologian and philologist, who published a study of the Latin scriptural text in the time before the Vulgate and the *Itala* of Augustine.[7] According to Wiseman, the discrepancies in manuscripts and quotations and the multitude of divergent translations already lamented by the Church Fathers were the result of several independent adaptations of a single translation; according to Ziegler, the correspondences between the divergent testimonies of the ancient Latin translation were the result of a secondary alignment of independent translations (see further chap. 1).

The discussion as to when the first Latin translations of biblical texts became available received new impetus in the last quarter of the nineteenth century with the discovery and publication of the complete text of the Acts of the Scillitan Martyrs (held in Carthage in 180 CE). Hermann Usener (1834–1905) had first edited the text from a Greek manuscript and identified it as a translation from Latin.[8] A little later, the newly discovered Latin text was edited by Joseph Armitage Robinson (1858–1933).[9] Since the text bears witness to Latin-speaking Christianity in North Africa in the last quarter of the second century, and mentions *libri et epistulae Pauli uiri iusti* ("books and letters of Paul, a righteous man"), it was seen as proof that Latin translations of the biblical scriptures were widespread at that time. Peter Corssen (1856–1928) found confirmation for this in the Latin biblical quotations in the *Passio Perpetuae* (1899; see Corssen

---

[6] Nicholas Wiseman, *Two letters on some parts of the controversy concerning 1. John V.7, containing also an enquiry into the origin of the first Latin version of Scripture, commonly called the Itala* (Rome: Salviucci, 1835).

[7] Leo Ziegler, *Die lateinischen Bibelübersetzungen vor Hieronymus und die Itala des Augustinus. Ein Beitrag zur Geschichte der Heiligen Schrift* (Munich: Riedel, 1879).

[8] Hermann Usener (ed.), *Acta martyrum Scilitanorum Graece* (Bonn: Georgi, 1881).

[9] Joseph Armitage Robinson (ed.), *The Passion of S. Perpetua* (Cambridge: Cambridge University Press, 1891).

1900: 9f.). These quotations, as Armitage Robinson had shown in his edition, were close to those in Tertullian (ca. 160–220). Quotations and paraphrases of Old and New Testament texts in Tertullian received special attention as potential early evidence for an ancient Latin biblical text. Hermann Rönsch (1821–88), who compiled and edited all the material for the New Testament, believed that Tertullian was dependent on existing translations.[10] In contrast, Theodor Zahn (1838–1933), among others, maintained that a written Latin biblical text did not exist at the time of Tertullian.[11] Armitage Robinson observed an early use of a Latin biblical text in Gaul in the letter of the year 177 CE from the congregations in Lyons and Vienne quoted by Eusebius of Caesarea: a striking paraphrase of Ephesians 6:5 in this Greek text can only be satisfactorily explained as a re-translation from Latin.[12]

The Vulgate

Although Humfrey Hody (1659–1707) had compiled and published material for a comprehensive history of the Latin Bible in 1705, in the nineteenth century it was initially mainly Catholic theologians who contributed to further research into the history of the Vulgate.[13] Editions were limited to reprints of the Sixto-Clementine Vulgate with some corrections and supplementary information (Stummer 1928: 207f.). First came that of Leander van Ess (1772–1847), who provided the text of the 1592 edition with variants from the 1593 and 1598 editions as well as Sixtus V's edition of 1590.[14] Between 1849 and 1881, similar reprints were undertaken by Valentin Loch (1813–93), Carlo Vercellone (1814–69), and Suitbert Bäumer (1845–94).[15] The 1906 edition by Michael Hetzenauer (1860–1926) also stands in this line.[16] Van Ess also produced a history of the Vulgate, which combines an account of the beginnings of the Latin Bible with analyses of the Vulgate decree of the Council of Trent and the subsequent preparation of the official edition.[17] Following this, Franz Kaulen (1827–1907) in Bonn also published a history of the

---

[10] Hermann Rönsch, *Das Neue Testament Tertullian's aus den Schriften des Letzteren möglichst vollständig reconstruirt* (Leipzig: Fuess, 1871); see Stummer 1928: 11–14.

[11] Theodor Zahn, *Geschichte des Neutestamentlichen Kanons* (Vol. 1/1) (Erlangen: Deichert, 1888), 48–60; see the criticism in Corssen 1900: 13–15.

[12] Eusebius, *Historia Ecclesiastica* 5.1.1; Robinson, *The Passion of S. Perpetua*, 97–100. See also Fischer 1972: 6; Stummer 1928: 9–11; Corssen 1900: 11.

[13] Humphrey Hody, *De bibliorum textibus originalibus, versionibus graecis, & latina vulgata libri IV* (Oxford: Sheldonian, 1705): see Corssen 1900: 52.

[14] Leander van Ess (ed.), *Biblia Sacra vulgatae editionis* (3 vols.; Tübingen: Fues, 1822–1824).

[15] Valentin Loch (ed.), *Biblia Sacra vulgatae editionis* (4 vols.) (Regensburg: Manz, 1849); Carlo Vercellone (ed.), *Biblia Sacra vulgatae editionis* (Rome: Congregation for the Propagation of the Faith, 1861); *Biblia Sacra vulgatae editionis* (Turin: Marietti, 1881; Suitbert Bäumer as consultant for the text).

[16] Michael Hetzenauer (ed.), *Biblia Sacra vulgatae editionis* (3 vols.) (Innsbruck: Wagner, 1906).

[17] Leander van Ess, *Pragmatisch-kritische Geschichte der Vulgata im Allgemeinen und zunächst in Bezug auf das Trientische Decret* (Tübingen: Fues, 1824).

Latin Bible (1868) and an introduction to its language and style (1870).[18] In the year between these two volumes, a similar study by the Protestant theologian Hermann Rönsch appeared, taking into account the differences between the Vulgate and the Old Latin translation.[19]

Specialist studies of individual aspects of the history of the Vulgate complemented these overviews. The Dominican Heinrich Suso Denifle (1846–1905) examined medieval corrections to the text of the Vulgate in detail.[20] Richard Simon (1638–1712) had already drawn attention to these *correctoria*, and Carlo Vercellone had studied those in the Vatican Library.[21] The French Protestant theologian Samuel Berger (1843–1900) undertook further work on such *correctoria*, including a summary of his results in a major study of the history of the Vulgate in the early Middle Ages.[22] This had a decisive influence on further research, even though Berger's conception of the textual history of the Vulgate and his theory of a gradual spread from France to the rest of Europe was outdated (Fischer 1972: 2 n. 4; Stummer 1928: 207; Corssen 1900: 54f.). Another French scholar, Léopold Delisle (1826–1910), also made important contributions to the study of the medieval history of the Vulgate with works on the Theodulf Bible and the scriptorium of Tours.[23]

Luigi Maria Ungarelli (1779–1845), a Barnabite, played an important role in researching the origin of the official Roman edition of the Vulgate. He rediscovered a copy of the text produced by the commission set up by Sixtus V and led by Cardinal Antonio Carafa (Vatican City, BAV, Vat. lat. 12959–60; see Stummer 1928: 182–95; Colgiago 1987: 118–23). Comparing this with the first official edition of the Vulgate published in 1590 revealed the extent to which Sixtus V had not adopted the text of the commission.[24] This was investigated in more detail by his student and fellow Barnabite

---

[18] Franz Kaulen, *Geschichte der Vulgata* (Mainz: Kirchheim, 1868); Franz Kaulen, *Handbuch zur Vulgata. Eine systematische Darstellung ihres lateinischen Sprachcharakters* (Mainz: Kirchheim, 1870).

[19] Hermann Rönsch, *Itala and Vulgate. Das Sprachidiom der urchristlichen Itala und der katholischen Vulgata unter Berücksichtigung der römischen Volkssprache* (Marburg: Elwert, 1869); Hermann Rönsch, *Itala and Vulgate. Das Sprachidiom der urchristlichen Itala und der katholischen Vulgata unter Berücksichtigung der römischen Volkssprache* (2nd ed.) (Marburg: Elwert, 1875); see Corssen 1900: 75f.

[20] Heinrich Suso Denifle, "Die Handschriften der Bibel-Korrektorien des 13. Jahrhunderts," *Archiv für Literatur- und Kirchengeschichte des Mittelalters* 4 (1888): 263–311, 471–601. See Metzger 1977: 346f; Stummer 1928: 155–57; Corssen 1900: 64–67.

[21] Carlo Vercellone, "Dei correttori biblici della Biblioteca Vaticana," *Dissertazioni della Pontificia Accademia Romana di Archeologia* 14 (1860): 211–29 (presented in 1857).

[22] Samuel Berger, "Des essais qui ont été faits à Paris au XIIIe siècle pour corriger le texte de la Vulgate," *Revue de Théologie et de Philosophie* 16 (1883): 4–66; Samuel Berger, *Quam notitiam linguae hebraicae habuerint Christiani medii aevi temporibus in Gallia* (Paris: Berger-Levrault, 1893); Samuel Berger, *Histoire de la Vulgate pendant les premiers siècles du moyen âge* (Paris: Berger-Levrault, 1893).

[23] Léopold Delisle, "Les Bibles de Théodulf," *Bibliothèque de l'École des Chartes* 40 (1879): 5–47; Léopold Delisle, *Mémoire sur l'école calligraphique de Tours au IXe siècle* (Paris: Imprimerie nationale, 1885); see Corssen 1900: 59–61.

[24] Aloisius Maria Ungarellius, *Prælectiones de Novo Testamento et historia Vulgatæ Bibliorum editionis a concilio Tridentino* (Rome: Salviucciani, 1847).

Carlo Vercellone.[25] Franz Heinrich Reusch (1825–1900) in Bonn also followed up Ungarelli's preliminary work.[26] Important supplementary studies on the origin and publication of the Sixtine Vulgate were presented at the beginning of the twentieth century by Paul Maria Baumgarten (1860–1948), Johann Baptist Nisius (1853–1922), and Fridolin Amann (1882–1963).[27] For the Sixto-Clementine Vulgate of 1592, mention should be made of the works of Xavier-Marie Le Bachelet (1855–1925), the Benedictine Hildebrand Höpfl (1872–1934), and the Jesuit Karl Alois Kneller (1857–1942).[28]

Impetus from Editions of the Greek Bible

Although it became increasingly clear that the Sixto-Clementine Vulgate provided neither a critically responsible text nor the information on attestation in manuscripts and citations necessary for textual history, work toward a new critical edition progressed only hesitantly. It was textual criticism of the Greek New Testament that drove the need for an improved edition of the Vulgate. The eighteenth century had seen criticism of the accuracy and reliability of the *Textus Receptus*, the Greek text which predominated in New Testament editions and could be traced back as far as Erasmus of Rotterdam (1464/69–1536). Richard Bentley (1662–1742), an English philologist, attached particular importance to the Vulgate for determining the New Testament text. Accordingly, he planned to produce a reliable text of the New Testament Vulgate on the basis of manuscripts as a foundation for work on the text of the Greek New Testament, but neither saw the light of day.[29]

In the next century, Karl Lachmann (1793–1851) decided that, on the basis of the evidence then known, the oldest tangible form of the text of the Greek New Testament

---

[25] Carlo Vercellone, 'Studi fatti in Roma e mezzi usati per correggere la Bibbia Volgata,' in Carlo Vercellone, *Dissertazioni accademiche di vario argomento* (Rome: Spithoever, 1864), 57–78.

[26] Franz Heinrich Reusch, "Erklärung der Decrete des Trienter Concils welche sich auf die Vulgata betreten," *Der Katholik* 2, no. 3 (1860): 641–77; Franz Heinrich Reusch, "Zur Geschichte der Entstehung der officiellen Ausgabe der Vulgata," *Der Katholik* 2, no. 4 (1860): 1–24.

[27] Paul Maria Baumgarten, *Die Vulgata Sixtina von 1590 und ihre Einführungsbulle* (Alttestamentliche Abhandlungen 3.2) (Münster: Aschendorff, 1911); Paul Maria Baumgarten, *Neue Kunde von alten Bibeln* (2 vols.) (Rome: Krumbach, 1922–27); Johann Baptist Nisius, "Zur Geschichte der Vulgata Sixtina," *Zeitschrift für Katholische Theologie* 36 (1912): 1–47; 37 (1913): 681–89, 706–8, 878–89; Fridolin Amann, *Die Vulgata Sixtina von 1590* (Freiburger theologische Studien 10) (Freiburg: Herder, 1912).

[28] Xavier-Marie Le Bachelet, *Bellarmin et la Bible sixto-clémentine* (Etudes de théologie historique 3) (Paris: Beauchesne, 1911); Hildebrand Höpfl, *Beiträge zur Geschichte der sixto-klementinischen Vulgata, nach gedruckten und ungedruckten Quellen* (Biblische Studien 18) (Freiburg: Herder, 1913); Karl Alois Kneller, "Zur Geschichte der klementinischen Vulgata-Ausgaben," *Zeitschrift für katholische Theologie* 43 (1919): 391–438; Karl Alois Kneller, "Zur Vulgata Sixtus V.," *Zeitschrift für katholische Theologie* 46 (1922): 313–25, 468–79; 47 (1923): 154–59, 601–11; 48 (1924): 133–51; Karl Alois Kneller, "Neue Studien zur sixtinischen Vulgatabulle," *Zeitschrift für katholische Theologie* 59 (1935): 81–107, 268–90.

[29] See further his letters to Archbishop Wake (1716) and *Dr Bentley's Proposals for Printing a New Edition of the Greek Testament and St. Hierom's Latin Version* (London: Knapton, 1721).

was that of the fourth century, which also underlay Jerome's Vulgate.[30] This meant that the Vulgate was an important aid to New Testament textual criticism, once its original text had been recovered. Following his 1831 edition of the Greek text, Lachmann published a bilingual edition of the New Testament in which his text of the Vulgate was printed underneath the Greek and its apparatus.[31] The most important manuscripts he used for his text of the Vulgate were the sixth-century Codex Fuldensis (Vg F) and the eighth-century Codex Amiatinus (Vg A; for more details of these and the other manuscripts cited in this chapter, see the corresponding entry in Houghton 2016). His apparatus also presents Old Latin variants from Sabatier's edition. Another German philologist, Theodor Friedrich Heyse (1803–84) published an edition of the Vulgate for the Old Testament with Constantin von Tischendorf (1815–74). In this, the text of the Sixto-Clementine Vulgate was set out in sense-lines corresponding to those in Codex Amiatinus, with textual variants from this manuscript also recorded.[32] Using the Epistle to the Galatians, Peter Corssen attempted to show what a critical edition of the Vulgate of the New Testament might look like, taking into account the variants of Old Latin tradition.[33]

With the discovery of new manuscripts of the Greek New Testament, other and better witnesses to the fourth-century text became available. At the same time, it became apparent that witnesses to the Old Latin translation apparently preserved a form of the New Testament that was already widespread in the second century (sometimes termed the "Western text"), which some scholars believed preserved the original wording, at least in certain places (see further Fischer 1972: 80–92). Since the Old Latin translation and, to some extent, the Vulgate were considered important witnesses to New Testament textual history, their readings were recorded in major critical editions along with those of other early translations (Houghton 2016: 134f.; Parker 2008: 207–13; Aland and Aland 1989: 21–46).

Samuel Prideaux Tregelles (1813–75) examined and collated numerous manuscripts, including Latin ones, for his edition. This included the text of Codex Amiatinus parallel to the Greek text, with an indication of the variants of the Sixto-Clementine Vulgate, while in the critical apparatus he noted readings from Old Latin sources.[34] Tischendorf also gave a comprehensive account of the Old Latin translation and the Vulgate in the apparatus of the eighth edition of his critical text, followed a few decades later by the extensive edition of Hermann von Soden (1852–1914).[35] Brooke Foss Westcott (1825–1901)

---

[30] Karl Lachmann, "Rechenschaft über seine Ausgabe des Neuen Testaments," *Theologische Studien und Kritiken* 3 (1830): 817–45.

[31] Karl Lachmann (ed.), *Novum Testamentum Graece et Latine* (2 vols.) (Berlin: Reimer, 1842/1850); see Metzger 1977: 349.

[32] Theodor Heyse and Constantin von Tischendorf (eds.), *Biblia sacra Latina Veteris Testamenti* (Leipzig: Brockhaus, 1873).

[33] Peter Corssen (ed.), *Epistula ad Galatas ad fidem optimorum codicum vulgatae* (Berlin: Weidmann, 1885).

[34] Samuel Prideaux Tregelles (ed.), *The Greek New Testament* (London: Bagster, 1857–1879).

[35] Constantin von Tischendorf (ed.), *Novum Testamentum Graece* (editio octava critica maior) (Leipzig: Giesecke und Devrient, 1869/1872); Hermann von Soden (ed.), *Die Schriften des Neuen Testament in ihrer ältesten erreichbaren Textgestalt* (Göttingen: Vandenhoek und Ruprecht, 1902).

and Fenton John Anthony Hort (1828–92) attached special importance to the Old Latin as a witness to the "Western text." Where this offered a shorter text than the best witnesses of the Greek text, they believed that this should be taken as original (the "Western Non-Interpolations").[36]

As early as the end of the eighteenth century, Robert Holmes (1748–1805) in Oxford began a critical edition of the Septuagint based on all known material, continued and completed after his death by James Parsons (1762–1847).[37] The critical apparatus lists the early translations, including the Old Latin based on Sabatier's edition. Similarly comprehensive editions of the Septuagint, with references to Old Latin and Vulgate sources in the apparatus, followed in the twentieth century. Parts of the Cambridge edition of Alan England Brooke (1863–1939) and Norman McLean (1865–1947) appeared between 1906 and 1940, remaining unfinished.[38] Even more extensive was the Göttingen Septuagint of Rudolph Smend (1851–1913) and Julius Wellhausen (1844–1918), continued by Alfred Rahlfs (1865–1935), which is still ongoing.[39]

The Göttingen edition, and Septuagint research as a whole, benefited from the work of Paul de Lagarde (1827–91), a German Protestant theologian who was a student of Karl Lachmann (Jellicoe 1968: 5–9; Würthwein 1988: 71–73). Lagarde started from the assumption that all manuscripts (Greek and Latin) contained a mixed text, deriving from different traditions, and that the original form could be obtained through an eclectic process. One important step was the elimination of the dominant influence of Origen's Hexapla: as this postdated the initial Latin translation, the Old Latin witnesses were therefore particularly valuable for this (see chap. 2). Lagarde also realized that Sabatier's edition was no longer sufficient to provide a complete picture of Old Latin tradition. In 1885, he produced a sample based on the evidence for Psalms 1–17, but this approach did not initially meet with approval and was not taken further.[40]

Editions of Latin Biblical Manuscripts

The new critical editions of the Greek text of the Old and New Testaments were the result of the analysis of manuscripts already known and a search for further witnesses

[36] Brooke Foss Westcott and Fenton John Anthony Hort (eds.), *The New Testament in the Original Greek* (2 vols.) (London: Macmillan, 1881/1882).

[37] Robert Holmes and James Parsons (eds.), *Vetus Testamentum Graecum* (3 vols.) (Oxford: Clarendon, 1798–1823); see Jellicoe 1968: 2f.; Würthwein 1988: 88.

[38] Alan England Brooke and Norman McLean (eds.), *The Old Testament in Greek* (Cambridge: Cambridge University Press, 1906–40): see Jellicoe 1968: 21–24; Würthwein 1988: 88.

[39] Alfred Rahlfs et al. (eds.), *Septuagint. Vetus Testamentum Graecum* (Göttingen: Vandenhoek und Ruprecht, 1931–); see Jellicoe 1968: 9–21; Würthwein 1988: 88f.

[40] Paul de Lagarde, *Probe einer neuen Ausgabe der lateinischen Übersetzungen des Alten Testaments* (Göttingen: Dieterich, 1885); see Corssen 1900: 4.

that were as old as possible. During this systematic sifting through library holdings in the latter part of the nineteenth century, further important evidence was discovered for the Old Latin and Vulgate traditions. This led to the publication of separate editions of individual documents, often with collations providing details of variant readings in other manuscripts. The rapidly growing number of such editions made the text of more and more manuscripts accessible, providing an important initial step toward further work on critical editions and research into the textual history of the Latin Bible.

Ernst Ranke (1814–88), a theologian in Marburg, produced an edition of Codex Fuldensis (Vg F) in 1868, followed shortly after by a collation of Old Latin gospel fragments in Chur (VL 16).[41] Codex Fuldensis is of particular importance as a witness to a Gospel harmony based on Tatian's *Diatessaron* (see chap. 15 and Schmid 2014). In the same year as that edition, Albrecht Vogel (1822–90) published fragments of the Old Latin translation of Ezekiel from the monastery of St. Paul in Carinthia (part of VL 175) and of Proverbs from the Vienna Court Library (VL 165).[42] A third contemporary Protestant scholar, Leo Ziegler, was responsible for printing the fragmentary Old Latin texts of the Pauline Epistles and 1 John (VL 64) and a palimpsest of the Pentateuch (VL 104).[43] The Norwegian theologian Johannes Belsheim (1829–1909) was particularly productive, editing several manuscripts of the Old Latin Gospels and fragments of the Latin Old Testament. He also published the Old Latin text of the Acts of the Apostles and Revelation from the thirteenth-century Codex Gigas (VL 51), with a collation of the rest of the New Testament.[44] However, the quality and care of his editions was severely criticized, with Corssen condemning them as "sämtlich wissenschaftlich unbrauchbar" ("completely unusable for scholarship"; Corssen 1900: 19, n. 1).

Research on the Latin Bible in the Twentieth Century

The twentieth century is marked by the publication of the Oxford Vulgate, begun several years earlier, and the inauguration of two major projects, the Roman Vulgate and the *Vetus Latina* edition.

---

[41] Ernst Ranke, *Codex Fuldensis* (Marburg: Elwert, 1868); Ernst Ranke, *Curiensia Evangelii Lucani fragmenta Latinae* (Marburg: Koch, 1872).

[42] Albrecht Vogel, *Beiträge zur Herstellung der alten lateinischen Bibel-Uebersetzung* (Vienna: Braumüller, 1868).

[43] Leo Ziegler, *Italafragmente der Paulinischen Briefe nebst Bruchstücken einer vorhieronymianischen Übersetzung des ersten Iohannesbriefes* (Marburg: Elwert, 1876); Leo Ziegler, *Bruchstücke einer vorhieronymianischen Übersetzung des Pentateuch* (Munich: Riedel, 1883).

[44] Johannes Belsheim, *Die Apostel-Geschichte und die Offenbarung Johannis in einer alten lateinischen Übersetzung aus dem "Gigas librorum"* (Christiania: Malling, 1879).

The Oxford Vulgate (New Testament)

An official announcement of plans for a new, three-volume edition of the Vulgate edited by the Oxford scholar John Wordsworth (1843–1911) was made in 1882. Building on research that, in part, reached back into the eighteenth century, the goal of the edition was to provide an accurate representation of the Vulgate text at the beginning of the fifth century, as well as giving information about later forms of text and, for the Gospels, the Old Latin translation on which Jerome's revision was based. Following Wordsworth's appointment as Bishop of Salisbury, Henry Julian White (1859–1934) was appointed as co-editor in charge of the edition. The first fascicle, with the introduction and text of the Gospel of Matthew, appeared in 1889; volume one, comprising all four Gospels, was completed in 1898. Work continued with the initial fascicles of Acts (1905) and Romans (1913). The second volume, of the Pauline Epistles, was not completed until 1941, after the death both of White and his assistant Alexander Ramsbotham (1870–1932). It was seen through the press by Hedley Sparks (1908–96), who also completed the third volume and, thereby, the edition itself, in 1954.[45] In addition, White published a single-volume hand edition of the entire Latin New Testament in 1911, based on the work carried out to that point.[46]

As is customary, this substantial edition lists the manuscripts used and provides a critical apparatus with the attestation of the text and divergent readings. Detailed introductions are found only in the first volume on the Gospels and in the first fascicles of the other two volumes. The later contributions lack such introductions. Individual books are preceded by Jerome's prologues or those from other Church Fathers, as well as ancient outlines (lists of *sectiones* and *capitula*). The division of the text into sense-lines follows Codex Amiatinus (Vg A), which was considered the most important witness by the editors. Below the editorial text of the Gospels, the sixth-century Codex Brixianus (VL 10) is printed from Bianchini's edition (see above), as Wordsworth and White believed that this represented the Old Latin form underlying Jerome's revision. Overall, this three-volume edition of the Vulgate of the New Testament is a significant achievement. Nevertheless, some justified criticism has been made: particularly problematic are the assumption that Codex Amiatinus is a consistently excellent witness and the identification of Codex Brixianus as Jerome's model (see Fischer 1955: 180–85).

Parallel to work on the Vulgate, Wordsworth initiated the Oxford series of *Old-Latin Biblical Texts* in 1883, with editions of important manuscripts. He was responsible for editing the Old Latin text of Matthew in Codex Sangermanensis *I* (VL 7/Vg G) and an edition of the fourth-century Codex Bobiensis (VL 1), in collaboration with White and William

---

[45] John Wordsworth, Henry Julian White, et al. (eds.), *Nouum Testamentum Domini nostri Iesu Christi latine secundum Editionem Sancti Hieronymi* (3 vols.) (Oxford: Clarendon, 1889–1954).

[46] John Wordsworth and Henry Julian White (eds.), *Nouum Testamentum Latine, secundum editionem Sancti Hieronymi* (editio minor) (Oxford: Clarendon, 1911). See Metzger 1977: 350; Fischer 1972: 51f.

Sanday (1843–1920).[47] White edited the text of Codex Monacensis (VL 13) and the Bobbio palimpsest (VL 53).[48] Edgar Buchanan (1872–1932) presented new editions of two known Old Latin Gospel manuscripts, Codex Corbeiensis secundus (VL 8) and Codex Veronensis (VL 4); the former also included the fragments of the Fleury palimpsest (VL 55).[49] However, his subsequent four volumes of *Sacred Latin Texts* (1912–16), in which he published the text of further manuscripts of the Latin New Testament, met with criticism.[50]

The Roman Vulgate (Old Testament)

Work began in Rome at the beginning of the twentieth century on a critical edition of the Vulgate, commissioned by Pope Pius X (see Stummer 1928: 208f.; Metzger 1977: 351f.; Sainte-Marie 1987: 144–48). Carlo Vercellone had already compiled a collection of variants to the text of the Sixto-Clementine Vulgate from manuscripts for the Pentateuch and the books of Joshua to Kings, revealing the extent to which it was in need of revision.[51] The Pope's intention was to establish a scholarly basis for improving the official Vulgate text for use in the Roman Catholic Church. Since this could not be done by an individual, a request was made in 1907 to Abbot Hildebrand de Hemptienne (1849–1913) to see if the Benedictines would be willing to undertake this work. The assembly of the presiding abbots of the Benedictine Congregations decided to set up a commission for the revision of the Vulgate. Its leadership was entrusted to Francis Aidan Gasquet (1846–1929), an English Benedictine abbot. The commission was initially based in Sant'Anselmo, the Benedictine college and high school on the Aventine, but in 1933, the Abbey of St Jerome (San Girolamo) in Trastevere was built for its use (Cimosa 2006: 170). The central figure for almost two decades in this work toward a new Roman edition of the Vulgate was the French Benedictine Henri Quentin (1872–1935). After his death, Robert Weber (1904–80), a Benedictine from Luxembourg, took over responsibility. The edition only contains the books of the Old Testament: the first volume appeared in 1926 after extensive preliminary work, while the final, eighteenth volume was only published in 1995.[52]

---

[47] John Wordsworth (ed.), *The Gospel according to St. Matthew from the St. Germain MS* (Oxford: Clarendon, 1883); John Wordsworth, William Sanday, and H. J. White (eds.), *Portions of the Gospels according to St. Mark and St. Matthew from the Bobbio MS* (Oxford: Clarendon, 1886).

[48] Henry Julian White (ed.), *The Four Gospels from the Munich MS* (Oxford: Clarendon, 1888); Henry Julian White (ed.), *Portions of the Acts of the Apostles of the Epistle of St. James and the first Epistle of St. Peter from the Bobbio Palimpsest* (Oxford: Clarendon, 1897).

[49] E. S. Buchanan (ed.), *The Four Gospels from the Codex Corbeiensis . . . together with fragments . . . from the Fleury Palimpsest* (Oxford: Clarendon, 1907); E. S. Buchanan (ed.), *The Four Gospels from the Codex Veronensis* (Oxford: Clarendon, 1911).

[50] E. S. Buchanan (ed.), *Sacred Latin Texts* (4 vols.) (London: Heath Cranton and Ouseley, 1912–16): see Houghton 2016: 136.

[51] Carlo Vercellone, *Variae Lectiones Vulgatae Latinae Bibliorum* (2 vols.) (Rome: Spithoever, 1860/ 1864): see Corssen 1900: 74; Colgiago 1987: 126f., 132f.

[52] *Biblia sacra iuxta Latinam vulgatam versionem* (18 vols.) (Rome: Vatican Polyglot Press, 1926–95): see Metzger 1977: 351f.; Stummer 1928: 207–21.

The series *Collectanea Biblica Latina* was founded in 1912 for the publication of editions and studies that served the preparation of the edition or were related to it. Many of the volumes published in this series were from Benedictines and other Catholic theologians who played an important role in the study of the Latin Bible in the twentieth century. The first was by Ambrogio Amelli (1848–1933), who edited an unknown Old Latin translation of the Psalter, revised from Origen's Hexapla, from a manuscript at the Abbey of Montecassino Abbey.[53] In the following year, Heinrich Joseph Vogels (1880–1972), later professor in Bonn, edited Codex Rehdigeranus (VL 11), and Paul (Bernard) Capelle (1884–1961) presented a study of the text and history of the Old Latin translation of the Psalter in North Africa (1913).[54] Gasquet himself edited Codex Vercellensis (VL 3), while Donatien de Bruyne (1817–1935), a Benedictine from Belgium, printed the text of fragments of the Pauline Epistles (VL 64).[55]

Volume 6 of the series was particularly important, in which Quentin presented the principles of the new Vulgate edition for the books of the Octateuch.[56] Through comparison and statistical evaluation, the manuscripts were to be divided into groups based on a common archetype. From the comparison of the archetypes, the original reading was to be determined according to fixed rules. In this way, the constitution of the text was to be as objective as possible. The publication of Quentin's *Mémoire* led to a lively debate as to whether subjectivity could be eliminated in such a way. On the Protestant side, the contributions of Francis Crawford Burkitt (1864–1935) and the American Edward Kenneth Rand (1871–1945) should be mentioned; Catholic participants included Donatien de Bruyne and the English Benedictine John Chapman (1865–1933). In parallel with the publication of the edition of Genesis in 1926, Quentin presented further details and clarifications of his method in response to the criticisms.[57] There was a gap of almost two decades in the *Collectanea* after the sixth volume: later contributions were mostly by collaborators on the edition, including Pierre Salmon (1896–1982), Henri Marcotte de Sainte-Marie (1907–89), also, like Weber, Benedictines from Luxembourg. Weber himself published an examination of 2 Chronicles and the Old Latin versions of the Psalter.[58]

[53] Ambrogio Amelli, *Liber Psalmorum iuxta antiquissimam Latinam versionem nunc primum ex Casinensi cod. 557* (CBL 1) (Rome: Pustet, 1912).

[54] Heinrich Joseph Vogels, *Codex Rehdigeranus. Die vier Evangelien nach der lateinischen Handschrift R 169 der Stadtbibliothek Breslau* (CBL 2) (Rome: Pustet, 1913); Paul Capelle, *The Latin Psalter Text in Africa* (CBL 4) (Rome: Pustet, 1913).

[55] Francis Aidan Gasquet, *Codex Vercellensis* (CBL 3) (2 vols.) (Rome: Pustet, 1914); Donatien de Bruyne, *Les fragments de Freising* (CBL 5) (Rome: Pustet, 1921).

[56] Henri Quentin, *Mémoire sur l'établissement du texte de la Vulgate* (CBL 6) (Rome: Pustet, 1922); see Stummer 1928: 209–13.

[57] Henri Quentin, *Essais de critique textuelle* (Paris: Picard, 1926).

[58] Robert Weber, *Les anciennes versions latines du deuxième livre des paralipomènes* (CBL 8) (Rome: Abbey of St Jerome, 1945); Robert Weber, *Le psautier romain et les autres anciens psautiers latins* (CBL 10) (Rome: Abbey of St Jerome, 1953).

Connected with work on the Roman Vulgate were also two collections of summaries and prefaces to the Latin Bible compiled and anonymously published by Donatien de Bruyne.[59] Also related to the edition, at least indirectly, was the *Bulletin d'ancienne littérature chrétienne latine*, which appeared at irregular intervals from 1929 onward in the *Revue bénédictine* published by the monks of the Belgian abbey of Maredsous and whose first section gave information about publications on the Latin Bible.[60] The initial editor of the *Bulletin* was Paul (Bernard) Capelle, and its contributors included de Bruyne and André Wilmart (1876–1941), a French Benedictine who lived in England.

New Beginnings in Research on the Textual History of the Latin Bible

With the new editions of Old Latin manuscripts, alongside the two projects on the Vulgate, plans to update Sabatier's work with a new comprehensive edition gradually took shape. Intensive study of the history of the text of the Old Latin translation(s), which is attested in various forms, preceded this undertaking. The analysis of manuscripts and biblical quotations in early Christian writers gave rise to reflections about the principles on which an edition of the evidence of the Old Latin biblical text should be based, and how it might reliably provide information about the complex questions of its history and transmission (see Fischer 1972: 5–18; Frede 1972: 455–57, 477f.).

From the end of the nineteenth century, researchers endeavored to organize the many divergent forms in which the Old Latin translation is attested, and to differentiate between the nature of the Latin text in use at various times and particular places. The key methodological insights for this were formulated by William Sanday in a publication on an Old Latin manuscript of James (VL 66), having been developed in conjunction with White through their edition of Codex Bobiensis (VL 1).[61] With the help of quotations from Christian writers, it could be determined when and where a certain form of the text attested in manuscripts was in use. The aim was to work out the peculiarities of certain text forms in vocabulary and translation technique (known as "translation coloring" *Übersetzungsfarbe*) in order to be able to decide, where only quotations and no manuscripts were available, whether a quotation actually attested an Old Latin form or was a free (ad hoc) translation or loose quotation (Frede 1972: 457–72). Further investigations showed that a difference could be observed on the basis of translation technique and vocabulary between older African and younger European forms of the Old Latin biblical text.

---

[59] [Donatien de Bruyne], *Sommaires, divisions et rubriques de la Bible latine* (Namur: Godenne, 1914); [Donatien de Bruyne], *Préfaces de la Bible latine* (Namur: Godenne, 1920).

[60] *Bulletin d'ancienne littérature chrétienne latine* (Denée: Abbaye de Maredsous, 1929–93).

[61] William Sanday, "Some further remarks on the Corbey St. James (ff)," *Studia Biblica et ecclesiastica* 1 (1885): 233–63; Wordsworth, Sanday, and White, *Portions of the Gospels*.

This approach shaped the editions in the *Old-Latin Biblical Texts* and *Collectanea Biblica Latina* series. The contemporary writings of Burkitt are also worth mentioning.[62] Hans von Soden (1881–1945) reconstructed on this basis the Latin text of the New Testament used in North Africa before the middle of the third century.[63] Heinrich Joseph Vogels used the method, among others, to separate elements of the old African text from more recent European forms in the Old Latin gospel manuscripts Codex Palatinus (VL 2) and Codex Colbertinus (VL 6).[64] Vogels also deployed this technique to identify and reconstruct the Old Latin form of the text of the Gospels on which Jerome based his Vulgate revision.[65] He showed that Jerome's model followed a textual form preserved by Codices Veronensis (VL 4), Corbeiensis secundus (VL 8), Vindobonensis (VL 17), and Monacensis (VL 13), rather than Codex Brixianus (VL 10), as advocated by Wordsworth and White, or Codex Vercellensis (VL 3), as claimed by Alexander Souter (1873–1943).[66] With his study of Revelation, Vogels was the first to use the method to examine and present the textual history of the Latin translation as completely as possible for a biblical book.[67] His student Karl Theodor Schäfer (1900–74), later also a professor in Bonn, presented similar studies on Hebrews and Galatians.[68] In turn, Schäfer's own students (including Franz Tinnefeld, Ernst Nellessen, Udo Borse, Hermann Josef Frede, and Heinrich Zimmermann) produced similar studies on the textual history of the Latin translation of other Pauline Epistles (Fischer 1972: 3 n.9; Frede 1972: 477f.).

Mention should be made of several other important figures for the study of the textual history of the Latin Bible in the first half of the twentieth century. Johannes Schildenberger (1896–1990), a German Benedictine from the Archabbey of Beuron, investigated the early textual history of the Latin translation of the Book of Proverbs.[69] His encouragement for this investigation came from his colleague Alban Dold (1882–1960), responsible for a series of studies of Latin biblical manuscripts and particularly

[62] F. C. Burkitt, *The Old Latin and the Itala* (T&S 4.3) (Cambridge: Cambridge University Press, 1896); F. C. Burkitt, "Itala Problems," *Miscellanea Amelli* (Monte Cassino: Typographia Pontificia, 1920), 25–41.

[63] Hans von Soden, *Das lateinische Neue Testament in Nordafrika zur Zeit Cyprian* (Texte und Untersuchungen 3.3 [33]) (Leipzig: Hinrichs, 1909).

[64] Heinrich Joseph Vogels, "Übersetzungsfarbe als Hilfsmittel zur Erforschung der neutestamentlichen Textgeschichte," *Revue bénédictine* 40 (1928): 123–29; Heinrich Joseph Vogels, *Evangelium Palatinum* (Neutestamentliche Abhandlungen 12.3) (Münster: Aschendorff, 1926); Heinrich Joseph Vogels, *Evangelium Colbertinum* (2 vols.) (Bonner Biblische Beiträge 4–5) (Bonn: Hanstein, 1953).

[65] Heinrich Joseph Vogels, *Vulgatastudien* (Neutestamentliche Abhandlungen 14.2/3) (Münster: Aschendorff, 1928).

[66] Alexander Souter, 'The Type or Types of Gospel Text used by St. Jerome,' *Journal of Theological Studies* 12 (1911/12) 583–592. On the text of Jerome's exemplar, see also Chapter 3.

[67] Heinrich Joseph Vogels, *Untersuchungen zur Geschichte der lateinischen Apokalypse-Übersetzung* (Düsseldorf: Schwann, 1920).

[68] Karl Theodor Schäfer, *Untersuchungen zur Geschichte der lateinischen Übersetzung des Hebräerbriefs* (Freiburg: Herder, 1929).

[69] Johannes Schildenberger, *Die altlateinischen Texte des Proverbien-Buches* (Beuron: Beuroner Kunstverlag, 1941).

well known for his work on palimpsests.[70] As director of the Palimpsest Institute of the Archabbey of Beuron, Dold developed methods to make scraped and overwritten text in manuscripts visible through photographic processes. Schildenberger also received encouragement from his teachers in Rome, the Jesuits Alberto Vaccari (1875–1965) and Augustinus Merk (1869–1945), both of whom published editions of the Latin Bible.[71] Arthur Allgeier (1882–1952), a Catholic theologian in Freiburg associated with Alban Dold, studied the Latin translations of the Psalms.[72] Cuthbert Turner (1860–1930) was responsible for an edition and study of the gospel text of the oldest surviving manuscript of the Vulgate (Vg S), which was published posthumously by Alexander Souter.[73]

Building on the research of the nineteenth and early twentieth centuries, work began in the 1940s at the Archabbey of Beuron under the direction of Bonifatius Fischer (1915–97) on a new critical edition of the Old Latin translation of the Bible (see further chap. 24). The initial basis of this research was material that the Catholic priest Josef Denk (1849–1927) had compiled in Munich.[74] Around the same time, work began in Spain under the direction of Teófilo Ayuso Marazuela (1906–62) on an edition of the characteristic Spanish form of the Old Latin translation, although this was never completed.[75] Even before World War II, Adolf Jülicher (1857–1938) began to prepare a critical edition of Old Latin gospel manuscripts, distinguishing between an African and a European form of the text. Following Jülicher's death, Walter Matzkow (1909–42) completed the volumes for Matthew and Mark, while Kurt Aland (1915–94) later saw the volumes of Luke and John through the press and subsequently produced second editions of the first three Gospels.[76]

---

[70] Alban Dold, *Prophetentexte in Vulgata-Übersetzung* (Beuron: Archabbey, 1917); Alban Dold, *Konstanzer altlateinische Propheten- und Evangelienbruchstücke* (Beuron: Archabbey, 1923); Alban Dold, *Getilgte Paulus- und Psalmentexte unter getilgten ambrosian liturgiestücken aus Cod. Sangall. 908* (Beuron: Archabbey, 1928); Alban Dold, *Lateinische Fragmente der Sapientialbücher aus dem Münchener Palimpsest CLM 19105* (Beuron: Archabbey, 1928); Alban Dold, *Zwei Bobbienser Palimpseste mit frühestem Vulgatatext* (Beuron: Archabbey, 1931).

[71] Alberto Vaccari, *Studii critici sopra le antiche versioni latine del Vecchio Testamento* (Rome: Pontifical Biblical Institute, 1914); Alberto Vaccari and Gianfranco Nolli (eds.), *Biblia sacra Vulgatae editionis* (4 vols.) (Rome: Officium Libri Catholici, 1955); Augustinus Merk (ed.), *Novum Testamentum Graece et Latine* (Rome: Pontifical Biblical Institute, 1933).

[72] Arthur Allgeier, *Die altlateinischen Psalterien* (Freiburg: Herder, 1928); Arthur Allgeier, *Bruchstücke eines altlateinischen Psalters aus St. Gallen* (Heidelberg: Winter, 1929); Arthur Allgeier, *Die Überlieferung der alten lateinischen Psalmenübersetzungen und ihre kulturgeschichtliche Bedeutung* (Freiburg: Herder, 1931); Arthur Allgeier, *Die Psalmen der Vulgata* (Paderborn: Schöningh, 1940); see also Alban Dold, *Der Palimpsestpsalter im Codex Sangallensis 912* (Beuron: Archabbey, 1933).

[73] C. H. Turner [and Alexander Souter], *The Oldest Manuscript of the Vulgate Gospels* (Oxford: Clarendon, 1931).

[74] Joseph Denk, *Sabatier redivivus. Die altlateinische Bibel in ihrem Gesamtbestande vom 1.–9. Jahrhundert* (Leipzig: Fock, 1914): see Frede 1972: 476f.

[75] Teófilo Ayuso Marazuela (ed.), *Vetus Latina Hispana* (Madrid: Instituto Francisco Suárez, 1953ff); see Houghton 2016: 127.

[76] Adolf Jülicher, Walter Matzkow, and Kurt Aland (eds.), *Itala. Das Neue Testament in altlateinischer Überlieferung* (4 vols.) (Berlin: De Gruyter, 1938–63); see Houghton 2016: 125–27; Metzger 1977: 321f.; Fischer 1972: 3.

FURTHER LINES OF INQUIRY

The account of research on the Latin Bible presented in this chapter has been largely restricted to a listing of the most important names and works. Significant aspects and questions of detail have, in part, been left to one side.[77] Greater detail could have been provided about discussions regarding the language of the Old Latin translation, resulting in the conclusion that the peculiarities of biblical and Christian Latin did not originate in a (North African) provincial language but in the general vernacular (see Corssen 1900: 81–83 and, further, chap. 28). Investigations of Jerome and his work on the biblical text of the Bible would also require a separate presentation. By the early twentieth century, it had been recognized that only the text of the Gospels in the New Testament Vulgate could be attributed to Jerome, with a lively debate over the identity of the reviser of the other writings (see chap. 6).[78] Following the work of Vogels, it has become clear that Jerome, in his work on the Latin Bible, by no means consistently observed and applied the principles he formulated (Metzger 1977: 354f.; see also chap. 3). This must be taken into account in the textual criticism of the Vulgate. For the textual criticism of the Bible, it is also important to realize that due to the long coexistence of the Old Latin translation and the Vulgate, a mixture of both these forms of text is present in many manuscripts (Fischer 1972: 22; Corssen 1900: 28f.). Another question that has been much discussed since the early twentieth century is the possibility of an early Latin translation of Marcion's *Evangelion* and *Apostolos*, and its potential relation to the quotations in Tertullian and the oldest Latin biblical texts.[79] The role of the Latin witnesses in research on the *Diatessaron*, mentioned briefly with regard to Codex Fuldensis, has been a further line of inquiry during this period (see chap. 15).

BIBLIOGRAPHY

Aland, Kurt, and Barbara Aland. 1989. *Der Text des Neuen Testaments. Einführung in die wissenschaftlichen Ausgaben und in die Theorie wie Praxis der modernen Textkritik*. 2nd ed. Stuttgart: Deutsche Bibelgesellschaft. [English trans. *The Text of the New Testament*, Grand Rapids: Eerdmans, 1987.]

Cimosa, Mario. 2008. *Guida allo studio della Bibbia latina. Dalla Vetus Latina, alla Vulgata, alla Nova Vulgata*. Rome: Istituto patristico Augustinianum.

---

[77] Indications of these are to be found in the bibliographical listings of Corssen 1900, Metzger 1955, the *Bulletin d'ancienne littérature chrétienne*, and its successor the *Bulletin de la Bible latine*.

[78] E.g., Donatien de Bruyne, "Étude sur les origines de notre texte latein de saint Paul," *Revue Biblique* 12 (1915): 358–92; see also Stummer 1928: 95; Corssen 1900: 56–58.

[79] Most importantly in Adolf von Harnack, *Marcion. Das Evangelium vom fremden Gott* (2nd ed.) (Texte und Untersuchungen 45) (Leipzig: Hinrichs, 1924); see further Roth 2009; Fischer 1972: 25 n.78, 30 n.88.

Colgiago, Virginio. 1987. "I barnabiti Luigi Ungarelli e Carlo Vercellone e la revisione della Volgata." In *La Bibbia "Vulgata" dalle origini ai nostri giorni*, edited by Tarcisio Stramare, 118–36. CBL 16. Rome: Abbey of St Jerome.

Corssen, Peter. 1900. "Bericht über die lateinischen Bibelübersetzungen." *Jahresbericht über die Fortschritte der klassischen Altertumswissenschaft* 101: 1–83.

Fischer, Bonifatius. 1955. "Der Vulgata-Text des Neuen Testaments." *Zeitschrift für die neutestamentliche Wissenschaft* 46: 178–96.

Fischer, Bonifatius. 1972. "Das Neue Testament in Lateinischer Sprache." In *Die alten Übersetzungen des Neuen Testaments, die Kirchenväterzitate und Lektionare*, edited by Kurt Aland, 1–92. ANTF 5. Berlin: De Gruyter.

Frede, Hermann Josef. 1972. "Die Zitate des Neuen Testaments bei den lateinischen Kirchenvätern." In *Die alten Übersetzungen des Neuen Testaments, die Kirchenväterzitate und Lektionare*, edited by Kurt Aland, 455–78. ANTF 5. Berlin: De Gruyter.

Houghton, H. A. G. 2016. *The Latin New Testament. A Guide to its Early History, Texts, and Manuscripts*. Oxford: Oxford University Press.

Jellicoe, Sidney. 1968. *The Septuagint and Modern Study*. Oxford: Oxford University Press.

Metzger, Bruce M. 1955. *Annotated Bibliography of the Textual Criticism of the New Testament 1914–1939*. Studies and Documents 16. Copenhagen: Munksgaard.

Metzger, Bruce M. 1977. *The Early Versions of the New Testament. Their Origin, Transmission and Limitations*. Oxford: Oxford University Press.

Parker, D. C. 2008. *An Introduction to the New Testament Manuscripts and Their Texts*. Cambridge: Cambridge University Press.

Roth, Dieter T. 2009. "Did Tertullian Possess a Greek Copy or Latin Translation of Marcion's Gospel?" *Vigiliae Christianae* 63: 429–67.

Sainte-Marie, Henri de. 1987. "Storia dell'edizione critica della Volgata." In *La Bibbia "Vulgata" dalle origini ai nostri giorni*, edited by. Tarcisio Stramare, 144–48. CBL 16. Rome: Abbey of St Jerome.

Schmid, Ulrich B. 2014. "The Diatessaron of Tatian." In *The Text of the New Testament in Contemporary Research. Essays on the Status Quaestionis*, edited by Bart D. Ehrman and Michael W. Holmes, 117–42. 2nd ed. NTTSD 42. Leiden: Brill.

Stummer, Friedrich. 1928. *Einführung in die lateinische Bibel. Ein Handbuch für Vorlesungen und Selbstunterricht*. Paderborn: Schöningh.

Würthwein, Ernst. 1988. *Der Text des Alten Testaments. Eine Einführung in die Biblia Hebraica*. 5th ed. Stuttgart: Württembergische Bibelanstalt. [English trans. *The Text of the Old Testament* (3rd ed.)], Grand Rapids: Eerdmans, 2014.

CHAPTER 24

THE VETUS LATINA INSTITUTE

THOMAS JOHANN BAUER

HISTORICAL BACKGROUND

THE rediscovery and gradual collection of the remains of the older Latin translations of the Bible, formerly grouped under the term *Itala* but now most commonly known as the *Vetus Latina*, began in the last quarter of the sixteenth century. When official editions of the Septuagint and the Vulgate for the Roman Catholic Church were prepared in Rome under the direction of Antonio Carafa (1538–91), it became apparent that biblical quotations in the Latin Church Fathers often deviated strikingly from the text of the Vulgate, and were close to the Greek text of the Septuagint in the Old Testament Scriptures. Over time, it was recognized that these passages were not the result of textual corruption, free quotations, or ad hoc translations but that they preserved an older Latin text which, unlike the Vulgate, was translated from the Septuagint. The early text of the Latin Bible, about whose diversity and contradictions Augustine, Jerome, and others had repeatedly complained, had not disappeared after the appearance of the Vulgate but had remained in use for a considerable time, leaving identifiable traces in a few manuscripts as well as biblical quotations in Christian writers (see chap. 1 and Stummer 1928: 28f., 181–83).

Early attempts to collect evidence for the early Latin text of the Bible have already been described in chapter 23. These began with the edition of the Old Testament published in Rome in 1588 by Flaminio de' Nobili (1532–90), continuing in the subsequent century with publications by Giuseppe Maria Tomasi (1649–1713) and Jean Martianay (1647–1717).[1] However, the first edition that met scholarly standards and took into account as much

---

[1] Flaminius Nobilius (ed.), *Vetus Testamentum secundum LXX Latine redditum et ex auctoritate Sixti V. pont. max. editum* (Rome: Ferrarius, 1588); Giuseppe Maria Caro [Tomasi] (ed.), *Sacrorum Bibliorum iuxta editionem seu LXX interpretum seu B. Hieronymi veteres tituli siue capitula sectiones et stichometriae*

of the known material as possible was that of Pierre Sabatier (1682–1742), a Benedictine of the Congregation of Saint Maur. Sabatier carefully documented the attestation of the old Latin translation for each verse of the Old and New Testaments, setting it out in a column next to the text of the Vulgate, which permitted the direct comparison of the two versions. It was only after his death that the three large volumes of the edition saw the light of day (1743–49).[2] At the same time, Giuseppe Bianchini (1704–64) produced a compilation of the text of four Old Latin gospel manuscripts.[3] Even though this was on a much smaller scale than Sabatier's edition, it clearly demonstrated that the text of the older Latin translation survived in widely divergent forms, thereby raising the question as to how meaningful it would be to reconstruct a single original translation from the available material.

Further research in the latter half of the nineteenth and early twentieth centuries made it increasingly clear that Sabatier's edition was in need of a thorough reworking. The discovery of further manuscript witnesses with an Old Latin affiliation, along with scholarly texts of Christian writers replacing those in the *Patrologia Latina* (1844–55), which was largely based on earlier editions, provided new and improved evidence.[4] The inadequacy of the material presented by Sabatier was also shown by work on critical editions of the Greek New Testament and the Septuagint and two major projects to edit the Vulgate: the Oxford Vulgate (for the New Testament) and the Roman Vulgate (for the Old Testament) were both accompanied by the examination and publication of important Old Latin manuscripts.[5] As early as 1885, Paul de Lagarde (1827–91), one of the great experts on the text and textual history of the Septuagint, presented samples for a new and improved edition of Sabatier, but this was not taken further.[6]

The systematic collection of all evidence for a Latin biblical text deviating from the Vulgate in manuscripts and quotations from Christian writers was initiated by Josef Denk (1849–1927), a Catholic priest in Munich. The inspiration for this project may have come from Eduard Wölfflin (1831–1908), the founder of the *Thesaurus Linguae Latinae* at the Bavarian Academy of Sciences in Munich. However, a comprehensive edition of the remains of the Old Latin Bible was to prove too extensive and too difficult for a single

---

(2 vols.) (Rome: Corbelletti, 1688); Johannes Martianay (ed.), *Sancti Eusebii Hieronymi Stridonensis Presbyteri Divina Bibliotheca* (Vol. 1) (Paris: Roulland, 1693).

[2] Petrus Sabatier (ed.), *Bibliorum Sacrorum Latinae versiones antiquae, seu Vetus Italica, et ceterae quaecunque in Codicibus Mss. & antiquorum libris reperiri potuerunt: quae cum Vulgata Latina, & cum Textu Graeco comparantur. . . .* (3 vols.) (Rheims: Florentain, 1743[–1749]; 2nd unaltered ed., Paris 1751).

[3] Josephus Blanchinus (ed.), *Evangeliarium quadruplex Latinae versionis antiquae seu veteris Italicae. Nunc primum in lucem editum ex codicibus manuscriptis . . .* (2 vols.) (Rome: Rubeis, 1749).

[4] The major series for the publication of these texts are the *Corpus Scriptorum Ecclesiasticorum Latinorum* (since 1864), *Sources chrétiennes* (since 1942), and the *Corpus Christianorum* (since 1953); see "Introduction."

[5] All these editions are described in chapter 23.

[6] Paul de Lagarde, *Probe einer neuen Ausgabe der lateinischen Übersetzungen des Alten Testaments* (Göttingen: Dieterich, 1885).

researcher. Denk published a sample fascicle with the Book of Ruth and the Epistle of Jude in 1914, announcing at the same time the imminent publication of the complete work in four volumes, but apart from a few related studies the project did not go further.[7] The enterprise, in which Denk had also invested his entire private fortune, ended in financial and personal catastrophe.

In 1921, the impoverished Denk moved to the Benedictine Archabbey in Beuron in the Upper Danube valley, whose Palimpsest Institute, founded in 1913, had become renowned for research into the manuscripts, text, and history of the Latin Bible. However, tensions and discord quickly arose, with Denk leaving Beuron in 1923 and returning to Munich. Through the initiative and commitment of Alban Dold (1882–1960), the director of the Palimpsest Institute, it was possible to save the material collected by Denk and to secure it permanently in the Archabbey of Beuron after his death in 1927 (see *Arbeitsbericht* 1988: 13f.). This consisted of well over half a million index cards on which Denk had recorded, verse by verse, not only the variants of biblical manuscripts but also as many quotations as could be identified from available editions of Christian writers of the first millennium. This collection, the so-called Denk-Kasten ("Denk boxes"), became the basis for the work on a new comprehensive edition of the remains of the Old Latin biblical text.

The Foundation and Development of the Institute

The Vetus Latina Institute (*Vetus Latina-Institut* in German) was established in Beuron in 1945 by Archabbot Benedikt Baur (1877–1963). Its purpose was to sift through the material left by Denk and to prepare an edition of the remains of the Old Latin Bible. The Institute was built up and strongly influenced by the Beuron monk Bonifatius Fischer (1915–97), whom Baur appointed as its director and entrusted with the edition of the *Vetus Latina*.[8] Under Fischer's direction, the collection begun by Denk was continually expanded and at the same time systematically checked and revised. Biblical quotations in Christian writers were updated and supplemented on the basis of the most recent editions of their works. In addition, variants from newly identified manuscripts with Old Latin biblical text were added to the index (see *Arbeitsbericht* 1953: 7f.). The number of index cards increased to about one million. In addition, the Institute began to assemble a collection of special photographs of all Bible manuscripts relevant to the Old Latin text, in order to check their wording or to record the text of manuscripts not yet

---

[7] Joseph Denk (ed.), *Sabatier redivivus. Die altlateinische Bibel in ihrem Gesamtbestande vom 1.–9. Jahrhundert* (Leipzig: Fock, 1914); Joseph Denk, *Der neue Sabatier und sein wissenschaftliches Programm* (Leipzig: Fock, 1914). On Denk and his work, see Haffter 1967: 139–44; and Dittmann 1957: 600f.

[8] An overview of the Institute's early history is given in *Arbeitsbericht* 2004: 8–15.

published. This collection today remains the Institute's second fundamental tool, along-side the "Denk-Kasten," for researching the Old Latin biblical text and producing the Beuron edition of the *Vetus Latina*. There are still no reliable editions for many manuscripts of the Latin Bible, and still more have not yet been digitized and made available in databases.

Parallel to work on the "Denk-Kasten" and the collection of photographs of manuscripts, the compilation of an inventory of manuscripts and editions of the Christian authors relevant to the edition was begun. This process led to the develop-ment of a system of *sigla*, numerals identifying the manuscripts and abbreviations for Latin writings. Both these indexes were printed for the first time in 1949, and they were continually expanded and published in new editions as the edition progressed.[9] The *Repertorium* with the *sigla* for Christian writings, providing information about the editions used for each book of the *Vetus Latina*, has grown to two volumes in the cur-rent fifth edition from 2007.[10] The *Register* of Manuscripts, now published separately, also comprises two volumes: the second volume (2004) contains the manuscripts of the Psalter and various indexes; the first volume (1999) the manuscripts for the other bib-lical books.[11]

Fischer, as director of the Institute, worked out the basis and methods for the planned new edition and the principles for presenting the material in the most meaningful way (see fig. 24.1). The first volume of the Beuron edition, the text of Genesis, appeared in four fascicles from 1951 to 1954. The introduction to the volume briefly outlines the ed-itorial practices of the edition.[12] Fischer's intention was not only to set out the evidence as completely and clearly as possible but also to reflect the diversity and development of the Old Latin tradition. Therefore, it was not appropriate to reconstruct a single, hy-pothetical, initial Latin text but rather to provide information about the various forms in which the text was used or is attested from different places and at different times. The Beuron edition thus develops the presentation that Adolf Jülicher (1857–1938) had already followed for his edition of Old Latin gospel manuscripts, in which he distin-guished between an older African and a younger European form of the text, each with a set of variant readings.[13]

With the arrival at the Institute in 1952 of Walter Thiele (1923–2016), a Protestant theo-logian, work began on the edition of the Catholic Letters. These were published in seven fascicles from 1956 to 1969, followed by Thiele's editions of the Wisdom of Solomon

---

[9] Bonifatius Fischer, *Verzeichnis der Sigel für Handschriften und Kirchenschriftsteller* (VL 1; Freiburg im Breisgau: Herder, 1949).

[10] Roger Gryson and Hermann Josef Frede, *Répertoire général des auteurs ecclésiastiques latins de l'antiquité et du haut moyen âge* (VL 1.1A–B; 2 vols; Freiburg im Breisgau, Herder, 2007); see Houghton 2016: 118–120.

[11] Roger Gryson, *Altlateinische Handschriften/Manuscrits vieux latins: Répertoire descriptif* (VL 1.2A–B; 2 vols; Freiburg im Breisgau: Herder, 1999 and 2004); see Houghton 2016: 117f..

[12] Bonifatius Fischer, *Genesis* (VL 2; Freiburg im Breisgau: Herder, 1951–1954), 22*–28*.

[13] Adolf Jülicher, Walter Matzkow, and Kurt Aland (eds.), *Itala. Das Neue Testament in altlateinischer Überlieferung* (4 vols.) (Berlin: De Gruyter, 1938–63; 2nd ed., 1972–76); see further chap. 23.

FIGURE 24.1. Bonifatius Fischer presenting the layout of the *Vetus Latina* edition. Courtesy of the Archive of Mariendonk Abbey.

(1977–85) and the first part of Ecclesiasticus (Sirach 1–24; 1987–2005). In 1958, the Catholic theologian Hermann Josef Frede (1922–98) joined the Institute. He had trained in Bonn with Heinrich Joseph Vogels (1880–1972) and, above all, Karl Theodor Schäfer (1900–74), two central figures in the field of research on the Latin Bible. Frede initiated work on the Pauline Epistles, publishing the Epistle to the Ephesians (1962–64), the Epistles to the Philippians and Colossians (1966–71), the Epistles to the Thessalonians and Timothy (1975–82), and the Epistles to Titus, Philemon, and Hebrews (1983–91). Along with Fischer, Thiele and Frede became the authoritative and formative figures of the Institute, establishing Beuron as the leading research center for the history and text of the Latin Bible. When Fischer retired as director of the Institute at the end of 1972, Archabbot Ursmar Engelmann (1909–86) first entrusted Thiele with its direction on a provisional basis, before Frede was appointed director of the Institute and editor of the *Vetus Latina* series in 1974.

On the initiative of the publisher Theophil Herder-Dorneich (1898–1987), the Vetus Latina Stiftung, a charitable foundation, was established in 1951 in Freiburg im Breisgau, in order to acquire additional financial resources for the work of the Institute (*Arbeitsbericht* 2004: 15). Its board was to include the director of the Herder publishing house, with which the Institute has close ties, the Archabbot of Beuron, and an expert in the field of Catholic theology and exegesis. Herder-Dorneich was succeeded as chairman in 1980 by his son Hermann Herder (1926–2011) and in 2011 by his grandson Manuel Herder. As Archabbot of Beuron, Benedikt Baur was a member of the board until 1955. The Archabbey was then represented by the Prior before the election of Benedikt Reetz (1897–1964) as Archabbot in 1957. He was followed by Damasus Zähringer from 1965, Ursmar Engelmann from 1968, Hieronymus Nitz from 1980, Theodor Hug from 2001, and Tutilo Burger from 2011. Academic theology was initially represented by Heinrich Joseph Vogels, professor of New Testament in Bonn, then by his successor Karl Theodor Schäfer from 1961, and by Rudolf Schnackenburg (1914–2002), professor of New Testament in Würzburg, from 1975. Hermann Josef Frede took over this role as director of the Institute in 1989: he was succeeded in 1999 by Erich Zenger (1939–2010), professor of Old Testament in Münster in Westphalia, and in 2011 by Ferdinand R. Prostmeier, professor of New Testament in Freiburg im Breisgau.

Members of the foundation's board of trustees represent its interests (and those of the Institute) in the wider ecclesiastical and political sphere. Among these have been scholars whose research is closely related to the work of the Institute: Kurt Aland (1915–94), founder of the *Institut für neutestamentliche Textforschung* in Münster; the American textual critic Bruce M. Metzger (1914–2007); the historian and philologist Bernhard Bischoff (1906–91); Joseph Ziegler (1902–88), famous for his work on the Göttingen Septuagint; Eligius Dekkers (1915–98), the founder of the *Corpus Christianorum*; the English theologian Henry Chadwick (1920–2008); and Jacques Fontaine (1922–2015), the French historian, Latinist, and medievalist. The board has also included three cardinals known for their theological research: Carlo Maria Martini (1927–2012), Karl Lehmann (1936–2018), and Walter Kasper (b. 1933).

From the beginning of the 1950s, the personnel and resources of the Institute were continuously funded by the German national research agency (the *Deutsche Forschungsgemeinschaft*; see *Arbeitsbericht* 1981: 11f.). When its funding scheme for long-term projects was no longer available, the foundation and the Archabbey sought support for the Institute's work from the Heidelberg Academy of Sciences and Humanities. The cooperation began in 1984 and lasted until the end of 2000 (see *Arbeitsbericht* 1984: 7f.; 2000: 8; 2004: 37–40). The director of the *Vetus Latina* Commission at the Heidelberg Academy was initially the classical philologist Viktor Pöschl (1910–97) and, after his death, Manfred Fuhrmann (1925–2005) from Konstanz (see *Arbeitsbericht* 1997: 21). The publication of the edition of the Song of Songs, undertaken by Eva Schulz-Flügel, could not be continued and completed after the end of the cooperation, although its first fascicle had appeared in 1992.

After the death of Hermann Josef Frede in 1998, Roger Gryson (born 1938), professor of patrology in Louvain-la-Neuve, became the new director of the Institute.

He had produced the *Vetus Latina* edition of Isaiah (1987–97) and was a member of the board of trustees. As director, he took over the edition of Revelation (2000–3), completing the work already begun by Thiele and Beda Paulus (1909–94) and later continued by Gerhard Balharek (1934–95). Under Gryson, the focus of the work shifted from the Institute to collaborators in and outside Germany (see *Arbeitsbericht* 2004: 40–47). Decades earlier, Gryson himself had established the *Centre de recherches sur la Bible Latine* at the Université Catholique de Louvain (see *Arbeitsbericht* 1985: 18–20), where Jean-Claude Haelewyck prepared his editions of Esther (published 2003–8) and the Gospel of Mark (published 2013–18). Also in Louvain-la-Neuve, Pierre-Maurice Bogaert, a Benedictine monk of Maredsous who was an editor of the *Revue bénédictine* and responsible for the *Bulletin de la Bible latine*, began work on the edition of Judith (2001; completed by Haelewyck in 2020).

In 2002, David Parker and Philip Burton at the University of Birmingham made contact with Gryson in order to take responsibility for the *Vetus Latina* edition of John (2011–), alongside Parker's work on the *Novum Testamentum Graecum Editio Critica Maior* of the same gospel. In 2009, Birmingham's Institute for Textual Scholarship and Electronic Editing was given permission by the board of the foundation to continue the partially begun editions of the Epistles to the Romans and the Corinthians, as well as Galatians (currently being overseen by Hugh Houghton). In Mainz, the classical philologist Wilhelm Blümer took over the preparation of the edition of the Acts of the Apostles, for which preliminary work had already been undertaken at the Institute. Bonifatia Gesche, a Benedictine nun at Mariendonk, delivered the editions of Ruth (2005) and 1 Esdras (2008–16), while Anthony J. Forte, a Jesuit in Rome, resumed work on the latter part of Ecclesiasticus (2014–). In order to make the material more easily accessible to those working outside the Institute, the "Denk-Kasten" were digitized on the initiative of Roger Gryson and made available online in 2002 as the *Vetus Latina Database* by Brepols publishers (see *Arbeitsbericht* 1999: 24; 2000: 8; 2002: 44).

In 2014, Thomas Johann Bauer, professor of New Testament in Erfurt, was appointed as the fourth director of the Institute. The current focus remains the continuation of ongoing projects and collaborations, as well as the start of work on the Gospels of Matthew and Luke.

LAYOUT OF THE BEURON EDITION OF THE *VETUS LATINA*

The methods and principles developed by Bonifatius Fischer were based on preliminary work by William Sanday (1843–1920) and Henry Julian White (1859–1934), which was later developed by Francis Crawford Burkitt (1864–1934), Hans von Soden (1881–1945), Bernhard (Paul) Capelle (1884–1961), and Donatien De Bruyne (1871–1935).[14] The

---

[14] For detailed information, see Fischer 1972: 5–18, supplemented by Metzger 1977: 320–22.

Beuron edition of the *Vetus Latina* aims to document and take full account of all known evidence from manuscripts and quotations, including liturgical tradition. The edition reflects the variety of different forms in which the Old Latin translation existed and is preserved in surviving witnesses. Its foundation is therefore the systematic comparison of the direct and indirect transmission of the Latin biblical text, with the principle that the direct tradition is decisive for the determination of the wording, and the indirect tradition for the chronological and geographical classification of the different forms of text. The goal is to determine, on the basis of meaningful correspondences with biblical quotations in Christian writers, when and where a particular text form in Old Latin manuscripts was first in use and, possibly, originated (see also chap. 1). Indirect tradition is important because the place where a manuscript was copied and its subsequent locations do not normally enable firm conclusions to be drawn about the origin and age of its biblical text. Even if it is known when and where a manuscript was created, it usually remains unclear where the exemplar came from that was used for its production. Moreover, when manuscripts were produced, several sources may have been used and compared. This can be clearly seen in biblical codices in which some of the books follow the Vulgate and some the *Vetus Latina*. The age of a manuscript therefore normally gives little indication about the age of the form of the biblical text it attests.

This line of approach is particularly important when the text of the Old Latin translation of a book or a passage is transmitted in more than one manuscript and the text of the surviving manuscripts differs considerably. Biblical quotations provide clues for the geographical and chronological classification of the variants, if clear correspondences can be established. When a particular variant is isolated for the first time in a Christian writing, the place and time of the author's activity make it possible to identify when and where a particular form of the Old Latin translation was, at the least, in use at an early stage. Ideally, the chronological sequence of the different forms of the Old Latin translations and their regional distribution can thus be determined. In this way, the Beuron *Vetus Latina* edition seeks to present and provide a reliable basis for establishing the (earlier) textual history of the Latin Bible.

However, a straightforward comparison of direct and indirect tradition is not always possible. Not all biblical books, and certainly not all verses, are preserved in both traditions. In addition, the direct and indirect attestation of a particular text may differ so much that the Old Latin form in a biblical manuscript cannot be classified geographically and chronologically by means of quotations. In such places, assistance is given by noting the characteristics of different forms of the Old Latin text with regard to their choice of words and translation technique where both direct and indirect transmission continue to be extant. This may reveal certain terms or practises typical of certain regions and times. On the basis of such peculiarities in vocabulary and translation technique, it becomes possible to classify the text of a manuscript when indirect evidence is not available, and also to establish whether a particular quotation may be assigned to a certain Old Latin text-type or whether it is a loose form of citation.

The Beuron edition of the *Vetus Latina* does not attempt to reconstruct an "original text" (*Urtext*) of the Old Latin Bible for individual Old and New Testament writings. The aim and characteristic of the edition are to set out the remains of the Old Latin biblical text as fully as possible, to document the diversity of its forms, and to illustrate its development up to the text of the Vulgate. These concerns determine the layout of the edition, with a typical page being divided into three sections (see further Houghton 2016: 115–25; Cimosa 2008: 156–70; fig. 24.1).

The upper area of the page contains the so-called *schema*. Here, different forms of the text are set out below each other in several lines. Rows that belong together are connected by a curly bracket in the left margin or demarcated by a continuous horizontal line. The first of these rows provides the Greek text: for the Old Testament, this is the Septuagint, following either the Göttingen edition or, if this is not available, the hand edition of Rahlfs; for the New Testament, this is the current edition of the Nestle-Aland *Novum Testamentum Graece*. Where they are necessary for understanding the Latin tradition, variants to the Greek text are given below the first row. At the bottom of the next set of rows is the Latin text of the Vulgate. This initially followed the Oxford Vulgate and Roman Vulgate, but from 1969 the text of the Stuttgart Vulgate has been used for both the Old and New Testaments. Between the Greek text and the Vulgate there are one or more lines of Latin text. Each of these represents a form of the Latin text that arose or was in use at a particular time and place, as identified by the editor. These lines, each of which has its own set of variants, are ultimately only a kind of guide and not the reconstruction of a fixed text.

The rows in the *schema* are based on the insights gained through the comparison of direct and indirect transmission, identifying different forms or types of Old Latin biblical text partly through their vocabulary and translation technique, partly through their Greek model. The Beuron edition generally distinguishes between an early and a later African text-type, as well as an earlier European text-type and a more developed one, with further subtypes. A text-type is attested in Augustine that stands between the African and European texts. Very early witnesses such as Tertullian are given as a separate line, as the extent to which they depend on a preexisting Latin translation is uncertain. In the case of the Old Testament, Jerome's adaptation of the Old Latin based on Origen's Hexapla is also given as a separate line where it exists. From top to bottom, the rows in the *schema* in sequence map the development from the earliest forms to the text of the Vulgate. The number of lines and the text-types identified make it easy to see for each verse (and each book), the variety and age of the forms of the Old Latin translation preserved in direct and indirect witnesses and how they differ.[15]

Below the *schema* is the critical apparatus, which provides information on the attestation of the variants. The critical apparatus also lists additional variants in the witnesses that do not belong to Old Latin tradition. When necessary, the critical apparatus also gives supplementary information about the Greek text or the text of the Vulgate. At the bottom of the page is the witness apparatus. Here, verse by verse, the

---

[15] For an overview of the different text-types in the Beuron edition, see Houghton 2016: 120f., chap. 1 and chap. 2; a criticism of this scheme is found in a short note in Schäfer 1957: 22.

complete text of all the witnesses is given: first the manuscripts, then quotations and paraphrases in Christian writers. The witness apparatus makes it possible to examine the considerations which underlie the *schema* and its text-types. At the same time, the apparatus provides information about how frequently individual verses of the Bible were used, thus allowing conclusions to be drawn about their relevance to the history of theology. For some verses, no or only a few citations are given; for others, the witness apparatus extends over several pages.

The beginning of each book of the edition presents and discusses the tradition and attestation of the Old Latin translation in manuscripts, quotations, and liturgical texts, as well as the approach to reconstructing the text-types. The editor also addresses the question whether the various forms of the Old Latin translation can be traced back to a single initial translation, or whether there were multiple early translations that subsequently influenced each other and were harmonized (see Houghton 2016: 12–14; Schäfer 1957: 24f.; Stummer 1928: 50–56). This question must be answered separately for each biblical book. However, in all the books edited thus far, the editors have concluded that the evidence points to a single initial translation which was continually reworked: vocabulary was adapted in order to match developments in ecclesiastical terminology, and the text was corrected and adjusted on the basis of Greek sources.

Although it preserves the tripartite division of the page, the edition of the Gospel of John deviates significantly from the principles for the rest of the series. Due to the large number of quotations in Latin writers, the editors decided not to print the text of allusions or paraphrases in full in the witness apparatus (although they are present in an online database). Moreover, they refrain from identifying and reconstructing text-types and offer only the text of the manuscripts in the *schema*.

OTHER ACTIVITIES OF THE INSTITUTE

From the beginning, the work of the Vetus Latina Institute in Beuron has focused on the preparation and completion of the edition of the remains of the text of the Old Latin Bible. Nevertheless, the significance of the Institute and its achievements over the last seventy-five years should not be measured solely by progress on this edition. Bonifatius Fischer published multiple studies of the history and tradition of the Latin Bible, correcting misapprehensions and making a lasting contribution to research on the history of the Latin Bible in the early Middle Ages and at the time of Charlemagne (Fischer 1985, 1986). Hermann Josef Frede and Walter Thiele both produced important studies of various problems in the Latin biblical text (listed in Gryson 1993: 1–15). This is no less true of Roger Gryson (see Gryson 2008: xxxv–xlvi). Valuable contributions to research, including editions of patristic and medieval sources relevant to the edition of the *Vetus Latina*, have appeared in the series *Aus der Geschichte der lateinischen Bibel* ("From the history of the Latin Bible"), which the Institute has published since 1957 (see Houghton 2016: 124f.).

FIGURE 24.2. The Editors of the Stuttgart Vulgate in Beuron in 1969.
Left to right: Robert Weber, Walter Thiele, Jean Gribomont, Hedley Sparks, Bonifatius Fischer. Courtesy of Anthony Forte.

The Institute was a noteworthy collaborator on the hand edition of the Vulgate, planned and published by the *Württembergische Bibelanstalt* (and now known as the Stuttgart Vulgate). The first consultations on this edition took place in Beuron in 1959: those invited included Robert Weber (1904–80), who was in charge of the Roman Vulgate (*Arbeitsbericht* 1969: 7–16), and Hedley Sparks (1908–96), who had overseen the completion of the Oxford Vulgate. Weber took responsibility for the Old Testament and Fischer, together with Thiele, edited the New Testament for the hand edition, which was published in 1969 (see fig. 24.2).[16] Fischer then began work on a concordance to the Vulgate, based on the text of the second edition, both of which appeared in 1975.[17] The Vetus Latina Institute has been involved in all subsequent editions of the Stuttgart Vulgate, up to the current, fifth edition of 2007, overseen by Gryson.

---

[16] Robert Weber (ed.) *Biblia Sacra iuxta vulgatam versionem* (adiuvantibus Bonifatio Fischer, Johanne Gribomont, H.F.D. Sparks, W. Thiele) (2 vols.) (Stuttgart: Deutsche Bibelgesellschaft, 1969); see also Houghton 2016: 127–29; Fischer 1972: 50–52; Metzger 1955: 351.

[17] Bonifatius Fischer, *Novae concordantiae bibliorum sacrorum iuxta vulgatam versionem critice editam* (5 vols.) (Stuttgart: Deutsche Bibelgesellschaft, 1977): see *Arbeitsbericht* 1975: 21f.; *Arbeitsbericht* 1968: 12–15.

Under Fischer, the Institute was also involved in projects on the Greek text of the Bible. As early as 1967, an initial conversation was held with Kurt Aland and other members of the *Institut für neutestamentliche Textforschung* about the project of an *Editio Critica Maior of* the Greek New Testament, for which Fischer became a member of the editorial board (Aland 1989: 34f.; *Arbeitsbericht* 1968: 18f.; 1969: 26–30). At the same time, the Institute agreed to collaborate on new editions of the United Bible Society's *Greek New Testament* (third edition) and the Nestle-Aland *Novum Testamentum Graece* (twenty-sixth edition) (Aland 1989: 40–46, 53–56; *Arbeitsbericht* 1969: 30f). The Institute was responsible for preparing the information on the Latin textual witnesses for all three of these editions.

Bibliography

Vetus Latina. Die Reste der altlateinischen Bibel nach Petrus Sabatier (neu gesammelt und herausgegeben von der Erzabtei Beuron, unter der Leitung von Bonifatius Fischer/Hermann Josef Frede/Roger Gryson/Thomas Johann Bauer); Freiburg im Breisgau: Herder, 1949–.

Arbeitsbericht: The Vetus Latina Institute regularly publishes a report on the status of the edition and work in progress. From 1952 to 1965, this took the form of an annual report of the Vetus Latina Foundation, with a separate report (*Bericht*) of the Institute between 1967 and 1969. Since 1971, the two reports have appeared jointly (beginning with the 15th *Arbeitsbericht* of the Foundation and the 4th *Bericht* of the Institute); in 2007, the Foundation report was renamed the *Bericht* and the Institute report the *Forschungsbericht*. The publication has been biennial since 2015.

Aland, Kurt, and Barbara Aland. 1989. *Der Text des Neuen Testaments. Einführung in die wissenschaftlichen Ausgaben und in die Theorie wie Praxis der modernen Textkritik.* 2nd ed. Stuttgart: Deutsche Bibelgesellschaft. [English trans., *The Text of the New Testament*, Grand Rapids: Eerdmans, 1987.]

Cimosa, Mario. 2008. *Guida allo studio della Bibbia latina. Dalla Vetus Latina, alla Vulgata, alla Nova Vulgata.* Sussidi patristici. Rome: Istituto patristico Augustinianum.

Corssen, Peter. 1900. "Bericht über die lateinischen Bibelübersetzungen." *Jahresbericht über die Fortschritte der klassischen Altertumswissenschaft* 101: 1–83.

Dittmann, Georg. 1957. "Denk, Josef." In *Neue Deutsche Biographie* 3, 600f. Munich: Historischen Kommission bei der Bayerischen Akademie der Wissenschaften. https://www.deutsche-biographie.de/pnd116072407.html#ndbcontent

Fischer, Bonifatius. 1955. "Der Vulgata-Text des Neuen Testaments." *Zeitschrift für die neutestamentliche Wissenschaft* 46: 178–96.

Fischer, Bonifatius. 1972. "Das Neue Testament in Lateinischer Sprache." In *Die alten Übersetzungen des Neuen Testaments, die Kirchenväterzitate und Lektionare*, edited by Kurt Aland, 1–92. ANTF 5. Berlin: De Gruyter.

Fischer, Bonifatius 1985. *Lateinische Bibelhandschriften im frühen Mittelalter.* AGLB 11. Freiburg im Breisgau: Herder.

Fischer, Bonifatius. 1986. *Beiträge zur Geschichte der lateinischen Bibeltexte.* AGLB 12. Freiburg im Breisgau: Herder.

Frede, Hermann Josef. 1972. "Die Zitate des Neuen Testaments bei den lateinischen Kirchenvätern." In *Die alten Übersetzungen des Neuen Testaments, die Kirchenväterzitate und Lektionare*, edited by Kurt Aland, 455–78. ANTF 5. Berlin: De Gruyter.

Gryson, Roger, ed. 1993. *Philologia Sacra. Biblische und patristische Studien für Hermann Josef Frede und Walter Thiele zu ihrem 70. Geburtstag*. AGLB 24. Freiburg im Breisgau: Herder.

Gryson, Roger. 2008. *Scientiam Salutis. Quarante années de recherches sur l'antiquité chrétienne*. BETL 211. Leuven: Peeters.

Haffter, Heinz. 1967. "Der Italaforscher Joseph Denk und der Thesaurus linguae Latinae." *Zeitschrift für die neutestamentliche Wissenschaft* 58: 139–44.

Houghton, H. A. G. 2016. *The Latin New Testament. A Guide to its Early History, Texts, and Manuscripts*. Oxford: Oxford University Press.

Metzger, Bruce M. 1977. *The Early Versions of the New Testament. Their Origin, Transmission and Limitations*. Oxford: Oxford University Press.

Schäfer, Karl Theodor. 1957. *Die altlateinische Bibel. Rede zum Antritt des Rektorates der Rheinischen Friedrich Wilhelms-Universität zu Bonn am 17. November 1956*. Bonner Akademische Reden 17. Bonn: Hanstein.

Stummer, Friedrich. 1928. *Einführung in die lateinische Bibel. Ein Handbuch für Vorlesungen und Selbstunterricht*. Paderborn: Schöningh.

CHAPTER 25

....

THE NOVA VULGATA

....

KEVIN ZILVERBERG

HISTORICAL OVERVIEW

THE Latin Church has expected its sacred Scriptures accurately to reflect the original biblical languages for both Old and New Testaments, especially since the reception of Jerome's new translation of the Old Testament from Hebrew. For better or worse, this displaced venerable, Greek-based Old Latin versions and established the Masoretic Hebrew text as the standard (as discussed in chap. 4). Although the Old Latin Gospels had often been revised on Greek models, Jerome's more definitive revision of the Gospels eventually displaced its predecessors as well, and the same goes for the rest of the New Testament which was revised in a similar manner (see chap. 3 and chap. 6). The combination of these revised texts into a complete Bible, circulating in one- and two-volume editions, constituted the "Vulgate" text. It was commonly understood *in toto* as the work of Jerome, even though he was only responsible for a large portion of it. What is more, the statement of the commission from Pope Damasus presented by Jerome in the preface to the Gospels meant that the Vulgate was seen to enjoy papal backing from its inception. Nevertheless, discrepancies from one manuscript to another diminished its authority, and there were multiple attempts throughout the Middle Ages to restore the Vulgate to its pristine form, typically taking Jerome's competence for granted. A new Latin translation from the original languages was usually out of the question.

Even before the Renaissance, however, there were a few instances of biblical scholars using the Hebrew Old Testament to improve the Vulgate, which might be considered as forerunners of the Neo-Vulgate. The Cistercian abbot Stephen Harding completed his Vulgate revision by 1112, and some thirteenth-century Dominicans in Paris also corrected from Hebrew texts (see chap. 22). For the most part, however, ignorance of Hebrew and Greek during the Middle Ages prevented this sort of criticism. The Renaissance saw revived interest in the biblical source languages, which led to increasing dissatisfaction with the Vulgate. The Italian Humanist Giannozzo Manetti

(1396–1459) set out to retranslate the Bible from the original languages, with the encouragement of Pope Nicholas V. In the late 1450s, he wrote a theoretical treatise entitled *Apologeticus* to accompany his psalter, in which he implicitly criticizes Jerome and puts forward his own work as a replacement (McShane and Young 2016: xviii–xxi).[1] Manetti's edition had three columns, setting his own psalter from the Hebrew alongside Jerome's two surviving versions (the Hexaplaric and the *iuxta Hebraeos*). Manetti also translated the New Testament from Greek into Latin. Not surprisingly, he was attacked for daring to imply that Jerome's hallowed translation could be improved upon; he died before translating the rest of the Old Testament. His contemporary Lorenzo Valla (1406–57) composed a set of groundbreaking *Adnotationes in Novum Testamentum* in 1505, which in 1516 were published by Erasmus and inspired him to revise the Vulgate New Testament. From then on, scholars increasingly understood the Vulgate's limitations even though it was often unclear whether its discrepancies from its sources resulted from corruption within the Latin manuscript tradition, Jerome's reliance on different originals, or his limitations as a translator.

In the sixteenth century, there was a proliferation of Latin and vernacular Bibles, including many Vulgate editions, and polemics raged over which text to use. The Italian Benedictine Isidoro Chiari produced a predecessor to the Neo-Vulgate in 1542 by using Hebrew and Greek to correct the Vulgate. He strove for moderation and recognized the importance of maintaining continuity with the received text, even as he claimed to have made eight thousand interventions.[2] Chiari's Bible, however, was just one among many editions that did not gain approval for liturgical use. Less than a generation later, the Portuguese Dominican and inquisitor Jerónimo de Azambuja (Hieronymus ab Oleastro) dared to propose similar biblical emendation, for which he himself eventually fell foul of the Inquisition (Coelho 2001: 107–11).[3] Similarly, the 1564 edition of the papal *Index of Prohibited Books* called for the removal of the prologue and prolegomena in Chiari's Bible, where he had expressed his outrage that no one had yet corrected the Vulgate's "innumerable errors."[4] The acceptance of the decree of the Council of Trent on the Vulgate curtailed such efforts in the Counter-Reformation church, effectively excluding the possibility of Vulgate corrections beyond its own manuscript tradition, and leading to the authoritative edition of the Sixto-Clementine Vulgate (as described in chap. 19).

---

[1] The Psalter remains in three manuscripts in the Vatican (BAV, Pal. lat. 40, Pal. lat. 41, and Urb. lat. 5).

[2] Isidoro Chiari (ed.), *Vulgata aeditio Veteris ac Noui Testamenti* (Venice: Schoeffer, 1542). For the interventions, see Jacques Le Long, *Bibliotheca sacra in binos syllabos distincta quorum prior qui jam tertio auctior prodit . . .* (Vol. 1) (Halle an der Saale: Gebaverus, 1723), 259.

[3] Jerónimo de Azambuja, *Commentaria in Mosi pentateuchum iuxta m. Sanctis Pagnini . . . interpretationem* (Lisbon: Barrerius, 1556; Repr., Antwerp: Stelsius, 1569). Scans are available of both the copy held by the Complutense University of Madrid (<https://books.google.com/books/ucm?id=Rz4Hu2tb744C&pg=PP9>), in which the passage calling for Vulgate revision has been thoroughly crossed out, and the copy held in the Biblioteca Nacional of Lisbon (<https://books.google.com/books?id=rCTSA AAAMAAJ&pg=PP18>), which has written warnings in the margin to prevent the reader from falling into error.

[4] See Le Long, *Bibliotheca sacra in binos syllabos distincta . . .*, 259.

The Latin Bible remained stable over the following centuries, but its insufficiencies became more keenly felt as the biblical sciences progressed. Pope Pius X finally intervened in 1907 by calling upon the Benedictines to establish the Abbey of St. Jerome in Rome for the purpose of printing a new, critical edition of the Vulgate from the best manuscripts. Abbot Pierre Salmon, president of the commission for this edition on the eve of the Second Vatican Council, would explain that it was always the commission's intention to produce the critical text as a preparation for subsequent revision (1965: 551) (i.e., a new Vulgate corrected with recourse to the original biblical languages). In any case the monks progressed slowly, releasing Genesis in 1926 and completing the Old Testament only in 1995 (see chap. 23). The commission for the Neo-Vulgate would use the completed editions as well as the two-volume critical edition of the whole Vulgate produced in 1969 by one of these monks, Robert Weber.

As the Benedictines released their Vulgate book by book, calls increased for a revised Psalter (Bea 1946: 15–21). In fact, a more intelligible Latin psalter approved for daily recitation had long remained a desideratum, and unofficial Latin psalters had continued to be published since the time of Manetti. When Pius XII established a commission in 1941 to produce a new Psalter from the Hebrew, he looked not to the Benedictines but rather to the Jesuits at the Pontifical Biblical Institute in Rome. They finished their work by 1945, eight years prior to the 1953 release of the critical edition of the Vulgate (Gallican) psalter. The pope approved his new "Pian" Psalter, alongside the traditional Gallican one, for private and public recitation of the Divine Office; it met fierce criticism and rejection above all for its strong classicizing tendency (Van Puyvelde 1949; Ziegler 1951: 13–14). The desire for a revision had been nearly unanimous (Ziegler 1951: 5), yet the Pian Psalter fell far short of the high expectations. This failed experiment at a time of strong momentum for the Catholic Liturgical Movement, however, resulted in a burst of reflection on how best to revise the Latin Psalter (Bea 1946: 171–73; Van Puyvelde 1949).

In 1959, early in the next pontificate, Pope John XXIII set in motion preparations for the Second Vatican Council (1962–65). Among the myriad proposals for the Church was the call by numerous clerics for the Psalter to be revised again; some even sought a revision of the whole Latin Bible (Secretariat 1961: I.18–20; II.312–13). About the same time that he called the council, John XXIII also approved efforts to begin revising the Pian Psalter (Bea 1962: 411). This led to Robert Weber's *Psalterii secundum Vulgatam Bibliorum versionem nova recensio* (1961) just before the Second Vatican Council, a work that would garner praise in the council hall (Martin 1972: 136) and pave the way for the Neo-Vulgate version eight years later. The preparatory commission for the conciliar document on divine revelation considered calling for a biblical revision but refrained from doing so, apparently because this would not fit the document's character as a dogmatic constitution (Ottaviani 1965: 536–37). The constitution on the sacred liturgy, however, did call for completion of the psalter revision already "happily begun" (Secretariat 1966: 43 = *Sacrosanctum Concilium* §91), a reference to the process set in motion by the production of the Pian Psalter. Its revision had already been in progress for some four years by the time the document was issued in late 1963. In early 1964, just weeks after the constitution's promulgation, Pope Paul VI publicly established the commission to revise the Psalter for the second time in a quarter of a century.

It was soon realized, however, that this further revision would lack coherence with the rest of the Bible, since the liturgical psalter also includes canticles from numerous books. Accordingly, in the next year, the Pope acceded to the long demand for the first-ever thorough revision and correction of the Vulgate as official Bible of the Roman Catholic Church (cf. *Nova Vulgata* 1986: vi). Paul VI named Cardinal Agostino Bea chair of the commission,[5] the same man who had overseen the production of the Pian Psalter and strenuously defended it once printed. The two commissions worked in parallel until the group revising the Psalter was merged into the Neo-Vulgate Commission in late 1967 (*Nova Vulgata* 1986: x).

When Bea assumed leadership he was already in his mid-eighties and had a long career of biblical and theological scholarship behind him, as well as significant experience in administration. He supervised the project for just a few years before his death in late 1968 gave his former student, Piero Rossano, the opportunity to take over. The latter's profile as a scholar of the Bible and classical languages, and his closeness to Bea, are likely to have been key factors in his nomination (Ciciliot 2017). Like Jerome, the commission gave precedence to the Psalms and dedicated special attention to them, for the revised text would be the only approved Latin one for the postconciliar liturgy to be sung in choir and privately recited every day around the world. Indeed, the council had mandated the clergy's continued use of Latin for the *Liturgy of the Hours* (Secretariat 1966: 45–46 = *Sacrosanctum Concilium* §101). The *Liber Psalmorum*, without the canticles, was incorporated into the new lectionary schema, the *Ordo lectionum Missae* (1969), released the same year and followed by the *Lectionarium* itself (1970–72). In April 1970, the commission published a draft of the Gospels, followed in September by the volume containing the Pauline and Catholic Epistles, and then Acts and Revelation in January 1971 (Schick 1972: 346).

At this point, Eduard Schick, an auxiliary bishop of Fulda in his mid-sixties, took over from Rossano to oversee the Old Testament revision. Schick had taught New Testament exegesis for many years when in 1962, Pope John XXIII named him a bishop in order for him to participate fully in the Second Vatican Council (Müller 2003). In that same year, he took on the leadership of the German translation known as the *Einheitsübersetzung*, so by his nomination in 1971 to head the Neo-Vulgate Commission, he already had long experience of coordinating a biblical translation project. During his tenure, the new divine office, the *Liturgia Horarum* (1972), employed the revised Psalms; the latter received a light revision in 1974. The other Old Testament books went through two sets of drafts: the first, printed in 1974–77, consisted of ten fascicles marked "pro manuscripto" on the cover, and privately distributed to about one hundred experts (which continue to

---

[5] A list of the commission's members and consultors was published each year in the Holy See's *Annuario Pontificio*, beginning with just twelve members in the 1966 edition. By the time Eduard Schick took over the presidency, more than forty consultants had been named, as listed in the 1972 edition, to assist the members.

be available in certain libraries); the second, printed in 1976–77, consisted of four hard-bound, public editions similar to those of the Psalms and New Testament.[6] These, unlike the Psalms, were not yet approved for liturgical use. The commission continued to solicit feedback from Catholic and non-Catholic scholars until the project's completion, when the newly elected John Paul II approved the release of the official, single-volume *Nova Vulgata* in 1979. This became the basis for the second edition of the *Liturgia Horarum* (1985–87) and the instructions for producing the lectionary in all languages, the *Ordo lectionum Missae* (1981).

Only minor changes were made to the Neo-Vulgate text for the 1986 second edition (cf. Zilverberg 2017: 115–16), enlarged by a preface and appendix as well as an introduction taken from those given in the draft volumes. One example of the revision is a punctuation change at Psalm 11:1–3 (Psalm 10:1–3 LXX). In the 1979 edition, this appeared as *Quomodo dicitis animae meae: "Transmigra in montem sicut passer? . . . iustus quid faciat?"* ("How do you say to my soul, 'Pass over to the mountain like a sparrow? . . . what should the just one do?'"). The first question mark was deemed to be confusing to the reader, and was emended to an exclamation mark in the revision ("Pass over to the mountain like a sparrow!"). The 1986 version also changed *homo* ("man") to *Adam* ("Adam") in Genesis 2–4 and, in keeping with the text's liturgical purpose, revised *Iahveh* ("Yahweh") to *Dominus* ("Lord") at Exodus 3:15 and Exodus 15:3. The Vatican Press produced a newly typeset edition in 1998 but otherwise left the text unchanged.[7]

TEXTUAL CHARACTER OF THE TRANSLATION

The commission claimed that it began with Weber's two-volume Vulgate (Weber and Fischer 1969), except for the Psalms and the deuterocanonical books, and corrected it with recourse to critical editions in the original biblical languages and related textual witnesses. The determination of the Latin base texts used for revision is more complicated than presented in the Neo-Vulgate prefaces, which only mention Weber for the Hebrew canon of the Old Testament (Commission 1977b: 7) and Weber along with occasional use of the Clementine Vulgate for the New Testament (Commission 1970–71: I.vii–ix). The issue will be treated in greater detail in the subsections that follow.

Bardski has estimated that 17 percent of the Bible's words were changed (2006: 22, n. 15). The preface of the second edition of the Neo-Vulgate provides the most synthetic account of the principles followed for revising the whole Bible (*Nova Vulgata* 1986: xi–xiv). The *Liber Psalmorum*, the first book commissioned and the first completed, set the basic

---

[6] New Testament drafts were likewise distributed to some fifty experts of various religious confessions (Vallainc 1968; Rossano 1970a), but their absence from library catalogues leads one to believe that they were not bound as fascicles. So, too, for the Psalms an unpublished draft was sent in January 1969 to more than a hundred experts around the world (Schick 1972: 346; cf. Gribomont 1987: 194).

[7] That is, except for the numerous typographical errors introduced. See Zilverberg 2017: 117, n. 111.

methodological standard for the rest of the Bible; its introduction offers the first detailed elaboration of the principles of emendation (Commission 1969: vii–xi). The Gallican Psalter was corrected, primarily with recourse to the Hebrew text. Christian Latin expressions were preserved (e.g., *confitemini Domino, levavi animam meam, salutare vultus mei, sacrificium iustitiae*), and the vocabulary for corrections was sought in the Vulgate itself, Jerome's commentaries, and contemporary patristic writings.

Numerous authors have compiled examples of Neo-Vulgate emendation, many of which have been noted in a selective compilation of such "improvements" (Zilverberg 2017: 112–16). A couple of examples from each Testament are provided here. The Neo-Vulgate renders a confusing Semitism less so at Psalm 95:11 (Psalm 94:11 LXX), where it reads *iuravi in ira mea: Non introibunt in requiem meam* ("I swore in my anger: They will not enter into my rest"); the corresponding passage in the Gallican Psalter (Psalm 94:11 LXX) reads *iuravi in ira mea: Si introibunt in requiem meam* ("I swore in my anger: If they will enter into my rest"; see also chap. 28). The Hebrew-based revision of Isaiah 54:5 binds it more closely to the recurring biblical theme of God marrying his people: *Qui enim fecit te, erit sponsus tuus* ("For he who made you will be your husband"), versus the Vulgate: *Quia dominabitur tui qui fecit te* ("For he who made you will rule over you"). At Romans 8:37, the revisers looked to the Latin Fathers Tertullian, Cyprian, Ambrose, and Augustine to restore a more precise rendering: *Sed in his omnibus supervincimus* ("But in all these things we more than conquer"), where the Vulgate verb is *superamus*, "we overcome"). The Neo-Vulgate omits the Johannine Comma of 1 John 5:7–8, a Trinitarian gloss absent from the Greek text but present in the Clementine Vulgate (see chap. 18).

Old Testament

For the Old Testament the revisers sometimes also consulted, in addition to Weber's two-volume Vulgate, the partially completed *editio maior* of the Roman Vulgate (Abbey of St. Jerome 1926–95). The edition by the same Abbey of the Clementine Vulgate was also taken into account (Abbey of St. Jerome 1965). The fascicles of the *Biblia Hebraica Stuttgartensia* supplied a modern, critical Hebrew text for the entire Hebrew canon as they were printed during the years 1968–76.

For the Old Testament, Stramare claims that the Clementine Vulgate was normally taken as the textual basis (1979b: 124; cf. 1979a: 447, n. 21), in contrast to the official claim that Weber's edition was normally used. As for the New Testament, the revision began prior to the release of Weber's edition (Weber and Fischer 1969; Vallainc 1968), and it seems that at least for this early period, Stramare's claim holds true. The revisers had apparently received the Isaiah fascicle of the *Biblia Hebraica Stuttgartensia* by 1967 (Thomas 1968; Stramare 1979b: 124; Schick 1980: 192) and used the Clementine edition as the base text to be corrected. Facsimiles of three corrected pages of Clementine Isaiah corroborate the use of the publisher Marietti's edition of the Clementine Vulgate as the base text for revision (Stramare 1975: 9; Schick 1978: 208; Garofalo 1979). The same base text for Ecclesiasticus, a special case, has also been confirmed (Stramare 1979a: 447, n. 21; Elwolde 2016–18: 13.86).

The introduction to the final Pentateuch draft names only Weber's edition (Commission 1977b: 7), which matches one account by the commission's president Eduard Schick (1980: 192). In 1972, however, Schick had affirmed that many Old Testament books were near completion and listed both the Benedictine *editio maior* and Weber's edition, in that order, as the principal Latin sources (Schick 1972: 346–47; cf. Castellano 1967). He would repeat the same account around the time of the revision's completion, giving preference to the *editio maior* when available (Schick 1977: 15; cf. Schick 1978: 205). Albert-Louis Descamps states, ambiguously, that for the whole Bible the commission began from the critical Vulgate text resulting principally from the work of the Abbey of St. Jerome (Descamps 1979: 602). Since the abbey's critical text only covered part of the Old Testament, perhaps Descamps intended to signify the Weber Vulgate. Weber was, after all, a monk of that abbey, and his edition benefited from the Old Testament books thus far collectively edited in critical editions.

Deuterocanonical Books

The deuterocanonical books presented difficulties owing to their impressive textual plurality and the imperfect state of our knowledge of their textual histories. Jerome dedicated little or no time to these, so their Latin texts were most in need of correction (see chap. 7). He did revise Tobit and Judith but took liberties with these that he did not allow himself for those books he considered canonical (Skemp 2000: 455–70; Bogaert 2012: 111–23). The Neo-Vulgate commission judged the Old Latin versions more pristine, so the eleventh-century manuscript in Vercelli (Archivio Capitolare Eusebiano, 22; VL 123) provided the starting point for a corrected Tobit, and one of the ninth century in Bern (Burgerbibliothek 533; VL 153) for Judith. All the Neo-Vulgate revisers indicated departures from a book's principal non-Latin source when making corrections. In Esther, the deuterocanonical additions that Jerome relegated to the end of the book and marked with obeli were reintegrated as required by the Greek narrative and the obeli removed, in accordance with the Tridentine affirmation that they are fully canonical and inspired. Likewise for the additions to Daniel, the obeli were removed but without changing to the usual Greek and Old Latin ordering (Susanna, then Daniel with the additions to the third chapter, and finally, Bel and the Dragon). Instead, the commission preserved Jerome's Hexaplaric ordering: Daniel (including additions to chapter three), Susanna, and Bel and the Dragon.

The rest of the deuterocanonicals, Ecclesiasticus, Wisdom, Baruch, and 1–2 Maccabees, were not revised by Jerome. Of these, Ecclesiasticus presents the most difficulties. Stramare describes in some detail the process that led to choosing the Clementine Vulgate as the base text for this book (Stramare 1979a: 447). Giuseppe

Scarpat reviewed the Wisdom of Solomon and concluded that its maladroit reviser used the Clementine Vulgate as well (1987: 188). The commission did not specify the Latin base text used for Baruch (or any of the prophets), which has virtually no introduction and just one critical note (Baruch 6:71, i.e., Epistle of Jeremiah 71). For 1–2 Maccabees, the last volume of the Roman *editio maior* had not yet been prepared. The "Vulgate," without further specification, served as the base text; perhaps Weber's edition might be implied by the claim that the revision of the historical books follows the same principles as previous Neo-Vulgate drafts (Commission 1977a: 7).

New Testament

For the New Testament, the Greek text was provided from the United Bible Societies' *Greek New Testament* (Aland et al. 1966), including advance material from the forthcoming third edition (Aland et al. 1975; Rossano 1970b). As mentioned above, the New Testament prefaces indicate that the Latin base text for emendation was that of Weber (1969), along with occasional use of the Clementine Vulgate. Nevertheless, Tarcisio Stramare claimed that for the New Testament, the base text was supplied first by the Wordsworth–White edition (1889–1954) and then by Weber, while still taking the Clementine Vulgate into account (Stramare 1979b: 120). Since the preface of the first volume of the New Testament mentions no critical edition other than Weber's (Commission 1970–71: I, vii; cf. Rossano 1970a), the primacy accorded to Wordsworth–White may be chronological, with the commission making use of it before the release of Weber's edition the year prior to the first public Neo-Vulgate drafts. An initial examination of minor discrepancies between the two critical editions suggests that the revisers preferred Wordsworth–White for the Gospel of Matthew but Weber for Romans.[8] Further investigation is required to verify this in the other books. Eduard Schick, writing just after the completion of the New Testament, implied that Weber's edition took precedence in general but affirmed that Wordsworth–White and other editions were also consulted (Schick 1972: 347).

The lack of clarity about the base Latin text being revised may reflect some flexibility accorded the revisers, as well as a methodological adjustment required by the appearance of Weber's edition after revision was already underway. This applies not just to the New Testament but to the whole Bible. Critical examination of each book in order to

---

[8] The evidence from my initial study consists of readings that satisfy two conditions: (1) Wordsworth-White differs from Weber, and (2) Greek variants either do not exist or, if they do, they are unlikely to account for the difference. The Neo-Vulgate follows Wordsworth-White at Matthew 2:22 *illuc*, 4:14 *impleretur*, 6:9 *es in caelis*, 6:10 *adveniat*, 12:15 *secessit*, 12:24 *daemonum*, 14:2 *operantur*, 17:18 *eum*, 24:26 *penetralibus*, 25:35. 43 *collegistis*, 25:41 *praeparatus*, 26:47 *missi*, and 27:31 *clamyde*. There are only a handful of counterexamples in which the Neo-Vulgate follows Weber's Matthew against Wordsworth-White. The Neo-Vulgate follows Weber at Romans 1:20 *divinitas ut*, 9:16 *miserentis Dei*, 13:9 *tamquam*, and 14:23 *non ex* (2nd occurrence in verse), with no counterexamples in this epistle.

identify each one's textual dependencies remains a desideratum. The commission's papers remain classified in the Archivio Apostolico Vaticano, Vatican City, but it is to be hoped that their eventual release will shed light on the matter.

In any case, the revisers looked for instances in which the Latin text diverged from the critical Greek text and intervened to render it accurately and clearly in Latin. Out of respect for the hallowed Vulgate, they sometimes did not conform it fully to the Greek text (Commission 1970–71: I.viii-ix). Likewise, they allowed bland but intelligible Vulgate readings to stand, even when more precise Old Latin readings were available. So, comparing the Neo-Vulgate Gospels to the examples that Philip Burton adduces to illustrate Jerome's translation technique (Burton 2000: 192–99), none of Jerome's "unfocused" renderings have been corrected. Among the etymologizing ones, the three most confusing (Luke 11:53, 12:29) or imprecise (Matthew 9:38) are emended. When available, Old Latin readings that precisely render the Greek text replace unsatisfactory Vulgate ones (Rossano 1970a; compare Romans 8:37 above); otherwise the revisers compose emendations according to the vocabulary and style of the Vulgate.

Reception

The revision of the Vulgate lost much of its urgency during the period of its preparation (1964–79), for the Roman Catholic Church turned to vernacular liturgy quickly and decisively from the late 1960s onward. The Second Vatican Council had called for the retention of Latin and the limited introduction of the vernacular into certain parts of the rites, while requiring all clergy to continue praying the divine office in Latin. In practice, however, the nearly wholesale abandonment of Latin in the postconciliar liturgy meant that most of the faithful never heard of the Neo-Vulgate and most clerics never read it. Catholics suspicious of the conciliar reforms likewise had no interest in an updated Vulgate. Some resisted all postconciliar liturgical innovations and sought out the still-surviving preconciliar rites, which, naturally, employed the Clementine Vulgate.

Although the first edition of the Psalms became official in 1969, the rest of the Neo-Vulgate achieved this status with the 1979 release of the single-volume edition, lightly revised and augmented by a preface and introduction in 1986 (Zilverberg 2017: 115–16). Since the 1979 first edition, the Holy See has employed the Neo-Vulgate when citing sacred Scripture in Latin documents, and especially in the sacred liturgy. There has been no further update to the text, but it was newly typeset for the 1998 printing.

Even though the Neo-Vulgate's projected influence and readership vastly diminished from the time of Pope Paul VI's 1965 mandate to revise the Latin Bible to Pope John Paul II's promulgation of the 1979 Neo-Vulgate, thousands of clergymen, consecrated religious, and lay faithful continue to pray daily from this biblical edition. They do so principally by exercising their option to recite or chant the postconciliar divine office in Latin (*Liturgia Horarum* 1972; 1985–87). This four-volume set of nearly seven thousand pages contains a vast amount of biblical text, so its readers encounter the Neo-Vulgate, especially the Psalter's psalms and canticles, up to seven times a day.[9] Every liturgical hour contains a few selections from the Psalter and another biblical pericope, with the hour called Office of Readings containing longer excerpts to guide the reader systematically through the Bible each year.

The typical edition of the postconciliar lectionary also employs the Neo-Vulgate, at least in theory. Although the Holy See updated its postconciliar schema for the Roman-rite lectionary following the official release of the Neo-Vulgate (*Ordo lectionum Missae* 1981), it never actually printed the book described therein. A publisher in the Chicago suburbs, Midwest Theological Forum, met this need in 2008 with an up-to-date Latin lectionary "according to the typical edition," but it is now out of print.[10] It serves de facto as the typical edition itself, since the Holy See had only ever published a single edition prior to the Neo-Vulgate, with readings derived from the Clementine Vulgate and Neo-Vulgate Psalms (*Lectionarium* 1970–72). Furthermore, the 2008 *Lectionarium* is the only means of establishing how to use the 1986 Neo-Vulgate in the lectionary, because the most recent *Ordo lectionum Missae* dates to 1981 and relies on the 1979 Neo-Vulgate. The Holy See's failure to produce a Latin lectionary indicates both a lack of demand for this as well as its unwillingness to promote such a volume.

As the Catholic Church now encourages biblical translations from the original languages (Secretariat 1966: 443 = *Dei verbum* §22; Congregation 2001 §24), the Neo-Vulgate has been little translated. In 1973, the Psalter received a French translation followed by a two-volume compilation of patristic commentaries on the Psalms (*Psautier Chrétien*; cf. Beauchamp 1974: 55–59). Paul Griffiths translated the Neo-Vulgate Song of Songs into English for his 2011 theological commentary on the book. Władyslav Chernyavsky et al. produced the first and only full Neo-Vulgate translation known to the present author, into Belarusian, revised by other Latinists for its 2012 publication by the Bible Society of the Republic of Belarus. The translators, in fact, began from a manuscript translation of the Clementine Vulgate and revised it to conform to the Neo-Vulgate (Elwolde 2016–18: 12.11).

As Elliott observes in chapter 27, the Neo-Vulgate text has been reproduced in various bilingual and polyglot editions. These include the Greek–Latin–Spanish *Nuevo Testamento trilingüe* (Bover and O'Callaghan 1977), two different editions with the title *Novum Testamentum Graece et Latine* (Nolli 1981; Aland and Aland 1984), the Navarre Bible in Spanish (Facultad 1997–2004) and its translations, and the American Bible Society's *Biblia polyglotta* (2008).

---

[9] The Vatican edition has been out of print for about a decade, but Midwest Theological Forum's six-volume edition remains in print (*Liturgia Horarum* 2010) and its 2018 reprint introduced very minor changes: two new saints in the general calendar and typographical corrections.

[10] Curiously, the Congregation for Divine Worship stipulated that this lectionary employ the 1969 first-edition Neo-Vulgate psalter, which had been updated in 1974, 1979, and 1986. This may have been done to make it correspond to the version of the Psalter used in older postconciliar editions. However, the Congregation used the 1979 psalter in its updated divine office (*Liturgia Horarum* 1985–87, 2000) and allowed the same Midwestern publisher to use the 1986 psalter in its own edition (2010, 2018). The differences from one liturgical book to another, albeit minor, annoy the attentive reader.

The Neo-Vulgate gained attention in 2001 when the Holy See's Congregation for Divine Worship called for biblical translations for vernacular liturgies to take the Latin edition as a reference point for canonicity and chapter and verse numbering, as well as the determination of which texts to translate (Congregation 2001: §§ 37–38). It also put forth the Neo-Vulgate as a model liturgical translation worthy of imitation (§§24, 41, 43). Some Catholic scholars have rejected this as unwarranted meddling in local church affairs and biblical scholarship, while others welcome the rules as an appropriately flexible basis for unity (Zilverberg 2017: 102–12). The prefect of the Congregation clarified the matter by reaffirming the autonomy of biblical translators while requiring at least minimal commonality among the myriad vernacular translations in Roman Catholic liturgical use (Medina Estévez 2001). Furthermore, the continued use in official liturgical editions of older Latin texts set to Gregorian chant, such as the invitatory psalm and the Magnificat, demonstrates Vatican moderation in the liturgical application of the Neo-Vulgate.

CONCLUSION

Although Vulgate revision according to original-language biblical manuscripts had sometimes been proposed and even attempted over centuries of Catholic history, it was the boldness of the Second Vatican Council that finally enabled its realization. The failure of the 1945 Pian Psalter, a new translation from the Hebrew, led to the much more conservative approach of taking the Vulgate as a starting point and preserving established Christian Latin forms. Like Jerome, the revisers applied their philological and exegetical acumen to produce a Bible translation that mediated the authority of the Hebrew and Greek texts. The Church's sudden shift to vernacular liturgy diminished the Neo-Vulgate's importance, but the thousands who daily pray the *Liturgia Horarum* and the fewer who employ the *Lectionarium* at Mass have received it as their Bible.

BIBLIOGRAPHY

Zilverberg (2017: 120–25) provides the most recent full Neo-Vulgate bibliography. Notable additions in the following bibliography are: Bardski 2006; Castellano 1967; Chernyavsky et al. 2012; Elwolde, 2016–17, 2018; Stramare 1975; Vallainc 1968; Zilverberg 2017.

Abbey of St. Jerome in Rome, ed. 1926–95. *Biblia Sacra iuxta latinam vulgatam versionem*. 18 vols. Rome: Vatican Polyglot Press.
Abbey of St. Jerome in Rome, ed. 1965. *Biblia Sacra vulgatae editionis*. 2nd edn. Turin: Marietti.
Aland, Kurt, Matthew Black, Bruce M. Metzger, and Allen Wikgren, eds. 1966. *The Greek New Testament*. 1st ed. New York: American Bible Society.
Aland, Kurt, Matthew Black, Carlo M. Martini, Bruce M. Metzger, and Allen Wikgren, eds. 1975. *The Greek New Testament*. 3rd ed. New York: American Bible Society.

Aland, Kurt, and Barbara Aland, eds. 1984. *Novum Testamentum Graece et Latine*. 23rd ed. Stuttgart: Deutsche Bibelgesellschaft.

American Bible Society, ed. 2008. *Biblia polyglotta*. New York: American Bible Society.

Bardski, Krzysztof. 2006. "Neo-Wulgata a tłumaczenie św. Hieronima." In *Ioannes Paulus II— In memoriam*, edited by Waldemar Chrostowski, 15–26. Warsaw: Uniwersytetu Kardynała Stefana Wyszyńskiego.

Bea, Agostino. 1946. *Il Nuovo Salterio latino*. 2nd ed. Scripta Pontificii Instituti Biblici 95. Rome: Pontificio Istituto Biblico.

Bogaert, Pierre-Maurice. 1988. "La Bible latine des origines au moyen âge. Aperçu historique, état des questions." *Revue Théologique de Louvain* 19: 137–59, 276–314.

Bogaert, Pierre-Maurice. 2012. "Jérôme hagiographe et conteur. La conversion d'Achior dans le livre de Judith." In *La surprise dans la Bible*, edited by Geert Van Oyen and André Wénin, 111–23. BETL 247. Leuven: Peeters.

Bover, José María, and José O'Callaghan, eds. 1977. *Nuevo Testamento trilingüe*. Madrid: La Editorial Católica.

Burton, Philip H. 2000. *The Old Latin Gospels: A Study of Their Texts and Language*. Oxford: Oxford University Press.

Castellano, Giorgio. 1967. "Problem Neo-Wulgaty." *Tygodnik Powszechny* 13: 4.

Coelho, Ilda Sobral. 2001. "Frei Jerónimo de Azambuja: Exegeta e hebraísta Português." *Cadmo* 11: 101–21.

Chernyavsky, Władyslav, et al., trans. 2012. Бiблiя. Кнiгi Святога Пiсання Старога i Новага Запаветаў. Minsk: Bible Society of the Republic of Belarus.

Ciciliot, Valentina. 2017. "Rossano, Pietro (Piero)." *Dizionario Biografico degli Italiani. Vol. 88: Robusti–Roverella*, 509–11. Rome: Istituto della Enciclopedia Italiana.

Commission for the Neo-Vulgate, ed. 1969. *Liber Psalmorum*. 1st edn. Vatican City: Vatican Polyglot Press.

Commission for the Neo-Vulgate, ed. 1970–71. *Novum Testamentum*. 3 vols. Vatican City: Vatican Polyglot Press.

Commission for the Neo-Vulgate, ed. 1974. *Liber Psalmorum*. 2nd ed. Vatican City: Vatican Polyglot Press.

Commission for the Neo-Vulgate, ed. 1977a. *Libri Historici*. Vatican City: Vatican Polyglot Press.

Commission for the Neo -Vulgate, ed. 1977b. *Pentateuchus*. Vatican City: Vatican Polyglot Press.

Congregation for Divine Worship and the Discipline of the Sacraments. 2001. "Instructio Quinta . . . De Usu Linguarum Popularium (*Liturgiam authenticam*)." *Acta Apostolicae Sedis* 93: 685–726.

Descamps, Albert-Louis. 1979. "La Nouvelle Vulgate." *Esprit et Vie* 89 (Nov. 15): 598–603.

Elwolde, John Francis. 2016–18. "A Text-Critical Study of the *Nova Vulgata* of Sirach 41." *Tamid* 12: 7–63; 13: 35–93.

Facultad de Teología. 1997–2004. *Sagrada Biblia*. 5 vols. Pamplona: Universidad de Navarra.

Garofalo, Salvatore. 1979. "L'Edizione tipica della nuova Bibbia latina." *L'Osservatore Romano*, 28 April, p. 3.

Gribomont, Jean. 1987. "La révision conciliaire du Psautier de la Néo-Vulgate." In *La Bibbia "Vulgata" dalle origini ai nostri giorni*, edited by Tarcisio Stramare, 192–97. CBL 16.Vatican City: Libreria Editrice Vaticana.

Lectionarium. 1970–1972. 1st ed. 3 vols. Vatican City: Libreria Editrice Vaticana.

Lectionarium. 2008. Edition according to the *editio typica altera*. 3 vols. Chicago: Midwest Theological Forum.

Liturgia Horarum. 1972. *Liturgia Horarum.* 4 vols. Vatican City: Libreria Editrice Vaticana. 2nd ed. 1985–87.

Liturgia Horarum. 2010/2018. Edition according to the *editio typica altera.* 6 vols; Chicago: Midwest Theological Forum.

Martin, J. Albert. 1972. "Relatio de schemate constitutionis de Sacra Liturgia (21 oct. 1963)." in *Acta Synodalia. Vol. II. Periodus Secunda. Pars III. Congregationes Generales L-LVIII,* edited by Archivum Concilii Vaticani II, 124–46. Vatican City: Vatican Polyglot Press.

McShane, Myron, and Mark Young. 2016. "Introduction." In *A Translator's Defense by Giannozzo Manetti,* vii–xxxviii. I Tatti Renaissance Library 71. Cambridge, MA: Harvard University.

Medina Estévez, Jorge A. 2001. "Litterae Congregationis, Prot. N. 2071/01/L, 5 Nov. 2001." *Notitiae* 37, no. 11–12: 521–26.

Müller, Michael. 2003. "Schick, Eduard." In *Biographisch-bibliographisches Kirchenlexikon. Band 22: Ergänzungen 9,* edited by Friedrich W. Bautz and Traugott Bautz, 1215–20. Nordhausen: Traugott Bautz.

Nolli, Gianfranco, ed. 1981. *Novum Testamentum Graece et Latine.* 1st ed. Vatican City: Libreria Editrice Vaticana.

Nova Vulgata Bibliorum Sacrorum Editio. 1979. 1st ed. Vatican City: Libreria Editrice Vaticana.

Nova Vulgata Bibliorum Sacrorum Editio. 1986. 2nd ed. Vatican City: Libreria Editrice Vaticana.

Ordo lectionum Missae. 1969. 1st ed. Vatican City: Libreria Editrice Vaticana.

Ordo lectionum Missae. 1981. 2nd ed. Vatican City: Libreria Editrice Vaticana.

Ottaviani, Alfredo. 1965. "Relatio de schemate constitutionis de Fontibus Revelationis (9 nov. 1961)." In *Acta et Documenta. Series II (Praeparatoria). Vol. II, Pars I,* edited by Secretariat of the Second Vatican Council, 532–37. Vatican City: Vatican Polyglot Press.

Psautier Chrétien. 1973. 3 vols. Paris: Téqui.

Rossano, Piero. 1970a. "Le Epistole di S. Paolo e Cattoliche." *L'Osservatore Romano,* 16 October, p. 3.

Rossano, Piero. 1970b. "Il Libro dei Vangeli." *L'Osservatore Romano,* 25–26 May, p. 3.

Salmon, Pierre. 1965. "Animadversio de schemate constitutionis de Fontibus Revelationis (10 nov. 1961)." In *Acta et Documenta. Series II (Praeparatoria). Vol. II, Pars I,* edited by Secretariat of the Second Vatican Council, 550–53. Vatican City: Vatican Polyglot Press.

Secretariat of the Second Vatican Council. 1961. *Acta et Documenta. Series I (antepraeparatoria). Appendix voluminis II. Analyticus conspectus.* 2 vols. Vatican City: Vatican Polyglot Press.

Secretariat of the Second Vatican Council. 1966. *Sacrosanctum Oecumenicum Concilium Vaticanum II.* Vatican City: Vatican Polyglot Press.

Scarpat, Giuseppe. 1987. "Osservazioni sul testo della *Sapientia* nella *Nova Vulgata.*" *Rivista Biblica* 35, no. 2: 187–94.

Schick, Eduard. 1972. "Eine Neuherausgabe der Vulgata." *Theologisch-praktische Quartalschrift* 120, no. 4: 345–47.

Schick, Eduard. 1977. "Bibel neu übersetzt. Nach zwölfjähriger Arbeit liegt eine neue Vulgata vor." *Bonifatiusbote* 49, no. 4: 14–15.

Schick, Eduard. 1978. "Die 'Neue Vulgata'. Anlass, Methode und Ziel der im Jahre 1977 abgeschlossenen Revision der Vulgata." In *Eine Bibel—viele Übersetzungen,* edited by Siegfried Meurer, 203–11. Bibel in der Welt 18. Stuttgart: Evangelisches Bibelwerk.

Schick, Eduard. 1980. "Die Neovulgata. Bericht über die Arbeit am neuen lateinischen Schrifttext." *Liturgisches Jahrbuch* 30, no. 3: 186–96.

Skemp, Vincent T. M. 2000. *The Vulgate of Tobit Compared with Other Ancient Witnesses.* SBL Dissertation Series 180. Atlanta: SBL.

Stramare, Tarcisio. 1975. "La Neo-Volgata. Una nuova Bibbia in lingua latina." *Tabor ns* 29, no. 1: 7–10.

Stramare, Tarcisio. 1979a. "Il Libro dell'Ecclesiastico nella Neo-Volgata." In *Kirche und Bibel. Festgabe für Bischof Eduard Schick*, edited by Hochschule Fulda, 443–48. Paderborn: Schöningh.

Stramare, Tarcisio. 1979b. "La Neo-Volgata: impresa scientifica e pastorale insieme." *Estudios Bíblicos* 38, no. 1–2: 115–38.

Thomas, D. Winton, ed. 1968. *Biblia Hebraica Stuttgartensia. 7. Liber Jesaiae.* Stuttgart: Württembergische Bibelanstalt.

Van Puyvelde, Clément. 1949. "Le Nouveau Psautier," *Les Questions Liturgiques et Paroissiales* 30/2: 49–52.

Vallainc, Angelo. 1968. "Lo stato dei lavori per la 'neo-Volgata.'" *L'Osservatore Romano*, 8 June, p. 2.

Weber, Robert, ed. 1961. *Psalterii secundum Vulgatam Bibliorum versionem Nova Recensio.* Clervaux: Abbaye S. Maurice et S. Maur.

Weber, Robert, and Bonifatius Fischer, eds. 1969. *Biblia Sacra iuxta vulgatam versionem.* 2 vols. Stuttgart: Württembergische Bibelanstalt.

Wordsworth, John, Henry Julian White, et al., eds. 1889–1954. *Nouum Testamentum Domini nostri Iesu Christi latine secundum editionem sancti Hieronymi.* 3 vols. Oxford: Clarendon.

Ziegler, Joseph. 1951. "Das neue lateinische Psalterium." *Zeitschrift für die alttestamentliche Wissenschaft* 63: 1–15.

Zilverberg, Kevin. 2017. "The Neo-Vulgate as Official Liturgical Translation." In *Verbum Domini: Liturgy and Scripture*, edited by Joseph Briody, 93–125. Wells: Smenos.

CHAPTER 26

···

VERNACULAR TRANSLATIONS OF THE LATIN BIBLE

···

OLIVER DY AND WIM FRANÇOIS

It is customary for contemporary Bible translators to adopt scriptural texts in Greek, Hebrew, or Aramaic as their source texts. The broader history of Bible translation, however, attests to vernacular translations that derive from the Latin Bible. Although the Vulgate is itself a translation, it nonetheless serves as a source text within the Catholic tradition of Bible translating. Its status as an authoritative version of Scripture was reaffirmed by the Council of Trent in its decree of April 8, 1546 (as quoted in chap. 19). Taken at face value, the conciliar decree specifies the normative importance of the Latin Vulgate in public uses of Scripture such as liturgical readings, theological debates, sermons, and biblical explanations. However, it is silent on whether or not, and to what extent, the Latin Vulgate should be used as a basis for translating Scripture given the existence of biblical texts in the original ancient languages. In determining the role and place of the Latin Vulgate in the work of biblical translation, Catholic Bible translators were shaped by, and in turn also helped shape, the prevailing hermeneutics regarding the Tridentine decree on the Vulgate.

HISTORY OF THE USE OF THE LATIN VULGATE AS A TRANSLATION SOURCE

Trent's *Insuper* decree (see chap. 19) highlights an issue peculiar to the Catholic tradition of Bible translating, namely, the tension between the Latin Vulgate and the biblical texts in the original languages as competing source texts of translation. This is part of a more complex and broader problem rooted in the nature of the Bible as a plural text (Tov 2002: 251; Pym 2007: 196–97). One ancient manifestation of this is the debate between Jerome and Augustine as to whether the Hebrew or Greek text should be considered of greater value in the translation and interpretation of the Old Testament (Gallagher 2016; Decock 2008). Another example is the more recent question of which among the various manuscripts and textual variants in the original biblical languages should be selected as the proper source texts when producing contemporary vernacular versions of the Bible (Tov 2008; Clarke 1999).

The tension between Latin and the original languages of Scripture in the arena of Catholic Bible translation can be seen as the historical result of the encounter between two intellectual-religious currents that impinged upon the world of Scripture from the sixteenth to the middle of the seventeenth century. On one hand, the proponents of biblical humanism considered the Vulgate philologically worthless and emphasized the primary importance of the original languages in the reconstruction and interpretation of Scripture. On the other hand, there was the process of "confessionalization" to which biblical exposition and translation had become subject (see chap. 20; Rummel 2008; Jenkins and Preston 2007).

A printed vernacular Bible could be identified with a particular Christian confession through a set of characteristic markers of identity such as particular formulations of contested passages of Scripture (e.g., Matthew 3:2, 4:17, 16:18; Luke 1:28; Romans 3:28; James 5:14) and "paratextual elements" (see François 2020b). On the Catholic side, such paratextual identifiers typically included the censorial *imprimatur*, the presence of deuterocanonical books in complete Bibles, a calendar of Feasts and Saints' Days with an apparatus allowing the reader to follow Latin liturgical readings in the vernacular, and a statement asserting that the translation had been principally made or revised from the Latin Vulgate. In contrast, translations in the vernacular Bibles of Protestants of whatever denomination were claimed or presumed to have been made directly from the original languages and embellished with elaborate annotations and registers that offered a "Protestant" reading of Scripture. In this way, the choice of the primary source text for biblical translation became a contested point that expressed and symbolized the confessional divide between Catholic and Protestant.[1]

In the encounter between "confessionalization" and biblical humanism in the wake of Trent's decree on the Vulgate, the former ultimately proved a more compelling force in shaping the choice and arrangement of source texts in Catholic vernacular Bibles. The need to assert the "authentic" Vulgate as the primary source of these translations for confessional reasons prevailed over the need to emphasize the original languages of Scripture as demanded by biblical humanism. The complete Douay-Rheims Bible serves as an illustration of this. In the preface to the first volume of 1609, "To the English Reader," the translators explain their choice of the Vulgate on the basis of inherited

---

[1] It should be noted that such confessional identification in vernacular Bibles does not necessarily reflect the translation's relation to earlier translations. The revision of selected key passages and the strategic addition of the appropriate paratexts could bestow a new confessional identity on an existing vernacular version (e.g., Ingram 2004). Some Catholic translations that claim to have been made from the Latin Vulgate are actually "vulgatized" versions of earlier Protestant translations dependent on original language texts, as discussed below.

presumptions about the comparative textual integrity between the derivative Latin, as "more pure" and the Hebrew and Greek originals as "fouly corrupted" (fol. 3v). The preference for the Vulgate is legitimized in text-critical terms, which also provide the basis for developing a definition of what is meant by the Vulgate's "authenticity." Nevertheless, the devaluation of original-language versions of Scripture is tempered by the claim in the title that the translation had also been "diligently conferred with the Hebrew, Greeke, and other editions in divers languages" (fol. 1r). Notwithstanding the allegations of their textual unreliability, the original-language texts are given a role and place, even if only as auxiliary sources for translation. Another key example is the controversial "Jansenist" *Nouveau Testament de Mons* of 1667 (see below). In its elaborate prologue, after explaining their choice of the "authentic" Vulgate as the primary source out of respect for Trent, the translators informed the reader that the places where the Greek and Latin are at variance with each other are systematically indicated in the translation. This was the translators' way of negotiating the Tridentine decree while giving as much prominence as possible to the Greek original in the composition and presentation of the translation.

With the development of biblical philology and textual criticism during the nineteenth century through the work of scholars such as Griesbach, Lachmann, Tischendorf, Westcott, and Hort, regard for the Latin Vulgate began to diminish among Catholic Bible translators. In response to the trends in biblical scholarship, the encyclical *Providentissimus Deus* was issued by Pope Leo XIII in 1893. This underscores the need for professors of biblical studies to "master those tongues in which the sacred Books were originally written" (§17) while giving due respect to the "authentic" Latin Vulgate. Not a few Catholic Bible translators took this statement to mean that the original texts rather than the Vulgate should be given greater priority in composing new translations or revising older ones.

The death knell for the use of the Vulgate as a translation source was sounded by the release of Pius XII's *Divino Afflante Spiritu* in 1943. This encyclical not only endorses the adoption of the historical-critical approach in interpreting Scripture in its original languages but also asserts that Trent's declaration of the Vulgate's authenticity was made not so much on text-critical as on juridical grounds (§21; see chap. 19). Support for this position came from the supplementary records of the Council of Trent published by the Görres Society (*Concilium Tridentinum* 1901–2001) in the aftermath of the opening of the Vatican Archives in 1880 (O'Malley 2013: 267). *Divino Afflante Spiritu* also specifies that Trent's decree on the Vulgate does not forbid one "to make translations into the vulgar tongue, even directly from the original texts themselves . . . as We know to have been already done in a laudable manner in many countries with the approval of the Ecclesiastical authority" (§22). This indicates a departure from the general impression that the Tridentine decree required Catholic translators to translate primarily from the Latin Vulgate (e.g., Schwarz 1955: 11; Neuner 2015: 542–48). Supported by advances in Catholic biblical scholarship and the new hermeneutic regarding the Council of Trent in general and the Vulgate's authenticity in particular, Catholic Bible translators found themselves belatedly turning to the methodology of prioritizing the original texts of Scripture which had long been maintained by their Protestant counterparts.

The preface to the New Testament in the *Catholic Revised Standard Version* of 1965 contains a crisp summary of how the grip of the legacy of "confessionalization" on the field of Catholic Bible translation with its attendant bias toward the Latin Vulgate was eventually dislodged by the modern successors of biblical humanism:

> For four hundred years, following upon the great upheaval of the Reformation, Catholics and Protestants have gone their separate ways and suspected each other's translations of the Bible of having been in some way manipulated in the interests of doctrinal presuppositions. It must be admitted that these suspicions were not always without foundation. At the present time, however, the sciences of textual criticism and philology, not to mention others, have made such great advances that the Bible text used by translators is substantially the same for all—Protestants and Catholics alike. Thus, for example, Catholics no longer make their translations from the Latin Vulgate; though it is arguable that before the development of textual criticism it was in certain respects a better way of making a translation than to make it from late and in some places corrupt Greek manuscripts, as was done by some of the Reformers. Today, and indeed since the appearance in 1943 of the Encyclical Letter, *Divino Afflante Spiritu*, encouraging biblical studies, Catholics like everyone else go back to the original languages and base their translations on the same critical principles.[2]

As a final move, Vatican II set its stamp of approval on the growing practice of reducing reliance on the Latin Vulgate as a source text for biblical translations. In *Dei Verbum* (1965), the Council stipulates that vernacular Bible translations for the use of the faithful should be produced "especially [*praesertim*] from the original texts of the sacred books" (§22). As a formally expressed conciliar norm, this serves as a definitive limit to the role and place of the "authentic" Latin Vulgate in Catholic Bible translating after Vatican II (Dy 2016: 154–55).

SELECTED VULGATE-BASED BIBLE TRANSLATIONS

To illustrate the extent of the employment of the "authentic" Latin Vulgate in Catholic Bible translating, this section examines a range of Bibles in German, French, English, and Dutch. These four target languages display long and relatively uninterrupted histories of Bible translation from the late medieval period to the present. The continuity of Bible production in these languages can be appreciated against the backdrop

---

[2] Catholic Biblical Association of Great Britain, *The New Testament of our Lord and Saviour Jesus Christ, Revised Standard Version Catholic Edition* (London: Thomas Nelson and Sons, 1965), vii–ix.

of the universal Catholic policy of censorship applied to vernacular Scriptures from the middle of the sixteenth to the middle of the eighteenth century. The Roman Inquisition had sought to limit and regulate access to vernacular Scriptures with its interpretation of the so-called Fourth Rule of the Tridentine Index of 1564 and its more rigid version of 1596. Accordingly, a de facto prohibition on vernacular Bible translations was implemented in territories and colonies under Italian, Spanish, and Portuguese rule. Ecclesiastical dispensations were, however, granted for geographical regions and localities in Northwestern and Central Europe with predominantly Protestant or mixed Catholic-Protestant constituencies. Only with the reform of the index of forbidden books in 1758 would this Roman policy of the censorship on the vernacular Scriptures become less restrictive (François 2013; Fattori 2014: 680–98).

The following five categories are employed to chart the choice and arrangement of the translation source texts as evidenced paratextually in Catholic Bibles in German, French, and English published following Trent's decree of 1546:

V	The Vulgate is the sole source text
Vo	The Vulgate is the primary source with original languages acting as secondary sources
V + O	The Vulgate and the original languages are coequal sources
Ov	The original languages are the primary sources with the Vulgate acting as a secondary source
O	The original languages alone are the source texts

Here, only Bible samples that contain at least the Pentateuch or Psalms (for the Old Testament) and the complete Gospels or Epistles (for the New Testament) are selected for the survey. The tabulated results in figure 26.1 and figure 26.2 reveal that the stated

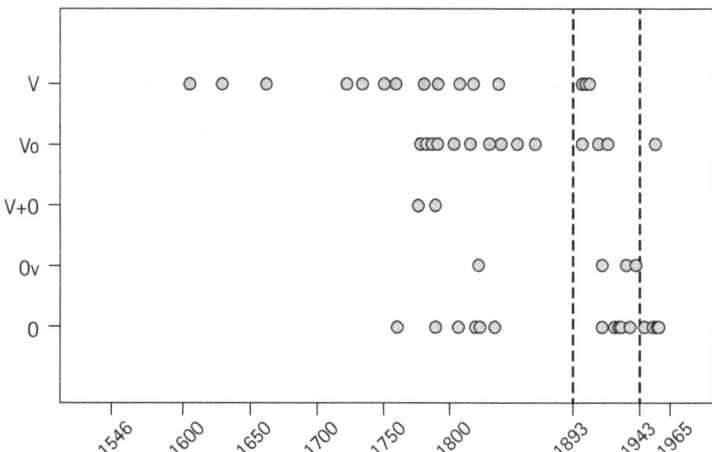

FIGURE 26.1. The choice and arrangement of the source texts of translation of Catholic vernacular bibles in English, French, and German (1546–1965): The Old Testament.

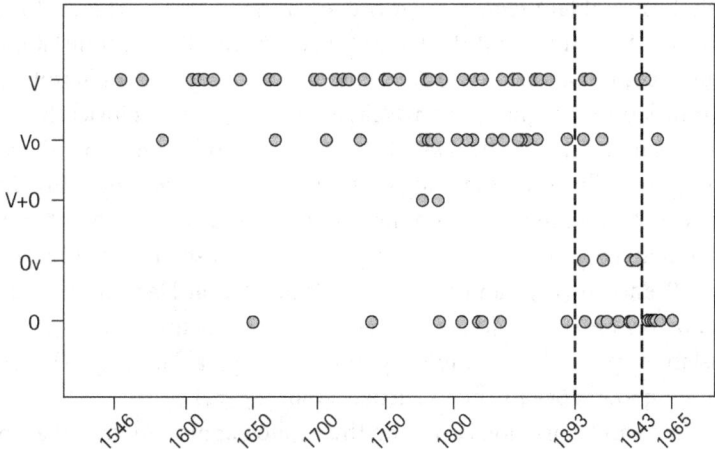

FIGURE 26.2. The choice and arrangement of the source texts of translation of Catholic vernacular bibles in English, French, and German (1546–1965): The New Testament.

use of the Vulgate as a source text was a general feature of Catholic vernacular Bibles until the late nineteenth century (Dy 2017: 215–17).

The sections that follow describe, in greater detail, the local histories of the use of the Latin Vulgate in the making of German, French, English, and Dutch Catholic Bibles.

German

During the late Middle Ages, Germany was the region of Europe where by far the most vernacular translations of the Bible were circulated and read. Eighteen complete Bibles and about seventy partial translations were printed between 1466 and the advent of Luther's New Testament (1522) and complete Bible (1534) translations based largely on the original languages. As was only to be expected, the earlier German versions were all made from the Vulgate. With the arrival and subsequent popularity of Luther's translations, Catholic translators chose to correct his work on the basis of the Vulgate rather than the more ambitious and laborious undertaking of producing independent translations. Three of the most notable of these *Korrektur-bibeln* are the New Testament of Jerome Emser (1527), its later revision in the complete Bible of the Dominican Johann Dietenberger (1534), and the Bavarian rewording of Luther's translation by Johann Eck (1537). Dietenberger's Bible came to be the most widely distributed, at least outside Bavaria and Austria, with multiple revisions and reissues especially following the release of the Sixto-Clementine Vulgate in 1592 (Köster 1995: 1–103; Fischer and Moger 2016; also Strand 1982). Other translations based on the 1592 Vulgate are those of Caspar Ulenberg (1630), the Mainz translators (1662), Thomas Aquinas Erhard (1723), an anonymous Strasbourg translator (1734), and Germanus Cartier (1751) (Dy 2017: 166–67; Köster 1995: 104–59).

The Catholic Enlightenment (*Katholische Aufklärung*) around 1750, with its increased openness to the Scriptures and the Church Fathers, resulted in translations based on the Vulgate in combination with texts in the original languages of Scripture. These include the translations of Ignatius von Weitenauer (1777–83), Heinrich Braun (1788 onward), and Johann Michael Feder (1803). The German "Bible movement" also produced translations primarily from the Vulgate such as the *Regensburg New Testament* of Georg Michael Wittmann (1808) and the *Munich New Testament* of Johannes Gossner (Scheuchenpflug 1997: 102–264). Others, including Joseph Lauber (1760 onward), Dominic of Brentano (1790 and 1797), Thaddaeus Anton Dereser (1815–28), Leander van Ess (1807 onward), and Johann Martin Augustin Scholz (1828–37), made or revised translations partially or completely from the original languages (Dy 2017: 174–89; Scheuchenpflug 1997: 265–401; also Gélébart 1986: 563–74).

The first German translations carrying the explicit approbation of the Apostolic See were produced by Joseph Franz von Allioli (1830–32), who revised the Braun-Feder translation using the Vulgate as his primary source but with regard to the original languages (Scheuchenpflug 1997: 19–101). The results were subject to several revisions, the most important of which was published by Augustin Arndt in 1899 and 1901 in the wake of the encyclical *Providentissimus Deus*. Sometimes known as the Allioli-Arndt edition, this was one of the more popular German translations and underwent several revisions. Other translations based mainly on the Vulgate but also considering original languages include those by Valentin Loch and Wilhelm Reischl (Dy 2017: 192–213).

A bilingual edition in five volumes of the complete Latin Vulgate with a German translation was released in 2018–19 by the De Gruyter publishing house in Berlin. It was made by Michael Fieger, Widu-Wolfgang Ehlers and Andreas Beriger from the Vulgata Verein Chur, and based on the fifth edition of the Stuttgart Vulgate (Weber and Gryson 2007).

French

Vernacular Bible translations were made, copied, and read in France throughout the High Middle Ages, even during the period of "heresies" (Cathars, Waldenses, and heterodox beguines) that prompted ecclesiastical authorities and theologians to become suspicious of such translations (Bogaert 1991: 13–46; Sneddon 2012). The early sixteenth-century French reform movement aimed to make the liturgical readings of Scripture more accessible to the laity. One of the protagonists of this *évangélisme*, the biblical humanist Jacques Lefèvre d'Étaples, published his multivolume New Testament (1523) and Psalms (1524) in Paris. These Vulgate-based translations were subject to the censorship of the theologians of the Paris Faculty, who adopted a conservative position in the face of the emergent reforms. Fleeing to Strasbourg, Lefèvre continued his translation of the Old Testament and published it in Antwerp in 1528, followed by his first edition of the complete Bible in 1530. Both of these bore the endorsement of theologians based in Louvain (Bogaert and Gilmont 1991: 50–65; Paquin 2018: 55–72; see also chap. 18).

After Henten published his revision of the Vulgate in 1547, there appeared in 1550 a "new" French translation made by his colleague Nicolas de Leuze with the assistance of François de Larben. Known as the *Bible de Louvain*, this was largely a revision of the French text in Lefèvre's Bible of 1530 (and probably also its 1534 edition), with some additional borrowings from the 1540 Reformed *Bible à l'Épée* or the *Sword Bible* (Bogaert and Gilmont 1980, 1991: 87–90). A comparable French translation was published by the Paris priest and theologian René Benoist in 1566. Despite its claim to be based on Henten's edition, it was a "vulgatized" revision of the Reformed *Bible de Genève*, and accordingly was condemned by the Paris theologians and later the Pope. Nevertheless, Christopher Plantin published the Benoist New Testament in 1567 (first edition) with the second edition (1573) and the complete Bible in 1578 having removed the name of Benoist from the title page and inserted an approbation from the Louvain theologians written by Jacques de Bay. After the appearance of the Sixto-Clementine Vulgate, this *Bible des Théologiens de Louvain* (not to be confused with the 1550 *Bible de Louvain*) was subject to further revisions by Pierre de Besse (Paris, 1608; Rouen, 1611), Jean-Claude Deville (Lyons, 1613–14), and especially Pierre Frizon (Rheims, 1620–21). It became the standard French Vulgate translation until the beginning of the eighteenth century (Bogaert and Gilmont 1991: 91–101; Chédozeau 1991: 137–40; Ingram 2004).

Strikingly, it was in France that the idea became prevalent as early as the seventeenth century that Bible translations should be based upon the Greek and Hebrew originals, and that the laity had the right to read them. Witnesses to this evolution were the New Testaments published by François Véron (1647) and Michel de Marolles (1649). Far more popular was a version of the New Testament, commissioned by the *Assemblée du Clergé*, made by the Oratorian Denis Amelote on the basis of the Vulgate but with the Greek as a secondary source, and published in 1666. A competing group of translators, connected to the Jansenist Abbey of Port-Royal, from 1665 onward issued various editions containing the Psalms, translated on the basis of the Hebrew and/or the Vulgate. Their version of the New Testament, the *Nouveau Testament "de Mons,"* actually printed in Amsterdam in 1667, was based upon an array of sources: even though the Latin Vulgate was the primary text, reference was made throughout to Greek, and textual variants between the two sources were indicated in the margins. This text also became known by the name of its main compositor, Louis-Isaac Lemaistre de Sacy, and was followed by a translation of the Old Testament on the basis of the Vulgate (1672–93) along with a revised version of the New Testament (1696–1708). These translations, amounting to thirty-two volumes and accompanied by long explanations taken from the Fathers, became the famous *Bible de Port-Royal*. It was, however, in its version with *notes courtes* ("brief notes") and also because of its literary qualities that the *Bible de Port-Royal* or *Bible de Sacy* became extremely popular (Al-Faradzh 2020; Chédozeau 2007). In reaction against Sacy's "Jansenist" New Testament, the Jesuit Dominique Bouhours, assisted by his confreres Michel Le Tellier and Pierre Besnier, published a New Testament translation mainly based on the Latin Vulgate (1697–1703). Between 1713 and 1725 Jacques-Philippe Lallemant, another Jesuit, published a revised edition of his confreres' New Testament with the Latin of the Vulgate, and provided with extensive *Réflexions morales*, as a reply to Pasquier Quesnel's eponymous but Jansenist-inspired work. The *Bible de Port-Royal* and these later "Jesuit" translations remained popular in their respective spiritual communities until the nineteenth century (Chédozeau 2012: 11–63, 105–8).

The first part of the eighteenth century saw the questioning of the primacy of the Vulgate in the light of the development of historical-critical exegesis. One of its most famous protagonists, the (former) Oratorian Richard Simon, nonetheless felt obliged to follow the text of the Vulgate in his 1702 translation of the New Testament, relegating Greek variants to the marginal notes (Chédozeau 2012: 65–79). In these heydays of French Catholic Bible fervor, reference should also be made to the multi-volume French Vulgate version that Louis de Carrières based upon the *Bible de Sacy*. Published between 1701 and 1716, in the New Testament it gave the variants from the Greek between brackets, and was furnished with extensive commentaries (Chédozeau 1991: 151–63; also Chédozeau 2012: 103–4).

Innumerable Bible translations were produced in the nineteenth century, including revisions of the Sacy Bible by Catholic scholars such as Jean-Nicolas Jaeger (1838–44, 1846) and, especially, Louis-Claude Fillion (1888–95, 1904), who also considered Greek sources. The multiple-volume French Bible by Antoine-Eugène de Genoude (1821 and 1824) was based upon original-language texts, although his bilingual edition (1822) takes the Vulgate as the main source of the translation. Other Vulgate translations that had a considerable influence were produced by Jean-Baptiste Glaire, a Hebraist and biblical scholar, published in 1834–36, and Jean-Jacques Bourassé and Pierre-Désiré Janvier (first edition 1865–66).

The translations of Augustin Crampon are worthy of special mention because they illustrate the change in attitude in the nineteenth century. His 1864 Gospel translation was based on the Vulgate, with "the rare and small differences in the Greek text . . . indicated in a note."[3] Likewise, his complete New Testament published in 1884 was based on the Vulgate. After the release of *Providentissimus Deus* in 1893, however, Crampon began revising his earlier translations based on the original texts of Scripture, with the Vulgate playing only a secondary role (Dy 2017: 152–53; Savart 1985: 19–34).

English

In the 1370s, John Wycliffe and the Lollards initiated a translation into English based on the Vulgate as part of a broader European movement which sought religious "ressourcement" based upon the reading and interpretation of the Scriptures. But whereas the "Netherlandish" *Devotio Moderna* remained largely "orthodox," the Wycliffite and Hussite movements in, respectively, England and the Czech lands were eventually condemned as heretical. In this regard, the Oxford Constitutions of 1407–9

---

[3] "Les rares et légères differences du texte grec sont indiquées en note," in *Les Quatre Evangiles. Traduction nouvelle accompagnée de notes et de dissertations*, ed. Augustin Crampon, ix (Paris: Tolra and Haton, 1864).

forbade any new translation of the Bible into English or any other vernacular language without prior approval from the local bishop or a provincial council (Poleg 2013; Marsden 2012). With the advent of the Reformation and Protestant Bible translations such as those of Tyndale and Coverdale, no English Catholic Vulgate translation was published until the famous Douay-Rheims version. This was attributed to a group of translators led by Gregory Martin and connected to the English College, home of the refugee Catholic academic community in Douai and Rheims. The New Testament was released in Rheims in 1582 and the two-part Old Testament in Douai in 1609–10. The word choice and syntax of the Douay-Rheims Bible are clearly dependent on the Latin Vulgate, though attention was also paid to Greek and there are similarities with the 1538 Latin-English diglot New Testament by Miles Coverdale. Further research is needed to identify the textual basis of the Douay-Rheims translation, as it is neither the Louvain nor the Sixto-Clementine Vulgate (Swift and McKinney 2010: xiv–xv).

The Douay-Rheims Bible became the standard Catholic translation in English, undergoing various revisions which sought to smooth its literal renderings of the Vulgate and mitigate the oddness of the vocabulary and syntax in some parts of the translation. The most important revision was by Richard Challoner in 1749–52. Challoner was a Catholic convert from Protestantism, where he had been raised with the King James Version of 1611. He claimed to have made his revisions on the basis of the Sixto-Clementine Vulgate, but they also appear to reflect the renderings of the King James Version (which for its part had also been influenced by the Douay-Rheims version). Other revisions to the Douay-Rheims-Challoner text were made in the following centuries (Walsham 2014: 285–314; Bobrick 2003: 189–96). In Dublin, Bernard MacMahon published a series of editions from 1783 to 1810 in which he emended Challoner's 1752 edition to reduce its similarities with the King James version. These various Dublin versions were the basis of many, but not all, Douay-Rheims Challoner versions printed in the United States in the nineteenth century. Editions printed in England occasionally follow one of MacMahon's New Testament revisions but more often rely on Challoner's earlier editions of 1749 and 1750 (Dy 2017: 101).

At the end of the eighteenth and in the course of the nineteenth century, several translators in the English Catholic world departed from the idea that a Bible should be primarily or exclusively based upon the Vulgate. Among them were Alexander Geddes, whose 1792 version of the Old Testament has largely fallen into oblivion, and John Lingard (Gospels, 1836). Francis Patrick Kenrick edited the Douay-Rheims-Challoner Bible with a view to the original languages (New Testament from 1849; Old Testament from 1857). The Dominican Francis Aloysius Spencer took the Greek as his primary source while keeping an eye on the Vulgate in his Gospels translation of 1898 (Dy 2017: 101–8). In general, however, the Vulgate maintained a stronger position among English-speaking Catholics than among their French or German co-religionists.

In the English-speaking world, *Providentissimus Deus* was first taken as a reassertion of Trent's decree on the Vulgate, and English Bible translations based primarily on the Vulgate continued to be produced and circulated. Emblematic of this is the New Testament published in 1941 by the American Confraternity of Christian Doctrine, which is still based on the Douay-Rheims-Challoner version but with some attention paid to Greek texts. In contrast, the revision of the Old Testament issued by this same body of scholars between 1948 and 1969 was predominantly founded on the original languages. It was the encyclical *Divino Afflante Spiritu* that prompted this shift to the Hebrew and Greek texts as the primary sources of translation (Dy 2017: 110–15, 218). Nevertheless, Monsignor Ronald Knox undertook a new translation on the basis of the Vulgate at the request of the Bishops of England and Wales. The work was published in 1945 (New Testament) and 1950 (Old Testament). The editions of the so-called *Knox Bible* of 1954/55 are still Vulgate-based, even though there was also by then an acknowledgement of the original languages as secondary source texts. Both the *Confraternity Bible* and the *Knox Bible* were approved vernacular versions to be used in the lectionary readings for Mass from 1965 to the early 1970s. After this, new English Bible versions exclusively based upon the original languages, such as that of Kleist-Lilly which appeared in 1954, had become the common editions (Dy 2017: 111–13).

A six-volume Latin-English version of the Bible was published in 2010–13 by Edgar Swift and Angela Kinney in the Dumbarton Oaks Medieval Library series. For the English translation, a version of the Douay-Rheims-Challoner Bible was used alongside a modern Vulgate text which attempted to reconstruct (in part) the pre-Clementine Vulgate version that served as the basis for the Douay-Rheims translation.

Dutch

In the Netherlands, the High Middle Ages saw the production of several Bible versions, due to the impetus of the *Devotio Moderna* and an increasingly literate urban culture—editions that were invariably based upon the Vulgate (Den Hollander 2016; Desplenter 2015: 31–202). Triggered by the movements of humanism and Reformation and the vernacular Bible versions published in their wake, the Catholic authorities in the Netherlands—with the Louvain Faculty of Theology as the religious-intellectual heart—aimed to provide the faithful with a "trustworthy" Vulgate translation. The *Vorsterman Bible* (1528–45) preserved an eclectic text typical of the preconfessional period, but had the theologically crucial passages of Scripture "vulgatized" with effect from its New Testament of 1529. The *Leuvense Bijbel* or *Louvain Bible* (1548) made by the Louvain Augustinian canon Nicolaus van Winghe, based on the Latin Vulgate of 1547, was intended to supersede the *Vorsterman Bible* but nevertheless borrowed heavily from it. A later *Leuvense Bijbel*, revised on the basis of the Sixto-Clementine Vulgate, was published in 1599 by Jan Moerentorf (Moretus) in Antwerp (François 2020a: 191–202). The *Moerentorf Bible* was subject to constant but limited updates of its language and style, such those by the Jesuit Franciscus Costerus and, especially, Henricus van den Leemputte. It remained the standard version for Catholics in Belgium and the Netherlands until the late nineteenth century (Agten 2020: 134–46).

Jansenist circles in the Netherlands modeled themselves on developments in France and took the Bible editions of Port-Royal, especially the *Nouveau Testament de Mons*, as a source of inspiration. The degree to which this New Testament of Mons and its reliance upon the Greek was used, alongside the Vulgate, in the production of three Dutch "Jansenist" Bibles around 1700 remains a source of debate. The first of these was by Aegidius de Witte; the second, by Andreas van der Schuur and Hendrick van Rhijn, was adopted as the official version of the "schismatic" Church of Utrecht; the third was the work of Philippus Laurentius Verhulst (Agten 2020: 258–375). These continued to be used well into the nineteenth century.

Epilogue

Despite the widespread disregard for the Vulgate and Vulgate-based translations in the contemporary era, translations of the Vulgate and "vulgatized" versions remain a significant part of the heritage of Catholic Bible translation. Even so, there was controversy when the encyclical *Liturgiam Authenticam* in 2011 officially prescribed the Vulgate as an "auxiliary tool" (§24) for constructing the vernacular texts of Scripture in the liturgical books of the Roman rite (Dy 2016). Vulgate-based translations continue to be cherished or rediscovered by traditionalist Catholics. The most recent projects to translate the Vulgate into English and German show that, even today, vernacular translations based on this Latin source text continue to exercise an attraction for readers and scholars of the Bible.

Bibliography

Agten, Els. 2020. *The Catholic Church and the Dutch Bible: From the Council of Trent to the Jansenist Controversy (1564–1733)*. Leiden: Brill.

Al-Faradzh, Elizaveta. 2020. "Salvation in the vernacular: the New Testament of Mons and Post-Tridentine piety." *Early Modern French Studies* 42, no. 1: 38–54.

Bobrick, Benson. 2003. *The Making of the English Bible*. London: Phoenix.

Bogaert, Pierre-Maurice. 1991. "La Bible française au moyen âge." In *Les Bibles en français. Histoire illustrée du moyen âge à nos jours*, edited by Pierre-Maurice Bogaert, 14–46. Turnhout: Brepols.

Bogaert, Pierre-Maurice, and Jean-François Gilmont. 1980. "La première Bible française de Louvain (1550)." *Revue Théologique de Louvain* 11: 275–309.

Bogaert, Pierre-Maurice, and Jean-François Gilmont. 1991. "De Lefèvre d'Étaples à la fin du XVIe siècle." In *Les Bibles en français. Histoire illustrée du moyen âge à nos jours*, edited by Pierre-Maurice Bogaert, 47–106. Turnhout: Brepols.

Chédozeau, Bernard. 1991. "La Bible française chez les Catholiques." In *Les Bibles en français. Histoire illustrée du moyen âge à nos jours*, edited by Pierre-Maurice Bogaert, 134–68. Turnhout: Brepols.

Chédozeau, Bernard. 2007. *Port-Royal et la Bible. Un siècle d'or de la Bible en France 1650-1708*. Paris: Nolin.

Chédozeau, Bernard. 2012. *Le Nouveau Testament autour de Port-Royal: Traductions, commentaires et études (1697-fin du XVIIIe siècle)*. Paris: Champion.

Clarke, Kent. 1999. "Original Text or Canonical Text? Questioning the Shape of the New Testament We Translate." In *Translating the Bible: Problems and Prospects*, edited by Stanley Porter and Richard Hess, 281–322. Sheffield: Sheffield Academic.

Concilium Tridentinum: diariorum, actorum, epistularum, tractatuum. 1901–2001. Freiburg im Breisgau: Herder.

Decock, Paul. 2008. "Jerome's Turn to the Hebraica Veritas and His Rejection of the Traditional View of the Septuagint." *Neotestamentica* 42: 205–22.

Dei Verbum. 18 November 1965. <http://www.vatican.va/archive/hist_councils/ii_vatican_council/documents/vat-ii_const_19651118_dei-verbum_en.html>.

Desplenter, Youri. 2015. "Part 1: Middeleeuwen (tot 1522)." In *De Bijbel in de Lage Landen. Elf eeuwen van vertalen*, edited by Paul Gillaerts, Henri Bloemen, Youri Desplenter, Wim François, and August den Hollander, 31–202. Heerenveen: Jongbloed.

Dy, Oliver. 2016. "The Latin Vulgate as an 'Auxiliary Tool' of Translation: Historical Perspectives on Liturgiam Authenticam." *Questions Liturgiques* 97: 141–70.

Dy, Oliver. 2017. "Latin Vulgate vs. Original Texts: The Changing Norms in Choosing and Prioritizing the Biblical Source Texts of Translation." PhD diss., Catholic University of Leuven.

Fattori, Maria Theresia. 2014. "Vernacular Bible Translations and the Roman Inquisition in Italian History Between the XVI and XVII Centuries." *Revue d'Histoire Ecclésiastique* 109, no. 3–4: 656–97.

Fischer, Roman, and Jourden Travis Moger. 2016. "Johannes Dietenberger and his Counter-Reformation German Bible." *Journal of the Bible and its Reception* 3: 279–302.

François, Wim. 2013. "The Catholic Church and Vernacular Bible Reading, before and after Trent." *Biblicum Jassyense* 4: 5–37.

François, Wim. 2020a. "Bible Production and Bible Readers in the Age of Confessionalisation: The Case of the Low Countries." In *Lay Readings of the Bible in Early Modern Europe*, edited by Erminia Ardissino and Elise Boillet, 191–216. Leiden: Brill.

François, Wim. 2020b. "Traducciones vernáculas de la Biblia y formación de identidad en las regiones multiconfesionales de la Europa temprano moderna." In *La Reforma protestante desde el margen. A 500 años del evento banal que revolucionó la cultura de Occidente*, edited by Santiago Francisco Peña, Constanza Cavallero, Ismael del Olmo, and Carolina Losada, 33–53. Buenos Aires: SB Editorial.

Gallagher, Edmon. 2016. "Augustine on the Hebrew Bible." *Journal of Theological Studies ns* 67: 97–114.

Gélébart, Yves-Claude. 1986. "La Bible dans l'*Aufklärung* catholique." In *Le siècle des Lumières et la Bible*, edited by Yvon Belaval and Dominique Bourel, 563–77. BTT 7. Paris: Beauchesne.

Hollander, August den. 2016. "Late Medieval Vernacular Bible Production in the Low Countries." In *Basel 1516. Erasmus' Edition of the New Testament*, edited by Martin Wallraff, Silvana Seidel Menchi, and Kaspar von Greyerz, 43–58. Tübingen: Mohr Siebeck.

Ingram, Elizabeth Morley. 2004. "Dressed in Borrowed Robes: The Making and Marketing of the Louvain Bible (1578)." In *The Church and the Book*, edited by R. N. Swanson, 212–21. Woodbridge: Boydell.

Jenkins, Allan K., and Patrick Preston. 2007. *Biblical Scholarship and the Church: A Sixteenth-Century Crisis of Authority*. Aldershot: Ashgate.

Köster, Uwe. 1995. *Studien zu den katholischen deutschen Bibelübersetzungen im 16., 17. und 18. Jahrhundert*. Münster: Aschendorff.

Leo XIII. 18 November 1893. "Providentissimus Deus." <http://w2.vatican.va/content/leo-xiii/en/encyclicals/documents/hf_l-xiii_enc_18111893_providentissimus-deus.html>.

Marsden, Richard. 2012. "The Bible in English." In *New Cambridge History of the Bible: Vol. 2. From 600 to 1450*, edited by Richard Marsden and E. Ann Matter, 217–38. Cambridge: Cambridge University Press.

Neuner, Peter. 2015. "The Reception of the Bible in Roman Catholic Tradition." In *New Cambridge History of the Bible: Vol. 4. From 1750 to the Present*, edited by John Riches, 537–62. Cambridge: Cambridge University Press.

O'Malley, John. 2013. *Trent: What Happened at the Council*. Cambridge, MA: Belknap Press.

Paquin, René. 2018. *L'Évangile à l'Index? Pierre Viret et la crise entourant la publication et la censure de la Bible en langue vulgaire (1540-1562)*. Paris: Hermann.

Pius XII. 30 September 1943. "Divino Afflante Spiritu." <http://w2.vatican.va/content/pius-xii/en/encyclicals/documents/hf_p-xii_enc_30091943_divino-afflante-spiritu.html>.

Poleg, Eyal. 2013. "Wycliffite Bibles as Orthodoxy." In *Cultures of Religious Reading in the Late Middle Ages: Instructing the Soul, Feeding the Spirit and Awakening the Passion*, edited by Sabrina Corbellini, 71–91. Turnhout: Brepols.

Pym, Anthony. 2007. "On the Historical Epistemologies of Bible Translating." In *A History of Bible Translation*, edited by P. A. Noss, 195–215. Rome: Storia e letteratura.

Rummel, Erika. 2008. *Biblical Humanism and Scholasticism in the Age of Erasmus*. Leiden: Brill.

Savart, Claude. 1985. "Quelle Bible les catholiques français lisaient-ils?" In *Le monde contemporain et la Bible*, edited by Claude Savart and Jean-Noël Aletti, 19–34. BTT 8. Paris: Beauchesne.

Scheuchenpflug, Peter. 1997. *Die Katholische Bibelbewegung im frühen 19. Jahrhundert*. Würzburg: Seelsorge/Echter.

Schwarz, Werner. 1955. *Principles and Problems of Biblical Translation: Some Reformation Controversies and their Background*. Cambridge: Cambridge University Press.

Sneddon, Clive R. 2012. "The Bible in French." In *New Cambridge History of the Bible: Vol. 2. From 600 to 1450*, edited by Richard Marsden and E. Ann Matter, 251–67. Cambridge: Cambridge University Press.

Strand, Kenneth A. 1982. *Catholic German Bibles of the Reformation Era: The Versions of Emser, Dietenberger, Eck, and Others*. Naples, FL: Ann Arbor.

Swift, Edgar, and Angela M. Kinney, eds. 2010–13. *The Vulgate Bible, Douay-Rheims Translation*, 6 vols. Cambridge, MA: Harvard University Press.

Tanner, Norman 1990. *Decrees of the Ecumenical Councils: Vol. 2. Trent to Vaticanum II*. London: Sheed & Ward.

Tov, Emanuel. 2002. "The Status of the Masoretic Text in Modern Text Editions of the Hebrew Bible." In *The Canon Debate*, edited by Lee Martin McDonald and James A. Sanders, 234–51. Peabody, MA: Hendrickson.

Tov, Emanuel. 2008. "The Textual Basis of Modern Translations of the Hebrew Bible: The Argument against Eclecticism." In *Hebrew Bible, Greek Bible, and Qumran: Collected Essays*, 92–106. Tübingen: Mohr Siebeck.

Walsham, Alexandra. 2014. *Catholic Reformation in Protestant Britain*. Aldershot: Ashgate.

Weber, Robert, and Roger Gryson, eds. 2007. *Biblia Sacra: Iuxta Vulgatam Versionem*. 5th ed. Stuttgart: Deutsche Bibelgesellschaft.

CHAPTER 27

....

LATIN TRADITION AND THE
GREEK NEW TESTAMENT

....

J. K. ELLIOTT

THE critical apparatus to printed editions of the Greek New Testament normally contains evidence from early translations and patristic citations of biblical passages in addition to the readings of Greek continuous-text and lectionary manuscripts. The oldest Christian translations are those in Syriac, Latin, and Coptic; several editions also include evidence from the Gothic version in the Gospels. The Latin Codex Fuldensis which has a harmonized version of the Gospels, comparable to Tatian's *Diatessaron* (see chap. 15), may also occasionally be located in an apparatus. Other, later witnesses in languages such as Georgian, Armenian, Ethiopic, and Slavic (Old Church Slavonic) are sometimes found in critical editions, albeit used only sparingly. Latin witnesses are often extensively cited, reflecting both the dominance of Latin in Western scholarship and, until recently, the exclusive reading of the Latin Bible in Roman Catholicism.

The Roman edition of the Latin Old Testament, the *Vetus Latina* volumes, the Oxford Vulgate (commonly called Wordsworth–White after its first two editors), and the Stuttgart Vulgate (Weber and Gryson 2007) are the main Latin Bibles. "Popular" editions of bilingual (Greek–Latin) New Testaments edited by Merk (1992), Bover (1977), and Vogels (1955) have gone through many editions in the twentieth century. Such scholarship can trace its significance back to Erasmus (who saw himself as a Jerome *redivivus*); his own Latin translation of the New Testament was printed by Froben in Basle in 1516 and was the first published Greek New Testament (originally entitled *Novum Instrumentum*). The Greek text was provided alongside Erasmus's own new Latin translation only to demonstrate his Latin translation's validity and closeness to the underlying "original" Greek of its biblical authors; it also enabled scholars to assess the importance of the Latin. As is well known, Erasmus retranslated the ending of Revelation from Latin into Greek as the Greek manuscript available to him lacked Revelation 22:16–21. This resulted in the faulty reading "*book* of life" at Revelation 22:19. Other readings for which he was criticized included *sermo* rather than the traditional *uerbum* in John 1:1, and *mysterium* for *sacramentum* at Ephesians 5:32 where the church's teaching on the sanctity of marriage was deemed to be thereby threatened.

Ironically, it was Erasmus's Greek text that came to dominate New Testament textual scholarship thereafter. A later but derivative edition by the Elzevir (or Elzevier) family promoted itself and came to be known as the *Textus Receptus* in 1633. That tag was subsequently applied to all editions by Erasmus and other editors. In contrast to the Roman Catholic emphasis on the Latin text, these editions were increasingly promoted by Protestants by virtue of their underlying Luther's German New Testament of 1522 and Tyndale's English New Testament of 1525–1626 (and, through that edition, the English "Authorized" Version in 1611). In fact, the *Textus Receptus* and other comparable editions dominated the future of biblical scholarship for 350 years, in the same way that the Latin Vulgate attributed to Jerome had dominated Christianity for at least a thousand years previously (Elliott 2016).

The *Textus Receptus* was toppled from its dominant position in 1881 when Westcott and Hort printed a Greek New Testament representing what they termed the "original" Greek. This text differed not only from the *Textus Receptus* but also from the Vulgate. Protestant scholars such as Kurt Aland tried to coerce Roman Catholic colleagues to promote a Latin translation that paralleled the Greek New Testament, that is, the text of Nestle, which he disingenuously stated was indeed that requisite standard text (as in the introduction to NA26 or the Preface to the fifteenth edition of his German synopsis). Carlo-Maria Martini, one-time Rector of the Pontifical Biblical Institute in Rome and later Cardinal Archbishop of Milan, served on the board of the United Bible Societies edition, which served to commend its text to the Catholic hierarchy. The *Nova Vulgata* was an attempt to produce a Latin text that matched this "standard" Greek text (see chap. 25). Following the approval of this Latin version in a papal encyclical of 1979, Aland printed a bilingual edition with NA26 alongside the *Nova Vulgata* in 1984.[1] This text now finds little support and is of no text-critical value.

Modern scholarship correctly tries to place the Vulgate into its proper context, in conjunction with the Old Latin versions that preceded it. Jerome's biblical revisions were not as extensive as previously assumed (see chap. 3, chap. 4, and chap. 6). Earlier scholars had often repeated the dictum that, having been commissioned by Pope Damasus, Jerome duly set out to translate the whole of the New and Old Testaments (or at least the Hebrew Bible). It is now clear that, as far as the New Testament is concerned, the task was one of emendation rather than a fresh translation, and even these changes were not always successful, popular, or accepted. Regular usage had fixed much vocabulary in a believer's mind; the pious are often notoriously reluctant to embrace change. The revisions thus often failed to hit their intended mark, leading to many so-called mixed texts (see chap. 1). These may reflect deliberate resistance to change or merely the

---

[1] A second edition appeared seven years later (Aland 1991). A review of the first edition by Frans Neirynck in *Ephemerides Theologicae Lovanienses* (1986) complained that the Alands failed to disclose the changes made compared with previous editions: the *apparatus* in the second edition displays differences between the *Nova Vulgata* and eleven other Latin versions.

accidental reintroduction of familiar wording. Many manuscripts classified as Old Latin or Vulgate are in fact a mixture of both, as will be noted below.

EDITIONS OF THE GREEK NEW TESTAMENT

Editions of the Greek New Testament may be divided into hand editions, synopses, bilingual editions, and major editions.

Hand Editions

The two current hand editions of the Greek New Testament most frequently used by scholars are the twenty-eighth edition of Nestle-Aland (NA28) and the United Bible Societies' fifth edition (UBS5). Recent competitors (the *SBL Greek New Testament* and the *Tyndale House Greek New Testament*) do not cite any Latin evidence, in keeping with their stated editorial policies. Full details of the Old Latin manuscripts cited in NA28 are given on pages 68*–69* and Appendix 1B.[2] This list indicates the "Beuron" numbers assigned by the Vetus Latina Institute for each witness (Gryson 1999-2004), which provide a means of avoiding the obvious ambiguity of the alphabetical systems in which one letter can refer to different manuscripts. This nomenclature should be adopted in all future *apparatus*. UBS5, on pages 31*–33*, provides a similar list. Table 27.1 gives the number of witnesses apparently cited in the five sections of the New Testament in these editions.

The total of manuscripts in NA28 seems to be sixty-seven, but in fact it is only fifty-four because several manuscripts are listed in more than one section. These are as

Table 27.1 Number of Old Latin Manuscripts Listed in Greek Hand Editions

Section	NA28	UBS5
Gospels (e)	28	28
Acts (a)	11	17
Pauline Epistles (p)	14	18
Catholic Epistles (c)	9	8
Revelation (r)	5	5
Total	54	63

[2] The page numbers given relate to the English introduction. NA26 and earlier editions included an Appendix IV: *Textuum Differentiae:* as Parker indicates, the use of this apparatus in conjunction with Scrivener's edition, which lists the differences between the *Textus Receptus* and Lachmann, permits one to "chart the varying decisions of most of the important editions of the critical era" (2008: 213).

follows: 5/d (*eac*); 56/τ/t (*apcr*);[3] 55/h (*acr*); 53/s, 67/l (*ac*); 51/gig, 74/sin (*ar*); and 64/r, 65/z (*pc*). UBS5 takes a slightly different approach: it gives a full list of sixty-three manuscripts, yet the precise contents are not given for all of these and in some cases are misleading. For instance, 109/comp contains *eapcr* but only *p* is Old Latin, and so the other sections are not listed here—presumably because they are considered Vulgate and not cited in the edition. However, in the case of 59/dem, the manuscript is listed as *eacp* even though it is predominantly Vulgate throughout. 5/d is only listed as containing *ea* and not *c*, even though it is Old Latin in all sections. It remains to be verified whether all the manuscripts actually occur in the apparatus for each of the categories in which they are listed.[4] It should also be noted that not all the witnesses are continuous-text biblical manuscripts. For example, 89/b and o are the text of the Pauline Epistles from commentary manuscripts; 24/p, 57/r, 74/sin and 87/s are fragments from lectionaries. The *testimonia* collection known as the *Speculum*, however, is cited as a patristic witness in both editions, despite the earlier practice of assigning it the siglum *m*. Very few Old Latin manuscripts are extant for complete sections of the New Testament.

The problem of mixed-text manuscripts affects both NA28 and UBS5. The following manuscripts are not Old Latin throughout but include Vulgate texts in some of the sections (indicated within square brackets):

6/c *ea*[*pcr*].
51/gig [*e*]*a*[*pc*]*r*
54/p [*e*]*a*[*pcr*]
58/w [*e*]*a*[*pcr*]
61/ar [*e*]*ap*[*c*]*r* (but this manuscript is not cited in NA28 in *p* and *r*).

Even within a single section, the affiliation of a manuscript may vary. For instance, 15/aur is predominantly Vulgate in Matthew but has a more significant Old Latin element in the other Gospels, while both Matthew and Mark are Vulgate in 11/l. The majority of the ten manuscripts listed in UBS5 but not NA28 are mixed or predominantly Vulgate texts or small fragments (25/v, 43/φ, 59/dem, 60/sa, 61/ar [not in *pr*], 62/ro, 63/ph, 65/z [not in *c*], 87/s, 109/comp). NA28 cites the fragment 80/p in Romans 5. Despite their disagreements, both editions include the oldest and most important Old Latin witnesses, including seven gospel manuscripts copied in the fourth or fifth century (3/a, 1/k, 2/e, 4/b, 8/ff2, 12/h, 7/i), the fifth-century Codex Bezae (5/d) in the Gospels, Acts,

[3] The Beuron number for this manuscript is 56 (not supplied in NA28); in the Catholic Epistles, it is listed as *t* rather than τ.

[4] It may be noted, however, that UBS5 is an improvement on UBS3, where several manuscripts are listed in the introduction yet do not feature in the apparatus. These include 61/ar, 51/gig, m/Speculum and 26/r[2] in the Gospels, 7/g[1] in *apcr*, 67/l, 54/p in *ap*, 59/dem in Acts, 83/w in Paul and 5/d in the Catholic Epistles (perhaps explaining its absence from the introduction from UBS5).

and part of the Catholic Epistles and the fifth- or sixth-century Codex Claromontanus (75/d) in the Pauline Epistles. Nevertheless, the latter are both bilingual witnesses (along with 76/e, 77/g, 78/f), and NA28 explicitly notes that the Latin texts of these manuscripts "are cited only when their witness differs from that of their accompanying Greek texts" (NA28: 69*), although neither NA28 nor UBS5 seems to include 76/e. No individual Vulgate manuscripts are cited in NA28 or UBS5, but only editions: references to readings found in one or more Vulgate manuscripts (vg^{ms} or vg^{mss}) need to be cross-referenced in those editions (normally the Oxford Vulgate). Care must be taken here to disambiguate these from Old Latin witnesses, especially in the case of 7/g^1 which is listed as G for most of the New Testament in Vulgate editions.

A couple of peculiarities regarding Latin evidence in earlier editions of the Greek New Testament deserve a mention, showing that inconsistencies are by no means restricted to the current hand editions. In the second edition produced by the British and Foreign Bible Society (1958), there are multiple examples of sundry manuscripts mentioned in the apparatus which lack a reference in the introductory listing! These include, in the Gospels: p, s and t; in Acts: c and e; in Paul: c, dem, t, v; in the Catholic Epistles: e, q; in Revelation: c, dem, t. In Souter's second edition (1947), the *Speculum* collection of *testimonia* is cited (with the siglum m) as well as Latin witnesses with the sigla r and δ. Although such witnesses are often difficult to identify, some help is offered in the concordances prepared by Houghton (2016: 283–89).

Synopses

The most recent edition of the gospel synopsis by Aland (2001: xxxiii–xxiv) lists the following thirty-three manuscripts:

> 3/a 16/a^2 15/aur 4/b 26/β 6/c 5/d 2/e 10/f 9/ff^1 8/ff^2 7/g^1 51/gig 12/h 55/h 17/i 22/j 1/k 11/l 44/λ 45/μ 16/n 16/o 20/p 54/p 18/π 13/q 14/r^1 28/r^2 24/ρ 21/s 19/t 25/v.

Of these, however, 20/p, 18/π, and 28/r^2 are apparently absent from the apparatus. The English translation of an earlier edition (1979) includes also 29/g^2 30/gat 33 m/Speculum 28/r^2 7/g^2 51/gig 55/h 54/p.

The Huck-Greeven synopsis contains fifty Old Latin manuscripts (1981: xix–xx, xxxi–xxxii):

> 3/a 16/o 4/b 26/β 6/c 5/d 27/δ 2/e 10/f 8/ff^2 9/ff^1 7/g^1 29/g^2 12/h 17/i 22/j(z) 1/k 11/l 16/n 16/o 20/p 18/w(π) 13/g 14/r^1 15/z 28/r^2 21/s 19/t 25/v 23 30/gat 31 32 36 37 38 39 40 41 42 43 56/t 59/dem 61/ar 65/z plus 75/d 76/e 77/g 78/f (in 1 Corinthians) and 250 (in the Psalter).

This synopsis is carefully executed: for example, 27/δ, 29/g^2, and 30/gat are cited only when they differ from the Vulgate, and d/5 only where it differs from its Greek text.

Bilingual Editions

Aland's bilingual edition with the *Nova Vulgata* as the Latin text has already been discussed. The sixth edition of Bover (1977) is a trilingual edition, including a Catalan version by O'Callaghan. The introduction (xxiii–xxvii) lists the Latin manuscripts, but several of these are not used in the apparatus (see Elliott 1984). What is worse, and typical of a cavalier and derisory attitude to editing in bilingual editions, are witnesses that appear in the apparatus but are not listed in the introduction. These include g^2, o, and r^2 in the Gospels, g^2 in Acts, c and p in Paul, and d in the Catholic Epistles. The thirteenth edition of Merk (1992) gives extensive initial lists of Latin manuscripts, divided into Old Latin and Vulgate witnesses. Again, this features some witnesses never cited in the apparatus, whereas other sigla appear in the apparatus, although absent from these lists (Elliott 1984). The same is true of Vogels (1955). These editions list the Vulgate manuscripts and those manuscripts thought predominantly to contain the *Vetus Latina*. The critical apparatus that includes individual manuscripts of the Old Latin accompanies only the Greek text in the editions originally by Vogels and by Bover. Merk's text has the *Vetus Latina* and the Vulgate together beneath each Latin page. Patristic evidence (Greek and Latin Fathers) appears in all three editions.

Major Editions of the Gospels

The introductions to the editions of Mark and Matthew prepared for the Critical Greek Testament project (Legg 1935, 1940) list twenty-one and twenty-two Old Latin manuscripts, respectively, although in the apparatus these are often referred to as *it rell* ("the rest of the *Itala*"; on this term see chap. 1). The Mark edition includes m/Speculum, 19/t, 29/g^2 and 27/δ, as well as 7/g^1 even though this manuscript is only Old Latin in Matthew. In Matthew, the list includes 51/gig (another Vulgate witness) and includes the gospel harmony of Codex Fuldensis at the end of the list.

The edition of Luke prepared by the International Greek New Testament Project (IGNTP; *Luke*, 1984–1987) includes eighteen Old Latin manuscripts: 3/a, 16/a^2, 15/aur, 4/b, 26/β, 6/c, 5/d, 10/f, 8/ff^2, 7/g^1, 30/gat, 17/i, 11/l, 44/λ, 18/π, 13/q, 14/r^1, 21/s. Old Latin evidence is grouped under the siglum Lvt, and the Vulgate is Lvg. Versional evidence comes from the Syriac (Ss Sc Sp Sh Sj), two diatessaronic witnesses (Dta Dtp), and Coptic (Cs Cb), Armenian, Georgian (Ggl II2-4 III), Ethiopic, Gothic, and Slavic (OS).

Editio Critica Maior

The two volumes of this edition currently available are the Catholic Epistles (Strutwolf et al. 2013) and the Acts of the Apostles (Strutwolf et al. 2017). In the Catholic Epistles, the following (often only partly) Old Latin manuscripts are listed: 56/t (plus other texts from the *Liber Comicus* tradition: 70, 72, 73, 189), 57/r, 61/ar, 67/l, 74/sin. The majority of the Latin evidence in the critical apparatus of the edition is grouped under the text-types reconstructed by Thiele in the *Vetus Latina* edition (see chap. 1 and chap. 24). This therefore includes Latin patristic evidence, although no account is taken of the Latin witnesses in the CBGM (Coherence-Based Genealogical Method) and other online resources.

In Acts, for which the *Vetus Latina* edition has yet to appear, the following Old Latin manuscripts are cited: 5/d, 50/e, 51/gig, 53/s, 54/p, 55/h, 56/t, 57/r, 58/w, 61/ar, 67/l, four lectionaries (70, 72, 73, 74), and 189 (Codex Cavensis). Four Vulgate manuscripts are cited at a single point of variation (Acts 16:12; see Strutwolf et al. 2017: 3.137 where further details are given of the selection of Old Latin material). The Greek patristic material includes the Latin translations of Irenaeus's *Aduersus Haereses* (IrLat), Origen (OrLat), and Pseudo-Clement of Rome (PsClemLat). Tertullian (Tert) is treated as a Greek writer because of the possibility that the majority of his biblical quotations were translated directly from a Greek source (see chap. 1). Seven Latin Fathers are also cited in the critical apparatus as witnesses to Latin tradition: Ambrose of Milan, Hilary of Poitiers, Marius Victorinus, Augustine, Cyprian, Quodvultdeus, and Lucifer of Cagliari. Fortunatianus of Aquileia is absent from the apparatus, but his citations of Acts are analyzed in the volume of studies, which also presents the text of lengthy citations of Acts in Augustine's early writings (Strutwolf et al. 2017: 4.68–72).

The Use and Limitations of Latin Evidence in an *Apparatus Criticus*

As far as biblical scholars and textual critics of the Greek New Testament are concerned, versional evidence is of paramount significance in a critical apparatus. Readings may be found in extant Latin witnesses older than any surviving Greek evidence. This is true not only for continuous-text manuscripts but for patristic citations too. The latter may add to our stock of readings that differ from Jerome's Vulgate, as even late writers may use or quote from a version independent of Jerome's revision. The Old Latin survived longest in Ireland and Spain because of the isolation of these two countries from the rest of Christendom, and the Vulgate consequently only gradually made inroads there. Obviously, all citations need to be carefully examined in the light of each writer's reliability and the overall context of every quotation. However, we may gain proof from patristic citations when and where a certain form of a text was current.

Most of the early Latin versions seem to have been literal renderings of the underlying Greek. Some Latin words are mere transliterations (e.g. *agape, anastasis,* and *eremus*), whereas other words from an early Latin rendering (such as *angelus, martyr, hypocrite, baptisma,* and *thesaurus*) survived the revisions by Jerome and his successors. Although overliteral translations have sometimes been described as dubious Latin or unliterary forms, they remain important linguistic documents. Burton's study of the language of the Old Latin Gospels shows what can, and should, be achieved (Burton 2000; see also chap. 28).

As to the limitations of using Latin, or any early version for that matter, to bolster the stock of Greek textual readings in the New Testament, the contribution by Bonifatius Fischer in Metzger (1977) is essential reading. In a study of the Greek text, it is necessary to eliminate from the apparatus purely inner-versional variants—that is, readings that most plausibly belong to the later development of the version itself rather than a Greek source text. The evidence of versions is often very limited in cases concerning the addition or omission of particles, word order, conjunctions, and possibly even tenses. Latin, of course, lacks the subtleties of the Greek aorist or perfect; the optative and middle voice, rare though those may be in biblical Greek are absent from Latin. Definite articles are common in Greek but do not exist as such in Latin. Certain plurals are also to be viewed with extreme caution. Similarly, we must be alert to the special use of participles with the verb "to be" in Greek. Differences in prepositions, especially those that seem to be synonymous (e.g. ἀπό/ἐκ, ἐν/ἐπί) can mislead the unwary. Other synonyms may cause similar problems, and there is always the possibility that some versional readings merely coincidentally agree with a Greek reading. We may be on surer ground if a version (or some manuscripts) happens to support either longer or shorter readings. Similarly, where several witnesses from versions in different languages agree in support of one reading we may wish to add that versional evidence in favor of a Greek reading. Nevertheless, it is also important to realize that versional evidence should not be counted in the same way as Greek manuscripts, as no matter how many versional manuscripts support a particular reading, it may only represent one point of contact with Greek tradition. Overall, then, the conclusion must be to urge caution when considering a Latin versional reading in support of a Greek variant.

BIBLIOGRAPHY

Aland, Kurt, ed. 1991. *Nestle-Aland: Novum Testamentum Graece et Latine*. 2nd ed. Stuttgart: Deutsche Bibelgesellschaft.

Aland, Kurt, ed. 1994. *Kurzgefasste Liste der griechischen Handschriften des Neuen Testaments*. 2nd ed. ANTF 1. Berlin: De Gruyter.

Aland, Kurt, ed. 2001. *Synopsis Quattuor Evangeliorum*. 13th ed. Stuttgart: Deutsche Bibelgesellschaft. (*A Synopsis of the Four Gospels*. Stuttgart: United Bible Societies, 1979 [Eng. trans.]).

Bover, J. M. 1977. *Nuevo Testamento Trilingüe*. Madrid: Biblioteca autores cristianos.

British and Foreign Bible Society. 1958. Η Καινη Διαθηκη. 2nd ed. London: British and Foreign Bible Society.

Burton, P. H. 2000. *The Old Latin Gospels: A Study of their Texts and Language*. Oxford: Oxford University Press.

de Hamel, Christopher. 2001. *The Book: A History of the Bible*. London: Phaidon.

Elliott, J. K. 1984. "Old Latin Manuscripts in Printed Editions of the Greek New Testament." *Novum Testamentum* 26: 225–48. Repr., Elliott. *A Survey of Manuscripts Used in Editions of the Greek New Testament*, App. II. Leiden: Brill, 1987.

Elliott, J. K. 1987. *A Survey of Manuscripts Used in Editions of the Greek New Testament*. Supplements to *Novum Testamentum* 57. Leiden: Brill.

Elliott, J. K. 1992. "The Translations of the New Testament into Latin: The Old Latin and the Vulgate." In *Aufstieg und Niedergang der römischen Welt*. II *Principat*, 26/1 *Religion*, edited by Wolfgang Haase, 198–245. Berlin and New York: De Gruyter.

Elliott, J. K. 2016. "'Novum Testamentum editum est': The Five-Hundredth Anniversary of Erasmus' New Testament." *The Bible Translator* 67: 9–28.

Gryson, Roger. 1999–2004. *Altlateinische Handschriften/Manuscrits vieux latins*. VL 1/2A and 1/2B. Freiburg im Breisgau: Herder.

Houghton, H. A. G. 2016. *The Latin New Testament: A Guide to Its Early History, Texts, and Manuscripts*. Oxford: Oxford University Press.

Huck, A. 1981. *Synopse der drei ersten Evangelien/Synopsis of the First Three Gospels*. 13th ed. Tübingen: J.C.B. Mohr (Paul Siebeck).

International Greek New Testament Project. 1984/1987. *The New Testament in Greek*. III. *The Gospel according to St. Luke*, edited by the American and British Committees of the International Greek New Testament Project. 2 vols. Oxford: Clarendon.

Legg, S. C. E., ed. 1935. *Novum Testamentum Graece: Evangelium secundum Marcum* Oxford: Clarendon.

Legg, S. C. E., ed. 1940. *Novum Testamentum Graece: Evangelium secundum Matthaeum* Oxford: Clarendon.

Merk, A., ed. 1992. *Novum Testamentum Graece et Latine*. Scripta pontificii istituto biblici 65. 13th ed. Edited by J. O'Callaghan. Rome: Pontifical Biblical Institute.

Metzger, Bruce M. 1977. *The Early Versions of the New Testament: Their Origins, Transmission and Limitations*. Oxford: Clarendon.

Parker, D. C. 2008. *An Introduction to the New Testament Manuscripts and their Texts*. Cambridge: Cambridge University Press.

Souter, Alexander, ed. 1947. *Novum Testamentum Graece*. 2nd ed. Oxford: Clarendon.

Strutwolf, Holger, et al. eds. 2013. *Novum Testamentum Graecum Editio Critica Maior*. IV *Catholic Letters/Die katholischen Briefe*. 2nd ed. 2 vols. Stuttgart: Deutsche Bibelgesellschaft.

Strutwolf, Holger, et al. eds. 2017. *Novum Testamentum Graecum Editio Critica Maior*. III *Acts of the Apostles/Die Apostelgeschichte*. 4 vols. Stuttgart: Deutsche Bibelgesellschaft.

Vogels, Heinrich Joseph, ed. 1955. *Novum Testamentum Graece et Latine*. 4th ed. Freiburg im Breisgau: Herder.

Weber, Robert, and Roger Gryson, eds. 2007. *Biblia Sacra iuxta Vugatam versionem*. 5th ed. Stuttgart: Deutsche Bibelgesellschaft.

Wordsworth, John, Henry Julian White, et al. eds. 1889–1954. *Nouum Testamentum Domini nostri Iesu Christi latine secundum editionem sancti Hieronymi*. 3 vols. Oxford: Clarendon.

CHAPTER 28

LATIN BIBLES AS LINGUISTIC DOCUMENTS

PETER STOTZ

CHARACTERISTICS OF BIBLICAL LATIN

BIBLICAL Latin is only one of several components whose contributions shaped the language of Christians and of the Church, but it is likely to be the most important. Its first molding stems from outside the sphere of influence of high literature: the impact of everyday language (*sermo cotidianus*) is often discernible, as is the ubiquitous nature of the biblical Greek from which the texts were initially translated. Although the translators did not slavishly follow a word-for-word (*uerbum de uerbo*) style of translation, they still strove for the highest possible fidelity with regard to the original. The outcome of these factors was that the biblical language of Christians would have had a disconcerting effect on educated pagan Romans which would nearly have been equal to that produced by Christian teachings. The difference in handling language compared to the general standard was clearly perceived and voiced, for instance, by Augustine of Hippo.

Only a selection of characteristics of the Latin biblical language can be presented here.[1] Moreover, many of the linguistic phenomena it shares with Late Antique or Vulgar Latin texts must be left out of consideration. Among the manifold peculiarities of the *Vetus Latina*, we mainly cover those that also, later, entered into the Vulgate. As the specific vocabulary of the Latin Bible is most striking, the first section treats different aspects of the lexicon. This is followed by sections on morphology, syntax, and stylistics.

---

[1] Each of the phenomena mentioned is treated in several studies or dictionaries. The linguistic form of the *Vetus Latina* has been especially thoroughly studied: Rönsch 1875 is a foundational work; Vineis 1971–74 is valuable but little known; Burton 2000 is a thorough study of a subfield. For basic information about biblical or Christian Latin, see Stotz 1996–2004:1.35–62 (and *passim*): most peculiarities mentioned in the present chapter can easily be found in Stotz's index.

In conclusion, this chapter makes some observations on the importance of biblical Latin in Late Antiquity, the Middle Ages, and the Early Modern period.

The Lexicon

Lexical characteristics of the Latin Bible include loanwords from Greek, Hebrew, and Aramaic, semantic calques based on Greek and Hebrew, other semantic innovations and new coinages.

Loanwords from Greek

Many of the Greek loanwords are terms that were of great importance in the life of Christian communities, such as *apostolus* ("apostle"), *episcopus* ("bishop"), *euangelium* ("gospel"), *eleemosyna* or *elemosina* ("alms"), *baptizare* ("baptize"), or *blasphemare* ("blaspheme"). Many of them gave birth to an entire word family. On the one hand, some related terms were also borrowed from the Greek, such as *apostolicus, euangelicus, euangelizare, euangelista, baptismus/baptisma, baptista, blasphemia,* and *blasphemus*; on the other hand, numerous further words were derived with the usual Latin suffixes. Many of these words have left a rich progeny in modern languages, for instance *episcopus* as Spanish *obispo,* Italian *vescovo,* French *évêque,* English *bishop,* German *Bischof.* Further borrowings include *angelus* ("messenger, angel") and *psalmus* ("psalm"). Other words were shared with Judaism, such as *presbyter* ("elder," later "priest"), *proselytus* ("proselyte, stranger"), *synagoga* ("synagogue"), *ecclesia* ("community, church") or *gazophylacium* ("treasury; offertory box"). *Diabolus* ("devil") is probably a calque of the Hebrew word that also entered Latin as *Satan(as)*. The verb *iudaizare* ("live like a Jew") joins the ranks of numerous coinages formed with the borrowed suffix *-izare.* Some words are already attested in pagan texts but become common only through biblical usage, like *diaconus* ("assistant"), *propheta* ("prophet"), or *hymnus* ("hymn"). In the Bible and in Christian texts the feminine noun *eremus* ("wasteland," often spelled *heremus*) is well attested, occasionally also as a masculine (cf. Spanish *el yermo*).

   Some words of Greek origin are only used rarely in the Bible but gained much ground subsequently, for example, *teloneum* ("toll booth"), *paracletus* ("advocate, Holy Spirit"), *schisma* ("schism"), *parasceue* ("[Good] Friday"), *pentecoste* ("Pentecost" or "Whitsuntide"), *neophytus* ("neophyte"), *allophylus* ("of another stock"), or *zizania* ("weeds" or "darnel," used figuratively for "discord"). In certain cases, it will not have been the resonance of a biblical passage as much as the usage around it that was decisive, as in *martyr* ("martyr") or *apostata* ("apostate"). Some biblical Graecisms found their way mostly into poetical language, such as *abyssus* ("abyss") or *paracletus* (as mentioned above). The word *charisma* ("God-given gift"), borrowed from the Greek Bible, became common in the Latin Bible and elsewhere but was finally superseded by *donum* or *gratia*:

it remained an erudite rather than a regular Christian term. A few loanwords are found in *Vetus Latina* texts but stayed out of the Vulgate. These too sometimes had a rather erudite character, such as *logion/logium* ("the breastplate of the ephod"), *polyandr(i)um* ("mass grave," later also "cemetery" or "ossuary"), or *choicus* ("earthly").

Loanwords from Hebrew and Aramaic

Through the Septuagint and the Greek New Testament, a number of words of Hebrew or Aramaic origin entered into biblical Latin. Among these are terms for cosmic powers, such as *cherub*, plural *cherubim* (or *cherubin*), for winged companions of the Godhead, and *Satan(as)* ("adversary, enemy"), which became the proper name of a power seen as the adversary of God. (Compare also the Greek loanword *diabolus*.) Three expressions of prayer and liturgical language remain important among Christians: *alleluia, amen,* and *osanna*. Two designations of time have become fundamental in the Christian world: *sabbatum*—the word for the Israelites' weekly rest day became the name of a normal weekday ("Saturday")—and *pascha*, the name of the Passover, subsequently applied to the Christian Easter feast. Both words live on in the Romance languages.

Certain expressions that were initially confined to single biblical passages later became more common. The Israelites were sated with bread falling from the sky during their wandering through the desert: the Semitic word was taken over into Greek as μάννα ("manna"), then as *manna* in Latin. This term was often used with an allegorical or typological meaning, for instance, with regard to the Eucharist. An Aramaic toponym became the designation of an eschatological place of punishment: the biblical borrowing of γέεννα/*ge(h)enna* ("Gehenna") came to stand for the concept of a fiery Hell. A Hebrew legal term designating the one year in fifty that arable land was to lay idle and to be returned to the original owners, the Year of Jubilee, was translated into Greek in the Septuagint and does not seem to occur in the *Vetus Latina* texts either. The Hebrew word, which was only Hellenized at a late stage as ἰωβηλαῖος, entered into Latin texts as *annus iubeleus* (or similar, sometimes as a noun), for instance in Jerome's Bible at Leviticus 25:12–21 and Joshua 6:13. In the later Middle Ages, *iubilaeum* meant "remission, indulgence" and periodically proclaimed "holy years" were also denoted by it, hence the familiar meaning of jubilee. An Aramaic word for "possession, wealth" appears as μαμ(μ)ωνᾶς in the Gospels ("Mammon"; e.g. Luke 16:9–13). This word, standing for deleterious wealth, also enters biblical and Christian Latin as *mam(m)ona(s)*. Finally, the Semitic term for an inebriating drink appears in biblical Greek as σίκερα and in Latin as *sicera*. The word lives on in French *cidre* (cf. English *cider*).

Semantic Calques from Greek

Semantic calques from biblical Greek are of no less importance than outright borrowings. Many native Latin words adopted new functions in Latin Bible translations and in Christian language generally, following a semantic broadening in their Greek models. This applies to doctrinal concepts, such as *fides* which (analogously to πίστις) came to denote faith and trust in God's salvific activity. The word *gratia* ("favor"), like χάρις, was broadened to mean divine grace. Christian salvation is denoted by *salus* (like σωτηρία), a word that originally meant "well-being, safety." Although ἀγάπη ("love") is at first often rendered in *Vetus Latina* texts by *dilectio*, a specifically Christian coinage, in the Vulgate there is a preference for *caritas*, a word already common; *amor* is found occasionally. The word *redemptor,* a term from the economic and juridical sphere (e.g., as "contractor"), in the Latin Old Testament represents the Greek λυτρωτής. In Christian Latin, it denotes Christ as the "Savior," to which *redemptio* "salvation" is joined. Like κόσμος ("world"), the Latin Bible uses the word *mundus* to denote the earthly, transient world from which Christians separate themselves. A similar meaning is attributed to *(hoc) saeculum* which, analogous to αἰών, originally meant "lifetime, generation, age." *Paenitentia* ("penitence") is used like μετάνοια with the sense of a radical conversion or change of mind, often in the syntagm *paenitentiam agere* (later coming to mean "do penance"). Semantically related to this is remorse, for which the word *contritio* became established in Christian literature from the Old Testament, especially the prophetic writings: its original, literal meaning is something like "a grinding." *Confusio* and *confundere* denote "pouring together" or "a mixing of substances" and then encompass "disarray." In the Bible, this word pair is used with the same meaning as αἰσχύνη—(κατ)αισχύνειν (respectively, "disgrace" and "to wreck").

For the fundamental Christian task of authoritative preaching, the verb *praedicare* ("herald, praise") was chosen as an equivalent to κηρύσσειν. *Eruct(u)are* means "belch forth" but also, in a more general sense, "cast forth": in biblical and Christian Latin, however, the word is used for "bring forth through speech" or "utter," often with reference to prophecy, on the model of Greek (ἐξ)ἐρεύγεσθαι. Along with κτίσις, *creatio* ("creation") is used from the *Vetus Latina* onward metonymically for all that was created, as is *creatura* in the Vulgate. In some cases, there was a further semantic borrowing from Greek for a word which had already been adopted in Latin. For instance, ὑποκριτής was first borrowed as "actor" in the form *hypocrita*, but in the Synoptic Gospels the word denotes a "hypocrite," whose appearance is a pretense.

Some of these calques gave rise to derived words, such as verbs or adjectives from nouns, or agent nouns fom verbs. Many live on in modern languages, as in the case of *praedicare* leading to French *prêcher*, German *predigen*, English *to preach*. Moreover, it is noteworthy that some took on further differentiated special meanings. For instance, in the monastic perspective, *saeculum* and its derivative *saecularis* denote the (equally Christian) world outside the monastery.

Semantic Calques from Hebrew

The Greek of the Septuagint was significantly influenced by Hebrew, and some of the terms in the Latin Bible taken from biblical Greek stem ultimately from this language.

This is true of *caro* in the sense of "flesh" as opposed to "spirit"; *omnis caro* denotes the sum of all living creatures, or at least all human beings. This harks back to σάρξ as a designation for creaturely weakness or sinfulness, based on Hebrew *bāśār*. The adjective *gentilis* originally means "from the same clan or tribe (*gens*)," but in the Latin Bible it stands for Ἕλλην ("Greek") and for ἐθνικός ("pagan"): the background to this is the Hebrew *gōyim* ("peoples, heathen"), for which the Latin Bible uses *gentes*. The word δόξα ("opinion") also gained in biblical Greek the meaning "glory, glamor," under the influence of the Hebrew *kābôd*; the oldest Latin Bible translations usually render this by *gloria*. New shades of meaning were introduced for the glory of martyrdom or for participation in God's glory. The confession of sins or of Christ is often expressed by the verb *confiteri*, in which the sense of praising and thanking is conspicuous: this can be traced back to ἐξομολογεῖσθαι in biblical Greek, and indirectly to the Hebrew *tôḏāh*, which means both "acknowledge" and "praise." *Parabola* had already been borrowed in the first century CE as a technical term in rhetoric, from παραβολή ("comparison," "parable"): the considerable semantic wealth of *māšāl* was added to the term by means of the Greek Bible.

Other Semantic Innovations

For some words, semantic nuances arose through the language of the Latin Bible that contrasted with their common usage but had no discernible external stimulus. In the case of the conceptual pair "pray, prayer," the use of *preces/precari* for Greek (προσ)εὔχεσθαι—προσευχή would have seemed natural, but this was out of the question since, at least initially, pagan sacral terminology was shunned. Instead, *orare* was used, whose original meaning was "to speak (solemnly)" but had also denoted "pray, ask" from olden times. The corresponding verbal substantive *oratio*, with the sense of "prayer," is a Christian innovation. Some popular nonliterary words seem to have been (as it were) ennobled through biblical usage. Although the verb *manducare* ("chew") had already acquired the meaning "eat" in contemporary Vulgar Latin, its enormous spread is certainly not unrelated to its occurrence in the Bible (cf. Italian *mangiare*; French *manger*). Sometimes, semantic changes can be subtle, for instance, when compounded verbs change the meaning of their prefix. *Supplere* usually means "complete, supply," but in James 2:23 (as well as a *Vetus Latina* version of Matthew 13:35) *suppleri* means "to be fulfilled," even though *impleri* is normally used of a prophecy: this meaning is also seen in the Middle Ages. To the numerous semantic nuances of *sustinere* ("receive, suffer, keep back," etc.) biblical Latin adds those of "expect, stay, persevere."

Some semantic peculiarities of the *Vetus Latina* did not enter the Vulgate but nonetheless had a lasting impact, as in the case mentioned above of *creatio* in the sense of "creature." The verb *gratificari* ("do a favor"), derived from *gratus* and used in the *Vetus Latina* in the sense of "to thank," was replaced by *gratias agere* in the Vulgate, yet the earlier use continued as well, as did the employment of *gratificare* with the sense of "to bless." *Deuenire* ("to come from somewhere, reach something") occasionally signifies "become" in the *Vetus Latina*, a meaning which continues in medieval Latin (cf. Italian *divenire*; French *devenir*). A change in the semantic structure of a compound can be observed in the case of *caelicola* ("inhabitant of Heaven," from *colere* "dwell"): in some passages in the *Vetus Latina*, this signifies "striving for Heaven," based on the sense of *colere* as "revere" and translating σεβόμενος.

New Coinages

Time and again in certain fields—such as the reception of Greek philosophy—intra-Latin coinages imposed themselves. Christianity was a movement that, together with its novelty of thought and experience, also produced a renewal of language. Whereas neologisms were generally spurned in the sphere of literary language, such concerns were set aside by the Christians. The vocabulary needed to express the content of the new teachings was freely created, mainly during the translation of biblical texts from Greek. Among these are dogmatic and soteriological key terms: for instance, the verb *saluare* ("save") for σώζειν, formed from the established *saluus*; to this was added *saluator* ("savior") for σωτήρ. Augustine uses this term to illustrate the significance of such creation of new words among Latin Christians: there would always have been room for the word in Latin by itself, but it remained irrelevant as long as the designated person, the Savior, had not yet appeared.[2] A calque was made of παλιγγενεσία ("rebirth, re-creation") as *regeneratio*. The Pauline differentiation between σαρκικός ("carnal, earthly, temporal") and πνευματικός ("spiritual") became *carnalis—spirit(u)alis*; even if these adjectives are occasionally also used differently, by and large they belong to biblical language. The same is true for *incorruptibilis* as "imperishable" (ἄφθαρτος) and *immarcescibilis* as "unwitherable" (ἀμάραντος). Although the established adjective *mundanus* was occasionally used for the Christian interpretation of *mundus* ("world"), in the *Vetus Latina* the neologism *mundialis* appears (rendering κοσμικός), a new term that spread far. *Magnalia* ("mighty works," usually of God's deeds) was coined to render μεγάλα or μεγαλεῖα. In order to translate εὐδοκεῖν (or a syntagm with εὐδοκία) the verb *beneplacere* ("to please well") was coined in the *Vetus Latina*: likewise, *iustificare* was developed for δικαιοῦν ("justify"), while *clarificare* and *glorificare* (imitating the common *magnificare*) were introduced for δοξάζειν ("glorify") and subsequently became very common; *mirificare* was used for the semantically similar θαυμαστοῦν ("to marvel").

Even though some neologisms do not concern core topics of Christian faith but incidental matters, they nonetheless became very common. This is true for *gaudimonium* ("gaiety"), which also occurs in Petronius, and *congaudere* ("rejoice together"), based on συγχαίρειν. The Latin *pinnaculum*, rendering πτερύγιον, appears in the *Vetus Latina* as

---

[2] E.g., *Sermo* 299.6 and *De trinitate* 13.10, although it may be noted that *saluator* also appears in the Old Testament.

meaning both "little wing" and "pinnacle (of a building)," but it began to be used in other meanings as well (cf. Italian *pennacchio* "spandrel"). The verb *appretiare* ("appreciate"), coined to render τιμᾶν, became common in the Middle Ages with additional meanings. *Amaricare* ("embitter"), formed in accordance with παραπικραίνειν, was also commonly used (cf. Italian *amaricare*; Spanish *amargar*). Somewhat lesser posterity was enjoyed by *manicare* ("come in the morning"), a calque based on ὀρθρίζειν from *mane* ("early in the morning"). Similar nontechnical words include *dementare* ("deceive"), *adpropiare* ("approach"), *principare/principari* ("rule"), and the adjective *cornupeta* ("pushing with the horns," of a bull). The compound σπερμολόγος in Acts 17:18, meaning "idle babbler," was imitated in the Vulgate as *seminiuerbius*: however, its semantic significance was subsequently reversed and it came to have the positive signification of "preacher." Some coinages in the *Vetus Latina* are absent from Jerome's translations yet were adopted all the same, for instance, *indisciplinatus* ("undisciplined") for ἀπαίδευτος (with *indisciplinatio* for ἀπαιδευσία) and *indultor* ("who condones"). Other occasional forms hardly found any resonance, such as Hesychius's invention of *manufactile* ("created by human hands") to render χειροποίητα in Leviticus 26:1.

Among the points of contact between biblical and Vulgar Latin are univerbations of one preposition with another or with an adverb. These new words often define a relative position, locally or temporally. Besides established particles such as *exinde* ("thence, from that time") or *insuper* ("on top, besides"), new ones appeared in imperial times. Many of these, indeed, first occur in the *Vetus Latina*, in which the threshold for the written adoption of popular usage was especially low. Some coinages later proliferated in Romance languages, such as *abante* ("in front of, frontally"), which first occurs as preposition or adverb in the Latin Bible (cf. Italian *avanti*, French *avant*). The adverb *deintus* ("[from] inside; within"; cf. French *dans*) is first attested in the *Vetus Latina*, very profusely, and then in other texts, although the Vulgate tends to avoid it. *Deforis* is used on multiple occasions in the *Vetus Latina* and elsewhere as an adverb ("outside"; cf. Italian *difuori*; French *dehors*); it is also sometimes used as a preposition in the Bible. Also first attested in the *Vetus Latina* is *depost* ("behind, after"), a word that later became very widespread (cf. Portuguese *depois*; Italian *dopo*): similar cases are *deprope* ("close by"), rare at first but becoming more common in the Middle Ages, as well as *delonge* ("far") and *alonge* ("[from] afar"). Other such coinages seem only to have enjoyed a minimal existence (e.g., *deex* "from").

MORPHOLOGY

Numerous peculiarities in inflectional morphology can be observed in biblical Latin. Many are unknown to school grammar, even though some are rather common. *Vetus Latina* texts often provide early, or even the earliest, written evidence of these: as noted above, this is because these versions were prepared to commit certain linguistic usages to writing which were avoided elsewhere.

The first examples concern the declension of nouns and pronouns. Instead of the usual *infirmus/-a/-um* "weak," *infirmis/-e* is quite common in the *Vetus Latina* and other texts of a Vulgar Latin complexion. Sometimes complete new paradigms were created from single inflectional nominal forms. From *retia*, the nominative and accusative plural of the noun *rete* ("net"), a new feminine *retia, -ae* was shaped. Common in the *Vetus Latina*, this is absent from Jerome's Bible but still appears in later texts. For many Greek loanwords, the Greek accusative in *-a* became the springboard for an inflection as a feminine noun. The *Vetus Latina* offers the first attestation of *apsida (absida)* instead of *apsis* ("apse") and—apart from some uncertain Early Latin instances—*lampada* instead of *lampas* ("torch, lamp"). These variants subsequently became very common. An adjective *praestus/-a/-um* to the adverb *praesto* ("ready"; cf. Italian *presto*; French *prêt*) was formed in Late Antiquity and, again, appears first in the *Vetus Latina*. Inflected forms of *nequam* ("good for nothing") are occasionally found in the Latin Bible and later texts. Although pronouns have their own declensions in Latin, there were already many exceptions to this in Early Latin, which may also be observed in Late Antiquity, particularly in biblical texts. For instance, the frequent use of *illum* and *istum*, respectively, instead of *illud* and *istud* ("that") is first attested in the *Vetus Latina*.

Substantives constitute a border area between morphology and syntax. Noteworthy in the *Vetus Latina* are feminine declensions of *imber* ("rain") or *grex* ("herd"; cf. Spanish *la grey*). *Gens* ("race, clan") is often used in the plural to mean "people": under the influence of *homines* or *populi* in the *Vetus Latina* (and later on) *gentes* is often used as a masculine (cf. French *les gens*). In the transition from Vulgar Latin to Romance, the neuter was abandoned as an independent category and its role was usually taken over by the masculine. Traces of this are found in the *Vetus Latina*—for example, *hic uerbus* ("this word"), *retem plenum* ("full net"), *regnum uenientem* ("the kingdom to come"). As an aside, the word *uirgo* ("virgin") is also used for men, following biblical Greek παρθένος: its original application was only to women, but in the light of Revelation 14:4 it was extended within Christianity to men. There are many cases of double comparison, for which just one example will suffice: the form *plurior(es)* as a comparative of *plus* in the *Vetus Latina* and elsewhere (cf. French *plusieurs* < **plusiores*).

The conjugation of verbs, likewise, provides plenty of evidence for innovation in the Latin Bible. The *Vetus Latina* features a number of metaplasms, such as *uocitus* instead of *uocatus* ("called"). Besides *florere* ("blossom"), it frequently has popular forms based on *florire*, especially *florie(n)t* (cf. Italian *fiorire*; French *fleurir*). Augustine acknowledged that these forms were incorrect, but he believed they could not be removed from popular usage, especially in song.[3] Similarly, variants of *fodere* ("dig") and its compounds as *fodire* had existed since Early Latin, and continued to spread in the Middle Ages (cf. French *fouir* "scrape"). The Latin Bible contains forms of *perfodire* ("dig through"), which, in defense against the norms promoted by secular grammarians

---

[3] *quod iam auferre non possumus de ore cantantium populorum* (*De doctrina christiana* 2.13.20).

in the Middle Ages, were claimed to be sanctified by this occurrence. Even more frequent was the replacement of some stems in biblical Latin. The *Vetus Latina* and other
texts exhibit forms such as *lauauisse* instead of *lāuisse* for *lauare* ("wash"), *sonauisse*
instead of *sonuisse* for *sonare* ("sound"), and *increpauisse* instead of *increpuisse* for
increpare ("chide"). Another such case is *sileuit* instead of *siluit* from *silere* ("be silent").
Sometimes the marker of the perfect stem was dropped, whether sigmatic or formed
by reduplication: for *cedere* ("retreat") and its compounds, perfect forms in *-cedisse* instead of *-cessisse* are common from imperial times onward, including the *Vetus Latina*.
The same is true of forms without reduplication such as *spondisti* or *sponderit* for
spondere ("promise"). The verb "to go" (*ire*), and especially its compounds, were often
inflected like normal verbs of the fourth conjugation, particularly in the future tense.
Such forms proliferated among Christian authors and in the Middle Ages: the Latin
Bible thus has *circumiet, exies, peries, prodiet,* and *transiet*. Another common feature
of this verb in these sources is the "normal" inflection of its present participle, for example. *abientes* and *exientes*. Some verbs of the third and fourth conjugation exhibit
future forms in *-bo, -bis* instead of *-am, -es* (e.g., *intendebis, metuebitis, obliuiscebor* and
custodibo, scibit, and *sepelibit*); conversely some second conjugation verbs have futures
in *-am, -es* (*amoueam, appareas, deleam* etc.).

Syntax

Numerous syntactic peculiarities of the *Vetus Latina* were retained in the Vulgate. Some
of them are characteristic of biblical language. As a matter of course, biblical texts share
many other Late Antique linguistic features, especially those of Vulgar Latin. One example of the latter is the very common use of *in* plus ablative with an instrumental
meaning, both in biblical texts and elsewhere.

There are some striking uses of cases. Isolated emphatic nominatives are frequent, in
which the pertinent main term is prepended to the sentence and then integrated into the
sentence structure by a pronoun in an oblique case. This is exemplified in the following
two verses: *Filii hominum dentes eorum arma et sagittae* ("The children of men, their
teeth are weapons and arrows"; Psalm 56:5 LXX); *Omnis . . ., qui confitebitur me coram
hominibus, confitebor et ego eum coram patre meo* ("Everyone who will confess me before men, him will I too confess before my Father"; Matthew 10:32). Another instance
of a nonconstrued nominative (or vocative) is found in expressions of labeling, such as
Vocauit nomen loci illius Temptatio ("He called the name of that place 'Temptation'";
Exodus 17:7), *Inposuit Simoni nomen Petrus* ("He gave to Simon the name Peter"; Mark
3:16), and *Vos uocatis me magister et domine* ("You call me master and Lord"; John
13:13). Nonconstrued *dicens/dicentes*, like λέγων/λέγοντες, is typical for introducing direct speech in biblical language, and ultimately goes back to Hebrew. One *Vetus Latina*
form of Genesis 22:20 has *et nuntiatum est Abrahae dicentes* ("And it was announced to
Abraham, [them] saying").

Biblical texts often exhibit peculiarities in case usage. For example, *inter* with ablative is first attested in a *Vetus Latina* version of the Angelic Greeting (Luke 1:28): *benedicta tu inter mulieribus* ("blessed are you among women"). Augustine cites this phenomenon as an example of a harmless solecism: *Utrum . . . "inter homines" an "inter hominibus" dicatur, ad rerum non pertinet cognitorem* ("Whether it says 'among humans' [acc.] or 'among humans' [abl.] makes no difference to the one who understands matters").[4] The construction of the genitive of quality (*genitivus qualitatis*), common in biblical language, can be traced back to Hebrew (via Greek). Thus the phrase "unjust judge" at Luke 18:6, *iudex iniquitatis* (literally, "judge of injustice") is taken over from ὁ κρίτης τῆς ἀδικίας: the Apostle Paul's description as a "chosen instrument" (*uas electionis*) (literally, "instrument of choosing") matches σκεῦος ἐκλογῆς at Acts 9:15. Following such biblical uses, this construction became extremely widespread. Another Hebrew feature is the genitive of intensity, such as *rex regum* ("king of kings") or *cantica canticorum* ("song of songs"). This kind of intensification of a term which emphasizes one noun among its equals is common in many languages and cultures, but in biblical language it follows the Hebrew precedent. The most frequent syntagms of this sort are *caeli caelorum* ("the heaven of heavens") and *in saecula saeculorum* ("for the ages of ages" [i.e., "for ever and ever"]).

There are some unusual features in the comparison of adjectives in biblical Latin. The positive is sometimes used with the function of a comparative in the *Vetus Latina*, for example, in Ecclesiasticus 16:4: *utile mori sine filiis quam relinquere filios impios* ("it is *proper* to die without children than to leave behind godless children"). In the Vulgate, this is seen in Psalm 117:8 (LXX): *bonum est confidere in domino quam confidere in homine* ("it is *good* to trust in the Lord than to trust in a human"). A comparative form is often used in the *Vetus Latina* for a Greek superlative, but these are phenomena that may also be observed in other texts. The same is true for the pleonastic comparison with both *plus/magis* and a comparative—for example, 2 Samuel 6:22: *uilior fiam plus quam factus sum* ("I shall become *more cheaper* than I have been made"), or Matthew 12:12: *quanto magis melior est homo ove* ("how much *more better* is a human than a sheep?"). The indication of the comparative with *ab* instead of *quam* is due to a Hebraism mediated by Greek—as in Psalm 8:6 (LXX): *Minuisti eum paulo minus ab angelis* ("You have made him little lower *from* the angels"). The use of *super* in this function is also an indirect Semitism—for example Psalm 18:11 (LXX): *desiderabilia super aurum . . . et dulciora super mel et fauum* ("More to be desired *above* gold . . . and sweeter *above* honey and honeycomb").

With regard to verbs, a typical feature of biblical language is the use of perfect forms with present meaning, again reflecting a Hebraism mediated by Greek. In Genesis 22:2, a *Vetus Latina* text has: *Accipe filium tuum illum unicum, quem dilexisti* ("take your son, that only one, whom you loved"). Especially famous is Psalm 1:1: *Beatus uir, qui non abiit in consilio impiorum et in uia peccatorum non stetit* ("Blessed is the man who did not set off in the plan of the ungodly and did not stand in the path of sinners"). Certain deponent verbs are used with an active meaning. The *Vetus Latina* seems to have been

---

[4] *De doctrina christiana* 2.13.19.

responsible for such a use of *confitere* ("confess"). Conversely, *paenitere* ("do penance"), following the impersonal *paenitet*, is very often used in the Latin Bible as a deponent, as in Mark 1:15: *paenitemini et credite euangelio* ("Repent and believe the good news"). The use of *lacrimari* ("weep") as a deponent is first and frequently attested in the *Vetus Latina*—for example, John 11:35: *et lacrimatus est Iesus* ("And Jesus wept").

Indirect declarative clauses formed with conjunctions occurred frequently in Late Antiquity, in place of the accusative and infinitive: these became dominant in the Romance languages and beyond. Clauses following verbs of speech or thought (*verba dicendi/sentiendi*) were initially introduced by *quod*. Subsequently, mainly as a result of translations of biblical and other texts from Greek (in which such clauses were introduced by ὅτι), the prevalence of *quia* increased greatly, followed later by *quoniam* ("since, seeing that"). In particular, the use of *quoniam* after *scire, putare, uidere*, and *dicere* has a very biblical ring. The use of ὅτι also led to the use of *quia* and *quod* (and more rarely *quoniam*) to introduce direct speech: this is first seen in the *Vetus Latina* but continues in the Vulgate New Testament.

Two further examples from the plethora of biblical characteristics may suffice to conclude this section. The first is the use of the preposition *in* before a predicate (*in praedicativum*), a Hebraism mediated through Greek (εἰς) that subsequently became common. It usually has a consecutive or resultative character, as in *factus est homo in animam uiuentem* ("The human became *into* a living soul"; Genesis 2:7) or *enutriuit eum sibi in filium* ("she brought him up *into* a son for herself"; Acts 7:21). The second is the use of *ut quid* in elliptically shortened questions, which acquired the meaning "wherefore" or "why." This biblical peculiarity, based on the Greek ἵνα τί, later spread widely.

STYLISTICS

Some linguistic features are most conveniently treated as elements of style. As has already been seen, many of these are indirect Hebraisms. One example is the expression of finite verbs by a circumlocution with an agent noun and *esse* or *fieri*. Thus it is said in Acts 10:34, *non est personarum acceptor* ("God is no receiver of persons"), while in Hebrews 11:6, *inquirentibus se remunerator fit* ("God is the rewarder for those who seek him"). This kind of expression subsequently caught on more broadly. The same is true of the juxtaposition of a verb with its present participle, as in *multiplicans . . . multiplicabo semen tuum* ("multiplying . . . I will multiply your offspring"; Genesis 16:10) or, in the *Vetus Latina, nisi benedicens benedicam te et implendo implebo semen tuum* ("yet blessing will I bless you and by filling will I fill your offspring"; Genesis 22:17). There are similar pleonastic uses of verbs of movement and speech, as *uadens reuertar ad locum meum* ("going I shall return to my place"; Hosea 5:15) or *Dixit . . . Isaac ad Abraham . . . dicens* ("Isaac said to Abraham, saying"; Genesis 22:7 [*Vetus Latina*]). Sometimes a pleonastic pronoun is seen in a relative clause with the same referent as the relative pronoun itself—for example, *Non . . . erat domus, in qua non erat in ea mortuus* ("there was no house in which there was not a dead man in it"; Exodus 12:30 [*Vetus Latina*]) or *Beata gens, cuius est Dominus Deus eius* ("Blessed is the people of whom the Lord God is theirs"; Psalm 32:12 LXX).[5] The use of *si* ("if") to stand pragmatically for a negation is a complex phenomenon. It goes back to a petrified aposiopesis in the Hebrew Old Testament and thence entered the Septuagint. Thus in Psalm 94:11 (LXX) God says: *ut iuraui in ira mea: "si intrabunt in requiem meam"* ("As I swore in my anger, *If* they will [i.e. they will not] enter into my rest"; compare also Mark 8:12). Following this, *si* was occasionally used as a negation in the Middle Ages. An even more striking Hebraism is a formula of affirmation common in the Old Testament: *uiuit Dominus quia . . .* ("as truly as the Lord lives is it that . . .").

CONCLUSION: THE IMPACT OF BIBLICAL LATIN

The effect of biblical language on Latin usage up to the early modern period can hardly be overestimated. Just as biblical ideas and teachings permeated the thought of Christian authors, so did biblical diction mark their way of writing. A *consuetudo scripturarum* ("scriptural custom") had arisen, as Augustine observes (*De doctrina christiana* 2.14.21). This comprised not only linguistic phenomena such as those discussed above but also the charging of "common" words with Christian content: *uita* signified "(eternal) life" and *mors* "(spiritual) death," *dominus* ("lord") implied God or Christ, while *aduersarius* ("enemy") meant the devil. Potent biblical imagery was also evoked by expressions such as *petra* ("rock"), *ouis* ("sheep"), or *cedrus* ("cedar"), as noted above for *zizania*. Christians developed a kind of natural attachment to biblical language: it was not so much perceived as beautiful in itself, but Christians were steeped in it and adopted its linguistic patterns in their own use. This tendency was reinforced by the paratactic style of biblical narrative and the fact that many of its characteristics were familiar from the developing Romance languages. While Christian Latin practice in general was strongly shaped by the Bible, sometimes there are instances of what might be called "mimetic biblical style": the methodical and purposeful incorporation of biblical traits into one's own writing in order to achieve particular effects.

In patristic times, as a result of the confrontation with critics of biblical language, a rich metalinguistic dossier was accumulated and bequeathed to posterity. This enabled medieval scholars to acquire a notion of the historicity of language. Again and again, the idiosyncrasies of biblical language were defended against classical norms.[6]

---

[5] This phenomenon became one of the *loci classici* in the discussion about faithful translation, *sermo humilis*, and linguistic correctness (see *De doctrina christiana* 2.13.20).

[6] For the following, see Stotz 2015: 17–24, and the discussion of *florire* and *perfodire* above.

Sometimes the allocation of certain linguistic features to individual stages in the development of Latin was erroneous. In addition, the language of the Bible was believed to be removed from the norms of grammarians because it had arisen from the Holy Spirit. Discussion of the Latin Bible often proceeded as if it were itself the *Urtext*, and not the result of translation processes. There were even attempts to make it the basis of Latin language teaching. At any rate, for many generations the Bible (especially the Psalms) was the most important means to acquire the knowledge of Latin.

Even so, in the Middle Ages many were aware of the distance between the *consuetudo*, the familiar text-form, and the *ueritas*, the original wording. The question whether it was licit to intervene in the text in the name of *grammatica*, correct usage, was also discussed (see Linde 2012: 199–239). Finally, Renaissance humanists broke with some of the phenomena of traditional Christian language: *saluator* was replaced by *seruator, praedicare* by *contionari*. Some of the more ecclesiastically minded scholars (such as Erasmus), despite their general critical attitude, continued to respect the shape of biblical language. Others, however, felt a vocation to oppose the Vulgate, deeply anchored in ecclesiastical life, through a radically alternative approach. One such was Sebastian Castellio, a Protestant (Stotz 2018; see chap. 21). His new translation of the Bible changed *timor Domini* ("fear of the Lord") to *Iouae metus* ("dread of Jove"); instead of *angelus* he used *genius*, instead of *baptisma*, *lotio*; declarative clauses with conjunctions were changed to accusative and infinitive; the paratactical style and the immediacy of direct speech was reduced. Yet this revolutionary approach met with heavy criticism, not least from other Protestants. It thus provides valuable testimony of how far the language and concepts of the Latin Bible had shaped Christian thought and experience, even transcending confessional differences, across many centuries.

Bibliography

Braun, René. 1985. "L'influence de la Bible sur la langue latine." In *Le monde latin antique et la Bible*, edited by Jacques Fontaine and Charles Pietri, 129–142. BTT 2. Paris: Beauchesne.

Burton, Philip. 2000. *The Old Latin Gospels. A Study of their Texts and Language*. Oxford: Oxford University Press.

Kaulen, Franz. 1904. *Sprachliches Handbuch zur biblischen Vulgata*. 2nd ed. Freiburg: Herder.

Linde, Cornelia. 2012. *How to Correct the Sacra Scriptura? Textual Criticism of the Latin Bible between the Twelfth and Fifteenth Century*. Oxford: Society for the Study of Medieval Languages and Literature.

Rönsch, Hermann. 1875. *Itala und Vulgata. Das Sprachidiom der urchristlichen Itala und der katholischen Vulgata unter Berücksichtigung der römischen Volkssprache*. 2nd ed. Munich: Hueber.

Sheerin, Daniel. 1996. "Christian and Biblical Latin." In *Medieval Latin. An Introduction and Bibliographical Guide*, edited by F. A. C. Mantello and A. G. Rigg, 137–56. Washington, DC: Catholic University of America.

Stotz, Peter. 1996–2004. *Handbuch zur lateinischen Sprache des Mittelalters*. 5 vols. Munich: Beck.

Stotz, Peter. 2015. *Die Bibel auf Latein–unantastbar?* 3rd ed. Zürich: Chronos.

Stotz, Peter. 2018. "Castellios neues lateinisches Sprachkleid für die Bibel – was hat es dem *sermo piscatorius* voraus?" In *Sebastian Castellio (1515–1563)–Dissidenz und Toleranz*, edited by Barbara Mahlmann-Bauer, 103–29. Göttingen: Vandenhoeck & Ruprecht.

Vineis, Edoardo. 1971–74. "Studio sulla lingua dell'Itala." *L'Italia dialettale* 34: 137–248; 36: 287–372; 37: 154–66.

....

CHAPTER 29

THE LATIN BIBLE AND LITURGY

....

ASHLEY BECK

LATIN IN THE LITURGY OF THE ROMAN CATHOLIC CHURCH

....

FOR Roman Catholics, one of the most significant events of the twentieth century was the Second Vatican Council between 1962 and 1965. One of its first teaching documents, and arguably one of its most important, was the constitution on the Sacred Liturgy, known by its Latin opening words *Sacrosanctum Concilium*. This text affirmed the importance of what had become known as the "Liturgical Movement" and built on reforms made to the liturgy in the 1950s by Pope Pius XII. It called for further reforms to the mass and the celebration of other sacraments, while at the same time affirming the place of Latin in the public worship of the Church. Based on its teaching that hearing the Word of God read in the mass is one of the four ways in which Jesus Christ is encountered in the liturgy, *Sacrosanctum Concilium* sought to promote a revision of the cycle of readings read at mass to enable Catholics to hear more of the Bible.

By the Middle Ages, and in the *Missale Romanum* of Pope Pius V (1570), readings from the Old Testament were largely restricted to the different Mass texts for each weekday of the season of Lent. These included the long readings known as "prophecies" also read on the penitential days during the year known as the *Quattuor Temporum*, or Ember Days, as well as the chosen lections for the Easter Vigil and Pentecost Vigil.[1] What this meant was that, until the new lectionary was published in 1969, most Catholics hardly ever heard the Old Testament read at Mass. The introduction of the

---

[1] So, for example, the Saturday Ember day in September has two readings from Leviticus 23, one from Micah 7, one from Zechariah 8, together with the epistle (Hebrews 9) and gospel (Luke 13).

three-yearly cycle of readings for Sundays and the two-year weekday lectionary significantly changed their awareness of the Bible, as did the growing adoption of vernacular translations. Permission was given in some countries at the time of World War II for the Latin scripture readings on Sundays also to be read in local languages: this had been adopted in America as early as the Baltimore Synod of 1791 (Pecklers 2003: 26–27). Following the Second Vatican Council the vernacular was even more widely adopted. At the same time, the council also promoted the revision of Latin biblical texts, leading eventually to the *Nova Vulgata* (see chap. 25). On its appearance in 1979, this was used to revise some of the official Latin texts of the Mass and the other sacramental celebrations and the Divine Office (see below). However, the 1962 edition of the *Missale Romanum,* which is the only form of the "Extraordinary Form" of the Roman rite permitted by Pope Benedict XVI's 2007 document *Summorum Pontificum,* uses the earlier form of the Vulgate, in keeping with other liturgical books in use at that time.

Debates continue, at least in some quarters of the Catholic Church, about the reforms to the liturgy ushered in by the council, often with a polemical and divisive tone. Defenders of the "Old Rite" argue that the twentieth-century reformers overlooked the ways in which the Order of Mass was very rich in scripture, beyond the cycle of epistles and gospels. The present chapter is not concerned with such polemic but instead will examine the ways in which the Latin Bible is used in the whole of the liturgy, including versions that precede Jerome's Vulgate; many of these are still to be found in the Latin version of the 1970 Missal and its revisions.[2]

The Earliest Latin Liturgies, the Lectionaries, and the Psalter

In the time of Hippolytus, a presbyter in Rome in the middle of the second century, clergy and most other Christians in the capital city of the Empire were still speaking Greek, but this soon began to change. The fourth-century rhetorician Marius Victorinus quotes Greek texts from the Canon of the Mass in the middle of a Latin text, although slightly later the source conventionally known as "Ambrosiaster" (fl. 366–84) quotes the same basic text in Latin.[3] The earliest Christians had taken the reading of

---

[2] References from the Latin Bible in this chapter are normally to the Clementine Vulgate for the Old Testament (Colunga and Turrado 1982), and for the New Testament to the *editio minor* of the Oxford Vulgate (Wordsworth and White 1920) or, where noted, the *Nova Vulgata.* Translations from the Vulgate are taken from Knox 1955. For the Latin text of the Ordinary form of the Roman Rite the *tertia editio* is used (*Missale Romanum* 2002; official translation *Roman Missal* 2010), while the "Old Rite" is taken from *English Missal* 1958.

[3] *Hinc oratio oblationis intellectu eodem precatur deum:* σῶσον περιούσιον λαὸν ζηλωτὴν καλῶν ἔργων ("This is why the prayer of oblation prays to God with the same meaning: 'Save a people of

scriptures during their meetings from Jewish practice (cf. Luke 4:16–21; Acts 13:27). Justin Martyr observes that the first part of the Christian Eucharist included readings from "the memoirs of the apostles or the writings of the prophets" (*First Apology* 67). In most liturgies in the early Church, three or more readings were read on Sundays. Normally two were taken from the New Testament, one from the Epistles or Acts, and one from a Gospel, although the former seems to have gradually to have fallen out of the Roman liturgy from the fourth century onward (Jungmann 1951–54: I.395ff.; Chavasse 1958: 190–97). There is some uncertainty as to *how* the selection of readings was made. In some places, there was a continuous reading of texts, perhaps reflected in patristic commentaries on texts which seem to have been originally preached as sermons (see chap. 9). Elsewhere, it appears that a choice was made by the bishop, although the readings for major feasts seem to have been established early on (Cobb 1992: 226; Willis 1968: 10).

Generally, readers were expected to locate the passages chosen as liturgical readings in a continuous-text manuscript.[4] A few Latin lectionary manuscripts indicate that compilations of these passages were also created at a relatively early period. The oldest Latin lectionary from the Iberian Peninsula is the *Liber comicus* produced between the seventh and ninth centuries (Morin 1893).[5] This combines Old Latin forms of text (e.g., the Epistle for the feast of the Epiphany; Titus 2:11–3:7) with others from the Vulgate (e.g., the Gospel for Christmas Day; Luke 2). A similar mixture is found in the Luxeuil lectionary, whose text dates from around 700 (Salmon 1944, 1953). This gives us a good idea of the Latin Bible used in the liturgy in Merovingian Gaul, with readings designated for Mass throughout the year and for the daily Hours.

Even more than the gospels, the part of the Bible most used and known in Latin throughout the history of the Church is the Psalms. Jerome's second revision of the text of the Psalms, known as the *Psalterium Gallicanum*, was used almost universally until the twentieth-century revision of the Vulgate (see chap. 5). Given the extent to which the psalter dominates liturgical worship, particularly in the use of music, the importance of this biblical book is hard to exaggerate. The Gallican Psalter was not replaced until the Psalter of Pope Pius X (see chap. 25).

---

your own, who are zealous for good deeds' [cf. Titus 2:14]." Marius Victorinus, *Aduersus Arium* 2.8 [PL 8: 1094D]); for Ambrosiaster, see CSEL 50: 268 (although this includes an erroneous reference to Pseudo-Augustine).

[4] This underlies the instruction as late as the Missal of 1570 that the reader of the gospel announces it with the words *Sequentia sancti evangelii secundum* . . . ("the continuation of the Holy Gospel according to . . .").

[5] The term is derived from the noun *comes* (with a short "o") meaning a companion; so it would be a book used "with companions" or in a community. The appellation is often used for Latin lectionaries, especially in Spanish tradition.

THE LATIN BIBLE IN THE 1570 MISSAL
OF PIUS V

The lectionary for readings at Mass in the Missal of 1570 is essentially that which was used in most Latin rites from the early Middle Ages. Most of the readings were the same in the Sarum Missal, which formed the basis for the readings in the Anglican Book of Common Prayer: Thomas Cranmer made few changes in this respect, apart from replacing the Latin with an English translation (Procter and Frere 1902: 116ff.). In contrast to all modern liturgies, this lectionary was a one-year cycle consisting of readings from the Epistles and Gospels. Beyond the lectionary, however, all Christian liturgies are imbued with the phrases and theology of Scripture. In many cases, this is so ingrained that the scriptural origins are no longer noticed: for example, the priest's salutation *Dominus vobiscum* is biblical in origin (Ruth 2:4 and 2 Chronicles 15:2), replaced at the beginning of every Mass celebrated by a bishop with the risen Christ's greeting to his disciples *Pax vobis* (John 20:19, etc.). Such use of the Bible differs from the varying passages chosen as lections: these are not readings intended for edification but forms of prayer and praise (as seen in parts of the Bible itself). The following paragraphs consider some of the most important citations and uses of Scripture from the *Ordo Missae* in the 1570 Missal. Occasional comments are made on differences between this and the "new rite" of the 1970 Mass, although the latter is the subject of its own section (The Latin Bible in the 1970 Missal of Pope Paul VI) below.

The Mass begins with the *Introitum*, read by the priest on arrival at the altar. This consists of an antiphon, a psalm, and the *Gloria Patri*. The antiphon consists of Psalm 42:4 (LXX), *Introibo ad altarem Dei: ad Deum qui laetificat iuventutem meam*, ("There I will go up to the altar of God, the giver of triumphant happiness"),[6] which precedes the reading of the whole of this Psalm. In the 1570 Roman Rite, this Psalm is said at the foot of the altar by the celebrating priest, alternating verses with the deacons and subdeacon or (more often) with a single altar server; in some liturgies, it is said in the sacristy. Its use seems to have originated in Frankish-Gallic rites from 1000. It is worth noting that, until its removal in the 1964 revision of the Missal, this Psalm would have been the most substantial Latin biblical text that a participant in the Mass other than the celebrating priest would have been expected to learn by heart.

The ancient hymn *Gloria in excelsis Deo* is central to this initial section, although both the *Gloria* and Psalm 42 are omitted in times of penitence (e.g., Passiontide) and from Requiem Masses. The opening words of this hymn, from Luke 2:14, are taken not from the Vulgate (in which they are *Gloria in altissimis Deo*) but from the *Vetus Latina*. Although it is customary for the entire text to be called "the angelic hymn," only the first

---

[6] As in certain other passages cited in this chapter, the official English translation sometimes moves beyond a literal correspondence to the Latin text.

words are directly from Scripture; the composition of the Latin version is traditionally attributed to the fourth-century bishop Hilary of Poitiers.

The prayer which the deacon or priest says before reading the Gospel, *Munda cor meum ac labia mea, omnipotens Deus, qui labia Isaiae Prophetae calculo mundasti ignito* . . . ("Cleanse my heart and my lips, almighty God, who didst cleanse the lips of the prophet Isaiah with a live coal . . .") recalls the scene and the language of Isaiah 6:6–7. In the new rite the prayer is simply *Munda cor meum ac labia mea, omnipotens Deus, ut sanctum Evangelium tuum digne valeam nuntiare* ("Cleanse my heart and my lips, almighty God, that I may worthily proclaim your holy gospel").

At the Offertory, after offering the bread and wine, the priest bows and says the prayer *In spiritu humiliatis et in animo contrito suscipiamur a te, Domine; et sic fiat sacrificium nostrum in conspectu tuo hodie, ut placeat tibi, Domine Deus* ("In a humble spirit, and with a contrite heart, may we be accepted of thee, O Lord: and so let our sacrifice be offered in thy sight this day, that it may be pleasing unto thee, O Lord God."). The opening phrase draws on Daniel 3:39 (*sed in animo contrito, et spiritu humilitatis suscipiamur*). Even so, the reversal of the two elements suggests that it is taken from an earlier, pre-Vulgate version of this book.

At High Mass, the priest says a different prayer to bless the incense at the Offertory from that used at the beginning of the Mass, *Per intercessionem beati Michaeli Archangeli, stantis a dextris altaris incensi, et omnium electorum suorum, incensum istud dignetur Dominus benedicere* . . . ("Through the intercession of blessed Michael the Archangel, standing at the right hand of the altar of incense, and of all his elect, may the Lord vouchsafe to bless this incense."). The reference to Michael is intriguing, as the angel present at the altar of incense in the gospels is not Michael but Gabriel (Luke 1:19; see also Daniel 8:16, 9:21). While censing the altar, the priest recites part of Psalm 140 (LXX): *Dirigatur oratio mea sicut incensum in conspectu tuo; elevatio manuum mearum sacrificium vespertinum* ("Welcome as incense-smoke let my prayer rise up before thee; when I lift up my hands, be it acceptable as the evening sacrifice"). There follows Psalm 25:6–12 (LXX), *Lavabo inter innocentes manus meas et circumdabo altare tuum* ("With the pure of heart I will wash my hands clean, and take my place among them at thy altar"), recited by the priest as his fingers are washed. In the 1970 Mass, no prayers are provided for either the blessing of incense or the censing, and Psalm 25 is replaced by a brief prayer.

The ancient acclamation known as the *Sanctus* draws on a text of Isaiah 6:13 in pre-Vulgate sources: *Sanctus, sanctus, sanctus Dominus Deus Sabaoth; pleni sunt caeli et terra gloria tua* ("Holy, Holy, Holy Lord God of Hosts. Heaven and earth are full of thy glory"). The Vulgate reads *Sanctus, sanctus, sanctus Dominus, Deus exercituum; plena est omnis terra gloria eius.* The following phrase, *Benedictus qui venit in nomine Domini* (Psalm 117:26 LXX, "Blessed is he who cometh in the name of the Lord") is quoted at Jesus's entry to Jerusalem in Matthew 21:9. As in the *Gloria*, the word *excelsis* marks a difference between the *Vetus Latina*, on which the Liturgy draws, and the text of the Vulgate. These acclamations also show the way in which scriptural verses were reworked and spliced together in the canon of the Mass. Protestant reformers were uncomfortable with this, and in Cranmer's Second *Book of Common Prayer* of 1552, the *Benedictus* was removed, even though it is entirely scriptural.

The Eucharistic Prayer in the Roman rite, known as the *Roman Canon,* was fixed by the end of the sixth century at the latest. Apart from the Preface, which changes according to the season, its fixed character defines it as the "Great Prayer which is absolutely essential and quite indispensable in the celebration of any Eucharist" (Hope and Woolfenden 1992: 268). As the only Eucharistic Prayer in the Western Mass for over thirteen hundred years, its importance is hard to exaggerate. In the Eucharistic theology of the Catholic Church, the point at which the elements of bread and wine are consecrated as the Body and Blood of Christ is the account of the Last Supper, known usually as the "Institution Narrative."[7] It is significant that this narrative does not follow closely any of the Gospels or the account in 1 Corinthians but rather conflates all of them.[8] Some phrases are not in the text of Scripture, such as *accepit panem in sanctas ac venerabiles manus suas, et elevatis oculis in caelum* ("he took bread into his holy and venerable hands, with eyes raised to heaven") and *accipiens et hunc praeclarum calicem in sanctis ac venerabiles manus suas* ("taking also this excellent Chalice into his holy and venerable hands"). Devotional embellishments of this kind would not have seemed odd in the early Church. The words of institution are not in the prayer to reproduce historical narrative, but to effect an act of God, and Scripture serves as a "tool" at the service of the worship of God, not simply a source for quotations.

There remains a debate as to whether or not the words of the Canon of the Mass, and the words of Christ in particular, should be said audibly. The earlier practice was to recite the Canon in a whisper, apart from the words *Nobis quoque peccatoribus* ("To us sinners also"), but the instruction in the 1970 Mass is for the whole Canon to be said or sung aloud. Given that the practice adopted affects the audibility of many of the citations or allusions to the Latin Bible in the Liturgy, caution should be exercised in arguing about their broader application, as those present may not have been able to hear what the priest was saying. Nevertheless, the Latin words of the Institution narrative (*Hoc est Corpus Meum* and *Hic est Calix Sanguinis Mei*) have a particular force associated with the moment of consecration. On occasion, these have been treated superstitiously or as a form of mockery or abuse: the latter is seen in the phrase "hocus pocus" or the dance known as the "Hokey-cokey."

A further example of scriptural allusion in the Canon occurs in a paragraph after the Consecration, in which the priest says:

> *Supra quae propitio ac sereno vultu respicere digneris, et accepta habere, sicuti accepta habere dignatus es munera pueri tui iusti Abel, et sacrificium Patriarchae nostrae Abrahae: et quod tibi obtulit summus sacerdos tuus Melchisedech, sanctum sacrificium, immaculatam Hostiam.*

---

[7] In contrast, the key point in most Eastern liturgies is the *Epiclesis,* the point at which the Holy Spirit is invoked. This is lacking from the Roman Canon.

[8] For studies of this, see Jungmann 1951–54: III.111, n. 2

("Upon which vouchsafe to look with a favourable and gracious countenance: and to accept them, even as thou didst vouchsafe to accept the gifts of thy just servant Abel, and the sacrifice of our Patriarch Abraham: and the holy sacrifice, the spotless victim, which thy high priest Melchisedech offered unto thee.")

This succinct text combines three distinct sacrifices from Genesis and Hebrews. Abel is not called "just" in the Bible, but it is inferred from the favor showed to him by God (cf. Genesis 4:4). In Genesis 22, the "sacrifice" by Abraham of his son Isaac does not actually happen but is replaced by that of a ram (cf. Hebrews 11:17). In terms of the Eucharist, the climactic figure in this passage is the mysterious Melchisedek who offers bread and wine (Genesis 14:18). The early Church interpreted these figures as typological for the sacrifice of Christ and the Eucharist (for illustrations, see Jungmann 1951–54: 149ff.). Although this part of the Canon does not quote the Latin Bible directly, some of the vocabulary is the same, such as the verb *obtulit*.

Before the giving of the *Pax*, the priest says the prayer *Domine Jesu Christe, qui dixisti apostolis tuis: Pacem relinquo vobis, pacem meam do vobis*. This is a direct quotation of John 14:27, *Pacem relinquo vobis, pacem meam do vobis* ("Peace is my bequest to you, and the peace which I will give you is mine to give"): the text matches the Vulgate although the Old Latin witnesses are similar. This prayer is said at Low Masses where the Peace is not shared, and was retained unchanged in the 1970 missal.

One final characteristic of the 1570 rite is the reading of the "Last Gospel," after a blessing and a dismissal. This is usually, but not always, the opening section of John (1:1–14). The suitability of this passage for a celebration of mass is in its expression of the doctrine of the Incarnation: the priest genuflects during the final verse, *Et verbum caro factum est, et habitavit in nobis* ("And the Word was made flesh, and came to dwell among us"). In the reforms to the mass in the late 1950s, the Last Gospel was deleted if another liturgical action was to follow immediately (such as the Absolutions at a Requiem Mass) and in 1964 it was removed altogether.

THE LATIN BIBLE IN THE MASS AND THE "APOSTROPHIC VOICE"

Catherine Pickstock's classic, *After Writing: On the Liturgical Consummation of Philosophy*, remains one of the most interesting and original studies of the medieval Latin Mass, with a focus on the 1570 Rite. The use of Latin is perhaps intrinsic to the specific character of the mass as identified by her exploration. In Pickstock's overall analysis, the rite has a "stuttering" quality which defies logical or neat treatment (hence her negative view of what is seen as a "tidying up" in the postconciliar reforms). The source of this is portrayed as the use of *apostrophe*, or verbal exclamations, made by the priest in many of the prayers. This characteristic is seen particularly in the Canon of the Mass, as well as in the syntax of the Latin in various places. Sometimes it relates to what the priest is trying to do in the liturgy, while elsewhere it is simply gratuitous. She observes that "the apostrophic voice calls in order to be calling, or in the hope of a further calling, and is thus situated within an expectant and passionate order of language: *Confiteor tibi in cithara, Deus meus*" (Psalm 42:5 LXX; Pickstock 1998: 193). Here, and in other examples, it is possible to identify alliteration and repetition which appear to be natural to the Latin. Liturgical language has many purposes beyond simply conveying meaning, which is one reason why Latin is such a good medium for choral music (see chap. 30).

Later on, in a complex and rich discussion, Pickstock (1998: 223) makes a similar point in relation to the Latin syntax found particularly in the Canon. This builds up her picture of a unique liturgical time which is encountered in the mass. Looking at the words of Jesus in the Institution Narrative—which, as noted above, do not follow closely the scriptural texts—and other passages in this prayer, she shows how the use of conjunctions and relative pronouns create a different liturgical world. She identifies the result of this as an "intensified complication of language" and a "narrative attenuation and obsessiveness" (1998: 224). In some ways, this is the last thing one would expect in liturgical language: it is not grand, solemn, or conventionally sacred, and one might argue that the use of Latin is intrinsic to this picture, as only the terseness and grammatical compactness of Latin fulfils such a role. This is shown in the rather forced character of the 2010 translation of the 1970 Missal, which attempts to reproduce the function of relative pronouns such as *quam* in a literal English form (see further below).[9]

THE LATIN BIBLE IN THE 1970 MISSAL OF POPE PAUL VI

Among Roman Catholics there is a spirited debate about the extent to which the liturgical changes that took place very quickly after the Second Vatican Council closed in 1965 reflected the Council's wishes as expressed in *Sacrosanctum Concilium*. In the context of the present chapter, however, it was certainly not the intention that the celebration of the mass in Latin should die out. The *editio typica* of the reformed rite was issued in Latin in 1970, exactly four hundred years after the publication of the Missal of Pius V. This has undergone two subsequent minor revisions in 1972 and 2002, the second of which incorporated biblical texts from the *Nova Vulgata* published in 1979. Quite apart

---

[9] It is also worth noting that there has existed for some time a complete translation of the missal into what may be called "Cranmerian" English, known as *The English Missal*. This still used in some Anglo-Catholic communities in the Church of England despite arguably always being illegal in England (although at one point it was officially authorized for use in the Anglican diocese of Guyana). The emphasis in the discussion above on the use of Latin suggests that the insights of Pickstock's work cannot be applied to this translation in a straightforward manner. I am grateful to Ian Coleman for his observations here and elsewhere.

from the intention that it should continue to be used on occasion, the Latin text remains authoritative for translations into vernacular languages.

Many of the prayers from the 1570 Rite which contain scriptural allusions remain unchanged in the present *Missale Romanum*. The Roman Canon itself, *Eucharistic Prayer I*, remains unchanged apart from the addition of St. Joseph to the first list of saints (promulgated by St John XXIII) and the relocation of the phrase *mysterium fidei*: in the 1970 Missal, this serves as the invitation to the acclamation inserted after the elevation of the chalice.[10] Other prayers have been shortened, often with the reduction of the scriptural element (as noted in the analysis of the 1570 Rite). The Offertory prayer *In spiritu humilitatis* has not been altered, despite the change from *animo contrito* to *anima contrita* at Daniel 3:39 in the *Nova Vulgata*: although variable texts in the Missal and the Divine Office published after 1979 reflect this new edition of the Latin Bible, the texts from the Ordinary of the Mass were not updated. This indicates the way in which the awareness of these passages as biblical references has largely been superseded by their deployment as liturgical texts.

One of the richest texts in the 1970 Mass is *Eucharistic Prayer IV*. This is rarely used, because it is significantly longer than the second and third canons, but it contains a variety of scriptural references. For example, the phrase *salutem evangelizavit pauperibus, redemptionem captivis, maestis corde laetitiam* ("To the poor he proclaimed the good news of salvation, to prisoners, freedom, to the sorrowful of heart, joy") refers to Luke 4:17–19, itself dependent on Isaiah 61:1–2. Even more powerfully, after the invocation of the Holy Spirit, the words of institution are prefaced by a strong echo of the Johannine Farewell Discourse: *Ipse enim, cum hora venisset ut glorificatur a te, Pater sancte, ac dilexisset suos qui erant in mundo, in finem dilexit eos* ("For when the hour had come for him to be glorified by you, Father most holy, he loved them to the end"; cf. John 12:27 and 13:1).

Other often-neglected scriptural elements in the modern Roman Rite are two Eucharistic Prayers for Reconciliation, originally written for the Holy Year of Reconciliation in 1975, and the four Eucharistic Prayers "for use in Masses for Various Needs" (originally composed in the 1980s for the Church in Switzerland). In the first prayer for Reconciliation, there is a direct quotation of Ephesians 2:4 in the phrase *cum sis dives in misericordia* ("being rich in mercy").[11] Toward the end of the second Reconciliation Prayer, the words *ad perpetuae unitatis convivium, in caelis novis et terra nova* ("to the unending banquet of unity in a new heaven and a new earth") offer an allusion to Revelation 21:1 (itself drawing on Isaiah 65:17). All the Eucharistic Prayers for Various Needs include the phrase *concede, ut virtute Spiritus caritatis tuae, inter Filii tui membra, cuius Corpori communicamus et Sanguini, nunc et in diem aeternitatis numeremur* ("Grant that, by the power of the Spirit of your love, we may be counted

[10] In the Apostolic Constitution *Missale Romanum*, introducing this Missal, Pope Paul VI writes: "The words *Mysterium Fidei*, taken from the context of the words of Christ our Lord, and said by the priest, serve as an introduction to the acclamation of the faithful" (§3).

[11] This prayer predates St. John Paul II's encyclical *Dives in Misericordia*.

now and until the day of eternity among the members of your Son in whose Body and Blood we have communion"), recalling 1 Corinthians 12:27. The second prayer ("God Guides His Church along the Way of Salvation") has in its preface the line *In manu potenti et brachio extento populum tuum Israel desertum duxisti* ("With mighty hand and outstretched arm you led your people through the desert"), reflecting a range of Old Testament verses, such as Deuteronomy 4:34 and 26:8 as well as Psalm 136:12 in the *Nova Vulgata* (Psalm 135 LXX). The third prayer ("Jesus, the Way to the Father") says *ille via est quae nos ad te ducit, veritas quae nos liberat* ("He is the way that leads us to you, the truth that sets us free"), drawing on John 8:32 and 14:6.

The English Translation of the Missal (2010)

There has been greater awareness among English-speaking Roman Catholics of the Latin character of the text of the Mass since 2010, when a new translation of the missal was published. In accordance with the directives of the Holy See (which have since been modified considerably by Pope Francis), this text follows the Latin more closely than any earlier translations. In some places, Latin word order has been maintained, as in the opening words of the Roman Canon [Eucharistic Prayer I]: *Te igitur, clementissime Pater* . . . is rendered as "You, therefore, most merciful Father . . .". Such insights into Latin sentence structure are, however, of limited value to most Catholics. Elsewhere, the choice of English words in order to connect the translation to its Latin source results in some strange usages, such as the archaic use of the word "confess" to mean "believe" in the Nicene Creed.

The new translation also affects biblical texts in the 1970 Missal. For example, the Communion Antiphon for the Second Sunday of Easter, based on John 20:27, reads as follows: "Bring your hand and feel the place of the nails, and do not be unbelieving but believing, alleluia." Although the Latin is *et noli esse incredulus sed fidelis*, the translation in fact appears to reflect the contrast in Greek between ἄπιστος and πιστός. Similarly, the Communion Antiphon for the Common of Religious, which draws on Mark 10:29–30, is translated as: "Amen, I say to you, that you who have left all and followed me will receive a hundredfold and possess eternal life." This use of Amen, although also found in the Douay-Rheims Bible, is at some distance from its normal English usage at the end of prayers.

The ideological gulf between two approaches to translation (literal vs. "dynamic equivalence") has thus been powerfully reignited within the domain of English Catholicism, and there are parallel disputes in other language groups. It is, however, undeniable that the result has drawn greater attention to the underlying Latin source, sometimes with the recovery of the original imagery. One of the best examples of this is found at the opening of Eucharistic Prayer III, which includes a phrase from Psalm 112:3 (LXX): *a solis ortu usque ad occasum oblatio munda offeratur nomini tuo*, rendered as "from the rising of the sun to its setting a pure sacrifice may be offered to your name." This literal translation is not only closer to its scriptural source but, in replacing the earlier English text "so that from east to west a perfect offering may be made to the honour of your name," it removes the somewhat Eurocentric exclusion of global differences which operate from north to south.[12] Another indication of the intention that the 2010 translation should enable people to recover knowledge of the Latin text of the Mass is seen in the printing of the Latin texts, with music, of the *Gloria, Sanctus, Benedictus, Pater Noster*, and *Agnus Dei* alongside the English versions in the Ordinary of the Mass.

THE BIBLE IN OTHER LITURGICAL SERVICES

Outside the Mass, acts of worship involving the other sacraments before the Second Vatican Council involved far less biblical material. The rites for Confession, Infant Baptism, or Extreme Unction, for example, contained no provision for a formal Scripture reading. Following the reforms, a reading from the Bible has been included at Baptism and Unction, although it is probably still unusual for a priest in the confessional to follow the direction to read a formal extract from Scripture to the penitent. The modern rite for the Visitation and Care of the Sick (*De Visitatione et Cura Infirmorum*) includes a choice of readings from three psalms (Psalms 90, 15, and 50) and gospels (Matthew 8:5–13, Mark 16:14–18, and John 1:1–14). Even in communities where the Ordinary rite of the Mass is celebrated regularly in Latin, however, the use of Latin in these sacraments has become much less common during the course of the twentieth century.[13]

The exclusion of a formal scripture reading from the earlier rite of Extreme Unction reflects the emphasis on administering the rite quickly, before the sick person should die. Nevertheless, in the Latin text of the rite for commending the Soul (*Ordo Commendationis Animae*), there are numerous biblical allusions, especially in the prayer *Suscipe Domine*.[14] The vast majority of these are to instances of God's liberation of figures in the Old Testament, naming Enoch, Elijah, Noah, Abraham, Job, Isaac, Lot, Moses, Daniel, Susanna, and David, with details of the troubles that beset them. Only one clause refers to the New Testament, mentioning Peter and Paul, while the last in the list, Thecla, is from the Apocryphal Acts. As has already been noted, prior to the twentieth-century liturgical reforms of the liturgy most Catholics would have had minimal knowledge of the Old Testament because it was absent from the standard Mass

---

[12] Another example of improvement is the more literal translation of the ancient Latin chant known as the *Exultet*, proclaimed by the deacon at the Easter Vigil, in which the original imagery has been restored; this includes the wax of the candle as the work of "mother bees."

[13] For instance, in *Collectio Rituum* (1960) most of the order of Infant Baptism may be said in English or Gaelic rather than Latin.

[14] Many of these are reproduced, in Latin, in John Henry Newman's poem *The Dream of Gerontius* (1865).

lectionary: even if they understood the Latin, then, they were unlikely to be familiar with many or most of these references.[15]

Unlike the Mass, the daily prayer of clergy and religious known as the *Breviary* was frequently revised, as were the monastic offices on which it was based. While the changes after Vatican II led to a notable increase in the number of scriptural readings in the mass and the sacramental offices, the opposite was the case in the 1970 revision of the Daily Office. These reforms reduced the amount of material in order to make the office more practical for clergy and others working in parishes. Thus, although the 1931 Roman Breviary has five psalms in each of the morning and evening offices of Lauds and Vespers, there are only two psalms and a canticle in the revised version. Likewise, depending on the day it was being recited, the earlier form of the office of Matins could include up to nine more psalms and a substantial Scripture reading (divided into three parts), not to mention up to two nonscriptural readings. Again, for each of the four "little Hours" it prescribed a further three psalms, with three more in Compline at the end of the day. These were reduced in the 1970 revision to three psalms or sections of a psalm at the single "Prayer during the Day," and to one or two psalms at Compline.

The Latin Bible in the Liturgy of the Church of England

For many centuries, it has been the custom for the University of Oxford to celebrate the Eucharist in the University Church of St. Mary the Virgin at the beginning of each full term from the Book of Common Prayer of the Church of England, but in Latin.[16] This version was prepared in 1560, early in the reign of Queen Elizabeth I. One aim of the translators may have been to win over the more conservative University Fellows to the new liturgy. Other claims for the purpose of the Latin text were that it fixed the meaning of the words (see Harford and Stevenson 1925: 813ff.), that it enabled scholars in continental Europe to assess the progress of the English Reformation, and that it assisted clergy and laypeople who could not speak English (principally in Ireland, although presumably also in parts of Wales and Cornwall at this time). The last of these suggestions, however, relies on the rather unlikely presupposition that such people were more conversant in Latin than English! This Latin text follows the English text of the First Prayer Book of Edward VI, issued in 1549, rather than the later, more Protestant versions produced in 1552 and 1559. It seems to have been used in college chapels in Oxford and Cambridge, the public schools of Winchester and Eton, and meetings of the Convocation of Clergy. There are other Latin versions of the First Prayer Book. The 1670 version by Durel is the official text, which follows the medieval Sarum rite. In this, the Psalms, Epistles, and Gospels are from the Vulgate, but not the Canticles (for which the existing Latin text was kept). There

[15] It is perhaps unsurprising that this prayer is completely omitted from the Irish *Collectio Rituum* (1960).

[16] The text is available in Bright and Goldsmith (1869); see also <http://justus.anglican.org/resources/bcp/Latin1560/BCP_Latin1560.htm>.

is also a 1713 Latin version by Parsel, without authorization, which uses Castellio's Latin Bible of 1551 instead of the Vulgate (see further chap. 21).

One major scriptural feature distinguishes the liturgy of Cranmer's Second Prayer Book (followed in the 1662 Book of Common Prayer) from the Catholic Mass, namely, the substitution of the *Kyrie Eleison* with the reading of the Ten Commandments from Exodus 20 and Deuteronomy 5. Although the Latin text follows the Vulgate, it has been abbreviated in places. Another strikingly new use of the Bible in the Book of Common Prayer was the "Offertory Sentences": in place of the Catholic focus on the bread and wine at this point, Cranmer recast these as exhortations for the people to be generous in their financial giving, drawing on texts from the Sermon on the Mount, 1 and 2 Corinthians, Galatians, 1 Timothy, and Hebrews, together with Tobit, the Psalms, and Proverbs. Further scriptural verses introduced in the Book of Common Prayer include allusions to Luke 14 and 1 Corinthians 11, as well as the "Comfortable Words" before the confession, which are direct quotations from the Sermon on the Mount and other parts of the New Testament.

Conclusion: Latin Liturgy Today

Although the use of Latin in public worship has declined significantly, along with knowledge of the Latin Bible and the Latin language itself, there is still a place for it, particularly in the Roman Catholic community. Public worship remains the place where the largest number of people encounter the Latin Bible in spoken or sung form (compare chap. 30). For example, the Ordinary Form of the Roman Rite is celebrated daily in Latin in Westminster Cathedral and the London Oratory, and regularly elsewhere. Since the extension of the celebration of rites from the 1962 Missal by Pope Benedict XVI, the use of the older liturgy (the "Extraordinary Form") has become a significant part of the life of the Catholic Church. Celebrations of mass in Latin broadcast by the Vatican or other Catholic networks also serve to increase the availability of liturgical worship in Latin. Moreover, in June 2019, Vatican Radio launched a five-minute weekend news bulletin spoken entirely in Latin, entitled *Hebdomada Papae* ("The Pope's week"): perhaps at some stage, this will involve biblical quotations. The liturgy remains one of the most important contexts for the ongoing use of the Latin Bible, both in terms of the fixed readings from the lectionary and the more flexible treatment of scriptural material which imbues earlier and current rites. Indeed, the history of liturgy in the Western Church is intertwined with the history and reception of the Latin Bible.

Bibliography

Breviarium Romanum. 1931. 13th ed. 4 vols. Ratisbon: Pustet.
Bright, William, and Peter Goldsmith, eds. 1869. *Liber precum publicarum Ecclesiae Anglicanae.* London: Rivington.

Chavasse, Antoine. 1958. *Le sacramentaire gélasien, Vaticanus Reginensis 316. Sacramentaire presbytéral en usage dans les titres romains au VII* siècle*. Paris: Desclée.

Cobb, Peter G. 1992. "The Liturgy of the Word in the Early Church." In *The Study of Liturgy*, edited by Cheslyn Jones, Geoffrey Wainwright, Edward Yarnold, and Paul Bradshaw, 219–29. Rev. ed. London: SPCK.

Collectio Rituum 1960. *Collectio rituum: ad instar appendicis Ritualis Romani, pro omnibus dioecesibus Hiberni*. Dublin: M. H. Gill.

Colunga, Alberto, and Lorenzo Turrado, eds. 1982. *Biblia Sacra iuxta Vulgatam Clementinam, nova editio*. Madrid: Biblioteca de Autores Cristianos.

English Missal. 1958. *The English Missal for the Laity*. 3rd ed. London: Knott.

Harford, G., and M. Stevenson. 1925. *The Prayer Book Dictionary*. Bath: Pitman.

Hope, D. M., and G. Woolfenden. 1992. "The Medieval Western Rites." *The Study of Liturgy*. edited by Cheslyn Jones, Geoffrey Wainwright, Edward Yarnold, and Paul Bradshaw, 264–85. Rev. ed. London: SPCK.

Jungmann, Josef A. 1951–54. *The Mass of the Roman Rite: Its Origins and Development* (= *Missarum Solemnia*). New York: Benziger.

Knox, Ronald A. 1955. *The Holy Bible: A Translation from the Latin Vulgate in the Light of the Hebrew and Greek Originals*. London: Burns and Oates.

Missale Romanum. 2002. *Missale Romanum tertia editio*. Vatican City: Libreria Editrice Vaticana.

Morin, Germain. 1893. *Liber Comicus, sive Lectionarius Missae quo Toletana Ecclesia ante annos mille et ducentos utebatur*. Maredsous: Abbaye.

Newman, John Henry. 1865. *The Dream of Gerontius*. London: Simpkin, Marshall.

Nova Vulgata. 1986. *Nova Vulgata Bibliorum Sacrorum Editio*. 2nd ed. Vatican City: Libreria Editrice Vaticana.

Pecklers, Keith F. 2003. *Dynamic Equivalence: The Living Language of Christian Worship*. Collegeville: Liturgical Press.

Pickstock, Catherine. 1998. *After Writing. On the Liturgical Consummation of Philosophy*. Oxford: Blackwell.

Procter, Francis, and W. H. Frere. 1902. *A New History of the Book of Common Prayer*. London: Macmillan.

Ratcliff, E. C. 1971. "The Eucharistic Institution Narrative of Justin Martyr's First Apology," *Journal of Ecclesiastical History* 22, no. 2: 97–102 .

Roman Missal. 2010. *The Roman Missal*. London: Catholic Truth Society.

Salmon, Pierre. 1944–53. *Le lectionnaire de Luxeuil (Paris, ms. lat. 9427)*. 2 vols. Rome: Abbey of St. Jerome.

Willis, G. G. 1968. *Further Essays in Early Roman Liturgy*. Alcuin Club 50. London: SPCK.

Wordsworth, John, and Henry J. White, eds. 1920. *Novum Testamentum Latine. Editio minor emendata*. Oxford: Clarendon.

....

CHAPTER 30

MUSICAL SETTINGS OF LATIN BIBLICAL TEXTS

....

SIOBHÁN DOWLING LONG

GREGORIAN CHANT

....

Gregorian Chant, also known as plainchant and plainsong, is the monophonic liturgical music of the Roman Rite that has inspired numerous compositions of Western art music through the centuries.[1] It is also known as the "sung Bible," since many of its sacred texts are taken from the Latin Bible (Light and Boynton 2014: 6). From earliest centuries to the present day, it has been used in the recitation of the Mass (Ordinary and Proper), the Requiem Mass (*Missa pro defunctis*), and the Liturgy of the Hours (also known as the Divine Office, the Office, the Canonical Hours, or Breviary). Each of these is considered in sequence in the following sections (for more on the scriptural content of each, see chap. 29).

The Ordinary of the Mass

Most fourteenth-century polyphonic settings of the Ordinary of the Mass from Tournai, Toulouse (incomplete), Barcelona, and the Sorbonne (incomplete) comprise a compilation of settings of the five movements of the Mass.[2] These are the *Kyrie* (cf. Matthew 17:15), *Gloria* (cf. Luke 2:14), *Credo*, *Sanctus* (Isaiah 6:3) and *Benedictus* (Matthew 21:9), and the *Agnus Dei* (cf. John 1:29). Unlike later settings of the Mass, such settings were not unified by any underlying musical theme. In contrast, at some point in the fourteenth century, Guillaume de Machaut composed the first complete and unified polyphonic

---

[1] For a discussion of the beginnings of Gregorian chant and other rites outside of the Roman tradition, see Hiley 2009: 83–120.

[2] More details of Mass settings are given in Saulnier 2009: 19–28 and Hoppin 1978: 116–42.

setting of the Ordinary of the Mass, entitled *Messe de Nostre Dame*. Scored in six movements (including a final *Ite Missa est*), and set for four voice parts, it is regarded as a work of great historical significance: Arlt states that it is "outstanding in terms of artistic merit and belongs among the most impressive works of the Middle Ages" (Arlt 2001: §6). Four of its movements make use of the *Ars nova* isorhythmic technique. The polyphonic Mass is thought to be a precursor of the cyclic mass: the latter became the norm in the fifteenth and sixteenth centuries, and was pioneered by two English composers, John Dunstable (ca. 1390–1453) in his *Missa "Gaudiorum premia"* and his contemporary Leonel Power (d. 1445) in his *Missa "Alma redemptoris mater."* It was later imitated by Guillaume Dufay (1397–1474), Gilles Binchois (1400–60), and their successors.

The Parody Mass was a type of setting that made use of secular tunes in the *cantus firmus*. Well-known examples include Dufay's *Missa Face Ay Pale* and *L'homme armé*. The latter, a French secular song tune from the Renaissance, inspired more than forty mass settings. These include two works by the French composer Josquin des Prez (d. 1521), entitled *Missa L'homme armé super voces musicales* and the *Missa L'homme armé sexti toni* (see Grout and Palisca 1960: 191–98). Over time, certain musical practices such as the more frequent appropriation of secular tunes in sacred music, as well as elaborate polyphonic settings that gave priority to the music rather than the words, resulted in general dissatisfaction at local church councils and the threat of an outright ban on polyphonic music by the Council of Trent.[3] Legend has it that Palestrina's *Missa Papae Marcelli*, with its "linear beauty, contrapuntal mastery, harmonic lucidity and control and clarity of text" saved polyphonic music from the ban (see Lockwood 1957: 342–71; Unger 2010: 293). A gradual decline in the composition of Mass settings around 1600 reflected the more general move away from polyphonic music in favor of new genres.

The seventeenth century witnessed the rise of the polychoral Mass in the compositions of Andrea Gabrieli (d. 1585) and his nephew Giovanni Gabrieli (d. 1612) in Venice and Marc-Antoine Charpentier (1643–1704) in France. This was followed by eighteenth-century masses in the Neapolitan *stilus mixtus*, also known as the Cantata Mass, which mixed old contrapuntal styles in the chorus with a new style of music incorporating solo arias. One of the most famous examples is the Mass in B minor (BWV 232) by Johann Sebastian Bach (1685–1750). In the eighteenth century, "the summit of Catholic church music" (Dyer 2001: §5) was reached in the orchestral masses of Joseph Haydn (1732–1809). A notable example is Haydn's *Missa Cellensis in honorem* (BVM HXXII:5), which represented a new genre of mass composition, namely, the "grand *missa solemnis.*" The *Landmesse* (Country Mass) was another genre of mass composition in Latin that was intended, although not exclusively, for performance by a small number of amateur singers within the setting of a parish church. In contrast, the nineteenth century saw the composition of large-scale symphonic masses, usually intended for performance in secular venues. This continued in the twentieth century, with Latin Mass settings by composers

---

[3] For an account of the conciliar and synodal decrees which prepared the way for the decisions of the Council of Trent on church music, see Fellerer 1953: 576–94.

such as Leoš Janáček (1854–1928), Zoltán Kodály (1882–1967), Igor Stravinsky (1882–1971), Frank Martin (1890–1974), Jean Langlais (1907–91) Benjamin Britten (1913–76), and James Macmillan (1959–).

The Requiem (Missa pro defunctis)

The earliest reference to a polyphonic Requiem features in the will of Guillaume Dufay, although the music is lost. The first extant Requiem is one by Dufay's younger contemporary, the Franco-Flemish composer Johannes Ockeghem (ca. 1410–97). This comprises five movements: *Introitus, Kyrie, Graduale: Si ambulem* (Psalm 22:4 LXX), *Tractus: Sicut cervus* (Psalm 41:1–3 LXX), and *Offertorium*. The *Missa pro Defunctis* was standardized by Pope Pius V after the Council of Trent, in the *Missale Romanum* of 1570 (see chap. 29), and codified to comprise the following eleven movements: (1) Introit (*Requiem aeternam*), (2) *Kyrie*, (3) Gradual (*Requiem aeternam*), (4) Tract (*Absolve Domine*), (5) Sequence (*Dies Irae*), (6) Offertory (*Domine Jesu Christe*), (7) *Sanctus*, (8) *Agnus Dei*, (9) Communion (*Lux aeterna*), (10) Responsory (*Libera me*), and (11) Antiphon (*In paradisum*).

In nineteenth-century music, the liturgical Requiem evolved into a much longer and more elaborate concert piece. In many of these settings, the poetry of the Sequence hymn (*Dies irae–Quantus Tremor–Tuba mirum* [vv. 1–3] and *Rex Tremendae–Confutatis* [vv. 8–9]) featured as "ripe material for dramatic settings" (Chase 2004: 238). The modification or exclusion of certain Requiem texts is a feature of works by composers such as Berlioz, Cherubini, Dvořák, Verdi, Bruckner, and Duruflé. The British composers Benjamin Britten and Howard Goodall each juxtaposed Latin texts from the *Missa pro Defunctis* with English poetry. Britten's *War Requiem* (Op. 66, 1961–62) drew on a selection of Wilfred Owen's war poems (see Dowling Long 2013: 185–216). Goodall's *Eternal Light: A Requiem* (2008) not only employs English poetry and John Henry Newman's hymn "Lead, Kindly Light" alongside Latin excerpts from the Requiem but also sets two passages from Revelation 8 taken from Theodore Beza's sixteenth-century Latin version (see further chap. 21).

Liturgy of the Hours

Many of the Latin psalms and biblical canticles from the services of Matins, Lauds, Prime, Terce, Sext, None, Vespers, and Compline have inspired musical compositions, predominantly for liturgical use. Among these, the three New Testament canticles hold pride of place: the *Benedictus* (Song of Zechariah: Luke 1: 68–79), *Magnificat* (Song of Mary: Luke 1:46–55), and *Nunc Dimittis* (Song of Simeon: Luke 2:29–32). The revolutionary tone of the *Magnificat* made it popular among liberation theologians in Latin America, while Dietrich Bonhoeffer described it as "the most revolutionary Advent hymn ever sung . . . a hard, strong and relentless hymn about the toppling of thrones and the humiliation of lords of this world" (Bonhoeffer 2012: 116). A notable Latin setting is Arvo Pärt's *Magnificat* (1989) for five voices in his *tintinnabuli* style, where the use of dissonance captures the unsettling nature of Mary's revolutionary words.

A discussion of plainchant would be incomplete without a mention of Hildegard of Bingen, whose collection of seventy-seven liturgical chants entitled *Symphonia Harmoniae Caelestium Revelationum* ("Symphony of the Harmony of Heavenly Revelations") is found in two twelfth-century manuscripts, the Dendermonde Codex or Villarenser Codex 9 (ca. 1174/75) and the Riesenkodex (Wiesbaden, Hessische Landesbibliothek, Hs. 2; ca. 1180–85). Many of these were inspired by Latin biblical texts.

LATIN HYMNS AND SEQUENCES

Christian hymns have been composed since apostolic times, with a later development of sequences connected to liturgical gospel reading.

Hymns

The fourth century saw the deployment of hymnody in Latin for the promotion of theological doctrines, such as Augustine's *Psalmus contra partem Donati* ("Psalm against the Faction of Donatus") following an earlier hymn by the Donatist Parmenianus (Van Geest 2016: 22–29; on its performance see Hunink 2011: 397–400). Hilary of Poitiers (d. 367) is identified as one of the first Latin Christians to have composed a "Book of Hymns" (*Liber Hymnorum*).[4] Although many hymns have been attributed to Hilary, only three are regarded as authentic (Feder 1916: 209–16). Another hymn associated with Hilary, *Hymnum dicat turba fratrum*, recounting the life of Jesus in seventy-four lines, was popular in Ireland, and features in the Bangor Antiphonary (Trinity College Dublin, MS 1441). This late eleventh-century "service book" in Latin and Irish comprises forty hymns and canticles that were used in the services of the early Celtic church.

Regarded as the father of Latin hymnody, Ambrose of Milan (340–97) created a model known as the Ambrosian hymn-form, comprising eight stanzas each with four lines of iambic dimeters (i.e., eight syllables per line). Fourteen hymns are generally attributed to Ambrose (Fontaine 1992), many of which have been translated into English and German. Martin Luther's chorale *Nun komm der Heiden Heiland*, used extensively by Johann Sebastian Bach, is an adaptation of Ambrose's hymn *Veni Redemptor gentium* ("Come thou Redeemer of the earth") with a reshaping of its Gregorian melody.

---

[4] This is mentioned in Jerome, *De uiris illustribus* 100. See also Messenger 1953: 1 and Apel 1990: 40.

The great hymn of praise known as the *Te Deum* is traditionally ascribed to Ambrose but is almost certainly from an earlier date.[5] Morin (1894) has suggested that its author was Nicetas of Remesiana (d. post-414). The hymn follows the pattern of the Apostles' Creed, drawing on Isaiah's vision (Isaiah 6) and several Psalms, including Psalm 144 (LXX) (Dowling Long and Sawyer 2015: 233).

Another notable early hymn writer is Prudentius, whose hymn *Corde natus ex parentis* ("Of the Father's heart begotten"), considered to be one of the oldest Christmas carols, includes allusions to the Creation narrative of Genesis 1, the Nativity story, and Alpha and Omega (Revelation 1:8). The Christian poet Sedulius, author of the biblical epic known as the *Carmen Paschale* ("Easter Song"), was also responsible for two hymns: *A solis ortus cardine* ("From the point of the sun's rising") and *Cantemus, socii, Domino* ("Let us sing, companions, to the Lord"). The first of these is an abecedarius, a special type of acrostic in which the first letter of every verse follows the order of the alphabet. There are twenty-three stanzas of iambic dimeter which tell of the life of Christ, including a reference to the Wedding at Cana (John 2). This hymn became extremely well known, being cited by Bede in *De arte metrica* 21, in the *Parker Chronicle* (Cambridge, Corpus Christi College, MS 173, fol. 79v), and in a mediaeval English macaronic carol "A Babe is Born." Later versions include a German translation by Luther and many other settings, from Gilles Binchois in the fifteenth century to James Healey Willan in the twentieth.

Sequences

The Sequence (*Sequentia*), known also as the *Prosa*, is a type of hymn sung on special feast days as an introduction to the proclamation of the Gospel. As the centuries progressed, their further elaboration and greater length contributed to longer and more stylized masses. As part of the reforms promulgated by Pope Pius V, a vast number of sequences were pruned back to a group of four in the *Missale Romanum* of 1570: *Victimae paschali laudes* (Easter); *Veni Sancte Spiritus* (Pentecost), also known as the "Golden Sequence" and inspired by Acts 2:1–13; *Lauda Sion* (Corpus Christi) attributed to Thomas Aquinas; and the *Dies Irae* (as mentioned above in the Requiem Mass), attributed either to Thomas of Celano or Latino Malabranca Orsini, and based on Zephaniah 1:15–16 and Revelation 20:11–15. In 1727, a fifth sequence, which had been removed from the liturgy by the Council of Trent, was revived by Pope Benedict XIII for the two feasts of the Seven Sorrows of Our Lady. This is the *Stabat Mater*, once attributed to the Italian poet, Jacopone da Todi (d. 1306), but now thought to be of thirteenth-century Franciscan origin (Caldwell 2001). Describing the suffering of Mary, the mother of Jesus, at the Crucifixion, its twenty stanzas only have one quotation of the biblical text

---

[5] The Golden Legend (*Legenda aurea*) of Jacobus de Voragine (ca. 1228–98) ascribes the *Te Deum* jointly to Ambrose and Augustine.

(Luke 2:35). All five sequences have enjoyed numerous musical settings by well-known composers across the ages.

FROM TROPES TO PASSIONS

Tropes flourished from the tenth to the twelfth centuries, developing into musical settings of the Passion from the thirteenth century onwards.

Tropes

Tropes are significant in the history of music for their contribution to liturgical drama (see Hoppin 1978: 182–86). Antiphons from the mass were interpolated in three distinct ways: first, as newly composed textual additions to existing plain-chant melismas; second, as musical extensions to existing plainchant melismas or as newly composed melismas; and third, as newly composed textual and musical ma-terial placed before or after the chant. Tropes functioned to enrich and deepen the meaning of the verses of a given antiphon by alluding to or referencing other biblical texts or episodes.

The Introit antiphon for Easter Day, *Resurrexi et adhuc tecum sum* ("I have risen, and still am with you"; Psalm 138:18 LXX) is regarded as one of the most important introits of the Gregorian repertoire. Christians understood it as Christ's words to his Father at his rising—that is, the Resurrection, as seen in the ninth-century *Liber Officialis* of Amalar of Metz. The untroped version of this antiphon comprises three verses of this psalm (vv. 18, 5, 6), each with an alleluia (see fig. 30.1). The antiphon's verse is taken from the same psalm (vv. 1–2): *Domine probasti me, et cognovisti me.* The musical setting is in Mode 4, which was deemed to have mournful characteris-tics appropriate to a context of death: this is expressed in a Latin inscription on one of the capitals of the abbey church of Cluny III: *Succedit quartus simulans in carmine planctus* ("There follows the fourth [mode], which imitates lament in a song"; see Ambrose 2004: 157).

Of all the "*Resurrexi*" tropes, the most famous is the three-line *Quem quaeritis* trope that was first inserted into the *Resurrexi* introit in the early tenth century. This was in-spired by the Gospel accounts of the visit of the three women to the tomb on Easter Sunday morning and their dialogue with the angel guarding the tomb (Matthew 28:1–7; Mark 16:2–7; Luke 24:1–18). Over the passage of time, variations of the *Quem quaeritis* dialogue assumed greater length, being performed on a set (an empty tomb) along with stage directions.[6] Even more elaborate performances and extended versions of

---

[6] These are noted in the *Regulis Concordia*, a foundational document of English Benedictine reform probably written by Aethelwold, Bishop of Winchester (963–84): see Yorke 1997.

FIGURE 30.1. Plainsong Introit for Easter Sunday (*Resurrexi et adhuc tecum*).

Gregorian Missal, 349; Graduale Romanum, 240–41; Liber Usualis, 777–78.

the *Quem quaeritis* became known as the *Visitatio Sepulchri*. In order to enable staged performances during the liturgy, the drama was moved at some point from the beginning of the Mass on Easter Day to the end of Matins (Bjork 1980: 46–49; Shaqrir 2010: 64).

The *Visitatio Sepulchri* also features in the Fleury Playbook (Orléans, BM, 201, ca. 1200), a medieval collection of ten Latin liturgical dramas associated with the Benedictine abbey of St. Benoît-sur-Loire in Fleury. As with the *Quem quaeritis* dialogue, these dramas were intended to be sung, and were notated with neumes on four lines in the style of Gregorian plainchant (compare fig. 30.1). Of the ten music-dramas in the Fleury Playbook, six are inspired by New Testament texts: two focus on the Nativity, the *Officium Stellae* also known as the Play of Herod (*Ordo ad Representandum Herodem*), and the *Ordo Rachelis* depicting the Slaughter of the Innocents (*Interfectio Puerorum*; cf. Jeremiah 31:15, Matthew 2); two treat the Resurrection, a *Visitatio Sepulchri,* and a *Peregrinus* play based on the appearance at Emmaus (Luke 24:13–35); the two others are the Conversion of Paul (*Conversio Sancti Pauli*; Acts 9:1–27), and the Raising of Lazarus (*Resuscitatio Lazari*; John 11:1–44). These plays highlight the pathos of certain female biblical characters, such as Mary Magdalene and her dramatic expression of grief and loss at Christ's death, and the grief of the mothers whose children were massacred by Herod's soldiers. The Play of Herod also contains a version of the *Quem quaeritis* trope, this time an extra-biblical dialogue between the midwives in attendance at the birth of Christ and the shepherds. There is much debate as to whether these plays, including others like them such as the thirteenth-century *Beauvois Danielis,* were precursors to the miracle and medieval mystery plays of later centuries (Petersen 2018; Bjork 1980).

Interest in the *Quem quaeritis* dialogue inspired musical compositions, most notably in the seventeenth and early eighteenth centuries in a genre known as the *Sepolcro*. Performed mainly in Vienna during Holy Week and written by Habsburg court composers, this was similar to an oratorio (see below), but with some exceptions in that it was staged with costumes, scenery, and actions. The composer Antonio Draghi (ca. 1634–1700) composed twenty-six such works, while Emperor Leopold I wrote several *Sepolcri,* including *Il sagrificio d'Abramo* based on Genesis 22, which were intended for performance before a sepulchre. A modern *Visitatio Sepulchri* was composed by the Roman Catholic composer James MacMillan in 1992–93, based on a fourteenth-century text from Notre Dame Cathedral in Paris. Scored for seven soloists, a seven-part chorus, and chamber orchestra, it is set in three sections: an orchestral prelude captures the violence of the Crucifixion, before the *Quem quaeritis* dialogue, which is then followed by a setting of the *Te Deum* (see above).

Passions

Richard Davy's setting of the Passion according to Saint Matthew (Matthew 26–27), composed in 1500–5, is the earliest extant polyphonic setting of the Passion by a known composer (Eton College, MS 178). Here the words of Jesus and the Evangelist are chanted to the traditional Sarum recitation tone, while the words of the *synagoga* (i.e., the dialogues of the disciples, Pilate, and the crowd) are set in polyphony. Anonymous Passions predating that by Davy include two versions in the thirteenth-century *Carmina Burana* (Munich, BSB, Clm 4660), and fourteenth-century Passions according to Matthew and Luke in the Windsor manuscript (London, BL, Egerton MS 3307), both scored for three voices. The genre of the Passion in Latin reached a highpoint in the polyphonic works of the Renaissance composers Orlando di Lassus (see below) and Tomás Luis de Victoria (d. 1611).

Dietrich Buxtehude's *Membra Jesu Nostri* (BuxWV75), a "cycle of seven concerto-aria cantatas" (Snyder 2001) composed in 1689, is another early type of Passion, not unlike an oratorio. It is based on a medieval poem attributed variously to Arnulf of Leuven and Bernard of Clairvaux, which is a meditation on the seven wounds of Christ's crucified body, quoting biblical verses: *Ad pedes* (Nahum 1:15), *Ad genua* (Isaiah 66:12), *Ad manus* (Zechariah 13:6), *Ad latus* (Song of Songs 2:13–14), *Ad pectus* (1 Peter 2:2–3), *Ad cor* (Song of Songs 4:9), and *Ad faciem* (Psalm 30:17 LXX). Also in the seventeenth century, Marc-Antoine Charpentier composed a meditative work on the Passion entitled *Méditations pour la Carême* (H. 380–89), comprising ten *petits motets* for three male voices and continuo, with texts taken from a variety of sources: the Old and New Testaments (nos. 4, 5, 6, 10), Responses (nos. 2, 7), the *Stabat mater* (no. 8) and a poem, *Sola vivebat in antris* (No. 9). The final motet, *Tentavit Deus Abraham*, based on Genesis 22, ends at the point where Abraham takes the knife in his hand to slay Isaac (v. 10). Through the music, and at the dramatic highpoint of this biblical narrative, listeners are encouraged to reflect on Abraham's obedience to God's command.

Other notable Passions in Latin from the seventeenth century include the *Johannespassion* (ca. 1770) by Alessandro Scarlatti, in which the words of Christ, the four-part chorus, the Judas scene, and the death of Jesus are accompanied by strings. In the eighteenth century, Haydn's Seven Last Words of Christ (*Die sieben letzten Worte unseres Erlösers am Kreuze*, Hob. XX:1A; 1786) features a Latin title at the head of each of the seven sonatas in the initial orchestral version to describe the content of each movement (e.g., I. *Pater, dimitte illis, quia nesciunt, quid faciunt* ["Father, forgive them because they know not what they do"], II. *Hodie mecum eris in paradiso* ["Today you will be with me in Paradise], III. "*Mulier, ecce filius tuus*" ["Woman, behold your son"] etc.). The work opens with an *Introduzione* in the doleful tonality of D minor, and closes with *Il terremoto*, a movement based on the earthquake scene from Matthew 27:51. A decade later, he arranged a version of it for soloists, chorus, and orchestra (Hob. XX:2, 1796). Sonata VI, *Consummatum est* ("It is finished"), is initially set in G minor and concludes in G major, pointing perhaps to the joyful news of the resurrection.

Later works on a similar theme include *Via Crucis* by Liszt (S. 53, 1876–79), a retelling of the story of Christ's Passion through the fourteen stations of the cross; the oratorio *Passio et Mors Domini Nostri Jesu Christi Secundum Lucam* (1966) by Krzysztof Penderecki; and *Passio* (1982) by Arvo Pärt based on John 18–19. Although James MacMillan's *St. John Passion* (2007) is mostly in English, the narrative is interpolated with Latin text in each of the sung movements, which the composer claims offers "a more objective and detached reflection" (MacMillan 2008).

MOTETS

The motet developed from the *clausula*, which in turn originated from *organum*, the earliest form of polyphony, in which a plainchant melody was embellished though the addition of one or more vocal lines above or below the original plainchant. The earliest type of *organum*, called "parallel *organum*," consisted of an organal voice (the added voice), called a *duplum*, placed note-against-note at an interval of a fourth or fifth below a voice part singing the original plainchant. In the eleventh century, in what is known as "free *organum*," composers placed the organal voice part above the principal voice part (i.e., the part with the plainchant). By the twelfth century, composers abandoned the note-against-note style for what became known as "melismatic" or "florid *organum*." The principal voice, now called the tenor (from the Latin, *tenere*, "to hold"), held the plainchant, whose rhythm had been altered to sound in long notes which became known as the *cantus firmus*. The voice above sang an elaborate part that moved in shorter, free-flowing unmeasured notes to each syllable of a given word in the chant.

The great flowering of *organa* occurred in the compositions of Léonin (1150–1201) and Pérotin (1160–1230) from the Notre Dame School. Léonin composed many *organa* on chants for church festivals such as Easter and Christmas. One well-known example is the ancient Christmas gradual, *Viderunt Omnes Fines Terrae* based on Psalm 97:2 (LXX) in Léonin's *Magnus Liber Organi de graduali et antifonario*, a work which is no longer fully extant (see Bonds 2003: 66–67). The composers of Notre Dame introduced a new element into their *organa*, namely, the *clausula*. At the point of the melisma in a given chant, a polyphonic section of discant *organum* was composed and inserted in place of the existing melisma. In this section, the composer set the tenor part in a quicker rhythm (triple time) using notes from the chant which this voice part had previously articulated in long extended notes. Many composers, including Pérotin and Léonin, composed *clausulae*, which could then be substituted into the appropriate section of an existing work of *organum*. For example, the Florence manuscript of the *Magnus liber organi* (BML, Pluteus 29.1) has ten different *clausulae* based on the words *in saeculum* of the Gradual *Haec Dies* (from Psalm 117:24 LXX). Singers were free to include in their performance of this chant any one or more of the ten *clausulae*, in whatever combination they desired. Bonds observes that "the impetus for these works was to provide a layer of commentary above the plainchant" (Bonds 2003: 67). Pérotin, who edited the *Magnus Liber Organi*, embellished Léonin's works by adding a third (*triplum*) and fourth (*quadruplum*) voice part above the plainchant.

In the thirteenth century the *duplum* became known as the *motetus*, when some unknown composers substituted text in the vernacular in place of Latin in the *duplum* of an existing *clausula*. These new works were performed outside the liturgy of the Church (see Bonds 2003: 67). Likewise, in polytextual motets of this time, known as Petronian motets, it was not unusual to find a different text assigned to individual voice parts, such as a Latin biblical text in the *motetus* juxtaposed with a French secular text, such as a love poem, in the *triplum*. Many motets from this period are preserved in the Montpellier Codex (Bibliothèque Inter-Universitaire, H196), the Bamberg Codex (Staatsbibliothek Msc. Lit. 115), and the Las Huelgas Codex (Monastery of Las Huelgas near Burgos) (Bonds 2003: 68).

Without doubt, the highpoint of the motet's development was in the late fifteenth and sixteenth centuries, when composers such as Josquin, Tallis, Palestrina, Lassus, and Byrd composed motets based on or inspired by biblical texts. For example, Josquin's *Miserere mei, Deus* for five voices (published in 1519), a setting of Psalm 51 (50 LXX), was one of the most famous settings of this Psalm in the entire Renaissance. The same text inspired other well-known settings, such as Allegri's seventeenth-century version for two choirs of four and five voices. This was performed exclusively by the Papal Choir in the Sistine Chapel in complete darkness at the end of the Tenebrae Service in Holy Week, right up to the 1870s. In the eighteenth and nineteenth centuries, there were many legends in circulation about Allegri's *Miserere* which did as much to inflate the reputation and mystique of the Sistine Chapel choir as they did to promote the reputations of others. Most famous is that of the child prodigy Mozart who supposedly risked excommunication for transcribing the ornamentations (*abbellimenti*) following a visit to the Sistine Chapel in 1770; the work was published for the first time by the travel diarist Charles Burney in London in 1771, whose story was conflated with that of Mozart's illegal transcriptions. Monsignor Giuseppe Baini (1775–1844), the director of the Sistine Chapel Choir, perpetuated the myth about Mozart and Allegri's *Miserere* in the nineteenth century, leading to its incorporation in writings by famous literary figures such as Goethe, Mary Shelley, and Charles Dickens (who failed to gain admission into the Sistine Chapel to hear the *Miserere*), as well as composers Ludwig Spohr, Felix Mendelssohn, Fanny Mendelssohn, and Franz Liszt among others (Bourcy 1993: 278–325).

Giovanni Pierluigi da Palestrina (1525–94) composed hundreds of motets. His fourth book, published in 1584, was entitled *Canticum Canticorum Salomonis*, a cycle of twenty-nine motets for five voices based on the Song of Songs. The sensual biblical text, interpreted allegorically as an expression of Christ's love for the Church or the Soul, is vividly illustrated with word painting. *O Magnum Mysterium* is another well-known motet, taken from the fourth responsorial chant for Matins on Christmas Day, which highlights the mystery of Christ's incarnation among the lowly animals (Habakkuk 3:2; Isaiah 1:3) and the adoration of the Blessed Virgin (Luke 1:28). Popular in the sixteenth century, the text continues to be set today, with recent compositions by Francis Poulenc (1952), Morten Lauridsen (1994), and Judith Bingham (1995).

Orlando di Lassus (1532–94) composed five hundred motets, as well as a setting of the Penitential Psalms (*Psalmi Davidis poenitentiales*), which was the first to set all seven psalms as a single unit. He also wrote two motet cycles based on the Latin text of Job, *Sacrae lectiones novem ex Propheta Iob* (1560; published 1565), and *Lectiones sacrae novem, ex libris Hiob excerptae* (1582), along with two versions of the Book of Lamentations, *Lamentationes Hieremiae Prophetae* (1585). Lassus's swan song, *Le Lagrime di San Pietro* (1594), a collection of twenty spiritual madrigals based on Luigi Tansillo's poetic text in Italian and a concluding motet in Latin, was inspired by Peter's threefold denial of Christ (Luke 22:61–62).

In England at this time, Thomas Tallis (1505–85) and William Byrd (1538–1623) published jointly their *Cantiones sacrae*.[7] This was a major collection of music published

---

[7] Other collections with the same Latin title were produced by various composers from this period. For example, the Protestant composer Heinrich Schütz dedicated a collection of *Cantiones sacrae* consisting of motets and madrigals to a Catholic Prince of Protestant lineage, Hans Ulrich von Eggenberg (1568–1634).

in England in 1575 to celebrate the seventeenth year of the reign of Queen Elizabeth I, with each composer contributing seventeen motets. Two of the motets by Tallis in this collection were *In Jejunio et Fletu*, based on Joel 2:12 and 17 (sung as a Matins response in the Roman Rite for the first Sunday of Lent), and *In Manus Tuas*, based on Christ's last words (Luke 23:46; cf. Psalm 31:5). Tallis's famous *Spem in Alium*, for forty voices, is based on a Matins response from the Sarum rite, adapted from Judith's prayer (Judith 9). The occasion of its composition has not been identified, but it may have been composed for the fortieth birthday of Queen Mary in 1556 or Queen Elizabeth I in 1573. Tallis is also renowned for his Latin setting of the *Lamentations of Jeremiah*.

In his motets telling of the destruction of Jerusalem and the captivity of the children of Israel, William Byrd reflected the suffering and plight of English Catholics during the reigns of Queen Elizabeth I and James I. In 1583, the Flemish composer Philippe de Monte, who was Kapellmeister to the Holy Roman Emperor, sent Byrd a copy of his eight-part setting of the first four verses of *Super Flumina Babylonis* (Psalm 136 LXX), as an expression of concern for a fellow Catholic composer during this time of religious persecution. Byrd responded a year later with an eight-part motet based on the same Psalm, beginning where de Monte had left off: *Quomodo cantabimus* ("How shall we sing the Lord's song in a foreign land?" [Psalm 136:4 LXX]; see Dowling Long and Sawyer 2015: 228). Byrd's last motet, *Plorans Plorabit*, inspired by Jeremiah 13:17–18, was published in book one of *Gradualia ac cantiones sacrae* (1605). In this too, he depicted through expressive word painting Jeremiah's prophecy about the Babylonian exile, as well as Byrd's own lamentation over the state of the Catholic Church in Elizabethan England.

Oratorios and Other Large-Scale Works

Performances of the Oratorio Latino began in Rome, deriving in part from the genre of the *laude.* These were songs that accompanied the "spiritual exercises" of the *Congregazione dell'Oratorio* (also known as the Oratorians) led by Philip Neri in the oratory of San Girolamo della Carità. When Neri and his disciples moved in 1576 to a new church, the Chiesa Nuova (also known as Sancta Maria in Vallicella), the oratories of these two churches became centers for the performances of oratorios which were intended primarily for the edification of the common people. Later on, Giacomo Carissimi (1605–74), the "Father of Oratorio," who was a Jesuit priest and director of music in the German College of Rome, composed oratorios for a noble audience at the *Arciconfraternita del Santissimo Crocifisso.* Carissimi set Latin texts taken primarily from the Old Testament (*Jephte, Abraham et Isaac, Oratorio de Daniele profeta, Ezechias, Diluvium universale, Historia di Job, Jonas, Balthazar, Historia Davidis and Jonathae, Cum reverteretur David, Judicium Salomonis, Vanitas vanitatum, Sponsa canticorum*), although two come from the New Testament (*Historia dei pellegrini di Emmaus* and *Judicium extremum*; see further Dixon 1986).

To take one example, the *Historia di Abraham et Isaac* remains largely faithful to the biblical story of the Sacrifice of Abraham in Genesis 22:1–19 (see Dowling Long 2013: 136–55). The anonymous librettist mirrors the structure of the biblical story by retaining the same plot and sequence of events, as well as two of the biblical narrative's three monologues (vv. 2, 16–17) and one of the three dialogues (vv. 7–8), in addition to selected narrations (vv. 1, 3, 10, 15). Textual omissions, such as Abraham's monologue to the two servants (v. 5), "eliminated the troublesome reference of Abraham's 'deception' of the two servants, protected Abraham's moral integrity, and ensured listeners would imitate only Abraham's moral actions" (Dowling Long 2013: 143). To complete the creative retelling of the story, the librettist incorporated a duet (*O felix nuntium*) following the angel's monologue (v. 12) expressing Abraham and Isaac's mutual delight on hearing the angel's good news, which Carissimi set in the key of G major as a song of jubilation, along with a chorus comprising religious instruction.

Oratorios in Latin were also popular in Bologna, Modena, Florence, and Venice. In Paris, Marc-Antoine Charpentier, a student of Carissimi, also composed oratorios in Latin. The Old Testament themes included *Judicium Salomonis*, *Judith sive Bethulia liberata*, *Historia Esther*, *Mors Saulis et Jonathae*, and *Josue*, while on the New Testament he wrote *In nativitatem Dominum*, *Filius prodigus*, and *Le Reniement de Saint Pierre* ("The Denial of St Peter"). Charpentier also composed many motets and settings of the *Te Deum* and *Magnificat*, into which he incorporated the majestic characteristics of the Versailles grand motet style. Other noteworthy Latin oratorios include *Davidis Pugna et Victoria* by Alessandro Scarlatti (1660–1725), a *Dramma sacrum* for soloists and five-part orchestra inspired by the story of David and Goliath (1 Samuel 17). It concludes with the laments of the Philistines juxtaposed with the rejoicing of the Israelites following the death of Goliath.

From the early nineteenth century, the majority of large-scale religious choral works began to be written in the vernacular, with Latin texts in decline. Two exceptions by French composers are the *Oratorio de Noël* (Op. 12, 1858) by Camille Saint-Saëns, inspired by nine biblical texts from Luke, Psalms, and Isaiah, and Charles Gounod's *Mors et Vita* (1885), dedicated to Pope Leo XIII and drawing on various New Testament texts including lengthy extracts from the book of Revelation. Nevertheless, the twentieth century saw numerous large-scale settings of the Latin texts of the *Requiem*, *Magnificat*, *Te Deum*, and Psalms. Composers such as Benjamin Britten and Vaughan Williams also used Latin texts in other major compositions. For example, Britten inserted the Gregorian Chant *Hodie Christus Natus Est* at the beginning and end of "A Ceremony of Carols" (Op. 28, 1942). *Cantata Misericordium*, also by Britten, sets a Latin text by Patrick Wilkinson which tells the story of the Prodigal Son in humanist terms, without direct reference to Luke 15:11–32. Ralph Vaughan Williams included the *Agnus Dei* in his cantata *Dona Nobis Pacem*, written as a plea for peace in 1936. This combines three poems by Walt Whitman with various Old and New Testament texts. Other large-scale works in Latin include *Beatus Vir* (Op. 38, 1979) by Henryk Górecki (drawing on Psalms 142, 30, 37, 66, and 33), commissioned by Cardinal Karol Wojtyła (later Pope John Paul

II), and the 1967 piece by Krzysztof Penderecki known as the "Auschwitz Oratorio" (*Dies irae: oratorium ob memoriam in perniciei castris in Oświęcim necatorum inexstinguibilem reddendam*) based on quotations from Revelation, 1 Corinthians, and the Psalms, as well as the composer's Latin translations of contemporary Polish and French poetry.

CONCLUSION

From earliest centuries to the present day, singing and the reception of Gregorian Chant in classical and popular music have been partly responsible for keeping the Latin Bible alive in the minds and memories of people down through the centuries, during liturgical celebrations, and in concert halls where Latin biblical texts are regularly performed. Recently, there has been a resurgence of popular interest in Gregorian Chant as performed by religious communities such as the Benedictine Monks of Santo Domingo de Silos and the Cistercian Monks of Stift Heiligenkreuz in Southern Austria, who have sold millions of CDs worldwide. This interest extends to the sell-out performances of the German group "Gregorian," which mixes ancient Gregorian Chant with modern-day hits.[8] There is no doubt that music such as this as well as the many choral masterpieces composed over the last five hundred years will continue to keep the Latin Bible alive in the minds and memories of all who hear it performed, both within and outside the Church.

ACKNOWLEDGMENTS

I wish to acknowledge the support of research funding for this chapter from the College of Arts, Celtic Studies and Social Studies, University College Cork, Ireland.

BIBLIOGRAPHY

Ambrose, Kirk. 2004. "Visual Poetics of the Cluny Hemicycle Capital Inscriptions." *Word and Image* 20, no. 2: 155–64.
Apel, Willi. 1990. *Gregorian Chant*. Bloomington: Indiana University Press.
Arlt, Wulf. 2001. "Guillaume de Machaut." In *Grove Music Online*, edited by Deane Root. Oxford: Oxford University Press. https://doi.org/10.1093/gmo/9781561592630.article.51865.
Bonds, Mark Evan. 2003. *A History of Music in Western Culture*. 3rd ed. Upper Saddle River: Prentice Hall.
Bonhoeffer, Dietrich. 2012. *The Collected Sermons of Dietrich Bonhoeffer*. Translated from German by Douglas D. Scott et al., edited by Isabel Best. Minneapolis: Fortress.

---

[8] See the group's website at https://www.gregorian.de/.

Bourcy, Richard. 1993. "The Mystique of the Sistine Chapel Choir in the Romantic Era." *Journal of Musicology* 11, no. 3: 277–329.

Bjork, David A. 1980. "*Quem quaeritis* and the *Visitatio Sepulchri* and the Chronology of their Early Sources." *Comparative Drama* 41, no. 1: 46–69.

Caldwell, John and Malcolm Boyd. 2001. "Stabat mater dolorosa." In *Grove Music Online*, edited by Deane Root. Oxford: Oxford University Press. https://doi.org/10.1093/gmo/978156 1592630.article.26489 .

Chase, Robert. 2004. *Dies irae. A Guide to Requiem Music.* Lanham: Scarecrow Press.

Dowling Long, Siobhán. 2013. *The Sacrifice of Isaac. The Reception of a Biblical Story in Music.* The Bible in the Modern World 54. Sheffield: Sheffield Phoenix.

Dowling Long, Siobhán, and John F. A. Sawyer. 2015. *The Bible in Music: A Dictionary of Songs, Works and More.* Lanham: Rowman and Littlefield.

Dixon, G. 1986. *Carissimi.* Oxford: Oxford University Press.

Dyer, Joseph. 2001. "Roman Catholic Church Music." In *Grove Music Online*, edited by Deane Root. Oxford: Oxford University Press. https://doi.org/10.1093/gmo/9781561592630.article.46758 .

Feder, A., ed. 1916. *Hilarius Pictaviensis, Tractatus mysteriorum, Collectanea antiariana, Ad Constantium imperatorem, Hymni, Fragmenta.* CSEL 65. Vienna: Tempsky.

Fellerer K. G., and Moses Hadas. 1953. "Church Music and the Council of Trent." *The Musical Quarterly* 39, no. 4: 576–94.

Fontaine, Jacques, et al. eds. 1992. *Ambroise de Milan, Hymnes.* Paris: Cerf.

Grout, D. J., and C. V. Palisca. 1960. *A History of Western Music.* 4th ed. London: Dent & Sons.

Harper, John. 1991. *The Forms and Orders of Western Liturgy from the Tenth to the Eighteenth Century. A Historical Introduction and Guide for Students and Musicians.* Oxford: Clarendon.

Hayburn, Robert F. 1979. *Papal Legislation on Sacred Music: 95 A.D. to 1977 A.D.* Collegeville: Liturgical Press.

Hiley, David. 2009. *Gregorian Chant.* Cambridge Introductions to Music. Cambridge: Cambridge University Press.

Hoppin, R. H. 1978. *Medieval Music.* London: W. W. Norton.

Hunink, Vincent. 2011. "Singing Together in Church. Augustine's Psalm against the Donatists." In *Sacred Words: Orality, Literacy and Religion*, edited by A. P. M. H. Lardinois, J. H. Blok, and M. G. M. van der Poel, 389–403. Leiden: Brill.

Light, L. and S. Boynton, 2014. *Sacred Song. Chanting the Bible in the Middle Ages and Renaissance.* New York: Les Enluminures.

Lockwood, Lewis H. 1957. "Vincenzo Ruffo and Musical Reform after the Council of Trent." *The Musical Quarterly* 43, no. 3: 342–71.

MacMillan, James. 2008. *St John Passion: Composer's Notes.* Online https://www.boosey.com/cr/music/James-MacMillan-St-John-Passion/49500.

Messenger, Ruth Ellis. 1953. *The Medieval Latin Hymn.* Washington, DC: Capital.

Morin, Germain. 1894. "Nouvelles recherches sur l'auteur du Te Deum." *Revue bénédictine* 11: 49–77, 337–45.

Petersen, Nils Holger. 2018. "Liturgical Drama and Mystery Plays II. Music." In *The Encyclopedia of the Bible and its Reception*, edited by Christine Helmer, Steven L. McKenzie, Thomas Römer, Jens Schröter, Barry Dov Walfish, Eric Ziolkowski. Vol. 16: 868–71. Berlin: De Gruyter.

Saulnier, Daniel. 2009. *Gregorian Chant: A Guide to the History and Liturgy.* Brewster: Paraclete Press.

Shaqrir, Iris. 2010. "The *Visitatio Sepulchri* in the Latin Church of the Holy Sepulchre in Jerusalem." *Al-masāq* 22, no. 1: 57–77.

Snyder, Kerala J. 2001. "Buxtehude, Dietrich." In *Grove Music Online*, edited by Deane Root. Oxford: Oxford University Press. https://doi.org/10.1093/gmo/9781561592630.article.04477.

Smither, H. E. 1987. *A History of the Oratorio. Vol. 3. The Oratorio in the Classical Era*. Oxford: Clarendon.

Unger, Melvin P. 2010. *Historical Dictionary of Choral Music*. Lanham, Plymouth: Scarecrow.

Van Geest, Paul J. J. 2016. "Space in Coercive Poetry. Augustine's Psalm against the Donatists and his Interpretation of the Fear of God in *Enarrationes in Psalmos*." *Perichoresis* 14, no. 2: 21–37.

Yorke, Barbara, ed. 1997. *Bishop Aethelwold: His Career and Influence*. Cambridge: Boydell and Brewer.

CHAPTER 31

....

LATIN BIBLES: MATERIALITY AND ART HISTORY

....

MICHELLE P. BROWN

MATERIALITY, MAKING, AND MEANING
....

THE materiality of the Latin Bible reflects the broader practices of post-Roman Europe and the Near East. Local traditions were enhanced by the use of distinctive scripts (Brown 1999), decoration, and bindings or containers. Sacred codices became cultural icons and could be worn, brandished, visited, and venerated—as well as read (Watts 2013; Brown 2006a, 2011). Such books were designed to impress, for it probably seemed natural to patrons to accord the Word of God the same honor as traditionally accorded to the emperor, signaled by the same visible consumption of resources. By the 380s Jerome was already complaining that Christian patrons were spending money on ostentatious purple-dyed manuscripts of Scripture written in gold and silver inks, instead of using it for the good works advocated therein (*Epistula* 22). At the same time, cycles of narrative imagery were starting to convey the new religion's message (Brown 2006a).

Treasure bindings survive from Byzantine, Armenian, Irish, Anglo-Saxon, Carolingian, Ottonian, and High Medieval contexts. Particularly important examples in Latin tradition include the Lombardic Theodolinda Gospels from around 600 CE and the Lindau Gospels, begun under Insular influence in eighth-century Austria. Roman consular diptychs and Early Christian ivories sometimes adorned early medieval bindings, or contemporary covers were carved from walrus ivory, such as the Carolingian Lorsch Gospels cover (Needham 1979; van Regemorter 1992; Lowden 1997, 2012; van Regemorter 1992). Book shrines are found in Eastern tradition from the sixth century onward, and this practice was soon transmitted to the West. This is shown by the Lough Kinale book shrine (Old Irish *cumdach*), made in Ireland around 800. Its dimensions and its translation into metal of a cross-carpet page design suggest that it once contained a gospel book, yet it was designed never to open because the book within had become the relic of a founding saint (Kelly 1994).

Sacred books were displayed at shrines and high altars, sometimes being carried on circuit to proclaim the authority and property ownership of a religious community.

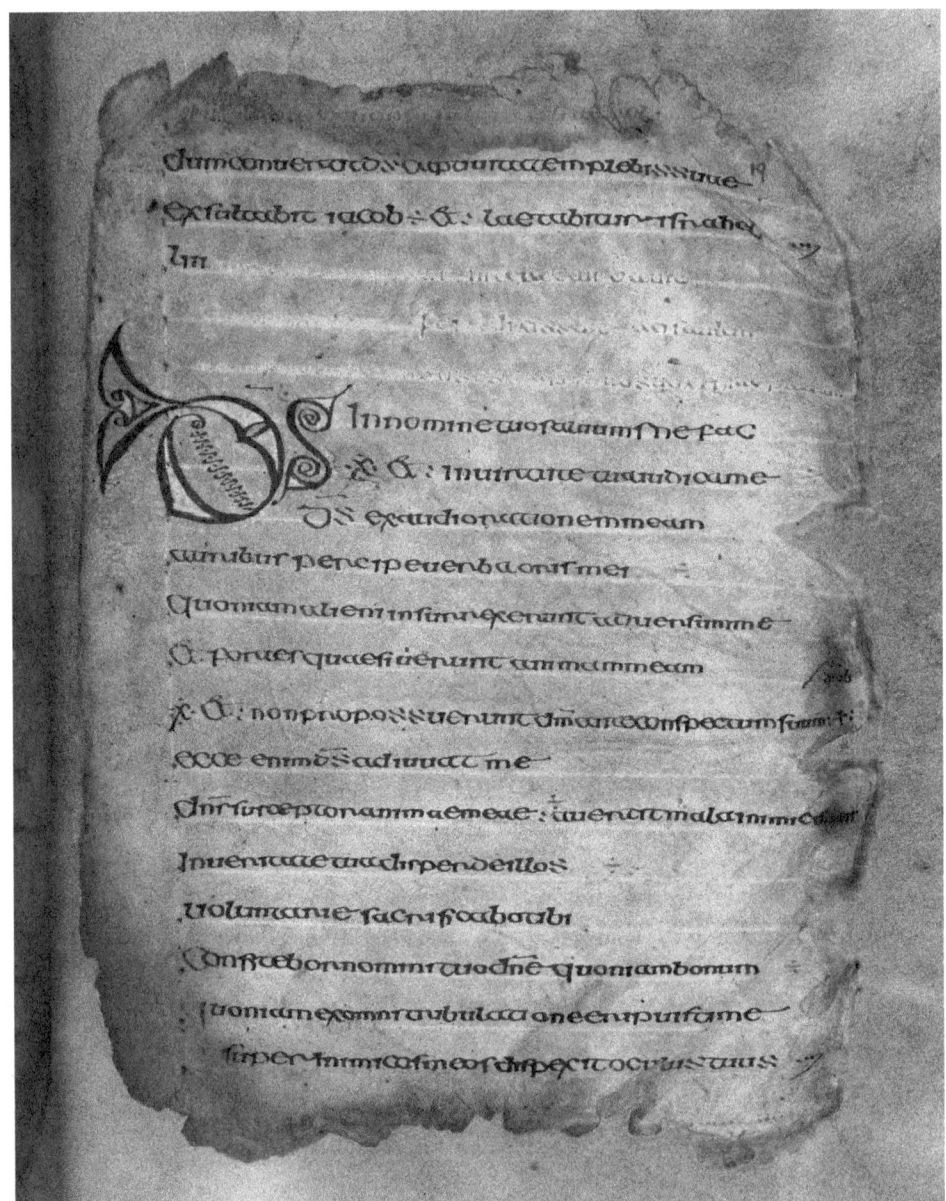

FIGURE 31.1. The Cathach (Royal Irish Academy MS 12.R.33, fol. 19r). Ireland, ca. 560–600. By permission of the Royal Irish Academy © RIA.

Later in the Middle Ages, a Psalter long thought to be by St. Columba's own hand, gained its name, the "Cathach" or "battler" of Columcille, from the fact that its hereditary keepers carried it before them into battle (see fig. 31.1).[1] Names were given to two

---

[1] The naming of books and their being carried into battle was also an Armenian practice: see Nersessian 2001; for the Cathach, see also chap. 10.

other Irish Latin biblical codices, the "Domnach Airgid" and "The Garland of Howth." A seventh-century copy of the Gospel according to John, now known as the Cuthbert Gospel, exerted its authority from its concealment within the coffin of St. Cuthbert, while the Lindisfarne Gospels, made in 715–20 CE, served as his cult's book of the high altar. Historic books were used for the swearing and enacting of legal transactions, including the freeing of slaves. The earliest recordings of such manumissions were written in the margins and decorated pages of the Chad Gospels in mid ninth-century Wales and in the Bodmin Gospels in early tenth-century Cornwall, and are among the earliest examples of the written vernaculars of those regions. It seems fitting that, as embodiments of God incarnate, such books played a role in places of public assembly and helped transform society (Brown 2003, 2008b).

Narrative and Illustration

In a letter to Bishop Serenus of Marseilles written around the year 600, Pope Gregory the Great censured the destruction of images on the grounds that:

> It is one thing to adore a picture, another to learn what is to be adored through the history told by the picture. What Scripture presents to readers, a picture presents to the gaze of the unlearned. For in it even the ignorant see what they ought to follow, in it the illiterate read.[2]

Gregory thereby opened the door to the use of figural imagery for sacred themes in the West, at a time when idolatry was a topic of debate (Chazelle 1990; Brown 2011). In 599 CE, he sent emissaries to the Greek Orthodox monastery of St. Catherine's, Sinai, home of some of the greatest early icons, which may have shaped his views (Brown 2018a). The St. Augustine Gospels, thought to have accompanied Augustine of Canterbury's mission from Rome to England in 597 CE (Brown 2016), are highly didactic in their display of narrative scenes from the Life of Christ, arranged in strips and set like an eastern iconostasis screen or the carved doors of the Roman basilica of St. Sabina, flanking the portrait of St. Luke as an antique author (see fig. 31.2).

This mode of figural narrative was perpetuated a century later by Benedict Biscop, founder of the influential Northumbrian monasteries of Wearmouth and Jarrow in 674 and 682, of whom Bede relates that:

> He brought back many holy pictures of the saints to adorn the church of St Peter he had built . . . Thus, all who entered the church, even those who could not read, were able, whichever way they looked, to contemplate the dear face of Christ and His

---

[2] Gregory the Great, *Epistula ad Serenum Massiliensem episcopum* (PL 77: 1128C); translation from Ayerst and Fisher 1977: 101–2.

FIGURE 31.2. Image of Luke in the St. Augustine Gospels (Cambridge, Corpus Christi College MS 286, fol. 129v). Italy, sixth century. By permission of the Parker Library, Corpus Christi College, Cambridge.

saints, even if only in a picture, to put themselves more firmly in mind of the Lord's Incarnation and, as they saw the decisive moment of the Last Judgement before their very eyes be brought to examine their conscience with all due severity.[3]

Around 685 CE, he returned from his fifth visit to Rome with

a large supply of sacred books and no less a stock of sacred pictures than on previous journeys. He brought back paintings of the life of Our Lord for the chapel of the Holy Mother of God which he had built within the main monastery, setting them, as its crowning glory, all the way round the walls. His treasures included a set of pictures for the monastery and church of the blessed apostle Paul, consisting of scenes, very skilfully arranged, to show how the Old Testament foreshadowed the New . . . the Son of Man up on the cross was paired with the serpent raised up by Moses in the desert.[4]

The images displayed at Wearmouth-Jarrow visually summarized the relationship between the Old and New Testaments, illustrated by means of didactic typology, a genre favored by Jerome and Bede (Brown 2003).

EARLY ILLUMINATED BIBLICAL TEXTS IN THE WEST

"Illumination" has come to embrace not only decoration made to scintillate by the incorporation of gold but visual ornamentation and illustration, which assist in navigating and articulating the text, didactically narrating it, and penetrating deeper into its meaning.[5] Some of the finest illustrated early Christian books are copies of the Greek Septuagint: the early fifth-century Cotton Genesis, and the Vienna Genesis made in Syria in the first half of the sixth century. The images in these two manuscripts contain extratextual details derived from popular elaborations and Jewish commentaries which led to the postulation of a Judaeo-Hellenic background for such cycles, comparable to the biblical frescoes painted in 244 CE in the synagogue at Dura Europos in Syria (Levin 1985). It is likely, given Jerome's criticism of decorated copies of Scripture, that deluxe Latin manuscripts also existed, as seen in the Quedlinburg Itala fragment. These six folios from Samuel and Kings, made in Rome during the 420s–30s feature four illusionistically painted images per page, some illustrating minor episodes, suggesting that the cycle would have been immense (see also chap. 8).

---

[3] Bede, *Vita Beatorum Abbatum* 6 (ed. Plummer [1896: 369]); see Farmer 1983: 194.
[4] Bede, *Vita Beatorum Abbatum* 9 (ed. Plummer [1896: 373]).
[5] On Late Antique, Early Christian and Early Medieval illumination and its application to the biblical books, see, for example, McKendrick and Doyle (2007); Kauffmann (2003); Lowden (2012, 1997); de Hamel (2001, 1997); Webster and Brown (1997); Nordenfalk (1988); Pächt (1986); and Weitzmann 1970.

Cycles of illustrations in the Gospels are also seen first in Eastern tradition, as seen in the Syriac Rabbula Gospels, the first dated illuminated manuscript, whose colophon states that it was made at Beth Zagba in 586 CE (Weitzmann 1970). Contemporary with this are the Greek Rossano Gospels and the Codex Sinopensis (or Sinope Gospels), both also copied on purple parchment in the sixth century. These images prefigure scenes in the margins of tenth- and eleventh-century Byzantine Psalters, while the typological juxtaposition of prefatory cycles of scenes from the lives of King David and of Christ in later Anglo-Saxon and medieval Gothic Psalters, such as the Tiberius Psalter (see fig. 31.3) and the Oscott Psalter, is probably indebted to them in part (Brown 2006a).

Western literacy levels contracted in the post-Roman period and book production generally shifted from secular scribes and publishers to the Church. Cassiodorus's founding of the Vivarium, devoted to studying, editing, and copying Scripture, effectively created a monastic publishing house. Cassiodorus set out a series of influential injunctions to scribes in his *Institutiones*, and his various editions of the Bible included illustrations and diagrams in late Antique style, a recollection of which may be preserved in the Codex Amiatinus.[6] To help preserve cultural and political identity, the Lombards fostered their own Beneventan minuscule script along with a Germanic love of zoomorphic ornament. The eighth-century Codex Beneventanus, a splendid gospel book with canon tables set within classical marble columns resembling those of Byzantium, is a tribute to their book production and perpetuation of late Antique elements in combination with the robust "barbarism" of the North (Brown 1999, 2006a). The Visigoths likewise preserved their minuscule script and ornament in the face of Islamic occupation (Brown 1999). The deployment of script, illumination, codicological practices, binding, and textual recension could all be imbued with geoethnic, political, and ecclesiological meaning.

Ireland received Christianity during the fifth century and significantly developed the arts of the book. Irish copyists introduced word separation and systematic punctuation to clarify legibility and began enlarging and decorating initials to mark text divisions, reinventing a hierarchical system of scripts which, like that of the Roman Empire, was based on form and function: Insular half-uncial script was developed for Scripture, while calligraphic minuscule was used for less formal purposes (Brown 1999). Their enthusiastic recognition of this potential gave the illuminated book much of its distinctive appearance and apparatus, and stemmed from an interest in the use of graphic devices to enhance legibility during the process of embracing written (as opposed to a sophisticated oral) literacy and of learning Latin as a foreign language. The Anglo-Saxons, whom the Irish helped to convert, added their own artistic motifs, including zoomorphic interlace, and further developed the range of scripts, under renewed influence from Rome via centers such as Canterbury and Wearmouth-Jarrow.

---

[6] Part of Cassiodorus's library is thought to have been incorporated into that of the monasteries of Wearmouth-Jarrow, responsible for this eighth-century pandect (Brown 2003; Meyvaert 1996).

FIGURE 31.3. The Harrowing of Hell in the prefatory cycle of images in the Tiberius Psalter (British Library, Cotton MS Tiberius C.VI, fol. 14r). Canterbury, mid-eleventh century. © British Library Board.

FIGURE 31.4. King David in the Vespasian Psalter (London, British Library, Cotton MS Vespasian A.I, ff. 30v–31r). Kent, 720s. © British Library Board.

The appearance of the Insular book was striking, highly distinctive, and indebted to varied cultural sources (Webster and Brown 1997; Brown 2006a; see also chap. 8). Gospel books such as the Book of Durrow (perhaps made on Iona around the 670s), the Lindisfarne Gospels (715–20), and the Book of Kells (probably Iona ca. 800) blended influences from Celtic, Germanic, European, Byzantine, Coptic, and Near Eastern art. The word explodes across the page as an iconic image in their Incipit pages, carpet pages recall their Coptic counterparts and prayer mats (sometimes used in northern Europe as well as the Middle East), arcaded Canon Tables evoke church chancels, and Evangelist miniatures feature author portraits or their apocalyptic symbols. Iconic and aniconic responses are combined in ways that are sensitive to the ongoing debate concerning images of the divine. Hierarchies of initials, line-fillers, and runover symbols articulate text layout. The Insular "historiated" (storytelling) initial, integrating text and image, first appeared in the Kentish Vespasian Psalter made in the 720s, which favors modeled late antique-style figures. It also features a full-page image of King David, depicted as a contemporary ruler (see fig. 31.4). Other miniatures, in works such as the Codex Amiatinus and the Book of Kells, adopt a characteristic multivalent approach in which literal, narrative meaning is complemented by layers of allegorical and exegetical meaning (Brown 2003, 2011, 2016).

ICONIC AND ANICONIC REPRESENTATION AND ICONOCLASM

The highly visual nature of the way in which the word is adorned in the Lindisfarne Gospels is the key to its enduring impact. Its mode of visual discourse is largely ornamental and symbolic rather than narrative, yet wonder, complexity, and technical awe are every bit as impressive to a newly converted audience as visible consumption of wealth. It is iconic in its aniconic visual language. It is perhaps no coincidence that, at the time of its production, idolatry was still being actively discussed not only in Judaic and Islamic but also in Christian circles: the Iconoclast controversy prevailed in Byzantium from the 720s until 787 CE, with only the book and the cross being acceptable public manifestations of belief.

The iconographies of the Virgin and the Crucifixion also began to grow in popularity during this period, encapsulating the points of greatest intersection between the human and divine wills. Originating in the East, they rapidly spread westward, inspiring Insular responses such as the Virgin and Child in the Book of Kells and the Durham Gospels Crucifixion. The iconic stylized Eastern figuralism of the Durham Gospels contrasts with its aniconic counterparts, such as the cross carpet pages in the Lindisfarne Gospels (see fig. 31.5). The aniconic and oblique iconographic solutions adopted to depicting the divine in the face of such controversy was a distinctive, subtle aspect of the Insular approach to imagery.

FIGURE 31.5. St Luke's Gospel cross-carpet page and Incipit page. The Lindisfarne Gospels (British Library, Cotton MS Nero D.iv, ff. 138v–139r). Holy Island, Northumbria, ca. 715–20. © British Library Board.

The Lindisfarne Gospels' evangelist portraits also indicate concern with such debates. They sit like framed Eastern icons on the page, their captions in Greek transliterated into Latin lettering. Two are of a Byzantine bearded type, while the two youthful clean-shaven evangelists rely upon Roman models. This is a theologically inspired choice. The bearded Matthew and Luke symbolize in exegesis the human aspects of Christ—incarnation and sacrifice—and are mortal and aging, while the clean-shaven Mark and John represent kingship or Resurrection and Second Coming and are divine and eternally youthful. This forms a neat visual summary of the adherence of the Insular Church to international Orthodoxy, and a refutation of the Monothelite controversy as to how Christ could be simultaneously both human and divine: a meeting in 679 CE at Hatfield near London had preceded the debate on this topic at the Sixth Ecumenical Council in Constantinople in 681 CE (Brown 2017).

The Carolingian stance on imagery perpetuated the iconoclasm debate. The official response took the form of the *Libri Carolini* compiled by Theodulf of Orleans. Coming from iconoclastic Mozarabic Spain, Theodulf was extremely cautious about images but found space for creative collaboration with the pro-image Alcuin of York, active in Tours. The result was a statement in which the primacy of the word was asserted over images which, although permitted, were deemed to possess no inherent holiness, and their use as icons was proscribed. Copies of Scripture produced from this time until around 810 CE (when the Lorsch Gospels once more dared to feature an image of Christ in Majesty) are noticeably devoid of pictures of the divine, preferring biblical illustrations or evangelist portraits (Kessler 1977). This left ample scope for the development of Carolingian and subsequently Ottonian ruler iconography, which was often set within biblical image cycles, as seen in several of the Alcuin Bible pandects from Tours, notably the Bible of San Paolo fuori le Mura, the Second Bible of Charles the Bald, and the Moutier-Grandval Bible (fig. 31.6; Mutherich and Gaehde 1976; Kessler 1977; Mayr-Harting 1999).

MULTIVALENCE

In medieval art, visual symbols, motifs, and iconographies were often used as a trigger to unlock other points of reference which enabled a deeper level of "reading" and mnemonic retention. This functioned rather like hypertextuality and intertextuality in the digital age. Such reading strategy was only as deep as the pool of knowledge to which the audience had access and would have varied between viewers. The key to reading much medieval imagery lay in the principle of multivalence: why settle for the literal, meaning when you can also explore other allegorical meanings (Brown 2011, 2016)?

The famous "Ezra" miniature in Codex Amiatinus may accordingly be read on multiple levels (see fig. 31.7). Not only does it offer a narrative illustration of the great preserver of the Judaic Scriptures, Ezra the Scribe, committing them to writing from memory following the destruction of the Temple by the Babylonians, but it also has a

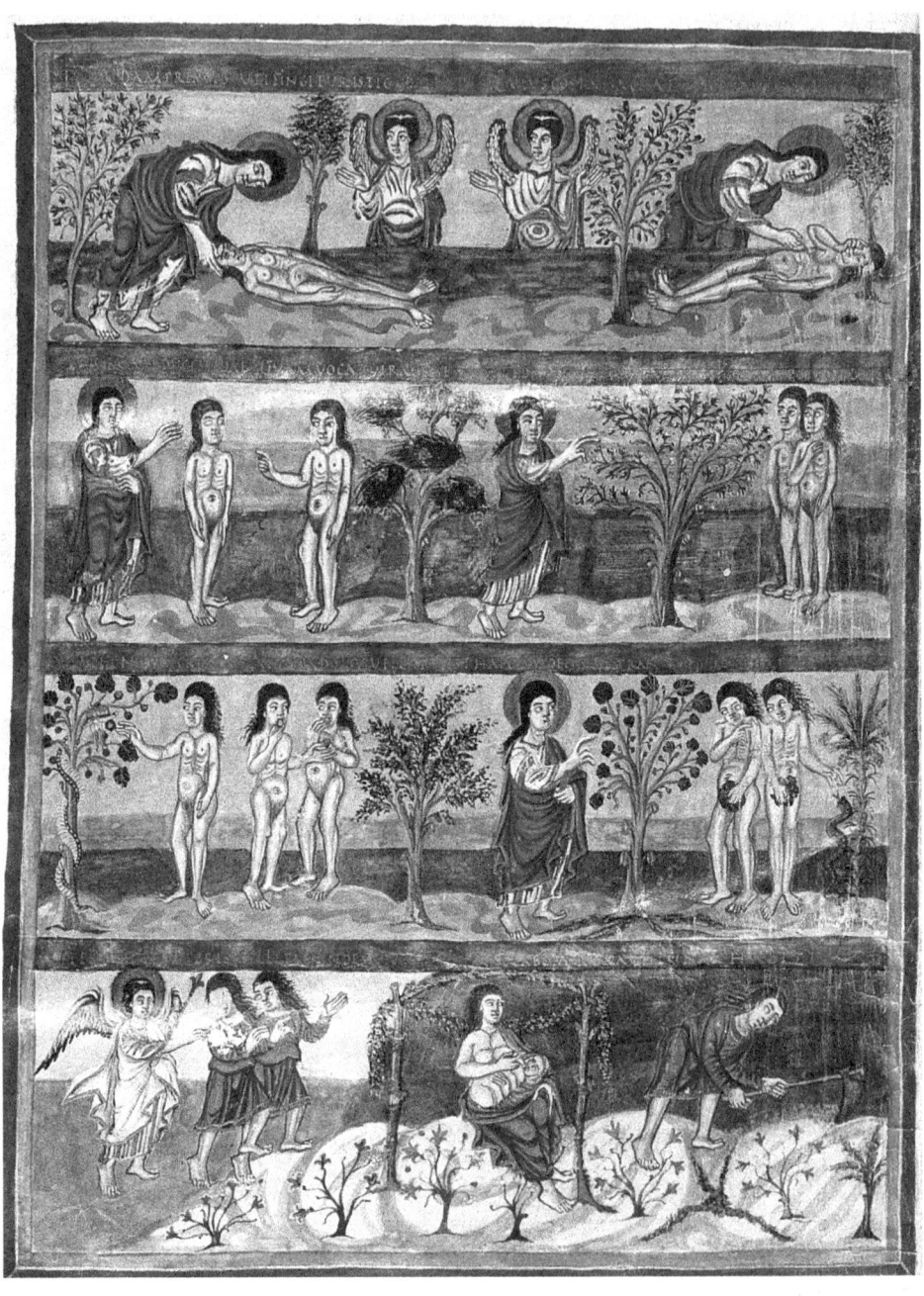

FIGURE 31.6. The Creation and Fall of Adam and Eve. The Moutier-Grandval Bible (British Library, Add. MS 10546, f. 5v). Tours, 830s–40s. © British Library Board.

FIGURE 31.7. Ezra the Scribe: A sacred *figura* of biblical transmission. Codex Amiatinus (Florence, Biblioteca Medicea Laurenziana, MS Amiatino 1, f. Vr). Wearmouth-Jarrow, ca .700–16. Reproduced with permission of MiBAC. Further reproduction by any means is prohibited.

multivalent image depicting Cassiodorus, signaled by the inclusion of the *armarium* containing the *novem codices*, his nine-volume edition of the Bible. The names of scriptural writers inscribed on the spines of these books extends the scope of the image further, turning it into an homage to the ongoing process of transmission, rediscovery, and emendation of sacred text inspired by the Spirit. The central figure of the scribe is thus Ezra, Cassiodorus, Jerome, other early biblical editors, Ceolfrith, Bede, and others who worked on the Ceolfrith Bibles. It is also an open invitation to those who look upon it to perpetuate the process of transmission (Meyvaert 1996; Brown 2017). Those responsible for the Ceolfrith Bibles were not attempting "authorized" editions, but authoritative ones, drawing together the best sources they could find. It would have been anathema to them to view their work as the "last word," for the process of transmission and exploration was divinely inspired and perpetual.

John Cassian, a founding figure of Eastern and Western monasticism, advocated the deployment of three sorts of spiritual knowledge in order to understand Scripture: allegory, anagoge, and tropology (see also chap. 9 and chap. 17). History deals with real past events which have a literal meaning, whereas allegory relates to prefigured mysteries. Anagoge goes beyond such mysteries to penetrate the secrets of heaven, while tropology interprets all three for the moral edification and instruction of the present. This approach was also favored by Jerome and Gregory the Great, with the latter observing:

> First we lay the foundation of history, then through typical signification we build the fabric of the mind into a stronghold of faith; last we clothe the edifice through the grace of morality, as if with overlaid colour. Clearly what else must the words of Truth be believed to be except food for rebuilding the mind?[7]

The same method was adopted by Bede in his work on rhetoric, *De schematibus et tropis*. Such layered meaning might be difficult for others than learned scholars to "read," although the taste for riddles and conundrums probably inclined people toward it. Art, however, rendered it more accessible. In terms of visual exegesis, it meant that the representation of historical episodes in Scripture (*figurae*) should be interpreted and imbued with Christian moral meaning.

An example of the Insular espousal of this threefold approach can be found in the Temptation of Christ in the Book of Kells (fig. 31.8; see Brown 2003, 2016). At a literal level, this illustrates the gospel passage, but it is not placed near it and can thus also be interpreted as a sacred *figura* (the representation of Scripture's "shapes"), embodying the theological concept of the Communion of Saints. Christ is the head of the Church, flanked by onlookers symbolizing the Church Militant (those believers currently alive), while angels representing the Church Triumphant (those already in heaven) hover above; the Church Expectant (those awaiting liberation from hell/limbo) inhabit a lower realm, presided over by Osiris, God of the Dead. The moral injunction is for the

---

[7] Gregory the Great, *Moralia in Iob* (CCSL 143; I.3.110–15).

FIGURE 31.8. The Temptation of Christ in the Book of Kells (Dublin, Trinity College MS 58, fol. 202v). Ireland, ninth century. By permission of the Board of Trinity College Dublin.

faithful to participate in the unity of eternal communion and do the work in the world during life.

Aquinas later taught that humans became literate with the help of mental images (*phantasmata*) stored while reading (*Quaestio* 85; see Buettner 1992: 79). Gregory the

Great's approach to the didactic and mnemonic role of imagery (cited above) presaged this thirteenth-century scholastic view, and the Anglo-Saxons and Celts were likewise no strangers to *phantasmata*, even if their images were traditionally received aurally: their literatures are replete with them.

Balancing *Traditio* and *Innovatio*

Around the year 1000, the figural narrative trend peaked in Anglo-Saxon England with extensive picture cycles in vernacular books such as Junius 11 and the Old English Hexateuch, with their Genesis and Exodus cycles. In Latin tradition, this is seen in the Harley Psalter (fig. 31.9), whose complex illustrations also serve as picture poems, forming visual tropes on the cycle of illustrations in its exemplar, the Carolingian Utrecht Psalter made in the diocese of Reims in the 830s (van der Horst 1996; Brown 2016). Such pictorial narratives are ultimately indebted to Early Christian cycles. Aelfric, the Anglo-Saxon homilist, instructed the lay (possibly female) patron of his Old English paraphrase of the Hexateuch how to excavate the hidden treasures of Scripture by employing spiritual understanding: examples of this were provided in a cycle of 550 illustrations, such as Joseph saving the people from starvation being a type of Christ who saves humanity from the hungers of hell.

The challenges of producing an extensive integrated cycle of images and text engrossed the Christ Church Canterbury scriptorium for two centuries from the time it began work on the Harley Psalter in the early eleventh century (van der Horst 1996). Usually the scribes undertook the initial layout of the page, but the primacy of the illustrations here led the illuminators to do so. However, the version of the Psalms used in the Carolingian Empire was the Gallican Psalter, while that in Canterbury was the Roman, so the words differed, as did the script: the version of caroline minuscule employed in England was considerably smaller than the Utrecht Psalter's classicizing rustic capitals. The scribes rebelled and took over the process of ruling the pages, as they could not fit the words into the spaces, at which point the artists floundered. The book remained unfinished, although the scriptorium continued to work on it and produced several other versions, notably the Romanesque mid-twelfth-century Eadwine Psalter. The latter applied the image cycle to a complex comparative and glossed text layout, containing three Latin versions of the Psalms, with Old English, and Anglo-Norman translations.

The process of producing these deluxe illuminated manuscripts with integrated image and text cycles proved very instructive (Kauffmann 2003). While the *traditio* of the scenes in such books may have been based upon early Christian cycles, it also permitted a degree of *innovatio*. Iconographic details could be tweaked to bestow new theological emphases or details of contemporary dress and artifacts, thereby siting the contemporary Anglo-Scandinavian population within the timeless biblical landscape. For example, Noah's Ark in the Old English Hexateuch is depicted as a dragon-prowed Viking longship (Brown 2016).

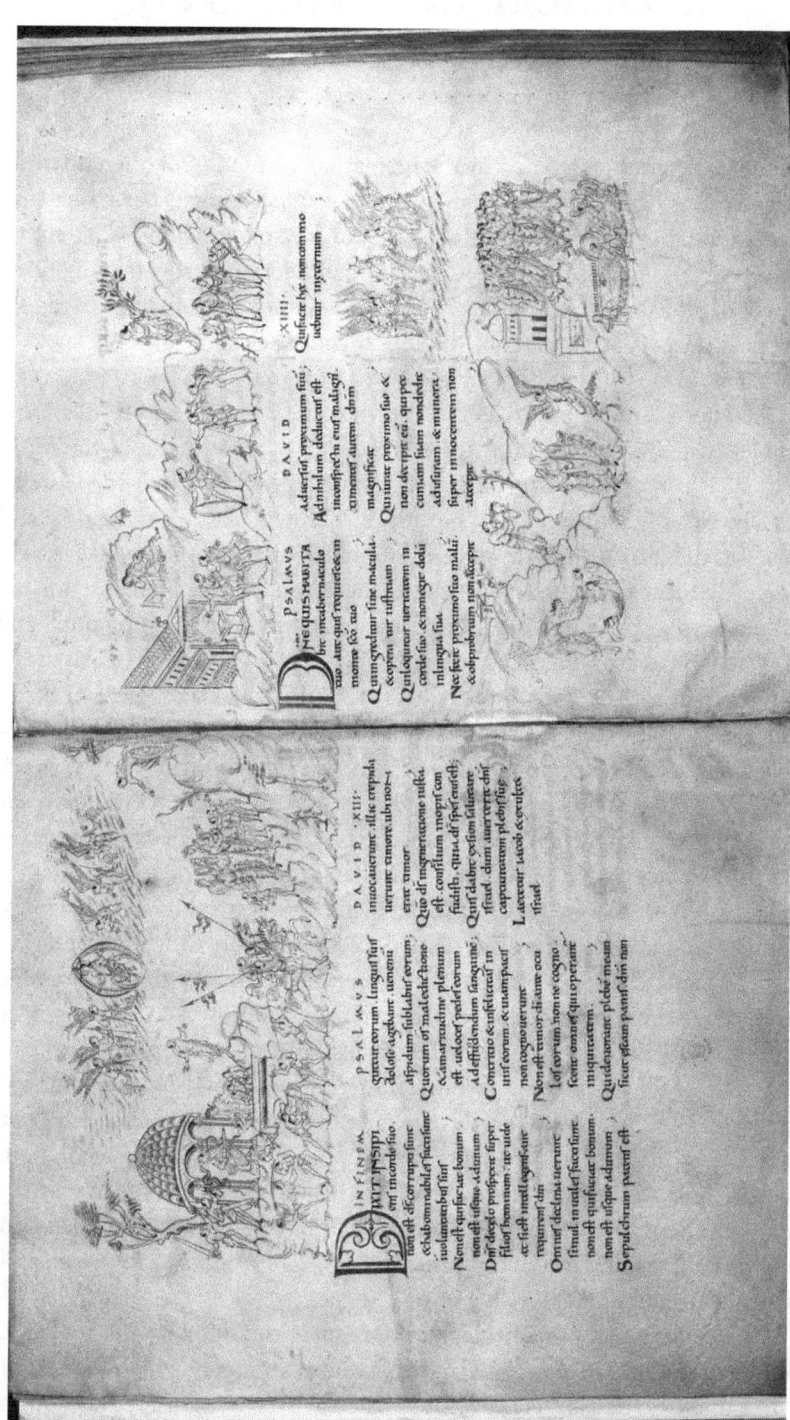

FIGURE 31.9. Psalms 13, 14, and 15. The Harley Psalter (British Library, Harley MS 603, ff. 7v–8r). Christ Church Canterbury, early eleventh century. © British Library Board.

LITURGICAL AND DEVOTIONAL
MANUSCRIPTS

Biblical volumes were supplemented by the increased production of often luxurious liturgical manuscripts from the ninth century onward. Gospel books gave way to gospel lectionaries, and readings from Scripture were incorporated into books used in the enactment of services, such as the Carolingian Drogo Sacramentary, the Anglo-Saxon Benedictional of St. Ethelwold, and the Ottonian Sacramentary of Henry II, as well as deluxe personal gospels and psalters (Mutherich and Gaehde 1976; Kauffmann 2003; Mayr-Harting 1999).

During the later eleventh and twelfth centuries, the large-format Romanesque or Atlantic Bibles, usually divided into two or three parts, were made in the monastic scriptoria of the Rhine and Meuse (see chap. 13). Fine examples include the Floreffe and Stavelot Bibles. Heavily illustrated and beautifully painted versions were also made in England, such as the Bury, Lambeth, and Dover Bibles (Kauffmann 2003; de Hamel 1997, 2001). A detached leaf from another of these, the Winchester Bible made for Bishop Henry of Blois, graphically illustrates the internationalism of the twelfth century and the exchange of influences stimulated by travel during pilgrimage and the Crusades. This leaf, now in the Pierpont Morgan Library in New York, depicts scenes from the life of King David and was painted by artists who are also thought to be responsible for frescoes (now sadly damaged) at Sigena, in northeast Spain. The Psalter of Henry of Blois reflects his Eastern-facing interests born of the Crusades, and features what is essentially a manuscript icon of the Virgin and Child in Byzantine style. The marriage of Emperor Otto II to the Byzantine princess Theophano in 972 CE had provided another important route for the transmission of Eastern artistic influences into Western manuscript sacred art. A further illuminated book reflecting international collaboration is the Melisende Psalter, made for the Armenian princess of that name who was married to the crusader Fulk of Anjou. Produced in the Latin kingdom of Jerusalem, its hybrid style is the work of artists from the local region, Byzantium, and the Latin West, whilst its covers are plates of ivory carved with delicate foliate rinceaux forming roundels containing Davidian imagery.

Psalters were the principal vehicle for private devotion. Particularly opulent illuminated copies include the St. Alban's Psalter, perhaps made in the second quarter of the twelfth century as a gift from the monastic community to anchoress Christina of Markyate (Kauffmann 2003; de Hamel 1997, 2001). Prayer books were also made from at least the eighth century, and by the 1230s the first Books of Hours began to appear in the context of urban production.

The rise of the university book trade in centers such as Bologna, Salerno, Paris, and Oxford hastened the spread of certain trends in bookmaking, in which the Latin Bible featured prominently (de Hamel 1997, 2001). The Parisian book trade was dominated in the late twelfth century by the making of copies of biblical commentaries by Peter Lombard and others, arranged in complex wraparound formats which enabled text and commentary to be compared. The size of script, with the use of decorated initials, colored paragraph marks, running titles, and the like, helped the reader to navigate the text. Hugh of Saint Victor advocated using the shape of the text as a means of keying its content into the reader's memory (Carruthers 1990: 94–95). During the thirteenth century, Paris went on to develop compact single-volume study Bibles, with tiny script, decorated or historiated initials, and decorative apparatus (see chap. 16; de Hamel 1997). Subsequent developments included the resplendent *Bible Moralisée* as well as the *Bible Historiale* and *Speculum humanae salvationis* (see chap. 13). Each of the surviving *Bibles Moralisées* contains some thirteen thousand images, arranged in roundels like contemporary stained-glass windows, which convey moralistic didactic typology designed to foster royal piety and good government (Lowden 2000).

The earliest example of a Book of Hours is the de Brailes Hours (fig. 31.10; Donovan 1991), made around 1240 in Oxford and illuminated by William de Brailes, a clerk in minor orders who co-owned a workshop with his wife Selina. These devotional aids became one of the most prolific and popular of medieval books. They were designed to enable laypeople to participate in an abbreviated cycle of devotions throughout the year based upon the Divine Office practiced by professional religious (Wieck 1999). The price varied according to pocket, catering for a wide social range of buyers. Their imagery focused upon scenes from the life of Christ, on the Virgin Mary, and on the obsequies of the Office of the Dead, with calendars featuring the late Roman cycles of the labors of the months, the zodiac signs, and images of the saints. They normally reflected the devotional practice of a particular region, and could be customized to feature the town and countryscapes of the place in which they were made and the life and pursuits of the patron, as in the deluxe Books of Hours produced for Jean Duc de Berry in the early fifteenth century.

Illustrated copies of the Book of Revelation, known as Apocalypses, had emerged by around the year 800. The earliest extant copy is the Valenciennes Apocalypse, a Carolingian copy of a book from Wearmouth-Jarrow, where panel paintings from Rome depicting this and other subjects were hung on the church walls (see above; Klein 2009). The Trier Apocalypse, from ninth-century Tours, is also thought to preserve an early Christian image cycle (Snyder 1964). During the eleventh and twelfth centuries vibrant, colorful copies with highly stylized imagery (consistent with Islamic rule over the Christian mozarabs) were made in northern Spain, as part of the process of Christian reconquest of the territory. Perhaps the most splendid of these is the Silos Apocalypse, produced in Silos itself between 1091 and 1109, with a bright palette of primary colors and its Picasso-esque figures (fig. 31.11; Williams 1994–2002). A vogue for copies of Revelation often accompanies times of social unrest and perceived threat (Klein 2018), and during the late thirteenth and fourteenth centuries, when the Tartars and the ambitions of the Holy Roman Emperor were causing unease, many illuminated copies were made in England and France, mostly for secular patrons. Their text is in Latin or French, and they contain elegant narrative picture cycles.

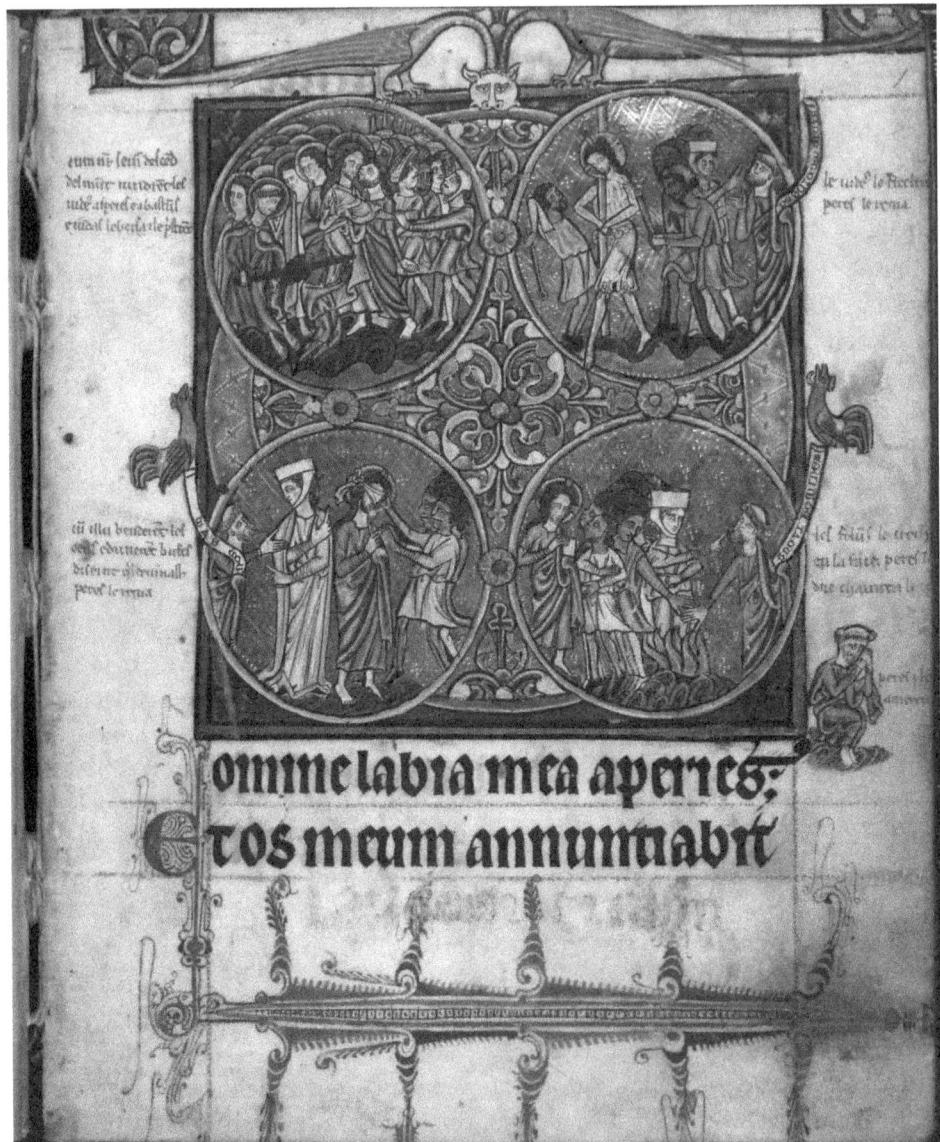

FIGURE 31.10. Christ's betrayal, scourging, and mocking and Peter's denial. The De Brailes Hours (British Library, Add. MS 49999, fol. 1r). Oxford, ca. 1240. © British Library Board.

In the 1320s or 1330s an enterprising maker of *opus anglicanum* embroidered vestments, John Fifhide, who had a workshop beside St Paul's Cathedral in London, took it upon himself to make a book in which the Creation, Christ's Life, and the Book of Revelation were all brought together and conveyed in pictures, with captions composed in a curious hybrid of Church Latin, Court French, and everyday Middle English. He depicted himself as a witness to and recipient of the process of salvations portrayed.

FIGURE 31.11. The woman clothed with the sun, the beast of the Apocalypse, and Lucifer bound. The Silos Apocalypse (British Library, Add. MS 11695, ff. 147v–148r), Silos Abbey, Spain, ca. 1100. © British Library Board.

This, the Holkham Bible (fig. 31.12; Brown 2008a) was the first of the "Poor Man's Bibles" (*Biblia Pauperum*). By the fifteenth century, these were being produced in opulent illuminated copies for noble patrons (such as the British Library *Biblia Pauperum*, made for Count Albrecht of Holland or his wife, Margaret of Cleves, in the Hague around 1405), and in cheap versions illustrated by woodblock prints. Images were the prime means of conveying the biblical narrative and message of redemption, complementing the imagery encountered on church walls, in liturgical drama and mystery plays, and in the often heavily visual language of preachers.

Commissioned manuscripts often provide windows into the context from which they come. Among the most highly customized is the Luttrell Psalter, created in the 1330s for the Lord of the Manor of Irnham in Lincolnshire, Sir Geoffrey Luttrell (fig. 31.13; Brown 2006b). A player in unsettled times, his hopes and fears for eternity are manifest in the program of marginalia in which his achievements and faults, and those of his society, are held up for scrutiny (if often obliquely portrayed) against the age-old backdrop of the cry *De Profundis* and the alleluias of the Psalms (Brown 2008a; Camille 1992). The rigorous

FIGURE 31.12. Salome's dance, with the artist looking on behind Herodias. The Holkham Bible (British Library, Add. MS 47682, fol. 21v). Pater Noster Row, London, 1320s–30s. © British Library Board.

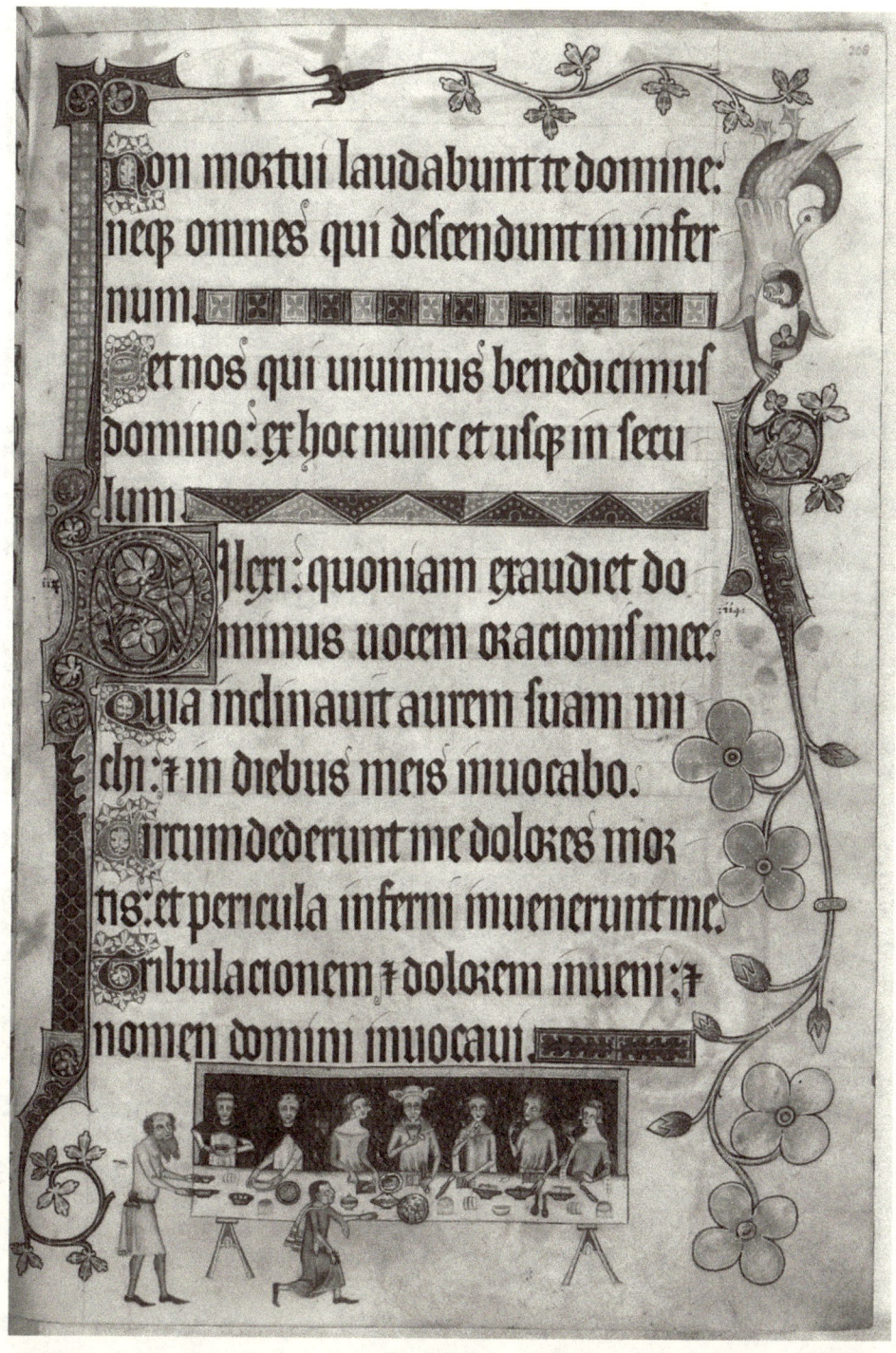

on mortui laudabunt te domine:
neca omnes qui descendunt in infer
num.

et nos qui uiuimus benedicimus
domino: er hoc nunc et ufca in secu
lum

Ileri: quoniam eraudiet do
minus uocem orationis mee.

Quia inclinauit aurem suam mi
chi: 7 in diebus meis inuocabo.

ircumdederunt me dolores mor
tis: et pericula inferni muenerunt me.

Tribulacionem 7 dolorem mueni: 7
nomen domini inuocaui.

FIGURE 31.13. Sir Geoffrey Luttrell, his family, and his Dominican confessor feasting. The Luttrell Psalter (British Library, Add. MS 42130, fol. 208r). Norwich and Irnham (Lincs.), 1330–40s. © British Library Board.

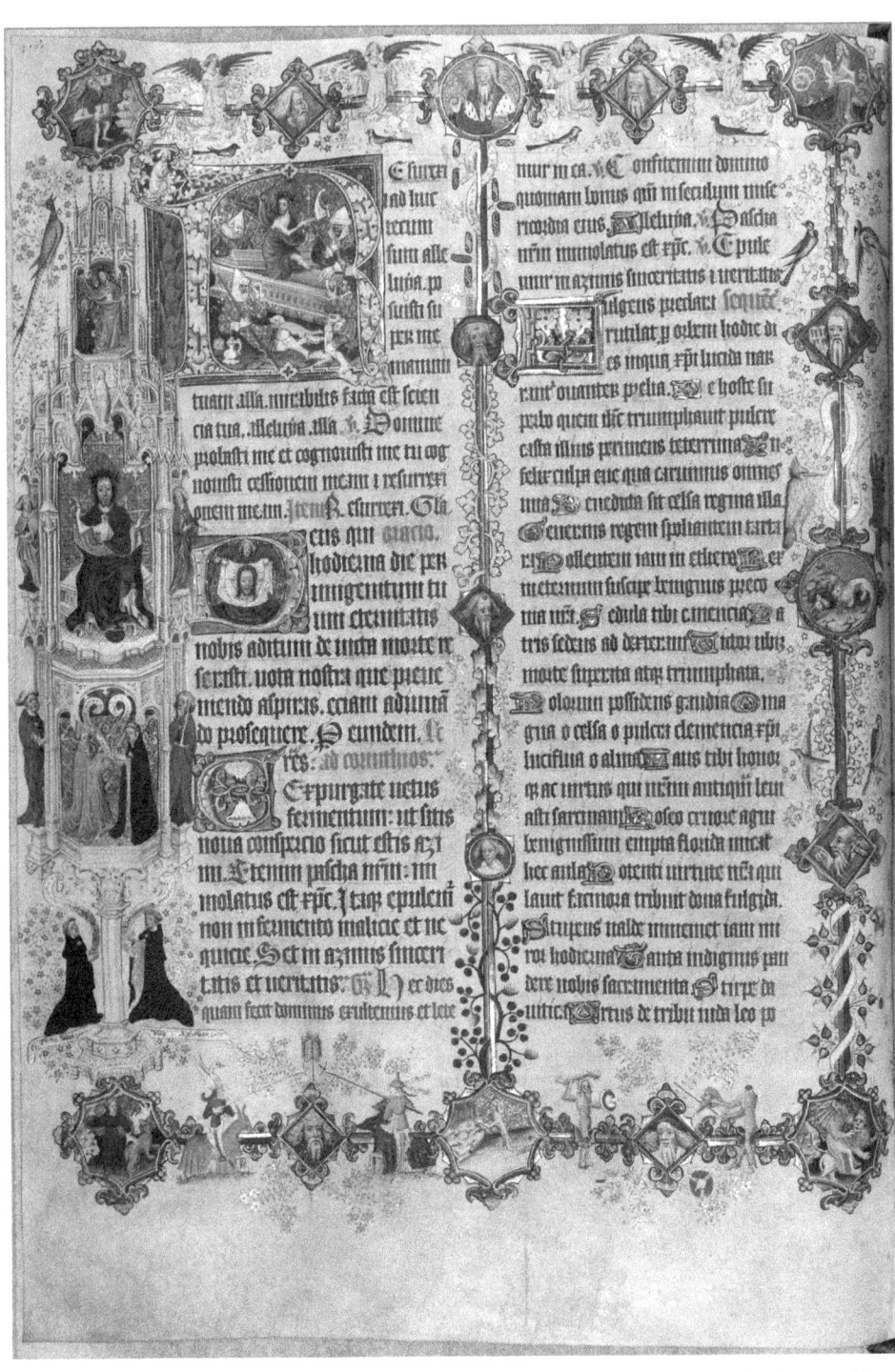

FIGURE 31.14. The Sherborne Missal (British Library, Add. MS 74236, p. 216). Sherborne Abbey, Dorset, ca. 1400–1407. © British Library Board.

spiritual program of self-examination and of exhortation to good works, and much of the intimate coded iconography, was probably the work of his confessor, the Dominican William of Fotheringay. A century later, the Sherborne Missal, made at the Benedictine abbey there, is one of the greatest acts of corporate sponsorship of the late Middle Ages (fig. 31.14). Commissioned by Abbot Robert Bruyning, the book abounds with depictions of him, his overlord the Bishop of Salisbury, the itinerant Dominican artist John Siferwas, and the monk John Whas, son of a local cottar. The liturgy throughout the year is enlivened by an opulent program of illumination in which the historical primacy of Sherborne is proclaimed by virtue of its post-Roman and Anglo-Saxon origins.

The International Gothic style of the Sherborne Missal reflects the confluence of the art of the late Middle Ages with that of the early Italian and Northern Renaissance (Alexander 1978; Kren and McKendrick 2003). The humanist revival of classical texts and script styles was complemented by the reappearance of classical figural naturalism and neoclassical motifs. Manuscript miniaturists might also be panel or fresco painters, such as Giovanni di Paolo (who illuminated Dante's *Paradiso* and *Inferno*) and Gerard David. Illuminators such as Gerard Horenbout and Simon Bening might achieve artistic fame for illuminating deluxe works (including Books of Hours) for leading patrons. Splendid illuminated service books and music manuscripts continued to be made too.

THE RISE OF PRINT

Around 1500, the urban craftspeople who had traditionally made medieval manuscripts morphed, seamlessly in some cases, into the publishers of early printed books. The previous century had seen a trend toward diversification, with specialist illuminators, scribes, and binders increasing the ranges of skills available and moving in on the territory of the entrepreneurial stationers (*libraires* or *cartolai*) responsible for subcontracting out work or commissioning it for sale in their own shops. This variety of interconnected urban specialists gradually consolidated their operations to become the publishing houses of early modern Europe (Alexander 1992). Such trends helped increase access to books, but it would not be until the educational reform acts of the late nineteenth century that real mass literacy would be achieved.

Early printed books, such as the Gutenberg Bibles, were generally distributed unbound, cutting transport costs and allowing their bindings to be customized as required (see chap. 18). Color, which had played a significant role not only in decorating medieval manuscripts but in helping to navigate their texts, was often added by hand to incunables. Where it was absent, some volumes were given even more extensive cycles of marginal engraved imagery in compensation, while in fifteenth- to sixteenth-century manuscripts woodblock prints of sets of miniatures painted elsewhere were sometimes pasted in. A high-point in early biblical print history was Albrecht Dürer's Apocalypse series of 1498 (Bartrum 2002). That deluxe illuminated manuscripts were not immediately ousted by print is shown by the Prayer Book of King Henry VIII (fig. 31.15; Carley 2009), in which the "Defender of

Sed sperauit in multitudine diuitiaᶻ
suarum: & preualuit in vanitate sua.
Ego autem sicut oliua fructifera in
domo Dei speraui in misericordia Dei
in eternum, & in seculum seculi.
Confitebor tibi in seculum quia fecisti
& expectabo nomen tuum quoniam bonū est
in conspectu sanctorum tuorum Gloria
patri Sicut erat.

Dixit
insipiēs
in corde
suo nō
est Deꝰ
Cor=
ruptisūt

FIGURE 31.15. King Henry VIII as King David, with his fool. The Prayerbook of King Henry VIII (British Library, Royal MS 2 A XVI, fol. 63v). London, ca. 1540. © British Library Board.

the Faith" (and spoliator of monasteries and their libraries) had himself portrayed as King David composing the Psalms, with his jester as audience.

Many illustrated printed Bibles have been produced, but one of the most influential was the Doré Bible, with illustrations by French artist Gustave Doré (Kaenel 2014). This large folio edition, with 238 pictures, was published in 1866 by Cassell, Petter, and Galpin: although the text was in French, as a translation of the Vulgate it stood at only one remove from the Latin Bible. This costly production was intended to become a family treasure: for the nineteenth-century bourgeoisie, to possess a Doré Bible was like owning a cycle of masterpieces. It could be purchased in installments (the London publication appeared in sixty-four parts at four shillings each, while in New York the thirty parts came at two dollars apiece) or complete, at prices varying from eight to fifteen pounds. It achieved long-lasting success in the United States and helped to shape the public's mental image of Bible stories.

Hand coloring and lithographic printing helped to bring color flooding back into biblical book illustration, not to mention facsimile editions of manuscripts themselves. Even so, something had been lost with the decline of the art of illumination (revived for a time in the "printed manuscripts" of the visionary poet William Blake, the socialist designer William Morris, and the Kelmscott Press), for *illuminare* means "to light up" and light is revelatory.

MAKING COPIES OF SCRIPTURE AS A DEVOTIONAL ACT

The patristic concept of the "inner library" advocated the necessity for each believer to make themselves a library of the divine Word, a sacred responsibility which the Irish sage Cummian's letter *De Controversia Paschale* referred to as "entering the Sanctuary of God" by studying and transmitting Scripture. To be entrusted with the transmission of the Word could be viewed, in some areas, as a priestly calling in the early Christian age, akin to that of the Jewish *sofer*. Books are the vessels from which the believer's ark, or inner library, is filled.

In the prologue to his Commentary on Luke, Bede says that "I have subjected myself to that burden of work in which, as in innumerable bonds of monastic servitude which I shall pass over, I was myself at once dictator, notary, and scribe."[8] This revealing passage shows not only that he regarded such work as an expression of his religious profession but also that he differentiated between the functions of author, note taker, and formal copyist. Cassiodorus describes each word written by the monastic scribe as "a wound on Satan's body," thereby ascribing to the scribe the role of *miles Christi* (soldier of Christ).[9]

---

[8] *dictator simul notarius et librarius* (Bede, *In Lucae evangelium expositio* prol. 95 [CCSL 120: 7]).

[9] *tot enim uulnera Satanas accipit quot antiquarius Domini uerba describit* (Cassiodorus, *Institutiones* 1.30.1 [ed. Mynors 1960: 75.13]).

In the same passage, he observes that the scribe could "preach with the hand and un-leash tongues with the fingers," imitating the action of the Lord who wrote the Law with his all-powerful finger, and calling to mind the pointing hand of God in later Anglo-Saxon evangelist miniatures.[10]

The production of the Lindisfarne Gospels indicates that this ethos could also be extended to the artistic adornment and visual exploration of Scripture. This complex book is the work of a single artist-scribe, probably Eadfrith, Bishop of Lindisfarne from 698–721 (Brown 2003). Modern scribes estimate that at least two years of full-time work in optimum physical conditions would be required to produce it, even without undertaking such a task alongside the other time-consuming monastic duties. The only other Insular illuminated manuscripts that favored such solitary working patterns are the Book of Durrow and the Durham and Echternach Gospels (Brown 2016). This may have represented a distinctive Insular outworking of the call to meditation and contemplation: if the act of copying and transmitting the Gospels was to glimpse the divine, then this may have been seen as a solitary undertaking on behalf of the com-munity rather than a communal collaboration, like many other aspects of Celtic ere-mitic monasticism. In the monastic federation of St. Columba, the production of such books was the preserve of the *seniores*, the most experienced and venerable members, who often held respected positions such as bishop, abbot, or anchorite. Columba him-self is said to have made holy books single-handedly as a Lenten penitential exercise (Brown 2003).

Female religious were also responsible for the production of books. St. Melania the Younger and the nun Lydia of Thessaloniki are both said to have written books single-handedly, "in the manner of men" in the Early Christian period.[11] Abbess Eadburh and the nuns of Minster-in-Thanet in Kent supplied books to St. Boniface in the German mission fields during the early eighth century, including some adorned with gold to impress poten-tial converts. They may have helped furnish books for major English churches, just as the nuns of Jouarre, Chelles, and Faremoutiers-en-Brie did in Merovingian Gaul. The output from Minster-in-Thanet included the mid-eighth-century Stockholm Codex Aureus (VL 15; Brown 2016), an early medieval version of the late antique *codex purpureus*. The role of such nunneries decreased somewhat after 900, although there were some exceptions presided over by remarkable female scholars such as Hildegard of Bingen: it may, however, be reflected in the fact that only in the book-related professions could women trade inde-pendently in an urban milieu during the high Middle Ages.

---

[10] *manu hominibus praedicare, digitis linguas aperire* (Cassiodorus, *Institutiones* 1.30.1 [ed. Mynors 1960: 75.10]). Examples of the hand of God may be seen in the added miniature to London, British Library, Royal MS 1 E VI (fol. 30v) and the York Gospels (York Minster, Chapter Library, MS Add. 1, ff. 22v, 60v, 85v).

[11] This is recounted in the *Life of Melania the Younger*, ch. 26, E. A. Clark, *The Life of Melania the Younger* (New York: Edwin Mellen, 1984), 46 (Eng. trans.), and the *Life of St Macarius of Alexandria*, C. Butler, *The Lausiac History of Palladius I* (Cambridge: Cambridge University Press, 1898), 150(Eng. trans.). See Brown 2011: 24.

The devotional impetus for bookmaking was perpetuated in the coenobitic environment of monastic and cathedral scriptoria, whose work was part of the *opus dei* with its daily round of the Divine Office, *lectio divina*, and manual labor. The mendicant orders also concerned themselves with the production and study of books as part of their mission of preaching and pastoral care of souls. Urban craftspeople and patrons, too, would often have seen their involvement in the making and commissioning of sacred tomes as a devotional endeavor, even if a commercialized one. Across the ages, the making and owning and giving of books, especially finely produced and costly ones, has also been an adjunct of social and political power play, positioning, and messaging.

A more recent glimpse of the devotional impact upon the scribe of writing, adorning, and embodying the words of Scripture is to be gained from the St. John's Bible (1998–2011), the first handwritten and illuminated complete Bible to be made since print became established.[12] It was commissioned by St. John's Abbey and University, Minnesota, from the British calligrapher Donald Jackson. The illustrations continue the process of adapting traditional iconographies and imbuing them with continued social relevance, such as the inclusion of a holocaust mass grave as an illustration. Jackson commented on his experience:

> I loved the feel of the pen as it touched the page and the breathtaking effect of coloured ink as its wetness caught the light. Those sensations, which I still experience as I work, are what seem to direct the shapes and colours of my designs and letters. The quill and the brush, not my conscious thinking, make the choice. The continual process of opening up and accepting what may reveal itself through hand and heart on a crafted page is the closest I have ever come to God.[13]

There remains a deep psychological and spiritual dimension to the process of transmitting the Bible through the physical labor of writing, and of beautifying it and digging deeper into the meanings and social relevance of text through imagery.

BIBLIOGRAPHY

Alexander, J. J. G. 1978. *The Decorated Letter*. London: Chatto and Windus.

Alexander, J. J. G. 1992. *Medieval Illuminators and Their Methods of Work*. New Haven: Yale.

Ayerst, David, and A. S. T. Fisher. 1977. *Records of Christianity* II. Oxford: Blackwell.

Bartrum, G. 2002. *Albrecht Dürer and his Legacy*. London: British Museum.

Brown, M. P. 1999. *A Guide to Western Historical Scripts from Antiquity to 1600*. Rev. ed. London: British Library & Toronto University.

Brown, M. P. 2003. *The Lindisfarne Gospels: Society, Spirituality and the Scribe*. London: British Library.

Brown, M. P. 2006a. *In the Beginning: Bibles before the Year 1000*. Washington, DC: Smithsonian Institute.

---

[12] See www.saintjohnsbible.org.

[13] Interview in Brown 2021, ch. 30.

Brown, M. P. 2006b. *The Luttrell Psalter: A Facsimile*. London: British Library & Folio Society.

Brown, M. P. 2007. "The Triumph of the Codex: the manuscript book before 1100.'" In *The Blackwell Companion to the History of the Book*, edited by S. Eliot and J. Rose, 179–93. Oxford: Blackwell.

Brown, M. P. 2008a. *The Holkham Bible: A Facsimile*. London: British Library & Folio Society.

Brown, M. P. 2008b. "The Lichfield/Llandeilo Gospels Reinterpreted." In *Authority and Subjugation in Writing of Medieval Wales*, edited by R. Kennedy and S. Meecham-Jones, 57–70. New York: Palgrave Macmillan.

Brown, M. P. 2011. *The Book and the Transformation of Britain, c.550-1050: A Study in Written and Visual Literacy and Orality*. The Sandars Lectures in Bibliography 2009. London: British Library & Chicago University.

Brown, M. P. 2016. *Art of the Islands: Celtic, Pictish, Anglo-Saxon and Viking Visual Culture c.450-1050*. Oxford: Bodleian.

Brown, M. P. 2017. "Reading the Lindisfarne Gospels: Text, Image, Context." In *The Lindisfarne Gospels*, edited by R. G. Gameson, 79–90. Leiden: Brill.

Brown, M. P. 2018a. "The Bridge in the Desert: towards establishing an historical context for the newly discovered Latin manuscripts of St Catherine's Sinai." In *Palaeography Between East and West*, edited by A. d'Ottone Rambach, 73–98. *Rivista degli Studi Orientali* Supplement. Pisa: Serra.

Brown, M. P., rev. by Elizabeth Teviotdale and Nancy K. Turner. 2018b. *Understanding Illuminated Manuscripts: A Guide to Technical Terms*. 2nd ed. Los Angeles: J. Paul Getty Museum.

Brown, M. P. 2021. *Christian Art*. Oxford: Lion Hudson.

Brown, T. J., ed. 1969. *The Stonyhurst Gospel*. London: Roxburghe Club.

Buettner, B. 1992. "Profane Illuminations, Secular Illusions: Manuscripts in Late Medieval Courtly Society." *The Art Bulletin* 74, no. 1: 75–90.

Camille, M. 1992. *Image on the Edge: The Margins of Medieval Art*. London: Reaktion.

Carley, J. P. 2009. *King Henry's Prayer Book*. London: Folio Society.

Carruthers, M. 1990. *The Book of Memory*. 1st ed. Cambridge: Cambridge University Press .

Chazelle, C. 1990. "Pictures, Books and the Illiterate: Pope Gregory I's Letters to Serenus of Marseilles." *Word and Image* 6, no. 2: 138–53.

de Hamel, Christopher. 1997. *A History of Illuminated Manuscripts*. London: Phaidon.

de Hamel, Christopher. 2001. *The Book: A History of the Bible*. London: Phaidon.

Donovan, C. 1991. *The de Brailes Hours: Shaping the Book of Hours in Thirteenth-Century Oxford*. Toronto: University of Toronto.

Farmer, D. H., ed. 1983. *The Age of Bede*. Rev. ed. Harmondsworth: Penguin.

Ganz, David. 1990. *Corbie in the Carolingian Renaissance*. Sigmaringen: J. Thorbecke.

Kaenel, P. 2014. *Doré: Master of Imagination*. Paris: Flammarion.

Kauffmann, C. M. 2003. *Biblical Imagery in Medieval England 700-1500*. London: Harvey Miller.

Kelly, E. P. 1994. "The Lough Kinale Shrine: the Implications for the Manuscripts." In *The Book of Kells*, edited by Felicity O'Mahony, 280–89. Aldershot: Scolar.

Kessler, H. 1977. *The Illustrated Bibles from Tours*. Princeton: Princeton University Press.

Klein, P. 2009. *Apocalypse of Valenciennes. Valenciennes, Bibliothèque de Valenciennes, Ms. 99*. Madrid: Orbis Mediaevalis.

Klein, P. 2018. "Circulation, Popularity and Function of Illustrated Apocalypses from the Late Antiquity to High Medieval Europe." In *Medieval Europe in Motion: La Circulación de Manuscritos Iluminados en la Península Ibérica*, edited by A. Miguélez Cavero and F. Villaseñor Sebastian, 201–14. Madrid: CSIC.

Kren, T., and Scot McKendrick. 2003. *Illuminating the Renaissance. The Triumph of Flemish Painting in Europe*. Los Angeles: Getty Trust.

Levin, I. 1985. *The Quedlinburg Itala: The Oldest Illustrated Biblical Manuscript*. Leiden: Brill.

Lowden, John. 1997. *Early Christian and Byzantine Art*. London: Phaidon.

Lowden, John. 2000. *The Making of the Bibles Moralisées*. Philadelphia: Pennsylvania State University.

Lowden, John. 2012. "The Word Made Visible: the Exterior of the Early Christian Book as Visual Argument." In *The Early Christian Book*, edited by W. Klingshirn and L. Safran, 13–47. Washington, DC: Catholic University of America.

Mayr-Harting, H. 1999. *Ottonian Book Illumination*. London: Harvey Miller.

McKendrick, Scot, and Kathleen Doyle. 2007. *Bible Manuscripts: 1400 Years of Scribes and Scripture*. London: British Library.

Meyvaert, Paul. 1996. "Bede, Cassiodorus and the Codex Amiatinus." *Speculum* 71: 827–83.

Mutherich, F., and J. Gaehde. 1976. *Carolingian Painting*. New York: George Braziller.

Needham, P. 1979. *Twelve Centuries of Bookbindings*. New York: Pierpont Morgan Library.

Nersessian, V., ed. 2001. *Treasures of the Ark: 700 Years of Armenian Christian Art*. London: British Library,

Nordenfalk, C. 1988. *Early Medieval Book Illumination*. New York: Rizzoli.

Pächt, O. 1986. *Book Illumination in the Middle Ages*. London: Harvey Miller.

Snyder, James. 1964. "The Reconstruction of an Early Christian Cycle of Illustrations for the Book of Revelation: The Trier Apocalypse." *Vigiliae Christianae* 18, no. 3: 146–162.

van der Horst, K. 1996. *The Utrecht Psalter in Medieval Art*. Leiden: Hes & De Graff.

van Regemorter, B. 1992. *Binding Structures in the Middle Ages*. Leiden: Brill.

Watts, J. W., ed. 2013. *Iconic Books and Texts*. Sheffield: Equinox.

Webster, L., and M. P. Brown, eds. 1997. *The Transformation of the Roman World*. London: British Museum.

Weitzmann, K. 1970. *Late Antique and Early Christian Book Illumination*. London: Chatto and Windus.

Wieck, R. S. 1999. *Time Sanctified: The "Book of Hours" in Medieval Art and Life*. New York: George Braziller.

Williams, J. 1994–2002. *The Illustrated Beatus: A Corpus of the Illustrations of the Commentary on the Apocalypse*. 5 vols. London: Harvey Miller.

Index of Manuscripts

For the benefit of digital users, indexed terms that span two pages (e.g., 52–53) may, on occasion, appear on only one of those pages.

Tables and figures are indicated by *t* and *f* following the page number. For the common names of manuscripts, see the Index of Subjects.

Index of Biblical Books and Passages

For the benefit of digital users, indexed terms that span two pages (e.g., 52–53) may, on occasion, appear on only one of those pages.

---

[1] All Psalm references are given to the Vulgate Gallican Psalter (LXX). For cross-references to the Hebrew Psalter, *Nova Vulgata*, and modern translations see Table 1.1.

Index of Subjects

rabbinic exegesis, 252, 264–65, 283–84, 286,
    333, 334, 336–37, 339, 343
Rainaud of Saint-Eloi, 248–49
Ramism, 314
Ramsbotham, Alexander, 357
Rand, Edward Kenneth, 359
Ranke, Ernest, 225n.1, 356
Rashi. *See* Solomon, Rabbi
Ravenna, 107–8, 162
refectory, 106–7, 192–93, 277
Reformation, 101, 293, 311–12, 315–16, 320,
    324–25, 400–1, 402, 440–41
    See also Gregorian reform
relics. *See* veneration of manuscripts
renderings, xxxi–xxxii, 9–10, 43, 62, 66, 70,
    85–86, 383, 401, 412–13
    etymologizing renderings, 44, 386
    See also translation
Renner, Franz, 276–77
Requiem Mass, 443, 445, 455–56
Reticius of Autun, 123
Reuchlin, Johannes, 284, 334–35, 342, 343
Reusch, Franz Heinrich, 352–53
revision
    of biblical text, xxx, 6–7, 8, 10–12, 20, 40–41,
        56–59, 83, 85–86, 171
    of translation, 10–11, 20, 66–67, 80–81, 82,
        86, 87–88, 99
rhetoric, 60, 123, 128, 129–30, 134–35, 222, 259,
    264–65, 268, 307–8, 311–12, 418–19, 472
Richard of Saint-Victor, 249, 340
Richard of Thetford, 259–60
Robert of Basevorn, 259–60
Robert of Melun, 217–18, 249, 269–70
Robinson, Joseph Armitage, 350–51
Rocca, Angelo, 300–1
Rönsch, Hermann, 350–52
Roland of Cremona, 251
Roman Catholicism, xxix–xxx, 305–10, 386, 387,
    388, 392–95, 429–30, 436–37, 438, 441, 454
Roman Psalter. *See* Psalter, Roman
Roman Vulgate, xxxiii, 91, 286–88, 358–60,
    366, 373, 375, 380, 383, 406–7
Rome, 56–57, 66, 107, 135, 161, 189, 191, 276–77,
    307, 454–55
    place of Bible revision, 14, 300
    lectionary, 115–16

Rossano, Piero, 381
Rosslyn Missal. *See* Edinburgh, NLS, 18.5.19
rubrication, 188–90, 274–75, 277, 278–79
Rufinus of Aquileia, 14, 68–69, 84
Rufinus the Syrian, 82, 84, 85, 86, 87
Rusch, Adolf, 279
Rushworth Gospels. *See* Oxford, Bodl.,
    Auct. D.II.19

Sabatier, Pierre, xxviii–xxix, xxxiii, 15, 69, 349,
    355, 365–66
sacra pagina, 208, 217–18, 221
sacredness of Bible. *See* inspiration of
    Scripture
    See also veneration of manuscripts
Sacy. *See* Lemaistre de Sacy
    See also Bible de Sacy
St. Alban's Psalter. *See* Hildesheim,
    Domschatz, St. God. 1
St. Augustine Gospels. *See* Cambridge, Corpus
    Christi, 286
St. Gall, 164, 165
St. John's Bible, 487
Saint-Germain Bible. *See* Paris, BnF,
    lat. 11937
Saint-Germain Psalter [VL 303]. *See* Paris,
    BnF, lat. 11947
Saint-Jacques, Paris, 244, 246, 251, 338
Salmon, Pierre, 359, 380
Salomon of Troyes. *See* Solomon, Rabbi
Samaritan Pentateuch, 309–10, 314–15
Samuel ben Meir, 334
Sanday, William, 357–58, 360, 371–72
Sardinia, 11, 13–14, 161
Schäfer, Karl Theodor, 361, 368–69, 370
Schick, Eduard, 381–82, 384
Schildenberger, Johannes, 361–62
Schnackenburg, Rudolf, 370
schools, 51, 123, 131–32, 139–40, 146–47,
    182, 193–94, 209, 211–12, 217, 241–42,
    250–51, 253, 267, 281, 296–97, 335,
    336–37, 440–41
Schott, Johann, 321–22
Schulz-Flügel, Eva, 15, 370
scribes. *See* copyists
scriptoria, 117, 169, 173, 187–89, 474, 476,
    486–87